Montana & Wyoming

Includes Yellowstone and Glacier National Parks

Alli Rainey Wendling

interior photographs by the author

The Countryman Press ✳ Woodstock, Vermont

FIRST EDITION

DEDICATION

To the memory of the people who lived in Montana and Wyoming long before
my ancestors ever set foot in your land—I hear the whispers of your presence and
catch glimpses of your spirits everywhere I turn. May we someday regain comprehension of even the tiniest bit of the remarkable and balanced way you lived on
and loved the land, for the good of all beings and the future of the planet.

We welcome your comments and suggestions. Please contact Explorer's Guide
Editor, The Countryman Press, P.O. Box 748, Woodstock, Vermont 05091, or
e-mail countrymanpress@wwnorton.com.

ISBN 0-88150-619-2
ISSN 1556-2042

Maps by Moore Creative Designs, © 2005 The Countryman Press
Book design by Bodenweber Design
Text composition by PerfecType, Nashville, TN
Interior photographs © Alli Rainey Wendling
Cover photograph of Highway to the Sun, Glacier National Park
    © Peter French/Inside Stock Imagery

Published by The Countryman Press, P.O. Box 748, Woodstock, Vermont 05091

Distributed by W. W. Norton & Company, Inc., 500 Fifth Avenue, New York,
NY 10110

Printed in the United States of America

10 9 8 7 6 5 4 3 2 1

Montana & Wyoming

EXPLORE WITH US!

Welcome to the first edition of *Montana & Wyoming: An Explorer's Guide*. All attractions, activities, lodgings, and restaurants in this guide have been selected on the basis of merit, not paid advertising. The organization of the book is simple, but the following points will help to get you started on your way.

WHAT'S WHERE

In the beginning of each state's section, you will find an alphabetical listing with thumbnail sketches of special highlights and important information for travelers.

ORGANIZATION

This guidebook is organized roughly north to south and west to east, starting with Montana (six regions), followed by Wyoming (five regions). Following an introduction that provides interesting background information on the region while highlighting some of its more noteworthy attractions, you'll find details about that region's attractions listed in a consistent, uniform fashion. These listings will help you plan your exploration of the region accordingly. For each region, you'll find first a selection of area attractions (under *To See, To Do,* and *Wilder Places*), followed by suggestions about where to sleep (under *Lodging*) and where to eat (under *Dining Out* and *Eating Out*), and, finally, a selection of that area's annual events (under *Special Events*). As certain attractions fit in several categories, every attempt to provide helpful cross-references has been made.

LODGING

Lodging establishments are selected for mention in this book based on merit; no business owner or innkeeper was charged for inclusion. When making reservations, ask about the establishment's policy on children, pets, smoking, and credit cards.

Rates: Please don't hold us or the respective innkeepers responsible for the rates listed as of press time in 2005. Some changes are inevitable. State and local room taxes (7 percent in both states, plus any local taxes) are not included in lodging prices unless specifically noted. Unless otherwise noted, all rates included are for double occupancy.

RESTAURANTS

In most sections, please note a distinction between *Dining Out* and *Eating Out*. By their nature, restaurants listed under *Eating Out* are generally less expensive, featuring mainly entrée selections under $10, while the majority of entrée selections for the restaurants listed under *Dining Out* will be $10 or more. Please note that due to the seasonal nature of tourism in Montana and Wyoming, many restaurants change their hours or close entirely in the off-season, accounting for the lack of business hours in this guide. If your sights are set on a particular venue, it's best to call ahead for the most up-to-date hours of operation.

KEY TO SYMBOLS

🎗 **Special value.** The blue ribbon denotes establishments of exceptional value for a reasonable price.

✐ **Child friendly.** The crayon symbol appears next to lodgings, restaurants, and activities that welcome families with children.

♿ **Handicapped access.** The wheelchair symbol appears next to lodgings, restaurants, and attractions that are partially or completely handicapped accessible. While every effort has been made to ensure accuracy, it's best to double-check with establishments before your arrival.

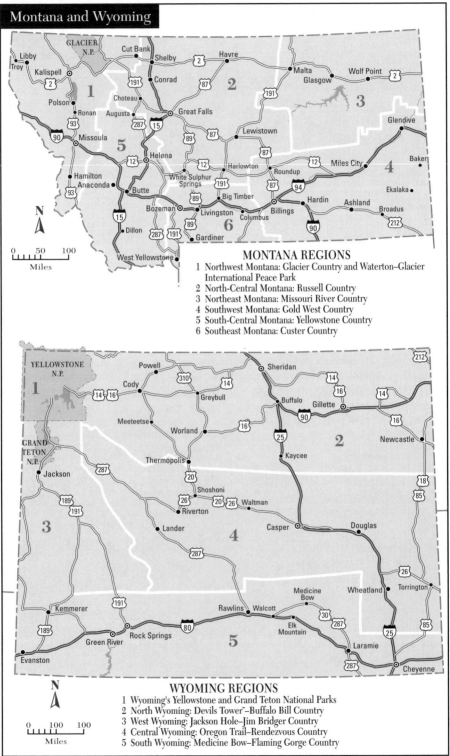

Montana and Wyoming

MONTANA REGIONS
1 Northwest Montana: Glacier Country and Waterton–Glacier International Peace Park
2 North-Central Montana: Russell Country
3 Northeast Montana: Missouri River Country
4 Southwest Montana: Gold West Country
5 South-Central Montana: Yellowstone Country
6 Southeast Montana: Custer Country

WYOMING REGIONS
1 Wyoming's Yellowstone and Grand Teton National Parks
2 North Wyoming: Devils Tower–Buffalo Bill Country
3 West Wyoming: Jackson Hole–Jim Bridger Country
4 Central Wyoming: Oregon Trail–Rendezvous Country
5 South Wyoming: Medicine Bow–Flaming Gorge Country

CONTENTS

ACKNOWLEDGMENTS

Ultimately, this book would not have been possible to write without the inspiration provided by the incomparable states of Montana and Wyoming and all of the wonderful attractions found within each of them. This book would also not have been possible without The Countryman Press, particularly without the direction provided first by Dale Hetsko, and then by Kermit Hummel, as well as all of the people there who helped me put this project together and make it a reality.

I'm especially grateful for the support of the remarkable Cody crew, including Tad Anderson, for his calming presence and for dragging me out to climb on the coldest of winter's days; Leslie Paul, for reminding me to lighten up and laugh at myself and for the awesome girl power; Mike Snyder, for all of the beta, laughter, and bouldering; Meg Snyder, for the great conversation and the inspiration and strength she inspires; Mark DeVries, for the comfortable place to crash many nights; and Jeremy Rowan, for his quiet and supportive presence, providing me with a willing ear to listen and a shoulder to cry on when I needed it most. I love you all from the depths of my soul. Thank you.

More than anyone else, my dear husband, Matt Wendling, made this book possible. Without his tolerant and patient support, his willingness to stop traveling for a time so I could buckle down and write, his consistent love, and his unique ability to make me laugh and see things from a different perspective, I doubt I could have ever undertaken such a monstrous task, much less completed it. Matt, you are a magical, mysterious source of inspiration in my life, and I will love you always.

INTRODUCTION

Finally, an *Explorer's Guide* to not just one, but to two of the wildest and most wondrous states in the West—Montana and Wyoming—compiled by an individual whose wanderlust and compulsion for travel are driven by an undying passion to embrace and fully appreciate all of the unique smells, sights, sounds, ambience, and flavors of this area of the United States. From the gorgeous and more familiar vistas of Glacier National Park, Yellowstone National Park, and Grand Teton National Park to lesser-known but equally worthy travel destinations in both states, you'll find in these pages an honest effort to guide you to the finest, most intriguing, and most awe-inspiring attractions modern-day Montana and Wyoming have to offer.

Rich natural history and an impressive record of human habitation characterize both of these states. Long before explorers of European ancestry ever crossed into their borders, humans inhabited the areas now known as Montana and Wyoming; in fact, ancient people dwelled in these lands more than 10,000 years ago, a testament to the lavish abundance of both flora and fauna that has long existed in this region, enabling people to live here despite often inhospitable weather conditions. Later, many tribes of Native Americans called these lands home, including the Assiniboine, Blackfeet, Cheyenne, Crow, Gros Ventre, Kalispel, Kootenai, Pend d'Oreille, and Salish in Montana; and the Arapaho, Arikara, Bannock, Blackfeet, Cheyenne, Crow, Gros Ventre, Kiowa, Nez Perce, Sheep Eater, Sioux, Shoshone, and Ute in Wyoming.

Both Wyoming and Montana received their earliest visits from explorers in the first decade of the 19th century. This is when the Lewis and Clark expedition crossed Montana (1804–6), and a man named John Colter discovered an area in 1807 that he deemed Colter's Hell. (Less than a century later, in 1872, this area became Yellowstone National Park—the world's first park of its kind.) Soon after the first explorers passed through these areas, Montana and Wyoming became favored stomping grounds for fur trappers and traders, who strove to meet the demand for beaver hats, which had become the latest fad in fashionable European society. As this demand waned in the middle of the century, the gold rush picked up, bringing a fresh onslaught of pioneers headed west on the Oregon Trail and other pioneer trails to seek their fortunes in Montana and Wyoming, where gold had been found, or traveling through to California in pursuit of the gold there. Still others passed this way on their journey to claim a plot of the rich land rumored to be found in Oregon and thereabouts. Bands of Mormons came, too, traveling west on the Mormon Trail in an effort to escape religious persecution.

Conflicts between pioneers and Native Americans continued throughout the 19th century, as the struggle for land and resources became pointed and the traditional ways of living for the Native Americans came under siege from the combined effects of alcohol, new diseases, new people, and a new system of trading, among other stressors. Some of the most horrific and bloody battles between Native Americans and the encroaching settlers occurred in Montana and Wyoming; by the close of the 19th century the Native Americans were forced onto reservations for the most part. The vast herds of buffalo, too, that once roamed the area dwindled into virtual oblivion, unable to maintain their numbers in the face of the massive, wanton slaughtering undertaken by the newcomers.

Montana became a state in 1889; Wyoming in 1890. Both states developed strong agricultural bases, particularly through ranching of both sheep and cattle (though these two different types of ranching served as the basis for historical conflicts as well), but also in the growing of crops. Both states developed strong economic dependence on the mineral extraction industry as well, with the creation of such mining powerhouses as Montana's Anaconda Copper Company. Founded by Marcus Daly in the late 19th century, it became the world's largest mine of its type. The vast quantities of coal in Wyoming prompted the building of the transcontinental railroad across the southern part of the state in the mid- to late 19th century, leaving behind a legacy of coal mining that still contributes to the state's economy today.

Throughout the 20th century and into the present time, both states have continued to rely economically to a certain extent on mining and agriculture— mining still ranks as the greatest economic contributor in Wyoming, while agriculture ranks number one in Montana. Nonetheless, both states have also undergone a gradual and significant shift in economic dependence on these traditional sources as tourism to the region has grown, with both states now counting tourism as the second-greatest contributor to their economies. With so much focus on making these states friendly and worthy travel destinations, not to mention the enormous quantity of fantastic attractions, then, you can't go wrong in planning a visit!

If you've never visited either state, you're in for a true treat; perhaps more than any other area of the country, these two western locales retain a strong, vibrant frontier spirit, embodied by the rugged, but for the most part welcoming, individuals whom you'll undoubtedly encounter during your travels, as well as by the vast tracts of public lands contained within the states themselves. In Montana lie more than 28 million acres of national lands, including one national park; more than 8 million acres of land administered by the Bureau of Land Management (BLM); and state-owned lands that include 42 state parks. Wyoming contains almost 15 million acres of national lands, including two national parks; more than 18 million acres of land administered by the BLM; as well as state-owned lands including 12 state parks, a state recreation area, and numerous state historic sites.

Perhaps this vast inland sea of relatively untrammeled wildness is what made me fall in love with Wyoming and choose it as my home, after years of feeling placeless and unable to answer the inevitable "Where are you from?" question that comes up in standard introductory conversations. Born in New York City, I was so young when I moved that I can no longer remember the place, spending my childhood in Seattle, Phoenix, and Boston. I moved west a year after finishing college, traveling for two months before settling in Colorado for a time. But it wasn't until I traveled up to Wyoming that I discovered a place that I really wanted to say I was from and to call my home, a place that continues to wow and amaze me the more I explore and learn about it, from the stark beauty of its badlands and the colorful, sudden blooms of its spring wildflowers in its canyons and mountains to the roughly 500,000 individuals (the smallest population of any state in the nation) scattered across its vast territory—Wyoming ranks ninth in area among all of the states.

Having been a converted Wyomingite for several years made it easy, then, to decide to catalog not only its attractions but the worthy sights and scenes of its neighbor to the north as well. Montana, the nation's fourth-largest state in area (but 44th in population, with under a million hearty souls), also appealed to the explorer in me, with the promise of endless natural sights to discover and behold as well as numerous cultural, historical, and recreational resources. As a visitor to this great and mysterious tract of land, I have made my best effort to unearth and share here some its finest treasures and attractions, which I discovered during my months of initial forays into a place to which I shall undoubtedly return many times in the future. Over time, as I increase my knowledge of and intimacy with Montana, I aim ultimately to include additional valuable information about this place—and about Wyoming, too—in future editions of this guide.

For now, though, I will leave you to start your exploration, hoping that in Wyoming and Montana you will discover, as I have, a treasure trove of fantastic and wonderful opportunities that will leave you yearning to return again and again.

Montana

WHAT'S WHERE IN MONTANA

AGRICULTURE With roots reaching back into Montana's pioneer days, agriculture continues to be the mainstay of this state's economy, bringing in revenues of more than $2 billion annually. The state's number-one industry relies on the production of beef and dairy cattle, sheep, swine, and honey, as well as crops of hay, wheat, cherries, and barley, among others. What may surprise you is that Montana ranks second in the nation for agricultural lands, with nearly 60 million acres of farmland (making up 22,000 farms) carved out of its total 93 million acres of land. Despite this huge percentage of lands devoted to agricultural endeavors, farmers and ranchers account for only about 5 percent of the state's population.

AIRPORTS Montana has several international airports, including **Billings Logan International Airport** (406-238-3420; www.flybillings.com) in Billings; **Great Falls International Airport** (406-727-3404; www.gtfair port.com) in Great Falls; **Glacier Park International Airport** (406-257-5994; www.glacierairport.com) in Kalispell; and **Missoula International Airport** (406-728-4381; www.msoairport.org) in Missoula. The state also has many regional, county, and municipal airports. For more listings, see www.airnav.com/airports/us/mt.

AMTRAK Amtrak (1-800-872-7245; www.amtrak.com) has 12 stations in northern Montana, all of which lie along its 75-year-old Empire Builder line, which travels from Chicago to Seattle. Key Montana attractions that lie along the line include Fort Benton, the Lewis and Clark Interpretive Center, and Glacier National Park.

ANTIQUES If your travels include searching for antiques, a good resource for finding antique dealers in Montana is *The Antiques & Collectibles Guide* online listings for Montana, available at www.acguide .com/ShopsLocMT.html. You can find an online list of Montana's annual antique shows by visiting www.visit mt.com/tripplanner/events and selecting "Antique Shows."

AREA CODE Montana has a single area code—**406.**

BEARS Many of the outdoor attractions listed in this guide are home to bears—both grizzlies and black bears. Though seeing a bear can be quite a thrill, you need to remember at all times that bears are wild animals and that you should keep your distance and respect them as such. In order to take proper precautions should you enter a bear habitat (usually, such areas are signed and have information about how you should behave), you should educate yourself about the areas where you will recreate. It is your responsibility to help keep bears wild by not habituating them to receiving food from human sources, including garbage.

BICYCLING Bicycling opportunities abound in Montana for both the avid road rider and the serious mountain biker, as well as for less serious cyclists of either genre. In this guide, rides mentioned tend to cater to the latter. A list of 33 selected rides varying in difficulty from easy to experienced, complete with route descriptions, maps, and directions, is available for free at www.visitmt .com/virtualvisitor/biking. Other good resources for cyclists include **Bike Plan Source's** Montana page (www .bikeplan.com/mt.htm) and **Montana Cycling** (www.montanacycling.org).

BIRD-WATCHING Montana's almost 400 species of birds in more than 40 families include the state bird, the

western meadowlark, as well as the trumpeter swan, sage grouse, and whooping crane, among many others. Bird-watchers visiting the state can start their trip by visiting the Web site www.camacdonald.com/birding/us montana.htm for a list of birds, great places to see them, and more. You'll find an array of places listed in various sections throughout this guide that mention bird-watching opportunities, particularly under *Wilder Places* in each chapter.

BOATING Eleven reservoirs in Montana under the management of the Great Plain Region of the **United States Bureau of Reclamation** (USBR) account for more than 1 million visitors annually, many of them boating enthusiasts. The latest information on these reservoirs is available by calling the **Montana Area Office** at 406-247-7298 or visiting www.usbr .gov/gp/mtao/index.cfm. In this guide, most of the listings under *To Do—Boating* provide information about bodies of water (lakes and reservoirs) suitable for motorized watercraft in addition to human-powered craft. Listings for rivers—even those that allow motorized watercraft—will be found under *To Do—Fishing* and *To Do—Paddling/Floating*, though they are usually cross-referenced at the end of the *To Do—Boating* section in relevant chapters.

BUREAU OF LAND MANAGEMENT (BLM) LANDS

BLM Montana–Dakotas (406-896-5000; www.mt.blm.gov) has seven field offices that help administer the 8 million acres of BLM lands in the state (as well as one for each Dakota). Responsibilities also include the management of nearly 50 million subsurface acres of mineral estate in the three states, as well as recreational management, wild horse management, and more.

BUS SERVICE

Three private bus services serve Montana: **Greyhound** (1-800-229-9424; www.greyhound.com); **Powder River Trailways** (1-800-442-3682); and **Rimrock Trailways** (1-800-255-7655; www.rimrocktrailways.com). Billings, Butte, Great Falls, Kalispell, and Missoula also have city bus services. For more information, contact the **Montana Department of Transportation** (406-444-6200; www.mdt.state.mt.us).

BYWAYS

When you get right down to it, nearly every long-distance drive in Montana is scenic, but a sampling of the state's designated scenic byways include the **Beartooth Scenic Byway** (which dips into Wyoming) in the southeastern part of the state; the **Pioneer Mountains Scenic Byway** in the southwest; and the **Kings Hill Scenic Byway** in the central part of the state. For detailed suggestions in addition to those listed in this book, you can look to www.visitmt.com/tripplanner/wheretogo/drive.htm.

CAMPGROUNDS

The majority of campgrounds listed under *To Do—Camping* in this guidebook lie on public lands, as it's my opinion that such camping adventures tend to be a little more outdoorsy and adventuresome (in keeping with that explorer's spirit) than staying at a full-service campground in a town or a city. You should know that in addition to those campgrounds listed, primitive camping is permissible on much of the public land in the state as well. Please note that the dates given for when a campground is open often mean that this is when a fee is charged to stay there and when all services (water, garbage pickup, camp hosts, restrooms) are provided. Often, free camping is permitted at these locations in the off-season so long as they are accessible, though no services are provided. Of course, Montana has scads of private campgrounds, too. For a free, comprehensive guide to Montana's campgrounds, visit www.visitmt.com/tripplanner/campandlodge/camp.htm and click on "Complete Listings," or order a hard copy, contained in the free **Montana Travel Planning Kit** (1-800-VISIT MT; www.visitmt.com).

CITIES

Montana has seven incorporated cities with populations of more than 10,000, of which **Billings** is the largest (roughly 90,000 people live there). The state capital, **Helena,** has a population of about 26,000 people.

CLIMATE

Unless snow sports or cold temperatures appeal to you, your best bet is to plan your vacation to Montana for the summer months (July is the warmest), when warmer daily highs in the 60s to 80s tend to prevail statewide. If you want to avoid the crowds but still be comfortable, early autumn is a good time to visit as well;

although tourism declines considerably when the kids are back in school, many seasonal services remain open for a time. The average annual precipitation in Montana is only 15 inches, but of course some areas receive considerably more than this—often in the form of snowfall.

COFFEE Coffee lovers, never fear—in Montana you'll find more than just the gas station variety of your favorite brew. Along with the cafés and shops listed in this guide (and those omni-present little drive-through coffee huts), Montana boasts fine coffee roasters of its own, including **Montana Coffee Traders, Inc.** (1-800-345-5282; www.coffeetraders .com) in Whitefish and **Hunter Bay Coffee Roasters** (1-866-835-5589; www.hunterbay.com) in Lolo.

CONSERVATION GROUPS Montana has many conservation groups, including the **Montana Conservation Corps** (406-587-4475; www.mtcorps .org), **Montana Conservation Voters** (406-254-1593; www.mtvoters.org),

and **American Wildlands** (406-586-8175; www.wildlands.org). To find a list of links to Montana conservation and environmental organizations, visit www.mcvedfund.org/group_contacts .html.

COUNTIES Montana has 56 counties.

DUDE RANCHES Whether a working cattle ranch or an upscale guest ranch with luxurious amenities—or something in between—one of Montana's many guest ranches can provide you with just the right level of comfort and a balance between work and play to suit your vacationing tastes. From the full-flavored ranching experience to cushy resort ranches, the **Montana Dude Ranchers' Association** (www.montanadra.com; e-mail: office@montanadra.com) lists a wide variety of ranches in locales around the state that cater to guests. To help you out, this guide lists under *Ranch Vacations* (see *To Do—Unique Adventures* in each region) a number of dude and guest ranches offering this type of adventure.

EMERGENCIES Dial **911** statewide in case of emergency. In addition, phone numbers and addresses for regional medical facilities are provided under *Guidance* in each region of this guidebook.

EVENTS Montana's events span all seasons and tastes, and locating and listing them all would be a monumental task. Luckily, it's been done for you, courtesy of **Travel Montana,** from the **Montana Department of Commerce** (www.visitmt.com). Click on "Plan a Montana Vacation," and then click on the link for "Events," to find the most up-to-date listings of the latest goings-on in the state. Additionally, you'll find selected events listed under *Special Events* in each region of this guidebook.

FARMER'S MARKETS Montana boasts a number of annual farmer's markets around the state, as well it should, considering the role that agriculture plays in the state's economy. For a comprehensive list of the state's markets, including dates of operation, hours, and contact information, see www.ams.usda.gov/farmers markets/states/montana.htm, or call 406-444-2402.

FISHING Montana has long been a well-known destination among anglers, for good reason. Fantastic trout fishing can be found in rivers, streams, and lakes throughout the state, with fishing for other species, including bass and yellow perch, available in many locales as well. A comprehensive online interactive guide, with information on regulations, where to fish, and everything else you could possibly need to know before planning a trip to fish in Montana, is available courtesy of **Montana Fish, Wildlife and Parks** (406-444-2535; www.fwp.state.mt.us/fishing/default.aspx). If you want to hire a

guide, a good place to start is **Fishing Outfitters Association of Montana** (406-763-5436; www.FOAM-Montana .org). Another great resource is **Big Sky Fishing.com** (www.bigskyfishing.com). You'll find regional fishing spots of note listed under *To Do— Fishing* throughout this guidebook.

GAMBLING Gambling is legal in the state of Montana, and you won't have to look too hard to find places to try your luck. Off the Indian reservations, the maximum bet you can make is $2, and the most you can win is $800. Legal live games include **bingo, bridge, cribbage, hearts, keno, panguingue, pinochle, pitch, poker, raffles, rummy, shake-a-day, solo,** and **whist. Video bingo,** and **poker machines** are also legal.

GEOGRAPHY At 630 miles long and 280 miles wide, Montana's 145,552 square miles of land make it the fourth-largest state in the nation. Montana can be divided into two basic geographic regions, with the western two-fifths being part of the **Rocky Mountain region** and the eastern three-fifths being in the **Great Plains region.** The **continental divide,** a 3,100-mile-long imaginary line that separates waters that drain into the Atlantic from those that drain into the Pacific, passes through Montana's Rocky Mountain region. Montana is the only state whose rivers drain into the Gulf of Mexico, the Hudson Bay, and the Pacific Ocean.

GEOLOGY Montana presents a veritable geologic wonderland for the explorer. Wind- and water-eroded formations and glacial till abound in the eastern plains portion of the state, while in the west, you'll discover glacier-carved mountains, lifted up and folded by plate tectonics. With its abundance of mineral wealth, Montana is also home to "the richest hill on earth" (near the Mineral Museum in Butte), as well as many active and prolific dig sites that continue to unearth dinosaur remains and other fossils hearkening back to prehistoric times. To augment those geological attractions highlighted throughout this work, consider picking up a copy of *Roadside Geology of Montana,* by David Alt and Donald W. Hyndman (Mountain Press Publishing Company, 1986) to beef up your knowledge on the fly as you drive around the state.

GOLF COURSES More than 70 courses await the golf lover visiting Montana, including the Jack Nicklaus signature **Old Works Golf Course** (406-563-5989; www.oldworks.org) in Anaconda, among other options, both rustic and refined. For a complete list of Montana's golf courses and additional information, visit the **Montana State Golf Association** Web site (www.montana.net/msga).

GUIDES AND OUTFITTERS The **Montana Outfitters and Guides Association** (406-449-3578; www.moga-montana.org) lists almost 200 member organizations that can take you on the hunting or fishing adventure of a lifetime. **OutfittingMontana.com** (www.outfittingmontana.com) offers another terrific resource, including listings for not only qualified hunting and fishing guides but also horseback riding, hiking, kayaking, and more.

HIGHWAYS Montana's major north–south highways include **US 93** in the west, **I-15** in the west-central area, and **US 191** in the east-central area, which meets **US 87.** Major east–west routes include **US 2** in the north and **I-94** to **I-90** in the south.

HIKING You've probably already figured out that you could spend every day of your Montana vacation exploring its great hiking opportunities and barely scratch the surface of what the state has to offer. If you're a serious hiker, your best bet is to pick up one of the many detailed hiking guidebooks out there that will take you to the finest trails in the area or areas you're planning to visit, as the hikes detailed in this book (in the *Hiking* sections) for the most part are short jaunts to special sights as well as sites that will be accessible to travelers of almost any age and fitness level.

HISTORICAL MARKERS AND TRAILS Montana led the way in this department back in 1935, becoming the first state to utilize historical markers to memorialize important events that took place in its past. Of particular note are the markers indicating Lewis and Clark's passage, the **Bozeman Trail,** and those of Native American import, among others. For a detailed tour of the state's historical markers, pick up a copy of *Montana's Historical Highway Markers*, recently updated by the Montana Department of Transportation's Jon Axline. It's available for $10.95 plus shipping through the **Montana Historical Society** by calling 1-800-243-9900.

HISTORY Montana's citizens have long been interested in documenting its history, from the time long before pioneers first traveled to the state to the present. In fact, the state's historical society came into being in 1865—24 years before Montana became a state! In addition to the historical facts, figures, and tidbits about Montana woven throughout this guidebook, you'll find recommendations for selected historical attractions under *To See—Towns, To See—Museums,* and *To See—Historic Landmarks, Places, and Sites,* among other places. To delve more deeply into Montana's history, contact the **Montana Historical Society** (406-444-2694; www .his.state.mt.us), which publishes the magazine *Montana: The Magazine of Western History* and is home to the Montana Historical Society Press, which publishes numerous books on Montana history.

HOT SPRINGS You can visit a number of hot (or warm) springs—some with developed amenities such as therapeutic massage and steam rooms, some au naturel—in Montana, making for a great way to unwind and relax after a busy day of playing. You'll find selected hot springs listed in some regions covered in this guidebook. For a complete listing of all of the state's hot springs, see www.hot springsenthusiast.com/mt.htm.

HUNTING If you want to hunt big game, you can't beat Montana as a destination of choice. Known for its fantastic **elk, deer,** and **antelope** hunting, Montana also sells licenses for hunting **black bear, mountain goat, bighorn sheep,** and other big-game animals, as well as smaller game. Hunting is regulated by **Montana Fish, Wildlife and Parks** (406-444-2535; www.fwp.state.mt.us/hunting/default.aspx), and you'll find detailed information about regulations and more by calling or visiting the Web site.

INDIAN RESERVATIONS Montana has seven Indian Reservations—**Blackfeet, Crow, Flathead, Fort Belknap, Fort Peck, Northern Cheyenne,** and **Rocky Boy's**— which represent the state's 11 tribes— **Assiniboine, Blackfeet, Chippewa-Cree, Crow, Gros Ventre, Kootenai, Northern Cheyenne, Pend d'Oreille, Salish,** and **Sioux.** On Indian lands, tourists will find a variety of attractions, from camping, fishing, and boating opportunities to cultural resources including museums and historic sites, as well as certain annual events that are open to the public, such as powwows and rodeos. Selected Native American attractions and events are highlighted throughout this book; for detailed information visit www.indiannations.visitmt.com.

LEAVE NO TRACE Leave No Trace (1-800-332-4100; www.lnt.org) is a "national nonprofit organization dedicated to promoting and inspiring responsible outdoor recreation through education, research and partnerships." These seven principles of Leave No Trace are general guidelines for minimizing your impact on the land while you travel: "plan ahead and prepare; travel and camp on durable surfaces; dispose of waste properly; leave what you find; minimize campfire impacts; respect wildlife; and be considerate of other visitors." Detailed information on these principles, as well as other relevant information, can be found by calling the organization or visiting the Web site.

LIBRARIES Need to check your e-mail? That seems to be one of the primary functions of public libraries for travelers these days—though don't forget, libraries can be great places to learn about local events and history, to catch up on the latest news, or just to relax and unwind with a great book. You can search for a library near the places you're visiting via the handy directory under "Patron Resources" on the **Montana Library Network's** Web site (http://montana libraries.org).

LICENSE PLATES Montana's most recently issued license plate came out in March 2000. The plate features standout aspects of the state's two distinctive geographical regions: the rugged mountains of the west and the sweeping plains of the east, illustrated in hues of deep bluish purple and gold.

LODGING Lodgings described in this book are focused away from traditional hotels and motels and and instead feature unique offerings in each region, whether the area in question has bed and breakfasts, lodges, resorts, or other types of facilities. The reason for this is that you probably already know what to expect if you book reservations at a typical hotel or motel. When you do find listings for motels in this guide, assume that unique or unusual lodgings are rare or nonexistent in that particular area. For a free, detailed guide to Montana's lodging options, visit www .visitmt.com/tripplanner/campand lodge, or order a hard copy, contained in the free **Montana Travel Planning kit** (1-800-VISITMT; www.visit mt.com).

MAPS If you like to get topographically intimate with the states in which you travel (or you just like looking at detailed maps), pick up a copy of *Montana Atlas & Gazetteer* (DeLorme; available at www.delorme .com), which will guide you to public and private lands, back roads and byways, and even ski areas and fishing spots—and much, much more.

MICROBREWERIES The **Montana State Brewers Association** (www.montanabrewers.org) lists 16 microbreweries located around the state for a tasting treat, including the **Yellowstone Valley Brewing Company** (www.yellowstonevalleybrew .com), "brewed from the waters of the Yellowstone River," in Billings, and the **Kettlehouse Brewing Company** (www.kettlehouse.com) in Missoula, home to hemp beer and more.

MILEAGE Please remember during your trip planning that all mileages given in this book are approximate and subject to a number of inaccuracies due to differences in odometers, source errors, or pilot errors—or all three (yikes!). That having been said, to avoid future misadventures by others, the report of any gross inaccuracies you find would be greatly appreciated; and if you do find yourself off in the middle of nowhere in the middle of the night, you might want to recheck your map and the directions—unless, of course, you planned it that way (which is always a possibility in Montana).

MUSIC You'll find no shortage of music festivals and events to keep you humming and drumming to the beat in Montana, whether you prefer orchestral concerts, bluegrass, rock, choral music, or something else. One annual event of note is the **Bitterroot Valley Bluegrass Festival** (406-363-1250; www.bluegrassfestival.org), in Hamilton, which has been putting on a great show for visitors and families for more than 15 years. In addition to music festivals highlighted under *Special Events* throughout this book, you can find an up-to-date listing of upcoming venues at www.visitmt.com/tripplanner/events by selecting "Music/Concerts" from the drop-down menu under "Select a Type of Event."

NATIONAL FORESTS Montana became one of the first areas in the country to have its forests protected, via an 1897 proclamation by President Grover Cleveland that created 13 timberland preserves (future national forests), three of which lie partially or wholly in Montana: **Bitterroot, Flat-head,** and **Lewis and Clark.** Today, 10 national forests exist within Montana: **Beaverhead–Deerlodge** (southwest; 3.3 million acres), **Bitterroot** (southwest; 1.6 million acres), **Custer** (south-central and southeast; 2.5 million acres), **Flathead** (northwest; 3.6 million acres), **Gallatin** (south-central; 1.7 million acres), **Helena** (west-central; 975,000 acres), **Kootenai** (northwest; 2.2 million acres), **Lewis and Clark** (central and north-central; 1.8 million acres), and **Lolo** (west; 2.1 million acres). Montana also has two national recreation areas: **Bighorn Canyon National Recreation Area** (southeast; 120,000 acres, three-quarters of which lie in Montana, the rest in Wyoming); and **Rattlesnake National Recreation Area** (west; 59,000 acres). Detailed information about all of these forests can be found in the appropriate regional section of the text.

NATIONAL PARKS AND MONUMENTS With a bit more than 1 million acres of land within its boundaries, **Glacier National Park** has been a premier Montana destination since its designation as a national park in 1910. The park's name derives not from the small glaciers found there today (which are melting at an alarmingly quick rate and are likely to vanish completely in a generation or two) but from the giant glaciers responsible for carving out the park's remarkable geological features about 20,000 years ago. Together with **Waterton Lakes National Park** in Canada, Glacier National Park is known as **Waterton–Glacier International Peace Park,** the first park of this type in the world.

In addition to Glacier National Park, 168,707 acres of **Yellowstone**

2513) or **Beartooth Paddler's Society** (406-252-3724; www.sun shine-sports.com/events/club/43). A great online resource is available at **Big Sky Fishing.com** (www.bigsky fishing.com), which describes rivers in great detail, including potential put-in points located along each river. There are also many books that detail paddling destinations throughout the state, such as *Paddling Montana*, by Hank and Carol Fischer (Falcon, 1999).

National Park (which has 2.2 million acres of land in total, most of which lie in Wyoming) and three of the park's five entrances lie in southwestern Montana. Montana is also home to the **Little Bighorn Battlefield National Monument, Pompeys Pillar National Monument,** and the **Upper Missouri River Breaks National Monument.**

PADDLING/FLOATING Whatever kind of paddling or floating you're interested in, be it kayaking class V whitewater, canoeing on a pristine lake, or paddling down a mellow river in an inflatable raft, Montana's rivers and lakes will certainly provide you with ample opportunities to float your boat. Most of the adventures described under the *To Do—Paddling/Floating* headings of this book are suitable for the mere dabbler in the aforementioned genres and often include a recommended local guiding service as well. If you're a serious kayaker, rafter, or canoeist—or you want a recommendation on where to take a lesson or reserve a guided trip—a good place to find information and other like-minded souls is by contacting **Montana Paddlers** (406-994-

PUBLIC LANDS In Montana lie more than 28 million acres of national lands, including one national park; more than 8 million acres of land administered by the **Bureau of Land Management** (BLM); and plentiful state-owned lands that include 42 state parks. (See also *Bureau of Land Management (BLM) Lands, National Forests,* and *State Parks* in this section.)

REST AREAS The **Montana Department of Transportation** (MDT) lists 51 rest areas around the state at www .mdt.state.mt.us/travinfo/restarea.html.

RIVERS More than 15 rivers carve pathways throughout Montana, including two nationally designated **Wild and Scenic Rivers,** the **Flathead** and the **Missouri** (for more about Wild and Scenic Rivers, visit www.nps.gov/rivers/about.html), as well as too many creeks and streams to enumerate. Many of Montana's rivers feature prime fishing, rafting, and paddling opportunities, but they are also in need of protection and preservation for future generations. For more information about Montana's rivers, contact **Montana River Action** (406-587-9181; www.montana riveraction.org).

ROAD REPORTS The **Montana Department of Transportation (MDT) Traveler Information** Web site (www.mdt.state.mt.us/travinfo) provides current information about travel advisories, road closures, accidents, and much, much more, including live images from cameras around the state. You can also call 1-800-226-7623 for statewide road conditions.

ROCK CLIMBING Though it's not a rock climbing hot spot—not yet, anyway—Montana does offer plenty of vertical terrain for the visiting climber, from boulder gardens to lengthy alpine traditional routes, and everything in between. For details on Montana's rock climbing opportunities, a good resource to begin with is **RockClimbing.com's** (www.rockclimbing.com) listing for Montana. Want to hire a guide? One option is **Reach Your Peak Guiding and Instruction** (406-578-2155; www.climbmontana.com), P.O. Box 78, Wilsall 59086.

ROCKHOUNDING Rockhounding—and even gold panning—opportunities abound in Montana, as evidenced by its historical ties to the mining industry. **BLM Montana Dakotas** has a specific Web page devoted to

rockhounding rules and regulations: www.mt.blm.gov/faq/rockhound.html. A terrific general resource for rockhounders can be found online at www.fs.fed.us/oonf/minerals/rockhound.htm, with details on rules and regulations for rockhounds. For help on finding great places to rockhound in Montana, a copy of *Rockhounding Montana,* by Robert Feldman (Falcon, 1996), should help you get started.

RODEOS If the idea of watching bucking broncos, bull riders, and barrel racers in action sounds like a fun time to you (as it does to many Montanans and visitors alike), you'll find no shortage of action of this type to entertain you in Montana. The state hosts numerous rodeos throughout the year around the state, with events happening almost daily in the summer season. The **Northern Rodeo Association** Web site (www.northernrodeo.com) provides an updated schedule of its sanctioned events. You'll find listings for more Montana rodeos at www.visitmt.com/tripplanner/events. Select "Rodeos" from the drop-down menu.

RV PARKS If you have a home on wheels, you probably already know some of the best resources for finding RV parks around the country—the Internet is rife with listings. A great place to start your search for a place to park and hook up is the **Campground Owners Association of Montana** (www.campingmontana.com), which provides an interactive map to help you narrow your choices. **Travel Montana** (www.visitmt.com) has a listing of RV dump stations on the Web site under "Getting Around." (See also *Campgrounds* in this section.)

SNOW SPORTS Montana offers plenty in the way of winter activities, including skiing—both downhill and cross-country—snowmobiling, snowboarding, ice-skating, ice fishing, and dogsledding, among others. In addition to the individual entries you'll find listed under *To Do—Snow Sports* in this book, **Montana Winter** (www.wintermt.com) provides detailed, updated information about all of your favorite snow sports, as well as comprehensive information about planning a trip to Montana in the winter. You can also order a hard copy of the **Montana Winter Planning Kit** online at the Web site or by calling 1-800-847-4868.

SPEED LIMITS AND SEAT BELTS On the interstate, both day and night, the speed limit in Montana is 75 miles per hour, with the exception of urban areas (Billings, Great Falls, and Missoula), where it drops to 65 miles per hour. On two-lane highways, the speed limit is 70 miles per hour in the daytime and 65 miles per hour at night. US 93 is the exception to this rule, with the speed limit being 65 miles per hour at all times. Seat belts are required to be worn at all times by every occupant of a vehicle. Please be courteous—if you're driving exceptionally slowly (say, 10 miles per hour below the speed limit), and traffic builds up behind you, make an effort to pull over safely and allow the other drivers to pass.

STATE CAPITAL Helena is the capital of Montana.

STATE PARKS Montana has 42 state parks administered by **Montana Fish, Wildlife and Parks' State Parks Division** (406-444-2535; www.fwp.state.mt.us/parks/default.aspx), all of which are free of charge for residents of Montana (and only $2 to $5 a day, and $25 for an annual permit, for nonresidents). Many of these lovely places are highlighted under *To See* and *To Do* throughout this work, as they provide opportunities, including camping, fishing, hiking, picnicking, learning, and much, much more.

STATE THIS AND THAT Every state has them—those symbols, officially designated somethings, and nicknames that distinguish them. Some of Montana's include: nickname—**Treasure State;** motto—*Oro y Plata* (Spanish for "gold and silver"); state flower—**bitterroot;** state animal—**grizzly bear;** state bird—**western meadowlark;** state tree—**ponderosa pine;** state gemstones—**agate and sapphire;** state fish—**cutthroat trout;** and state fossil—*Maiasaura,* or **duck-billed dinosaur.**

STATISTICS Montana is the fourth-largest state in area at 145,556 square miles. The state ranks 44th in population, with 902,195 residents (according to the 2000 census). It ranks 48th in the United States in population density, with six people per square mile. The highest point in Montana is

Granite Peak at 12,799 feet; the lowest is where the Kootenai River flows into Idaho at 1,820 feet. Montana became the 41st state to be admitted to the union, on November 8, 1889.

TOURIST RAILROADS In addition to **Amtrak's Empire Builder** line (see *Amtrak* in this section), Montana has several other tourist railroads for those who enjoy such outings. You'll find selected rail tours listed for specific areas under *To Do—Unique Adventures*. For more information, go to www.visitmt.com/tripplanner/thingstodo and click on "Rail Tours," or call 1-800-847-4868.

TRAVEL INFORMATION The best resource for statewide travel information is **Travel Montana** (1-800-847-4868; www.visitmt.com), which offers free vacation packets and a plethora of additional resources for travelers. For local and regional contacts to specific areas of the state, look to the *Guidance* sections of this book. Montana has easily accessed visitor information centers spread around the state, some of which operate seasonally (May through September) and some year-round. For a complete listing and contact information, go to www.visitmt.com/tripplanner/planning assistance/vic.htm or call 1-800-847-4868.

WEATHER The most reliable resource I've found for accurate weather forecasts is the **National Weather Service** (www.nws.noaa.gov). Just enter the city and state name, and you'll have an up-to-date forecast and current conditions at your fingertips. The highest temperature recorded in Montana was 117 degrees Fahrenheit in Glendive back in 1893; the lowest

was –70 degrees Fahrenheit at Rogers Pass in 1954. (See also *Climate* in this section.)

WILDERNESS AREAS Montana has 15 nationally designated wilderness areas, providing numerous recreation opportunities in pristine settings; be sure you know the rules and regulations governing each one, and the necessary outdoors skills, before you visit. As a general guideline, you should practice the principles of **Leave No Trace** (1-800-332-4100; www.lnt.org; see entry in this section) when visiting wilderness areas. You can find a complete list of Montana's wilderness areas by going to www .wilderness.net, clicking on "Explore Wilderness Data," and entering *Montana* in the search criteria. You'll get a list of live links to all of Montana's designated wilderness areas, each of which yields detailed information about the area in question.

WILDFLOWERS If you love wildflowers and other native plants, Montana's lush abundance of both will delight you, from the pink hues of the state flower, the lovely **bitterroot,** to the bright yellow **arrowleaf balsamroot**

and deep indigo of **lupine,** among many others. You'll find many of these flowers—and other flora of the state—in the excellent book *Plants of the Rocky Mountains,* by Linda Kershaw, Andy MacKinnon, and Jim Pojar (Lone Pine, 1998). For those with an amateur interest in plants and flowers, this book will be an indispensable resource, with its high-quality photography, its keys to plants and flowers, and its well-written descriptions about each plant, which include interesting trivia about historical uses and more. **Montana Plant Life** (www.montana.plant-life.org) provides a fantastic, interactive online resource with a guide to 250 species in the state, including edible, poisonous, native, and introduced plants. They also sell a CD ($19.95 plus $3.95 for shipping and handling) with more than 750 species detailed (and more than 3,000 images), available for purchase on the site or via U.S. mail by sending a check or money order to Montana Plant Life, P.O. Box 1144, Emigrant 59027.

WILDLIFE Montana's abundance of wildlife (Montana claims to have greater variety than any other state in the Lower 48) means that you'd be hard-pressed—or just plain distracted —to escape the state's borders without multiple sightings of the birds and beasts that inhabit its lands. Some residents include **mountain goats, bighorn sheep, elk, deer, bison, pronghorn, bears, wolves, loons, eagles, geese** . . . the list goes on and on. If wildlife-watching tops your agenda, don't leave home without reading "Seeing Wildlife Wonders in Montana," provided by **Travel Montana** at www.wildlife.visitmt.com; it includes guidelines for wildlife view-

ing, as well as what, how, and where to watch. Another great resource, provided by the **Montana Fish, Wildlife and Parks' Wildlife Division** (406-444-2535), can be found at www.fwp.state.mt.us/wildthings/ default.asp.

WILDLIFE REFUGES Montana is home to more than 20 designated wildlife refuges (14 of which are national wildlife refuges) and numerous additional wildlife management areas. In addition to those refuges highlighted in this book (usually under *Wilder Places*), detailed information about each national refuge, including directions, recreation opportunities, contact information, and more, can be found by clicking on "MT" at http://refuges.fws.gov/ profiles/bystate.cfm. Another good source of information, provided by **Travel Montana** (1-800-847-4868), can be found at www.visitmt.com/trip planner/wheretogo/refuge.htm.

WINERIES For those who love their wine, at least four wineries lie in Montana: **Lolo Peak** (406-549-1111; www.lolopeak.com), near Missoula; **Mission Mountain Winery** (406-849-5524; www.missionmountain winery.com), near Polson; **Painted Rocks Winery** (406-349-9463; www.paintedrocks-winery.com), near Darby; and **Rolling Hills Winery** (406-787-5787; www.rollinghills winery.com), near Culbertson. Detailed information can be found under the appropriate *To See— Wineries* sections in this book.

WOMEN'S FIRSTS In 1916, **Jeannette Rankin** of Montana became the first woman to be elected to the U.S. House of Representatives.

ZOOS The state's zoos and nature centers are distinctive in their attention to creating quality natural habitats for the inhabitants and in their drive to educate visitors about those inhabitants, many of which include native Montana wildlife specimens that cannot be returned to the wild for a variety of reasons. You'll find listings for individual zoos and nature centers under *To See—For Families* in this book. For more information, go to www.visitmt.com/tripplanner/thingstodo/zoo.htm.

NORTHWEST MONTANA: GLACIER COUNTRY AND WATERTON–GLACIER INTERNATIONAL PEACE PARK

GLACIER COUNTRY

First and foremost, Glacier Country probably makes you think of Glacier National Park, which together with Canada's Waterton Lakes National Park forms Waterton–Glacier International Peace Park—undoubtedly the region's most popular and visited destination. Thus this region includes two chapters, and the second one details specific resources that will help you plan a visit to the "Crown Jewel of the Continent," with all of the typical information included in this book for each of Montana's travel regions. Listings for East Glacier Park, St. Mary, and West Glacier Park appear in this special section on the park, as most people staying in these towns are probably visiting this region primarily to experience Waterton–Glacier and all it has to offer.

Beyond Waterton–Glacier International Peace Park, however, lies a vacation wonderland for travelers with all sorts of interests, whether you're an outdoor activity junkie, a history buff, or a leisure seeker. Thus it would almost be criminal to forgo exploring beyond the boundaries of the park if you will be in the region for any significant amount of time; you would most certainly miss out on an incredible array of interesting, one-of-a-kind, and/or exhilarating attractions—most with a lot fewer people than you'll see in the park.

For those with an interest in history, Glacier Country is rife with both Native American and more recent pioneer history. Two enormous Indian reservations lie within this area: the Blackfeet Indian Reservation, home to the Blackfeet Nation; and the Flathead Indian Reservation, home to the Confederated Salish and Kootenai Tribes. Both of these tribes once roamed much larger expanses of territory in this area, and now they strive to preserve their traditions and cultures, often in the face of adversity, in today's modern world. Visitors can learn a tremendous amount about the area's Native Americans through a wide array of attractions, including museums such as The People's Center and the Museum of

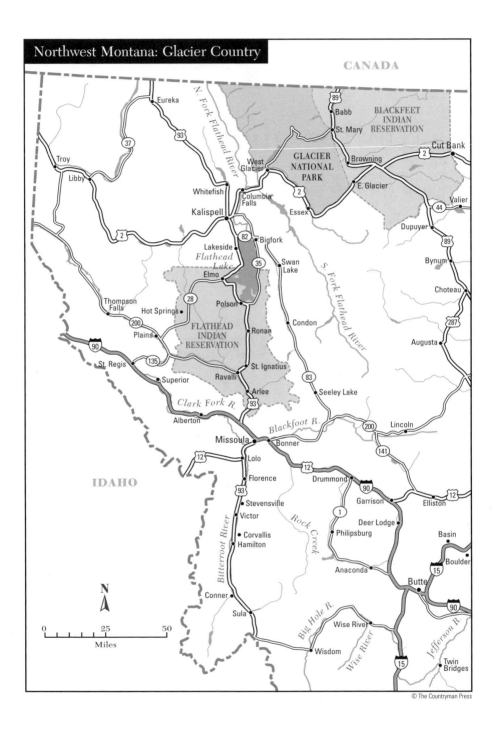

Northwest Montana: Glacier Country

CANADA

Eureka

N. Fork Flathead River

89
Babb
St. Mary
BLACKFEET
INDIAN
RESERVATION

37

93

Troy

Libby

GLACIER
NATIONAL
PARK

West
Glacier

Browning

Cut Bank

2

E. Glacier

Whitefish

Columbia
Falls

2

Valier

Kalispell

Essex

44

2

Dupuyer

82
Bigfork

89

Lakeside
Flathead
Lake

35
Swan
Lake

S. Fork Flathead River

Bynum

Elmo

Choteau

Thompson
Falls

Hot Springs

28

Polson

Condon

287

200

Plains

Ronan

Augusta

90

135

FLATHEAD
INDIAN
RESERVATION

St. Regis

Superior

Ravalli

St. Ignatius

83

Seeley Lake

Arlee

93

Clark Fork R.

Alberton

Blackfoot R.

Lincoln

Missoula

Bonner

200

12

Lolo

141

Florence

12

Drummond

Elliston

12

93

Stevensville

IDAHO

Garrison

90

Victor

1

Deer Lodge

Corvallis

Philipsburg

Basin

Hamilton

Rock Creek

Boulder

Anaconda

15

Butte

Conner

Bitterroot River

Sula

Wise River

Big Hole R.

Wise River

90

Wisdom

15

Jefferson R.

Twin
Bridges

N

0   25   50
Miles

© The Countryman Press

the Plains Indian, places such as Council Grove State Park and the National Bison Range, and unique cultural adventures and events such as Native Edventures and the Annual North American Indian Days.

More recently, this area saw exploration from the Lewis and Clark expedition. You can walk in the footsteps of the Corps of Discovery at Camp Disappointment and Travelers' Rest State Park. Truly avid enthusiasts can stay a night or a week at the Lolo Trail Center, which includes numerous exhibitions and even Lewis and Clark–related children's activities; join with Missoula-based Rocky Mountain Discovery Tours for a multiday, multistate tour following the trail of the explorers; or attend Cut Bank's Lewis and Clark Festival, held in July.

Following the explorations by Lewis and Clark, this area saw a gradual influx of white settlers, starting with the establishment of the first permanent white settlement in Montana—St. Mary's Mission—in 1841, at the present-day location of Fort Owen State Park. The influence and impact of the early settlers—and their interactions, both positive and negative, with the native population—are in evidence throughout this region. You'll find their stories chronicled in museums and at historic sites, including an array of museums and building at historic Fort Missoula, located in the region's largest city, Missoula.

With just under 60,000 inhabitants, Missoula is a big city for Montana; but like most of Montana's "big cities," it retains a small-town feel. The charming, bustling downtown is clean and friendly, with a plethora of fine dining and casual eating establishments, shopping opportunities, cultural attractions, and its very own carousel and distinctive play area that certainly shouldn't be missed, no matter what your age (I saw more heads of gray than of any other color riding the merry-go-round on my visit!). A wonderful riverside path parallels the Clark Fork River as it runs through the city, making for an easy way to get a sense of where things are while also getting some exercise.

If you want more exercise than a jaunt on a riverside path, you'll have plenty of opportunities in Glacier Country, no matter what the season—no fewer than five downhill ski areas offer you a range of skiing opportunities, including Montana Snowbowl, just northwest of Missoula. You can enjoy a full-service resort with all of the amenities by planning a vacation to Big Mountain Ski and Summer Resort, north of Whitefish; or you can escape crowds and frills both and test yourself on the mostly expert terrain of Turner Mountain Ski Area, located in the remote northwestern corner of the state. If you're not into downhill skiing, you'll find a ton of additional winter recreation activities, such as an abundance of cross-country ski trails and snowmobile trails crisscrossing the more than 8 million acres of land contained in the four national forests of this region—which of course provide tremendous hiking, mountain biking, and horseback riding opportunities in warmer weather.

In summer and winter alike, anglers will find a lifetime's worth of waters to explore in Glacier Country. Due to the vast quantity of fishable waters, only basic information—contact information, general location, access information, paddling or floating options, and major species of fish present—are listed for five of the largest rivers in this region. You'll also find information about rivers in the *To Do—Paddling/Floating* section, as well as within the text for each of the five major rivers selected. For lakes, turn to the *To Do—Boating* section—but be aware that once again, the lakes included there are by no means inclusive; instead, they feature some of the region's more developed recreation areas. The "See also" listings at the end of the section point you to further options, but a look at any map of the region will show you hundreds and hundreds of other boating and fishing destinations, many of them more remote.

Likewise, with so many camping options available in national forests and state parks, not to mention within Glacier National Park, as well as dispersed camping opportunities and private campgrounds, all of them cannot be included. Under *To Do—Camping*, then, is a basic list of the national forest camping opportunities (as well as cross-references to other developed campgrounds). For each national forest, you'll find information about the number of campgrounds in each ranger district, detailed information about one selected campground, and the contact information for that ranger district. If you know in advance that most campgrounds are open only seasonally (usually May or June through the beginning or end of September) and arm yourself with a decent road atlas, you should have no trouble locating other campgrounds in each district—once you know the general location in which you'd like to spend the night. You can always simply call the ranger district for detailed information as well.

By now, you probably realize that this is a region packed full of incredible outdoor attractions beyond the main draw of Waterton–Glacier International Peace Park. In fact, were it not for Waterton–Glacier, you would most likely have heard of this region due to Flathead Lake (if you've never heard of it, skip down to *Natural Wonders* to fill yourself in), which hosts its own complete array of tourist services and attractions. Or perhaps you'd have caught wind of the Seeley-Swan Scenic Drive with its corridor of lakes and all of their related activities and services. Then again, maybe the giant cedars of Ross Creek Cedar Grove Scenic Area would have captivated your attention . . . So whatever your travel plans are, visit Waterton–Glacier, for sure, but try to budget time to explore the lesser-known but similarly fantastic terrain and attractions to be found throughout the region known as Glacier Country.

GUIDANCE **Bigfork Area Chamber of Commerce** (406-837-5888; www .bigfork.org), 8155 MT 35, P.O. Box 237, Bigfork 59911.

Bitterroot Valley Chamber of Commerce (406-363-2400; www.bvchamber .com), 105 E. Main Street, Hamilton 59840.

Blackfeet Nation–Town of Browning (town: 406-338-2344; nation: 406-338-7406; 406-338-7521; www.blackfeetnation.com and www.browningmontana .com), 124 2nd Avenue NW, P.O. Box 469 (town) or P.O. Box 850 (nation), Browning 59417.

Columbia Falls Chamber of Commerce (406-892-2072; www.columbia fallschamber.com), US 2, 1 mile north of intersection with MT 206, P.O. Box 312, Columbia Falls 59912.

Confederated Salish and Kootenai Tribes (1-888-835-8766; 406-675-2700), 51383 US 93 N., P.O. Box 278, Pablo 59855.

Cut Bank Area Chamber of Commerce (406-873-4041; www.cut

bankchamber.com), 725 E. Main Street, P.O. Box 1243, Cut Bank 59427.

Eureka Chamber of Commerce (406-889-4636; www.welcome2 eureka.com), P.O. Box 186, Eureka 59917.

Flathead Convention and Visitor Bureau (406-756-9091; www.fcvb .org), 15 Depot Park, Kalispell, 59901.

Flathead Indian Reservation. See Confederated Salish and Kootenai Tribes, above.

LOGAN CREEK IN GLACIER NATIONAL PARK

Glacier Country Regional Tourism Commission (1-800-338-5072; www .glaciermt.com), 836 Holt Drive, Suite 320, P.O. Box 1035, Bigfork 59911.

Hot Springs Chamber of Commerce (406-741-2662; 406-741-2751; www .ronan.net/~hscofc), 216 Main Street, P.O. Box 580, Hot Springs 59845.

Kalispell Chamber of Commerce (406-758-2800; www.kalispellchamber .com), 15 Depot Park, Kalispell 59901.

Lakeside–Somers Chamber of Commerce (406-844-3715; www.lakeside chamber.com), P.O. Box 177, Lakeside 59922.

Libby Area Chamber of Commerce (406-293-4167; www.libbychamber.org), 905 W. 9th Street, P.O. Box 704, Libby 59923.

Mineral County Chamber of Commerce (406-822-4891; www.thebigsky.net/ MineralChamber), 100 2nd Avenue E., P.O. Box 483, Superior 59872.

Missoula Chamber of Commerce (406-543-6623; www.missoulachamber .com), 825 E. Front Street, P.O. Box 7577, Missoula 59807.

Missoula Convention and Visitors Bureau (406-532-3250; www.missoula cvb.org), 1121 E. Broadway, Suite 103, Missoula 59802.

Plains–Paradise Chamber of Commerce (406-826-4700), 108 E. Railroad (Rocky Mountain Bank), P.O. Box 1531, Plains 59859.

Polson Chamber of Commerce (406-883-5969; www.polsonchamber.com), #4 2nd Avenue E., P.O. Box 667, Polson 59860.

Ronan Chamber of Commerce–Mission Mountain County Visitor's Center (406-676-8300), 207 Main Street SW, Ronan 59864.

St. Ignatius Chamber Visitor Center (406-745-3501), P.O. Box 236, located in the Stoneheart Inn Bed & Breakfast at 26 N. Main Street, St. Ignatius 59865.

Seeley Lake Area Chamber of Commerce (406-677-2880; www.seeley lakechamber.com), MT 83 mile marker 12.5 (just south of town), P.O. Box 516, Seeley Lake 59868.

Swan Lake Chamber of Commerce (406-886-2080), MT 83, P.O. Box 5199, Swan Lake 59911.

Thompson Falls Chamber of Commerce (406-827-4930), P.O. Box 493, Thompson Falls 59873.

Troy Chamber of Commerce (406-295-1064), P.O. Box 3005, Troy 59935.

Whitefish Chamber of Commerce (1-877-862-3548; 406-862-3501; www .whitefishchamber.org), 520 E. 2nd Street, Whitefish 59937.

GETTING THERE Missoula lies along I-90. Hamilton is south of Missoula on US 93. From south to north, St. Ignatius, Ronan, Polson, Lakeside, Somers, Kalispell, and Whitefish lie north of Missoula on US 93. From east to west, Cut Bank, Browning, Glacier National Park, Columbia Falls, Kalispell, Libby, and Troy lie on US 2. The Flathead Indian Reservation lies north of Missoula, with US 93 and MT 28 running through it. The Blackfeet Reservation lies just east of Glacier National Park, with US 2 and US 89 as the major roads through it. US 2 and US 89 also lead to Glacier National Park. Bigfork is southeast of Kalispell on MT 35. Swan Lake and Seeley Lake are south of Kalispell on MT 83. Plains and Thompson Falls lie on MT 200, northwest of Missoula.

See also *Airports, Amtrak, Bus Service,* and *Travel Information* in "What's Where in Montana."

MEDICAL EMERGENCY **Blackfeet Community Hospital** (406-338-6194), Hospital Circle, Browning.

Clark Fork Valley Hospital (1-800-826-3601; 406-826-4800), 110 Kruger Road, Plains.

Community Medical Center (406-728-4100), 2827 Fort Missoula Road, Missoula.

Kalispell Regional Medical Center (406-752-5111), 310 Sunnyview Lane, Kalispell.

Marcus Daly Memorial Hospital (406-363-2211), 1200 Westwood Drive, Hamilton.

Mineral Community Hospital (406-822-4841), 1208 6th Avenue E., Superior.

Northern Rockies Medical Center (406-873-2251), 802 2nd Street SE, Cut Bank.

North Valley Hospital (1-888-815-5528; 406-863-3500), 6575 US 93 S., Whitefish.

St. John's Lutheran Hospital (406-293-0100), 350 Louisiana Avenue, Libby.

St. Joseph Medical Center (406-883-5377), 6 13th Avenue E., Polson.

St. Luke Community Hospital (406-676-4441), 107 6th Avenue SW, Ronan.

St. Patrick Hospital and Health Sciences Center (406-543-7271), 500 W. Broadway, Missoula.

✳ To See

TOWNS **Bigfork** lies on the northeast shore of Flathead Lake on MT 35. If you love original artwork, you need to schedule a stop or a stay in Bigfork, for this small town plays host to numerous contemporary artists of note. Throughout the town you'll find **art galleries galore** in which you'll discover original artwork on display and for sale. Bigfork is also home to a **live summer theater,** fine restaurants, and lodgings. It also provides access to surrounding outdoor recreational opportunities, making it a great vacation base if you prefer to split your time between cultural and outdoor pursuits.

Browning, situated at the junction of US 2 and US 89, serves as the unofficial eastern gateway to Glacier National Park. Located on the 1.5-million-acre Blackfeet Indian Reservation, Browning is the reservation's administrative center as well as an activity hub for visitors. The town is home to the **Museum of the Plains Indian** (see *Museums*), hosts **North American Indian Days** (see *Special Events*), and also provides access to abundant recreational opportunities both on and off the reservation.

Hot Springs, southwest of Flathead Lake via MT 28, is well worth the side trip if you enjoy sampling the supposed healing powers of natural mineral waters bubbling from deep within the earth. Located on the Flathead Indian Reservation, this town is home to hot springs that have been likened to the more well-known waters of Germany's Baden-Baden. Long used by Native Americans, the waters of the mineral springs that gave this town its name can be accessed today via several privately owned businesses, as well as at a public facility on the edge of town (limited maintenance; for contact information, see *Guidance*). (See also **Hot Springs Spa** and **Symes Hot Springs Hotel** under *To Do—Hot Springs.*)

Libby lies at the junction of US 2 and MT 37 in the northwest corner of Montana, smack-dab in the midst of the gorgeous **Kootenai National Forest** (see *Wilder Places—Forests*), with its plethora of developed Forest Service campgrounds (see *To Do—Camping*). Among other recreational pursuits, incredible fishing and paddling/floating opportunities await the visitor to this area—first and foremost, in the **Kootenai River** (see also *Fishing* and *Paddling/Floating* under *To Do*). **Rock climbers** will find 200 established routes at Stone Hill, located on MT 37. Below you'll find listed a number of other outdoor activities in the area surrounding Libby. The town also has a seasonal **Heritage Museum** (406-293-7521), 1367 US 2 S., which details local history.

Pablo, south of Polson on US 93, is the administrative center for the 1.3-million-acre **Flathead Indian Reservation,** home of the Confederated Salish and Kootenai Tribes. The reservation includes a portion of **Flathead Lake** (see *To Do—Boating*), as well as the **National Bison Range** (see *Wilder Places—Wildlife Refuges and Areas*). Striving to preserve cultural heritage is a top priority for both tribes. Visitors can learn more by stopping at **The People's Center** (see *Museums*) or the **Flathead Indian Museum and Trading Post** (406-745-2951), located south of Pablo at 1 Museum Lane in St. Ignatius.

Polson is a lakeshore community on the southern end of Flathead Lake, at the junction of US 93 and MT 35. In addition to providing easy access to the surrounding recreational opportunities of the Flathead Indian Reservation, Polson is home to an abundance of shopping, lodging, and dining facilities. At the **Polson–Flathead Historical Museum** (406-883-3049), 708 Main Street, and the

Miracle of America Museum, Inc. (406-883-6804), 58176 US 93, you can learn about the area's culture and history.

Seeley Lake is northeast of Missoula on MT 83, a road that provides a scenic, slower route through lake-riddled forests and wilderness areas to the Kalispell area and Glacier National Park. In and around Seeley Lake, you'll find **all-season recreational opportunities,** including boating, camping, fishing, hiking, horseback riding, mountain biking, paddling/floating, swimming, skiing, snowmobiling, and more. Seeley Lake makes a great base from which to experience all that this outdoor-lover's paradise has to offer, with numerous lodging options, dining facilities, and additional in-town amenities, including a golf course and shopping.

MUSEUMS ⅋ **Aerial Fire Depot Smokejumper Visitor Center** (406-329-4934; www.fs.fed.us/fire/people/smokejumpers/missoula), 5756 W. Broadway Street, Missoula. Open daily Memorial Day through Labor Day 8:30 AM–5 PM (call for off-season hours and reservations); free. Here at the largest base in the United States, learn about the courageous men and women who jump from planes to fight forest fires. The visitor center includes dioramas, videos, and exhibits explaining various aspects of fire suppression and the role of smoke jumpers. Guided tours (45–60 minutes; free) to the parachute loft and training facilities are available as well.

⅋ **Art Museum of Missoula** (406-728-0447; www.artmissoula.org), 335 N. Pattee Street, Missoula. Open Tuesday through Friday 10 AM–5 PM, Saturday 10 AM–3 PM; free. Until the 2006 completion of renovations and expansion of the museum's Carnegie Library building on Pattee Street, the art museum will be temporarily housed on a floor of the Florence Building (111 N. Higgins Street). Here you can view a rotating contemporary art exhibition, and the museum holds educational programs. The renovated and expanded facility will provide increased visitor services as well as increased exhibition space, where the museum will display items from its own collection—including its distinguished Contemporary American Indian Art Collection—as well as from the Missoula County Art Collection.

⅋ **Glacier County Historical Museum** (406-873-4904; www.glaciercountymt .org/museum), 107 Old Kevin Highway, Cut Bank. Open Tuesday through Friday 10 AM–5 PM, Saturday noon–5 PM; free. This regional museum, run by the Glacier County Historical Society, details the history of longtime area residents, the Blackfeet Indians, as well as the area's original homesteaders and the 1930s oil boom. The main museum building contains exhibits relating to these topics. In addition, several historic structures around the museum include an oil derrick and a windmill.

⅋ **Historical Museum at Fort Missoula** (406-728-3476; www.fortmissoula museum.org), Building 322 at Fort Missoula, enter via South Street (across from Big Sky High School), Missoula. Open Memorial Day through Labor Day Monday through Saturday 10 AM–5 PM, Sunday noon–5 PM; open Labor Day through Memorial Day Tuesday through Sunday noon–5 PM; $3 adults, $2 seniors, $1 students, $10 maximum per family. More than 30 years ago a collective community effort resulted in the formation of this museum, which preserves the remains of historic Fort Missoula—including 13 structures—on 32 acres of land. The fort was constructed in 1877 as a permanent military outpost. Since that time, it has also served as a military training center, as regional headquarters for the Civilian Conservation Corps (CCC), and as an alien detention center, as well as a place for holding soldiers court-martialed following World War II. Today the museum's historic collection exceeds 20,000 artifacts, many of which are included in its long-term exhibits. The museum also regularly displays temporary exhibits. (See also Montana Natural History Center and Rocky Mountain Museum of Military History, below; and Northern Rockies Heritage Center under *Historic Landmarks, Places, and Sites.*)

HISTORICAL MUSEUM AT FORT MISSOULA

& Hockaday Museum of Art (406-755-5268; www.hockadaymuseum.org), 302 2nd Avenue E., Kalispell. Open Monday through Saturday 10 AM–6 PM, Sunday noon–4 PM (summer); open Tuesday through Saturday 10 AM–5 PM (off-season); $5 adults, $4 seniors, $2 students, $1 children ages 6–18, children 5 and under free. Housed in the historic Carnegie Library building (a registered historic site), Kalispell's art museum rotates exhibitions on a monthly basis, featuring works by local, regional, national, and international artists of note. The museum also has a permanent collection focused on regional artists that includes works by the museum's namesake, Hugh Hockaday, as well as Leonard Lopp and Bob Scriver, among others. Children will find the museum's hands-on Discovery Room a welcome haven for interactive art-related fun. (See also Arts in the Park in *Special Events.*)

& Montana Natural History Center (406-327-0405; www.thenature center.org), Building T-2, Fort Missoula, enter via South Street (across from Big Sky High School), Missoula. Open Monday through Friday 9 AM–5 PM; free. Dedicated to educating the public about Montana's natural history and the importance of protecting, preserving, and understanding nature, this museum includes a native plant garden, a self-guided nature trail, and natural history exhibits. The

HOCKADAY MUSEUM OF ART

museum itself is housed in the historic Post Headquarters Building at Fort Missoula. (See also Historical Museum at Fort Missoula, above; Rocky Mountain Museum of Military History, below; and Northern Rockies Heritage Center under *Historic Landmarks, Places, and Sites.*)

Museum of the Plains Indian (406-338-2230; www.doi.gov/iacb/museum/museum_plains.html), junction of US 2 and US 89, Browning. Open daily June through September, 9 AM–4:45 PM; open October through May Monday through Friday 10 AM–4:30 PM; $4 adults, $1 students ages 6–12, children 5 and under free, $1 per person for groups of 10 or more. If you are interested in Native American culture, past and present, a stop at this museum is essential—and convenient, as it's right on the way to Glacier National Park. Founded in 1941, this museum's exhibits center around the artwork of regional Native Americans, both past and present. Peoples from the Northern Plains represented include Arapaho, Assiniboine, Blackfeet, Chippewa, Cree, Crow, Flathead, Nez Perce, Northern Cheyenne, Sioux, and Shoshone. Remember that in these cultures, artwork has been and continues to be functional as well, so you'll see not only art for art's sake but also horseback riding gear, clothing, bags, weapons, toys, and household implements, among other items. (See also Lodgepole Gallery and Tipi Village under *Lodging—Other Options.*)

& **Ninepipes Museum of Early Montana** (406-644-3435; www.ninepipes.org), 40962 US 93, Charlo (6 miles south of Ronan). Open daily Memorial Day through Labor Day 8 AM–6 PM; open Labor Day through Memorial Day Wednesday through Sunday 11 AM–5 PM; $4 adults, $3 students, $2 children ages 6–12, children 5 and under free. Established in 1998, this museum keeps alive the culture and heritage of the surrounding Flathead Indian Reservation as well as early Montanans. As such, exhibits include both Native American and early settler themes. The Gallery of the Art of the Old West includes works by C. M. Russell, E. S. Paxson, and others noted for depicting Montana in pioneer times. Native American culture is captured in an extensive collection of beadwork, a life-size diorama of an Indian camp, and an impressive collection that includes weaponry, clothing, and more. The grounds contain an old cabin, numerous buggies and wagons, and a short nature trail (handicapped accessible).

& **The People's Center** (1-800-883-5344; 406-675-0160; www.peoplescenter .org), Pablo. Open daily May through September, 9 AM–6 PM; open October through April Monday through Friday 9 AM–5 PM. This museum preserves the cultural heritage of the Salish, Kootenai, and Pend d'Oreille tribes while attempting to connect it to the present and preserve it for the future. Exhibits show how these tribes lived before ever having contact with those of European descent, how that contact ultimately disrupted and changed their traditional ways of living, and how they live in the present. (See also Native Ed-ventures under *To Do—Unique Adventures.*)

Rocky Mountain Museum of Military History (406-549-5346; www.geo cities.com/fortmissoula), Buildings T-310 and T-316 at Fort Missoula; enter via South Street (across from Big Sky High School), Missoula. Open daily June 1 through Labor Day noon–5 PM; open Sunday only Labor Day through Memorial Day noon–5 PM; free. Anyone interested in the U.S. military shouldn't pass up a visit to this museum, which contains artifacts, documents, and memorabilia relating to the nation's servicemen and -women, dating from the Old West to the present. Housed in buildings constructed by the Civilian Conservation Corps (CCC) during the Great Depression, the museum strives to broaden and deepen comprehension of the military's role in this country, both past and present. (See also Historical Museum at Fort Missoula and Montana Natural History Center, above; and Northern Rockies Heritage Center under *Historic Landmarks, Places, and Sites.*)

See also Libby, Pablo, and Polson under *Towns;* Conrad Mansion Museum under *Historic Landmarks, Places, and Sites;* and Lolo Trail Center under *Lodging—Other Options.*

HISTORIC LANDMARKS, PLACES, AND SITES Camp Disappointment is 12 miles northeast of Browning on US 2 at mile 233. Here you'll find an interpretive sign 4 miles south of the actual northernmost point attained by Lewis and Clark during the Corps of Discovery expedition (the actual site is on private land). On July 23, 1806, they arrived at Camp Disappointment, where their hopes of the Marias River extending north to 50 degrees latitude were dashed, as Lewis could clearly see the river flowing out of the mountains to the west. Thus the Louisiana Territory did not become extended as far north as they had hoped—hence the name of this site. A commemorative monument, erected in 1925 by the Great Northern Railroad, sits on the hillside above the sign. This site is on the National Register of Historic Places, as is the **Meriwether Lewis– Two Medicine Fight Site.** Also situated on private land, the Meriwether Lewis site lies 25 miles southeast of Browning, where Lewis and Clark's only violent encounter with Native Americans occurred during their entire expedition.

Conrad Mansion Museum (406-755-2166; www.conradmansion.com), on Woodland Avenue between 3rd and 4th Streets E., Kalispell. Open May 15 through October 15 Tuesday through Saturday 10 AM–5 PM for guided tours on the hour (last tour at 4 PM); $8 adults, $7 seniors, $3 children under 12. It's hard to imagine what it would be like to actually live inside the luxurious walls of this 13,000-square-foot 1895 mansion, a National Historic Site. Constructed for the founder of Kalispell, Virginia native Charles Conrad, the mansion's striking exterior landscaping and Victorian architecture are almost eclipsed by its interior grandeur—but only almost. The decor of the 26 rooms features original furnishings, from canopied four-poster beds to marble bathrooms, with added touches such as original toys and clothing.

CONRAD MANSION MUSEUM

Council Grove State Park (406-542-5500; www.fwp.state.mt.us/ parks/parksreport.asp?mapnum=31), Exit 101 off I-90 in Missoula, then south for 2 miles on Reserve Street, then west for 10 miles on Mullan

Road (MT 263). Open year-round for day-use only; free. This park marks the site where Isaac Stevens negotiated the fateful 1855 Hellgate Treaty with the Salish, Kootenai, and Pend d'Oreille Indians, establishing the 1.3-million-acre Flathead Indian Reservation to the north. Picnicking, hiking, and wildlife viewing are popular activities at this 87-acre park.

& **Daly Mansion** (406-363-6004; www.dalymansion.org), 251 Eastside Highway (MT 269), Hamilton. Open for tours daily April 15 through October 15, 10 AM–5 PM; open by appointment off-season; $7 adults, $6 seniors, $3 children ages 6–12, children 5 and under free. This lavish structure served as the summer home for Irish immigrant and copper-mining magnate Marcus Daly, who made his fortune by transforming the Anaconda silver mine into an enormously profitable copper mine. Built in 1896 in the Queen Anne style of Victorian architecture and remodeled under the direction of Daly's wife in 1910 (Marcus Daly died in 1900) to reflect a Georgian Revival style, the mansion is listed on the National Register of Historic Places. This huge and lavish structure includes more than 56 rooms for a total of 24,000 square feet—quite a summer home, by anyone's standards! The mansion has been fully restored, renovated, and furnished with appropriate period pieces. A tour will afford you the opportunity to learn more about not only the mansion itself but also the Daly family and the tremendous influence they had on shaping Montana.

& **Darby Historical Visitor Center** (406-821-3913), 712 N. Main Street, Darby. Constructed in the late 1930s, this building served as the Bitterroot National Forest's first official ranger station and was then used by the Bitterroot Hot Shot Fire Crew from 1965 to 1990. Now it serves visitors to the area as an information and interpretive center for the forest. (See also Bitterroot National Forest in *Wilder Places—Forests.*)

Fort Owen State Park (406-542-5500; www.fwp.state.mt.us/parks/parksreport .asp?mapnum=1), US 93, 25 miles south of Missoula to Stevensville Junction, then 0.5 mile east on MT 269. Open year-round for day-use only; free. On a single acre of land, you'll find some of the log and adobe structures that mark the site of the first permanent white settlement in Montana: St. Mary's Mission (see below). After encountering difficulties with the Blackfeet Indians, the Jesuit missionaries abandoned the mission until a later date. They sold the mission's mills and fields to Major John Owen, who established a trading center at the same location in 1850. Restored rooms in the east barracks furnished with period pieces and artifacts afford visitors a look back to the early days of Fort Owen. The site is on the list of National Historic Places.

Missoula County Courthouse (406-721-5700; www.co.missoula.mt.us), 200 W. Broadway, Missoula. Open Monday through Friday 8 AM–5 PM; free. Spanning an entire city block, this impressive edifice was constructed from 1908 to 1910 and is listed on the National Register of Historic Places. In addition to its lofty exterior, the building's south foyer contains eight murals painted from 1912 to 1914 by notable western artist Edgar S. Paxson.

Northern Rockies Heritage Center (406-728-3662; www.nrhc.org), headquartered in Building 30 at Fort Missoula (enter via South Street, across from

Big Sky High School), Missoula. Grounds open year-round; free. This organization works to protect and preserve 13 of Fort Missoula's historic buildings, its
water tower, and its parade grounds. A stroll around the well-cared-for grounds
allows you the chance to view these historic places and structures, all of which
are on the National Register of Historic Places. (See also Historical Museum at
Fort Missoula, Montana Natural History Center, and Rocky Mountain Museum
of Military History under *Museums.*)

& **St. Ignatius Mission** (406-745-2768), 2 blocks off US 93 in St. Ignatius (follow signs). Open in summer 9 AM–8 PM; open in fall through spring 9 AM–5 PM;
free. Catholic missionaries established this mission in 1854, and under their
direction, Native Americans constructed the church in the 1890s. Inside, Broth-
er Joseph Carignano, SJ, painted some 60 murals on the walls and ceilings, while
outside, the stunning backdrop of the Mission Mountains adds to the inspirational appeal of this registered National Historic Site. Sunday mass is held weekly at 9:15 AM.

& **St. Mary's Mission** (406-777-5734; www.saintmarysmission.org), west end of
4th Street (3 blocks from Main Street), Stevensville. Open for tours April 15
through October 15; $5 adults, $2 students. A registered National Historic Site,
St. Mary's Mission was the first permanent white settlement in Montana—though
this site was not its original location. Established by Father Pierre DeSmet, SJ, a
Belgian, in 1841, St. Mary's Mission closed down temporarily after troubles with
the Blackfeet Indians, who were traditional enemies of the mission-served Flathead Indians (see Fort Owen State Park, above). The mission reopened at this
new location in 1866. The construction of the chapel seen today ensued, and an
addition was built in 1879, doubling the chapel's size. The interior of the chapel
has been restored and features fur-
nishings designed by Father Anthony
Ravalli, SJ, Montana's first physician.
Chief Victor's cabin, on the grounds,
houses a Native American museum.
You can learn more about the mission
and its historical significance at the
visitor center, which includes an art
gallery, a museum, and more. Picnic
tables are located on the grounds (no
fee to picnic).

& **Tobacco Valley Historical Village** (406-297-7654), S. Main Street
(across from Riverside Park), Eureka.
Open Memorial Day through Labor
Day 1 PM–5 PM; free. Since importing
three doomed buildings slated to be
destroyed by the flooding caused by
the formation of Lake Koocanusa in
1971, Eureka's historic village has
grown to include many additional

ST. IGNATIUS MISSION

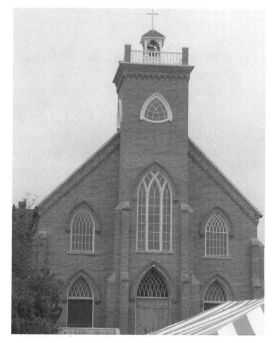

historic buildings. The town's original buildings—a general store, railroad depot, and church from Rexford—have been joined by a schoolhouse, caboose, hand-hewn house, historic cabin, library, and fire tower. Inside all of these historic structures, visitors can see memorabilia and artifacts from days gone by, displayed in realistic settings. Visitors can also access two hiking/biking trails along the banks of the Tobacco River from this area. (See also Eureka Montana Quilt Show under *Special Events.*)

& **Travelers' Rest State Park** (406-273-4253; www.travelersrest.org), 8 miles south of Lolo via US 93, then 0.25 mile west on Mormon Creek Road. Open daily June through October, 8 AM–8 PM; open November through Memorial Day 8 AM–5 PM; free. You are virtually certain to be walking the same ground as Lewis and Clark when you visit this park along the shores of Mormon Creek. The Corps of Discovery stayed at this site twice, once in 1805 and once in 1806. This is one of the few locations where archaeologists have unearthed physical evidence of the explorers' passage, including a fire ring and a latrine. This was also a much-used campsite and trail crossing for generations of Native Americans. Interpretive signs detail the park's significance.

See also Glacier County Historical Museum, Historical Museum at Fort Missoula, Hockaday Museum of Art, Montana Natural History Center, and Rocky Mountain Museum of Military History under *Museums;* Garnet National Back Country Byway under *Scenic Drives;* Symes Hot Springs Hotel under *To Do— Hot Springs;* 10,000 Waves Raft and Kayak Adventures under *To Do—Paddling/ Floating;* Pointer Scenic Cruises to Wild Horse Island State Park under *To Do— Unique Adventures;* Woodland Park under *Wilder Places—Parks;* Foxglove Cottage Bed and Breakfast, Garden Wall Inn Bed and Breakfast, Gibson Mansion Bed and Breakfast, and Goldsmith's Bed and Breakfast Inn under *Lodging—Bed & Breakfasts;* Double Arrow Resort under *Lodging—Lodges;* and Lodgepole Gallery and Tipi Village and Historic Kalispell Grand Hotel under *Lodging— Other Options.*

FOR FAMILIES ♂ **Big Sky Waterpark** (406-892-2139; www.bigskywaterpark .com), 7211 US 2 E., Columbia Falls. Open Memorial Day through Labor Day 10 AM–6 PM or until 8 PM in midsummer; $17.95 adults, $11.95 children 10 and under and seniors 60 and older (water park only); or $22.99 adults, $18.99 children 10 and under and seniors 60 and older (includes water park, round of mini-golf, carousel ride, and more). Reward the kids for their patience with a trip to Montana's largest water park, which features not only a number of thrilling waterslides, but also minigolf, a carousel, bumper cars, a video game arcade, and more.

& ♂ ☙ **A Carousel for Missoula** (406-549-8382; www.carrousel.com), 101 Carousel Drive, Missoula. Open June through August, 11 AM–7 PM; open September through May, 11 AM–5:30 PM; $1 adults, $.50 seniors, $.50 children under 19; free for those with disabilities. In 1991, Missoula cabinetmaker Chuck Kaparich agreed to facilitate the making of this incredible hand-carved carousel after the city council promised to never take it apart. Roughly 100,000 volunteer hours later, the carousel opened in 1995, and it has since become a beloved city treasure. Both young and old delight in selecting a colorful steed and then whirling around on this marvelous contraption.

🐉 🦎 **Dragon Hollow Playarea** (406-549-8382; www.carousel.com), 1 Caras Park, Missoula. Open year-round, dawn to dusk; free. Located next to A Carousel for Missoula (above), Dragon Hollow represents a genuine effort for adults to take children's desires into account when planning a really cool playground. Colorful green-and-yellow dragons are the theme, complete with tongues and teeth and googling eyes—a child's delight, for certain. The playground has obstacle courses, swings, slides, and musical instruments, as well as a special area for kids under 5.

A CAROUSEL FOR MISSOULA

See also Hockaday Museum of Art under *Museums; To Do—Horseback Riding;* Lolo Hot Springs Resort and Lost Trail Hot Springs Resort under *To Do—Hot Springs;* 10,000 Waves Raft and Kayak Adventures, Flathead Raft Company, and Pangaea Expeditions under *To Do—Paddling/Floating;* Big Mountain Ski and Summer Resort, Blacktail Mountain, and Lost Trail Powder Mountain under *To Do—Snow Sports;* Logan State Park and Woodland Park under *Wilder Places—Parks;* and Bitterroot Valley Bluegrass Festival, Huckleberry Festival, International Wildlife Film Festival, Lewis and Clark Festival, Loon and Fish Festival, Two Rivers Rendezvous, and Winterfest under *Special Events.*

SCENIC DRIVES **Garnet National Back Country Byway** covers 12 miles on Garnet Range Road; go northeast on MT 200 east of Missoula for 30 miles, then follow signs as you head southeast. Closed January 1 through March 31. This road gains 2,000 feet of elevation as it takes you into the **Garnet Mountain Range** (see *Wilder Places—Forests*), leading you right by **Garnet Ghost Town,** one of Montana's most well-preserved ghost towns. A visitor center (free) helps interpret the site. Additionally, you'll see breathtaking scenery, including views of the Swan Mountain Range, the Mission Mountains, and the Blackfoot River valley. This road (marked and groomed by the Bureau of Land Management from January 1

DRAGON HOLLOW PLAYAREA

to April 30) provides access to the 31.5 miles of snowmobile trails in the **Garnet National Winter Recreation Trail System,** as well as other trails suitable for hiking, biking, cross-country skiing, and horseback riding. Camping and fishing are also popular in this area. (See also 10,000 Waves Raft and Kayak Adventures under *To Do—Paddling/Floating.*)

Lake Koocanusa Scenic Byway runs 67 miles from Libby to Eureka via MT 37, or alternately via F.R. 228 on the west side of the lake. This route takes you along the eastern or western shore (or both) of Lake Koocanusa, formed in 1974 with the construction of the Libby Dam. At 90 miles in length, the lake and its shores are noted for their **excellent recreational opportunities,** including biking, fishing (species include rainbow trout and bull trout), camping (developed and undeveloped—see also **Kootenai National Forest** under *To Do—Camping*), boating (four ramps), wildlife viewing, and more. The lake's original name resulted from a contest held to name it—a woman from nearby Eureka suggested it, as it combines three letters each from *Kootenai* (after the Kootenai Indian tribe, *Canada* (which is home to part of the reservoir), and, of course, *USA*. (See also Lake Koocanusa Loop under *To Do—Biking.*)

Quartz–Loon Scenic Drive, 37 miles; start in Libby and follow MT 37 for 0.5 mile north to River Road (F.R. 853). Go west 4.4 miles to Quartz Creek Road (F.R. 600). Go north 18 miles to Loon Lake Road (F.R. 471). Go east 4.3 miles to Pipe Creek Road (MT 567). Proceed south 17 miles back to MT 37. This lovely loop drive at first parallels the Kootenai River before sending you north along Quartz Creek, providing access to the **Skyline National Recreation Trail** (see *To Do—Hiking*). You'll pass by **Loon Lake** and the **Turner Mountain Ski Area** (see *To Do—Snow Sports*) and then head south as the road parallels Pipe Creek. **Wildlife viewing** potential along this drive is tremendous, with white-tailed deer and ruffed grouse commonly sighted—though you might also see a moose, a black bear, or bighorn sheep, if you're lucky. (See also Kootenai National Forest under *Wilder Places—Forests.*)

St. Regis–Paradise National Forest Scenic Byway, 30 miles east on MT 135 starting in St. Regis to MT 200 in Paradise. This scenic road follows the path of the Clark Fork River through **Lolo National Forest** (see *Wilder Places— Forests*). If you're headed to Glacier National Park from the west on I-90, you might consider this as an alternate route if you have time to spare. The drive takes you through remarkably varied scenery, including views of the Coeur d'Alene Mountains as well as Montana flatlands. Anglers and boaters can take advantage of the easy access to the **Clark Fork River** (see *To Do—Fishing*). This is also a great way to access the **National Bison Range** (see *Wilder Places—Wildlife Refuges and Areas*).

Seeley–Swan Scenic Drive runs 90 miles along MT 83 from Seeley Lake to Swan Lake. Lakes, lakes, and more lakes—hundreds of them, in fact, in all shapes and sizes—mark this incredible drive through scenery that is pure Montana. From the time you leave Seeley Lake until you arrive at Swan Lake to the north, you will find yourself in the heart of a breathtaking valley filled with natural lakes and surrounded on both sides by mountain ranges—the Mission Mountains to the west, and the Swan Mountains to the east. Recreational opportunities throughout this corridor are endless, including access to **Holland Falls National Recreation Trail** (see *To Do—Hiking*) and the **Old Squeezer Loop Road,** a scenic loop road accessible 12 miles south of Swan Lake that is recognized by the Audubon Society for its bird-watching value. Boating, camping, fishing, hiking, horseback riding, cross-country skiing, and snowmobiling are also popular along this route.

Yaak Loop Scenic Tour, 90 miles; go west on US 2 from Libby, then north on Yaak River Road (MT 508), then south on Pipe Creek Road (MT 567) back to Libby. You should plan to take your time on this scenic loop through **Kootenai National Forest** (see also *Wilder Places—Forests*). Perhaps you'll even spend the night at one of the six Forest Service campgrounds along the way (or just off the main route, on a side road). Driving along the Yaak River through the Yaak Valley, you will encounter the incredible **Yaak Falls** 7 miles north of US 2 on MT 508; the falls will undoubtedly prompt you to pull over and take a closer look. If you don't have time to drive this entire loop, consider taking the shorter Quartz–Loon Scenic Drive listed above, which covers similar and some of the same terrain as this loop.

See also National Bison Range Complex under *Wilder Places—Wildlife Refuges and Areas.*

WINERIES Lolo Peak Winery, Inc. (406-549-1111; www.lolopeak.com), northwest corner of Reserve Street and Mount Avenue, Missoula. Open Monday through Saturday 10 AM–6 PM. During normal business hours, you can taste wine made only from the finest Montana agricultural produce. Ingredients include Mission Valley raspberries, Flathead Lake cherries, and apples from the Bitterroot Valley.

Mission Mountain Winery (406-849-5524; www.missionmountainwinery.com), on US 93 in Dayton, 23 miles north of Polson. Open May 1 through November 1, 10 AM–5 PM. Producing more than 6,000 cases of wine a year, the experienced winemakers here have plied this art since 1984. Some of the grapes used are grown in local vineyards, while others come from vineyards in Washington State. This winery has won some 50 awards, garnering even international recognition. Wine tasting is available during normal business hours.

Painted Rocks Winery (406-349-9463; www.paintedrocks-winery.com), 9747 W. Fork Road, Alta (south of Darby on US 93, then west on MT 473 for about 25 miles to Painted Rocks Lake, and then 5 more miles beyond the lake). Reservations are required; call ahead. This winery was changing hands at the time of publication. Call or e-mail for up-to-date information. If you're going to Painted Rocks State Park (see *To Do—Boating*) to boat or fish, this could be a fun side trip.

NATURAL WONDERS Flathead Lake lies along US 93 and MT 35 south of Kalispell and north of Missoula. This incredibly huge lake is in fact the largest natural freshwater lake west of the Mississippi River. It is located just south of Glacier National Park, which perhaps overshadows the attention it might otherwise garner, but you should take notice—with more than 200 square miles of water surface and 185 miles of shoreline, the lake is a water-lover's paradise, whether your passion is for fishing (species include lake trout, lake whitefish, and westslope cutthroat trout), boating, camping, water sports, or simply picnicking. The southern portion of the lake lies within the **Flathead Indian Reservation** (see the listing under *Guidance* for contact information), and you must purchase a tribal permit to recreate here. Scattered around the lake are a number of public access sites administered by Montana Fish, Wildlife and Parks (406-752-5501; www.fwp.state.mt.us), including fishing access sites as well as six separate locations that together make up **Flathead State Park,** including **Big Arm State Park** (406-849-5255; www.fwp.state.mt.us/parks/parksreport .asp?mapnum=35), 14 miles north of Polson on US 93. Open year-round for day-use, free for residents and $5 for nonresidents; May 1 through September 30 for camping, $15 per night. In addition to camping facilities, this location has a boat launch (close proximity to day-use, boat-access-only **Wild Horse Island State Park;** see Pointer Scenic Cruises to Wild Horse Island State Park under *To Do— Unique Adventures*), yurt rental ($25–35), and a nature trail. **West Shore State Park** lies farther north on US 93 (20 miles south of Kalispell). **Finley Point State Park, Yellow Bay State Park,** and **Wayfarers State Park** lie north of Polson on or just off MT 35. Camping is allowed at all of these locations.

Kootenai Falls are accessible 6 miles east of Troy along US 2. A stop at Kootenai Falls County Park garners you a view of these magnificent falls—the biggest waterfall in Montana that has not been dammed. Sacred to the Kootenai Tribe, the falls to them represent the center of the world, a place for peaceful meditation and spiritual communion and guidance. For the adrenaline junkie, a visit to this natural feature should include a walk across the Kootenai River on the swinging bridge, which stretches over the gorge at a height of 2,100 feet. Film buffs will be interested to learn that the movie *The River Wild* was filmed here. A short trail through the woods leads you down to the falls. Picnic tables, restrooms, and fishing access are available here, as is access to a mountain bike trail (requires a 1.5-mile bike carry/push across shale after crossing the bridge to access; or start at the opposite trailhead, which begins at the terminus of Kootenai River Road).

&. **Ross Creek Cedar Grove Scenic Area** lies southeast of Troy on MT 56. Since 1960, this 100-acre tract in Kootenai National Forest has been set aside for preservation and research, as well as public access and appreciation, due primarily to its abundance of old-growth western red cedars. Along the 0.9-mile interpretive nature trail, you'll have the opportunity to view these ancient behemoths close-up—and they are huge, with some measuring 8 feet in diameter and towering nearly 200 feet above the forest floor. You'll also learn about the other wildlife in the area. Fishing and picnicking are also available. (See also Kootenai National Forest under *Wilder Places—Forests.*)

See also *Scenic Drives;* National Bison Range Complex under *Wilder Places— Wildlife Refuges and Areas;* and "Glacier National Park"

☀ To Do

BICYCLING &. **Blue Mountain Recreation Area,** US 93 south of Missoula 2 miles, then west on Blue Mountain Road to the parking lot. If this recreation area were a person, it would truly be a jack-of-all-trades. At this kissing cousin to the city of Missoula, opportunities include not only great mountain biking trails (with lots of hills) but also a 1.5-mile accessible interpretive trail along the banks of the Bitterroot River and numerous additional trails for hikers, horseback riders, and cross-country skiers. You'll also find a folf (Frisbee golf) course, so bring your disc if you like to play.

& **Clark Fork Riverfront Trail System** is a partially paved, wide trail that runs along the river on both sides in Missoula. It is accessible from numerous places, including Caras Park (see A Carousel for Missoula under *To See—For Families*). Whether you go for a leisurely stroll, a jog, or a bike ride or you in-line skate, this trail provides a great way to see Missoula while you get fresh air and exercise. Picnic tables, benches, and parks are found along the path. (See also Kim Williams Nature Area Trail under *Hiking*.)

Kreis Pond Mountain Bike Trails are accessible from Kreis Pond Campground, Exit 82 off I-90, then MT 10 for 1.4 miles west to Remount Road, then 2.7 miles north to Ninepipe Ranger Station, then north on F.R. 476, then west on F.R. 456, and then south on F.R. 2176 to the parking area, in Lolo National Forest (see *Camping* and *Wilder Places—Forests*). Whether you're a novice mountain biker or you have a ton of experience, you'll find some terrain that challenges you in the 35 miles of trails and forest roads—four loops of varying lengths and degrees of difficulty—that depart from this campground. Brochures with maps are available at the Ninepipe Ranger Station, which you'll pass on the way to the area. You can also hike, horseback ride, fish, and camp here.

Lake Koocanusa Loop starts at the junction of MT 37 and Fisher River Road east of Libby, then goes north on MT 37 to the bridge across the lake, then south on F.R. 228 back to your starting point. This 80-mile ride will delight the experienced road biker, while those with less experience or fitness can choose to do a shorter out-and-back ride to get a sense of what it has to offer. The road goes up and down, twisting and turning, as you pedal your way through the Kootenai National Forest's captivating scenery (see *Wilder Places—Forests*). Many Forest Service roads and trails accessible off these main roads provide endless exploration of this area for mountain bikers as well. (See also Lake Koocanusa Scenic Byway under *To See—Scenic Drives*.)

Railroad–Daly Loop is a 16-mile mountain-bike loop ride in Bitterroot National Forest (see *Wilder Places—Forests*), which offers numerous additional trails and roads for riding. To access this ride, take US 93 south from Hamilton, then go east on MT 38 (Skalkaho Highway) for about 13 miles, and then turn southeast and park in the open area. Begin your ride up F.R. 75, proceeding 2 miles to its junction with F.R. 711. Follow this as it arcs around (stay on the main road to avoid getting lost or getting in over your head), bringing you back to MT 38 (now dirt). Turn left and proceed back to your vehicle. Though the trail presents little in the way of technical challenges, this ride nonetheless demands a better-than-average level of fitness, as its distance and vertical rise present a challenge.

Seeley Creek Mountain Bike–Nordic Ski Trails, accessed by taking MT 83 for 0.5 mile north of Seeley Lake, then heading west on Morrell Creek Road for about 1 mile to the parking area. This series of 1- to 6-mile loops in Lolo National Forest (see *Wilder Places—Forests*) is suitable for the not-so-experienced mountain biker, though you can lengthen your ride—and increase the difficulty —by linking up with other nearby trails and Forest Service roads. The trails are mostly forested and provide little in the way of technical challenges, allowing beginners to test their mettle without the terror of tight turns and loose terrain. In winter, these trails are groomed for skate skiers.

See also Tobacco Valley Historical Village under *To See—Historic Landmarks, Places, and Sites;* Garnet National Back Country Byway under *To See—Scenic Drives;* Kootenai Falls under *To See—Natural Wonders;* Morrell Falls National Recreation Trail under *Hiking;* Big Mountain Ski and Summer Resort under *Snow Sports; Wilder Places—Forests;* and Swanson Lodge under *Lodging— Lodges.*

BOATING Hungry Horse Reservoir lies in Flathead National Forest (see *Wilder Places—Forests*) south of US 2 (exit between West Glacier and Columbia Falls) via West Side Road (F.R. 895) or East Side Road (F.R. 38). Ten boat ramps around the shores of this almost 24,000-acre reservoir (formed by the 1953 construction of the Hungry Horse Dam) provide you with easy access to launch your watercraft. In addition to water sports and swimming, fishing (mountain whitefish and west-slope cutthroat trout) is a popular activity. With no fewer than 14 developed campgrounds around the reservoir's shores, not to mention dispersed camping, you shouldn't have much trouble finding a place to spend the night. (See also Flathead National Forest under *Camping.*)

&. **Lake Como Recreation Area** lies in Bitterroot National Forest (see *Wilder Places—Forests*), via US 93 south of Missoula. Open for day-use year-round; $2; and camping (see *Camping*). Boating is so popular here that on weekends in the peak season (July and August), the area often exceeds its capacity. The boat launch area features 30 parking spots that accommodate a vehicle and a boat. In addition, Lake Como has a roped-off swimming and beach area, a horseback riding camp, fishing (mountain whitefish, rainbow trout, and west-slope cutthroat trout), Woods Cabin ($50 per night), and access to the Lake Como National Recreation Loop Trail, a 7-mile, easy trail that circles the lake, among other trails.

&. **Painted Rocks State Park** (406-542-5500; www.fwp.state.mt.us/parks/parks report.asp?mapnum=43). Take US 93 for 17 miles south of Hamilton, then 23 miles southwest on MT 473. Open year-round for day-use and camping; free. This remote park in Montana's southwest "peninsula" of land that is surrounded by Idaho features a reservoir with a boat ramp and a dock, making it a great spot for water sports. Fishing (trout and mountain whitefish), swimming, and camping are also popular here. (See also Painted Rocks Winery under *To See— Wineries.*)

&. **Placid Lake State Park** (406-677-6804; www.fwp.state.mt.us/parks/parks report.asp?mapnum=34). Take MT 83 for 3 miles south of Seeley Lake, then go 3 miles west on Placid Lake Road (F.R. 349). Open May 1 through November 30; day-use free for residents, $5 for nonresidents; camping $13–15. This lake is a popular destination for boaters, who enjoy a ramp, a dock, and 12 boat slips (first-come, first-served). In addition, the park is a great place for swimming and other water sports, as well as fishing (handicapped accessible; brown trout, kokanee salmon, largemouth bass, mountain whitefish, rainbow trout, west-slope cutthroat trout, and yellow perch). Camping is permitted.

&. **Salmon Lake State Park** (406-677-6804; www.fwp.state.mt.us/parks/parks report.asp?mapnum=33), 5 miles south of Seeley Lake on MT 83. Open for day-use May 1 through November 30; free for residents, $5 for nonresidents; open for camping May 1 through September 30, $15. Easy access and a gorgeous wooded setting make this lake a popular spot for boaters and water sports enthusiasts. A boat ramp and dock are available. Fishing (brown trout, kokanee, mountain whitefish, northern pike, rainbow trout, west-slope cutthroat trout, and yellow perch), swimming, and camping attract many visitors as well.

&. **Whitefish Lake State Park** (406-862-3991; www.fwp.state.mt.us/parks/ parksreport.asp?mapnum=40), 1 mile west of Whitefish on US 93, then 1 mile north to the park entrance. Open year-round for day-use; free for residents, $5 for nonresidents; May 1 through September 30 for camping, $15. This 3,000-acre lake is known by those who love water sports—since windy conditions are uncommon here, water skiing conditions are usually good. The park has a boat ramp and a dock and also provides opportunities for swimming and fishing (arctic grayling, brook trout, bull trout, coho salmon, cutthroat trout, kokanee salmon, lake trout, northern pike, rainbow trout, and west-slope cutthroat trout), as well as camping.

See also Lake Koocanusa Scenic Byway and Seeley–Swan Scenic Drive under *To See—Scenic Drives;* Flathead Lake under *To See—Natural Wonders;* Holland Falls National Recreation Trail under *Hiking; Paddling/Floating;* Pointer Scenic Cruises to Wild Horse Island State Park under *Unique Adventures;* Lake Mary Ronan State Park, Logan State Park, and Thompson Falls State Park under *Wilder Places—Parks;* and *Wilder Places—Forests.*

CAMPING &. **Bitterroot National Forest** stretches down the west side of US 93 south of Missoula, as well as southeast of Hamilton, east of US 93. The forest has four ranger districts. **Darby Ranger District** (406-821-3913) has six developed campgrounds, including two on Lake Como 4 miles north of Darby on US 93, then 5.3 miles east on C.R. 82 (handicapped accessible; open June through early Sept; $8 and $14; see also Lake Como Recreation Area under *Boating*). **Stevensville Ranger District** (406-777-5461) has three developed campgrounds, including **Charles Waters Campground,** 5 miles north of Stevensville, then 2 miles east on Bass Creek Road (handicapped accessible; open late May through early September; $9; see also Charles Waters Nature Trail under *Hiking*). The **Sula Ranger District** (406-821-3201) has six developed campgrounds, including **Spring Gulch Campground,** 3 miles northwest of Sula on US 93 (handicapped accessible; open May 15 through September 15; $12). The **West Fork Ranger District** (406-821-3269) has eight developed campgrounds, including **Alta Campground,** 4 miles south of Darby on US 93, then 30 miles southwest on MT 473 (open May through November; $7). The forest also has **five cabins** ($25–50) and **two historic fire lookouts** ($25–30) available for overnight rental. (See also the listing under *Wilder Places—Forests.*)

⚿ **Flathead National Forest** begins at the Canadian border west of Glacier National Park and reaches about 120 miles to the south, covering 2.3 million acres of land west of the continental divide. The forest has five ranger districts. **Glacier View Ranger District** (406-387-3800) has four developed campgrounds, including **Big Creek Campground,** 20.5 miles north of Columbia Falls via MT 486 and 2.5 miles south of the Camas Creek Entrance into Glacier National Park (handicapped accessible; open Memorial Day through Labor Day; $10). **Hungry Horse Ranger District** (406-387-3800) has 12 developed campgrounds, including **Lost Johnny Campgrounds,** 9–10 miles south of Hungry Horse via West Side Road (F.R. 895), on the shores of Hungry Horse Reservoir (see *Boating;* handicapped accessible; open mid-May through September; $10). **Spotted Bear Ranger District** (406-758-5376) has three developed campgrounds, including remote **Spotted Bear Campground,** 55 miles southeast of Martin City on East Side Road (F.R. 38) (handicapped accessible; open mid-June through mid-September; $10). **Swan Lake Ranger District** (406-837-7500) has four developed campgrounds, including **Swan Lake Campground,** 1 mile northwest of Swan Lake on US 83 (handicapped accessible; open mid-May through September; $12). **Tally Lake Ranger District** (406-863-5400) has four developed campgrounds, including **Tally Lake Campground,** 6 miles west of Whitefish on US 93, then 15 miles west on Tally Lake Road (F.R. 113) (handicapped accessible; open Memorial Day through Labor Day; $12). (See also the listing under *Wilder Places—Forests.*)

⚿ **Kootenai National Forest** encompasses 2.2 million acres of land in the northwest corner of Montana. The forest has five ranger districts. **Cabinet Ranger District** (406-827-3533) has six developed campgrounds, including **Bull River Campground,** 4 miles west of Noxon on MT 200 (handicapped accessible; open April 15 through November 30; $8). **Fortine Ranger District** (406-882-4451) has five developed campgrounds, including **North Dickey Lake Campground,** 5 miles south of Fortine on US 93, then 0.1 mile into the campground (handicapped accessible; open April 15 through November 30; $7). **Libby Ranger District** (406-293-7773) has seven developed campgrounds, including **McGregor Lake Campground,** 53 miles southeast of Libby or 32 miles southwest of Kalispell on US 2 (handicapped accessible; open May 15 through September 10; $8). **Rexford Ranger District** (406-296-2536) has seven developed campgrounds, including **Rocky Gorge Campground,** 26 miles south of Rexford and 38 miles north of Libby on MT 37 on the shores of Lake Koocanusa (see *To See—Scenic Drives*) (handicapped accessible; open year-round; $9). **Three Rivers Ranger District** (406-295-4693) has 10 developed campgrounds, including **Yaak River Campground,** 7 miles west of Troy on US 2 (handicapped accessible; open year-round; $9). The forest also has **four cabins** ($20–25) and **five historic lookout towers** ($25) available for overnight rental. Some campsites can be reserved through the National Recreation Reservation Service (1-877-444-6777; www.reserveusa.com). (See also the listing under *Wilder Places—Forests.*)

Lolo National Forest includes 2 million acres of land surrounding the city of Missoula and abutting other national forest lands in the region. The forest has five ranger districts. **Missoula Ranger District** (406-329-3750) has nine developed campgrounds, including **Lolo Creek Campground,** 15 miles west of Lolo on US 12 (open May through September; $10). **Ninemile Ranger District** (406-626-5201) has two developed campgrounds, including **Kreis Pond Campground,** Exit 82 off I-90, then MT 10 for 1.4 miles west to Remount Road, then 2.7 miles north to Ninepipe Ranger Station, then north on F.R. 476, then west on F.R. 456, then south on F.R. 2176 (see *Biking;* handicapped accessible; open April 1 through December 1; free). **Plains–Thompson Falls Ranger District** (406-826-3821) has seven developed campgrounds, including **Cascade Campground,** 8 miles south of Paradise on MT 135 (handicapped accessible; open late May through September; $10). **Seeley Lake Ranger District** (406-677-2233) has seven developed campgrounds, including **Seeley Lake Campground,** 4 miles northwest of Seeley Lake on F.R. 77 (handicapped accessible; open Memorial Day through Labor Day; $10). **Superior Ranger District** (406-822-4233) has three developed campgrounds, including **Quartz Flat Campground,** 11 miles east of Superior just off I-90 behind Quartz Flat Rest Area (handicapped accessible; open mid-May through September; $10). The forest also has **five cabins/houses** ($40–75) and **four historic lookout towers** ($25–30) available for overnight rental. (See also the listing under *Wilder Places—Forests.*)

See also *To See—Scenic Drives;* Flathead Lake under *To See—Natural Wonders; Boating;* Holland Falls National Recreation Trail and Morrell Falls National Recreation Trail under *Hiking;* Lolo Hot Springs Resort and Lost Trail Hot Springs Resort under *Hot Springs;* Lake Mary Ronan State Park, Logan State Park, and Thompson Falls State Park under *Wilder Places—Parks; State Forests* under *Wilder Places—Forests;* and North Fork Hostel (and Square Peg Ranch) under *Lodging—Other Options.*

FISHING ♿ **The Bitterroot River** (406-542-5500; www.fwp.state.mt.us), 84 miles along US 93 from Conner to Missoula. Species of fish include brook trout, brown trout, mountain whitefish, rainbow trout, and west-slope cutthroat trout. Ten state fishing access points lie along this route, some with camping and some handicapped accessible. With no whitewater, the river is easy to float and is suitable for paddlers of any ability level. (See also Time After Time Bed and Breakfast under *Lodging—Bed & Breakfasts.*)

♿ **The Blackfoot River** (406-542-5500; www.fwp.state.mt.us) flows about 130 miles from its origins near the continental divide west along MT 200 to its confluence with the Clark Fork River at Bonner. This renowned blue-ribbon stream's species include brook trout, brown trout, mountain whitefish, rainbow trout, and west-slope cutthroat trout. More than 30 miles of the lower part of the river has been designated the Blackfoot River Recreation Corridor, making access easy. Most of the river's 17 state fishing access points lie along this route, some with camping and some handicapped accessible. This river offers great opportunities for paddling and floating, particularly in the recreation corridor, including sections of class II and III rapids.

The Clark Fork River (406-542-5500; www.fwp.state.mt.us) flows northwest for about 350 miles right along I-90, from its headwaters at the confluence of

Silver Bow Creek and Warm Springs Creek, just west of Butte, to St. Regis, where it arcs along MT 135, then follows MT 200 before ending its journey at Lake Pend Oreille in Idaho. Though the Clark Fork still suffers from environmental damage due to mining tailings, it has recovered enough to be a decent fishery, with species including brook trout, brown trout, mountain whitefish, northern pike, rainbow trout, smallmouth bass, west-slope cutthroat trout, and yellow perch. The river has about 20 state fishing access sites, and its proximity to I-90 makes for many more easy access places. The river's floatability and paddling desirability is variable, ranging from slow and shallow near its origins to class III or IV rapids between Alberton and the Tarkio Access Site. (See also St. Regis–Paradise National Forest Scenic Byway under *To See—Scenic Drives.*)

The Flathead River (406-752-5501; www.fwp.state.mt.us) begins where the North Fork (the western border of Glacier National Park) and the Middle Fork (along US 2, the southern edge of Glacier National Park) of the Flathead River link up above Flathead Lake. They are joined by the South Fork, which flows north from the mountains northeast of Seeley Lake in Flathead National Forest to Hungry Horse Reservoir, then continues north to the confluence. After about 20 miles, the Flathead River flows into Flathead Lake on the north, and then exits the lake on the southwest, continuing 75 miles to its confluence with the Clark Fork River. The Flathead above and below the lake, as well as its three forks, have distinctive characteristics, and all provide good fishing opportunities. In the Flathead River proper, species include lake trout, lake whitefish, mountain whitefish, northern pike, rainbow trout, and west-slope cutthroat trout. Five state fishing access points are located north of Flathead Lake. Below the lake, you need to acquire a tribal permit, as the river is on the Flathead Indian Reservation (see *Guidance*). Floating and paddling north of Flathead Lake are relatively easy, with a swift current and just a few small rapids and riffles. South of the lake, the river is dammed at Kerr Dam, and the gorge below this can have class IV rapids, depending on the water flow.

FLATHEAD LAKE

The Kootenai River (406-752-5501; www.fwp.state.mt.us) begins in Kootenay National Park in Canada and then flows south into Lake Koocanusa, formed by the Libby Dam, which regulates its flow along MT 37 and US 2 before it exits the state into Idaho. This blue-ribbon stream's species include burbot, kokanee salmon, mountain whitefish, rainbow trout, and west-slope cutthroat trout. Easy fishing access can be found around Libby Dam, along MT 37, and near Kootenai Falls—but beware the potential for rapidly changing water levels, due to the dam. Floating and paddling on the Kootenai are popular for both anglers and adventure seekers—most of the river has a fast current, and it has only two major sections of rapids in Montana: China Rapids, class III rapids 26 miles from Libby Dam; and 2 miles of class III and IV rapids through a narrow gorge below Kootenai Falls. It is highly recommended that you do not paddle or float over the falls! (See also Kootenai Falls under *To See—Natural Wonders.*)

See also *To See—Scenic Drives;* Flathead Lake, Kootenai Falls, and Ross Creek Cedar Grove Scenic Area under *To See—Natural Wonders;* Kreis Pond Mountain Bike Trails under *Biking; Boating;* Holland Falls National Recreation Trail under *Hiking;* High Country Trails, Hole in the Wall Ranch, and Wildlife Adventures, Inc., under *Horseback Riding; Paddling/Floating;* Frenchtown Pond State Park, Lake Mary Ronan State Park, Logan State Park, and Thompson Falls State Park under *Wilder Places—Parks; Wilder Places—Forests;* Bighorn Lodge Bed and Breakfast under *Lodging—Bed & Breakfasts;* and The Blue Damsel on Rock Creek under *Lodging—Lodges.*

GOLF **Big Mountain Golf Course** (1-800-255-5641; 406-751-1950; www.golfmt .com/northernpines), 3230 US 93 N., Kalispell, 18 holes.

Buffalo Hill Golf Club (1-888-342-6319; 406-756-4530; www.golfbuffalohill .com), 1176 N. Main Street, Kalispell, 27 holes.

Cabinet View Country Club (406-293-7332; 406-293-8636), 378 Cabinet View Road, Libby, 9 holes.

Cedar Creek Golf Course (1-888-637-4443; 406-822-4443), 10 Wadsworth Lane, Superior, 9 holes.

Cut Bank Golf and Country Club (406-873-2574), 59 Golfcourse Road, Cut Bank, 9 holes.

Double Arrow Resort (1-800-468-0777; 406-677-2777; www.doublearrow resort.com), 2 miles south of Seeley Lake on US 83, 18 holes (see also *Lodging—Lodges*).

Eagle Bend Golf Club (1-800-255-5641; 406-837-7300; www.golfmt.com/ eaglebend), 279 Eagle Bend Drive, Bigfork, 27 holes.

Hamilton Golf Club (406-363-4251), 1004 Golf Course Road, Hamilton, 18 holes.

Highlands Golf Club (406-728-7360), 102 Ben Hogan Drive, Missoula, 9 holes. (See also Shadows Keep Restaurant under *Dining Out.*)

Kings Ranch Golf Course (406-626-4000), 17775 Mullan, off Exit 89 on I-90, Frenchtown, 9 holes.

Lake Mary Ronan Wilderness Golf Course (406-849-5459; www.lakemary ronan.com), 1283 Lake Mary Ronan Road, Proctor, 9 holes.

Larchmont Municipal Golf Course (406-721-4416), 3200 Fort Missoula Road, Missoula, 18 holes.

Linda Vista Golf Course (406-251-3655), 4915 Lower Miller Creek Road, Missoula, 9 holes.

Meadow Creek Golf Course (406-882-4474), 205 1st Street S., Fortine, 9 holes.

Meadow Lake Golf and Ski Resort (1-800-321-4653; 406-892-8700; www .meadowlake.com), 100 St. Andrews Drive, Columbia Falls, 18 holes.

Mission Mountain Country Club (1-800-392-9795; 406-676-4653; www.golf montana.net/missionmtn.htm), 640 Stagecoach Trail, Ronan, 18 holes.

Phantom Links Golf Club (406-532-1000; www.phantomlinks.com), 8500 Mullan Road, Missoula, 18 holes.

Polson Country Club (406-883-8230; www.polsoncountryclub.com), 111 Bayview Drive, Polson, 18 holes.

Rivers Bend Golf Course (406-827-3438), 46 Golf Course Road, Thompson Falls, 9 holes.

Trestle Creek Golf Course (406-649-2680), 1 Trestle Creek Golf Road, St. Regis, 9 holes.

University of Montana Golf Course (406-728-8629; http://grizzly.umt .edu/golf), 515 S. Avenue E., Missoula, 9 holes.

Village Greens (406-752-4666; www.golfmontana.net/villagegreens.htm), 500 Palmer Drive, Kalispell, 18 holes.

Whitefish Lake Golf Club (406-862-4000; www.golfwhitefish.com), US 93 N., Whitefish, 36 holes.

Whitetail Golf Course (406-777-3636), 4295 Wildfowl Lane, Stevensville, 9 holes.

Wild Horse Plains Golf Course (406-826-5626), 328 MT 200 W., Plains, 9 holes.

HIKING **Blodgett Overlook Trail** (#101) is accessed by going west on Hamilton's Main Street to Blodgett Camp Road (F.R. 476) and then taking Canyon Creek Road (F.R. 475) for 3 miles to the trailhead. Located in Bitterroot National Forest (see *Wilder Places—Forests*), this easy, 3-mile trail (round-trip) takes you to an impressive viewpoint overlooking dramatic Blodgett Canyon with views of the Selway–Bitterroot Wilderness as well. Use caution around the cliff edges at the overlook—don't become so carried away by the view that you forget you're standing on the brink.

Cascade National Recreation Trail (#242) is accessed by heading 8 miles south of Paradise on MT 135 to Cascade Campground in Lolo National Forest (see *Camping* and *Wilder Places—Forests*). A 1.4-mile round-trip on this educational adventure includes the opportunity to read 25 signs detailing ecologically pertinent information about the area. You'll also enjoy two scenic overlooks, getting a chance to view Cascade Falls. If you have more energy to burn, continue on Trail #242, which goes for 6.5 miles until reaching F.R. 97 and F.R. 194.

Charles Water Nature Trail is easily accessed from the parking area for Charles Waters Campground (handicapped accessible), located 5 miles north of Stevensville on US 93 and then 2 miles east on Bass Creek Road in the Bitterroot National Forest (see *Wilder Places—Forests*). This easy, 1-mile interpretive trail takes you on a journey through two distinctive and contrasting wildlife habitats—a dry ponderosa pine forest and a lush, creek-bottom area—allowing you the opportunity to view the creatures and vegetation that inhabit both environments. For those in search of a longer adventure, additional trails can be accessed from this parking area.

Holland Falls National Recreation Trail is accessible by driving 36 miles north on MT 83 from its junction with MT 200 and then turning right on Holland Lake Road (F.R. 44) and proceeding to the trailhead. This 3-mile round-trip hike features easy terrain, a view of the falls, scenic views of surrounding mountain ranges, and access to Holland Lake, with all of its recreational opportunities. In addition to more hiking trails, popular activities at the lake include boating, water sports, swimming, paddling, fishing (species include bull trout, kokanee salmon, and rainbow trout), and camping. Holland Lake Campground (handicapped accessible) is open mid-May through September; $12. (See also Flathead National Forest under *Wilder Places—Forests;* and Holland Lake Lodge under *Lodging—Lodges.*)

Kim Williams Nature Area Trail is accessible from the east end of 5th Street (Campus Drive) in Missoula. If you're visiting Missoula and you need a quick nature fix, this is an easy way to find one. This wide, flat, graveled trail follows an old railroad grade for 2.5 miles on the south side of the Clark Fork River. The trail goes through a 134-acre natural area, meaning you'll have the chance to view wildlife. It also connects with the **Riverfront Trail** (see *Biking*). If you're in the mood for a steeper jaunt, you can head up the **Mount Sentinel Trail,** which also departs from Campus Drive and takes you on a steep, 2.5-mile journey to the top of the mountain, providing sweeping views of the city and its surroundings.

RIVERFRONT TRAIL ALONG THE CLARK FORK IN MISSOULA

Leigh Lake Trail (#32), a 3-mile out-and-back trail, is in Kootenai National Forest (see *Wilder Places—Forests*). You can access this trail by driving 7 miles south on US 2 from Libby, then heading west for 3 miles on Bear Creek Road (F.R. 278); head right on Cherry Creek Road (F.R. 867) for 4 miles and head right on Leigh Creek Road (F.R. 4786) for approximately 2 miles to find the trailhead. Though the distance of this trail isn't long, the trail is steep, so be prepared. Your reward? Views of Snowshoe Peak, the Cabinet Wilderness (as well as access by trail to these attractions), and, of course, the sight of lovely Leigh Lake.

Morrell Falls National Recreation Trail (#30) is accessed by taking US 83 for 0.5 mile north of Seeley and then turning right on Morrell Creek Road. This soon becomes Cottonwood Lakes Road (F.R. 477). After 1.1 miles, take the left fork, W. Morrell Road (F.R. 4353), and go roughly 6 miles. Turn right on Pyramid Pass Road (F.R. 4381). After 0.25 mile, go left on Morrell Falls Road (F.R. 4364) and proceed about 1 mile to the trailhead. Located in Lolo National Forest (see *Wilder Places—Forests*), this popular trail takes you on an easy 5-mile round-trip to the base of the stunning cascades of Morrell Falls. With less than 200 feet of elevation gained on the entire journey, you can be guaranteed that you won't encounter any lung-burning steep climbs—just a lovely stroll among lodgepole pines, firs, spruces, and larches to Morrell Lake and the falls. Undeveloped camping is permitted in the parking area.

See also Montana Natural History Center and Ninepipes Museum of Early Montana under *To See—Museums;* Council Grove State Park and Tobacco Valley Historical Village under *To See—Historic Landmarks, Places, and Sites; To See—Scenic Drives;* Flathead Lake, Kootenai Falls, and Ross Creek Cedar Grove Scenic Area under *To See—Natural Wonders;* Blue Mountain Recreation Area, Clark Fork Riverfront Trail System, and Kreis Pond Mountain Bike Trails under *Biking;* Lake Como Recreation Area under *Boating;* Clearwater River Canoe Trail under *Paddling/Floating;* Big Mountain Ski and Summer Resort and Chief Joseph Cross Country Trails under *Snow Sports;* Pointer Scenic Cruises to Wild Horse Island State Park under *Unique Adventures;* Lake Mary Ronan State Park and Woodland Park under *Wilder Places—Parks; Wilder Places—Forests;* National Bison Range Complex under *Wilder Places—Wildlife Refuges and Areas;* and Swanson Lodge under *Lodging—Lodges.*

HORSEBACK RIDING ✔ **High Country Trails** (406-755-1283; www.horse rentals.com/highcountry.html), 2800 Foy's Lake Road, Kalispell. Trail rides are the specialty at this 800-acre family-owned ranch near Glacier National Park. If you ride for an hour, the fee is $25; for the day, it's $150. They offer a number of other horse-related adventures, including an evening ride followed by a dinner cookout ($75), private riding lessons ($40 per hour), group riding lessons ($25 per person per hour for two to five people), and overnight trips ($150). You can also enjoy a ride to an alpine lake for a fishing trip ($150).

✔ **Hole in the Wall Ranch** (1-800-683-6500; 406-542-8076; www.holeinthe wallranch.com), Exit 66 off I-90 in Alberton. This guest ranch offers its guiding services à la carte, including horseback rides by the hour ($45) or all day long ($100), among other options. In addition to riding, the ranch offers white-water rafting or kayaking on the Clark Fork River ($90 per person per day), guided river fishing ($300 for one or two people per day), and guided float trips ($75 per person per day). The ranch also has 12 cabins for rent ($100–225; children under 12 are free with parents), a dining room that serves lunch and dinner, and access to numerous on-premises amenities—including a hot tub and paddleboats—that come free of charge with your stay.

✔ **JM Bar Outfitters** (June through August: 406-825-4004; September through May: 406-825-3230; www.jmbaroutfitters.com), Exit 126 off I-90, Clinton. In business since 1975, JM Bar Outfitters has the experience to virtually guarantee you an expertly guided outdoor experience. In addition to guiding and outfitting big-game hunts, fishing trips, and snowmobile tours, this full-service outfitter also offers horseback rides by the hour ($30) or the day ($120), among other trip lengths.

⌀ 🐾 **O'Brien Creek Farm** (406-295-1809; www.mttrailrides.com), Kootenai National Forest (contact the farm for directions), Troy. Explore Montana's pristine forests via horseback with a guided trail ride from this local farm. You can ride by the hour ($20), but to fully experience what this outfit has to offer, you should consider a longer gig. An all-day ride ($80 per person) includes lunch and takes you to the summit of some of Montana's fantastic mountains, much faster than you could take yourself there by foot. You can also sample truly wonderful camp cooking (sourdough pancakes, anyone?) by choosing a breakfast ride ($40 per person) or a dinner ride ($50 per person)—or just book an overnight adventure to try out both meals ($225 per person). Rates are slightly less for children.

⌀ **Wildlife Adventures, Inc.** (1-888-642-1010; 406-642-3262; www.wildlife adventuresinc.com), 1765 Pleasant View Drive, Victor. This full-service guest ranch—which also runs an all-season bed & breakfast facility ($80–170)—offers horseback rides by the hour ($40) or the day ($150), among other options. The ranch also offers guided fishing (wade or float, $400 per day for one or two people), as well as guest ranch packages that include activities and meals from the dining room.

See also *To See—Scenic Drives;* Blue Mountain Recreation Area and Kreis Pond Mountain Bike Trails under *Biking;* Lake Como Recreation Area under *Boating;* Morrell Falls National Recreation Trail under *Hiking;* Lolo Hot Springs Resort under *Hot Springs;* Ranch Vacations under *Unique Adventures; Wilder Places— Forests;* The Timbers Bed and Breakfast under *Lodging—Bed and Breakfasts;* Holland Lake Lodge and Swanson Lodge under *Lodging—Lodges;* and Libby Nordicfest under *Special Events.*

HOT SPRINGS Hot Springs Spa (406-741-2283; www.ronan.net/~hscofc/spa .htm), 308 N. Spring Street, Hot Springs. Guests at this small motel–housekeeping apartment complex can enjoy mineral baths in some rooms, with waters from the springs that gave the town its name (see *To See—Towns*). Most rooms also have an attached kitchen. Massage and other spa therapies are available (extra charge) on the premises as well. Rooms $35–60.

& ⌀ **Lolo Hot Springs Resort** (1-800-273-2290; 406-273-2290; www.lolohot springs.com), 38500 US 12 W., Lolo. This full-service resort is close enough to Missoula for a day trip (37 miles), but its setting on 125 private acres right in the midst of Lolo National Forest (see *Wilder Places—Forests*) makes it feels worlds apart—and the mineral hot springs pools available for soaking sore bodies after a day spent playing out in the forest truly make any stay at this resort otherworldly. Kids will enjoy the bumper boats (think bumper cars on water). This resort also offers horseback riding, snowmobile rentals with access to 500 miles of groomed trails, cross-country skiing, and hiking, as well as a restaurant, bar, and casino.

You can stay in a cabin ($75) or a tipi ($25) or just set up camp in the camp-ground ($15–24).

&. ♪ **Lost Trail Hot Springs Resort** (1-800-825-3574; 406-821-3574; www .losttrailhotsprings.com), 8321 US 93 S., Sula. You probably won't have a prob-lem finding room to soak in the hot springs mineral pools at this resort, since one of them is an Olympic-sized swimming pool. The chemical-free pool is kept at 92° to 94°F year-round (and if you like it hotter, you can hop into the hot tub or sauna to really steam yourself up). The resort has plenty of lodging available in both lodge rooms and cabins ($55–120), as well as an on-premises, family-style restaurant. Camping is also an option ($10–25). Around the resort, you'll find easy access to nearby fishing, hunting, hiking, and skiing opportunities.

Quinn's Hot Springs Resort (1-888-646-9287; 406-826-3150; www.quinns hotsprings.com), 190 MT 135, Paradise. Guests enjoy access to the resort's clean, chemical-free hot spring mineral pools, whether they stay in one of 18 cabins ($99) or in one of 15 rooms in the lodge ($94). The cabins include two queen beds, while lodge rooms feature a king-sized bed, and both have private bath-rooms. The resort offers easy access to surrounding recreational activities, and it can help guests arrange for guide services if needed. It also features the on-premises, gourmet **Harwood House Restaurant,** offering prime rib among other options; as well as **Quinn's Tavern,** which hosts live entertainment on Sat-urday night.

Symes Hot Springs Hotel (1-888-305-3106; 406-741-2361; www.symeshot springs.com), 209 Wall Street, Hot Springs. This full-service, historic hotel has two connected outdoor mineral pools (101°–104°F) open to the public that are fed by the hot spring. Constructed in 1930 by businessman Fred Symes, the hotel retains much nostalgic decor from its early days in its 31 guest rooms, some with mineral baths, as well as its eight cabins and six apartments ($45–100). The hotel offers a full array of spa services for additional charges, including massage, hot rock therapy, wraps, and more. Also on the premises is the **Symes Bathhouse Grill,** serving breakfast, lunch, and dinner, as well as the **Daily Grind Espresso Bar.**

See also Hot Springs under *To See—Towns.*

PADDLING/FLOATING **Clearwater River Canoe Trail** starts 4 miles north of Seeley Lake via MT 83, then west 0.5 mile at the sign for the trail (F.R. 17597). Put-in is here, and takeout is 3.5 miles downstream at the Seeley Lake Ranger Station, where a 1-mile (30-minute) hiking trail takes you back to your starting point. The canoeing portion of the trip lasts 1 to 2 hours, depending on your speed. This designated water trail in Lolo National Forest (see *Wilder Places—Forests*) provides the canoeist of any level with the opportunity to get a more intimate view of the flora and fauna than one can by hiking (if you don't believe me, give it a try—it's incredible how much quieter and more discreet paddling can be). You'll have the chance to view birds, including kingfishers, loons, herons, and more, as well as beavers and turtles. Anglers will quite possibly be thrilled by the sight of large trout (brook, brown, rainbow, or west-slope cut-throat; the river also has mountain whitefish, northern pike, and yellow perch).

Need to rent a canoe? Try **Seeley Lake Fun Center** (406-677-2287) on MT 83 in Seeley Lake.

✍ **Flathead Raft Company** (1-800-654-4359; 406-883-5838; www.flatheadraft co.com), 1501 US 93, Polson. Whether you want to sit back and take it all in on a leisurely, scenic float or you want to paddle your way through thrilling white water, the Flathead Raft Company has a trip for you. This is the sole rafting company operating on this portion of the Flathead River, so you know that you won't be crashing into other rafts, as can happen on more crowded rivers. The Flathead River is warmer than most rivers in Montana, so you won't need a wet suit if it's the river that interests you. A half-day rafting trip costs $40 ($32 for kids). You can also book a white-water kayaking adventure, kayaking lessons, a scenic or fishing float trip, a sea kayaking adventure on the river or Flathead Lake, multiday trips, or a Native American Interpretive Trip: a paddle or float that includes cultural and historical guidance from a tribe member accompanying you on your adventure.

✍ **Pangaea Expeditions** (1-877-239-2392; 406-239-2392; www.pangaea -expeditions.net), 608 Railroad Street, Alberton. This guiding service's focus is rafting the wild and wooly rapids of the Alberton Gorge (Clark Fork River). A full-day adventure is $73 ($58.40 for children and seniors), which includes lunch and a wet suit. You can also take multiday and customized trips. Pangaea also rafts the Blackfoot River.

Silver Moon Kayak Company (406-752-3794; www.silvermoonkayak.com), 1215 N. Somers Road, Kalispell. Silver Moon offers a number of guided specialty trips by sea kayak—most requiring no previous kayaking experience whatsoever. One popular adventure is the summer moonlight paddle, in which participants paddle in the evening for a few hours with their guide on either the Flathead River or Flathead Lake, also enjoying hors d'oeuvres and drinks ($50). You can also sign up for formal kayaking instruction, rent a kayak (or canoe), or even purchase a kayak, a canoe, or paddling gear.

✍ **10,000 Waves Raft and Kayak Adventures** (1-800-537-8315; 406-549-6670; www.10000-waves.com), 1311 E. Broadway, Missoula. Whether you want to take to the river in a raft or in a kayak, 10,000 Waves has the experience and expertise to make sure you do it safely—and that you have fun. First, choose your river (the Blackfoot, the Clark Fork, and the Bitterroot are all options). Next, select your mode of transportation (Raft? Sit-on-top kayak? Inflatable kayak?). Finally, choose the time you want to spend on the river (from 2 hours to 2 days). A full-day rafting adventure costs $78, or $63 for children (kayaks are a few dollars more). You can also take kayaking lessons or book a guided tour of historic Garnet Ghost Town (combined with a paddling trip, if you like). (See also Garnet National Back Country Byway under *To See—Scenic Drives.*)

See also Flathead Lake under *To See—Natural Wonders; Fishing; Boating;* Holland Falls National Recreation Trail under *Hiking;* Hole in the Wall Ranch under *Horseback Riding;* Frenchtown Pond State Park, Lake Mary Ronan State Park, and Logan State Park under *Wilder Places—Parks; Wilder Places—Forests;* and Holland Lake Lodge under *Lodging—Lodges.*

Ice Fishing

Opportunities are practically endless in this region. Flathead Lake (see *To See— Natural Wonders*) proves as good a starting place as any. You can also test the frozen waters at Placid Lake, Salmon Lake, and Whitefish Lake (see *Boating*), Holland Lake (see *Hiking*), as well as at the chain of lakes between Seeley Lake and Swan Lake (see Seeley–Swan Scenic Drive under *To See—Scenic Drives*), among many other spots.

Ice-Skating

Ice-skating is available in winter months all around this region as its lakes and ponds freeze. For ideas about where to don your blades, start with Missoula's **Glacier Ice Rink** (406-728-0316; www.glaciericerink.com), 1101 S. Avenue W. (in the county fairgrounds); or **Whitefish Ice Rink** (406-863-2477; 406-863-2470), 725 Wisconsin Avenue (on the way to Big Mountain Ski and Summer Resort) in Whitefish. (See also Woodland Park under *Wilder Places—Parks;* and Holland Lake Lodge and Swanson Lodge under *Lodging—Lodges.*)

Skiing

Bear Creek Trail, accessible by driving 7 miles south of Libby on US 2, then going west on Bear Creek Road (F.R. 278), is one of many cross-country skiing trails in **Kootenai National Forest** (see also *Wilder Places—Forests*). The groomed trail does not allow snowmobiles. *Trails:* 5.5K of trails—2.3K easy, 1.8K intermediate, 1.4K advanced.

✁ & **Big Mountain Ski and Summer Resort** (406-862-1900; www.bigmtn .com), 3840 Big Mountain Road, Whitefish. Located in **Flathead National Forest** (see *Wilder Places—Forests*), Big Mountain lives up to its name, with more than 3,000 acres of skiable terrain—making it one of the largest ski resorts in both the United States and Canada. In addition to killer downhill skiing and snowboarding (including a terrain park) in winter, the resort also has 16K of groomed Nordic ski trails, a lift-served tubing hill, snowshoeing, and sleigh rides, among other seasonal activities. In summer, mountain bikers delight in the 20 or so miles of trails, and hikers can choose to tromp to the top of the mountain on one of the trails included in the Danny On Memorial National Recreation Trail. Dining and lodging opportunities abound at and near the resort. *Lifts:* two high-speed quads; one quad, five triple chairlifts, one double chairlift, two T-bars. *Trails:* 91 trails—20 percent beginner, 50 percent intermediate, 30 percent expert. *Vertical drop:* 2,500 feet. *Facilities:* 10 restaurants, including cafeterias, cafés, coffee shops, bars (Hellroaring Saloon & Eatery), and fine dining (Café Kandahar). *Ski school:* Snowsports Center offers ski and snowboarding lessons for all ages and ability levels. *For children:* Kiddie Korner day care for newborns–11; variety of group lessons for different ability levels. *Rates:* $49 adults, $39 college students and seniors, $36 juniors (7–18), children 6 and under free; also half-day and multiday rates. (See also Meadow Lake Golf and Ski Resort under *Golf.*)

✁ & **Blacktail Mountain** (406-844-0999; 406-844-0991; www.blacktail mountain.com), 7225 US 93 S., Lakeside. Montana's newest ski area makes an effort to be a family-friendly destination, with lesson programs for children and free skiing for kids 7 and under. Access to 40K of groomed cross-country ski trails (mostly easiest terrain) is adjacent to the mountain in **Flathead National Forest** (see *Wilder Places—Forests*). *Lifts:* one triple and two double chairlifts, one handle-tow. *Trails:* 24 trails—15 percent beginner, 70 percent intermediate, 15 percent expert. *Vertical drop:* 1,440 feet. *Facilities:* Lodge at base of mountain has cafeteria and full-service restaurant and pub. *Ski school:* Offers ski and snowboarding lessons for all ages and ability levels. *For children:* Young Fawns for ages 4–7 years, Young Bucks Racing for ages 7–13, Young Blacktails for ages 8–15 years. *Rates:* $30 adults, $22 college students (with ID), $20 teens (13–17), $13 children (8–12), seniors 70 and up and children 7 and under ski free; half-day and multiday rates available.

Chief Joseph Cross Country Trails, accessible at Chief Joseph Pass north of MT 43, about 40 miles south of Hamilton via US 93. Groomed weekly in-season by the Bitterroot Ski Club, this trail system is one of many in **Bitterroot National Forest** (see *Wilder Places—Forests*). It features eight loops of varying difficulty and a warming hut open December 1 through May 15. Maps are available at the trailhead, as is plowed parking for more than 50 vehicles. *Trails:* 24.6K of trails—8K easy, 14.5K intermediate, 2.1K difficult.

&. ♂ ♞ **Lost Trail Powder Mountain** (406-821-3211; www.losttrail.com), just off MT 43 and US 93 at the Idaho border, Conner. Open Thursday through Sunday in-season. This mountain ski area in **Bitterroot National Forest** (see *Wilder Places—Forests*) caters to families with its reasonable rates. *Lifts:* five double chairlifts, three handle-tows. *Trails:* 40 trails—20 percent beginner, 60 percent intermediate, 20 percent expert. *Vertical drop:* 1,800 feet. *Facilities:* day lodge with cafeteria. *Ski school:* Offers ski and snowboarding lessons for all ages and ability levels. *For children:* All Mountain Program meets weekly on Saturday or Sunday for 7 weeks. *Rates:* $25 adults, $17 seniors $60–69, $15 children (6–12), 70 and up and 5 and under free; half-day and multiday rates available.

♂ ♞ **Montana Snowbowl Ski Area** (1-800-728-2695; 406-549-9777; www .montanasnowbowl.com), take Exit 101 off I-90, then go north on Grant Creek Road, then left on Snowbowl Road; 12 miles northwest of Missoula. Proximity to Missoula makes this ski area a popular destination for a single day or weekend of skiing—but you can also plan a fun family vacation here. The slope-side **Gelandesprung Lodge** offers ski 'n' stay package deals, or you can stay in town and commute to the mountain in little time. *Lifts:* two double chairlifts, two handle-tows. *Trails:* 39 trails—20 percent beginner, 40 percent intermediate, 40 percent advanced. *Vertical drop:* 2,600 feet. *Facilities:* three mountain eateries— Double Diamond Café, Grizzly Chalet, and Last Run Inn. *Ski school:* Offers ski and snowboarding lessons for all ages and ability levels. *For children:* 6-week programs include Polar Bears for ages 4–8, Powder Hounds for ages 6–12, Team Extreme for ages 8–12, Boardheads for ages 10–16, Shred for ages 10–16. *Rates:* $33 adults, $30 seniors and students, $14 children (6–12), children under 6 free; half-day and multiday rates available.

♞ **Turner Mountain Ski Area** (406-293-4317; www.skiturner.com), 22 miles north of Libby on Pipe Creek Road. Open Friday through Sunday in-season.

"Steep, deep, and cheap" is an appropriate slogan for this ski area in northwest Montana. No frills or fancy stuff here—just lots of snow and lots of steep! *Lifts:* one double chairlift. *Trails:* 20 trails—10 percent beginner, 20 percent intermediate, 70 percent expert. *Vertical drop:* 2,110 feet. *Facilities:* snack bar in day lodge. *Ski school:* available sometimes. *Rates:* $24 adults, $19 junior and seniors. (See also Quartz–Loon Scenic Drive under *To See—Scenic Drives;* and Kootenai National Forest under *Wilder Places—Forests.*)

Snowmobiling

Snowmobiling opportunities can be found all over this region, particularly in the national forests (see *Wilder Places—Forests*). In Kootenai National Forest, for example, you'll find 135 miles of groomed and marked snowmobile trails, including the East Fork Pipe Creek Loop (30 miles), accessed via Pipe Creek Road (MT 567), 21 miles north of Libby. If you need to rent a snowmobile, you can try **Montana Recreation Station** (406-892-2386) in Columbia Falls or **Seeley Lake Fun Center** (406-677-2287) in Seeley Lake, among other providers. (See also *To See—Scenic Drives;* Morrell Falls National Recreation Trail under *Hiking;* Lolo Hot Springs Resort under *Hot Springs;* and Holland Lake Lodge under *Lodging—Lodges.*)

See also Garnet National Back Country Byway under *To See—Scenic Drives;* Blue Mountain Recreation Area and Seeley Creek Mountain Bike–Nordic Ski Trails under *Biking;* Cabinet View Country Club under *Golf;* Lolo Hot Springs Resort under *Hot Springs; Wilder Places—Forests;* The Timbers Bed and Breakfast under *Lodging—Bed & Breakfasts;* and Holland Lake Lodge and Swanson Lodge under *Lodging—Lodges.*

UNIQUE ADVENTURES Native Ed-ventures (1-800-883-5344; www.peoples center.org/edventure.htm), run by The People's Center (see *To See—Museums*) in Browning. Delve a little deeper—or a lot deeper—into the history, culture, and lifestyles of the people who lived in this area long before any person of European descent set foot here. A number of Ed-ventures are available, all of which bring you closer to "the People" (Salish, Kootenai, and Pend d'Oreille Tribes) of the Flathead Indian Reservation with the help of your informative and educational Native American guide. Choose from a number of programs, including visiting the National Bison Range Complex (see *Wilder Places—Wildlife Refuges and Areas*) with a guide; attending a powwow with a guide to help interpret the dances and their significance; or learning how to set up a traditional Native American tipi and camping out for the night. You can also customize your adventure to cater to your interests. Rates are reasonable (in the range of $30 for 3 hours) and depend on the tour.

Northwest Connections (406-754-3185; www.northwestconnections.org), Swan Valley. If you'd like to do something worthwhile and educational with your vacation time, consider taking a course from this "community-based education and conservation" organization. You can sign up for a number of college-credit field-work courses that involve activities that will enhance conservation efforts in the area. Options include everything from a 2-day Animal Tracking Clinic ($125) to the weeklong Alpine Field Studies ($550), to the 2-month semester course

Landscape and Livelihood, in which participants learn about ecology and community-based conservation ($6,900 in-state; $8,900 out-of-state).

Pointer Scenic Cruises to Wild Horse Island State Park (406-837-5617; www.glacieradventure.com/pointer/index.htm), 452 Grand Drive, Bigfork. Open May through November Monday through Saturday; $60 per hour for the entire boat (not per person), which can seat nine adults. Even if you don't give the folks at Pointer Scenic Cruises much advance warning of your arrival, they can usually accommodate your wishes to ride on board one of their charter boats to scenic, historic **Wild Horse Island State Park** (406-752-5501; www.fwp.state .mt.us/parks/parksreport.asp?sitenum=1558) in Flathead Lake. Once Salish-Kootenai Indians pastured horses on this 2,000-acre island to keep them from being stolen by other tribes. Today the primitive, day-use-only state park is accessible solely by boat to protect and preserve this historic site, which is home to endangered native prairie and abundant wildlife, including a herd of bighorn sheep and several wild horses. The experienced people at Pointer Scenic Cruises can fill you in on the island and details about the surrounding area while you enjoy the cruise. On the island, you can have a picnic or go for a hike. Pointer also offers catered cruises, including twilight and moonlight cruises. (See also Flathead Lake under *To See—Natural Wonders.*)

Ranch vacations. These vacations usually allow you to participate to a certain extent in various aspects of ranch life, often including cattle herding and branding. The ratio of work time to leisure time varies from ranch to ranch, as do the additional activities and amenities offered, but most ranches include horseback riding, lodging, and meals in a package deal. In this region, providers include **Alta Meadow Ranch** (406-349-2464), Darby; **Bear Creek Guest Ranch** (406-226-4489), East Glacier Park; **Chief Joseph Ranch** (406-821-0894), Darby; **Diamond R Guest Ranch** (1-800-597-9465; 406-862-5905), Whitefish; **Flathead Lake Lodge** (406-837-4391), Bigfork; **Laughing Water Ranch** (1-800-847-5095; 406-882-4680), Fortine; **McGinnis Meadows Cattle & Guest Ranch** (406-293-5000), Libby; **Pepperbox Ranch** (406-349-2920), Darby; **Rich Ranch** (1-800-532-4350; 406-677-2317), Seeley Lake; and **Triple Divide Ranch Outfitters** (406-338-5048), Babb (near Glacier National Park); among others.

Rocky Mountain Discovery tours (1-888-400-0048; 406-721-4821; www .rmdt.com), 248A N. Higgins Avenue, Missoula. Headquartered in Missoula, Rocky Mountain Discovery tours provide the ultimate adventure for any Lewis and Clark enthusiast. Retrace the steps of the famous explorers for days on end, immersing yourself in the history and culture of the expedition. You can book a 9-day tour through Montana and Idaho ($1,800 per person) or go all the way and ride for 20 days through all 11 states that the expedition explored between 1804 and 1806 ($3,800 per person). Prices include lunch, dinner, lodging, attractions, and guides and speakers. Participants must pay for transportation to the departure point and transportation home from the endpoint.

Trailsend Tours (406-387-5763; www.trailsendtours.com), Coram. Want to see the **Bob Marshall Wilderness** (see Flathead National Forest under *Wilder Places—Forests*) from the air? If you can find seven other like-minded souls, you can book an adventure of a lifetime with Trailsend Tours. Along with a scenic, 45-minute flight by helicopter, your day will include a 3-hour guided scenic and interpretive hike, as well as a 2-hour guided scenic, cultural, and interpretive van tour ($225 per person). Trailsend offers a wide array of additional unique adventures, including guided trail rides, western history tours, chartered bus tours, hunting and fishing pack trips, and wildlife tours.

See also Flathead Raft Company, Silver Moon Kayak Company, and 10,000 Waves Raft and Kayak Adventures under *Paddling/Floating;* and Lodgepole Gallery and Tipi Village under *Lodging—Other Options.*

✳ Wilder Places

PARKS See also "Glacier National Park."

♿ **Frenchtown Pond State Park** (406-542-5500; www.fwp.state.mt.us/parks/parksreport.asp?mapnum=32), 15 miles west of Missoula on I-90 to Exit 89, then 1 mile west on Frenchtown Frontage Road. Open May through September for day-use only; free for residents, $5 for nonresidents. A small, clean, spring-fed lake is the central attraction at this park (no pets allowed!). Surrounded by grassy shores and only about 10 feet deep at its deepest, the lake is a great place for swimming, paddling, bass fishing, and picnicking.

Lake Mary Ronan State Park (406-849-5082; www.fwp.state.mt.us/parks/parksreport.asp?mapnum=36), from US 93 in Dayton (west shore of Flathead Lake), head northwest on MT 352 for 7 miles. Open May through March for day-use; free for residents, $5 for nonresidents; May through September for camping; $10–12. If you're driving along the west side of Flathead Lake and you want a quick diversion to a remote natural setting, Lake Mary Ronan will delight you. Your 7-mile side trip will bring you to this wooded little lake, which, though dwarfed by its massive neighbor, holds its own with an array of recreational opportunities belying its smaller size. Here you can boat, paddle, swim, and fish (kokanee salmon), or if you're more of a landlubber, you can pick up trails into the surrounding Flathead National Forest (see *Forests*) or grab a campsite for the night.

WOODLAND PARK

♿ 🐾 **Logan State Park** (406-293-7190; www.fwp.state.mt.us/parks/parksreport.asp?mapnum=38), 45 miles west of Kalispell on US 2. Open year-round; day-use free for residents, $5 for nonresidents; camping $13–15. On the shore of Middle Thompson Lake—part of the Thompson Chain-of-Lakes that also includes Upper and Lower Thompson Lakes—this state park provides great opportunities for water lovers, including boating (boat ramp and dock), water sports, swimming, paddling, and fishing (rainbow trout). The park also has a playground, picnicking facilities, and a campground.

Thompson Falls State Park (406-752-5501; www.fwp.state.mt.us/parks/parks report.asp?mapnum=37), 1 mile northwest of Thompson Falls on MT 200. Open May through September; day-use free for residents, $5 for nonresidents; camping $12. On the shore of the majestic Clark Fork River (see *To Do—Fishing*), this state park provides seasonal recreational opportunities, including boating (one ramp), swimming, picnicking, and fishing (brook trout, brown trout, mountain whitefish, northern pike, rainbow trout, smallmouth bass, west-slope cutthroat trout, and yellow perch). The park also has a campground.

✆ **Woodland Park,** at Conrad Drive and Woodland Drive, Kalispell. This delightful city park invites you to take a stroll along its 2 miles of paved paths (with steps) through its well-kept gardens. You can stop and observe the domestic and Canada geese among the other birds gathered on the park's pond or, in winter, possibly ice-skate there yourself. The park also has a public swimming pool. It's amazing to think that this park was once a scary and feared locale, a place where parents forbade their children to go. In the early days of Kalispell, Woodland Park used to be a swamp surrounded by a thick stand of pines and other trees, making it a favorite spot for transients who rode in on the freight trains that began passing this way in the early 1890s. The park has fortunately undergone major improvements since that time more than a century ago, transforming it into the beautiful park it is today.

See also Council Grove State Park, Fort Owen State Park, and Travelers' Rest State Park under *To See—Historic Landmarks, Places, and Sites;* Flathead Lake and Kootenai Falls under *To See—Natural Wonders;* Painted Rocks State Park, Placid Lake State Park, Salmon Lake State Park, and Whitefish Lake State Park under *To Do—Boating;* and Pointer Scenic Cruises to Wild Horse Island State Park under *To Do—Unique Adventures.*

FORESTS

National Forests
Bitterroot National Forest (406-363-7100; www.fs.fed.us/r1/bitterroot), 1801 N. 1st Street, Hamilton. The 1.6 million acres of the Bitterroot's lands stretch down the west side of US 93 south of Missoula, including a large portion that lies across the Idaho border. A tract of the Bitterroot also lies southeast of Hamilton, east of US 93. Almost half of the forest's lands are designated wilderness, including the **Selway–Bitterroot, Anaconda–Pintler,** and **Frank Church–River of No Return wildernesses.** Recreational opportunities include boating, camping, fishing, hiking (along 50 miles of the 3,100-mile **Continental Divide National Scenic Trail**), horseback riding, mountain biking, paddling/floating, picnicking, rock climbing, snow sports, and wildlife-watching. (See also Darby Historical Visitor Center under *To See—Historic Landmarks, Places, and Sites;* Railroad–Daly Loop under *To Do—Biking;* Lake Como Recreation Area under *To Do—Boating;* the listing under *To Do—Camping;* Blodgett

Overlook Trail and Charles Water Nature Trail under *To Do—Hiking;* and Blacktail Mountain, Chief Joseph Cross Country Trails, and Lost Trail Powder Mountain under *To Do—Snow Sports.*)

Flathead National Forest (406-758-5204; www.fs.fed.us/r1/flathead), 11935 3rd Avenue E., Kalispell. From the Canadian border west of Glacier National Park, this forest stretches south for roughly 120 miles west of the continental divide, bordered on its eastern side by Lewis and Clark National Forest (see *Wilder Places—Forests* in "North-Central Montana: Russell Country") and encompassing 2.3 million acres of lands within its boundaries. Almost half of the forest's lands are designated wilderness, including the **Bob Marshall, Great Bear,** and **Mission Mountains wildernesses.** Also of interest is the 15,000-acre **Jewel Basin Hiking Area,** east of Kalispell in the northern portion of the Swan Mountain Range, which is designated for use by hikers and campers only. The forest provides numerous recreational opportunities, including boating, camping, fishing, hiking, horseback riding, huckleberry picking (no permit required—10-gallon limit per adult), mountain biking, paddling/floating, picnicking, snow sports, and wildlife-watching. (See also Hungry Horse Reservoir under *To Do—Boating;* the listing under *To Do—Camping;* Holland Falls National Recreation Trail under *To Do—Hiking;* Flathead Wild and Scenic River under *To Do—Paddling/Floating;* and Big Mountain Ski and Summer Resort and Blacktail Mountain Ski Area under *To Do—Snow Sports.*)

Kootenai National Forest (406-293-6211; www.fs.fed.us/r1/kootenai), 1101 US 2 W., Libby. This forest encompasses 2.2 million acres of land in the northwest corner of Montana (with about 50,000 of those acres in neighboring Idaho). The pristine **Cabinet Mountains Wilderness** accounts for more than 94,000 acres of this forest. You'll also discover tremendous hiking, horseback riding, and fishing in the gorgeous 19,100-acre **Northwest Peaks Scenic Area** (mostly primitive; accessible by heading north on F.R. 338 just west of Yaak) and 15,700-acre **Ten Lakes Scenic Area** (89 miles of trails; accessible via US 93 south of Eureka by taking F.R. 114 northeast to F.R. 319, a 20-mile trip). Recreational activities include boating, camping, fishing, hiking, horseback riding, mountain biking, paddling/floating, picnicking, rock climbing, snow sports, and wildlife-watching. (See also Quartz–Loon Scenic Drive and Yaak Loop Scenic Tour under *To See—Scenic Drives;* Ross Creek Cedar Grove Scenic Area under *To See—Natural Wonders;* the listing under *To Do—Camping;* Leigh Lake Trail under *To Do—Hiking;* and Turner Mountain Ski Area under *To Do—Snow Sports.*)

Lolo National Forest (406-329-3750; www.fs.fed.us/r1/lolo), Fort Missoula, Building 24, Missoula. The 2 million acres of land in this forest surround the city of Missoula and abut other national forest lands in the region. Step back in time with a visit to the **Ninemile Historic Remount Depot** (406-626-5201) in Huson, a ranger station that has served the forest since the 1920s and continues to do so to this day. Outdoor recreational activities include boating, camping, fishing, hiking, horseback riding, mountain biking, paddling/floating, picnicking, snow sports, and wildlife-watching. (See also St. Regis–Paradise National Forest Scenic Byway under *To See—Scenic Drives;* Kreis Pond Mountain Bike Trails and Seeley Creek Mountain Bike–Nordic Ski Trails under *To Do—Biking;* the listing under *To Do—Camping;* Cascade National Recreation Trail and Morrell Falls National Recreation Trail under *To Do—Hiking;* and Clearwater River Canoe Trail under *To Do—Paddling/Floating.*

State Forests

State forests in this region include **Clearwater** (around Greenough and Seeley Lake), **Coal Creek** (north of Whitefish), **Stillwater** (northwest of Whitefish), **Sula** (north of Sula), **Swan River** (south of Swan Lake), and **Thompson River** (northeast of Thompson Falls). The managing body for these entities is the **Department of Natural Resources and Conservation** (406-542-4300; www .dnrc.state.mt.us). These represent six of the seven established state forests in Montana, all of which were set aside with a twofold aim: to secure timber production and to preserve watershed covers. Recreational opportunities include boating, camping, fishing, hiking, wildlife viewing, and hunting. Most of the lands surrounding these designated tracts are national Forest Service lands.

WILDLIFE REFUGES AND AREAS & **National Bison Range Complex** (406-644-2211; http://bisonrange.fws.gov), north of Dixon and northwest of St. Ignatius on MT 212 in Moiese. Open year-round; hours of refuge and visitor center vary seasonally (high season is mid-May through October); $4 per vehicle. Once, veritable seas of bison trammeled and trampled the lands of Montana and all of the American West, before a widespread and wanton slaughter caused them to dwindle almost to the point of extinction. Though no longer in imminent danger of extinction today, they also are not likely to ever rebound to their former numbers, due in large part to the lack of available habitat. Thus they primarily dwell within wildlife reserves and refuges like this one. Established in 1908, the National Bison Range is one of this nation's oldest wildlife refuges. It is home to 350 to 500 American Bison, as well as numerous other animals, including elk, bears, eagles, and coyotes. The refuge has two auto tour routes: the Prairie Drive–West Loop, a 5-mile gravel route suitable for RVs that takes you by the bison pasture; and the 36-mile scenic round-trip Red Sheep Mountain Drive, suitable for smaller vehicles, which gains 2,000 feet and is open mid-May through late October only. The refuge also has a few short, developed trails (walking off trails is prohibited), as well as a picnic area.

The National Bison Range Complex includes not only the National Bison Range but also four national wildlife refuges (NWRs): **Lost Trail NWR** (about 40 miles from Kalispell; limited recreational access and use); **Ninepipe NWR** (5 miles south of Ronan on US 93; fishing and wildlife viewing); **Pablo NWR** (2 miles south of Polson on US 93; fishing and wildlife viewing); and **Swan River NWR** (1 mile south of Swan River on MT 83; wildlife viewing); as well as the **Northwest Montana Wetland Management District,** responsible for managing a number of smaller land tracts. (See also St. Regis–Paradise National Forest Scenic Byway under *To See—Scenic Drives.*)

& **Wolf Keep Wildlife Sanctuary** (406-244-5207; www.wolfkeep.com), via Sunset Hill Road, on the south side of MT 200 just west of its intersection with MT 83 (follow signs). Open year-round Thursday through Sunday 10 AM–7 PM. Opened in 1996, Wolf Keep used to be a private sanctuary for a pack of wolves.

ROCKY MOUNTAIN ELK FOUNDATION
WILDLIFE VISITOR CENTER

In 2002 the nonprofit sanctuary began allowing the public to come and view its inhabitants, a pack of 10 arctic and gray wolves. A visit to this wolf safe haven not only affords you the chance to observe the wolf pack but also to learn more about wolves, including their intriguing and complicated social structure and behaviors.

OTHER WILD PLACES 🌿 **Rocky Mountain Elk Foundation Wildlife Visitor Center** (1-800-CALL-ELK; 406-523-4545; www.rmef.org), 2291 W. Broadway (look for the elk statue), Missoula. Open Memorial Day through Labor Day Monday through Friday 8 AM–6 PM, Saturday and Sunday 9 AM–6 PM; open Labor Day through Memorial Day Monday through Friday 8 AM–5 PM, Saturday and Sunday 10 AM–4 PM; free. For any wildlife lover, this is a must-see stop—whether you're an avid elk hunter or just generally interested in the animal life of Montana. A captivating display of animal mounts illustrates the diversity of the fauna prevalent in Montana's natural world, while an impressive collection of record-setting elk also draws your attention. Extensive interpretive information helps explain animals' predicaments as humans encroach on their terrain, as well as more general information about various animals (with a focus on elk, of course). People who don't believe that hunters are among the world's most staunch and committed conservationists might change their minds after visiting this educational center.

✳ Lodging

BED & BREAKFASTS

Bigfork 59911

Beardance Inn and Cabins (1-888-443-2699; 406-837-4551; www.bear danceinn.com; mailing address: 439 Grand, #20), 135 Bay Drive. Peaceful accommodations await you at Beardance, where guests stay in cabins rather than individual bedrooms. Each cabin features at least one double bed, a kitchen, and a private bathroom—but no phones or televisions, so that your stay is quiet and worry-free. A delicious and full breakfast featuring fresh, seasonal fare is served daily in the 1940s main lodge, which also provides you with access to homemade cookies and coffee all day long ($95–158).

Candlewycke Inn Bed and Breakfast (1-888-617-8805; 406-837-6406; www.candlewyckeinn.com), 311 Aero Lane. Set on 10 wooded acres 3 miles from the charming town of Bigfork, this rustic yet elegant B&B offers you the opportunity to get away from it all in fine style. After a day spent exploring your surroundings, you can soak in the hot tub and then wrap yourself in a complimentary terry robe before you shower in your private bathroom and crawl under the covers of a queen- or king-size pillow-top bed. Morning brings with it a full breakfast, with your specific dietary needs taken into account, should that be necessary ($100–195).

Columbia Falls 59912

Bad Rock Country Bed and Breakfast (1-888-892-2829; 406-892-2829; www.badrock.com), 480 Bad Rock Drive. Choose from eight different rooms at this award-winning bed & breakfast, located on 10 acres of land just a stone's throw from Glacier National Park. In addition to the four lovely bedrooms (each with private bath and private phone) in the main house, four additional bedrooms are located in the nearby **Bad Rock Junction**—two gorgeous log buildings with two rooms each, and each room features a private entrance, private bath, private phone, and gas log fireplace, with close access to the hot tub in the main house. A full breakfast served daily features a creative and ever-changing selection, ensuring that you won't leave the table hungry ($98–168).

Elmo 59915

Wild Horse Hideaway Bed and Breakfast (1-866-880-6161; 406-849-6161; www.wildhorsehideaway.com), 79466 Old US 93. Montana may not be known for its beaches, but after you stay at this B&B, you might wonder why. Situated on its own private beach on the shores of Flathead Lake, the Wild Horse Hideaway boasts a beautiful surrounding thicket of trees, including cherry trees, for which the

area is known. You'll wake up to enjoy a full breakfast every morning, after you rise from the comfort of your Montana-made log bed in your lakeside room, and perhaps you'll finish each evening with a dish of homemade ice cream ($129).

Eureka 59917

&. **Heron House Bed and Breakfast** (1-888-734-0297; 406-889-3373; www.northwestmontanavacation rentals.com/hh_bednbreakfast.html), 175 Garrison Drive. With 200 feet of lakefront property, 3 private acres of land, four gorgeous bedrooms with private bathrooms, and easy access to an amazing lifetime's worth of outdoor recreation, Heron House is an obvious choice for the outdoor adventurer with a taste for pampering. After spending your day playing in the wilds, you'll spend your nights snug under the sheets of a luxurious bed and wake up each morning to a full or continental breakfast ($85–100).

Hamilton 59840

Big Sky Bed and Breakfast (1-800-953-3077; 406-363-3077; www.bigsky bandb.com), 703 Mariah Lane. With only two bedrooms available—both of which feature a queen-size bed and a private bath—you'll be assured of personal attention at this modern bed & breakfast, constructed in 2003. The two guest rooms each come with a view—one faces the Sapphire Mountains, while the other faces the Bitterroot Mountains—and share a common room in between them. In addition to the delicious, full breakfast served daily, snacks and beverages are served in the evening, followed by a homemade dessert later on ($85).

See also **Roaring Lion Inn** under *Lodges.*

Kalispell 59901

Cottonwood Hill Farm Inn (1-800-458-0893; 406-756-6404; www.cotton woodhillfarm.com), 2928 Whitefish Stage Road. Antique four-poster beds and eclectic, unique travel-related decor define each of this B&B's three guest rooms, all of which have private baths and televisions. A full, gourmet breakfast is served daily to guests April through September, while a continental breakfast is provided in the off-season. During the high season, guests also enjoy afternoon hors d'oeuvres, an evening dessert, and snacks and beverages available all day, included in the nightly rate ($65–135).

The Master Suite Bed and Breakfast (406-752-8512; www.mastersuite bedandbreakfast.com), 354 Browns Road. The perfect spot for a romantic getaway, The Master Suite features roughly 1,500 square feet of interior living space (set on a 15-acre property) dedicated to the lucky couple booked as the B&B's sole guests. Featuring a handsome sleigh-style queen-size bed, 1.5 bathrooms, a TV/VCR, a glass atrium, a partial kitchen, and exercise equipment, The Master Suite boasts incredible views from its windows; among the sights are Glacier National Park, Flathead Lake, and the Rocky Mountains. You can choose to take your gourmet breakfast (and your afternoon hors d'oeuvres and cocktails) in your suite or on one of three outdoor patios/decks ($140–195).

See also **Historic Kalispell Grand Hotel** under *Other Options*.

Libby 59923

The Huckleberry House (406-293-9720; www.thehuckleberryhouse .com), 1004 Main Street. Four comfortable bedrooms (two with shared bathroom) are available for guests at this cute B&B in Libby, where you'll enjoy the traditional country furnishings as well as easy access to attractions, both in-town and all around. Breakfasts do justice to the lodging's name, featuring delicious selections made from the inn's namesake tart little berries, including waffles and coffeecake ($70–90).

Marion 59925

At the Lake Bed and Breakfast (406-858-2456; 406-250-3522; www .vrbo.com/21177), 250 McGregor Lane. You'll know you're in the right place not only by the sign announcing it but also by the beauty and splendor of McGregor Lake's placid waters rippling nearby. Solitude and privacy are easy to find here: each of the two guest suites features its own private entrance, a private bathroom (with jetted tub), and private deck. Guests can also take the canoe or rowboat out for no extra charge. Full breakfasts are provided for nightly guests ($135 and up). Weekly and monthly rates are available as well.

Missoula

Foxglove Cottage Bed and Breakfast (406-543-2927; www.foxglove cottage.net), 2331 Gilbert Avenue, Missoula 59802. Surrounded by a charming Victorian garden, 100-year-old Foxglove Cottage has four distinctively decorated bedrooms, all with queen-size beds and TV/VCRs—so you can unwind in the privacy of your room with a video selected from the B&B's library of more than 500 movies. Two of the rooms have private baths, while two share a bath (these can be combined for a two-bedroom suite as well). Continental breakfast is included in the rate ($75–125).

Gibson Mansion Bed and Breakfast (1-866-251-1345; 406-251-1345; www.gibsonmansion.com), 823 39th Street, Missoula 59803. Any B&B that advertises its breakfast as a true "Wreck your diet" experience warrants, in my book, a closer look as a lodging selection, For a tempting, tantalizing, tasteful treat—and I'm not talking about the morning meal only—stay at this fully restored 1903 mansion, with its marvelous, majestic exterior columns framing the doorway that leads you into a comfortable, luxurious interior. Designed by architect A. J. Gibson (who also designed the Daly Mansion; see *To See—Historic Landmarks, Places, and Sites*), this B&B has four guest bedrooms outfitted in period furniture, and all have private baths, a TV/VCR, and phone and Internet access ($99–149).

Goldsmith's Bed and Breakfast Inn (1-866-666-9945; 406-728-1585; www.goldsmithsinn.com), 809 E. Front Street, Missoula 59802. Along the bank of the Clark Fork River on the path of Lewis and Clark, you can stay in one of seven bedrooms at this stately 1911 brick home. All of the rooms have private baths and telephones, and four come with suites that feature private balconies as well. Enjoy your complete gourmet breakfast inside or outside, depending on the season. This is not only the sole riverfront B&B in Missoula but also the closest B&B to the University of Montana ($69–154).

Noxon 59853
✦ **Bighorn Lodge Bed and Breakfast** (1-888-347-8477; 406-847-4676; www.bighornlodgemontana.com), #2 Bighorn Lane. Near the border of Idaho in northwest Montana, you'll find this great country getaway. The lodge has five guest rooms ($125), all of which come with private baths and access to a hot tub, as well as a separate, completely furnished and equipped vacation house (great for families), the River House ($250). Rates include a complete breakfast and use of outdoor equipment, including boats and mountain bikes. For an extra fee, you can add on dinners ranging from family-style to gourmet, as well as fishing guide services on the nearby Kootenai and Bull rivers.

Ronan 59864
The Timbers Bed and Breakfast (1-800-775-4373; 406-676-4373; www .timbers.net), 1184 Timberlane Road. Situated on 21 acres of land, The Timbers proves hard for many guests to leave—after all, why drive anywhere, when you can hike, ride, or ski right on the property? Nonetheless, should you wish to explore further, a stay at this location gives you close proximity to area attractions while accommodating you in one of two bedrooms (rental of the entire suite is possible, too). If you have horses, they have a place for your four-footed friends to stay, too ($95–160).

Twin Creeks Bed and Breakfast (1-877-524-8946; 406-676-8800; www.twincreeksbb.com), 2295 Twin Creeks. One of seven guest rooms at this B&B might tempt you, but if you really want to have a unique experience, why not stay the night in one of its three tipis, instead? Tipis come with sleeping bags, fire pits, and use of the bathhouse and hot tub, as well as a full breakfast ($60). Rooms in the lodge, each named for an important Montana historic figure, include a full breakfast as well, and some come with private baths ($80–125).

Somers 59932
Outlook Inn Bed and Breakfast
(1-888-857-8439; 406-857-2060; www
.outlookinnbandb.com), 175 Boon
Road. No matter which of the four
guest rooms you stay in, you'll enjoy a
fabulous, 20-mile-long view of Flathead Lake, as well as your own private bathroom. Sleep comes quickly
in the comfort of a hand-peeled log
bed in your Montana-themed guest
room, and no Montana experience
would be complete without a sample
of the finest local fare—a must-do
made easy by eating your full breakfast here, where the menu almost
always features Montana-made goodies that might include huckleberry
jam and buffalo sausages ($71–105).

Stevensville 59870
**Big Creek Pines Bed and Break-
fast** (1-888-300-6475; 406-642-6475;
www.bigcreekpines.com), 2986 US
93. A stay in this award-winning B&B
nestled deep in the incomparable Bitterroot Valley will provide you with
nothing less than an extraordinary
lodging experience. Four nature-
themed rooms, each with a private
bathroom, all have gorgeous views of
the surrounding Montana landscape.
The complete, gourmet breakfast
served each morning features three
separate courses, ensuring that you
will never leave the table without
feeling satisfied ($80–90).

Thompson Falls 59873
**Thompson Falls Bed and Break-
fast** (1-866-325-5722; 406-827-0282;
www.thompsonfallsbnb.net), 10
Mountain Meadows Lane. Surrounded by national forest lands, Thompson
Falls lies near the border of Idaho on
the banks of the Clark Fork River. A
peaceful night's sleep in this locale is
easy to come by when you stay in one

of three guest rooms at Thompson
Falls B&B, all of which include private bathrooms. Full breakfast is
served Sunday through Friday, and
Saturday morning features a breakfast
bar complete with fresh, home-baked
bread. To remember your visit, you
might even purchase a piece of original artwork from the B&B's on-
premises art gallery ($65–95).

Troy
See **Swanson Lodge** under *Lodges*.

Victor 59875
**Time After Time Bed and Break-
fast** (406-642-3258; www.treasure
state.com/timeaftertime), 197 Pistol
Lane. This rustic B&B has three bedrooms, two with a shared bath and
one with a private bath. Guests who
fancy fishing can enjoy practicing
their casting skills on a private pond
located on the 10-acre property, as
well as easy access to the nearby Bitterroot River. A full breakfast is
included, as well as snacks served
every evening ($80).

See also **Wildlife Adventures, Inc.,**
under *To Do—Horseback Riding.*

Whitefish 59937
**Garden Wall Inn Bed and Break-
fast** (1-888-530-1700; 406-862-3440;
www.gardenwallinn.com), 504
Spokane Avenue. The in-town location of this acclaimed B&B means
that you'll enjoy easy access to all of
the dining, shopping, and entertainment opportunities available in
Whitefish—while knowing that when
you've had enough activity, you can
escape it all in the comfort and elegance of your well-appointed guest
room. This 1920s home has been
fully restored, with five guest rooms
all decorated with period antiques, all
with private baths, and all with added

touches that make your stay truly special. The delicious three-course breakfast served daily features fresh, local ingredients prepared creatively by the chefs-owners ($125–155).

Gasthaus Wendlingen Bed and Breakfast (1-800-811-8002; 406-862-4886; www.whitefishmt.com/gast haus), 700 Monegan Road. For a unique twist on your western adventure, stay at this B&B, which features a "German-Western" theme. Situated on 8 acres of property just 2 miles outside Whitefish, the B&B provides you with a delicious breakfast prepared daily from family recipes, plus decor featuring family collectibles and antiques mixed with western influences—all in a setting that is undeniably western. You'll stay in one of four bedrooms (some with private baths) and enjoy access to the steam room ($60–125).

Hidden Moose Lodge Bed and Breakfast (1-888-733-6667; 406-862-6516; www.hiddenmooselodge.com), 1735 E. Lakeshore Drive. This B&B is renowned for its excellent guest accommodations, which all include private bathrooms, cable television, a DVD player, a minirefrigerator, and Montana-themed decor. A number of rooms feature private Jacuzzis in the bathroom as well. An outdoor hot tub is available for all guests. The lodge's main room features a huge river-rock fireplace and comfortable chairs for relaxation and socializing. A full and hearty breakfast served daily is included ($89–159 and up).

See also **Good Medicine Lodge** under *Lodges.*

Yaak 59935
River Bend Bed and Breakfast (406-295-5493; www.geocities.com/yaak59935/page1.htm), mile marker 40.8 on Yaak River Road (F.R. 92) 11 miles north of Yaak. Remote? You bet. Escape into the beauty and solitude of northwestern Montana, where you'll find a lifetime's worth of outdoor recreation at your fingertips. The Yaak River and Kootenai National Forest surround you at this rustic B&B, where you'll start each day with a hearty country breakfast before heading out to explore your incredible surroundings ($50–75).

LODGES *Browning 59417*

& **Aspenwood Country Inn and Campground** (406-338-3009; www.aspenwoodcamp.com), 9.5 miles west of Browning on US 89. Open June 15 through September 15, by reservation only after September 15. This country inn features three rustic, lodge-style rooms for travelers, all with private bathrooms ($70–90), as well as a cabin rental—Beaver Lodge ($150)—a campground with a bathhouse ($15–20), and teepee rentals ($35–45). Also on the property is the Sunshine Café, serving up healthy, homemade fare to both lodgers and passersby for breakfast, lunch, and dinner.

Clinton 59825
The Blue Damsel on Rock Creek (406-825-3077; www.bluedamsel.com), 1081 Rock Creek Road. Open March through December. Stay in one of five rooms in the lodge proper, or rent a small cabin on the property—it's your choice. Whatever option you go with, you'll be treated to 13 acres of private access to the blue-ribbon fishing stream of Rock Creek, making this lodge an angler's paradise (inclusive fly-fishing vacation packages are available). Constructed of Montana lodgepole pines, the modern lodge includes three rooms with

private Jacuzzi baths and two rooms that share a Jacuzzi bath. The lodge itself features gorgeous, artistic accents throughout, making for a delightful and inspiring locale. With the Full American Plan, you get a room, meals, and use of the lodge and grounds ($440).

Darby 59829

Rye Creek Lodge (1-888-821-3366; 406-821-3366; www.ryecreeklodge .com), on Rye Creek Road 1.3 miles east of US 93. Choose one of six private, luxurious log houses, all with stone fireplaces and private outdoor hot tubs, located adjacent to Bitterroot National Forest (see *Wilder Places—Forests*). You'll enjoy modern comforts that include satellite television, a private phone line, and a fully equipped kitchen. Step outside your door into a remote and wild wonderland, with mountains all around and Rye Creek meandering nearby—the perfect setting for viewing elk, deer, moose, and other wildlife that frequent the area ($200–500).

Hamilton 59840

&. **Roaring Lion Inn** (1-877-546-6466; 406-363-6555; www.roaringlion inn.com), 830 Timberbrook Lane. Each of the three rooms in this inn has a private entrance. Once you step inside, you'll be delighted to find a cozy gas-log fireplace to warm things up with its rosy glow, as well as a private bathroom and decor that combines rustic Montana flavor with antique collectibles. The cedar lodge itself is set in a pine forest, making it feel remote—yet it's only a 5-minute drive to Hamilton, which offers plenty of visitor services. A full breakfast served daily is included in the nightly rate ($95–135).

Missoula

See **Montana Snow Bowl Ski Area** under *To Do—Snow Sports*.

Seeley Lake 59868

Double Arrow Resort (1-800-468-0777; 406-677-2777; www.double arrowresort.com), 2 miles south of Seeley Lake on MT 83. Double Arrow's 5,000-square-foot main lodge was constructed more than 60 years ago, and the lustrous wood of its interior continues to create an aura of rustic yet elegant hospitality today. You can stay in one of the lodge's guest rooms or choose to stay in one of a number of well-appointed cabins situated on the 200-acre grounds ($80–168). Double Arrow also has entire houses for rent ($168–655). The main lodge houses the fine dining establishment **Seasons Restaurant** (see *Dining Out*). (See also *To Do—Golf*.)

Swan Valley 59826

&. **Holland Lake Lodge** (1-877-925-6343; 406-754-2282; www.holland lakelodge.com), 1947 Holland Lake Road. On the shores of Holland Lake near the border of the Bob Marshall Wilderness, you'll find this elegant and distinguished lodge nestled among the trees. The lodge has six cabins and nine lodge rooms available, all of which come with the Full American Plan (inquire about other plans if interested). This means that your nightly rate includes not only a place to sleep but also breakfast, lunch, and a four-course dinner; a 1-hour-per-day canoe or kayak rental; and drinks with meals, excluding alcoholic beverages and espresso ($190–230). The lodge offers horseback riding (a 2-hour ride is $45 per person) and canoe and kayak rentals ($8–10 per hour). In winter, guests can enjoy cross-country skiing trails (25K), snowmobiling, and ice-skating. (See also Holland Falls National Recreation Trail under *To Do—Hiking.*)

Troy 59935

Swanson Lodge (1-888-305-4555; 406-295-4555; www.swansonlodge .com), 1076 Swanson Lodge Road. With 100 acres abutting the Cabinet Mountain Wilderness, this lodge offers guests the opportunity to hike, mountain bike, ice-skate, and cross-country ski (equipment rentals available on-premises), as well as horse accommodations, all right on the property. You'll stay in one of six rooms featuring rich, lustrous wood walls and comfortable, Montana-themed country furnishings. A full breakfast served daily is included in the rates, and a five-course dinner is available (extra charge) by reservation on Friday and Saturday nights ($125).

Victor 59875

Bear Creek Lodge (406-642-3750; www.bear-creek-lodge.com), 1184 Bear Creek Trail. Operating under the American Plan, this lodge's rates include not only a room for the night but also three gourmet meals a day, snacks, beverages, an exercise and fitness room, fishing on nearby Bear Creek, a hot tub, and mountain bikes. The luxurious and beautiful modern lodge has eight rooms, all with private bathrooms and private entrances. A casual stroll from your door leads you into the Selway–Bitterroot Wilderness in minutes, offering year-round recreational opportunities ($390).

Whitefish 59937

&. ♪ **Good Medicine Lodge** (1-800-860-5488; 406-862-5488; www.good medicinelodge.com), 537 Wisconsin Avenue. Enjoy the flavor of the West at this cedar lodge that features Native American–influenced textiles among its interior decorations. Guests stay in one of nine rooms, all of which feature custom-crafted log beds, private baths, and vaulted wood ceilings, and some of which have mountain views and private balconies. Additional amenities include an outdoor spa, a ski room with a boot and glove dryer, and laundry facilities. A full breakfast served daily is included in the rate; children under 10 can stay for free in their parents' room ($85–150).

OTHER OPTIONS

Alberton

See **Hole in the Wall Ranch** under *To Do—Horseback Riding.*

Bigfork

See **Coyote Roadhouse Restaurant** under *Dining Out.*

Browning 59417

Lodgepole Gallery and Tipi Village (406-338-2787; www.blackfeet culturecamp.com), P.O. Box 1832. Located 2.25 miles north of Browning on US 89. Stay the way the Native Americans used to stay—in your own tipi. Each tipi has its own central fireplace, and firewood is included—but you'll need to bringing a sleeping bag or rent a sleeping setup from your hosts ($6; advance notice required). Continental breakfast is included in the rate ($60). You can also book a 2-night stay and take part in a Blackfeet Journey, a cultural and historical tour that takes you to tipi rings, buffalo jumps, and the former Mission School, as well as providing a guided tour through the Museum of the Plains Indian (see *To See—Museums*). Lodging for 2 nights, two full buffet breakfasts, and two dinners (one of traditional buffalo) are included in the rate ($380).

Columbia Falls
See **Meadow Lake Golf and Ski Resort** under *To Do—Golf.*

Hot Springs
See **Hot Springs Spa** and **Symes Hot Springs Hotel** under *To Do— Hot Springs.*

Kalispell 59901
✐ **Historic Kalispell Grand Hotel** (1-800-858-7422; 406-755-8100; www .kalispellgrand.com), 100 Main Street. The only remaining downtown hotel of the eight hotels that once stood in downtown Kalispell, this fully reno- vated structure features not only modern, comfortable rooms with pri- vate baths and high-speed Internet connections but also a home-baked continental breakfast served daily to guests in the spacious Grand Lobby. Families are welcome here—the hotel

HISTORIC KALISPELL GRAND HOTEL

actually has suites called Family Rooms, some of which include a room with a king bed connected to a room with two twin beds. ($65–130) Guests can also take advantage of the on- premises Spa at the Grand, which features a full array of treatments including massage therapy, as well as delicious meals at the **Painted Horse Grille** (see *Dining Out*).

Lolo
&. ✐ **Lolo Trail Center** (406-273- 2201; www.lolotrailcenter.com; mailing address: P.O. Box 386, Stevensville 59870), 38600 US 12 W. This unique center features not only three different-sized room options for modern lodging accommodations but also a gift shop and a large museum and interpretive center with exhibits focused around the Lewis and Clark Corps of Discovery expedition. Rooms all include private baths but not private telephones and televisions (though both are available on the premises), in an effort to let overnight guests enjoy true peace and quiet (call for current lodging rates). Plenty of children's educational activities are on hand, from Lewis and Clark–related computer games to puzzles. The Lolo Trail Center also has a dinner theater presentation.

See also **Lolo Hot Springs Resort** under *To Do—Hot Springs.*

Paradise
See **Quinn's Hot Springs Resort** under *To Do—Hot Springs.*

Polebridge 59928
✿ **North Fork Hostel (and Square Peg Ranch)** (406-888-5241; www .nfhostel.com), 80 Beaver Drive. Open May 1 through January 14. Not only is a stay at this hostel inexpen- sive, but also you'll enjoy its proximity

to Glacier National Park. Situated on the western edge of the park (accessible via MT 486), the North Fork Hostel provides rustic accommodations with no electricity but, rather, kerosene and propane to brighten your nights. You'll be surprised to know, then, that two giant batteries make e-mailing and recharging personal batteries possible on the premises. The hostel has an assortment of recreational equipment available for rent as well. A bed in the hostel is $15 per person; small cabins at the hostel are $30 per night; camping is $10 per person; and larger log homes up the road at Square Peg Ranch are $65 per night.

St. Ignatius 59865
🦌 **St. Ignatius Campground and Hostel, Inc.** (406-745-3959; www .camp-hostel.com), P.O. Box 321. Located at 33076 US 93. Whether you're camping or staying inside, this place will not bust your budget. The hostel is called an Earthship, meaning that it was constructed from recycled tires and cans. Heat comes via passive solar power as well as from a woodstove in colder seasons. Up to 16 people can sleep inside in the bunk-style accommodations ($14 per person), with close access to the heated bathhouse. Tipi rentals, tent camping, and RV camping are available as well ($14–20).

Seeley Lake 59868
The Lodges on Seeley Lake (1-800-900-9016; 406-677-2376; www .lodgesonseeleylake.com), P.O. Box 568. South of Seeley Lake on MT 83, then west on Boy Scout Road for 1.4 miles. Seclusion awaits guests staying in one of 12 lakeshore lodges, six of which date back to the 1920s. Whichever cabin you choose, a full

kitchen and fireplace are standard, as is access to recreational equipment, including paddleboats, canoes, rowboats, and more. Several cabins come with a private Jacuzzi as well. The property includes a sandy beach with a dock and a fire ring perfect for marshmallow roasts or just warming up on chilly nights ($91–275).

Sula
See **Lost Trail Hot Springs Resort** under *To Do—Hot Springs.*

Whitefish 59937
Lakeshore Rentals (1-877-817-3012; 406-863-9337; www.lake shorerentals.us), 1750 E. Lakeshore Drive. Providing quality vacation rental properties by the night, week, or month, Lakeshore Rentals has a wide assortment of well-appointed accommodations for you to choose from. Selections include charming, private cabins; modern, poolside condos; and luxurious lakeside homes ($99–350).

See also Bitterroot National Forest, Kootenai National Forest, and Lolo National Forest under *To Do—Camping;* and Big Mountain Ski and Summer Resort under *To Do—Snow Sports.*

✳ Where to Eat
DINING OUT

Bigfork
♿ **Coyote Roadhouse Restaurant** (406-837-1233; 406-837-4250; www .coyoteroadhouse.com), 600 and 602 Three Eagle Lane. Open seasonally; reservations required. This critically acclaimed restaurant is the proud recipient of numerous awards and recognitions—with good reason. To start with, diners choose from a

unique, handpicked selection of wines from small Italian wineries. The menu changes frequently, as the chef-owner creates marvelous entrées nightly featuring Tuscan, Southwestern, Mayan, and Cajun influences. Dishes can include veal, seafood, chicken, game, steak, lamb, and more. Salads, appetizers, and desserts are made fresh daily as well. The Coyote Roadhouse also has an inn and cabins for rent.

La Provence (406-837-2923; www .bigforklaprovence.com), 408 Bridge Street. Yes, you can find authentic Provençal cuisine in Montana! A native of southern France, the chef–co-owner of La Provence graduated from Marie Curie College of Culinary Arts, and his entrées reflect the cuisine of his native country, touched with the artistic hand of an expert chef. If you wish, you can forgo choosing from the menu yourself and select a six-course blind tasting menu—a great option for the adventurous diner who wishes to experience authentic French food. If you're not feeling so daring, you can read through the menu and choose a single entrée, with selections including seafood, chicken, game, lamb, beef, and pork. Be sure to save room for a handcrafted dessert. An excellent wine list is offered as well. A gourmet deli on the premises, La Petite Provence, offers lunchtime sandwiches, soups, quiches, salads, and pastries for dining in or to go.

Hamilton

Spice of Life Café (406-363-4433; www.bitterroot.net/spice), 163 S. 2nd Street. Spice things up a little bit with a meal at this local restaurant, which specializes in using the finest fresh and locally grown ingredients in its creative takes on old standbys as well

as its original dishes. Beef and lamb come from the Hamilton area—and the meat is even organic, when possible. Burgers (veggie burgers, too), sandwiches, and an impressive assortment of salads are available for tighter budgets and/or lighter appetites, while full entrées provide an array of options featuring ethnic twists like Jamaican jerk chicken, Thai curry noodles, and Cajun chicken fettuccine, as well as more traditionally American entrées. A children's menu is available.

Kalispell

Café Max (406-755-7687; www .cafemaxmontana.com), 121 Main Street. A frequently changing menu reflects the shifting of the seasons at this critically acclaimed restaurant, one of Kalispell's finest dining establishments. What doesn't change, however, is the focus on using the freshest and finest local and regional ingredients—an emphasis that extends to this restaurant's wine list, which always features wines from Oregon and Washington, as well as from around the world. Seafood, meat, poultry, and vegetarian options are prepared to perfection and presented beautifully, accompanied by fresh greens and a chef-selected side dish.

Painted Horse Grille (406-257-7035; www.paintedhorsegrille.com), 110 Main Street (in the Historic Kalispell Grand Hotel, see *Lodging—Other Options*). Serving lunch and dinner, the Painted Horse Grille features imaginative takes on favorites like salmon, seafood, poultry, duck, lamb, steak, and more. Fresh-baked breads are made daily from recipes created by the chef. Lunch options include sandwiches, entrée salads, and pastas. A complete wine list and a full selection of liquors are available, as are delectable desserts.

Missoula

The Red Bird (406-549-2906; www .redbirdrestaurant.com), 120 W. Front Street, #105 (in the historic Florence Building). Fine dining year-round in a historic setting characterizes The Red Bird, situated in the heart of downtown Missoula. The constantly changing menu features fresh, local fare whenever possible and can include such ingredients as Rocky Mountain lamb, buffalo tenderloin, and cheese made from Montana goat's milk. Vegetarian options are always available, as are salads and a wine list that features many northwestern wines.

♿ **Shadow's Keep Restaurant** (406-728-5132; www.shadowskeep.com), 102 Ben Hogan Drive. A traditional country-club dining experience awaits you at Shadow's Keep, situated on the foundations of the historic Mansion Restaurant, which burned to the ground in a mysterious fire in 1992. A year later, Shadow's Keep opened, with the new building carrying on the tradition of excellence established by its predecessor. The menu features time-tested, expertly prepared favorites such as shrimp scampi, chicken marsala, and top sirloin steak, among others, as well as several vegetarian options, nightly entrée and dessert specials, a complete wine list, and a full bar.

♿ **Zimorino's Red Pies Over Montana** (406-549-7434; www.zimorinos .com), 424 N. Higgins Avenue. If you're not drawn to this restaurant simply by dint of its original and somehow intriguing name, consider this: opened by two Italian brothers from New York, Red Pies has been a Missoula fixture for two decades, serving up authentic Italian entrées made with the recipes provided by Italian relatives and friends of the owners—as well as some Red Pies' originals. Classic pasta dishes include pasta primavera, spinach manicotti, and ravioli, among others, while meatier entrées include veal piccata, chicken marsala, and chicken parmigiana, to name a few. Everything on the menu is homemade, from appetizers to sauces to desserts. A children's menu is available.

See also **Highlands Golf Club** under *To Do—Golf.*

Paradise

See **Quinn's Hot Springs Resort** under *To Do—Hot Springs.*

Polson

Lake House Bar, Grill, and Casino (406-887-2115; www.lakehouse grill.com), 4161 E. Shore Route. One of the latest additions to the Flathead Valley dining scene is this lakeside restaurant, which provides diners with exceptional food in a premier location. Views of Flathead Lake (see *To See—Natural Wonders*) take center stage, providing a serene backdrop for those having a drink at the outdoor bar, as well as those seated to enjoy a full meal. The restaurant strives to use local, fresh ingredients whenever it can, including not only locally grown beef and vegetables but also wine from Mission Mountain Winery (see *To See—Wineries*) and beer from Glacier Brewing Company. Menu choices range from lighter fare (salads and sandwiches) to full entrées.

Seeley Lake

Seasons Restaurant (1-800-468-0777; 406-677-2777; www.double arrowresort.com/dining), 2 miles south of Seeley Lake on MT 83.

Located in the historic Double Arrow Resort (see *Lodging—Lodges*), this upscale restaurant features cuisine billed as "classic country," complemented by an excellent wine list. Steak and seafood creations dominate the menu, which is rounded out by selections featuring chicken, pork, duck, buffalo, and vegetarian themes. The classic, elegant atmosphere promotes relaxation and dining pleasure.

Whitefish

419 Wine Bar & Restaurant (406-862-9227), 419 E. 2nd Street. You'll find one of Whitefish's newest, most chic hangouts above the established Wasabi Sushi Bar (which might stop you in your tracks before you even make it upstairs). Don't worry—you can get sushi upstairs, too, as well as themed wine-tasting flights, 27 wines available by the glass, and a waitstaff well versed in pairing wines with meal selections (with 150 wines available by the bottle, most folks could use some help). Dining options include not only sushi but also fresh, raw oysters and classic, gourmet entrées prepared with steak, duck, lamb, and more. All of this is served in a contemporary, stylish setting, complete with jazz music, a fireplace, and remarkable views—a surefire recipe for romance if ever there was one.

Pollo Grille (406-863-9400; www .pollogrill.com), 1705 Wisconsin Avenue. For a unique fine dining experience, make reservations at the Pollo Grille, where the specialty of the house is—not surprisingly—chicken, as well as other poultry, which are cooked rotisserie style and served with your choice of two side dishes (veggies, potatoes, and rice). You can also select a number of entrée items from the grill, including steak, lamb,

seafood, and pork, which all come with the sides as well. Vegetarians can concoct a meal comprised solely of side dishes. Several pasta dishes and several entrée salads are also offered. A children's menu is available.

Tupelo Grille (406-862-6136; www .tupelogrille.com), 17 Central Avenue. You might have already guessed from its name that the Tupelo Grille's culinary wizardry involves top-notch Cajun, Creole, and southern cuisine—a true departure from the norm in northwestern Montana. Menu items include not only classic southern fare such as crawfish, shrimp, gumbos, jambalayas, and even grits but also steak, seafood, chicken, pastas, duck, and more, all expertly prepared with a distinctive southern flair. Vegetarians won't go hungry here. An award-winning wine list provides diners with a fine selection.

See also **Big Mountain Ski and Summer Resort** under *To Do— Snow Sports*.

EATING OUT

Bigfork

& **Brookies Cookies** (1-800-697-6487; 406-837-2447; www.brookies cookies.com), 191 Mill Street. Cookie and a cup of coffee, anyone? You'll find homemade cookies hot out of the oven all day long at this bakery— chocolate chip, peanut butter, snickerdoodle, ginger, and Java Jumble are just some of the kinds you might find. If you're not a big cookie eater, you can satisfy your sweet tooth with a fresh-baked cinnamon roll, muffin, or scone, among other options.

Showthyme (406-837-0707; www .showthyme.com), 548 Electric Avenue. For a deliciously prepared dinner in a casual, stylish setting, Showthyme fits the bill. Upscale American fare dominates the menu, with entrée options including duck, chicken, veal, lamb, steak, pastas, and more. For a unique experience, check out the Chicken Relleno "Montana," a Showthyme original featuring an entire Anaheim chili stuffed and surrounded with goodies, including cheese, chicken, shrimp sauce, tortilla, and rice. Desserts are decadent; drinks include a wine list, cocktails, and beers; and a children's menu is available.

& **The Village Well** (406-837-5251; www.villagewell.net), 260 River Street. This casual pub and restaurant will fill you up with any number of the favorites it offers, including burgers, pizzas, salads, sandwiches, wraps, and more. Vegetarians will find plenty to choose from on the menu. A selection of fresh microbrews will make beer aficionados happy. This restaurant also has games—table tennis, pool, and foosball—as well as a casino and live entertainment for listening to or dancing to on weekends. A children's menu is available.

& **Wild Mile Deli** (406-837-3354; www.wildmiledeli.com), 435 Bridge Street. This New York–style deli serves up freshly prepared American and German favorites for breakfast, lunch, and dinner daily from its extensive menu. German specialties include knockwurst, bratwurst, and bockwurst, among other selections, while American fare includes meatloaf (sandwich or dinner), prime rib, and vegetarian and chicken entrées. Also on the menu are egg dishes for breakfast and numerous salads, soups, and sandwiches, bagels, homemade desserts, homemade candies, and ice

cream. The deli also has wireless Internet, a big-screen television, takeout service, and a children's menu.

See also **La Provence** under *Dining Out*.

Browning
See **Aspenwood Country Inn and Campground** under *Lodging—Lodges*.

Hamilton
& **Nap's Grill** (406-363-0136), 220 N. 2nd Street. Popular with the locals, this restaurant has gained fame for its fantastic burgers that come with all of the fixings as well as its trademark friendly service. Other menu favorites include steaks and salads. Generous portions promise that nobody will leave the table hungry.

Hot Springs
See **Symes Hot Springs Hotel** under *To Do—Hot Springs*.

Kalispell
& **Bulldog Pub and Steakhouse** (406-752-7522), 208 1st Avenue E. If you're looking for the beef, you'll find it here, at this locals' favorite hangout. Steaks and prime rib are served up daily, prepared how you like 'em. The Irish-style pub also serves other entrées, including chicken, pastas, and seafood. Weeknights feature regular nightly specials as well. For a casual night on the town and a memorable meal, the Bulldog will not disappoint.

& **MacKenzie River Pizza** (406-756-0060; www.mackenzieriverpizza.com), 1645 US 93 S. This is one of the 11 MacKenzie restaurants that are now found around Montana. MacKenzie River Pizza claims to have first introduced Bozeman to the idea of gourmet pizza back when it opened its doors in 1993—and it has been a big hit ever since, as evidenced by its growth. You'll understand why if you choose to come in and check out their truly original and delicious pizzas. You can, of course, select one of the old standbys (cheese or pepperoni, anyone?), but why would you when you could sample a Polynesian, Branding Iron, or Rustler, among other specialties, all of which feature unique and exotic topping combinations? Also in Whitefish (9 Central Avenue; 406-862-6601).

&. **Vivienne's Fifth Street Café** (406-752-8436), 21 5th Street E. Specializing in breakfast and lunch, Vivienne's invites you to relax in the café's refreshing, comfortable decor while you enjoy your meal. Selections include plenty of choices for the health-conscious eater and for vegetarians—but hearty eaters will be satisfied as well. The menu features homemade soups, sandwiches, breads, and daily lunch specials. For a unique and distinctive treat, join Vivienne's on Wednesday or Thursday for a proper English afternoon tea, complete with scones, finger sandwiches, tarts—and, of course, tea.

Libby
Red Dog Saloon and Pizza (406-293-8347), 6788 Pipe Creek Road. If you're in search of sustenance and you love pizza, you're in luck. The Red Dog Saloon serves up freshly prepared, steaming-hot pies garnished with all of your favorite toppings—or none, if you're a cheese-only type of guy or gal—as well as some not-so-normal options for the more adventuresome pizza eater. Not into pizza? That's okay: Red Dog also delivers in the steak department—and the beer department, too.

Lolo
See **Lolo Hot Springs Resort** under *To Do—Hot Springs.*

Missoula
&. **The Bridge Bistro Restaurant** (406-542-0638; www.bridgebistro .com), 515 S. Higgins. A casual and relaxed atmosphere prevails at this local favorite, situated in a restored, turn-of-the-20th-century "dime-a-dance" hall, which has been under the same ownership for more than three decades. Sit back and order a drink from the antique bar, which has 10 local microbrews on tap as well as a full wine list, then peruse the extensive menu, which includes not only plenty of Italian favorites (pastas and pizzas) but also an assortment of unique and creative entrée specials with influences ranging from Thailand to Africa. Burgers, sandwiches, and specialty salads are available, as well as take-out food (call 406-542-0002 for takeout).

&. ❂ **HuHot Mongolian Grill** (406-829-8888; www.huhot.com), 3521 Brooks Street. Kids and adults will delight in selecting individual items, including vegetables, noodles, meats, seafood, poultry, and specialty sauces, which are then cooked on a grill and returned to the diner to enjoy with wraps and rice. This great concept allows picky eaters the option to go as bland as they wish, while more adventurous types will likely come up with some creative masterpieces.

❂ &. **Montana Club** (406-543-3200), 2620 Brooks Street. Exposed 100-year-old wooden beams and reproduced photos hanging on the walls enhance the authentic Montana feel of this lodge-style restaurant, which strives to make sure that its portions are so huge, you'll need a doggie bag for leftovers. Burgers, seafood, steaks, German entrées, a salad bar, and more fill up the dinner menu, and the breakfast menu features no fewer than eight choices for $1.99. A children's menu is available, as is a private gaming room.

&. **The Mustard Seed Asian Café** (406-542-7333; www.mustardseed asiancafe.com), 2901 Brooks Street (Southgate Mall). This acclaimed Asian restaurant started in Missoula in 1978, and it has since expanded to include locations not only around Montana but also in Washington and Idaho. The reason for this expansion can be explained only by the palate-pleasing, made-from-scratch Asian entrées that make up the menu, including black bean and lime halibut, chicken or beef teriyaki, and Asian glazed pork ribs, among others. Healthy, light sauces are made on the premises to complement the fresh meats and vegetables.

&. **The Raven Café** (406-829-8188; www.theravencafe.com), 130 E. Broadway. This cool hangout offers up all of your favorite coffee drinks, as well as loose-leaf teas and an array of microbrews and wines. Breakfast includes a selection of favorites such as omelets, skillets, and baked goods. Made-to-order sandwiches, homemade soups, fresh salads, and other deli-style entrées make up the lunch menu. At dinnertime, The Raven becomes Missoula's only tapas (little appetizers) bar, with an assortment of delicious, flavorful bites of creativity featured on the menu. Step in for a meal or a homemade dessert—and to enjoy a game of pool, use your Wi-Fi-enabled laptop, engage in stimulating conversation—or simply just relax, savor your food or drink, and take in the offbeat and eclectic environment.

Tipu's (406-542-0622; www.tipus tiger.com), 115½ S. 4th W. Perhaps the sole Indian restaurant in all of Montana, Tipu's also has the distinction of offering an entirely vegetarian menu—this in a state renowned for its beef. The restaurant serves no meat and has been a local favorite since it opened in 1997, which should tell you all you need to know about eating at Tipu's. The menu includes a reasonably priced selection of traditional Indian foods, including curries, rice dishes, and dals, along with chutneys and a variety of Indian breads. The restaurant also serves a critically acclaimed chai tea, which no diner should skip sampling—you can even purchase some of the mix to take home with you.

Polson

&. **Rancho Deluxe Steak House and Rio Café** (406-883-2300), 602 6th Street W. This local steakhouse has been around since the 1930s, and it continues to serve delicious prime rib and steak dinners (as well as other entrées, including seafood, pasta, and poultry options) in the tradition of excellence that the community has come to expect. The adjacent Rio Café features Southwestern fare in an appropriately decorated facility. Both restaurants have full-service cocktail lounges, and a casino adjoins them as well. Stop in to dine overlooking lovely Flathead Lake or simply to sip a beverage or to share a dessert in the company of friends.

Sula

See **Lost Trail Hot Springs Resort** under *To Do—Hot Springs*.

Whitefish

&. **Buffalo Café** (406-862-2833;

www.digisys.net/buffalocafe), 514 3rd Street. Sit down to breakfast or lunch and start your meal with freshly brewed coffee from a French press. The breakfast menu is so extensive that it would be surprising if you couldn't find your favorite breakfast fare, be it as simple as a bowl of granola or a more hearty meal of biscuits 'n' gravy, huevos rancheros, french toast, pancakes, a breakfast burrito . . . you get the idea. Lunch is no different, with a huge range of choices, including burgers done many ways, salads, sandwiches galore, burritos, quesadillas, and more. A children's menu is available.

Mambo Italiano (406-863-9600; www.glacieradventure.com/mambo), 234 E. 2nd Street. What makes this restaurant so popular among locals and visitors alike probably has a lot to do with the excellent Italian recipes prepared from scratch with the finest, freshest ingredients. The menu includes an array of creative pasta creations, such as gnocchi (potato dumplings) with meatballs or homemade noodles baked with ricotta, mozzarella, and meat sauce; as well as brick-oven pizzas, soups, salads, appetizers, and a children's menu. You'll also find a low-carb menu for those who subscribe to such a diet, as well as plenty of vegetarian options, a good wine list, and an assortment of traditional Italian desserts—truly, something for everyone.

See also **MacKenzie River Pizza** in the Kalispell listing above; and Big Mountain Ski and Summer Resort under *To Do—Snow Sports.*

❋ Special Events

January: ❧ **Winterfest,** Seeley Lake: action-packed festival takes place last two weekends of January; includes Nordic ski races and clinics, free dogsled rides, children's activities, a snow-sculpture contest, and a Christmas tree–fueled bonfire.

March: **Irish Fair,** Libby: celebration of Celtic heritage includes music, food, and more.

April: **Black Powder Shoot,** Libby: annual marksmen's contest featuring sharpshooting, knife throwing, tomahawk throwing, fire building, and dynamite shooting. **Montana Storytelling Roundup,** Cut Bank: storytellers, artists, and entertainers from around the country gather to trade tales and talent at the state's only annual storytelling event.

May: ❧ **International Wildlife Film Festival,** Missoula (406-728-9380; www.wildlifefilms.org): weeklong festival includes showings of award-winning films, the WildWalk Parade, and hands-on educational activities and workshops among other events. ❧ **Loon and Fish Festival,** Seeley Lake: Memorial Day festival celebrating local wildlife includes interpretive talks, kids' activities, an art show, and wildlife viewing.

July: **Annual North American Indian Days,** Blackfeet Indian Reservation: the largest event held by the Blackfeet Indians draws tribes from both the United States and Canada and includes drumming, dancing contests, arts and crafts, games, and more. **Arts in the Park,** Kalispell: 3-day celebration of the arts sponsored by Hockaday Museum of Art (see *To See—Museums*) includes an outdoor art show and sale. ❧ **Bitterroot Valley Bluegrass Festival** (406-363-1250; www.bluegrassfestival .org), Hamilton: annual family-friendly event features not only great music but also workshops for instrument players, arts-and-crafts vendors, and food. **International Choral Festival** (406-721-7985; www.choralfestival .org), Missoula: hundreds of choir singers from around the world converge in Missoula to share their love of choral music with concerts that are open to the public. *✔* **Lewis and Clark Festival,** Cut Bank: annual community celebration commemorating the explorers' travels through the region, including a children's parade, an all-ages parade, a farmer's market, free concerts, a talent show, an arts-and-crafts fair, and more. *✔* **Two Rivers Rendezvous,** Libby: all-ages event re-creating 1820s–'40s fur traders' camp and rendezvous, including shooting contests, games, and camping.

August: **Eureka Montana Quilt Show** (www.eurekaquiltshow.com), Eureka: annual quilt show includes workshops and sale of quilts made by local people; proceeds go toward upkeep of Tobacco Valley Historical Village (see *To See—Historic Landmarks, Places, and Sites*). *✔* **Huckleberry Festival,** Trout Creek: free celebration of huckleberries in the Huckleberry Capital of Montana includes a huckleberry pancake breakfast, arts-and-crafts vendors, fun run/walk, kids' games, a huckleberry dessert-making contest, and more.

September: **Festival of the Book** (406-243-6022; www.bookfest-mt.org), Missoula: 3-day celebration of the written word includes readings, workshops, literary contests, book signings, and more. *✔* **Libby Nordicfest** (1-800-785-6541; www.libbynordicfest.org), Libby: yearly celebration of Libby's Scandinavian heritage; including the distinctive International Fjord Horse Show, children's events, food vendors, a parade, an art show, and more.

WATERTON–GLACIER INTERNATIONAL PEACE PARK

Established in 1910, Glacier National Park and its environs have been deemed the Crown of the Continent. Long before it ever became a national park, the native people of the area, the Blackfeet Indians, referred to this definitive mountainous divide as the Backbone of the World. Both of these monikers aptly describe this distinctive locale. The continental divide is nowhere more dramatic and pronounced than here, where it bisects the park lengthwise, running from the northwest to the southeast. The surrounding glacier-carved terrain—including 175 mountains, 200 lakes, and more than 500 streams—that gives the park its name is nothing short of spectacular, offering some of the finest, most inspiring natural scenery you'll find anywhere. The park does have about 40 small glaciers inside its more than 1 million acres of territory, but the park's name is derived from the role played by the much more enormous glaciers of the past in sculpting it into its present configuration. In addition to its almost surreally gorgeous scenery, Glacier National Park has numerous attractions, including some 350 structures listed on the National Register of Historic Places, incredible fishing opportunities, and 730 miles of maintained hiking trails.

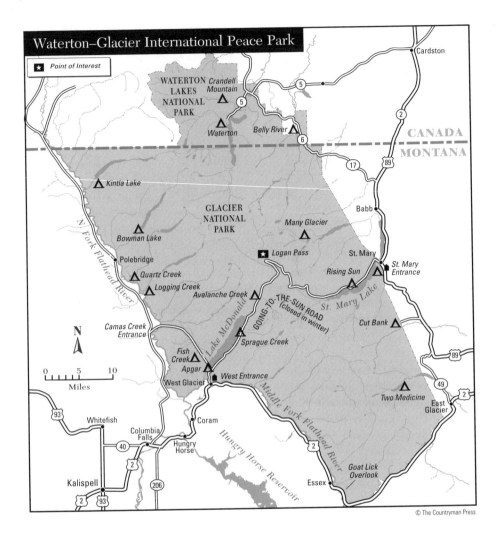

Waterton–Glacier International Peace Park

★ Point of Interest

WATERTON LAKES NATIONAL PARK

Crandell Mountain △ 5

△ Waterton

Belly River △ 6

Cardston

5

2

CANADA

MONTANA

17

89

△ Kintla Lake

GLACIER NATIONAL PARK

Babb

Many Glacier △

△ Bowman Lake

N Fork Flathead River

● Polebridge

△ Quartz Creek

△ Logging Creek

Avalanche Creek △

★ Logan Pass

St. Mary ●

Rising Sun △

St. Mary Entrance

St. Mary Lake

GOING-TO-THE-SUN ROAD (closed in winter)

Cut Bank △

Camas Creek Entrance

Fish Creek △

Apgar △

West Glacier ⬛ West Entrance

Lake McDonald

Sprague Creek △

Two Medicine △

East Glacier

49

2

N

0   5   10
Miles

93 Whitefish

Columbia Falls

40

Coram ●

Hungry Horse

Middle Fork Flathead River

Hungry Horse Reservoir

2

Kalispell

2 93

206

Essex ●

Goat Lick Overlook

© The Countryman Press

Since 1932, Glacier has also had the distinction of being part of Waterton–Glacier International Peace Park—the first such park in the world—in conjunction with its northern neighbor, Canada's Waterton Lakes National Park, established as a national park in that country in 1895. Glacier was designated as a World Biosphere Reserve in 1976; Waterton followed suit in 1979. Together, the single park received designation as a World Heritage Site in 1995. Today the park draws roughly 2 million visitors annually who come from around the world to see for themselves what no photograph or written words can adequately depict: a marvelous, lush, vibrant ecosystem characterized by impressive peaks, deep valleys, and water everywhere.

By no means a complete list of the incredible array of sites, services, and attractions available at Waterton–Glacier, the information provided in this guidebook should help you get started in planning your Peace Park vacation. As you enter the park, you'll receive several extremely informative and helpful documents published by the National Park Services that will provide further guidance. The park is in and of itself a natural wonder through and through, so in this chapter I've chosen to note a couple of "Wildlife Wonders" in lieu of "Natural Wonders"—since practically everywhere you look, you'll be wowed by the wonder of nature. Please note that fees for Waterton-based attractions are given in Canadian currency. Also, please note that because many of the park's dining establishments operate in conjunction with lodging establishments, these listings have been consolidated into a single section.

If you plan to cross the border, plan ahead—bring two forms of identification (one must be a government-issued photo ID, preferably a passport). As concerns about borders grow, changes are in the works even for crossing the U.S.–Canada border, so be sure you have the latest information on what you need to bring with you before you go. For more details about customs, in the United States, visit www.customs.gov/xp/cgov/travel, or call 250-887-3413; in Canada, call 406-889-3865.

GUIDANCE **East Glacier Chamber of Commerce** (406-226-4403; www.east glacierpark.org), P.O. Box 260, East Glacier Park 59434.

Glacier Adventure (406-862-3140; www.glacieradventure.com), 811 Kalispell Avenue, Whitefish 59937. This is an excellent source for online information about the park, including recommendations for dining, recreation, lodging, shopping, and more.

&. **Glacier National Park** (406-888-7800; www.nps.gov/glac), Park Headquarters, P.O. Box 128, West Glacier 59936. Located just before the park's west entrance station. Open all day every day (though many roads are impassable in fall, winter, and spring); $5 per person (7-day pass), $20 per vehicle (7-day pass), $25 per vehicle (12-month pass).

Glacier Park, Inc. (406-892-2525; www.glacierparkinc.com), P.O. Box 2025, Columbia Falls 59912. This full-service concessionaire authorized by the National Park Service is the one-stop place to call if you are interested in booking lodging, tours, transportation, or other guided tourism activities within the park. *Booking directly with Glacier Park, Inc., will save you the 10 percent reservation surcharge attached by many other companies booking activities within the park, as they will ultimately need to book your reservations by contacting Glacier Park, Inc.*

Trail of the Great Bear Central Reservations and Tours (1-800-215-2395; 403-859-2663; www.trailofthegreatbear.com), 114 Main Street, Waterton Lakes National Park, AB, Canada T0K 2M0. The sweep of this tourism organization is immense, as it can coordinate and book tours for you throughout the region, including not only Canada and Waterton–Glacier National Park but also much of Montana and Yellowstone National Park. This award-winning travel service provides one-stop shopping at its finest—they even have a gift shop in the park.

Waterton Lakes National Park of Canada (403-859-2224; www.pc.gc.ca/ waterton), Box 50, Waterton Park, AB, Canada T0K 2M0. Open daily, year-round;

$5 per person or $12.50 per vehicle (up to seven people) for 1-day pass; $30 per person or $63 for annual pass.

Waterton Lakes National Park Chamber of Commerce and Visitors Association (403-859-2224; www.watertonchamber.com), Box 55, Waterton Lakes National Park, AB, Canada T0K 2M0.

Waterton Park Information Services (403-859-2252; www.watertonpark.com or www.watertoninfo.ab.ca), Box 100, Waterton Lakes National Park, AB, Canada T0K 2M0.

GETTING THERE Glacier National Park lies on Montana's border with Canada, with Waterton Lakes National Park just to the north. From the south, Glacier can be accessed via US 93 and MT 83, which both feed into US 2, the major east–west road accessing the park. The Camas Creek Entrance and the Polebridge Entrance are accessed via the Outside North Fork Road (MT 486). From the north and south, US 89 also provides access to the park's Two Medicine, St. Mary, and Many Glacier entrance stations, as well as to the seasonal Chief Mountain International Highway (MT 17/AB 6; open mid-May through late September), the easiest way to access Waterton from the United States. Inside Canada, Waterton Lakes National Park can be accessed via AB 5 and AB 6.

See also *Airports, Amtrak, Bus Service,* and *Travel Information* in "What's Where in Montana."

MEDICAL EMERGENCY See *Medical Emergency* in "Glacier Country."

✳ To See

VISITOR CENTERS & **Apgar Visitor Center,** 2 miles north of West Glacier on the south side of Lake McDonald. Open daily May 1 through September 30, 9 AM–5 PM; open 8 AM–7 PM from the end of June to just after Labor Day; shorter hours in October and April; weekends only from November to March.

Logan Pass Visitor Information Center, 18 miles west of St. Mary on Going-to-the-Sun Road. Open daily early June through mid-October, 9:30 AM–4:30 PM; open 9 AM–7 PM from the end of June to just after Labor Day.

Many Glacier Ranger Station, west of Babb on US 89 via the Many Glacier Entrance. Open end of May through mid-September, 8 AM–5 PM.

Park Headquarters Building, located just before the park's entrance station at West Glacier. Open weekdays except holidays 8 AM–4:30 PM.

& **St. Mary Visitor Center,** just west of St. Mary off US 89. Open mid-May through mid-October 8 AM–5 PM; open 8 AM–9 PM from the end of June to just after Labor Day.

Two Medicine Ranger Station/Camp Store, west of US 49 at Two Medicine Junction. Open mid-May through mid-September 8 AM–4:30 PM.

Waterton Lakes Visitor Information Centre, in Waterton Park Village on AB 5. Open mid-May through early September 8 AM–4 PM.

HISTORIC LANDMARKS **Great Northern Railway Buildings National Historic Landmark** comprises five separate building complexes—**Belton Chalet, Granite Park Chalet, Many Glacier Hotel, Sperry Chalet,** and **Two Medicine Store,** which lie both within and outside Glacier National Park. Constructed from 1913 to 1915, this collection of buildings represents a distinctive style of architecture that was employed for park concessions in that time. Today, the Belton, Granite Park, and Sperry chalets are in good condition, **Many Glacier Hotel** is being renovated, and **Two Medicine Store** is slated for renovations in the near future. For more details, see individual listings in the *Lodging* section.

Lineham Discovery Well National Historic Site lies in Waterton Lakes National Park, about 5 miles west of the Waterton Townsite on Akamina Parkway (see *Scenic Drives*). This is the site of western Canada's first-ever oil-producing well, drilled in 1901. The well yielded 300 barrels a day for a time, and big plans were laid out to make the area into a rich, oil-producing locale, complete with a railroad line to the future Oil City. Due to a number of mishaps and circumstances, however, such lofty dreams had been dashed in a few short years, leaving the site deserted and derelict. Ultimately, the area's purported oil potential was not an actuality in fact, as the oil found was not indicative of the huge reserves expected.

See also Going-to-the-Sun Road under *Scenic Drives;* and Lake McDonald Lodge and Prince of Wales Hotel under *Lodging—Lodges.*

SCENIC DRIVES **Akamina Parkway** leads west for about 10 miles from just before the Waterton Townsite in Waterton Lakes National Park. This scenic drive takes you past the **Lineham Discovery Well National Historic Site** (see *Historic Landmarks*), past the original Oil City town site, and along Cameron Creek past Akamina Lake to Cameron Lake. The road is closed seasonally in late fall or early winter, becoming a favored place for cross-country skiing and snowshoeing.

Chief Mountain International Highway (MT 17/AB 6) is the major artery connecting Glacier National Park and Waterton Lakes National Park (30 miles from the junction of US 89 and MT 17 to the junction of AB 6 and AB 5 in Waterton Lakes National Park). It is open from mid-May to late September, with hours varying according to season (though it's never open overnight). You'll pass through scenic terrain on this drive from start to finish. Highlights include a sweeping view of the Front Range of the Rockies and a diverse landscape featuring grasslands, lakes, wetlands, and forests.

Going-to-the-Sun Road is a 52-mile adventure along a narrow, winding auto road that runs between St. Mary on the east side of the park and West Glacier on the west. If you have the time to spare, this is one scenic drive that should not be missed. Note, however, that portions of the road are closed in winter. The road itself is a National Historic Landmark that was 11 years in the making, with construction completed in 1932. Breathtakingly incredible scenery exists on a grand scale that is virtually indescribable, from the mountainsides streaming with waterfalls to the deeply carved, lush green valleys below. Nothing can prepare you for the renewed wonder for nature you may experience along this journey (it moved me to tears). Numerous pullouts, some with interpretive signs, enable you to stop and contemplate this natural wonderland. If you don't want to drive the distance yourself—or your vehicle is unsuitable to travel this road (vehicles longer than 21 feet or wider than 8 feet are banned from Avalanche Creek to Sun Point), you can take a guided auto tour. **Sun Tours** (1-800-786-9220) and **Glacier Park, Inc.** (406-892-2525) provide such tours. (See also *To Do—Bicycling.*)

Red Rock Parkway is a 9-mile journey northwest of the Waterton Townsite. Open early May through late October. The drive takes you through the valley along Blackiston Creek, with a number of pullouts featuring interpretive signs explaining areas of scenic, cultural, natural, and historic interest, including a buffalo jump site. The terminus for this drive is the Red Rock Canyon Day Use Area, where you can access the **Red Rock Canyon Trail** (see *To Do—Hiking*). In the months that this road is closed to auto traffic, it is a popular route for bikers, hikers, and cross-country skiers.

WILDLIFE WONDERS Bison Paddock, just west of AB 6 at the border of Waterton Lakes National Park. The bison paddock is home to a small herd of American buffalo, remnants of the vast and mighty herd that once freely roamed this area. A narrow road (not suitable for trailers) enables you to access the paddock for viewing—but remember: buffalo are wild animals and should not be approached.

Walton Goat Lick Overlook, along US 2 near Essex, is one of four popular spots for mountain goats in the park to gather when they feel the need to supplement their diets with the mineral salts of the cliffs. From spring to early summer, visitors can observe the goats gathering here (best viewing times are dawn and dusk), where they not only fill up on mineral salts but also interact with one another, sometimes violently.

See also Going-to-the-Sun Road under *Scenic Drives;* and Red Rock Canyon Trail, Running Eagle Falls Nature Trail, and Trail of the Cedars Nature Trail under *To Do—Hiking.*

VIEWS FROM GOING-TO-THE-SUN ROAD IN GLACIER NATIONAL PARK

✳ To Do

BICYCLING Glacier National Park restricts cyclists to roadways only, aside from a paved 2-mile hiker-biker trail from the Apgar Visitor Center (see *To See—Visitor Centers*) to West Glacier. Among other roads in the park, the Going-to-the-Sun Road (see *To See—Scenic Drives*) provides quite a challenge for cyclists, but you should be aware that portions of the road are closed to bike traffic during summer months, due to heavy vehicle traffic and the resulting safety concerns. These closures are 11 AM–4 PM from

June 15 to Labor Day and include the distance from the Apgar Visitor Center turnoff on the south side of Lake McDonald to the Sprague Creek Campground, as well as the distance (eastbound) from Logan Creek to the Logan Pass Visitor Center.

ST. MARY LAKE IN GLACIER NATIONAL PARK

Waterton Lakes National Park allows cycling on park roads. Chief Mountain International Highway (AB 6) and AB 5 are good options, as they have wide shoulders. Bikers must use caution, however, on the narrow, winding Akamina Parkway and on the Red Rock Parkway (see *To See—Scenic Drives*). In addition, cyclists can enjoy four backcountry trails: **Akamina Pass Trail** (3 km round-trip; steep but short), accessible near the terminus of the Akamina Parkway; **Crandell Loop** (20.6 km for a total loop, with shorter rides possible; advanced), accessible just past Crandell Mountain Campground off the Red Rock Parkway; **Snowshoe Trail** (16.4 km out-and-back; moderate), accessible from the Red Rock Day Use Area parking lot at the end of the Red Rock Parkway; and **Wishbone Trail** (21 km; easy for first half, then narrow and more challenging), accessible 0.5 mile south on Chief Mountain International Highway after its junction with AB 5. Need to rent a bike? Go to **Pat's Waterton** (403-859-2266) on Mountainview Road in the park.

BOATING Glacier National Park allows boating at Bowman Lake, located in northeastern Glacier National Park and accessible via the Inside or Outside North Fork roads; Lake McDonald, located just north of the West Entrance via Going-to-the-Sun Road; St. Mary Lake, located just west of the St. Mary Entrance; and Two Medicine Lake, located just west of the Two Medicine Entrance. All of these lakes have boat ramps and permit motorized, private boats. Hand-carried watercraft are permitted on many other lakes throughout the park. It is your responsibility to be sure to know all park rules and regulations before bringing your boat to Glacier National Park.

Glacier Park Boat Co. (406-257-2426; www.glacierparkboats.com) rents motorboats ($19) as well as canoes, sea kayaks, and rowboats ($10) in the park at five locations: Apgar, Lake McDonald, Many Glacier, St. Mary Lake, and Two Medicine (boat availability varies with location). This concessionaire also provides boat tours ($9.50–12; half price for children ages 4–12) on a number of the park's lakes, along with optional guided hikes.

Waterton Lakes National Park allows motorized boats only on Middle and Upper Waterton lakes, which both have boat launches. It is your responsibility to be sure to know all park rules and regulations before bringing your boat to Waterton Lakes National Park.

Waterton Shoreline Cruise Co. (403-859-2362; www.watertoninfo.ab.ca/m/cruise.html), in the village of Waterton. Open late April through early

October; $26 adults, $13 youths ages 13–17, $9 children ages 4–12, children 3 and under free. These 2.25-hour tours depart from Waterton and take you across Upper Waterton Lake into the United States to Goat Haunt. Your informative guide will provide information to help you learn about your surroundings. The company also provides round-trip hiker shuttle service ($13 adults, $6.50 children ages 4–12) to the trailhead for the popular Crypt Lake Trail, which features a 5.6-mile (one-way) adventure to Crypt Lake, including four waterfalls, a tunnel, and stunning views.

CAMPING **Glacier National Park** has 13 developed campgrounds and 66 backcountry campsites. Developed campgrounds include **Apgar** (handicapped accessible; open early May through mid-October; $15); **Avalanche** (handicapped accessible; open early June through early September; $15); **Bowman Lake** (open mid-May through mid-September; $12); **Cut Bank** (open late May through late September; $12); **Fish Creek** (handicapped accessible; open June 1 through early September; $17); **Kintla Lake** (open mid-May through mid-September; $12); **Logging Creek** (open July 1 through early September; $12); **Many Glacier** (handicapped accessible; open late May through late September; $15); **Quartz Creek** (open July 1 through early September; $12); **Rising Sun** (open late May through mid-September; $15); **Sprague Creek** (handicapped accessible; open mid-May through mid-September; $15); **St. Mary** (open late May through late September; $17); and **Two Medicine** (open late May through mid-September; $15). All of the developed campgrounds are first-come, first-served, except for Fish Creek and St. Mary, which can be reserved in advance by calling the **National Park Service Reservation System** (1-800-365-CAMP; http://reservations.nps.gov). Backcountry camping requires a permit ($4 per person per night).

Waterton Lakes National Park has three developed campgrounds and nine backcountry campsites. Developed campgrounds include **Waterton Townsite** (open mid-April through late October; $19–30); **Crandell Mountain** (open mid-May through early September; $17); and **Belly River** (open mid-May through mid-September; $13). Backcountry camping requires a permit ($8 per person per night). In winter (October through May), free camping is allowed at **Pass Creek Picnic Site,** located about 3 miles north of Waterton Townsite.

See also **Johnson's of St. Mary** under *Lodging—Other Options.*

FISHING **Glacier National Park** has numerous lakes, rivers, and streams, providing anglers with opportunities to catch arctic grayling, brook trout, bull trout, cutthroat trout, kokanee salmon, lake trout, mountain whitefish, rainbow trout, and northern pike, among other species. You don't need a permit or a fishing license of any kind to fish in Glacier National Park, but you do need to know the current regulations, which are available at any of the visitor centers listed under *To See,* as well as at ranger stations. Generally, the fishing season is open from the third Saturday in May to November 30, but there are exceptions to this rule. You are responsible for knowing all applicable rules and regulations before you fish in the park.

Waterton Lakes National Park requires a permit for fishing ($7 daily or $20 annually). You can fish in Upper and Middle Waterton lakes, Cameron Lake, Cameron Creek, Akamina Lakes, and Crandell Lake, among other spots. Species include bull trout, cutthroat trout, lake whitefish, lake trout, mountain whitefish, rainbow trout, and northern pike. The fishing season is open from mid-May to September 1 on the waters listed above and from July 1 to November 2 on other waters in the park that are not designated closed. You are responsible for knowing all applicable rules and regulations before you fish in the park, including those for closed waters.

See also **Summit Station Lodge** under *Lodging—Lodges.*

GOLF **Glacier Park Lodge and Golf Resort** (406-892-2525; 406-892-1115; www.glacierparkinc.com), US 2, East Glacier, 9 holes.

Glacier View Golf Club (1-800-843-5777; 406-888-5471; www.golfmontana .net/glacierview.htm), River Bend Drive, West Glacier, 18 holes.

Waterton Lakes Golf Course (403-859-2114; www.watertoninfo.ab.ca/m/ golf.htm), AB 5, Box 2000, Waterton Lakes National Park, 18 holes.

HIKING

Glacier National Park

Glacier Wilderness Guides (1-800-521-7238; 406-387-5555; www.glacier guides.com) offers guided day hikes ($55 per person) and backcountry hiking trips ranging from 3 to 10 days in length ($315 for a 3-day trip; $970 for 10-day trip) in Glacier National Park. Also available are hut trips, combination hiking and rafting trips with the Montana Raft Company (same ownership; see also *Paddling/Floating*), and customized trips designed to fit your interests. See also Granite Park Chalet under *Lodging—Other Options.*

Hidden Lake Nature Trail is a 3-mile round-trip route leaving from the Logan Pass Visitor Information Center. This moderate hike happens to be the park's most popular trail, and with good reason—it leads you to a stunning view of Hidden Lake, which lies in the valley 800 feet below. In spring and summer, you'll find abundant wildflowers after the snowmelt.

CEDARS NATURE TRAIL IN GLACIER NATIONAL PARK

Huckleberry Mountain Nature Trail is an easy 0.6-mile loop trail accessible via Camas Road in Glacier National Park or via Outside North Fork Road. The trail departs from the Camas Creek Entrance area, taking hikers on a self-guided interpretive trail through the site of a 1967 fire that lasted for more than a week. Today, the location is home to regenerating forests.

AVALANCHE GORGE IN GLACIER NATIONAL PARK

&. **Running Eagle Falls Nature Trail** is an easy, 0.4-mile out-and-back adventure accessible west of the Two Medicine Entrance. Stroll along Two Medicine Creek to the lovely Running Eagle Falls, which are in actuality two waterfalls, one falling above the other. To see the two-falls phenomenon, you'll have to time your visit right—too early in the season, and the massive water amounts will blend both falls together; too late, and the upper fall disappears entirely.

Sun Point Nature Trail is an easy 1.4-mile round-trip trail departing from a parking area west of St. Mary on Going-to-the-Sun Road. This self-guided, interpretive trail takes you to Baring Falls, which plummet 30 feet along the shore of St. Mary Lake. To extend this hike, you can continue for another mile to St. Mary Falls and then another 0.7 mile to Virginia Falls.

&. **Trail of the Cedars Nature Trail** is a 0.8-mile loop trail accessible just north of Avalanche Campground along Going-to-the-Sun Road. An interpretive self-guided journey through towering old-growth cedars and other trees leads you by Avalanche Gorge, a deep, narrow channel cut through stone by Avalanche Creek. Part of the trail features a beautiful wooden boardwalk. For a longer adventure you can take a 2-mile spur trail (not handicapped accessible) to Avalanche Lake.

Waterton Lakes National Park

Canadian Wilderness Tours (1-800-408-0005; www.whitemountainadventures .com), by **White Mountain Adventures,** #7, 107 Boulder Crescent, Canmore, AB, Canada T1W 1K9. If you want a guided hike along some of the nearly 200 miles of trails in the park, this is the place to contact. The service offers several regular hikes, including an evening wildlife-watching hike ($40 per person) and a breakfast hike ($40). You can also book half-day ($45 per person) and full-day ($90 per person) hikes, as well as privately guided hiking adventures.

&. **Linnet Lake Trail** is an easy 0.6-mile loop hike along a self-guided, interpretive trail on the shore of Linnet Lake near Waterton Village. Take a few minutes to enjoy a break from driving and learn a bit about the area before you head south to the village on this casual stroll—a perfect opportunity to stretch your legs.

Red Rock Canyon Trail is an easy, 0.7-mile loop trail accessible from the parking area at the Red Rock Day Use Area (see Red Rock Parkway under *To See—Scenic Drives*). This trail leads you through the stunningly colorful canyon area, with its unique and intriguing geological features. Self-guiding interpretive signs fill you in about the varying types of sedimentary rocks and other natural features of interest.

See also Red Rock Parkway under *To See—Scenic Drives;* Glacier National Park under *Bicycling;* Glacier Park Boat Co. and Waterton Shoreline Cruise Co. under *Boating;* and Sperry Chalet under *Lodging—Other Options.*

HORSEBACK RIDING

Glacier National Park
The park allows private horse owners to ride on most of the trails in the park, though horses are prohibited on paved roadways. You should check with the park (see *Guidance*) for the latest information and regulations before bringing your horse.

✐ **Mule Shoe Outfitters** (Lake McDonald: 406-888-5121; Many Glacier: 406-732-4203; winter: 928-684-2328; www.mule-shoe.com) offers guided trail rides in Glacier National Park, with facilities at Lake McDonald and at Many Glacier. You can ride for 2 hours ($47) or up to a full day ($115–120), with a number of scenic and historic rides to choose from.

Waterton Lakes National Park
The park allows private horse owners to ride on most of the trails in the park. You should check with the park (see *Guidance*) for the latest information and regulations before bringing your horse.

✐ **Alpine Stables** (403-859-2462; www.alpinestables.com), across from the golf course just north of the Waterton Townsite. Open May through September. Alpine Stables offers guided horseback rides in Waterton Lakes National Park that range in length from 1 hour ($25 per person) to all day long ($119 per person). Children ages 4 and up are welcome. Alpine Stables also can board your horse ($9 per night).

See also Glacier Park, Inc., under *Guidance*; and Summit Station Lodge under *Lodging—Lodges.*

PADDLING/FLOATING Cameron Lake, at the end of Akamina Parkway in **Waterton Lakes National Park** (see *To See—Scenic Drives*), offers the best paddling in Waterton. While the Waterton Lakes tend to have windier conditions, not to mention motorized watercraft on Middle and Upper lakes, Cameron Lake tends to be calmer and does not allow motorized watercraft. Boat rentals are available at Cameron Lake. Kayakers and other paddlers will find numerous other options in the park as well.

The Flathead River. The North Fork and the Middle Fork of the Flathead River together form the western border of **Glacier National Park.** Both rivers are suitable for floating and paddling, with the North Fork being a fairly tame river with several small rapids (though paddlers and floaters should beware downed trees and logjams, especially during high water). Species of fish in the North Fork include mountain whitefish and west-slope cutthroat trout. The popular Middle Fork is a much more serious paddling and floating prospect, with class II–IV rapids in the portion that is designated wilderness (no motorized watercraft) and more class II–IV rapids between Moccasin Creek and West

Glacier. Portions of the river are relatively tame and suitable for a casual float. Species of fish in the Middle Fork include mountain whitefish and west-slope cutthroat trout.

♪ **Montana Raft Company** (1-800-521-7238; 406-387-5555; www.glacier guides.com/rafting.asp) provides white-water adventures on the Middle Fork of the Flathead River, which forms part of the western border of **Glacier National Park.** Raft for half a day ($42.80 adults; $32.10 children), a whole day ($73.83 adults; $51.36 children), or several days, or combine your trip with a guided hiking trip. You can also book a combination white-water rafting and barbecue dinner trip, a mellow floating trip, or an inflatable kayak trip. (See also **Glacier Wilderness Guides** under *Hiking.*)

See also *Boating.*

SNOW SPORTS **Glacier National Park** has abundant opportunities for both **cross-country skiing** and **snowshoeing** during wintertime, though you'll find little in the way of marked or groomed trails. A good topographic map and a sound awareness of your surroundings, including the serious potential for avalanche danger, will go a long way in making your trip a safe one.

Waterton Lakes National Park has two designated cross-country ski trails, both of which are accessed off Akamina Parkway (see *To See—Scenic Drives*). The **Cameron Ski Trail** (5K round-trip; easy) is accessible from the Little Prairie Picnic Shelter and takes you to Cameron Lake. The **Dipper Trail** (5.5K round-trip; moderate) is accessible from the Row Trailhead, and it can easily be linked into the Cameron Ski Trail. In addition to these, there are numerous undesignated trails popular with cross-country skiers, as well as opportunities for **snowshoeing, ski touring, ice climbing,** and **sledding.**

See also Akamina Parkway and Red Rock Parkway under *To See—Scenic Drives.*

UNIQUE ADVENTURES **Glacier Park, Inc.,** and **Trail of the Great Bear** (see *Guidance*) can book any number of unique adventures for you in both parks, whether you're interested in auto tours, boat tours, fishing tours, scenic tours, evening entertainment, or even a massage.

See also Glacier Park Boat Co. and Waterton Shoreline Cruise Co. under *Boating;* and Canadian Wilderness Tours and Glacier Wilderness Guides under *Hiking.*

✳ Lodging and Eating Out

BED & BREAKFASTS

East Glacier Park
Bison Creek Ranch (1-888-226-4482; www.angelfire.com/mt/bison creek; summer mailing address and phone: Box 144, East Glacier Park 59434; 406-226-4482; winter mailing address and phone: 2811 MT 206,

Columbia Falls 59912; 406-892-0663), 20722 US 2 W. This rustic B&B provides you with easy access to the park's Two Medicine Entrance. Choose from housekeeping cabins ($45–60) or A-frame chalets ($70). You'll also enjoy exploring the ranch property itself, which includes a small stream that will interest anglers. The ranch's family-style restaurant also serves home-cooked dinners.

St. Mary

See **Johnson's of St. Mary** under *Other Options*.

West Glacier 59936

Paola Creek Bed and Breakfast (1-888-311-5061; 406-888-5061; www.paolacreek.com), P.O. Box 97. From mile marker 172.8 on US 2 E., go 0.25 mile on Paola Creek Road. For those seeking luxurious accommodations with easy access to Glacier National Park, this B&B is truly a gem. The handcrafted Montana log house features four bedrooms, each with a queen-size bed and private bath, as well as a suite with a king-size bed and private bath with a whirlpool. Guests can choose to read a book from the 1,000-volume library or socialize with other guests in front of the rock fireplace in the common room—and, of course, enjoy a delectable full breakfast served each morning ($140–170).

A Wild Rose Bed and Breakfast (406-387-4900; www.awildrose.com), 10280 US 2 E. Surrounded by incredible mountains, you'll be only 6 miles from Glacier National Park when you stay in one of the four elegant rooms at A Wild Rose. Each room/suite features a unique blend of furnishings, including Victorian pieces and family antiques, that provide a lovely and eclectic setting, whether you stay in the Whirlpool Suite or the extremely private Balcony Suite. Breakfast is an all-you-can-eat affair, prepared fresh daily. Set on 7 private acres of land, this B&B offers ample opportunities for Montana adventures right out the front door ($120–150).

East Glacier Park 59434

Summit Station Lodge (406-226-4428; www.summitstationlodge.com), Marias Pass, US 2 W. (10 miles west of East Glacier Park). The Great Northern Railway constructed Summit Station back in 1906 to serve as—what else?—a train station. Located right on the continental divide, Summit Station today offers guests accommodations in five cabins that come with two queen-size beds, private baths, and a continental breakfast (or hot breakfast for $10 apiece) ($175). The main lodge serves as the center of social and dining activities, with incredible views of the surrounding area. The on-premises restaurant features exquisitely prepared cuisine from a menu that changes weekly, served in a fine dining atmosphere. Summit Station also provides guided fishing and horseback riding trips, among other services.

See also **Glacier Park Lodge and Golf Resort** under *To Do—Golf*.

Glacier National Park

Apgar Village Lodge (406-888-5484; www.westglacier.com), P.O. Box 410, West Glacier 59936. Located at the junction of US 2 and Going-to-the-Sun Road near the West Entrance. Open May through mid-October. This lovely, historic lodge includes both motel-style rooms and cabins in its accommodations, all of which have private baths ($66–151). The adjacent **West Glacier Restaurant and Lounge** provides family-style American dining, featuring homemade breads, soups, and pies; open for breakfast, lunch, and dinner.

& **Lake McDonald Lodge** (406-892-2525; www.glacierparkinc.com),

LAKE MCDONALD IN GLACIER NATIONAL PARK

P.O. Box 2025, Columbia Falls 59912. Located on Going-to-the-Sun Road, approximately 11 miles inside the west entrance to the park, off US 2 at West Glacier. The lodge is a National Historic Landmark located on the northeast shore of Lake McDonald. Built in 1913, the structure was originally a hunting lodge. Today, it provides an array of accommodations, including cabins, motel rooms, and lodge rooms ($101–152). The lodge still retains its cozy and rustic atmosphere, complete with much of the original decor. Guests enjoy amenities including two restaurants—**Russell's Fireside Dining Room** (handicapped accessible; fine dining, including breakfast, lunch, and dinner) and **Jammer Joe's Grill and Pizzeria** (casual dining, including lunch and dinner)—as well as the **Stockade Lounge** (drinks and bar menu), a gift shop, a camp store, and easy access to many park attractions.

St. Mary 59417

&. **The Resort at Glacier St. Mary Lodge** (1-800-368-3689; 406-732-4431; in the off-season: 208-726-6279; www.glcpark.com), US 89 (at the junction with Going-to-the-Sun Road). Open mid-April through mid-October. This lodge provides not only lodge-style accommodations but also motel-style rooms and cabins

($139–249). You'll enjoy easy access to the park, as well as numerous on-premises amenities, including a grocery store, a gas station, and laundry facilities. On-premises eateries include a fine dining establishment, the **Snowgoose Grille,** acclaimed for its expertly prepared buffalo dishes; the **Curly Bear Café,** a deli; **Coyote Cones,** an ice-cream and dessert parlor; **Rainbow Pizza Company; Glacier Park Espresso Bar and Fudge Shop;** and the **Mountain Lounge,** a cocktail bar.

Waterton Lakes National Park

✑ &. **Crandell Mountain Lodge** (1-866-859-2288; 403-859-2288; www.crandellmountainlodge.com), Box 114, 102 Mountview Road, Waterton Park, AB, Canada T0K 2M0; in Waterton Village. This homey, family-friendly lodging offers overnight accommodations, from single rooms to suites, that include a kitchen, fireplace, microwave, and more. You'll enjoy clean country living and tremendous hospitality ($89–199 CAN).

&. **The Kilmorey Lodge** (403-859-2334; www.kilmoreylodge.com), Box 100, Waterton Lakes National Park, AB, Canada T0K 2M0; in Waterton Village. Constructed in the 1920s, this historic lodge was one of the town site's original buildings. The decor reflects this, with numerous photographs of olden times, as well as antiques and collectibles. Guests stay in one of 23 comfortable rooms in the lodge ($83–200 US). Dining establishments include the **Lamp Post Dining Room,** serving internationally influenced cuisine for breakfast, lunch, and dinner in an elegant and relaxed setting; the **Ram's Head Lounge,** featuring a full bar and a bar menu; and the casual **Gazebo Café,** which serves casual café fare and has a full bar.

See also **Waterton Alpine Hostel** under *Other Options*).

West Glacier 59936
Belton Chalet & Lodge (1-888-235-8665; 406-888-5000; www.belton chalet.com), P.O. Box 206. Located at the West Entrance on US 2. This 1910 chalet is one of the buildings included in the Great Northern Railway Buildings National Historic Landmark (see *To See—Historic Landmarks*). Today, guests can stay in comfort in the lodge's newly renovated accommodations, which all include a queen-size bed and private bath ($130–155). Cabins are also available ($285). Remedies Day Spa, the **Belton Grill Dining Room** (fine dining), and the **Belton Chalet Tap Room** (bar-style menu) are also on the premises.

OTHER OPTIONS
East Glacier Park 59434
🍴 **Backpacker's Inn** (406-226-9392), 29 Dawson Avenue (behind Serrano's Mexican Restaurant). Open May through October. Nothing fancy here—just friendly, dorm-style accommodations in the three cabins at this hostel located behind a Mexican restaurant. Each cabin has its own bathroom. One co-ed cabin has bunk beds ($10 per person). The other two cabins are private, with queen-size beds ($30).

The Brown House Gallery and Museum (406-226-9385; www.glacierinfo.com/Brownhouse.html), 402 Washington Street. Open June through September. This former grocery store, constructed in the 1920s,

now serves as both a charming guest accommodation and an art gallery and museum. The owner is an accomplished potter and sculptor whose works are on display and for sale on the premises, as are the works of other Montana artists. Guests stay in one of two comfortably furnished bedrooms, complete with private baths and private entrances ($60).

🍴 ✦ **Brownies Grocery & AYH Hostel** (406-226-4426), 1020 MT 49. This popular lodging (read: make reservations in advance) features dorm-style or more private accommodations on the upper floor of a historical 1920s log building ($13–35). The first floor houses a **grocery store,** a **deli,** and a **bakery**—and the tantalizing aromas of the freshly made pastries and desserts might just lead you into temptation again and again during your stay. Upstairs, guests share bathrooms, a kitchen, a porch, and laundry facilities. Internet access is available as well.

Glacier National Park
Granite Park Chalet (1-800-521-7238; 406-387-5555; www.glacier guides.com), P.O. Box 330, West Glacier 59936. Open July through mid-September; reservations required. To stay at this chalet, you'll need to take a 7-mile moderate hike on the Highline Trail, accessible from about the midway point on Going-to-the-Sun Road. This chalet is one of the buildings included in the Great Northern Railway Buildings National Historic Landmark (see *To See—Historic Landmarks*). Constructed in 1914, today this historic structure provides comfortable overnight accommodations for hikers, with optional linen service and packaged meals for sale (about $70 per person per night).

&. **Many Glacier Hotel** (406-892-2525; www.glacierparkinc.com), P.O. Box 2025, Columbia Falls 59912. Located west of the Many Glacier Entrance. Open mid-June through mid-September. Many Glacier Hotel is a historic property constructed before 1920 on the shores of Swift-current Lake. It has more than 200 guest rooms, making it the largest lodging facility in the park. Guests enjoy fantastic views, original Swiss-themed decor, and access to numerous park attractions when they stay in one of the rooms or suites ($117–236). Dining options include the **Ptarmigan Dining Room** (handicapped accessible; fine dining, including breakfast, lunch, and dinner); **Swiss and Interlaken Lounge** (bar and lighter fare); and **Heidi's Convenience Store** (quick foods like hot dogs and desserts).

Sperry Chalet (1-888-345-2649; 406-387-5654; www.sperrychalet.com), P.O. Box 188, West Glacier 59936. The chalet is accessible via a 6.7-mile trail that departs from Lake McDonald Lodge (see the listing under *Lodges*). Open mid-July through mid-September; reservations required. This chalet is one of the buildings included in the Great Northern Railway Buildings National Historic Landmark (see *To See—Historic Landmarks*). The hike in is a serious proposition, involving 3,300 feet of elevation gain. Your reward is a comfortable night's sleep in a historic, scenic setting. The stone building, constructed in 1913 or thereabouts, provides private, rustic accommodations (no running water or electricity in the rooms). Breakfast, lunch, and dinner are included in the rate ($255 double occupancy).

St. Mary 59417

&. **Glacier Trailhead Cabins** (1-800-311-1041; 406-732-4143; www.glacier trailheadcabins.com), P.O. Box 122, Babb 59411. Located on US 89 N., 2.5 miles north of St. Mary. Open all year, the 12 cabins here offer one or two queen-sized beds, private bathrooms, and easy access to Glacier National Park in all seasons ($65–120).

✿ **Johnson's of St. Mary** (406-732-5565; 406-732-4207; www.johnsonsof stmary.com), HC 72-10, Star Route. Located 0.25 mile from the St. Mary Entrance to Glacier National Park. For more than half a century, this family-owned and family-operated lodging facility and restaurant. Johnson's includes a campground ($16–30), as well as cottages and a bed & breakfast facility ($75–100). The **on-premises restaurant** serves breakfast, lunch, and dinner, featuring fresh-baked bread and family-style specials daily. Guests enjoy a wide array of amenities, including laundry facilities, a gift shop, modem connections, and much more.

Waterton Lakes National Park
Prince of Wales Hotel (406-892-2525; within Canada: 403-236-3400; www.princeofwaleswaterton.com), P.O. Box 2025, Columbia Falls 59912. Located on the shores of Upper Waterton Lake. Open early June through mid-September. This National Historic Site also has the distinction of being one of the world's most photographed hotels. Its magnificent, eye-catching, architecture is matched by its incredible setting on a bluff overlooking the township below. Completed in 1927 and named for Britain's Prince Edward, the hotel carries on a British theme throughout, including the serving of afternoon tea;

English bone china is available for purchase in the gift shop. Dining facilities include the **Royal Stewart Dining Room,** serving breakfast, lunch, and dinner in a casual atmosphere with views of the lake; **Valerie's Tea Room,** serving a continental breakfast and afternoon tea; and **Windsor Lounge,** serving a variety of spirits. Rooms $179–799 US.

✍ 🐾 ♿ **Waterton Alpine Hostel** (403-859-2150; 403-859-2151; www .watertonlakeslodge.com/hostel.html), P.O. Box 4, Waterton Lakes National Park, AB, Canada T0K 2M0; in Waterton Village. Open year-round, this hostel located at and run by Waterton Parks Lodge offers inexpensive yet comfortable accommodations for both individuals and families. Individual guests can stay in bunk-style dorm rooms with up to three other guests ($31–35 per person). Families and couples can rent private rooms with private adjoining bathrooms ($93–105). Rooms in the lodge are available as well ($139–315). Dining facilities include fine dining at the **Beargrass Lodge,** as well as the more casual eatery called the **Bighorn Grill,** with its attached bar, **The Wolf's Den.**

West Glacier 59936

♿ **Silverwolf Log Chalet Resort** (406-387-4448; www.silverwolf chalets.com), 160 Gladys Glen Road. Open mid-May through mid-October, this adult-oriented resort features private, designer log chalets built for two, complete with queen-size beds, private baths, gas-log fireplaces, and satellite television. Every morning, guests enjoy a lavish continental breakfast in their cabin, included in the rates ($155–158).

Contact **Glacier Park, Inc.** and **Trail of the Great Bear Central Reservations and Tours** (listed under *Guidance*) for more lodgings throughout the park.

For *Special Events,* see "Glacier Country."

NORTH-CENTRAL MONTANA: RUSSELL COUNTRY

Sweeping oceans of rippling prairie grasses interspersed with rugged islands of mountains in its southern reaches characterize the terrain of Russell Country, with the dramatic and untamed Upper Missouri River Breaks National Monument bisecting the region from west to east. And while this region is home to the "big city" of Great Falls—with a population hovering around 60,000—you'll find that much of Russell Country's land remains uninhabited and wild, almost exactly as it was when Lewis and Clark passed this way some two centuries ago. Scattered throughout this vast and largely untrammeled area, an adequate network of towns and cities provides all of the amenities and attractions a traveler might want, from fine dining and lodging to historic sites, museums, and family activities. And yet it is the uninhabited terrain of Russell Country that makes this area possess a magical and distinctive character of its own.

Perhaps the most dominant feature of the region's landscape is the Missouri River, a designated National Wild and Scenic River for 149 miles, from Fort Benton to the James Kipp Recreation Area in the Charles M. Russell National Wildlife Refuge. Nearly 400,000 acres of land on the banks surrounding this incredible, free-flowing stretch of river has been incorporated into a national monument that is managed by the Bureau of Land Management. If you're seeking solitude and remarkable, one-of-a-kind scenery, you'll find it in this area of Russell Country, whether you choose to explore the Upper Missouri by car via the Missouri Breaks National Back Country Byway or an auto touring service (see Missouri River Breaks Tours in *To Do—Unique Adventures*), by paddling or floating, by keelboat (see Upper Missouri River Keelboat Company Expedition in *To Do—Unique Adventures*), by horseback, or on foot.

South of the Upper Missouri River, you'll discover that spaced among the region's grasslands are oases of forests, while on its western border lies the Rocky Mountain Front. Together, these areas make up Lewis and Clark National Forest, with its Bob Marshall Wilderness Area. Winter brings with it virtually limitless potential for outdoor fun and recreation here, from downhill skiing at one of the forest's remote, uncrowded ski areas to snowmobiling, cross-country skiing, and even ice fishing. Trails crisscross the forest, many with campgrounds

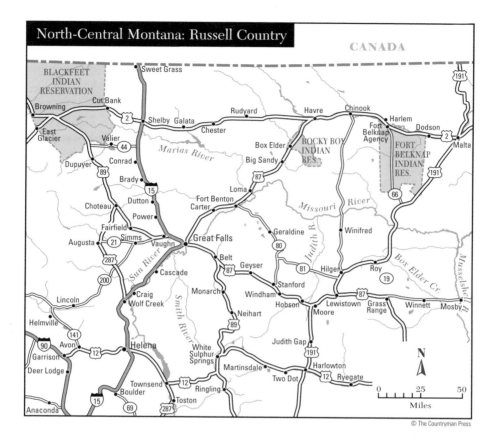

© The Countryman Press

serving as their starting point, making for easy access to activities popular during the warmer season, including hiking, horseback riding, and mountain biking.

In addition to the specific bicycling adventure detailed below, you'll discover that, given the relatively small amount of auto traffic, many of the area's paved and unpaved roads offer tremendous opportunities to explore the area via the power of your feet pushing those pedals. In addition, Lewis and Clark National Forest offers a plethora of more technically challenging trails suitable for more experienced riders. Your imagination is your sole limitation in plotting a ride, but be sure to prepare, as you'll likely ride on long stretches of Russell Country's roads with no services in sight.

If you prefer to play in or on the water rather than push on the pedals, you're in luck—water sports abound in Russell Country. Along with the Upper Missouri River, numerous other rivers flow through this region, providing the enthusiastic angler with myriad fishing opportunities. Those with a passion for casting should consider applying for a permit to float the remarkable and hard-to-access Smith River (see *To Do—Fishing* for details). A number of large lakes and reservoirs also serve as desirable boating and fishing destinations, even in winter, when ice fishing is the name of the game. In addition to the major destinations listed below under *To Do—Boating and Fishing*, boating enthusiasts and anglers with a sense of adventure will find many smaller, more remote bodies of water upon which to float their boats.

When you need a break from your outdoor adventures—or if outdoor adventures just aren't your thing—you'll still find plenty to occupy your time in Russell Country, both in the big city of Great Falls and in the smaller towns around the region. Great Falls has a variety of museums and cultural attractions—nine of them, in fact—that participate in April's Museum Sunday Sampler. A program that offers free admission, the Sunday Sampler gives folks a taste of the city's culture and history. In the Lewistown area, you can climb aboard the Charlie Russell Chew-Choo (see *To Do—Unique Adventures*) and enjoy a scenic train ride with a catered gourmet meal served on board. White Sulphur Springs provides the chance to soak in natural hot springs (see *To Do—Hot Springs*) and to learn about their interesting history.

From history to scenery, from forested mountain ranges to sweeping grasslands that do justice to the classic Montana nickname, Big Sky, Russell Country offers a chance to truly explore some of the nation's most vast and most remote terrain. Step into the shoes of Lewis and Clark . . . step back further and walk in the footprints of the Native Americans who once hunted buffalo here by the millions . . . or step far into the prehistoric past to commune with the bones of the dinosaurs who once walked this land.

GUIDANCE **Big Sandy Chamber of Commerce** (406-378-2418; www.big sandymt.com), P.O. Box 411, Big Sandy 59520.

RIVER'S EDGE TRAIL IN GREAT FALLS

Chinook Chamber of Commerce (406-357-3160; 406-357-2248; www.chinook montana.com). Visitor information available at the **Blaine County Museum** (406-357-2590), 501 Indiana Avenue, P.O. Box 744, Chinook 59523.

Chippewa Cree Business Committee (406-395-4282; http://tlc.wtp.net/ chippewa.htm), R.R. 1, Box 544, Box Elder 59521.

Choteau Chamber of Commerce (1-800-823-3866; 406-466-5316; www .choteaumontana.com), 35 1st NW, P.O. Box 897, Choteau 59422.

Conrad Area Chamber of Commerce (406-271-7791; www.conrad mt.com), 702 S. Main Street, Suite 1, Conrad 59425.

Fairfield Area Chamber of Commerce (406-467-2531), Drawer 9, Fairfield 59436.

Fort Belknap Tourism Office and Information Center (406-353-8471; 406-353-8473; http://tlc.wtp.net/fort
.htm), R.R. 1, Box 66, Harlem 59526.

Fort Benton Chamber of Commerce (406-622-3864; www.fortbenton.com), 11421 Front Street (in the Information Center), P.O. Box 12, Fort Benton 59442.

Great Falls Chamber of Commerce (406-761-4434; www.greatfallschamber .org), 710 1st Avenue N., Great Falls 59401.

Harlowton Chamber of Commerce and Agriculture (406-632-4694; www .harlowtonchamber.com), P.O. Box 694, Harlowton 59036.

Havre Area Chamber of Commerce (406-265-4383; www.havremt.com), 518 1st Street, Havre 59501.

Judith Basin Area Chamber of Commerce (406-566-2238; www.judithbasin .com), P.O. Box 102, Stanford 59479.

Lewistown Area Chamber of Commerce (406-538-5436; www.lewistown chamber.com), 408 NE Main Street, Lewistown 59457.

Liberty County Chamber of Commerce (406-759-4848), 15 E. Washington Avenue, P.O. Box 632, Chester 59522.

Meagher County Chamber of Commerce (406-547-2250; www.meagher chamber.com), P.O. Box 356, White Sulphur Springs 59645.

Rocky Boy Indian Reservation. See **Chippewa Cree Business Committee,** listed above.

Russell Country, Inc. (1-800-527-5348; www.russell.visitmt.com), P.O. Box 3166, Great Falls 59403.

Shelby Area Chamber of Commerce (406-434-7184; www.homestead.com/ shelbychamber), 102 Main Street, Shelby 59474.

Valier Area Development Corporation (406-279-3561; www.valier.org), P.O. Box 568, Valier 59486.

GETTING THERE Great Falls lies at the crossroads of I-15, US 87, and US 89. Shelby, Chester, Havre, Chinook, and Harlem lie from west to east on US 2. Shelby also lies on I-15, as does Conrad. White Sulphur Springs lies at the junction of US 89 and US 12. Harlowton lies at the intersection of US 191 and US 12. Lewistown lies on US 87 at its eastern junction with US 191.

See also *Airports, Amtrak, Bus Service,* and *Travel Information* in "What's Where in Montana."

MEDICAL EMERGENCY **Basin Medical Center** (406-566-2773), 76 Central Avenue, Stanford.

Benefis Healthcare (406-455-5200), 1101 26th Street S., Great Falls.

Big Sandy Medical Center (406-378-2188), 3 Montana Avenue, Big Sandy.

Central Montana Medical Center (406-538-7711), 408 Wendell Avenue, Lewistown.

Liberty County Hospital (406-759-5181), MT 223 and Monroe, Chester.

Marias Medical Center (406-434-3200), 640 Park Drive, Shelby.

Missouri River Medical Center (406-622-3331), 1501 Street Charles, Fort Benton.

Mountainview Medical Center (406-547-3321), 16 W. Main Street, White Sulphur Springs.

Northern Montana Hospital (406-262-1201), 30 13th Street W., Havre.

Pondera Medical Center (406-271-3211), 805 Sunset Boulevard, Conrad.

Teton Medical Center (406-466-5763), 915 4th Street NW, Choteau.

Wheatland Memorial Hospital (406-632-4351), 530 3rd Street NW, Harlowton.

✳ To See

TOWNS **Fort Belknap** is located at the junction of US 2 and MT 66 on the **Fort Belknap Indian Reservation.** Stop at the Fort Belknap Tourism Office and Information Center (see listing under *Guidance*) for information about the recreational and cultural activities on the reservation, which is inhabited by the Assiniboine and Gros Ventre tribes. This information center and rest area also has a campground, and the staff also gives tours of surrounding attractions that include the tribe's 10,000-acre **buffalo preserve, teepee rings, Mission Canyon, the Natural Bridge,** and **Devil's Kitchen,** among other sites.

Fort Benton lies northwest of Great Falls on US 87. This historic town marks the western border of the Upper Missouri National Wild and Scenic River. Established as a bustling crossroads for fur trading in the late 1840s by the American Fur Company, Fort Benton grew in importance and size with Montana's ensuing gold rush. This was a central spot for embarkation and debarkation during the steamboat era, and you can still walk along the old steamboat levee, which today forms a park that runs the length of the town. Many buildings constructed in the 1800s still stand in the downtown area—a **National Historic Landmark District**—including the remains of **Old Fort Benton** in City Park.

Harlowton lies at the junction of US 191 and US 12. This small town is home to **Chief Joseph Park,** which provides travelers with a campground, a picnic area, a playground, a fishing pond, and trails. Harlowton also has the **E-57B Electric Train Park,** which pays homage to the longest stretch of electric railroad in the world, as well as the **Upper Musselshell Museum,** which captures and preserves local history, memorabilia, and lore. To the east 20 miles on US 12, you'll find **Deadman's Basin Recreation Area,** which has camping (free), all-season fishing, a boat ramp, and seasonal ice-skating.

Havre, located along US 2 northeast of Great Falls, traces its roots to agricultural endeavors, as well as to the coming of the railroad. It is the largest city along Montana's major northern east–west throughway, US 2. To the southeast lie the **Bear Paw Mountains,** and the **Milk River** runs through town. Ample opportunities to explore can be found both by those in pursuit of outdoor recreation and by history buffs.

Lewistown, southeast of Great Falls on US 87, is the county seat of Fergus County—and the geographical center of Montana. Situated in the Judith Basin, Lewistown provides access to the **Judith Mountains** and the **Moccasin Mountains** to the north and the **Snowy Mountains** to the south. The town itself was the first Montana home for famed western artist Charles M. Russell, for whom this entire travel region was named. Lewistown is home to the **Lewistown Art Center** (406-538-8278), 801 W. Broadway, featuring 12 annual exhibits by local and regional artists; the **Central Montana Museum** (406-538-5436), 408 NE Main Street, a classic local history museum; and the historic residential **Silk Stocking District,** northeast of the downtown area (contact the chamber of commerce listed above under *Guidance* for a self-guided tour map). Along with the typical assortment of chain restaurants, in this town you'll also find many locally owned and locally operated eateries along Main Street.

Shelby lies north of Great Falls on I-15 and west of Havre on US 2. The county seat of Tooele County, this northern outpost provides a stopping point along one of the main routes into Glacier National Park, as well as prior to reaching the Canadian border 35 miles to the north. The **Burlington Northern–Santa Fe East and West Main Line** railroad tracks pass through Shelby, linking it to major cities like Seattle and Chicago. Shelby is home to an official **Montana State Visitor Center** on the east side of town on US 2 and the free **Marias Museum of History and Art** (406-434-2551), 206 12th Avenue N., with exhibits on local and regional history.

White Sulphur Springs lies south of Great Falls on US 89—the Kings Hill National Scenic Byway. Nestled in the Smith River Valley, the town is surrounded by the **Big Belt Mountains, Little Belt Mountains,** and **Castle Mountains.** This setting makes for a wealth of outdoor recreational pursuits, including fishing, hiking, camping, mountain biking, skiing, snowmobiling, and golfing—with the added bonus of **natural hot springs** in town that are open to the public for soaking sore bodies.

MUSEUMS **Castle Museum** (406-547-2324), 310 2nd Avenue NE, White Sulphur Springs. Open daily 10 AM–5:30 PM May 15 through September 15 (and by appointment in the off-season); $3 adults, $2 children or seniors. "The Castle" is worth a visit simply due to its historic value as a structure—but the added bonus is that it also houses the **Meagher County Museum.** Teams of oxen lugged the hand-cut granite blocks from the Castle Mountains to this site, where they were used to build this handsome Victorian mansion for Bryon Roger Sherman and his family in 1892. Today the mansion is filled with local pioneer-era memorabilia and antiques representing local history.

& **C. M. Russell Museum** (406-727-8787; www.cmrussell.org), 400 13th Street N., Great Falls. Open May 1 through September 30 Monday through Saturday 9 AM–6 PM, Sunday noon–5 PM; open October 1 through April 30 Tuesday through Saturday 10 AM–5 PM, Sunday 1 PM–5 PM; $6 adults, $5 seniors (60 and older), $3 students, children 5 and under free. Inside the museum, you can view an impressive, permanent collection of works by the renowned western artist Charles M. Russell, as well as pieces by other artists of note. In addition, the museum holds the Browning Firearms Collection, a series of miniature wagons, and numerous Russell personal items, such as illustrated letters. Stroll around the grounds before or after you go inside the museum—you'll see sculptures by Charles M. Russell and a sculpture of the artist, as well as his former log studio and his home that he shared with his wife, Nancy. (See also Museum Sunday Sampler under *Special Events.*)

&. **Fort Benton Montana's Heritage Complex** (406-622-5316; www.fort benton.com/museums), 1205 20th Street and/or Old Fort Park, Fort Benton. Open May 1 through September 30, 10 AM–5 PM; $4 per person (good for both museums). This complex of museums includes the **Museum of the Northern Great Plains** (1205 20th Street), detailing the story of human life on Montana's plains during the 19th century; and the **Museum of the Upper Missouri** (Old Fort Park), covering the unique role this area played in the migration to and set- tlement of the West. In addition, you can see the remains of Old Fort Benton at Old Fort Park or possibly tour them, if you make an appointment or the site has open hours (as it does in summer; call for details).

&. **H. Earl Clack Memorial Museum** (406-265-4000; www.theheritagecenter .com), 306 3rd Avenue, Havre. Open for tours Memorial Day through Labor Day Tuesday through Saturday 10 AM–5 PM; open Labor Day through Memorial Day Tuesday through Saturday 1 PM–5 PM; free. This museum houses educa- tional dioramas that help explain the local history of both Native Americans and settlers. You'll also see items recovered from the nearby Wahkpa Chu'gn Archae- ology Site on display here. The museum is located in the Heritage Center in downtown Havre, where you can find information about tour guides for historic Fort Assinniboine and Wahkpa Chu'gn Archaeology Site, as well as the offices of the Havre Historic Preservation Office.

&. **High Plains Heritage Center** (406-452-3462; www.highplainsheritage.org), 422 2nd Street S., Great Falls. Open Monday through Friday 10 AM–5 PM, Satur- day and Sunday noon–5 PM (summer); closed on all holidays and on Monday in winter; $2 per person, children 5 and under free. The 3-story, brick International Harvester Building, with its huge wooden beams and posts, conveys a sense of the heft required for the pro- duction of heavy industrial farm equipment—but its days as a building devoted to the manufacture of farm- related machinery are in the past. This structure is now dedicated to helping preserve the heritage of the Great Falls area, of which it is most certainly a part. The center is run by the Cascade County Historical Society and the Great Falls Genealogy Soci- ety, and the museum's third floor con-

CHARLES M. RUSSELL HOUSE, STUDIO, AND MUSEUM

tains an official records repository of archives that includes photographs, newspapers, and other significant documents. The **Great Falls Historic Trolley** (406-771-1100; www.greatfallshistorictrolley.com) departs from this museum June through September several times a day, giving riders a 2-hour narrated tour of the city ($20 adults, $5 children ages 2–12). (See also Museum Sunday Sampler under *Special Events*.)

PARIS GIBSON SQUARE MUSEUM OF ART

& **Lewis and Clark National Historic Trail Interpretive Center** (406-727-8733; www.fs.fed.us/r1/lewisclark/lcic), 4201 Giant Springs Road, Great Falls. Open daily Memorial Day through September 30, 9 AM–6 PM; open October 1 through Memorial Day Tuesday through Saturday 9 AM–5 PM, Sunday noon–5 PM; $5 adults, $4 students and seniors, $2 children 6 and older, children 5 and under free. Your tour of this interpretive center, situated on the banks of the Missouri River, should start with a stroll through the outdoor gardens. There you'll find plants that Lewis and Clark discovered during their exploratory mission, complete with explanatory plaques detailing both native uses of the plants as well as when and where Lewis and Clark encountered and gathered them. Inside, you'll learn all about the expedition of 1804–6 via costumed interpreters, audiovisual presentations, exhibits, and a film by noted filmmaker Ken Burns. (See also Museum Sunday Sampler under *Special Events*.)

Old Trail Museum (406-466-5332), 823 N. Main Street, Choteau. Open May 1 through September 30, 9 AM–6 PM; open October 1 through April 30 Tuesday through Saturday 10 AM–3 PM; free. The history of this area, known as the Rocky Mountain Front, is the focus of this museum, with exhibits covering both the natural world and the cultural aspects of the region. This museum strives to show all aspects of the colorful and interesting local history, from the days of the dinosaurs to the lives of Native Americans and the coming of settlers. If dinosaurs intrigue you, call ahead to schedule a walking tour (or a multiday educational adventure) on Egg Mountain, the site of a local paleontology dig located on the Nature Conservancy's **Pine Butte Preserve** (406-466-2158). For a special treat, grab a cone from the ice-cream parlor in the visitor center after you tour the museum.

& ❦ **Paris Gibson Square Museum of Art** (406-727-8255; www.the-square .org), 1400 1st Avenue N., Great Falls. Open Monday through Friday 10 AM–5 PM, Saturday and Sunday noon–5 PM, Tuesday evening 7 PM–9 PM; closed on Monday in winter; free. This museum's home is a striking, historic sandstone building constructed in 1896 and used as a school until 1975. Now, "the Square" houses a contemporary art museum featuring both Montana artists and other contemporary artists of note in its seven exhibition galleries. In addition, this community center offers classes, lectures, tours, art workshops, and performances on a regular basis. The **Bistro at the Square** serves up a gourmet lunch to patrons Tuesday through Friday each week. (See also Museum Sunday Sampler in *Special Events.*)

See also Harlowton, Lewistown, and Shelby under *Towns;* Bear Paw Battlefield and Havre Beneath the Streets under *Historic Landmarks, Places, and Sites;* and Timescale Adventures under *To Do—Unique Adventures.*

HISTORIC LANDMARKS, PLACES, AND SITES **Bear Gulch Pictographs** (406-428-2185; www.beargulch.net), 2749 Fairview Road, Forest Grove (27 miles southeast of Lewistown via MT 238). Open May through November for a daily tour at 10 AM; $10 per person or $25 per family, reservations accepted but not required. Take a tour to view some 2,000 pictographs and petroglyphs painted and etched onto the rocks by Native Americans at this site. Also in the works are construction of a campground and a visitor center.

Bear Paw Battlefield (406-357-3130; 406-689-3155; www.nps.gov/nepe), 16 miles south of Chinook via MT 240. Open year-round dawn to dusk; free. In this windswept, almost wistful setting on the Montana prairie, on a quiet day you can imagine that you hear the whispers of the violence—and ultimate defeat—that came to pass here on an autumn day in 1877. This battlefield marks the spot where the strong and noble Chief Joseph of the Nez Perce finally surrendered, ceasing his efforts to maintain his people's traditional ways of living, as well as their homelands. After a 1,300-mile retreat, this became the final stop on the Nez Perce Trail, which starts in Joseph, Oregon. "From where the sun now stands, I will fight no more forever," Chief Joseph proclaimed. At this site (one of 38 sites that together form the Nez Perce National Historical Park), you'll find an interpretive trail and picnic area. In nearby Chinook, the handicapped-accessible **Blaine County Museum** (406-357-2590), 501 Indiana Avenue, has exhibits and an audiovisual presentation on the battlefield and the Nez Perce Indians (open Memorial Day through Labor Day 8 AM–noon and 1 PM–5 PM; open Labor Day through Memorial Day, Thanksgiving, Christmas, and New Year's Day 1 PM–5 PM; free).

Cascade County Courthouse (406-454-6810; www.co.cascade.mt.us), 415 2nd Avenue N., Great Falls. Open Monday through Friday 8 AM–5 PM; free. If you love historic architecture on a grand scale, schedule a stop to view this imposing three-story courthouse constructed in the English Renaissance Revival style. Built between 1901 and 1903, the courthouse features a tall copper dome raised on columns, as well as four polished granite columns spanning the entrance to the building.

Fort Assinniboine Historic Site, Northern Agricultural Research Center (406-265-4000; 406-265-4383; www.ag.montana.edu/narc/fort.htm), 6 miles southwest of Havre on US 87. Open May through September for tours by appointment only through the H. Earl Clack Memorial Museum (see *Museums*); no other access permitted. From 1879 until 1911, this was the site of the largest military fort west of the Mississippi River, with more than 100 buildings in its 40-by-15-mile area. The reasons for its establishment lie primarily in an effort to prevent attacks from the Lakota Sioux Indians, led by Chief Sitting Bull, who had fled to Canada following the Battle of Little Bighorn. From this point, military patrols originated, and this fort even became Montana's military headquarters for a time. Abandoned as a military fort in 1911, this site became the home of a state agricultural experimentation station, and it retains that function today.

Havre Beneath the Streets (406-265-8888 www.havremt.com/attractions/beneath_the_streets.htm), 120 3rd Avenue, Havre. Tours daily in summer 9 AM–5 PM (first tour at 9:30 AM; last tour at 3:30 PM); tours in winter Monday through Saturday 10 AM–4 PM; $8 adults, $7 seniors, $4 children; reservations are required. Tours of the town's historic underground depart from the **Havre Railroad Museum** (free), which houses railroad-related displays, including model trains. A tour takes you straight into an intriguing page of Havre's past. When a fire destroyed most of the town in 1904, undaunted shopkeepers moved their businesses underground to keep them running until the surface could be rebuilt. This underground shopping district has been preserved for posterity, allowing today's visitors to step into the town's history by delving just beneath the surface. Included on your tour are visits to an opium den and to a bordello, as well as stops at more socially acceptable businesses. You can also take a walking tour of the aboveground historic buildings—which date from 1904, for the most part (maps are available at the museum). To complete your historic explorations of Havre, explore the 36-block **Havre Residential Historic District,** which is listed on the National Register of Historic Places and starts at the Heritage Center (306 3rd Avenue). Free walking-tour maps are available from the Havre Historic Preservation Office (by appointment only; 406-265-6233) located in the Heritage Center, which also provides free guided tours of the district on Saturday at 7 PM during the summer.

Historic ferries. Carter Ferry (406-454-5840), 26 miles north of Great Falls via US 87 to Carter, and then south on 3rd Avenue (Carter Ferry Road) to the crossing at Carter; **McClelland Ferry** (406-462-5513), north of Winifred on C.R. 300; **Virgelle Ferry** (1-800-426-2926; 406-378-3110), at Virgelle, northeast of Fort Benton and southwest of Big Sandy via US 87. Open April through October or November (depending on ice levels in the Missouri River); free. These three historic ferries provide ride-at-your-own-risk transportation across the river for you and your automobile. Ring a buzzer to call the ferry operator, and then watch as your car is hooked and hitched for secure passage.

Lewistown area ghost towns (406-538-5436; www.lewistownchamber.com), coordinated by the Lewistown Chamber of Commerce, 408 NE Main Street. With the discovery of gold in 1877, the former towns of Yogo City and Hoover City sprang up in Yogo Gulch, southeast of Utica on MT 239. The gold didn't pan out, and the populations dwindled until the discovery of sapphires in 1894. The original sapphire mine produced among the highest-quality sapphires in the world between 1895 and 1923, when the mine was damaged by rain; the mine never recovered economically. Today, Rancor, Inc., and Vortex Mining produce unique Yogo sapphires (marketing cut and finished products only) from this area. Also, individuals mine them from private lots in the small town of Sapphire Village; so, although Yogo City and Hoover City are no longer, the mining for these exceptional sapphires continues. More mining history lies northeast of Lewistown, where Gilt Edge, Kendall, and Maiden were all once bustling gold mining camps in their heydays in the late 1800s and early 1900s. Today all you'll find is a few buildings in disrepair and the crumbled remains of the rest of these towns. Stop at or call the Lewistown Chamber of Commerce for details and directions to each town site.

State of Montana's Lewis and Clark Memorial (406-622-3864; www.fort benton.com/l&c/index.htm), River Front Park, Fort Benton. Created by artist Bob Scriver, this is the state's official memorial commemorating the Corps of Discovery's leaders. It shows them seeking to pinpoint the way to the Pacific Ocean, accompanied by their famous Indian guide, Sacagawea, and her infant son.

& **Ulm Pishkun State Park** (406-866-2217; www.fwp.state.mt.us/parks/parks report.asp?mapnum=15), 10 miles south of Great Falls on I-15 to Exit 270, then north via Vaughn Road and Ulm Road. Open daily Memorial Day through September 30, 9 AM–5 PM; open October 1 through Memorial Day Wednesday through Saturday 10 AM–4 PM, Sunday noon–4 PM; residents: free; nonresidents: $2 adults, $1 children 6–12, children 5 and under free. Additional fees charged for special programs. This state park's interpretive visitor center explains the significance of this enormous buffalo kill site used by Native Americans for at least 2,000 years. Millions of buffalo remains lie at the bottom of the sandstone cliffs—evidence of the tremendous usefulness of this natural formation, over which the Indians would drive the buffalo to their death and then process their bodies for food, clothing, and shelter. In addition to exploring the visitor center, you can hike 2.5 miles of interpretive trails, see a black-tailed prairie-dog town, or have a picnic. (See also Museum Sunday Sampler under *Special Events.*)

Wahkpa Chu'gn Archaeology Site (406-265-6417; 406-265-7550; www.buffalo jump.org), 3993 6th Street W., Havre. Open June 1 through Labor Day for daily 1-hour tours 10 AM–5 PM and at 7 PM (except on Sunday); open and by appointment (weather permitting) the rest of the year; $5 adults, $4 students, $2.50 children 6 and older, children 5 and under free. Tours are given by the H. Earl Clack Memorial Museum (see *Museums*). A hands-on, up-close tour of this well-preserved site takes you some 2,000 years into the past, when Native Americans first used this area as a kill site for slaughtering buffalo, thus providing them with the necessary food, clothing, and shelter to survive. You'll see layers of campsites, arrowheads, and buffalo remains, showing that not one but actually three distinct groups of Native Americans used this area over time as a place for herding, corralling, and slaughtering buffalo as they jumped down the steep hillside to their death—killed by the plummet or by arrows fired upon them as they jumped or following the jump.

See also Fort Belknap, Fort Benton, Havre, and Harlowton under *Towns;* Castle Museum, C. M. Russell Museum, Fort Benton Montana's Heritage Complex, High Plains Heritage Center, and Paris Gibson Square Museum of Art under *Museums;* Gibson Park under *For Families;* Decision Point under *To Do—Hiking;* Timescale Adventures and Upper Missouri River Keelboat Company Expedition under *To Do—Unique Adventures;* Sluice Boxes State Park under *Wilder Places—Parks;* Collins Mansion Bed and Breakfast, Inn Dupuyer Bed and Breakfast, Stone School Inn Bed and Breakfast, and Symmes–Wicks House Bed and Breakfast under *Lodging—Bed and Breakfasts;* and Grand Union Hotel, Historic Hotel Calvert, and Pioneer Lodge under *Lodging—Other Options.*

FOR FAMILIES & ♪ **Children's Museum of Montana** (406-452-6661; www
.childrensmuseumofmt.org), 22 Railroad Square (behind the Civic Center),
Great Falls. Open Tuesday through Saturday 9:30 AM–5 PM; closed Fourth of
July, Thanksgiving, Christmas, and New Year's Day; $2.50 adults, children under
2 free. This museum caters to its most important visitors—your kids—with an
understanding of their innate desire to touch, probe, prod, grab, grasp, push,
and poke pretty much everything that comes within their reach. They'll find no
"hands-off" or "hush, hush!" here. Instead, they'll discover exhibits created with
interaction in mind, allowing them the freedom to explore, create, construct, and
play for hours (and you, too, if you're so inclined). (See also Museum Sunday
Sampler under *Special Events.*)

♪ **Electric City Water Park** (406-771-1265; www.ci.great-falls.mt.us/people_
offices/park_rec/ecwp/home.htm), 100 River Drive S., Great Falls. Open beginning of June through mid-August Monday through Friday 1 PM–8 PM, Saturday
and Sunday 11 AM–6 PM; all-access is $9 adults, $8 children 3–17, one child under
3 free with one paying adult, $1 for each additional child under 3; restricted-
access packages available as well. Enjoy a wild ride down one of the two slides of
the Power Tower Plunge, or surf the waves on a boogie board in the Flow Rider.
Small fry will enjoy the baby pool and interactive play structure at the Little
Squirts Soak Zone. Adults might prefer to hang out in Mitchell Pool, Montana's
largest outdoor heated public pool.

& ♪ **Gibson Park** (406-771-1265; www.ci.great-falls.mt.us/people_offices/
park_rec/parks.htm), along Park Drive between Central Avenue and 6th Street,
Great Falls. Open dawn to dusk year-round; free. This is the largest of Great
Falls's 53 city parks. It includes a playground, a duck pond (with ice-skating in
wintertime), statues (including one of Great Falls's founder, Paris Gibson), the
historic 1884 Vinegar Jones Cabin, a walking path (suitable for running, bicycling, and in-line skating as well) that links to the River's Edge Trail (see *To
Do—Bicycling*), and picnic areas. Gibson Park also has its own colorful flower
gardens, as well as the on-premises **Park & Ponder Coffeehouse.** The whole
family can relax in this lovely setting, enjoying a picnic lunch, a walk, a bike ride,
or the playground.

See also Lake Frances under *To Do—Boating;* Choteau City Park and Lake
Shel-oole Campground under *To Do—Camping;* Bull Run Guest Ranch,
DeBoo's Pine Ridge Ranch Adventures, Hitch'n Rail Ranch, and Sourdough
Ranch Adventures under *To Do—Horseback Riding;* Bear Paw Ski Bowl, Show-
down Montana Ski Area, and Teton Pass Ski Area under *To Do—Snow Sports;*
Timescale Adventures under *To Do—Unique Adventures;* Foxwood Inn Bed and
Breakfast, Our Home Bed and Breakfast, and Snowy View Bed and Breakfast
under *Lodging—Bed and Breakfasts;* Duvall Inn under *Lodging—Lodges;*
Grassy Mountain Lodge and Cabins under *Lodging—Other Options;* and Mon-
tana Chokecherry Festival, Central Montana Fair, Montana State Fair, Havre
Festival Days, and Montana Winter Fair under *Special Events.*

SCENIC DRIVES **Havre Badlands**, 5 miles along Road 534 northwest of Havre
and north of the Milk River. View the Havre area's version of the badlands on

this short scenic jaunt, which will also take you to the **Rookery Wildlife Management Area.** Much of this land is private property, but the road, which follows the former path of the Missouri River, allows you to view the dramatic, exposed geology before depositing you at a terrific place for wildlife viewing.

Kings Hill National Scenic Byway, 71 miles on US 89 from its junction with US 12 to its junction with US 87. During this drive, you'll twist and turn through Lewis and Clark National Forest's **Little Belt Mountains,** with the opportunity to explore the lovely terrain visible outside your windows via numerous side roads. A wealth of recreational opportunities awaits you, including camping, hiking, fishing, mountain biking, snowmobiling (200 miles of trails), cross-country skiing, and downhill skiing (see **Showdown Ski Area** under *To Do—Snow Sports*). But if you wish, you can simply sit back, relax, and enjoy driving or riding through some of the mountainous terrain that has made Montana famous.

Missouri Breaks National Back Country Byway, 80 miles total (note: you should not attempt this drive in poor or wet weather conditions, as the roads can become impassable; also, stock up on food and gas in Winifred, as you won't find either available along the drive). The byway starts in Winifred on MT 236 (38 miles north of Lewistown) and forms a loop via Knox Ridge Road and Lower Two Calf Road with an access road (NWR #200) to US 191, which deposits you at the **James Kipp Recreation Area** (see also *To Do—Camping*) in the **Charles M. Russell National Wildlife Refuge** (see *Wilder Places—Wildlife Refuges and Areas* in "Southeast Montana: Custer Country"). You'll find an interpretive kiosk at the junction of Knox Ridge Road and Lower Two Calf Road that provides background information about the area's incredible scenery. The northern route along the **Upper Missouri National Wild and Scenic River** takes you along a portion of the **Lewis and Clark National Historic Trail,** including two of their campsites. (See also Upper Missouri River Breaks National Monument–Wild and Scenic River under *Natural Wonders.*)

See also Benton Lake National Wildlife Refuge under *Wilder Places—Wildlife Refuges and Areas.*

NATURAL WONDERS & **Giant Springs State Park** (406-454-5840; www.fwp .state.mt.us/parks/parksreport.asp?mapnum=14), 4600 Giant Springs Road, Great Falls. Open year-round, day-use only; residents: free; nonresidents: $5 per vehicle. Lewis and Clark first observed this freshwater spring in 1805 during their expedition. Today, it remains one of the world's largest-known springs of this kind, flowing at 338 million gallons of water per day at a constant temperature of 54°F. You can hike some 15 miles of trails (4 of which both permit bicycles and are handicapped accessible), which link up with the River's Edge Trail (see *To Do—Bicycling*), as well as taking you to the Rainbow Falls Overlook. The park also contains a visitor center, state fish hatchery, playground, and picnicking facilities.

Square Butte (406-538-7461; www.nature.nps.gov/nnl/registry/usa_map/ states/montana/nnl/sb), MT 80 to Square Butte, then 2.5 miles on a signed county road to the monument. This feature, a designated National Natural Landmark, is a flat-topped, banded igneous butte that rises more than 2,000 feet from the surrounding plains, making it visible for 100 miles around. The grasslands vegetation atop the butte retains its natural state, providing ample forage for the herd of 80 mountain goats that make their home on the butte. A 1-mile hike takes you to the top of Square Butte.

Upper Missouri River Breaks National Monument–Wild and Scenic River (406-538-7461; www.mt.blm.gov/ldo/umnwsr.html) starts at Fort Benton on US 87, then spans 149 miles to end where the Fred Robinson Bridge on US 191 crosses the Missouri River. This section of the Upper Missouri River flows unimpeded for its entire length. Remote and inaccessible along much of this distance, this portion of the river looks nearly the same as it did in the time of Lewis and Clark, with abundant wildlife, including herds of elk and bighorn sheep, prairie-dog towns, raptors, antelope, deer, and sage grouse, among other nonhuman inhabitants. The monument includes more than 375,000 acres of land, administered by the Bureau of Land Management. Recreational opportunities include floating/paddling, camping, fishing, hiking, picnicking, and scenic drives. (See also Missouri Breaks National Back Country Byway under *Scenic Drives;* The Missouri River under *To Do—Fishing;* Hitch'n Rail Ranch and Sourdough Ranch Adventures under *To Do—Horseback Riding;* Upper Missouri River Breaks National Monument–Wild and Scenic River under *To Do—Paddling/ Floating;* and Missouri River Breaks Tours and Upper Missouri River Keelboat Company Expedition under *To Do—Unique Adventures.*)

See also Fort Belknap under *Towns;* and Old Trail Museum under *Museums.*

✴ To Do

BICYCLING ♿ **River's Edge Trail** (406-788-3313; www.thetrail.org), 25 miles along the Missouri River from Oddfellows Park (southwest) to Cochrane Dam (northeast), Great Falls. This lovely riverside trail system includes a total of 11 miles of paved trails and 14 miles of unpaved trails. The first 7.5 miles of the south side portion of the trail are paved and wheelchair-accessible. From Oddfellows Park, the trail winds along the riverfront through several city parks (see also Gibson Park under *To See—For Families*) before passing an old boxcar and caboose on display, Black Eagle Falls, and the Lewis and Clark National Historic Trail Interpretive Center (see *To See—Museums*). The trail then enters Giant Springs State Park (see *To See—Natural Wonders*), where it continues, still paved, to the Rainbow Falls and Cochrane Falls interpretive overlook areas. After that, it continues as a graveled single-track and double-track trail to the Cochrane Dam. The north side of the Missouri has 11 miles of graveled wide and single-track trails.

See also Windy Mountain Trail under *Hiking;* Beaver Creek Park and Sluice Boxes State Park under *Wilder Places—Parks;* and Lewis and Clark National Forest under *Wilder Places—Forests.*

BOATING ♿ **Fresno Reservoir** (406-266-2927; www.usbr.gov/gp/mtao/mt/ mtrec1.htm), 14 miles west of Havre via US 2, then north on access road. Boaters will find a concrete boat ramp here to help them get their adventures underway on the more than 7,000 surface acres of water in this reservoir (65 miles of shoreline). Water sports, swimming, picnicking, and fishing are popular as well. Fish species include northern pike, perch, and walleye. Camping is permitted (some handicapped accessible).

♿ **Lake Elwell and Tiber Dam State Recreation Area** (state office: 406-454-5840; www.fwp.state.mt.us), 10 miles south of Chester via MT 223, then 5 miles west on an unpaved road (recreation area access). Numerous additional access roads to the lakeshore south run off US 2 between Shelby and Chester. A marina, four boat ramps, and 181 miles of shoreline accessing the 17,678 acres of surface area make this reservoir a boater's paradise. Those interested in angling can potentially catch carp, ling, northern pike, perch, sauger pike, trout, and walleye (in winter, too). Other popular recreational activities include camping (some handicapped accessible) and swimming.

✏ **Lake Frances** (406-454-5840; www.fwp.state.mt.us), 6 blocks south of MT 44 via Teton Avenue–Lake Frances Road in Valier. Boating is just one of the many year-round recreational opportunities on this 3,618-acre natural lake, which is fed by mountain streams. Water-skiing, jet skiing, swimming, and, of course, fishing are popular as well. Species of fish present include northern pike, walleye, and yellow perch. Camping and picnicking are popular, and kids can enjoy the playground. In winter, ice-skating, ice fishing, ice tubing, and snowmobiling are popular here as well. (See also Lake Frances Ice Derby under *Special Events*.)

See also Harlowton under *To See—Towns;* Coal Banks Landing Recreation Site, James Kipp Recreation Area, and Judith Landing Recreation Area under *Camping;* the Missouri River, Pishkun Reservoir, and Willow Creek Reservoir under *Fishing;* Crystal Lake Shoreline Loop Trail under *Hiking;* Upper Missouri River Keelboat Company Expedition under *Unique Adventures;* Ackley Lake State Park and Beaver Creek County Park under *Wilder Places—Parks;* and Lewis and Clark National Forest under *Wilder Places—Forests.*

CAMPING ✏ **Choteau City Park** (406-466-2510). Turn east off Main Street in Choteau at the blinking light and proceed 2 blocks. Open year-round; $8. Water is available in summer months only at this city park, campground, and picnic area. The park has a playground and provides fishing access to Spring Creek. There is a 3-night-stay limit.

Coal Banks Landing Recreation Site (406-538-7461; www.mt.blm.gov/ldo), north of Fort Benton and south of Big Sandy off US 87 toward Virgelle on a gravel road. Open year-round; free. In the Upper Missouri Breaks National Scenic Monument (see *To See—Natural Wonders*), this recreation site has 5 acres of camping space, as well as picnic tables, hiking, fishing access, a boat ramp, and floating access. In fact, this is the main put-in point for those interested in boating the Upper Missouri River. (See also Upper Missouri River Breaks National Monument–Wild and Scenic River under *Paddling/Floating*.)

♿ **James Kipp Recreation Area** (406-538-7461; www.mt.blm.gov/ldo), where the eastern terminus (NWR #200) of the Missouri Breaks Back Country Scenic Byway (see *To See—Scenic Drives*) meets US 191. Open April 1 through

December 1; $6. This recreation area in the Charles M. Russell National Wildlife Refuge (see *Wilder Places—Wildlife Refuges and Areas* in "Southeast Montana: Custer Country") provides a popular take-out point and camping spot for those paddling or floating the Upper Missouri River. It has numerous single and group campsites as well as a warming unit, a boat ramp, restrooms, fishing access, and hiking. (See also Upper Missouri River Breaks National Monument–Wild and Scenic River under *Paddling/Floating.*)

Judith Landing Recreation Area (406-538-7461; www.mt.blm.gov/ldo), 26 miles northwest of Winifred via MT 236. Open late spring through early fall; free. This is a great place to spend the night—or a couple of nights—if you plan to drive the Missouri Breaks Back Country Scenic Byway (see *To See—Scenic Drives*), as both attractions are close to Winifred. Situated in the Upper Missouri River Breaks National Scenic Monument (see *To See—Natural Wonders*), this 3-acre Bureau of Land Management recreation area has 12 campsites, a boat ramp, hiking, and fishing access. (See also Upper Missouri River Breaks National Monument–Wild and Scenic River under *Paddling/Floating.*)

✒ **Lake Shel-oole Campground** (406-434-5222), 0.5 mile north of Shelby on I-15. Open May 1 through September 30; $15. This locally popular recreation area has 42 campsites with water and electricity, as well as a playground, fishing access, and walking trails. In winter, ice-skating and ice fishing are popular. You can also stay near Shelby at **Williamson Park Campground,** located 7 miles south of Shelby on the Frontage Road.

Lewis and Clark National Forest (406-791-7700; www.fs.fed.us/r1/lewisclark), 1101 15th Street N., Great Falls. In the **Rocky Mountain Division** of this forest, west of Great Falls, you'll find **10 campgrounds** (three are handicapped accessible), most of which lie west of Augusta or Choteau and are accessible via roads off US 287. One campground (Summit) lies 12 miles west of East Glacier on the border of Glacier National Park along US 2. Many of these campgrounds have trailheads allowing you to access the Bob Marshall Wilderness, as well as access to fishing locales. Most require a fee ($5–10), and all are open in either summer only or in summer and fall. The **14 campgrounds** (five are handicapped accessible) of the **Jefferson District** lie scattered throughout the parcels of land included within its jurisdiction (a good road atlas will usually show exact locations). Four of these are accessible from US 89 (Kings Hill National Scenic Byway; see *To See—Scenic Drives*). The rest can be found in the various additional smaller parcels. Most require a fee ($5–10) and are open in either summer only or in summer and fall, with the exceptions of Hay Canyon and Indian Hill (both southwest of Utica), which are both free and open year-round. The forest also has **five cabins** with various amenities (most somewhat primitive) available for overnight rental ($20–40). (See also Crystal Lake Shoreline Loop Trail, Mill Falls Trail, and Windy Mountain Trail–Briggs Creek Trail under *Hiking;* and Lewis and Clark National Forest under *Wilder Places—Forests.*)

See also Fort Belknap and Harlowton under *To See—Towns;* Upper Missouri River Breaks National Monument–Wild and Scenic River under *To See—Natural Wonders;* Fresno Lake and Lake Elwell and Tiber Dam State Recreation Area under *Boating;* the Missouri River, Pishkun Reservoir, and Willow Creek Reservoir under

Fishing; and Ackley Lake State Park and Beaver Creek County Park under *Wilder Places—Parks.*

FISHING Big Spring Creek (406-454-5840; www.fwp.state.mt.us), along MT 466 and MT 238 southeast of Lewistown, and along MT 426 northwest of Lewistown. From its origins near the state-run Big Springs Trout Hatchery to its confluence with the Judith River, this 30-mile, spring-fed creek features quality fishing for brown trout, mountain whitefish, and rainbow trout, particularly in its first 20 miles. Five state fishing access points lie along the creek, two southeast of Lewistown and three northwest of Lewistown. The lovely, tree-enshrouded area around the large spring from which the creek originates has a recreation area with wildlife viewing opportunities.

& **The Marias River** (406-454-5840; www.fwp.state.mt.us) flows 171 miles from near Cut Bank and Valier to Lake Elwell–Tiber Reservoir (see *Boating*), then southeast to join the Missouri River near Loma. During the Corps of Discovery expedition, Lewis named this Maria's River after his cousin, Maria Wood—and the apostrophe got lost at some point in the ensuing years. This river played a historic role in Lewis and Clark's travels, giving them pause while they determined the proper course to follow (see Decision Point Overlook under *Hiking* for details). Today, the river has one state fishing access site (with a boat ramp) at the Loma Bridge off US 87 near Loma, giving anglers a chance to catch brown trout, burbot, channel catfish, mountain whitefish, northern pike, rainbow trout, sauger, shovelnose sturgeon, and walleye. Access to the majority of the river is rather difficult, as it winds through remote prairie for much of its distance.

The Missouri River (406-538-7461; www.mt.blm.gov/ldo/fbframes.html) flows from Three Forks south of Great Falls on I-15 into the Missouri River Country at James Kipp National Recreation Area (see *Camping*). For 149 miles from Fort Benton to the Fred Robinson Bridge on US 191—the majority of its distance in this travel region—the Missouri River is a nationally designated wild and scenic river. The longest river in the country, stretching 2,341 miles in total, the Missouri provides incredible fishing opportunities in this travel region, particularly along I-15 south of Cascade to Holter Dam, where the trout fishing is at

THE MISSOURI RIVER

its finest. Along this stretch of river lie 10 state fishing access points (some handicapped accessible), some with camping and boat ramps. North of Cascade, there are four more state fishing access points to the Missouri in the Great Falls vicinity (no camping). There is one state fishing access point 27 miles north of Great Falls at Carter Ferry (no camping). Anglers visiting the Missouri River can catch black crappie, brown trout, burbot, channel catfish, lake whitefish, mountain whitefish, northern pike, paddlefish, rainbow trout, sauger, shovelnose sturgeon, smallmouth bass, walleye, and yellow perch. (See also Missouri Breaks National Back Country Byway under *To See—Scenic Drives;* Upper Missouri River Breaks National Monument–Wild and Scenic River under *To See—Natural Wonders;* Coal Banks Landing Recreation Site, James Kipp Recreation Area, and Judith Landing Recreation Area under *Camping;* DeBoo's Pine Ridge Ranch Adventures under *Horseback Riding;* Upper Missouri River Breaks National Monument–Wild and Scenic River under *Paddling/Floating;* and Missouri River Breaks Tours and Upper Missouri River Keelboat Company Expedition under *Unique Adventures.*)

 Pishkun Reservoir (406-454-5840; www.fwp.state.mt.us), US 287 0.5 mile south of Choteau, then 19 miles southwest on county roads (follow the signs). You can fish by boat (a boat ramp is at the access site) or from along the shoreline at this 1,550-acre reservoir, which is part of the Sun River Project. Species include kokanee salmon, northern pike, rainbow trout, and yellow perch. Camping is permitted. Pishkun Reservoir is a designated wildlife management area. (See also Willow Creek Reservoir below.)

The Smith River (406-454-5861; www.fwp.state.mt.us/parks/smith/default.asp), 121 miles from south of White Sulphur Springs north to its confluence with the Missouri River just west of Great Falls. Access to this river is severely limited, even though it's one of the finest and most famous of Montana's fishing destinations, but do not despair—with a little bit of forethought and advanced planning, you could find yourself experiencing the thrill of floating the river and catching some of its renowned brown trout and rainbow trout and possibly brook trout burbot, and mountain whitefish as well. From its origins to the first state access point north of MT 360 on Smith River Road—a distance of some 40 miles—the river runs through agricultural fields, has only a couple of access points, and tends to be too shallow for decent fishing in most seasons or too murky and turbulent in higher waters. The Smith River state fishing access point on Smith River Road provides the first truly worthwhile access point for anglers at most times of the year. Nine miles downstream lies Camp Baker, the last state fishing access site for nearly 60 miles. Both of these access points permit camping. The next state fishing access point is Eden Bridge, followed by the final point, Truly Take-Out (no camping permitted at either). While anglers can utilize these access points to fish the Smith, the best way to experience its fishing wonderland is to apply for a permit (due in February; $25 nonrefundable application fee) from Montana Fish, Wildlife and Parks to float or paddle the almost 60-mile stretch of river between Camp Baker and Eden Bridge. This trip generally takes 4 days, and June tends to be the best month, though May and July—and even April—are possibilities. Such a trip requires careful planning, from obtaining the permit to ensuring that you have the proper equipment and information regarding campsites, fishing rules, and so forth. You can also hire an outfitter to guide you on this trip—but be sure the outfitter is legal. A list of permitted outfitters, as well as all of the details about floating the Smith River that you'll need to properly plan your trip, can be found at the Web site listed above, or by calling the number listed above.

The Sun River (406-454-5840; www.fwp.state.mt.us), west of Great Falls along MT 200 to MT 21, and then to Willow Creek Reservoir and Gibson Reservoir (see below). From high in the mountains of Lewis and Clark National Forest's Rocky Mountain Division, the North Fork and South Fork of Sun River flow through the Sun River Game Preserve. They meet in Gibson Reservoir, and then the river flows through the Sun River Wildlife Management Area. The Sun River joins the Missouri River in Great Falls. One state fishing access point lies along the portion of the river not in the national forest: Fort Shaw, located 0.5 mile north of Fort Shaw, off MT 200 (look for the access sign). Species include brook trout, brown trout, mountain whitefish, and rainbow trout.

Willow Creek Reservoir (406-454-5840; www.fwp.state.mt.us), 5 miles northwest of Augusta via Willow Creek to Sun River Road, or continue 20 miles on Sun River Road to access **Gibson Reservoir.** Though technically in the Gold West region, Willow Creek Reservoir and Gibson Reservoir are in such close proximity to Pishkun Reservoir that they warrant being listed in this section; an angler visiting one of these spots might wish to check out all three. Willow Creek Reservoir's access site has a boat ramp and camping facilities. Species include kokanee salmon and rainbow trout. Gibson Reservoir's access site has two boat ramps and camping facilities. Species include brown trout, cutthroat trout, and rainbow trout.

See also Harlowton under *To See—Towns;* Giant Springs State Park under *To See—Natural Wonders;* Lake Elwell and Tiber Dam State Recreation Area under *Boating;* Choteau City Park and Lake Shel-oole Campground under *Camping;* Crystal Lake Shoreline Loop Trail and Windy Mountain Trail–Briggs Creek Trail under *Hiking;* Ackley Lake State Park and Beaver Creek Park under *Wilder Places—Parks;* Lewis and Clark National Forest under *Wilder Places— Forests;* Judith River Wildlife Management Area under *Wilder Places—Wildlife Refuges and Areas;* Pheasant Tales Bed and Bistro under *Lodging—Bed & Breakfasts;* Missouri River House and Prewett Creek Inn under *Lodging—Other Options;* and the Milk River under *To Do—Paddling/Floating* in "Northeast Montana: Missouri River Country."

GOLF **Anaconda Hills Golf Course** (406-761-8459; www.ci.great-falls.mt.us/ people_offices/golf/anaconda/index.htm), 2400 Smelter Avenue, Black Eagle (Great Falls), 18 holes.

Arrowhead Meadows Golf Course (406-547-3993), US 89 on the south side of White Sulphur Springs, 9 holes.

Beaver Creek Golf Course (406-265-4201; 406-265-7861), 5 miles west of Havre on US 2, 9 holes.

Chinook Golf Club (406-357-2112), John Stephens Memorial Road north of Chinook, 9 holes.

Choteau Country Club (406-466-2020), Airport Road, east of Choteau, 9 holes.

Eagle Falls Golf Club (406-761-1078; www.ci.great-falls.mt.us/people_offices/ golf/ro_speck/index.htm), 29 River Drive N., Great Falls, 18 holes.

Emerald Greens Golf Club (406-453-4844), 1100 American Avenue, Great Falls, 18 holes.

Gannon Ranch Golf Course (406-727-1206), 240 Sunflower Lane, Great Falls, 18 holes.

Harlem Golf Course (406-353-2213), on US 2 and 1.4 miles south of Harlem, 9 holes.

Harvest Hills Golf Course (406-467-2052), 0.5 mile south of Fairfield via US 89, 9 holes.

Jawbone Creek Golf Course (406-632-4206), N. Main Street, north end of Harlowton, 9 holes.

Judith Shadows Golf Course (406-538-6062), US 87 east, then north on Mercella Avenue, Lewistown, 18 holes.

Marias Valley Golf and Country Club (406-434-5940), 5 miles south of Shelby on I-15 to Exit 358, then 4 miles on marked Golfcourse Road, 18 holes.

Meadow Lark Country Club (406-454-3553), 300 Country Club Boulevard, Great Falls, 18 holes.

Pine Meadows Golf Course (406-538-7075), south on Spring Creek Road then east on Country Club Drive, Lewistown, 9 holes.

Pondera Golf Club (406-278-3402), west of Conrad, 9 holes.

Signal Point Golf Club (406-622-3666), northeast of Fort Benton on MT 387, 9 holes.

HIKING **A. B. Guthrie Memorial Trail,** a short, easy nature trail, is accessible via US 89, 5 miles north of Choteau, then west on Teton Canyon Road for 17 miles, then south across the Teton River, then straight for 3.5 miles, following signs to information kiosk. Located in the Nature Conservancy's **Pine Butte Swamp Preserve** (406-466-2158), this foot-traffic trail provides the only access to this natural area without reservations. Signs will direct you as you hike up a short path to a great vista point, with opportunities for wildlife viewing along the way. The preserve has numerous additional trails, but these can be accessed by prior arrangement only. The preserve is also home to **Pine Butte Guest Ranch,** which provides educational tours and ranch vacations.

Crystal Lake Shoreline Loop Trail, an easy 1.7-mile interpretive loop trail (#404), is accessible via US 87 west of Lewistown for 8.7 miles, then south on Crystal Lake Road for 16 miles (follow signs), then south on F.R. 275 for 8.5 miles to **Crystal Lake Campground** (handicapped accessible; $10). This trail loops

RIVER'S EDGE TRAIL

around the clear, shallow waters of 100-acre Crystal Lake, a popular spot for boating, fishing, and paddling, as well as snowmobiling in winter on the 5-mile **Crystal Lake Snowmobile Trail.** The **Crystal Lake Cabin,** available for rent October 15 through March 31 through Lewis and Clark National Forest ($25), is here as well. The shorter **Jack Milburn Trail** is handicapped accessible. Additional hiking and horseback riding trails leave from this campground, including the **Uhlorn Trail** (#493), a 16-mile hike (round-trip) that leads to year-round ice caves. (See also Lewis and Clark National Forest under *Camping* and *Wilder Places—Forests.*)

Decision Point Overlook is accessed via a 0.25-mile easy trail (0.5 mile round-trip) 11 miles north of Fort Benton along US 87. Take the time to step out of your car and hike this historic path up to the vantage point used by Lewis in an effort to solve the dilemma facing the Corps of Discovery. Confronted by two unknown rivers, now named the Marias and the Missouri, they experienced difficulty discerning which of the rivers was actually the Missouri and spent 9 days in this area before Lewis guessed correctly. This interpretive marker lies on the 3,700-mile **Lewis and Clark National Historic Trail,** which passes through 10 states in addition to Montana. (See also The Marias River under *Fishing.*)

Mill Falls Trail, an 0.1-mile easy hike departing from Mill Falls Campground (free), is accessible by taking US 287 north of Choteau for 17 miles to Teton River Road, then heading south across the Teton River, then west on F.R. 109 (34 miles total from Choteau). This short and casual jaunt takes you through a forest of fragrant Englemann spruce and cottonwood trees, leading you to scenic Mill Falls. If you're in search of a more rigorous outing, several other trails leave from this campground. One is the **Green Gulch Trail** (#127), which wanders for 5 miles through lush wildlife habitat and then links up with other trails in Lewis and Clark National Forest, including some that lead into the Bob Marshall Wilderness (see also *Wilder Places—Forests*).

Memorial Falls Trail, an easy 3-mile round-trip hike, is accessible via US 89, 37 miles north of White Sulphur Springs (just north of Neihart); the trailhead is on the east side of the road. If you're driving Kings Hill National Scenic Byway (see *To See—Scenic Drives*) in summer or early fall, consider stopping here to stretch your legs, take a break, and get a little exercise and Montana mountain air while you're at it. This trail (#438) follows the creek and leads to two waterfalls, separated by only 0.5 mile. (See also Lewis and Clark National Forest under *Wilder Places—Forests.*)

Windy Mountain Trail–Briggs Creek Trail (#454 and #431). Together these trails form a 6.5-mile moderate loop hike accessible by taking US 89 east from Great Falls 6 miles, then following MT 228 northeast for 13.9 miles to a stop sign, and then continuing straight on the gravel road, following signs for a total of 20 miles to **Thain Creek Campground** (handicapped accessible; $5; fishing access). Be prepared—you'll gain 1,200 feet in elevation as you hike your way up to the saddle on the south side of Windy Mountain. The scenic views should make the effort worthwhile, though, and then you get to enjoy a gradual descent to the Briggs Creek Trail. A stroll along this path takes you back to your starting point. (See also Lewis and Clark National Forest under *Wilder Places—Forests.*)

See also Harlowton under *To See—Towns;* Bear Paw Battlefield and Ulm Pishkun State Park under *To See—Historic Landmarks, Places, and Sites;* Gibson Park under *To See—For Families;* Square Butte and Upper Missouri River Breaks National Monument–Wild and Scenic River under *To See—Natural Wonders;* River's Edge Trail under *Bicycling;* Coal Banks Landing Recreation Site, James Kipp Recreation Area, Judith Landing Recreation Area, and Lake Shel-oole Campground under *Camping;* and Beaver Creek County Park under *Wilder Places—Parks.*

HORSEBACK RIDING ☙ **Bull Run Guest Ranch** (1-800-966-9269; 406-468-9269; www.bullrunguestranch.com), 719 Sheep Creek Road, Cascade. In addition to offering package deals on ranch-style vacations and nightly cabin rentals during the summer season, this guest ranch offers horseback riding trips. You can ride for an hour ($25), half a day ($75), or all day ($125). You can also sign up for a riding lesson, to learn more about proper riding techniques ($35 per hour), or sign up the whole family for a daylong trail ride followed by a gourmet dinner ($150 per person; minimum of four people).

☙ **DeBoo's Pine Ridge Montana Ranch Adventures** (406-472-3344; www .netclique.net/DeBoo/index.html), 2900 High Plains Road, Valier (27 miles west of town). It's best to make reservations for your ride at this family's working ranch. Whether your interest is just to take in the gorgeous scenery or to be taken to some of the finest fishing spots, a horseback riding trip with folks who have intimate knowledge of their surroundings promises to be a fun-filled adventure for the whole family. Call for rates.

☙ **Hitch'n Rail Ranch** (406-378-2571; www.trailridemontana.com), south of Big Sandy, downstream from Coal Banks Landing Recreation Site (see *Camping*). Take a tour of the Upper Missouri River Breaks National Monument (see *To See—Natural Wonders*) on horseback. Go for an hour, half a day, a day, or several days while experienced guides lead you on a customized journey through the landscape Lewis and Clark once explored. Your adventure will be tailored to the wishes expressed by you and your companions. Your journey can include canoeing as well, should you so desire. Call for reservations and rates.

☙ **Sourdough Ranch Adventures** (406-462-5422; www.sourdoughadventures .com), 106 3rd Avenue N., Winifred. Sign up the whole family for a daylong horseback riding adventure in the territory explored by Lewis and Clark. Before you hit the trail, you'll receive instruction on riding, so experience is unnecessary. A day trip ($200 adults; $150 children) includes lunch on the trail and dinner cooked over a campfire, not to mention the thrill of exploring the remote beauty of a portion of the Upper Missouri River Breaks National Monument (see *To See—Natural Wonders*). If you want to stay longer, you can book a weekend or weeklong adventure.

See also Crystal Lake Shoreline Loop Trail under *Hiking;* ranch vacations under *Unique Adventures;* Lewis and Clark National Forest under *Wilder Places—Forests;* and Rusty Spur Guesthouse and Gallery under *Lodging—Other Options.*

HOT SPRINGS Spa Hot Springs Motel (406-547-3366; www.spahotsprings .com), 202 W. Main Street, White Sulphur Springs (on US 89 and US 12). Open year-round, this miniresort has two hot springs–fed pools open to the public—one indoors (105°F) and one outside (95°F)—as well as 21 rooms for lodging, each with a private bathroom. The hot springs and their purported healing properties were long acknowledged by Native Americans before people of European origins knew of them. After learning about the springs in 1866, a man named James Brewer constructed a bathhouse at the springs in 1872, deeming the area Brewer's Springs. He sold his share of the springs to a Dr. Parberry in 1876, and it was Parberry who named them White Sulphur Springs. Another interesting piece of historic trivia is that John Ringling (of circus fame) owned the springs for a time and planned to transform this area into a lavish, upscale resort, only to be stymied by the Great Depression. Today, you can enjoy the more casual luxury of a small-town motel setting when you stop for a soak in the spring-fed pools. They remain free of chemicals—the pools are drained, cleaned, and refilled each night.

PADDLING/FLOATING **Upper Missouri River Breaks National Monument– Wild and Scenic River** (406-538-7461; www.mt.blm.gov/ldo/umnwsr.html) starts at Fort Benton on US 87 and spans 149 miles to end where the Fred Robinson Bridge on US 191 crosses the Missouri River. Floating the remote and wild section of the Missouri River within the monument is a popular activity in this region—with good reason. A float or paddle there brings you into intimate contact with terrain that is largely unchanged from the days when the explorers Lewis and Clark first laid their eyes upon it. The Web site listed above provides a long narrative of the incredible sites of natural and historic significance that you'll encounter along the way, as well as the information, including the regulations, necessary for planning your trip. If you want to, you can leave such details up to a local guiding service, of which there are many, including **Virgelle Merc & Missouri River Canoe Company** (1-800-426-2926; 406-378-3110; www .paddlemontana.com), Virgelle; **Montana River Outfitters** (1-800-800-8218; 406-761-1677; www.montanariveroutfitters.com), Great Falls; **Adventure Bound Canoe and Shuttle Company** (1-877-538-4890; 406-622-5077; www.montanarivertrip.com), Fort Benton; **Canoe Montana–Montana River Expeditions** (1-800-500-4538; 406-622-5882; www.canoemontana.net), Fort Benton; and **Upper Missouri River Guides** (1-866-226-6519; 406-563-2770; www.uppermissouri.com), Anaconda; to name a few. Many of these places rent equipment for floating or paddling the river. (See also Missouri Breaks National Back Country Byway under *To See—Scenic Drives;* Upper Missouri River Breaks National Monument–Wild and Scenic River under *To See—Natural Wonders;* Coal Banks Landing Recreation Site, James Kipp Recreation Area, and Judith Landing Recreation Area under *Camping;* the Missouri River under *Fishing;* Crystal Lake Shoreline Loop Trail under *Hiking;* Hitch'n Rail Ranch under *Horseback Riding;* and Missouri River Breaks Tours and Upper Missouri River Keelboat Company Expedition under *Unique Adventures.*)

See also the Smith River under *Fishing;* multiple additional listings under *Fishing;* Crystal Lake Shoreline Loop Trail under *Hiking;* Lewis and Clark National Forest under *Wilder Places—Forests;* and Riverbend Bed and Breakfast under *Lodging—Bed & Breakfasts.*

Ice Fishing

Opportunities for ice fishing in this region are prolific. For ideas of where to drop your line, see Harlowton under *To See—Towns;* Lake Frances under *Boating;* Lake Shel-oole Campground under *Camping;* Ackley Lake State Park and Beaver Creek County Park under *Wilder Places—Parks;* and additional listings under *Fishing* for ideas of where to go.

Ice-Skating

Ice-skating is available throughout this region when the temperatures dip low enough. For ideas of where to go, look to Harlowton under *To See—Towns;* Gibson Park under *To See—For Families;* Lake Frances under *Boating;* Lake Shel-oole Campground under *Camping;* and Ackley Lake State Park under *Wilder Places—Parks.*

Skiing

✿ **Bear Paw Ski Bowl** (406-265-8404; www.skibearpaw.com), 29 miles south of Havre via Beaver Creek Rd. (MT 234/BIA 114) to BIA 123 (watch for signs) in the Chippewa Cree Recreation Area on the Rocky Boys Indian Reservation. Open only on weekends during the season, this small ski area tucked in the Bear Paw Mountains is an affordable and fun place for the whole family to play for a day. *Lifts:* one double chairlift, one surface lift. *Trails:* 20 trails—25 percent beginner, 25 percent intermediate, 50 percent expert. *Vertical drop:* 900 feet. *Facilities:* On-site concession stand sells food and drinks. *Ski school:* certified ski school. *Rates:* $15 adults, $12 students 9–18, children 8 and under (with adult) and seniors 80 and older free.

♿ ✿ **Showdown Montana Ski Area** (1-800-433-0022; 406-236-5522; www .showdownmontana.com), 8 miles south of Neihart on US 89 (Kings Hill National Scenic Byway; see *To See—Scenic Drives*). Open Wednesday through Sunday in-season. Situated in the Little Belt Mountains of Lewis and Clark National Forest (see *Wilder Places—Forests*), Montana's oldest ski area offers not only downhill skiing but also 12K of groomed cross-country ski trails and 200 miles of groomed snowmobile trails (rentals available on-site from **Montana Snowmobile Adventures;** see *Snowmobiling* below). The area also rents snowshoes ($15 per day). *Lifts:* one triple chairlift, one double chairlift, two surface lifts. *Trails:* 34 trails—30 percent beginner, 40 percent intermediate, 30 percent expert. *Vertical drop:* 1,400 feet. *Facilities:* The base lodge offers a pro shop, a full-service restaurant (Kings Hill Grille), a saloon (Hole-in-the-Wall Saloon), and the T-bar Espresso Station. The summit has Top Rock Eatery, which offers snacks, hot drinks, and warmth (open weekends and holidays). *Ski school:* Ski and snowboarding lessons are available for all ages and ability levels. *For children:* Day care available on premises; reservations required for children 2 and younger. Snow Monsters for ages 4–6, Little Shredders for ages 7–10. *Rates:* $29 adults, $17 juniors (6–12), $17 seniors (70 and older), children 5 and under free; also half-day and multiday rates.

Silver Crest Ski Trail (406-236-5511; www.fs.fed.us/r1/lewisclark), 7 miles south of Neihart on US 89 (Kings Hill National Scenic Byway; see *To See—*

Scenic Drives). Park in the Kings Hill Recreation Area parking lot on US 89 to access the trails. This trail system features four loops (13.8K total) of easy to intermediate cross-country skiing trails. Groomed weekly, they allow you to glide inside the wintry wonderland of the Kings Hill area without needing too much expertise. Several warming huts along the trails get your blood flowing again if you become chilled. Numerous additional cross-country skiing trails lie through-out this region, both in the national forest and in other recreation areas. (See also Bear Paw Ski Bowl and Showdown Montana Ski Area, above; Teton Pass Ski Area, below; Beaver Creek County Park under *Wilder Places—Parks;* and Lewis and Clark National Forest under *Wilder Places—Forests.*)

Teton Pass Ski Area (406-466-2209; www.skitetonpass.com), 27 miles west of Choteau via US 89 to Teton River Road. Usually open only Friday through Sun-day during the season, this remote ski area on the Rocky Mountain Front offers not only downhill skiing but also cross-country skiing and snowmobile trails. The area rents snowshoes ($15 per day). *Lifts:* one double chairlift, one single chair-lift. *Trails:* 26 trails—25 percent beginner, 35 percent intermediate, and 45 per-cent expert. *Vertical drop:* 1,010 feet. *Facilities:* Base lodge has a bar and tavern. *Ski school:* Ski and snowboard lessons available for all ages and ability levels. *For children:* Dinos for ages 3–6, Teton Rangers for ages 7–12. *Rates:* $25 adults, $19 students (11–18), $13 children (6–10), $13 seniors (66 and older), children under 6 free; also multiday passes.

Snowmobiling

Snowmobiling along **Kings Hill National Scenic Byway** (406-236-5511; www.fs.fed.us/r1/lewisclark), 7 miles south of Neihart on US 89 (Kings Hill National Scenic Byway; see *To See—Scenic Drives*). Park in the Kings Hill Recreation Area parking lot to access the 200 miles of marked snowmobile trails in this part of Lewis and Clark National Forest (see *Wilder Places—Forests*). You can rent a snowmobile from **Montana Snowmobile Adventures** (406-236-5358), located at Showdown Montana Ski Area, listed above. Montana Snowmo-bile Adventures also offers guided tours. Numerous additional snowmobiling trails are available throughout this region, both in the national forest and in other recreation areas. (See also Lake Frances under *Boating;* Crystal Lake Shoreline Loop Trail under *Hiking;* Teton Pass Ski Area, above; and Beaver Creek County Park under *Wilder Places—Parks.*)

See also Lewis and Clark National Forest under *Wilder Places—Forests.*

UNIQUE ADVENTURES ꝕ **Charlie Russell Chew-Choo** (406-538-8721, ext. 312; www.lewistownchamber.com/chewchoo.htm). Boarding is 11 miles north-west of Lewistown via US 191 north for 3 miles, then 8 miles west on MT 346. Open June through September and for special seasonal events; $89.99 per per-son. Relax in the 1950s-vintage railroad cars and enjoy the beautiful scenery and wildlife of central Montana during this 3.5-hour train ride. You'll ride across three tall trestles, pass several ghost towns, and go through a tunnel more than 2,000 feet in length before the journey comes to a finish. While you ride, you'll be treated to a delicious, gourmet prime rib dinner catered by the **Yogo Inn** (1-800-860-9646; 406-538-8721), a well-respected 120-room hotel and conference center with an on-premises restaurant, which is located on Main Street in Lewistown.

Missouri River Breaks Tours (406-386-2486; www.fortbenton.com/mrbtours/index.htm), Big Sandy. Reservations required; tours run from 2 hours ($80) to 8 hours ($200). Let your experienced tour guide take the wheel for a while—in a touring vehicle—while you sit back and enjoy the stellar scenery of the Upper Missouri River Breaks. You'll spend several hours or the whole day exploring this beautiful area, with many opportunities to get out of the vehicle and hike to get a closer look at things (nonhiking tours are available as well). You will potentially view wildlife such as bighorn sheep, eagles, and antelope, as well as Indian artifacts, including pictographs and teepee rings. Your guide will fill you in on the history of the local area during your adventure. (See also Upper Missouri River Breaks National Monument–Wild and Scenic River under *To See—Natural Wonders.*)

Ranch vacations. These vacations usually allow you to participate to a certain extent in various aspects of ranch life, often including cattle herding and branding. The ratio of work time to leisure time varies from ranch to ranch, as do the additional activities and amenities offered, but most ranches include horseback riding, lodging, and meals in an inclusive package deal. In this region, providers include **Sky View Ranch** (406-378-2549), Big Sandy; **Bull Run Guest Ranch** (1-800-966-9269; 406-468-9269), Cascade; **Bonanza Creek Country Guest Ranch** (1-800-476-6045; 406-572-3366), Martinsdale; **Why Lazy Tee Ranch** (406-736-5416; 406-788-0365), Stockett, southeast of Great Falls via MT 227; **Homestead Ranch** (406-423-5301), Hobson; **Pine Butte Guest Ranch** (406-466-2158), Choteau; **Seven Lazy P Ranch** (406-466-2044), Choteau; **Grizzly Trails Ranch** (406-472-3301), Dupuyer; **Careless Creek Ranch Getaway** (1-888-832-4140; 406-632-4140), Shawmut near Harlowton; and **Heaven on Earth Ranch** (406-866-3316), Ulm, near Cascade; among others.

✐ **Timescale Adventures** (1-800-238-6873; 406-469-2211; www.tmdinosaur.org), 120 2nd Avenue S., Bynum (near Choteau). Join paleontologists at an active dinosaur dig site for 3 hours ($35 adults, $25 children 12 and under), for a day ($100 per person), for a week ($85 per person per day), or longer. These programs are run by the Two Medicine Dinosaur Center, a museum featuring many real and model dinosaur exhibits. No matter what the length, a Timescale Adventure focuses on a hands-on experience for you, the participant, as well as enjoyment and education. Depending on the length of your adventure, you'll learn the basics about fossils, geology, and local history; visit the dig site; and participate in digging, field preservation, fossil preservation and preparation, and more. Reservations are required.

Upper Missouri River Keelboat Company Expedition (1-888-721-7133; 406-739-4333; www.mrkeelboat.com), 4 miles east of Loma. Travel the Missouri River the way it used to be done—in a 38-foot keelboat. The *Gen. Wm. Ashley* is a replica of the keelboats that were once used prolifically by the fur trade that briefly dominated this area in the mid-1800s. The keelboat provides you with a comfortable, relaxing ride from which you can view the same type of terrain that Lewis and Clark witnessed during their exploration of this area. To help enhance the historic value of your experience, the crew of the boat dresses in period costumes; for multiday trips, you'll have the chance to see living-history presentations, take short and scenic hikes, camp where Lewis and Clark camped (though in much more comfortable setups), and even help pilot the boat, if you wish. Keelboats can accommodate from six to 10 people. Advance reservations are required; expeditions are priced according to length of trip and number of passengers. You can also book a 1- to 5-day guided canoe expedition if you wish. (See also Upper Missouri River Breaks National Monument–Wild and Scenic under *To See—Natural Wonders.*)

See also High Plains Heritage Center and Old Trail Museum under *To See— Museums;* Havre Beneath the Streets under *To See—Historic Landmarks, Places, and Sites;* the Smith River under *Fishing;* and Upper Missouri River Breaks National Monument–Wild and Scenic River under *Paddling/Floating.*

✳ Wilder Places

PARKS ⅙ **Ackley Lake State Park** (406-454-5840; www.fwp.state.mt.us/parks/ parksreport.asp?mapnum=13), 5 miles south of Hobson on MT 400, then 2 miles southwest to park entrance. Open year-round; free. This park's small lake (stocked with rainbow trout) provides opportunities for fishing, boating, and swimming in warm weather, as well as ice-skating and ice fishing when it's cold. Additional activities include camping and picnicking.

Beaver Creek County Park (406-395-4565), 20 miles south of Havre via Beaver Creek Road (MT 234). Open year-round. This 10,000-acre park is most likely the largest county park in the United States. Stretching for 17 miles in length across the foothills of the Bear Paw Mountains in a 1-mile-wide strip, the park features developed campsites (small fee), hiking and mountain biking trails, fishing, boating, and picnicking. It is also a popular winter recreation destination, with opportunities for snowmobiling, cross-country skiing, and ice fishing. The park's varied terrain makes it a wonderful place to see a diverse array of wildlife. Neighboring the park is the Rocky Boys Indian Reservation, with its abundance of recreational opportunities (see listing under *Guidance;* Bear Paw Ski Bowl under *To Do—Snow Sports;* and Rocky Boys Annual Powwow under *Special Events*).

Sluice Boxes State Park (406-454-5840; www.fwp.state.mt.us/parks/parks report.asp?mapnum=16), 8 miles south of Belt on US 89, then 0.5 mile to park entrance. Open year-round; free. This state park offers the visitor a rugged and remote experience, whether you come to hike, watch wildlife, fish in Belt Creek, or camp in the backcountry. A primitive trail provides access into the lovely northern portion of Belt Canyon, with its dramatic cliffs and scenery. But beware: the train bridges along the former railroad bed garnering access into the area have been removed, so you'll have to splash through the water to gain access— something that is possible only when water levels are low.

See also Ulm Pishkun State Park under *To See—Historic Landmarks, Places, and Sites;* Gibson Park under *To See—For Families;* and Giant Springs State Park under *To See—Natural Wonders.*

FORESTS Lewis and Clark National Forest (406-791-7700; www.fs.fed.us/r1/
lewisclark), 1101 15th Street N., Great Falls. Scattered in parcels mainly
throughout the southern portion of Russell Country, Lewis and Clark National
Forest accounts for 1.8 million acres of public lands. The forest has two major
divisions. The 680,000-acre **Rocky Mountain Division,** west of Great Falls,
abuts Flathead National Forest, Lolo National Forest, and Helena National Forest. Some 380,000 acres of this division form the **Great Bear–Bob Marshall–
Scapegoat Wilderness.** The **Jefferson Division** includes more than 1 million
acres of mountainous "islands" and the prairie lands surrounding them. This
division includes six mountain ranges and accounts for most of the forest's timber production and grazing. The forest's recreational opportunities include
mountain biking, boating, camping, fishing, hiking, horseback riding, paddling/
floating, skiing, snowmobiling, picnicking, and wildlife viewing. (See also Kings
Hill National Scenic Byway under *To See—Scenic Drives;* listing under *To Do—
Camping;* the Sun River under *To Do—Fishing;* Crystal Lake Shoreline Loop
Trail, Memorial Falls Trail, Mill Falls Trail, and Windy Mountain Trail–Briggs
Creek Trail under *To Do—Hiking;* and Showdown Ski Area and Silver Crest Ski
Trail under *To Do—Snow Sports.*)

WILDLIFE REFUGES AND AREAS Benton Lake National Wildlife Refuge
(406-727-7400; http://bentonlake.fws.gov), 922 Bootlegger Trail (12 miles north
of Great Falls via MT 225). Open year-round Monday through Friday 7:30
AM–4:30 PM; free. In reality a shallow marsh, the 5,000-acre Benton Lake and
the surrounding refuge (comprising 19 square miles) provide terrific wetlands
habitat for literally hundreds of thousands of waterfowl and migratory birds,
including ducks, geese, eagles, swans, and peregrine falcons. The "lake" was
scooped out by this continent's last inland glacier thousands of years ago. The
refuge is also home to numerous mammalian, reptilian, and amphibian species.
Visitors are welcome to view the wildlife by driving the 9-mile auto tour route
along **Prairie Marsh Wildlife Drive,** and limited hunting opportunities are
available as well.

Freezeout Lake Wildlife Management Area (406-467-2646; www.fwp
.state.mt.us/habitat/wma/freezout.asp), 40 miles west of Great Falls on US 89.
Open year-round; free. Montana's primary staging area for migrating snow geese
can host up to 300,000 of the birds during peak migration. The geese usually
reach this area in early March after a 1,000-mile flight from California, providing
visitors with incredible viewing opportunities. Tundra swans, raptors, shorebirds,
upland game birds, and waterfowl also reside here at various times of the year.
Public hunting is permitted.

Judith River Wildlife Management Area (406-454-5840; www.state.mt
.us/habitat/wma/judith.asp), 9 miles southwest of Utica via the main gravel road
north of the Judith River to Sapphire Village (southwest of Hobson, which is
southwest of Lewistown via US 87), then right on first road after the village for
1.5 miles. Open May 16 through November 30; free. This wildlife area strives to
protect winter vegetation forage for elk as well as other animals (hence the seasonal closure). Other wildlife viewed at this area includes antelope, deer, smaller

mammals, raptors, and birds. The Judith River, which flows for 127 miles from its origins in the Belt Mountains near this WMA to the Missouri River, gives anglers the chance to fish for brook trout, brown trout, burbot, channel catfish, mountain whitefish, rainbow trout, and sauger.

See also Old Trail Museum under *To See—Museums;* Havre Badlands under *To See—Scenic Drives;* Big Spring Creek, Pishkun Reservoir, and the Sun River under *To Do—Fishing;* A. B. Guthrie Memorial Trail under *To Do—Hiking;* and Charles M. Russell National Wildlife Refuge under *Wildlife Refuges and Areas* in "North-Central Montana: Custer Country."

OTHER WILD PLACES See also Missouri Breaks National Back Country Byway under *To See—Scenic Drives;* Upper Missouri River Breaks National Monument–Wild and Scenic River under *To See—Natural Wonders;* and Upper Missouri River Keelboat Company Expedition under *To Do—Unique Adventures.*

✳ Lodging

BED & BREAKFASTS

Big Sandy 59520
Raven Crest Bed and Breakfast (406-378-3121), 3002 Winchester Road, 10 miles west and north of Big Sandy on MT 432. A rustic retreat awaits you at Raven Crest, situated near the scenic White Cliffs of the Upper Missouri River. Located on a working grain ranch in Montana's prolific northern wheat-producing area, this B&B has two guest bedrooms and a shared bath. Guests enjoy a home-cooked ranch breakfast ($50–60).

Chester 59522
& **Great Northern Bed and Breakfast** (1-800-544-9936; 406-759-5900; www.greatnorthernbandb.com), 14 Monroe Avenue E. Solitude seekers, rejoice! You and your sweetheart (or just you) will have the whole place to yourselves if you stay at this charming, one-bedroom getaway in the tiny town of Chester. The cottage, constructed in 1909, features a stained-glass piece showing the Empire Builder train created by noted local artist Craig Waldron. This B&B is within walking distance of all of the

amenities of Chester, so you can enjoy the local flavor with ease and then return to the peace of Big Sky solitude and scenery. Breakfast included ($50–75).

Choteau
See **Styren Ranch Guest House** under *Other Options.*

Dupuyer 59432
& **Inn Dupuyer Bed and Breakfast** (406-472-3241; www.3rivers.net/ ~inndupyr), 308 Morton Avenue. If you're on your way to Glacier National Park through Russell Country or on your way back, you might want to consider spending a night in this wonderful 100-year-old house. This hand-hewn log abode still has its original fir floors that the homesteaders walked upon a century ago, as well as its porcelain doorknobs. Five individually decorated guest rooms each have their own private bath. Numerous guest common areas make for comfortable spots to kick back and relax, read a good book, or socialize. A full breakfast served daily and a self-serve hot beverage bar that offers tea, coffee,

espresso, and hot chocolate are included in the rates ($85).

Fairfield 59436
Viewforth Bed and Breakfast (406-467-3884; www.viewforth.com), 4600 US 287 (at its intersection with MT 408). Sweeping vistas of Montana prairies to the east and mountains to the west await the guest to this appropriately named B&B located on the Rocky Mountain Front. Numerous common areas allow guests to feast their eyes on the incredible natural views that surround the Viewforth, as well as the assortment of original artwork within the B&B. The two neatly decorated and comfortable guest rooms each have a queen bed and a private bath. Breakfast is a big deal here—every day you'll wake up to a different delectable selection made from the freshest possible ingredients, including fresh-baked breads and pastries, eggs from the owners' hens, and herbs from the kitchen garden ($80–85).

Fort Benton 59442
Riverbend Bed and Breakfast (406-622-5601; www.riverbendbb.com), P.O. Box 602. Located 5 miles west of Fort Benton on US 87, this country B&B offers guests two cozy bedrooms and a full or continental breakfast made daily from fresh ingredients. The property's setting in the tranquil Missouri River valley allows you to launch your own watercraft from private access points ($50–75).

♿ **Vixen Lane Guest House and Fox Cottage** (406-733-6791), 47 Vixen Lane, Shonkin 59450 (14 miles south of Fort Benton). Open March through November; reservations required. You have your choice between two distinctive lodging experiences: you can join the host's family for a little while by staying in one of the bedrooms at the Vixen Lane house (also called the Mickle House), or you can savor your solitude by choosing to stay at the private, three-bedroom Fox Cottage, a short walk from the main house. Either way, you can enjoy a full, delicious breakfast cooked daily and served in the main house ($75–90).

See also the Missouri River under *To Do—Paddling/Floating.*

Great Falls
Charlie Russell Manor (1-877-207-6131; 406-455-1400; www.charlie-russell.com), 825 4th Avenue N., Great Falls 59401. A 7,000-square-foot manor house offers guests accommodations in one of five bedrooms, each with its own private bath, data port, telephone, and Egyptian cotton linens. Two of the rooms are part of suites, one with a private Jacuzzi, the other with a fireplace. The manor has a number of common areas, including a 900-square-foot ballroom, a comfortable den with a big-screen television, and a grand dining room, among others. A full breakfast is included in the nightly rate ($85–145).

Collins Mansion Bed and Breakfast (1-877-452-6798; 406-452-6798; www.collinsmansion.com), 1003 2nd Avenue NW, Great Falls, 59404. Constructed in 1891 in the Victorian Queen Anne style of architecture, the Collins Mansion is listed on the National Register of Historic Places. Restored and renovated in 1998, it has five distinctively decorated guest rooms, each with a private bathroom and telephone. The mansion itself has gorgeously landscaped grounds, a circular front drive, a veranda with tremendous views of the city and mountains, and several common areas inside. A gourmet breakfast is included in the rate ($85–100).

Havre 59501
♪ Our Home Bed and Breakfast
(406-265-1055; www.hi-line.net/ ~donagh), 66 65th Avenue NW. Families, couples, and singles are welcome to stay at this home—which is truly the hosts' home—in Havre. The two guest bedrooms feature Native American decor and stunning views of the nearby Bear Paw Mountains. You'll sit down to enjoy a full breakfast each morning, with special dietary needs considered if you notify the hosts in advance ($55–65, plus $5 per child after double occupancy).

Lewistown 59457
Pheasant Tales Bed and Bistro
(406-538-6257; 406-538-2124; www .tein.net/pheasant), 1511 Timberline Road. A gourmand's delight, this bed & breakfast will serve you not only a full breakfast according to your schedule but also dinners certain to delight the most discriminating of palates, as long as you make reservations for meals in advance. If you're a hunter, they'll gladly include in the evening's menu the birds you bag, or you will have ample refrigerator or freezer space to keep them, as well as space for your dogs to stay. Six rooms are available, all with private bath, as well as access to a hot tub. You can also ask for guidance to great fishing spots on Big Spring Creek, as well as guidance to additional area attractions ($85).

♪ ❦ Snowy View Bed and Breakfast
(406-538-5538; www.snowyview .com), 1145 Timber Tracts Road. The perfect combination of country solitude close to small-town amenities awaits you at Snowy View, located 10 miles south of Lewistown at the base of the Snowy Mountains. You can spread out on the ground floor in a spacious suite with a queen bed, a sitting room, a porch, and a full, private bath—and send the kids up to sleep in the loft, with its two twin beds ($10 per child in addition to double occupancy rate). A full breakfast is included for all guests in the nightly rate ($75).

Symmes–Wicks House Bed and Breakfast
(406-538-9068), 220 W. Boulevard. In the heart of Lewistown's historic Silk Stocking District, you'll find this restored 1909 house, listed on the National Register of Historic Places. The three-story, sandstone B&B features distinctive shingle-style arts and crafts architecture on the outside and elegant Tiffany pieces and period antiques on the inside. Guests enjoy one of three bedrooms in the house (two with private baths), as well as a gourmet breakfast and afternoon tea served daily ($70).

Valier 59486
Stone School Inn Bed and Breakfast
(406-279-3796; www.stoneschool inn.com), 820 3rd Street. Listed on the National Register of Historic Places, this stone schoolhouse was constructed in 1911 to serve as an elementary school. The inside has undergone a makeover and now provides guests with a choice of five upstairs bedrooms, all of which have Internet access and private bathrooms. The bedrooms open up into a library. Common areas downstairs include a game room, a dining area, and a kitchen ($85–105).

White Sulphur Springs 59645
Foxwood Inn Bed and Breakfast

(1-888-547-2240; 406-547-2106; www.foxwoodinn.com), 52 Miller Road. Fourteen bedrooms to choose from? That's exactly what you'll find when you book a room at this 1890 Victorian home. Each room features its own distinctive decor, so it really depends on your tastes and needs— and the rooms' availability, of course. Four shared bathrooms include both modern showers and claw-foot bathtubs for those who wish to soak in old-fashioned comfort. A full breakfast is served daily in the elegant dining room ($50–75).

See also **Montana Mountain Lodge** under *Lodges*.

LODGES

Fort Benton 59442

& **Pioneer Lodge** (1-800-622-6088; 406-622-5441; www.pioneerlodgemt .com), 1700 Front Street. Listed on the National Register of Historic Places, this 10-room hotel originally served as the structure housing the Pioneer Mercantile Store, which was constructed in 1916. The interior has been remodeled to provide guests with comfortable, modern amenities, including queen beds, private bathrooms, and cable television—but to keep the past alive, each room's decor features a theme reflecting a piece of local history ($50–60).

Lewistown 59457

& ✐ **Duvall Inn** (406-538-7063; www .lewistown.net/~duvalinn), 612 Limekiln Road. In this lovely western lodge, you'll enjoy warm hospitality and good home cooking while you get away from it all in a peaceful mountain setting. Rooms feature queen beds and private baths. You can hang out in front of the stone fireplace and

socialize in the lodge's common area or explore the surrounding recreational opportunities before you come inside for some downtime. Breakfast is served daily, as are other meals, if you like ($75–90).

White Sulphur Springs 59645

Montana Mountain Lodge (406-547-3773; www.montanamountain lodge.com), 1780 US 89, 20 miles north of White Sulphur Springs. All of the area's recreational opportunities are at your fingertips when you stay in one of this lodge's five guest rooms, each with a private bath. If you want to just relax, read, watch wildlife, soak in the Jacuzzi, or warm up by a wood-burning stove, you can do that, too. Situated in the Little Belt Mountains of Lewis and Clark National Forest, Montana Mountain Lodge is open in all seasons. A full breakfast is included in the nightly room rate ($75–90).

OTHER OPTIONS

Cascade 59421

Missouri River House (406-442-1531; www.missouririverhouse.com), 68 Hill Brothers Road, Clancy 59634; 8 miles south of Cascade off I-15. Reservations are required to stay in this well-appointed guesthouse on the banks of the Missouri River. An angler's dream-come-true, this house has two full bedrooms (sleeping four to six guests), a loft (sleeps two) as well as a full kitchen, a living room, a dining area, satellite television, laundry facilities, a woodstove, and a deck with views of the Missouri flowing by. You can simply fish from the banks by the house, or the hosts will gladly hook you up with a guide; one of the proprietors is an experienced fishing guide himself ($275; 3-night minimum).

& **Prewett Creek Inn** (1-800-509-3943; 406-468-9244; www.prewett creekinn.com), 2468 Old US 91. Catering to anglers, this small creekside motel features rooms with two beds, refrigerators, rod racks, and places to hang waders—not to mention a gorgeous locale ($80). The hosts can help your arrange your entire fly-fishing trip on the world-class Missouri River, from setting you up with a guide service to shuttle service if you need it.

See also **Bull Run Guest Ranch** under *To Do—Horseback Riding;* and **Deerborn Inn** under *Dining Out.*

Choteau 59422

Styren Ranch Guest House (1-888-848-2008; 406-466-2008; www.styren guesthouse.com), 961 20th Road NW (10 miles north of Choteau). This three-bedroom guesthouse sits on the family's ranch. It can be rented "à la carte" by the bedroom (there are three of them), or you can rent the entire house. Guests enjoy the use of the full kitchen, which comes stocked with basic cooking ingredients as well as fixings for a simple breakfast. The house also has a laundry room, television, and phone. The entire house will sleep up to nine people (rooms: $70–85; entire house: $400 per week).

Fairfield 59436

Rusty Spur Guesthouse and Gallery (406-467-2700; www.rustyspur.net), 221 10th Lane SW. What a cool idea! You stay in the snug comfort of a two-bedroom house (sleeps three to five guests) in a gorgeous Montana setting, surrounded by a collection of western artwork—all of which is for sale, should one of the pieces happen to strike your fancy. You'll find pretty much everything you need for your home away from home—a full kitchen, a laundry room, a bathroom, satellite television, and even facilities for horses, if you need them ($70; $400 per week).

Fort Benton 59442

Franklin Street Guest House (406-733-2261; www.fortbenton.com/franklin/index.htm; mailing address: Dennis and June Bough, 6921 Shepherd Crossing Road, Highwood 59450), 1105 Franklin Street. This single-level guest home can comfortably sleep up to six people in three bedrooms and is available by the night, week, or month. It is fully furnished and has a full kitchen, a covered patio, 1.5 bathrooms, laundry facilities, cable television, a phone, and two attached garages, among other amenities ($100; 2-night minimum).

& **Grand Union Hotel** (1-888-838-1882; www.grandunionhotel.com), 1 Grand Union Square. Constructed in 1882 and listed on the National Register of Historic Places, the Grand Union is Montana's oldest operating hotel. Carefully restored and renovated, it provides guests the opportunity to experience a piece of Montana's history while enjoying modern amenities. The 26 rooms all have private baths and cable television. The **Union Grille,** on the premises, serves a sumptuous continental breakfast on weekdays and a weekend brunch, as well as offering a gourmet, fine dining experience on most evenings ($89–175).

Great Falls 59401

🐾 **Russell Country Inn** (406-761-7125; www.russellcountryinn.com), 2516 4th Avenue N. Whether you're staying for a night or a month, you'll find that this lower-level guest apartment has all that you could need to make your stay comfortable: a full kitchen, bedroom, living area, and bathroom, and it can sleep two to four people. Overnight guests can partake of a free continental breakfast. You also have the use of a laundry room, as well as the front yard and backyard—and a canoe and two bicycles ($60; weekly and monthly rates as well).

Lewistown 59457

🐾 **Historic Hotel Calvert** (406-538-5411; www.tein.net/~calvert), 216 7th Avenue S. Once a dormitory for the rural students of Fergus County High School, this 45-room hotel is listed on the National Register of Historic Places. It's nothing fancy, but if you want a roof over your head and a bed under your weary body, this place will surely fit the bill. None of the rooms are the same, and some share bathrooms ($18–30).

Leininger Ranch Log Cabins (1-866-306-5797; 406-538-5797; www.logcabinatlewistown.com), 5754 Lower Cottonwood Creek Road. Stay in one of three log cabins (sleeping four to nine people, depending on the cabin) on this working ranch 10 miles west of Lewistown. You'll enjoy all of the solitude you seek, while also enjoying a full kitchen, covered deck, a hot tub, and easy access to tons of outdoor recreation—not to mention splendid views. This is not a working ranch vacation—you're responsible for your own entertainment for the most part, though on occasion, those working on the ranch might have time to give you a tour of interesting ranch attractions ($85).

🕭 **Montana Bunkhouse and Paradise Cabin** (406-538-5543; www.montanabunkhouse.com; mailing address: The Montana Bunkhouse, HC 86 Box 19, Moore 59464), 12500 Beaver Creek Road, Moore. Situated 23 miles south of Lewistown in the Big Snowy Mountains, this 4,000-acre working ranch offers two cabins perfect for hunters or for those just wishing to savor the slower pace of life in Montana's mountains. The Bunkhouse (handicapped accessible) has two rooms, and each can sleep up to four people. It has a counter for food preparation (with a hot plate, a toaster, a coffeemaker, and dishes), as well as an outhouse; there is no running water (water is available at the ranch house). Paradise Cabin has two bedrooms, a full kitchen, running water, and a bathroom with a washer/dryer ($100–220).

Martinsdale 59053

🕭 🐾 **Crazy Mountain Inn** (406-572-3307; www.crazymountaininn.com), 112 Main Street. Rustic accommodations await at this century-old inn, where you can grab a room for the night (cash or check only) and grab a bite or, rather, a plateful to eat, too—all without putting much of a dent in your wallet. Experience the genuine hospitality of small-town Montana at this country lodging ($35–40).

White Sulphur Springs 59645

🌊 **Grassy Mountain Lodge and Cabins** (406-547-3357; 406-547-3973), 100 Grassy Mountain Road (south of White Sulphur Springs off US 12). You can rent one of three motel-style bedrooms in one of four cabins at this lodge—or rent a couple, so that the kids have a place of their own ($60). They'll also enjoy playing in the sandbox or on the playground. A restaurant on the premises (open to the public; seasonal hours) serves up delicious Montana fare ($60).

Montana Sunrise Lodge (1-866-685-6343; www.montanasunrise lodge.com), 2063 US 89. Bring the whole family or a bunch of friends to fill up this seven-bedroom haven of luxury, located 25 miles north of White Sulphur Springs in the Little Belt Mountains of Lewis and Clark National Forest (see *Wilder Places—Forests*). You'll enjoy easy access to all of the recreational activities the forest offers, while relaxing in the spacious living accommodations: four bathrooms, a full kitchen, laundry facilities, and a 37-inch satellite television and a well-stocked library of movies. The list goes on and on. ($1,800 per week June 1 through September 15; $200–300 per night in the off-season, except around Thanksgiving and Christmas–New Year's, when the rate is $2,100 per week).

See also A. B. Guthrie Memorial Trail under *To Do—Hiking;* Spa Hot Springs Motel under *To Do—Hot Springs; Charlie Russell Chew-Choo* and ranch vacations under *To Do—Unique Adventures;* and Lewis and Clark National Forest under *Wilder Places—Forests.*

☀ Where to Eat

DINING OUT

Cascade

& **Deerborn Inn** (406-468-2007; www.wereflyfishingmontana.com/restaurant.htm), #4 Cooper Drive. This upscale restaurant offers a number of different beef cuts, as well as a popular surf and turf. Whatever you choose, you can enjoy your meal in view of the gorgeous Rocky Mountains or the Missouri River. Depending on the season, you can relax after your lunch or dinner on the deck or by the fireplace, perhaps sipping a drink from the full bar. The Deerborn Inn also provides elegant lodging ($225).

Fort Benton

See **Grand Union Hotel** under *Lodging—Other Options.*

Great Falls

& ✿ **Bar S Supper Club** (406-761-9550), 8535 US 87, 5 miles north of the town center. This local favorite features enormous, perfectly prepared Montana beef entrées, from gigantic steaks (up to 30 ounces) to cuts suitable for the more mortal appetite. If your choice of meat (or chicken or seafood) isn't enough to fill you up, you can always count on the fresh salad bar, homemade soups, and fresh-baked breads to do the trick. A children's menu is available.

& **Indigo** (406-453-1760), 518 Central Avenue. Expensive? Yes. Worth it? *Yes.* Leave the little ones behind and head out for a romantic night on the town—and treat your taste buds to a sublime experience at this acclaimed "American bistro and martini bar." If you're not impressed by the chic decor, whatever items you select from the seasonally changing menu—will most certainly leave your mouth tingling with delight. Creative New American cuisine (featuring everything from barbecue to vegetarian fare) prepared with influences from, well, everywhere would perhaps be the best way to describe the culinary wizardry of Indigo.

Portofino Ristorante (406-453-7186), 220 Central Avenue. True Italian food aficionados will be delighted to discover this northern Italian eatery. Instead of just the usual and typical "American-Italian" entrées (think spaghetti and meatballs or chicken parmesan), you'll find a menu filled with many other choices that reflect a more genuine take on northern Italian cuisine—homemade gnocchi, anyone? The restaurant is attached to the Howard Johnson Hotel in Great Falls.

&. ⚓ **3D International Restaurant and Lounge** (406-453-6561), 1825 Smelter Avenue, Black Eagle (Great Falls). For nearly 60 years, this family-owned and family-operated restaurant has been a mainstay on the Great Falls dining scene. You can choose from a variety of cuisines, including Asian (Chinese, Thai, Mongolian grill), Italian, or American favorites like prime rib, steak, and seafood—making it a great choice if everyone's in the mood for something different. A children's menu is available.

See also **Paris Gibson Square Museum of Art** under *To See—Museums.*

Havre
&. **The Duck Inn's Mediterranean Room and Vineyard** (406-265-6111; www.havremt.com/duckinn/mediterranian_room.htm), 1300 1st Street. This elegant restaurant features not a salad bar but, rather, an impressive "salad garden," which you can order for your meal selection. It comes with a choice of homemade soups, as well as bread and butter. But I'm guessing you'll be tempted by more than one of the other tantalizing entrée options on the menu, which include specialty dinner salads, certified angus beef, pastas, chicken, ribs, and seafood, all prepared with expertise. If you want all of the taste in a more casual setting, you can dine at the **Vineyard,** which features the same menu in a lounge atmosphere—with a wine list and microbrews to

choose from, as well. A children's menu is available.

Lewistown
See **Charlie Russell Chew-Choo** under *To Do—Unique Adventures;* **Pheasant Tales Bed and Bistro** under *Lodging—Bed & Breakfasts;* and Lewistown under *To See—Towns.*

EATING OUT

Belt
Harvest Moon Brewery (406-277-3188), 7 5th Street S. For a decent brewpub-style meal, you can count on the Harvest Moon to fit the bill—but the real reason to stop here is to sample the critically acclaimed microbrews. Topping the list is the Pigs Ass Porter, followed by the Nut Brown Ale and the Beltian White, all of which draw rave accolades from both locals and visitors.

Choteau
&. **Buckaroo Coffeehouse and Eatery** (406-466-2667), 202 N. Main Street. Sick and tired of the same old greasy-spoon fare? Well, don't despair—at this Buckaroo's café, you'll find coffee, baked goods, and light-meal fare to save the day. In addition to a full spectrum of coffee specialty drinks, you can select from an assortment of homemade soups, salads, sandwiches, entrée items, and, of course, mouthwatering desserts.

Fort Benton
Bob's Riverfront Restaurant (406-622-3443), 1414 Front Street. You'll find plenty of delicious food at this local restaurant, which serves three meals a day. You should know, however, that Bob's claim to fame is a wonderful homemade blackberry cobbler, which is served with a generous dose

of warm cream—a sublime, melt-in-your-mouth taste experience for anyone with a sweet tooth.

&. **Expedition Pizza** (406-622-5102), 1050 22nd Street. Lewis and Clark would have probably appreciated being able to stop and enjoy a feast here during their expedition—and you'll probably appreciate this pizza place just as much when you stop on yours. In addition to pizza, the menu includes sandwiches, roasted chicken, and vegetarian options, among other selections. An array of drink options includes not only Italian sodas and espressos but also a wine list and microbrews.

Great Falls

Cattin's Family Dining (406-727-6874), 2001 10th Avenue S. This 24-hour restaurant can fill up the whole family whenever you need to stop—and the kids will be especially pleased to learn that they receive a free toy to accompany their meals. Basic, home-style cooking features burgers, steaks, and sandwiches . . . and desserts. Breakfast, lunch, and dinner are served any time of day. Takeout is available as well.

The Loft Family Restaurant (406-727-8988), 4800 10th Avenue S. A large, family-friendly restaurant, the loft has two stories—plenty of room to seat a crowd. The menu includes more than 15 varieties of omelets, as well as a full complement of burgers dressed up with all sorts of yummy toppings. For parents, there is also an espresso bar. Open for breakfast, lunch, and dinner.

MacKenzie River Pizza (406-761-0085; www.mackenzieriverpizza.com), 500 River Drive S. This is one of the 11 MacKenzie restaurants that are now found around Montana. MacKenzie River Pizza claims to have first introduced Bozeman to the idea of gourmet pizza back when it opened its doors in 1993—and it has been a big hit ever since, as evidenced by its growth. You'll understand why if you come in and check out one of their truly original and delicious pizzas. You can, of course, choose one of the old standbys (cheese or pepperoni, anyone?), but why would you when you could sample a Polynesian, Branding Iron, or Rustler, among other specialties, all of which feature unique and exotic topping combinations.

Penny's Gourmet to Go (406-453-7070), 815 Central Avenue. Specializing in delicious and healthy gourmet fare, this restaurant features sandwiches, pastas, pizza by the slice, soups, chili, salads, hot entrées, and desserts, to eat in or to go. Everything is made from scratch daily, and vegetarians will find options here as well. If you need something to drink, you can choose from an assortment of specialty coffee drinks, smoothies, or juice from the juice bar.

See also **Gibson Park** under *To See—For Families*.

Harlowton

&. **Snowy Mountain Coffee and Slow Rise Bakery** (406-632-6838; www.snowymountaincoffee.com), 124 N. Central Avenue. If you're a coffee lover, you shouldn't miss the chance to stop in at Snowy Mountain—where the coffee is fresh-roasted on the premises in a drum roaster, promising you a truly wonderful cup of java. The Slow Rise Bakery, also on the premises, bakes up a fine assortment of goodies, from muffins and cinnamon rolls to cookies and biscotti. The shop also sells sandwiches, if you're hungry for something a little more substantial. To top it all off, you can have a scoop or two of Wilcoxson's ice cream, a made-in-Montana favorite.

Havre

The Coffee Hound (406-265-8105), 4 1st Street. If you prefer your coffee a step—or a leap—up from standard service-station brew, a stop at the Coffee Hound will make you happy. You'll find freshly brewed coffee in both basic brew and specialty drinks, as well as chai and other such warming options. An assortment of fresh-baked goodies is always on hand as well.

PJ's Restaurant and Casino (406-265-3211), 15 3rd Avenue. Everyone will be happy with the menu at PJ's—since it has something for everybody, from lighter entrée choices, including salads and sandwiches, to hearty entrées featuring beef, chicken, seafood, and ribs; no one will be disappointed. And if gaming whets your whistle, you'll find plenty of that kind of entertainment, too. Breakfast, lunch, and dinner are served at PJ's every day.

✎ ♿ **Wolfer's Diner** (406-265-2111), 220 3rd Avenue, Suite 401 (in the Atrium Mall). Do you like big portions of old-fashioned, home-cooked food? If so, a stop at Wolfer's Diner will fill you up admirably, leaving you stuffed and content. All of the restaurant's beef is locally raised and ground fresh every morning. If you can manage it, save some space in your stomach for a delicious homemade dessert.

Lewistown

✎ **Ruby's 100 Percent Montana Burgers** (406-538-7450), 501 E. Main Street. For a true taste of Montana, look no farther than Ruby's, where the burgers come from beef raised by local ranchers and processed in Montana—they guarantee it. If beef just isn't your thing, the menu also includes chicken, hot dogs, sandwiches, and salads, as well as espresso, milk shakes, and smoothies. During the warmer months, you can enjoy your meal while seated outside or in. Ruby's also has a drive-through.

✎ ♿ **The Whole Famdamily** (406-538-5161), 206 W. Main Street. This local restaurant serves an assortment of traditional sandwiches, soups, and salads, as well as desserts. Sit back and relax in your comfortable surroundings while you enjoy a delicious sandwich piled high with toppings, or perhaps you'll choose one of the nightly specials—as is true in many towns in these western parts, the Friday-night prime rib is a local favorite. A children's menu is available.

See also Lewistown under *To See—Towns.*

White Sulphur Springs

♿ ✎ **Happy Days Café** (406-547-2223), 307 3rd Avenue SW. This small-town café claims to serve up the best—and biggest—hamburgers in the state. If you enjoy 1950s and '60s nostalgia, you'll certainly take pleasure in stopping here for a hearty American diner-style meal, perhaps topping off your tanks with a big slice of homemade pie. A children's menu is available.

✎ **Stageline Pizza and Video, and Strand Theatre** (406-547-3505), 210 E. Main Street. Located on the main drag, this pizza joint serves up piping-hot pies—and on Friday, Saturday, and Sunday, you can have your pizza brought to you in a booth at the

Strand Theatre while you watch a movie (reservations recommended).

See also **Grassy Mountain Lodge and Cabins** under *Lodging—Other Options.*

✳ Special Events

January: ✍ **Montana Winter Fair,** Lewistown (1-800-406-8841; 406-538-8841; www.centralmontanafair .com): statewide annual fair featuring livestock, horse show, free Sunday breakfast, chili cook-off, death by chocolate competition, vendors, and much, much more.

February: **Lake Frances Ice Derby,** Valier: annual competition for anglers, held by the local volunteer fire department and targeting northern pike and perch.

April: **Museum Sunday Sampler,** Great Falls: first Sunday in April; free entrance to nine museums and attractions in Great Falls, including Lewis and Clark National Historic Trail Interpretive Center, Children's Museum of Montana, C. M. Russell Museum, Galerie Trinitas, High Plains Heritage Center, Malmstrom Air Force Base Museum, Paris Gibson Square Museum of Art, Ulm Pishkun State Park, and the Ursuline Centre.

July: ✍ **Central Montana Fair,** Lewistown: (1-800-406-8841; 406-538-8841; www.centralmontanafair .com): fair featuring livestock, rodeo,

petting zoo, clowns, 4-H, horse show, and more.

July and August: ✍ **Montana State Fair,** Great Falls (406-727-8900; www.montanastatefair.com): state fair with carnival, livestock, rodeo, free entertainment, food, kids' activities, horse racing, and much more.

August: **Rocky Boys Annual Pow-wow,** Rocky Boys Indian Reservation: annual powwow celebrating Chippewa Cree culture, including Native American dancing, drumming, and costume competitions, as well as the sale of arts and crafts and food.

September: ✍ **Montana Chokecherry Festival,** Lewistown: annual celebration of chokecherries held on the first Saturday after Labor Day includes pit-spitting contests, a fun run/walk, a pancake breakfast, vendor booths, and free entertainment.
Brews and Blues Festival, Great Falls: annual festival featuring a blues concert with notable musicians, as well as food and local microbrews.
"What the Hay," Hobson, Utica, Windham: annual event in which these communities line the sides of MT 239 with decorated bales of hay.
✍ **Havre Festival Days,** Havre: mid-month community-wide event takes place over a weekend, featuring a parade, a quilt show, a barbecue, kids' and youth events, and a pancake breakfast.

NORTHEAST MONTANA: MISSOURI RIVER COUNTRY

Back in 1805, Meriwether Lewis and William Clark crossed what would one day be the border of Montana. They noted that this location would be the perfect spot for a trading post—and so it would, as it became the location of the Fort Union Trading Post (see *To See—Historic Landmarks, Places, and Sites*), now a National Historic Landmark. The explorers continued their journey from this point through northeastern Montana for more than a month. They passed through the land along the Missouri River (their route is now US 2) to the area around present-day Wolf Point and Glasgow and then dropped south to follow the river's course for 13 days through today's Charles M. Russell National Wildlife Refuge (see *Wilder Places—Wildlife Refuges*). During their expedition, they encountered wildlife with great frequency, including elk, antelope, buffalo, and grizzly bears, as they attempted, among other goals, to find a passage to the Pacific Ocean and to locate suitable sites for outposts.

You can follow in the tracks of this historic expedition as you wend your way through this still relatively pristine and sparsely inhabited area of Montana. You'll learn more about the historic journey of Lewis and Clark and their Corps of Discovery at the region's many museums and historic sites, supplementing and enhancing your experience and understanding of the terrain. At many of these locations, you'll also be able to increase your knowledge of the Native American Sioux and Assiniboine tribes, longtime residents of this area. In addition, you'll find information about the prehistoric creatures that made this region their home, as dinosaur fossils aplenty have been discovered here, particularly at Hell Creek Fossil Area (see *To See—Natural Wonders*). This is where a *Tyrannosaurus rex* fossil, among other notable finds, was unearthed in the early 1900s.

In this region of Montana, you'll also learn much about the country that Lewis and Clark passed through merely by watching out the window of your car, especially if you choose to drive one of the region's auto tour routes. In fact, today's flora and fauna still resemble to a certain degree the wildlife witnessed by the famous explorers—minus grizzly bears, which no longer inhabit the area.

Also creating a dramatic and distinctive change in the landscape since days past is Fort Peck Lake, a huge, 134-mile reservoir that came into being with the

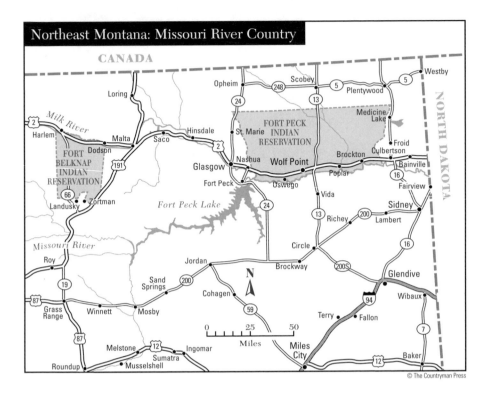

© The Countryman Press

construction of the Fort Peck Dam in the 1930s. Situated within the Charles M. Russell National Wildlife Refuge, this lake and the surrounding refuge provide abundant recreational opportunities, including fishing, hiking, paddling, floating, horseback riding, camping, wildlife viewing, bicycling, and more. For a peaceful night's sleep in a beautiful and remote setting, the Downstream Recreation Area (see *To Do—Camping*) provides shaded campsites and access to the Beaver Creek Nature Trail (see *To Do—Hiking*).

If you're looking for a real opportunity to get away from it all, then, you'll find it here in northeastern Montana—a place where elk still graze on their native prairie year-round, a place where lengthy stretches of river to float or paddle in solitude are easy to find, and a place rife with human history catalogued in numerous local museums as well as historic sites—but above all else, a place still relatively devoid of concentrated human habitation.

GUIDANCE Daniels County Chamber of Commerce and Agriculture (406-487-2061; www.scobey.org), 120 Main Street, Scobey 59263.

Fort Peck Indian Reservation (406-768-5155; www.fortpecktribes.org). Information available at the Fort Peck Tribal Museum (see *To See—Museums*), P.O. Box 1027, Poplar 59255.

Garfield County Chamber of Commerce (406-557-6158; www.garfield county.com), 434 Main Street, P.O. Box 370, Jordan 59337.

Glasgow Chamber of Commerce and Agriculture (406-228-2222; www .glasgowmt.net), 23 US 2, P.O. Box 832, Glasgow 59230.

Malta, Montana Chamber of Commerce (406-654-1776; www.malta chamber.com). Tourist Information Center located within the foyer of the Phillips County Museum (see *To See—Museums*); outdoor display at Malta Rest Stop (intersection of US 2 and US 191), P.O. Box 1420, Malta 59538.

Missouri River Country, Inc. (1-800-653-1319; www.missouririver.visitmt.com), P.O. Box 387, Wolf Point 59201.

Richey Chamber of Commerce (406-773-5634), 205 Antelope Avenue, P.O. Box 205, Richey 59259.

Sheridan County Chamber of Commerce and Agriculture (406-765-1733; www.plentywood.com), 501 1st Avenue W., P.O. Box 104, Plentywood 59254.

Sidney Area Chamber of Commerce and Agriculture (406-433-1916; www .sidneymt.com), 909 S. Central Avenue, Sidney 59270.

Town of Culbertson (406-787-5821; www.culbertsonmt.com). See Culbertson, Montana Museum Visitor Center under *To See—Museums*; offices at 11 Broadway Avenue, P.O. Box 351, Culbertson 59218.

Wolf Point Chamber of Commerce and Agriculture (406-653-2012; www .wolfpoint.com), 122 3rd Avenue S., Wolf Point 59201.

GETTING THERE US 2 is the main road through Montana's Missouri River Country, taking you to Culbertson, Wolf Point, Glasgow, and Malta. Plentywood and Scobey lie along MT 5. Sidney, Circle, and Jordan lie along MT 200. MT 24 runs north–south through this region intersecting US 2 at Glasgow. The Fort Peck Indian Reservation lies north of US 2, south of MT 5/MT 248, east of MT 24, and west of MT 16.

See also *Airports, Amtrak, Bus Service,* and *Travel Information* in "What's Where in Montana."

MEDICAL EMERGENCY **Daniels Memorial Hospital** (406-487-2296), 105 5th Avenue E., Scobey.

Frances Mahon Deaconess Hospital (406-228-3500), 621 3rd Street S., Glasgow.

Phillips County Medical Center (406-654-1100), 417 S. 4th E., Malta.

Roosevelt Memorial Medical Center (406-787-6281), 818 2nd Avenue E., Culbertson.

Sheridan Memorial Hospital (406-765-1420), 440 W. Laurel Avenue, Plentywood.

THE LITTLE ROCKY MOUNTAINS NEAR LANDUSKY AND ZORTMAN

Sidney Health Center (406-488-2100), 216 14th Avenue SW, Sidney.

Trinity Hospital (406-653-2100), 315 Knapp Street, Wolf Point.

✳ To See

TOWNS Culbertson is on US 2 near the North Dakota border. This friendly town of about 1,000 residents has its own museum (see also *To See—Museums*) detailing the area's past, a public swimming pool, and access to the Missouri River. The **Roosevelt County Fair** takes place in Culbertson (see also *Special Events*).

Fort Peck, south of US 2 on MT 24, is a small town that was constructed to facilitate the building of the enormous **Fort Peck Dam** in 1933. Today Fort Peck provides visitors with the opportunity to learn about the dam's construction, to enjoy an abundance of recreational opportunities, to visit the town's museum (see also *To See—Museums*), or to catch a show in the **Fort Peck Theater,** which hosts a summer theater company. Construction on the new **Fort Peck Dam Museum and Interpretive Center** was well underway at the time of this book's publication—stay tuned to a later edition for details.

Jordan lies along MT 200. It is the seat of Garfield County and home to its museum. This town sits in the midst of some of Montana's wildest lands, and the enormous **Charles M. Russell National Wildlife Area** is just to the north. The surrounding area has been the location of many findings of significance to paleontologists, including the 1904 discovery of a *Tyrannosaurus rex.* This historic town's Main Street still features many false-front buildings that are more than 80 years old.

Landusky and **Zortman** are located south of Malta off US 191, offering access to the Little Rocky Mountains, as well as being near to the **UL Bend National Wildlife Refuge** and the **Charles M. Russell National Wildlife Refuge.** These two refuges are the only places in Montana where elk continue to live on their native prairie all year long. The unincorporated towns of Zortman and Landusky are the former locations of historic mining camps established in the 1880s. (See also Camp Creek Campground and Montana Gulch Campground under *To Do—Camping;* and Buckhorn Store, Cabins, & RV Park and Whispering Pines Vacation Homes under *Lodging—Other Options.*)

THE LITTLE ROCKY MOUNTAINS OUTSIDE ZORTMAN

Westby is in the northeast corner of Montana on MT 5 near the border of North Dakota and Canada. If you really want to escape the madding crowds, you'll find plenty of space to relax and take it easy in this tiny town of fewer than 200 people. Originally the farthest point west in North Dakota, the town was moved into Montana with the construction of the Great Northern Railroad. (See also Hilltop House Bed & Breakfast Inn under

Lodging—Bed & Breakfasts; and Prairie Kitchen under *Eating Out.*)

PHILLIPS COUNTY MUSEUM

MUSEUMS ♿ **Culbertson, Montana Museum Visitor Center** (406-787-6320; www.culbertsonmt.com/museum.htm), 1 mile east of Culbertson on US 2. Open daily May and September 9 AM–6 PM, June through August 8 AM–8 PM, by appointment April and October; free. Life-size displays at this museum depict how life used to be lived in these parts from 1890 to 1940, including an old schoolhouse, saloon, doctor's office and drugstore, blacksmith shop, barber and beauty shop, and more. This museum also has a visitor information center to help guide you in your travels through the region and the state.

Fort Peck Tribal Museum (406-768-5155, ext. 392 and 328; www.fortpeck tribes.org), 605 Indian Avenue, Poplar. Open daily 8 AM–4:30 PM; free. Exhibits covering the histories and cultures of the Assiniboine and Sioux tribes are on display here, as are Native American–made arts and crafts.

♿ **MonDak Heritage Center Museum and Gallery** (406-433-3500), 120 3rd Avenue SW, Sidney. Open in summer Tuesday through Friday 10 AM–5 PM, Saturday and Sunday 1 PM–4 PM; in winter Wednesday through Friday 10 AM–4 PM, Saturday and Sunday 1 PM–4 PM; closed in January; $3 adults, $1 children 6–11, children 5 and under free. This art gallery and historic museum—the only one of its kind for some 150 miles around—has two viewing galleries featuring art by local, national, and international artists, as well as a replica of a pioneer village.

♿ **Phillips County Museum** (406-654-1037; www.maltachamber.com/museum), 431 US 2, Malta (0.3 mile east of the junction with US 191). Open mid-May through mid-September Monday through Saturday 10 AM–5 PM, Sunday 12:30 PM–5 PM; $3 adults, $1 children 5–12, children under 5 free. Located on the historic Lewis and Clark Trail, the Phillips County Museum features numerous exhibits chronicling the history of the area from prehistoric times through the pioneer days. Exhibits include a *Tyrannosaurus rex* skull, a restored 1903 house, an outlaw exhibit, and historical displays and artifacts related to both Native American inhabitants and pioneers.

Sheridan County Free Museum (406-765-2468; www.co.sheridan.mt.us/museum.htm), east of Plentywood at the junction of MT 5 and MT 16. Open daily Memorial Day through Labor Day 1 PM–5 PM, by appointment otherwise; free. The standout exhibit at this museum is a huge, 74-foot mural by local artist Bob Southland, depicting the history of the Sheridan County area from early Native American times to the present.

♿ **Valley County Pioneer Museum** (406-228-8692; www.valleycountymuseum .com), 816 US 2, Glasgow. Open Memorial Day through Labor Day Monday through Saturday 9 AM–7 PM, Sunday 1 PM–5 PM; free. This museum features a number of exhibits pertaining to local history, including materials detailing the expeditions of Lewis and Clark, cowboys and Indians (including a rare hide teepee and a chuck box and stove), the Great Northern Railroad (which came to this area in 1887), local artifacts dating from pioneer days into the mid-20th century, displays about Fort Peck Dam, a wildlife display, and a historic bar, among others.

See also **Daniels County Museum & Pioneer Town** and **Poplar Museum** under *To See—Historic Landmarks, Place, and Sites.*

HISTORIC LANDMARKS, PLACES, AND SITES Daniels County Museum & Pioneer Town (406-487-5965; 406-487-2061; www.scobey.org/museum.html), 7 W. County Road, Scobey. Open daily Memorial Day through Labor Day 12:30 PM–4:30 PM; open Labor Day through Memorial Day Friday 1 PM–4 PM and by appointment. Just 7 blocks west of Scobey's Main Street you'll find 35 restored turn-of-the-20th-century buildings on 20 acres of land. This pioneer town aims to give you a genuine feel for the way life was for early settlers in this part of Montana. You'll also find a collection of antique automobiles, tractors, and machinery. For a real history lesson, plan your visit during Pioneer Days (see *Special Events*).

Fort Peck Dam (406-526-3431; 406-526-3421; www.nwo.usace.army.mil/html/ Lake_Proj/fortpeck/welcome.html), 2 miles northeast of Fort Peck. The **Fort Peck Power Plant Visitor Center and Museum** is open year-round 9 AM–5 PM, and tours of the power plant are given 9 AM–5 PM daily Memorial Day through Labor Day. First learn about the history of this incredible engineering feat, and then take a tour to see how it operates. The completion of Fort Peck Dam, constructed from 1933 until 1940 to dam the Missouri River and create Fort Peck Lake, formed the fifth-largest artificial reservoir in the United States. At 134 miles in length with 1,520 miles of shoreline, today the lake provides wildlife habitat as well as numerous recreational opportunities, including boating, fishing, swimming, paddling, and camping along its shores. The lake is surrounded by the 1.1 million acres of the Charles M. Russell National Wildlife Refuge (see also *Wilder Places—Wildlife Refuges*).

& **Fort Union Trading Post National Historic Site** (701-572-9083; www.nps .gov/fous), 24 miles northeast of Sidney on ND 1804. Open Memorial Day through Labor Day 8 AM–8 PM (CST); open Labor Day through Memorial Day 9 AM–5:30 PM (CST); free. This historic trading post, constructed in 1828 by the American Fur Company, straddles the border between Montana and North Dakota just north of Fairview. It was here in 1805 that the Lewis and Clark expedition entered what would one day be Montana. Once the location of a bustling frontier outpost frequented by numerous Native American tribes as well as trappers and traders, the fort remained active until 1867.

FORT PECK DAM AND FORT PECK POWER PLANT VISITOR CENTER AND MUSEUM

Today, you can enjoy historic exhibits in the restored **Bourgeois House,** which also includes the visitor center, and tour the partially reconstructed grounds, which include teepees and an Indian trade house. (See also Bainville to Fort Union Trading Post National Historic Site on MT 327 under *Scenic Drives*).

Poplar Museum (406-768-5223), US 2, Poplar (across the street from the "Greets the Dawn" Fort Peck Community College Building). Open June 1 through Labor Day 11 AM–5 PM. This small museum is housed in the 1920s tribal jail, a historic site listed on the National Register of Historic Places. Displays include beadwork by Sioux and Assiniboine tribe members, much of which is for sale.

See also Charles M. Russell National Wildlife Refuge under *Wilder Places— Wildlife Refuges;* Fort Peck Hotel under *Lodging—Other Options;* and Fort Peck Summer Theatre under *Special Events.*

FOR FAMILIES ✍ ᵫ **Dinosaur Field Station** (406-654-2323; www.montana dinosaurdigs.com), at the intersection of US 2 and US 191 in Malta. Open May through September Monday through Saturday 10 AM–5 PM, Sunday 12 PM–5 PM; open in winter and on holidays by appointment; $5 adults, $3 children 12 and under. Watch scientists in action at this state-of-the-art field station, part of the Judith River Dinosaur Institute. Knowledgeable tour guides will lead you through the facility, explaining exactly what is going on in the laboratories as paleontologists work to preserve the specimens they have unearthed. Operated by the nonprofit Judith River Foundation, the field station provides the unique opportunity to view dinosaur specimens up close and to talk to the technicians working to prepare them for display and study. (See also Judith River Dinosaur Institute Dinosaur Digs under *To Do—Unique Adventures.*)

See also Gray's Coulee Guest Ranch under *To Do—Unique Adventures;* Charles M. Russell National Wildlife Refuge under *Wilder Places—Wildlife Refuges;* and *Special Events.*

SCENIC DRIVES **Bainville to Fort Union Trading Post National Historic Site on MT 327.** For 12 miles, you'll wind through lush farmlands along the Missouri River on a well-maintained gravel road as you make your way to the historic site (see *Historic Landmarks, Places, and Sites*). Idyllic agricultural scenes contrast sharply with the adjacent badlands, making this drive, though remote, well worth the effort.

Bitter Creek Wilderness Study Area. A map is available from the Bureau of Land Management (BLM) Glasgow Field Station (406-228-3750) for $4. The study area is accessible via US 2 west of Glasgow by taking Bristch

FORT UNION TRADING POST NATIONAL HISTORIC SITE

Road north for 15 miles. A high-clearance, four-wheel-drive vehicle is recommended for the unpaved portion of the route; travel in inclement conditions is not recommended due to the potential for getting stuck. Bristch Road traverses wild, lovely terrain with great potential for viewing wildlife (antelope, mule deer, grouse, coyotes, foxes, rattlesnakes, and more) before you reach pavement again and join MT 24 north of St. Marie. If you make the full loop, you'll drive through barren badlands, see tracts of aspen and cottonwoods, and perhaps, if you're lucky, stumble on a prehistoric teepee ring—evidence of human presence eons ago. Three other Wilderness Study Areas (WSAs) are accessible from near Glasgow as well, though they involve more driving and are not as easy to access: **Burnt Lodge WSA, Cow Creek WSA,** and **Antelope Creek WSA.** For more information, call the Glasgow BLM office or go to www.mt.blm.gov/mafo/wsapage.html.

Bowdoin National Wildlife Refuge Auto Tour Route (406-654-2863; http://bowdoin.fws.gov), 7 miles east of Malta on C.R. 2 (turn off US 2 at the sign for the refuge just east of Malta). You can pick up a guide to this 15-mile loop tour of the refuge at the headquarters on your way to starting the drive. You'll drive in a loop around Lake Bowdoin, enjoying the opportunity to view the area's abundant wildlife and variety of environments. Pronghorn, muskrats, waterfowl, and white-tailed deer are just some of the inhabitants you might encounter on your journey. Pullouts make it easy to stop and stretch your legs or to take a closer look. (See also *To Do—Bicycling* and *Wilder Places—Wildlife Refuges.*)

Charles M. Russell National Wildlife Refuge Auto Tour Route, NWR 101, located 55 miles south of Malta off US 191. This 20-mile, self-guided auto tour brings you a little bit closer to the wildlife of the refuge as well as to the historic Lewis and Clark expedition that came through this area in 1805. Astounding views of the Missouri Breaks as well as opportunities to see abundant wildlife, including birds, elk, deer, and antelope, make this drive a popular one.

See also Hell Creek Fossil Area under *To See—Natural Wonders.*

NATURAL WONDERS Hell Creek Fossil Area, located north of Jordan on MT 543. A scenic drive takes you north from Jordan about 20 miles to this National Natural Landmark. This is the site where a *Tyrannosaurus rex* was unearthed back in the early 1900s. This site has also yielded numerous other dinosaur remains, including a triceratops and an ancient alligator. (See also Hell Creek State Park under *Wilder Places—Parks*).

Medicine Lake Site, located in the Medicine Lake National Wildlife Refuge, 20 miles north of Culbertson (south of Plentywood) on MT 16. Heavy glaciation occurred at this National Natural Landmark some 15,000 years ago, forcing the Missouri River to find a new southward path. Abundant evidence of the glacial history of this locale exists to this day, including glacial tills, terrace deposits, outwash, twisting sand ridges known as eskers, and *kames* (stratified hills with steep sides). (See also *Wilder Places—Wildlife Refuges.*)

WINERIES Rolling Hills Winery (406-787-5787; www.rollinghillswinery.com), Culbertson (watch for signs on US 2). The owners of this relatively new winery

(2003) use native fruits—chokecherries, blueberries, and raspberries, to name a few—to craft their wines.

✳ To Do

BICYCLING Bowdoin National Wildlife Refuge (406-654-2863; http://bowdoin.fws.gov), 7 miles east of Malta on C.R. 2 (turn off US 2 at the sign for the refuge just east of Malta). Bicycling easy to moderate, paved terrain around Lake Bowdoin gains you a closer look at the refuge's incredible wildlife habitats and chances to view its more than 260 bird species. If you desire, you can start your ride to the west in Malta, or you can simply ride around the 15-mile loop road starting from the refuge's headquarters. (See also *To See—Scenic Drives* and *Wilder Places—Wildlife Refuges.*)

See also The Pines Recreation Area under *Camping;* and Charles M. Russell National Wildlife Refuge under *Wilder Places—Wildlife Refuges.*

BOATING Fort Peck Lake (406-526-3411; www.nwo.usace.army.mil/html/Lake_Proj/fortpeck/welcome.html), south of Glasgow via MT 24. This enormous, 134-mile lake is a boater's haven. A paved road at the west side of the dam affords larger vehicles access to the water via the Fort Peck Marina, while numerous smaller, concrete boat ramps around the lake provide additional places to launch. (See also Fort Peck Dam under *To See—Historic Landmarks, Places, and Sites;* and Charles M. Russell National Wildlife Refuge under *Wilder Places—Wildlife Refuges*).

CAMPING Camp Creek Campground, 1 mile northeast of Zortman on Dry Fork Road. Open year-round; small fee. Located on Bureau of Land Management (BLM) lands in the shadow of the Little Rocky Mountains, Camp Creek Campground gives you access to the Little Rocky Mountains with the convenience of a small grocery store and food available a scant 1 mile away. At this remote and wooded location you'll find sites with picnic tables, water, restrooms, and probably plenty of solitude.

DOWNSTREAM RECREATION AREA AND BEAVER CREEK NATURE TRAIL AT FORT PECK DAM

♿ ✎ Downstream Recreation Area (406-526-3224; www.www.nwo.usace.army.mil/html/Lake_Proj/fortpeck/5.html), south of Nashua on MT 117. Open late April through October 31; $10–12. You can make reservations by calling 1-877-444-6777 or going to www.reserveusa.com, or take your chances as a walk-in. On the northern shores of Fort Peck Lake, more than 70 wooded, spaced campsites are available as a base for exploring the surrounding area. Amenities include

hot showers, electrical hookups, a playground, drinking water, a nature trail, a visitor center, fishing ponds, a volleyball court, and more. (See also Fort Peck Dam under *To See—Historic Landmarks, Places, and Sites;* Beaver Creek Nature Trail under *Hiking;* and Charles M. Russell National Wildlife Refuge under *Wilder Places—Wildlife Refuges.*)

Montana Gulch Campground, 1 mile southwest of Landusky and 5 miles west of the junction between US 191 and MT 66 (watch for signs). Open year-round; small fee. This small campground in the Little Rocky Mountains features picnic tables and toilets, but no water. Plenty of trees make for a peaceful and restful camping experience away from the mainstream.

The Pines Recreation Area (406-526-3411; www.nwo.usace.army.mil/html/Lake_Proj/fortpeck/8.html), on Pines Road southeast of Fort Peck. Open year-round. This recreation area on the shores of Fort Peck Lake within the Charles M. Russell National Wildlife Refuge (see *Wilder Places—Wildlife Refuges*) offers 30 primitive campsites, along with vault toilets, water, picnic tables, fire rings, a playground, an interpretive display, a boat ramp, and access to cross-country skiing trails in winter. Recreational opportunities include hiking, fishing, boating, bicycling, and more. (See also Fort Peck Dam under *To See—Historic Landmarks, Places, and Sites;* and Charles M. Russell National Wildlife Refuge under *Wilder Places—Wildlife Refuges.*)

✎ **Trafton Park,** north of the rest stop at the intersection of US 191 and US 2 in Malta. Open May through November; $3. Shaded by cottonwood trees, Malta's city park makes a great place to stop for the night on the cheap. Public restrooms, water, and easy access to fishing and floating or paddling on the Milk River (see also *Paddling/Floating*), as well as a playground, picnic tables, horseshoe pits, and barbecue grills, will make your stay convenient and comfortable. If you're spending time in Malta, you'll find local attractions well within walking distance from the park, including the Phillips County Museum (see also *To See—Museums*).

See also Nelson Reservoir under *Fishing; Wilder Places—Parks;* and Charles M. Russell National Wildlife Refuge under *Wilder Places—Wildlife Refuges.*

FISHING Fort Peck Lake (406-526-3411; www.nwo.usace.army.mil/html/Lake_Proj/fortpeck/welcome.html), south of Glasgow via MT 24. In these plentiful waters, the avid angler has access to more than 50 species of fish, including walleye, northern pike, sauger, lake trout, smallmouth bass, and chinook salmon, as well as paddlefish—a large, flat-billed fish that has been around for some 70 million years and is found only in the Missouri and the Yellowstone rivers in the United States and in China's Yangtze River. (See also Fort Peck Dam under *To See—Historic Landmarks, Places, and Sites;* and Charles M. Russell National Wildlife Refuge under *Wilder Places—Wildlife Refuges.*)

The Lower Missouri River (406-454-5840; www.fwp.state.mt.us) flows from US 191 south of Zortman to the North Dakota border along US 2. This river originates in southwestern Montana where three rivers converge at Three Forks. The river then flows east roughly 700 miles across Montana before crossing the border into North Dakota. A 150-mile portion of the river, from near Fort Benton to the Fred Robinson Bridge (US 191) in the Charles M. Russell National Wildlife Refuge (see also *Wilder Places—Wildlife Refuges*) is designated Wild and Scenic (see "North-Central Montana: Russell Country" for details). At various points along the Missouri, anglers will find remarkable fishing opportunities. In this region, in addition to Fort Peck Lake and the area of the river within the refuge, there's great trout fishing just downstream from Fort Peck Dam and opportunities farther east to fish for warm-water species such as northern pike, walleye, catfish, and smallmouth bass. (See also Fort Peck Lake and the Lower Missouri River under *Paddling/Floating.*)

Medicine Lake National Wildlife Refuge (406-789-2305; http://medicine lake.fws.gov), 20 miles north of Culbertson (south of Plentywood) on MT 16. The northern, larger portion of this refuge is part of the Medicine Lake Wilderness, including Medicine Lake and five smaller lakes. Species include crappie, perch, walleye, and pike. No motorized boats are allowed on Medicine Lake. Be sure to check for opening dates at specific lakes before planning a trip, as they vary from lake to lake.

Nelson Reservoir (406-454-5840; www.fwp.state.mt.us), east of Malta off US 2. Species in this popular 4,000-acre reservoir include black crappie, burbot, channel catfish, lake whitefish, northern pike, smallmouth bass, walleye, and yellow perch. Access is available via the shoreline, but fishing improves greatly if you can paddle out onto the lake. Overnight, free camping is permitted here; amenities include toilets, water, and picnic tables.

See also **the Milk River** under *Paddling/Floating;* and **the Lower Yellowstone River** under *To Do—Fishing* in "Southeast Montana: Custer Country."

GOLF **Airport Golf Club** (406-653-2161), 3 miles east of Wolf Point on MT 25, Wolf Point, 9 holes.

Marian Hills Country Club (406-654-5527), 100 Doral, Malta, 9 holes.

Plentywood Golf Club (406-765-2532), 709 N. Sheridan Street, Plentywood, 9 holes.

Scobey Golf Course (406-487-5322; www.scobey.org/golfclub), Golf Course Road, Scobey, 9 holes.

Sidney Country Club (406-433-1894; 406-433-7460), MT 16 north of Sidney, Sidney, 18 holes.

Sunnyside Golf Club (406-228-9519), 95 Skylark Road, Glasgow, 18 holes.

See also Sleeping Buffalo Hot Springs under *Hot Springs.*

HIKING **Beaver Creek Nature Trail,** near Fort Peck Dam, departs from the Downstream Recreation Area (see *Camping*). This moderate trail, of varying distances depending on which path you take, leads you through wildlife habitat near Fort Peck Dam. Paved trails allow bicycles to cruise around as well, while riverside docks provide closer views of the nearby waterway. You'll likely see numerous bird species, with the potential for encountering mule deer as well.

This path is perfect for a quick morning stroll to get your nature fix before setting out on the road.

 ♿ **Bowdoin National Wildlife Refuge** (406-654-2863; http://bowdoin.fws .gov), 7 miles east of Malta on C.R. 2 (turn off US 2 at the sign for the refuge just east of Malta). This short loop trail leaves from just by the refuge headquarters, allowing you to stroll through a small wetland area. In addition, there is an accessible wildlife blind at Pearce Waterfowl Production Area near the northeast boundary, as well as an accessible pier next to Lake Bowdoin's main boat ramp. Additional hiking opportunities abound for those interested in longer excursions. (See also *Wilder Places—Wildlife Refuges.*)

See also Camp Creek Campground and The Pines Recreation Area under *Camping;* Hell Creek State Park under *Wilder Places—Parks;* and *Wilder Places—Wildlife Refuges.*

HORSEBACK RIDING See Charles M. Russell National Wildlife Refuge under *Wilder Places—Wildlife Refuges;* Tillmans Bed & Breakfast under *Lodging— Bed & Breakfasts;* ranch vacations under *Unique Adventures;* and Gray's Coulee Guest Ranch and Wolff Farms Vacation Home under *Lodging—Other Options.*

HOT SPRINGS Sleeping Buffalo Hot Springs (406-527-3370), HC 75 Box 460, Saco, 17 miles east of Malta and 10 miles west of Saco on US 2. Hours and prices vary; call in advance. With two indoor pools—a hot pool at 106°F and a warm pool at 90°F—as well as an outdoor pool with waterslides (100°F or so), you can soak at your leisure in the pool that most suits your temperature preference. This hot spring was discovered in 1922 by a man seeking oil—imagine his surprise at striking hot water at 3,200 feet instead! Legend has it that cowboys used to bathe with this water. Today you can do more than soak; you can play a round of golf at the 9-hole course or have a picnic at the picnic area.

SLEEPING BUFFALO HOT SPRINGS

PADDLING/FLOATING Fort Peck Lake (406-526-3411; www.nwo.usace .army. mil/html/Lake_Proj/fortpeck/ welcome.html), south of Glasgow via MT 24. Canoeists and kayakers will delight in paddling along the shoreline of this 134-mile-long reservoir, but beware of strong winds and motorized craft—venturing far from shore is not recommended. Small and versatile watercraft will allow more opportunities for wildlife viewing and exploration of the lake's hidden gems. You can rent canoes from an outfitter such as **Missouri River Outpost** (406-439-8438), located 1 mile south of Fort Peck Dam on MT 117. (See also

Fort Peck Dam under *To See—Historic Landmarks, Places, and Sites;* and Charles M. Russell National Wildlife Refuge under *Wilder Places—Wildlife Refuges.*)

The Lower Missouri River (406-454-5840; www.fwp.state.mt.us), stretching in this region from US 191 south of Zortman to the North Dakota border along US 2. Various put-in points above Fort Peck Lake allow access to the designated National Wild and Scenic portion of this river (see also *To Do—Paddling/Floating* in "North-Central Montana: Russell Country"); put-in points below the lake include an access site just after Fort Peck Dam and at the Culbertson Bridge just off US 2. Gorgeous solitude and ample wildlife viewing opportunities await you while you float or paddle your way toward the lake from Russell Country—but beware entering Fort Peck Lake. Due to its enormity, coupled with the potential for strong winds (see also *Fishing*), floating or paddling across it is not recommended. Below the lake, the cottonwood-lined river winds its way through Montana's rolling eastern prairies to the North Dakota border.

The Milk River (406-454-5840; www.fwp.state.mt.us), accessible off US 2 in Malta and at various points just off US 2, including near Hinsdale and Vandalia. This river originates in northwest Montana, travels up into Canada, and then reenters Montana almost 170 miles later. After recrossing the border, it meanders about, ultimately emptying into the Missouri River near Fort Peck Dam. The river has no real rapids, making it suitable for inflatable canoes and kayaks as well as rafts. The Milk River also offers opportunities for fishing for warm-water species such as smallmouth bass, catfish, sturgeon, whitefish, and pike.

See also **Nelson Reservoir** under *Fishing;* and Bowdoin Lake National Wildlife Refuge and Medicine Lake National Wildlife Refuge under *Wilder Places—Wildlife Refuges.*

SNOW SPORTS **Bowdoin National Wildlife Refuge** (406-654-2863; http://bowdoin.fws.gov), 7 miles east of Malta on C.R. 2 (turn off US 2 at the sign for the refuge just east of Malta). Come wintertime, this refuge transforms into a peaceful wonderland perfect for cross-country skiing adventures.

See also The Pines Recreation Area under *Camping;* and Tillmans Bed and Breakfast under *Lodging—Bed & Breakfasts.*

UNIQUE ADVENTURES ✇ **Gray's Coulee Guest Ranch** (1-866-270-6550; 406-774-3778; www.grayscoulee.com), 6 miles south of Lambert (about 20 miles west of Sidney). For a unique ranch experience, book a Learning Vacation at this working ranch. Natural history, archaeology, culture, geology, botany, farming, bird-watching, horseback riding, hiking, and more will be incorporated into a customized vacation (along with plenty of time for rest and relaxation) for you and your loved ones—but be sure to book your trip far in advance, so the ranch can plan your adventures. Lodging, meals, materials, horses, guides, and everything else you'll need for this fun, information-packed vacation is included in the daily fee ($175 per day for adults; $125 per day for children under 18 with an adult).

Judith River Dinosaur Institute Dinosaur Digs (406-654-2323; www .montanadinosaurdigs.com), P.O. Box 429, Malta 59538. Advance reservations required; call or visit the Web site for details and an application. A few times each summer, guests can sign up to accompany scientists on a 5-day educational expedition and dig for dinosaur bones in Montana. Though the digging is hard work, the rewards can be tremendous as you learn all about how paleontologists search for, map, dig for, and document dinosaur specimens. In addition to field-work, participants spend a day in the lab to learn about the latest preservation tech-niques. You must be at least 14 years old to participate ($850 per person; does not include lodging). (See also Dinosaur Field Station under *To See—For Families.*)

Ranch vacations. These vacations usually allow you to participate to a certain extent in various aspects of ranch life, often including cattle herding and brand-ing. The ratio of work time to leisure time varies from ranch to ranch, as do the additional activities and amenities offered, but most ranches include horseback riding, lodging, and meals in an inclusive package deal. In this region, providers include **Beaver Creek Trail Rides and Guest Ranch** (406-658-2111), Malta; **IOU Ranch** (406-557-2544), Sand Springs; **Old West Wagon Trains Inc.** (406-648-5536), Hinsdale; and **Sand Creek Clydesdales Ranch Vacations & Wagon Trains** (406-557-2865), Jordan; among others.

Sharp-Tailed Grouse Courtship Dancing Ritual (406-789-2305, ext. 101 or 109; http://medicinelake.fws.gov), at the Medicine Lake National Wildlife Refuge, 20 miles north of Culbertson (south of Plentywood) on MT 16. For a truly out-of-the-ordinary vacation experience, take a seat in the refuge's viewing blind between mid-April and the end of May, and watch how the male grouse tries to woo and impress his mate with an incredibly intricate dance. You'll need to reserve a time (available 7 days a week) and obtain directions from the head-quarters. Plan for an early day, as it's recommended that you arrive an hour before sunrise and stay until the day's dance is done, about 1 or 2 hours after sunrise.

✳ Wilder Places

PARKS ❧ **Hell Creek State Park** (406-232-0900; www.fwp.state.mt.us/ parks/parksreport.asp?mapnum=7), 25 miles north of Jordan via MT 543 (Hell Creek Road; see also Hell Creek Fossil Area under *To See—Natural Wonders*). Open year-round for day-use (free for residents, $5 nonresidents) and camping ($15 in-season, $13 off-season). This park, situated on Fort Peck Lake's Hell Creek Bay, provides opportunities for boating (four boat ramps), swimming, fish-ing, hiking, wildlife viewing, and picnicking, all after a scenic drive from Jordan (see also *To See—Towns*). Camping amenities include showers, flush toilets, water, picnic tables, barbecue grills, and even a grocery shop.

WILDLIFE REFUGES ❧ **Bowdoin National Wildlife Refuge** (406-654-2863; http://bowdoin.fws.gov), 7 miles east of Malta on C.R. 2 (turn off US 2 at the sign for the refuge just east of Malta). Established in 1936, this refuge both enhances and protects the native habitats of migratory waterfowl as well as numerous other animal inhabitants. The refuge's more than 15,000 acres contain saline and freshwater wetlands, native prairie, and shrubs. More than 260 bird species—such as pelicans, gulls, cormorants, and great blue herons—as well as more than 25 species of mammals make this area their home, as do some fish, amphibians, and reptiles. The best time to view migrating waterfowl flocks is in late fall or early spring, when literally thousands upon thousands of birds pass this way. Recreational opportunities include wildlife viewing, hiking, bicycling, paddling, cross-country skiing, an auto tour route, and bird hunting; no overnight camping is allowed. Unstaffed nearby refuges include **Black Coulee, Creedman Coulee, Hewitt Lake,** and **Lake Thibadeau national wildlife refuges.** (See also *To See—Scenic Drives;* and *Bicycling, Hiking,* and *Snow Sports* under *To Do.*)

✎ ♿ **Charles M. Russell National Wildlife Refuge** (406-538-8706; http://cmr.fws.gov), south of Glasgow on MT 24. This enormous refuge takes its name from the famous western artist who so often painted scenery from this area. Explored by the famous Lewis and Clark expedition, this area is also renowned for its plentiful yield of dinosaur fossils and other prehistoric fossils. Encompassing the gigantic 245,000-acre Fort Peck Lake with its 1,520 miles of shoreline, this 1.1-million-acre refuge features numerous wildlife habitats, including prairies, badlands, forests, and riparian environments. The refuge also has tremendous recreational opportunities, including bicycling (on numbered auto routes only), boating, fishing, hiking, horseback riding, camping (primitive camping as well as a number of developed campgrounds), swimming, playgrounds, and historic sites to view, including old homesteads. Within the refuge, the Missouri River is a designated National Wild and Scenic River from its western boundary to the Fred Robinson Bridge (US 191). (See also Charles M. Russell National Wildlife Refuge Auto Tour Route under *To See; To Do—Hiking;* Fort Peck Lake under *To Do—Boating, To Do—Fishing,* and *To Do—Paddling;* the listings for individual campgrounds under *To Do—Camping;* and Tillmans Bed and Breakfast under *Lodging—Bed & Breakfasts.*)

Medicine Lake National Wildlife Refuge (406-789-2305; http://medicine lake.fws.gov), 20 miles north of Culbertson (south of Plentywood) on MT 16. The northern, larger portion of this refuge is part of the Medicine Lake Wilderness, including Medicine Lake and five smaller lakes. To the south, Homestead Lake is also a part of the refuge. These protected areas provide migratory birds with a place to nest, rest, and breed. More than 270 species of birds can be seen, as well as numerous mammals, reptiles, amphibians, and fish. Recreational opportunities include wildlife-watching, hiking, paddling, hunting, and fishing; no overnight camping is allowed. (See also *To See—Natural Wonders, To Do— Fishing,* and *To Do—Unique Adventures.*)

UL Bend National Wildlife Refuge (406-538-8706; http://cmr.fws.gov), south of Malta and west of Jordan, located at an oxbow of the Missouri River and surrounded by the Charles M. Russell National Wildlife Refuge. More than 20,000 acres of this remote wildlife refuge have been designated a wilderness area (and this designation is also pending on another 160,000 acres), meaning no motorized vehicles are permitted. This refuge inside a refuge is a reintroduction site for the endangered black-footed ferret, which depends on the black-tailed prairie dog for food, thus accounting for the large population of these animals in the refuge. Exploration of this wild terrain will bring you into contact with some of Montana's truly wild and wonderful scenery.

OTHER WILD PLACES See **Bitter Creek Wilderness Study Area** under *To See—Scenic Drives.*

✳ Lodging
BED & BREAKFASTS

Froid 59226
🐾 **Sparks' Bed & Breakfast and Guest House** (406-963-2247), HC 61 Box 31. Located 13.5 miles east of Froid on MT 405. This bed & breakfast offers spacious, clean rooms in its guesthouse, along with two family rooms, a fully equipped kitchen, a pool, hookups for RVs, a game room, laundry facilities, kennels, and a continental breakfast. Opportunities for wildlife viewing abound, and the facility is open year-round ($50–75).

Malta 59538
🐾 **Tillmans Bed and Breakfast** (406-658-2514; 406-252-5537; www .tillmansofmontana.com; mailing address: 1512 Colorado, Billings, 59102), 17 miles south of Malta off of US 2 on US 191. Constructed in the early 1900s as a stopover for people on their way to and from Malta, Tillmans is now a fully restored roadhouse that can accommodate up to 10 guests ($50–75). Home-cooked meals are complemented by the area's array of recreational opportunities, including easy access to fishing on Fort Peck Lake and Nelson Reservoir (see also *To Do—Fishing*), wildlife viewing, hiking, cross-country skiing, and much more. This B&B also offers horseback riding, package hunting trips (call for rates), and a Lewis and Clark–oriented, guided day trip ($150 per person) into the Charles M. Rus-

sell National Wildlife Refuge (see also *Wilder Places—Wildlife Refuges*).

Westby 59275
Hilltop House Bed & Breakfast Inn (406-385-2533), 301 E. 2nd Street. If you happen to be in the very northeast corner of Montana, right at the border of North Dakota and near the border of Canada, you'll find this 1920s and '30s house—the perfect place to spend a night or two. Tremendous panoramic views from the B&B's windows bring a sense of peace and serenity complemented by the small-town atmosphere (less than $50). You'll find great places to walk, hike, bike, fish, and more nearby.

LODGES

Hinsdale 59241
♿ **Rock Creek Outfitters and Lodge** (406-648-5524; www.milk rivermontana.com), 1291 Rock Creek Road. An air-conditioned room and a private bathroom await all guests at this modern lodge in remote northeastern Montana, adjacent to the 60,000-acre Bittercreek Wilderness. Accommodation prices include not only lodging but also all home-cooked meals, horseback riding (horses provided), guided tours, entertainment, and airport transportation to the Glasgow airport ($400 per person per day, minimum stay is two people for 2 days; reservations required).

Wolf Point 59201

The Meadowlark (406-525-3289), 872 Nickwall Road. For a truly upscale vacation experience, stay at this fine guesthouse, where you'll enjoy not only a delicious, full breakfast every morning but also a scrumptious dessert to send you off to dreamland every night. The breakfast can even accommodate diabetics and gluten-intolerant individuals. Two suites of rooms are available for lodging, both of which include a bedroom and a private bath, as well as a variety of additional amenities ($95). There is also a primitive, well-appointed bunkhouse.

OTHER OPTIONS

Circle 59215

Wolff Farms Vacation Home (406-485-2633; 406-485-3523; www .midrivers.com/~ajw1), 1073 North Road. Located off MT 13 north of Circle. Stay at one of America's true food-producing ranches, located on the eastern Montana plains. Lodging rates include a private room, three meals daily, horseback riding and riding lessons, participation in farm life, wildlife viewing, picnics, local sightseeing, and hunting or fishing trips. Additional opportunities to recreate include nearby golfing, museums, and boating (not included in rates) ($125 per person).

Fort Peck 59223

Fort Peck Hotel (1-800-560-4931; 406-526-3266), 175 S. Missouri Street. Open April through December. This restored 1930s wooden hotel is listed on the National Register of Historic Places. Rooms feature a double and a single bed, private baths (some with a claw-foot bathtub), and all of the modern amenities necessary to make your stay comfortable. The hotel also features a dining room serving breakfast, lunch, and dinner, as well as easy access to the abundance of recreational opportunities available in the area ($50–75).

Jordan 59337

& ✿ **Hell Creek Marina** (406-557-2345; www.hellcreekmarina .com), P.O. Box 486. Located 25 miles north of Jordan on MT 543. Cabin rentals are available here, including nonsmoking accommodations. It is recommended that you make your reservations far in advance, as the cabins fill up quickly ($75–90).

Lambert 59243

✿ **Gray's Coulee Guest Ranch** (1-866-270-6550; 406-774-3778), C.R. 120, P.O. Box 252. Located 6 miles south of Lambert (about 20 miles west of Sidney). The remote location of this ranch will provide a true getaway, whether you choose to simply enjoy some R&R on the 6,000-acre farm ($80 single, $120 double, $45 for children under 18 with an adult; breakfast included in nightly lodging rates) or you book a ranch vacation or Learning Vacation (see *To Do—Unique Adventures*).

Zortman 59546

✿ & **Buckhorn Store, Cabins, & RV Park** (1-888-654-3162; 406-673-3162), 1st and Main Street. Located 7 miles off US 191. Seven rustic cabins with kitchenettes sleep up to six people each (less than $50). Also available are RV and tent sites, as well as a store that sells propane, gas, hunting licenses, and sporting goods.

Whispering Pines Vacation Homes (406-673-3304), 1100 Thompson Avenue. Enjoy privacy, comfort, and tremendous views in a two-bedroom, one-bathroom fully furnished vacation home with air-conditioning and television. Even your pets can enjoy these great accommodations near the Little Rocky Mountains. Recreational opportunities, including hiking, hunting, fishing, and cross-country skiing, abound in all seasons ($50).

✳ Where to Eat

DINING OUT

Glasgow

& ✐ **Sam's Supper Club** (406-228-4614; 406-228-4615), 307 Klein Avenue (turn off US 2 at the Big G Shopping Center). Locally owned and locally operated for more than a quarter of a century, this fine dining establishment specializes in serving large charbroiled steaks. A tasty array of seafood and pasta selections are on the menu as well, as are some vegetarian selections. A children's menu is offered.

Malta

& **Roger's Saloon and Chuckwagon** (406-654-9987), 147 S. 1st E. Daily specials round out a full menu that includes steaks, seafood, burgers, and sandwiches. Decor spotlights local history, with portraits of characters and scenery from Malta's past.

Plentywood

& ✐ **Dr. DeBelles** (406-765-2830; 406-765-2831), 1 mile east of Plentywood on MT 16. If the name of this fine dining establishment hasn't brought a smile to your face yet, it will when you learn that it's pronounced "doctor the belly"—which is this restaurant's avowed goal. A selection of delicious entrée items awaits your perusal, but your best bet is probably to stay local, since you're in the middle of prime cattle ranching country,

and go with a perfectly prepared steak. A children's menu is available.

Sidney

& **Cattle-Ac Niteclub, Casino and Steakhouse** (406-433-7174), 119 N. Central Avenue (MT 16). This distinctively decorated restaurant features entertainment nightly along with a terrific fine dining experience. Choose from a menu featuring an assortment of steak and seafood entrée items—this restaurant is a local favorite for its great food.

See also **South 40** under *Eating Out* and **Fort Peck Hotel** under *Lodging—Other Options*.

EATING OUT *Culbertson*

✐ **Wild West Diner** (406-787-5374), near the junction of US 2 and MT 16. Savor the flavors of home-style western cooking at this recently remodeled family restaurant, which specializes in homemade pies.

Fort Peck

& ✐ **Gateway Supper Club** (406-526-9988), 3 miles west of Fort Peck on MT 24. Enjoy the stunning lakeside setting and views as you dine on fresh-caught walleye or munch a buffalo burger. The whole family is welcome at this restaurant near Fort Peck Dam and Fort Peck Lake, where you'll enjoy the opportunity to relax and replenish after spending the day out recreating.

Missouri River Outpost (406-439-8438), 1 mile below Fort Peck Dam on MT 117. This famous restaurant and custom vacation outfitter features delicious steak and seafood meals cooked to perfection. They claim to serve the largest steak dinner available in the whole state of Montana and promise that if you can finish this meal in less than 1 hour, you won't pay a cent for it! If the thought of stuffing yourself to the gills isn't appealing, you can always settle for barbecued ribs, a burger, seafood, or another option.

Glasgow

& ✍ **Eugene's Pizza** (406-228-8552), 193 Klein Avenue (turn off US 2 at the Big G Shopping Center). In the mood for pizza? No? How about spare ribs—or a steak, chicken, a burger, or shrimp? Find something for everyone at Eugene's Pizza, known not only for its hand-tossed pizzas but also for its delicious "Only at Eugene's" ribs.

✍ **Johnnie Café** (406-228-4222), 433 1st Avenue S. Enjoy a taste of history when you dine in this local café, under new ownership since 2002. Originally constructed in 1914, the restaurant moved to its present location across the street from the Amtrak station in 1918, and it has been serving travelers and townspeople alike ever since. No matter what time of day you stop in, you'll always find a choice of homemade pies and caramel rolls to whet your appetite. A children's menu is available.

Jordan

✍ **Soda Fountain Jordan Drug Company** (406-557-6180), Main Street. Love ice cream? Love history? Then you should stop in at this historic downtown ice-cream parlor and drugstore, a Jordan mainstay since 1937. They will be happy to make you your favorite ice-cream concoction, whether you want a dish, a cone, a milk shake, or a soda.

Malta

✍ **Stretch's Pizza** (406-654-1229), 140 S. 1st E. This pizza parlor also

has a large game room—a surefire kid pleaser. In addition to pizzas, entrée selections include chicken, burgers, and sandwiches, as well as homemade pies and frozen yogurt.

Westside Restaurant (406-654-1555), US 2 on the west side of town. Known for its fantastic salad bar, this is a great place to stop if you're craving a fill-up on veggies. The restaurant's full menu (breakfast, lunch, and dinner) features award-winning beef as well.

Plentywood

✍ **Randy's Restaurant** (406-765-1661), 323 W. 1st Avenue. For breakfast, lunch, or dinner, you can stop and enjoy a home-cooked meal at this family-owned and family-operated establishment. Lunch and dinner specials are offered daily, and the restaurant prides itself in its fast and friendly service (you can even order your meal to go), allowing you to get back on the road quickly if you happen to just be passing through.

Poplar

✍ & **Buckhorn Bar** (406-768-5221), 203 2nd Avenue W. Stop here on Friday night if you can to take advantage of the weekly Indian taco special. You'll also find a great salad bar and a menu that includes prime rib and seafood selections, among other options. A children's menu is available.

Scobey

The Shirt Stop & Coffee Break (406-487-5902), 103 Main Street. Stop in for a cuppa joe and pick out a T-shirt while you're sipping your latte at this combination coffee and custom-design screen printing shop. They offer an array of drinks, including espresso and smoothies.

Sidney

& **The Bean Bag** (406-433-8388), 110 N. Central Avenue (MT 16). Coffee drinkers, rejoice! Pull up a chair at the Bean Bag to sip a cup of your favorite brew, and then purchase some gourmet coffee to take along on your travels. Espresso and espresso-based drinks are available as well.

& **M & M Café** (406-433-1714), south of Sidney on MT 16. Stop in at this local café that features home-cooked breakfast, lunch, and dinner, including daily specials as well as homemade pies, caramel rolls, and raisin rolls. Friendly service and affordable prices make for a great dining experience.

✈ **South 40** (406-482-4999; 406-482-4338), 209 2nd Avenue NW (1 block west of MT 16). For a delectable dining experience in a casual, rustic setting, you can't beat South 40. Slow-cooked, boneless, tender prime rib is a house specialty, but the menu features numerous additional entrée items, including seafood and burgers, to tempt your palate, along with an extensive soup and salad bar. A children's menu and a seniors' menu are available.

Westby

Prairie Kitchen (406-385-2404; 406-385-2317), 211 Main Street (MT 5). Westby's only café features home-style cooking in a family-friendly setting. You'll sit down to enjoy a meal complemented by delicious home-made mashed potatoes smothered in homemade gravy and home-baked bread. If you still have room, you can choose a homemade dessert. On Sunday, the kitchen offers a smorgasbord from 11:30 AM to 1:30 PM, which often includes a selection of three meats, a salad bar, and desserts.

Wolf Point

& **Old Town Grill** (406-653-1031), 400 US 2. Choose from a variety of Mexican and American entrée options at this clean, affordable restaurant. Daily specials and soups round out your choices, and you'll enjoy the comfortable window-side seating in booths as well as the friendly, attentive service.

& **The Pizza Place and Hideout Casino** (406-653-2577), 510 W. Blaine Street (just off US 2). Savor home-made pizza crust on your pizza or homemade bread that accompanies other items from the full menu. Choices include sub sandwiches, shrimp, chicken, burgers, and steaks. You can even escape to dine in the cool downstairs casino for some time in a quiet, adult-centered environment.

✳ **Special Events**

May: ✈ **Lewis & Clark Festival** (406-746-3200), Nashua: family-friendly festival celebrates and teaches about life in the 1800s with hands-on demonstrations, folklore, music, and more.

June: **Longest Dam Race,** Glasgow: 1K, 5K, and 10K road races; also includes a bicycle race. ✈ **Pioneer Days,** Scobey: held the last weekend of the month, this festival is home to the Dirty Shame Show, put on by five family-oriented variety acts; families can cool off in the nonalcoholic Dirty Shame Saloon; also has children's street games.

June through September: **Fort Peck Summer Theatre** (406-526-9943; www.fortpecktheatre.org), Fort Peck:

annual summer theater puts on productions of classic plays in a 70-year-old structure that is on the National Register of Historic Places.

July: **Wild Horse Stampede,** Wolf Point: Montana's oldest rodeo takes place the second week of July.

August: ✍ **Roosevelt County Fair,** Culbertson: traditional county fair featuring free lunch on Friday and Saturday, livestock auctions, Farmhand Olympics, vendors, a petting zoo, a fashion revue, a fun run, and more.

September: **Poplar Indian Days** (406-768-3826; 406-768-3351), Poplar: held Labor Day weekend, this powwow is open to the general public and features dancing, food, crafts, and fellowship.

SOUTHWEST MONTANA: GOLD WEST COUNTRY

A visit to Montana's Gold West Country brings you into the area of the state most known for its mineral wealth, both past and present. Here you'll find evidence of Montana's dependence on its mineral wealth almost anywhere you look, from "the richest hill on earth" to the myriad ghost towns scattered throughout the region. This area of the state more than any other sustained a vibrant mining culture beginning in the mid- to late 1800s, as discoveries of gold, copper, and sapphires, among other minerals, brought waves upon waves of immigrants to try their hands at striking it rich in Montana. Of course, only a few of the lucky—or smart—ones did, and they left an indelible legacy in their wake, not only in establishing productive mines and bolstering the economy but also in building among the most noteworthy historic mansions and structures that visitors come to see and tour today. And while Montana is significantly less dependent on mining today than it once was, mineral extraction is still an important contributor to the state's economy.

Perhaps the best place to begin a tour of Montana's Gold West Country is Butte, home of "the richest hill on earth." Butte's origins as a mining town stretch back to the mid-1800s, when gold seekers began placer mining for gold. After the area's gold potential petered out, silver mining took its place through the later years of the 1800s—that is, until a rich copper strike in the late 1880s turned Butte into a copper town above all else. Combined with developments in smelting, the proliferation of electricity (and the subsequent demand for copper to make wire), and the arrival of the railroad, Butte had all of the ingredients necessary to cook up a recipe for success, and succeed it did. The city became a mecca for copper magnates like Marcus Daly, who pushed production levels higher than ever before with the introduction of 24-hour-a-day mining operations. By the 1920s, the city boasted a population of more than 100,000—significantly more than the fewer than 40,000 people who live there today.

Mining-related sites to see in Butte include the Berkeley Pit (see *To See—Historic Landmarks, Places, and Sites*). This enormous water-filled pit, which is still used in a process for mining copper today, provides stark visual evidence of the environmental impact that mining has had and continues to have on the

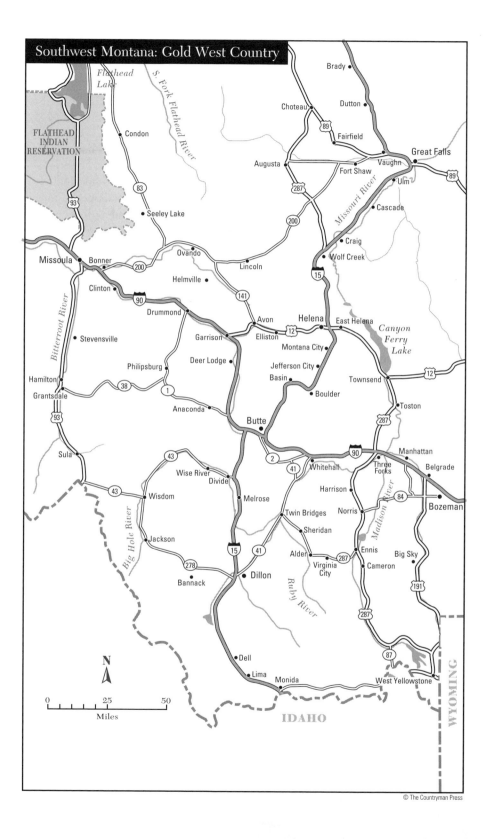

Southwest Montana: Gold West Country

Flathead Lake

S. Fork Flathead River

FLATHEAD INDIAN RESERVATION

Condon

Brady

Choteau

Dutton

Fairfield

89

Augusta

Fort Shaw

Vaughn

Great Falls

89

93

83

Seeley Lake

287

Ulm

200

Missouri River

Cascade

Craig

Wolf Creek

15

Missoula

Bonner

200

Ovando

Lincoln

Clinton

90

Helmville

141

Drummond

Avon

Helena

East Helena

Canyon Ferry Lake

Stevensville

Garrison

Elliston

12

Montana City

Philipsburg

Deer Lodge

Jefferson City

Townsend

12

Hamilton

38

1

Basin

Grantsdale

Anaconda

Boulder

Toston

93

Butte

287

Sula

43

2

Manhattan

Wise River

Divide

41

Whitehall

Three Forks

Belgrade

43

Wisdom

Melrose

Harrison

84

Bozeman

Jackson

Twin Bridges

Norris

Madison River

278

15

41

Sheridan

Alder

287

Ennis

Big Sky

Dillon

Virginia City

Cameron

Bannack

Ruby River

191

287

Big Hole River

Bitterroot River

N

0   25   50
Miles

Dell

Lima

Monida

West Yellowstone

WYOMING

IDAHO

© The Countryman Press

land. What you won't see might astonish you even more: beneath the surface in Butte lie some 3,000 miles of interlaced tunnels, stretching for nearly a mile below the ground. Butte is also home to the World Museum of Mining (see *To See—Museums*), a mandatory stop on your itinerary if mining interests you. Also of note is the Copper King Mansion (see *To See—Historic Landmarks, Places, and Sites*), the former residence of one of Butte's foremost historic copper magnates, William A. Clark. A plethora of additional mining-related and historical attractions draw visitors to the Butte area.

Travel a few miles west and north to visit another place strongly impacted by its mining history: the town of Anaconda, home of the Anaconda Copper Mining Company's famed smelter stack (see Smelter Stack State Park under *To See—Historic Landmarks, Places, and Sites*), the brainchild of copper baron Marcus Daly. Daly sought a location for the construction of an enormous smelter for the copper mined in Butte, and in 1882 he settled on Anaconda, for better or for worse. The better part was the positive impact on the local economy, as jobs were created at the stack until it closed in 1980. The worse part, of course, was the environmental impact, which resulted in heavy pollution of Silver Bow Creek and its surroundings (including the Clark Fork River), as they provided a convenient place for the disposal of mining wastes for more than a century. The cleanup efforts continue today, with 26 miles of the creek and the habitat surrounding it designated by the Environmental Protection Agency as a superfund site. Thus today's more environmentally aware Anaconda welcomes visitors not only to learn more about the community's historic ties to mining but also to explore the area's natural wonders, such as the Anaconda–Pintler Scenic Highway (See *To See—Scenic Drives*).

Continuing along its mining theme, throughout this region you'll find an array of ghost towns to explore, from those in total disrepair to those that have been restored and kept alive as tourist attractions, such as Bannack and Virginia City, Montana's former territorial capitals (see Virginia City and Nevada City under *To See—Towns;* and Bannack State Park in *To See—Historic Landmarks, Places, and Sites*). Activities at ghost towns range from photographing buildings from a distance to exploring them intimately, depending on the status of the town and the state of repair that the buildings are currently in. Some ghost towns also offer train rides, historic reenactments, museums, and more.

This region is also home to Montana's state capital, Helena, one of the prettiest and cleanest cities you'll find anywhere—and though it's not a ghost town in the least, it too has ties to mining. In the mid-1800s, Helena was

THE STATE CAPITOL IN HELENA

near the site of an incredibly prolific gold mine in the Last Chance Gulch, which produced more than $3 billion of wealth (in today's dollars) in only 20 years of mining. Vaulted to prominence, the city became the territorial capital in 1875 (stealing the title from Virginia City) and the state capital in 1898. Today the city features attractions hearkening to its mining past, such as the Spokane Bar Sapphire Mine (see sapphire mining under *To Do—Unique Adventures*), as well as numerous historic and current-day architectural attractions representative of its role as a capital city. These include the original Governor's Mansion, the State Capitol, and St. Helena Cathedral (see *To See—Historic Landmarks, Places, and Sites*). Surrounded by Helena National Forest (see *Wilder Places—Forests*), Helena also offers access to an incredible array of outdoor recreation, including the gorgeous Mount Helena City Park (see *To Do—Hiking*).

Beyond the history of mining, this region also witnessed the passage of Lewis and Clark during their famous Corps of Discovery expedition. In addition to a portion of the Lewis and Clark Trail, you'll find numerous related sites, such as Beaverhead Rock State Park and Clark's Lookout State Park (see *To See— Historic Landmarks, Places, and Sites*), Clark Canyon Reservoir (see *To Do— Boating*), Gates of the Mountains (see *To Do—Unique Adventures*), and Beaverhead County Lewis and Clark Festival (see *Special Events*).

Also a part of this region's history are the Native American peoples who once considered this area a part of their homelands. Several tribes traditionally hunted in the valley around Ennis (see *To See—Towns*) long before the arrival of white settlers. This region also saw the passage of the Nez Perce Indians along the Nez Perce Nee–Me–Poo Trail (see *To Do—Hiking*) as they fled the U.S. military in 1877, which was attempting to force them onto reservations. Along this trail lies the Big Hole National Battlefield (see *To See—Historic Landmarks, Places, and Sites*), where a battle took place on August 9 and 10 of that same year between the Indians and the military.

Finally, not to be overlooked are the abundance of recreational opportunities in this region, including world-class blue-ribbon fishing in the Madison River (see *To Do—Fishing*), as well as its incredible stretch of white water through Bear Trap Canyon (see *To Do—Paddling/Floating*). Also in this region lie three downhill ski areas and tremendous cross-country skiing and snowmobiling trails (see *To Do—Snow Sports*), as well as tons of outdoor warmer-weather recreational opportunities at sites such as Lewis and Clark Caverns State Park (see *To See—Natural Wonders*), where a guided hike will take you underground through gorgeous limestone caverns. You can even combine the area's mining history with an outdoor family activity at Crystal Park (see *Wilder Places—Parks*), getting everyone's hands dirty as you seek mineral wealth and perhaps experiencing a bit of the same spirit of adventure that motivated the original miners who ventured here so long ago.

GUIDANCE **Anaconda Chamber and Visitor Center** (406-563-2400: www .anacondamt.org), 306 E. Park Street, Anaconda 59711.

Beaverhead Chamber of Commerce and Dillon Visitor Information Center (406-683-5511; www.beaverheadchamber.org), 125 S. Montana, P.O. Box 425, Dillon 59725.

Butte–Silver Bow Chamber of Commerce (1-800-735-6814; 406-723-3177; www.butteinfo.org), 1000 George Street, Butte 59701.

Ennis Chamber of Commerce (406-682-4388; www.ennischamber.com), Main Street, P.O. Box 291, Ennis 59729.

Gold West Country (1-800-879-1159; 406-846-1943; http://goldwest.visitmt .com), 1155 Main Street, Deer Lodge 59722.

Greater Ruby Valley Chamber of Commerce and Agriculture (406-683-5511; www.rubyvalleychamber.com), P.O. Box 134, Twin Bridges 59754.

Helena Chamber of Commerce (1-800-743-5362; 406-447-1530; www.helena chamber.com), 225 Cruse Avenue, Suite A, Helena 59601.

Lincoln Valley Chamber of Commerce (406-362-4949; www.lincolnmontana .com), P.O. Box 985, Lincoln 59639.

Philipsburg Chamber of Commerce (406-859-3388; www.philipsburgmt .com), in the historic **Courtney Hotel** at 135 S. Sansome Street, P.O. Box 661, Philipsburg 59858.

Powell County Chamber of Commerce (406-846-2094; www.powellcounty montana.com), 1171 Main Street, Deer Lodge 59722.

Townsend Chamber of Commerce (406-266-4101), 415 S. Front, P.O. Box 947, Townsend 59644.

Virginia City Chamber of Commerce (1-800-829-2969; 406-843-5555; www .virginiacitychamber.com), P.O. Box 218, Virginia City 59755.

Virginia City Depot Information Center (406-843-5247; www.virginiacity mt.com), west end of Wallace Street (MT 287), P.O. Box 338, Virginia City 59755.

Whitehall Chamber of Commerce (406-287-2260; www.co.jefferson.mt.us/ communities/whhall.shtml), P.O. Box 72, Whitehall 59759.

GETTING THERE Helena lies at the junction of I-15 and US 287/US 12, north of Butte and south of Great Falls. Butte is on I-90 and I-15, where I-15 branches north from I-90. Deer Lodge is northwest of Butte on I-90. Anaconda is west of Butte via I-90 to MT 1 or MT 48. Philipsburg is north of Anaconda on MT 1. Dillon is south of Butte on I-15, at the junction with MT 41. Whitehall is east of Butte on I-90. Ennis is southeast of Butte on US 287.

See also *Airports, Amtrak, Bus Service,* and *Travel Information* in "What's Where in Montana."

MEDICAL EMERGENCY **Anaconda Community Hospital** (406-563-9644), 115 W. Commercial Avenue, Anaconda.

Barrett Hospital and HealthCare (406-683-3000), 1260 S. Atlantic Street, Dillon.

Broadwater Health Center (406-266-3186), 110 N. Oak Street, Townsend.

Granite County Medical Center (406-859-3271), off MT 1, Philipsburg.

Madison Valley Hospital (406-682-4222), 217 N. Main Street, Ennis.

Powell County Medical Center (406-846-2212), 1101 Texas Avenue, Deer Lodge.

Ruby Valley Hospital (406-842-5453), 220 E. Crofoot, Sheridan.

St. James Healthcare (406-723-2500), 400 S. Clark Street, Butte.

St. Peter's Hospital (406-442-2480), 2475 Broadway, Helena.

✳ To See

TOWNS **Dillon,** about 60 miles south of Butte on I-15, is the county seat of Montana's largest county—Beaverhead. The town dates back to the gold rush era, when it served as an important point for shipping goods south to Utah. The railroad, specifically the Utah and Northern Railroad, reached this town in 1880; however, the town took its name from a president of the Union Pacific railroad, Sidney V. Dillon. Attractions include the **Beaverhead County Museum** (406-683-5027; 15 S. Montana Street), which focuses on the area's historic role in mining as well as ranching; a self-guided, historical walking tour of the well-preserved downtown; and numerous outdoor recreation opportunities.

Ennis, about 75 miles northwest of Yellowstone National Park on US 287, is situated in the Madison River valley between three mountain ranges: the Tobacco Root Mountains to the northwest, the Gravelly Range to the southwest, and to the east, the Madison Range. For centuries, this valley served as fertile annual hunting grounds for tribes of Native Americans, including the Bannack, Flathead, and Shoshone Indians. The discovery of gold in nearby **Alder Gulch** in 1863 rapidly thrust the area into the limelight, and William Ennis settled here just two months later, starting the township that would take his name as its own. Today visitors to this last (or first) outpost before the 75-mile stretch southeast to Yellowstone National Park will discover a fly-fishing mecca (see **the Madison River** under *To Do—Fishing*), as well as the **Ennis National Fish Hatchery** (406-682-4847), 12 miles southwest of town, and the **Wildlife Museum of the West** (handicapped accessible; 406-682-7141) at 121 W. Main Street.

Lincoln, 60 miles northwest of Helena on MT 200, might be just the place for you if you're seeking a spot to really get away from it all and explore the great outdoors—particularly in wintertime. The **Scapegoat Wilderness Area** lies just to the north, while the **Blackfoot River** (see *To Do—Fishing* in "Northwest Montana: Glacier Country and Waterton–Glacier International Peace Park") runs just south of town. Also south of town is **Stemple Pass,** home to four ungroomed, marked cross-country ski trails, as well as the **Great Divide Ski Area** (see also *To Do—Snow Sports*). Snowmobiling is extremely popular here, too, and it's no wonder—the area around Lincoln features 250 miles of groomed trails.

Philipsburg is northwest of Anaconda on MT 1 (the **Pintler Scenic Route;** see *To See—Scenic Drives*). Established in the 1860s, this town and the surrounding area are the historic home to some of the finest sapphire and silver mines in the world. The town was named after Philip Deidesheimer, who invented square-set mine timbering (and you can probably guess why folks chose to use his first name rather than his last when they selected a name for the town). The renovated downtown is a National Historic District with impressive buildings, including a jailhouse, opera house, and school; also of historical interest is the **Granite County Museum and Cultural Center** (406-859-3020), in the historic **Courtney Hotel** at 135 S. Sansome Street, as well as the many ghost towns surrounding Philipsburg (contact the Philipsburg Chamber of Commerce, listed under *Guidance,* for details). (See also **sapphire mining** under *To Do—Unique Adventures.*)

Virginia City (and **Nevada City**) is 12 miles east of Ennis on MT 287. Virginia City was once the territorial capital of Montana back in the gold rush days of the 1860s. Though it has been called a ghost town, it really is anything but that. What you'll find today in Virginia City is the gold-mining era in as true-to-life a setting as anywhere, as the town is incredibly well preserved and kept up in comparison to most boom 'n' bust towns from that time—which is probably one of the reasons why it's a National Historic Landmark. Take a stroll on the wooden boardwalks; take a tour by foot, car, train, or horseback; or journey 1 mile west to see the **historic mining ghost town of Nevada City,** among other attractions. You can even catch a live theater performance during the summer, including the **Brewery Follies,** a cabaret and skit show at H. S. Gilbert Brewery; and the 19th-century melodrama presented by the **Virginia City Players** at the Opera House (1-800-829-2969; 406-843-5218; reservations recommended). (See also Bridger Outfitters under *To Do—Horseback Riding;* Alder Gulch Short Line Railroad under *To Do—Unique Adventures;* and **Gold Rush Fever Days** and **Heritage Days and Victorian Ball** under *Special Events.*)

MUSEUMS **Arts Chateau** (406-723-7600; www.artschateau.org), 321 W. Broadway, Butte. Open June through August Monday through Saturday 10 AM–5 PM, Sunday noon–5 PM; open September through May Monday through Saturday 11 AM–4 PM, Sunday noon–5 PM; donations gladly accepted. Two changing exhibitions, a permanent collection, a sales gallery, and a youth projects area are currently housed in this four-story, 26-room mansion constructed in 1898 for Charles W. Clark, son of Montana copper king William A. Clark. Guided tours take visitors through the home, which is decorated with 18th- and 19th-century antiques and textiles as well as artwork and collectibles. The museum is run by the Butte Silver Bow Arts Foundation, which also runs the community art center and coffeehouse, **Butte Silver Bow Art Center** and **Venus Rising Espresso,** located at 124 S. Main Street in Butte.

ARTS CHATEAU

Copper Village Museum and Arts Center (406-563-2422; 406-563-7722),

City Hall Cultural Center, 401 E. Commercial, Anaconda. Open Tuesday through Saturday 10 AM–4 PM; free. This museum is housed in a structure that was slated for destruction, then saved and renovated; it's now listed on the National Register of Historic Places. Inside you'll find exhibits featuring local, regional, and national artists of note. The center also holds community cultural events. In the same complex, you can visit the **Marcus Daly Historical Society Museum** (406-563-2220), open Tuesday through Saturday 1 PM–4 PM; a museum and archives detail the famed mining magnate's lifetime and his profound effect on the community and its surroundings.

& **The Mineral Museum** (406-496-4414; www.mbmg.mtech.edu/museum .htm), Montana Tech, 1300 W. Park Street, Butte. Open daily Memorial Day through Labor Day 9 AM–6 PM; open May, September, and October Monday through Friday 9 AM–4 PM, Saturday and Sunday 1 PM–5 PM; free. If you're on your way to or from the World Museum of Mining (see below), consider stopping at this free museum to round out your knowledge of the area's rich mineral history. Located on the Montana Tech campus, the museum displays samples of minerals extracted from the Butte area and its surroundings, a testament to the vast wealth of the area's underground mines. The museum also has numerous minerals on display from around the world.

& **Montana's Museum** (406-444-2694; 406-444-4710; www.his.state.mt.us/ museum/default.asp), 225 N. Roberts, Helena. Open May 1 through September 30 Monday through Saturday 9 AM–5 PM, Thursday until 8 PM; closed Sunday and holidays. Open October 1 through April 30 Tuesday through Saturday 9 AM– 5 PM, Thursday until 8 PM; closed Sunday, Monday, and holidays; $5 adults, $1 children, $12 per family. The museum of the Montana State Historical Society, Montana's Museum brings together artifacts, artwork, archaeology, geology, natural history, and more, all to tell a coherent story of the people, places, and things that collectively are Montana. Drawing together items of significance from both the past and the present, the museum weaves them together in an articulate and informative fashion, enabling visitors to leave with a broader, more in-depth perspective and understanding of Montana and its surroundings.

Powell County Museum (406-846-3111; www.pcmaf.org), 1106 Main Street, Deer Lodge. Open daily Memorial Day through Labor Day noon–5 PM; free. This county museum features exhibits on the local area's history, including a huge gun collection with firearms from frontier days and World Wars I and II, thousands of historic photos, an old jukebox and slot machine collection, and more. The museum is part of a larger complex of museums that includes the **Old Montana Prison.** Constructed in the late 19th century, this territorial prison's walls rise 24 feet above the ground and extend 4 feet below the ground as well, which served to prevent prisoners' tunneling to escape. Rumor has it that ghosts just might haunt the prison, so stop in and see for yourself. In addition to touring the prison and viewing the numerous exhibits detailing life behind bars, in the same complex you can also visit the **Montana Law Enforcement Museum, Frontier Museum, Desert John's Saloon Museum, Montana Auto Museum, Yesterday's Playthings** (doll and toy museum), and **Cottonwood City.**

OLD MONTANA PRISON MUSEUM

✦ **World Museum of Mining and Hell Roarin' Gulch** (406-723-7211; www.miningmuseum.org), 155 Museum Way, Butte. Open daily April 1 through October 31, 9 AM–5:30 PM (last ticket sold at 4:30 PM); open July through August Thursday 9 AM– 8:30 PM; $7 adults, $6 seniors over 65, $5 teens ages 13–18, $2 children ages 5–12, children 4 and under free. Step into the well-preserved past at the World Museum of Mining, where you can wander the cobbled streets of an 1880s mining camp called Hell Roarin' Gulch. Peer into windows of vintage shops that range from a Chinese laundry to a livery stable. Examine mining equipment and exhibits, including a walk through a mine tunnel, a mineral exhibit, old photographs and mine-related documents, and more. If you want to stop at one mining-related attraction during your stay in Montana, this is probably the one not to miss.

See also Dillon, Ennis, and Philipsburg under *Towns*.

HISTORIC LANDMARKS, PLACES, AND SITES Anaconda Smelter Stack State Park (406-542-5500; www.fwp.state.mt.us/parks/parksreport.asp?mapnum=28), visible off MT 1 in Anaconda; interpretive area on Smelter Road. Open year-round; free. Though you can view the Anaconda Copper Company's former smelter stack only from afar, it is nonetheless likely to make an impression. Taller than the Washington Monument, the 585-foot stack is one of the world's largest freestanding structures of brick. The top of the stack measures 60 feet in diameter, and you'll get a real sense of the immensity of this measurement when you stop at the interpretive site, where a ground-level ring of bricks 60 feet in diameter serves to show you just how huge this is. Completed in 1919, the smelter stack is listed on the National Register of Historic Places. A visit to the interpretive site will fill you in on its purpose, history, and effects on the town and area.

WORLD MUSEUM OF MINING

&. **Bannack State Park** (406-834-3413; www.bannack.org), I-15 south of Dillon 3 miles, then 20 miles west on MT 278, then 4 miles south on MT 5 (Bannack Road). Open year-round except December 24 and 25; open May through mid-October, 8 AM–9 PM; open mid-October through April 30, 8 AM–5 PM; free for residents, $3 adult nonresidents and $1 children ages 6–12. Open for camping year-round except December 24 and 25; $10–12, $25 for tipi rental. Visitor center open daily in summer 10 AM–6 PM. A National Historic Site, Bannack was Montana's first territorial capital. Named for the Bannock Indians (the *a* and *o* were later switched), the town grew up after John White's discovery of gold in the area in 1862. The very next year, however, gold discoveries near Virginia City prompted a mass move in that direction, and Virginia City became the new territorial capital shortly thereafter (see also Virginia City under *Towns*). Bannack today remains well preserved, with some 60 buildings still standing, most of which can be explored during your visit. The park celebrates Bannack's past in mid-July each year during Bannack Days. Picnicking and fishing are also available.

Beaverhead Rock State Park (406-834-3413; www.fwp.state.mt.us/parks/parksreport.asp?mapnum=25), on MT 41, 14 miles south of Twin Bridges. Open year-round for day-use only; free. On the National Register of Historic Places, this rock served as a landmark to Sacagawea in 1805 while she accompanied the Lewis and Clark expedition as a guide. The primitive park has no services, and you cannot walk up to the rock, but you can view it from afar and take photos.

♿ **Berkeley Pit** (1-800-735-6814; 406-723-3177; www.pitwatch.org), Continental Drive (at the east end of Park Street), Butte. Open March through November; free. See firsthand some of the effects of mining on this area at this enormous, water-filled pit on the edge of Butte. The pit began as an open-pit copper mine in 1955, and since that time, roughly 1.5 billion tons of material have been removed from it. Rapidly rising water levels in the pit aroused concerns about potential flooding and overflow; however, measures have been put in place to ensure that the water in the pit will never exceed the critical depth of 5,410 feet. After a hiatus, today the pit is once again being mined for copper by Montana Resources, which is recovering copper from the water in the pit.

♿ **Big Hole National Battlefield** (406-689-3155; www.nps.gov/biho), 10 miles west of Wisdom on MT 43. Open June through mid-September 9 AM–5:30 PM; mid-Sept through May 9 AM–5 PM; closed Thanksgiving, Christmas, and New Year's Day; $2 adults or $4 per family (fee charged only in summer months). This national battlefield is one of 38 sites scattered throughout Montana, Idaho, Oregon, and Washington that together make up the **Nez Perce National Historic Park** (www.nps.gov/nepe). These sites detail the lives, history, and culture of this noble people, including their struggle for survival in the face of insurmountable changes. On August 9 and 10, 1877, one of the battles of the five-month-long Nez Perce War took place at Big Hole. Throughout the war the Nez Perce Indians struggled to maintain their

BERKELEY PIT

traditional ways of living in opposition to the encroaching white settlers. A staffed visitor center provides interpretive displays, talks, and an audiovisual presentation to further your knowledge of what exactly took place here more than a century ago. You can also hike, picnic, and fish. (See also Nez Perce Nee–Me–Poo Trail in *To Do—Hiking*.)

Clark's Lookout State Park (406-834-3413; www.fwp.state.mt.us/parks/parks report.asp?mapnum=26). Take Exit 63 for MT 41 at Dillon, go east 0.5 mile, and then north 0.5 mile on old MT 91. Open year-round for day-use only; free. In 1806, William Clark used this hill as a lookout to survey the land ahead during the historic Corps of Discovery expedition. Today at this undeveloped park, you can follow in Clark's footsteps up the hill to overlook the land below.

Copper King Mansion (406-782-7580; www.copperkingmansion.com), 219 W. Granite Street, Butte. Once the home of one of Montana's foremost copper magnates, William A. Clark, this 34-room, three-story brick mansion today operates as both a historic house museum available for guided tours (May through September, 9 AM–4 PM, or by appointment off-season), as well as a year-round bed & breakfast accommodation ($65–100). Constructed in the 1880s, the privately owned mansion is listed on the National Register of Historic Places. Interior decor is true to the times and tastes of the original owner, with antiques, stained glass, frescoes on the ceilings, and much more.

Elkhorn State Park (406-495-3260; www.fwp.state.mt.us/parks/parksreport .asp?mapnum=20). Take Exit 164 off I-15 at Boulder, go 7 miles south on MT 69, then 11 miles north on the access road (F.R. 258). Open year-round; free. Most of the buildings you'll see at this location are privately owned, with the exception of two historic structures—**Fraternity Hall** and **Gillian Hall.** These two 19th-century buildings hearken back to the lucrative silver mining days of Montana's past. You can also take your mountain bike for a moderate ride up to the buildings and back on F.R. 258.

COPPER KING MANSION

Granite Ghost Town State Park (406-542-5500; www.fwp.state.mt.us/ parks/parksreport.asp?mapnum=41). Your best bet is to stop in Philipsburg and ask for directions. The road is marked "Granite" with a white sign, and can be accessed by taking either Contract Mill Rd. or Rosalind Rd. east of town. 4WD highly recommended. Open May 1 through September 30; free. You'll need a vehicle with good clearance to make your way out to this primitive park, which features the dilapidated remains of a once prospering silver miners' camp of the 1890s.

Grant–Kohrs Ranch National Historic Site (406-846-2070; www.nps.gov/grko), 266 Warren Lane, Deer Lodge. Open daily May 28 through September 1, 9 AM–5:30 PM; open September 2 through May 27, 9 AM–4:30 PM; closed Thanksgiving, Christmas, and New Year's Day; free. This ranch was established by Canadian John Grant in the late 1850s and expanded by cattleman Conrad Kohrs, who purchased the ranch from Grant in 1866. Today it takes you back into an earlier era, though you may be surprised to learn that it is still home to a working cattle ranch. Take a self-guided walking tour through the ranch buildings of this historic site, once the headquarters for a thriving 10-million-acre ranching dominion. You'll learn all about the lives and times of the men and women who lived and worked on this ranch from the 1850s through the 1970s, at this, the national park system's only site dedicated to preserving the country's unique ranching history. (See also Victorian Christmas at Grant–Kohrs Ranch under *Special Events.*)

Historic Uptown Butte (1-800-735-6814; 406-723-3177; www.butteinfo.org), on the hill, Butte. A stroll through the streets of well-kept uptown Butte will yield a plethora of historic buildings to both view and often read about as well, as many of them are listed on the National Register of Historic Places and have explanatory plaques detailing their pasts. These include the **Arts Chateau** (see *Museums*) and the **Copper King Mansion** (see above), as well as the **First Presbyterian Church** and **St. Lawrence O'Toole Church,** among many other sites. (See also Old No. 1 Trolley Tours under *To Do—Unique Adventures.*)

Montana State Capitol (1-800-243-9900; 406-444-2694; www.montanahistoricalsociety.org), 225 N. Roberts, Helena. Open daily 9 AM–5 PM for self-guided tours (closed holidays); free. Guided tours available hourly May 1 through September 30 Monday through Saturday 9 AM–3 PM, Sunday noon–4 PM; in even-numbered years, open October 1 through April 30 Saturday only 10 AM–2 PM. In odd-numbered years, open January 1 through April 30 Monday through Saturday 9 AM–3 PM, closed on Sunday and holidays. Completed in 1902, the capitol was constructed from sandstone and granite and topped with a copper dome upon which stands a statue representing liberty. The surrounding grounds feature exquisite landscaping, including an annual tribute to the state done in flowers; inside, attractions include a famous painting by Charles M. Russell depicting a Lewis and Clark encounter with Indians.

Original Governor's Mansion (1-800-243-9900; 406-444-4789; www.montanahistoricalsociety.org), 304 N. Ewing, Helena. Open May 1 through September 30 Tuesday through Saturday noon–4 PM; open October 1 through April 30 Saturday only, noon–4 PM; closed on Sunday, Monday, and holidays year-round; $4 adults, $1 children, $10 maximum per family. Tours begin on the hour each day, with the last tour departing at 4 PM.

GRANT–KOHRS RANCH NATIONAL HISTORIC SITE

Despite its name, this mansion was not originally constructed for the governor of Montana but for entrepreneur William A. Chessman. Chessman had the structure built in 1888 for his family, and several other families resided in the house before it became the property of the state of Montana in 1913. At that point, it became the first official residence for Montana's governors, a purpose that it continued to serve until 1959, having been called home by nine governors and their families. Today, the Queen Anne–style brick mansion has been fully restored and features decor from its heyday.

& **St. Helena Cathedral** (406-442-5825; 406-442-5754), 530 N. Ewing, Helena. Open daily year-round 7:15 AM–6 PM; free. Masses are held Monday and Friday at 7:15 AM; Tuesday through Thursday at 7:15 AM and noon; Saturday at 5:15 PM; and Sunday at 7:30 AM, 9 AM, and 11 AM. This turn-of-the-20th-century cathedral's twin spires rise 230 feet above the streets below; inside, an exquisite interior includes hand-carved oak pews and hand-forged bronze lighting fixtures. Constructed in the Geometric Gothic style of architecture, this gorgeous church was modeled after Austria's Votive Church of the Sacred Heart and is now listed on the National Register of Historic Places. Call ahead if you're interested in taking a 1-hour guided tour.

See also Dillon, Ennis, Philipsburg, and Virginia City under *Towns;* Arts Chateau, Copper Village Museum and Arts Center, Powell County Museum, and World Museum of Mining under *Museums;* Clark Canyon Reservoir under *To Do—Boating;* Boulder Hot Springs Bed and Breakfast under *To Do—Hot Springs;* Alder Gulch Short Line Railroad, Gates of the Mountains, Old No. 1 Trolley Tours, and sapphire mining under *To Do—Unique Adventures;* Barrister Bed and Breakfast, Bennett House Country Inn, Just an Experience, The Sanders—Helena's Bed and Breakfast, and Stonehouse Inn under *Lodging—Bed & Breakfasts;* Broadway Hotel, Celtic House Inn, and Historic Hotel Lincoln under *Lodging—Other Options;* On Broadway under *Dining Out;* and The Sweet Palace under *Eating Out.*

FOR FAMILIES See World Museum of Mining and Hell Roarin' Gulch under *Museums;* Upper Canyon Outfitters under *To Do—Horseback Riding;* Fairmont Hot Springs Resort and Norris Hot Springs under *To Do—Hot Springs;* Yellowstone Raft Company under *To Do—Paddling/Floating;* Discovery Basin Ski Area, Great Divide Snowsports, and Maverick Mountain under *To Do—Snow Sports;* Gates of the Mountains, sapphire mining, and

ST. HELENA CATHEDRAL

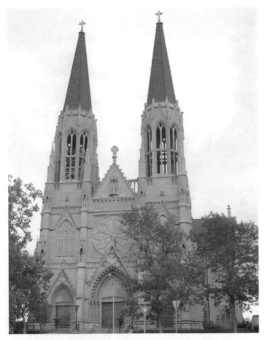

Wagon Ride Dinners at the Moose Meadow Tipi under *To Do—Unique Adventures;* Crystal Park under *Wilder Places—Parks;* The Sweet Palace under *Eating Out;* and Governor's Cup Road Race, Last Chance Stampede and Fair, and Victorian Christmas at Grant–Kohrs Ranch under *Special Events.*

SCENIC DRIVES Anaconda–Pintler Scenic Highway. This 63-mile adventure takes you from Exit 153 off I-90, along MT 1 through Philipsburg and Anaconda, and out to Exit 208 on I-90, making it an excellent alternative route if you're headed north on I-90 from Butte or south on I-90 toward Butte. From Drummond at Exit 153, you'll go south through historic **Philipsburg** (see also *Towns;* and **Granite Ghost Town State Park** under *Historic Landmarks, Places, and Sites*). Then you'll drive through the gorgeous natural terrain that leads up to the turnoff for the **Skalkaho Highway** (see below), then to **Discovery Basin Ski Area** (see *To Do—Snow Sports*), and then to **Georgetown Lake** (see *To Do— Boating*) and its surrounding recreational opportunities, with views of several mountain ranges and the Anaconda–Pintler Wilderness. Finally, you'll head east toward **Anaconda,** where you should stop and see the **smelter stack** (see Anaconda Smelter Stack State Park under *Historic Landmarks, Places, and Sites*), among other attractions.

Big Sheep Creek Backcountry Byway is a 50-mile alternative scenic route that starts off I-15 at Dell (Exit 23). Go south on the Frontage Road for 1.5 miles, and then go west on Big Sheep Creek Road (Road 302). Follow this road, a two-lane gravel road for much of its distance (with a short, one-lane dirt section), as it loops south and then turns back north, depositing you on MT 324 near **Clark Canyon Reservoir** (see *To Do—Boating*), at Exit 44 on I-15. You'll drive through solitude and incredible scenery in this remote area of Montana, with opportunities for trout fishing and camping, among other activities, along the way. Managed by the Bureau of Land Management (BLM), this area retains its primitive, pristine feel, with incredible potential for wildlife viewing (**bighorn sheep** in particular) as well as scenic views of mountains, valleys, and creeks. Adventure seekers can also explore the side roads that lead off the main road. The road is generally passable from May to late September.

Pioneer Mountains Scenic Byway takes you on a 50-mile partially paved, partially graveled journey through the mountains, starting by heading south off MT 43 (east of Divide, Exit 102 on I-90) at **Wise River** on F.R. 484 to MT 278. Note: In winter, the road is closed to autos, and it is a designated National Recreation Snowmobile Trail. On this byway, you'll travel the length of the **Pioneer Mountain Range,** gradually gaining an elevation of 7,800 feet and stopping to read interpretive signs along the way, if you like. **Blue-ribbon trout fishing** surrounds you, as do hiking trails, the majority of which are suitable for the serious hiker only (see **Blue Creek Trail** under *To Do—Hiking*). Road bikers will enjoy riding the portion from Wise River to **Crystal Park** (see *Wilder Places—Parks*). In addition, you'll drive through **Elkhorn Hot Springs** (see *To Do—Hot Springs*), past **Maverick Mountain Ski Area** (see *To Do—Snow Sports*), and by a number of campgrounds in **Beaverhead–Deerlodge National Forest** (see *To Do—Camping* and *Wilder Places—Forests*).

Skalkaho Highway is a 55-mile journey along MT 38 from about midway through the Anaconda–Pintler Scenic Highway (see above), just north of Georgetown Lake, to its junction with US 93 near Hamilton. You'll drive through incredible terrain in both **Beaverhead–Deerlodge National Forest** (see *Wilder Places—Forests*) and **Bitterroot National Forest** (see *Wilder Places—Forests* in "Northwest Montana: Glacier Country and Waterton–Glacier International Peace Park"), including the **Sapphire Mountains, Skalkaho Falls,** and **Skalkaho Pass.** Fantastic fishing opportunities lie along the drive, as do chances for wildlife viewing, camping, and hiking.

See also Red Rock Lakes National Wildlife Refuge under *Wilder Places— Wildlife Refuges and Areas.*

NATURAL WONDERS **Humbug Spires Wilderness Study Area** (406-533-7600; www.mt.blm.gov/bdo/pages/recsites.html#humbug), accessible via Exit 99 off I-15. This 11,775-acre roadless area is a favorite hangout for local rock climbers—with good reason, as it is characterized by 300- to 600-foot spires of granite. These exposed rock formations are part of the enormous **Boulder Batholith,** a 40-mile-wide granite formation resting mostly beneath the earth's surface that stretches from close to Helena to the Big Hole River, including the area around Butte. The result of volcanic activities, the granite came to rest fairly close to the surface, cracking as it cooled. Valuable metals, including gold, silver, and copper, seeped into these cracks, accounting for much of the area's mineral wealth. In the **Humbug Spires,** you will enjoy the opportunity to see a portion of the 70-million-year-old batholith aboveground. Recreational opportunities include hiking, fishing, rock climbing, camping (primitive), wildlife viewing, and horseback riding. The Bureau of Land Management (BLM) recommends that you bring a copy of the area brochure with you, available by calling the above number or writing Butte Field Office, BLM, 106 N. Parkmont, Butte 59701.

& **Lewis and Clark Caverns State Park** (406-287-3541; www.fwp.state.mt.us/ parks/parksreport.asp?mapnum=24), 19 miles west of Three Forks on MT 2. Open year-round; day-use $1 nonresidents, $5 residents; camping open year-round, $13–15. Open for cave tours (not handicapped accessible): from May 1 to June 14, the first tour leaves at 9 AM and the last at 4:30 PM; from June 15 to Labor Day, the first tour leaves at 9 AM and the last at 6:30 PM; from Labor Day to September 30 the first tour leaves at 9 AM and the last at 4:30 PM. Cave tours last 2 hours and involve a 2-mile hike; $10 adults, $5 children ages 6–11. The main attraction at this park is the incredible labyrinth of limestone caverns that lies hidden in the hillside above the campground. A guided tour takes you through the caverns, where you'll see amazing underground formations inside the caverns as you follow your informative guide. You'll have to hike a 2-mile round-trip to take the tour, which includes some easy sliding on your rear, careful stepping through the caverns, and the weird experience of total darkness when the guide turns out the lights for a few seconds while you're deep in the cave. The camping is lovely, with gorgeous views of surrounding mountains. You'll have access to 6 miles of hiking trails, and bikers will enjoy biking up and down the entrance road to the cavern tour area, which rests above the camping area. The park also has a café and gift shop (summer only), cabin rentals ($25–39), a visitor center, and fishing access.

Refrigerator Canyon is located in the **Gates of the Mountain Wilderness** in **Helena National Forest** (see *Wilder Places—Forests*), accessible via Beaver Creek Road (F.R. 138) northeast of Helena. A steep, narrow canyon, Refrigerator Canyon usually (and appropriately) has an ambient temperature of about 20°F lower than the air outside the canyon. You'll only have to hike a short distance—about 0.25 mile—on the Refrigerator Canyon Trail (#259) to get a real sense of its uniqueness, with its sheer limestone walls and trickling little creek. After 0.25 mile, you'll go through an opening and the terrain opens up around you. If you want to continue, you'll hike past Sheep Mountain and, at the 2-mile mark, meet a junction with Trail #260.

LEWIS AND CLARK CAVERNS STATE PARK

See also **Lost Creek State Park** under *Wilder Places—Parks.*

✳ To Do

BICYCLING **Mount Helena Ridge Trail** (#373), accessible at Mount Helena City Park (see *Hiking*), or via the Park City Trailhead, about 5 miles south of Helena on Grizzly Gulch Road. This 6-mile trail in Mount Helena City Park and Helena National Forest (see *Wilder Places—Forests*) takes you through lovely forest scenery just south of Helena, with some steep hill climbs (beginners may find themselves walking). Your reward is gorgeous mountain views and a great workout as you traverse the ridge.

Pear Lake Trail (#72), accessible north of Dillon on I-15 to Exit 74, then west on Birch Creek Road (Road 801) to the trailhead on the right. In Beaverhead–Deerlodge National Forest (see *Wilder Places—Forests*), this 12-mile out-and-back trail takes you mainly along an old four-wheel-drive road up to a remote and gorgeous mountain lake. You'll encounter strenuous and rocky portions along the way, but for the most part, beginners will be able to ride much of this journey—and there's even a small portion of single-track.

See also Elkhorn State Park under *To See—Historic Landmarks, Places, and Sites;* Pioneer Mountains Scenic Byway under *To See—Scenic Drives;* Lewis and Clark Caverns State Park under *To See—Natural Wonders;* Mount Helena City Park under *Hiking;* Potosi Hot Springs Resort under *Hot Springs;* Beaverhead–Deerlodge National Forest and Helena National Forest under *Wilder Places—Forests;* Red Rocks Lakes National Wildlife Refuge under *Wilder Places—Wildlife Refuges and Areas;* and Elkhorn View Lodge under *Lodging—Lodges.*

BOATING ⅄ **Canyon Ferry Lake** (406-475-3310; www.recreation.gov/detail
.cfm?ID=130), along US 12/US 287 southeast of Helena and MT 284 east of
Helena. Created by the Canyon Ferry Dam in 1955 and managed by the Bureau
of Reclamation, this enormous reservoir covers 33,535 acres, or roughly 25
miles, providing an incredible and popular recreational destination. Among the
lake's amenities, boaters will find more than 20 concrete boat ramps and three
marinas. Additional recreational opportunities include camping, fishing (brown
trout, burbot, rainbow trout, walleye, and yellow perch), hiking, picnicking,
swimming, and wildlife viewing (bald eagles in particular), as well as a state-run
wildlife management area and an informative visitor center run by the Bureau of
Land Management (BLM).

⅄ **Clark Canyon Reservoir** (406-683-6472; www.recreation.gov/detail
.cfm?ID=131), 11 miles south of Dillon on I-15. Managed by the Bureau of
Reclamation, this reservoir features 17 miles of shoreline and almost 5,000 acres
of surface area (varies according to water levels). Boaters will find concrete boat
ramps and a marina, as well as nine camping areas with nearly 100 sites total.
The reservoir is popular for fishing (brown trout, burbot, rainbow trout) and hiking, including the **Cattail Marsh Nature Trail,** an interpretive trail located in
the Cattail Marsh Recreation Area on the north end of the reservoir. The reservoir also enjoys the historical distinction of having been the place designated
Camp Fortunate by the Lewis and Clark expedition. Here they stayed on their
way west, stashing supplies and canoes for their return journey; and here Sacagawea and her people—the Lemhi Shoshone—were reunited.

Georgetown Lake is located in Beaverhead–Deerlodge National Forest (see
Camping and *Wilder Places—Forests*), west of Anaconda and south of Philipsburg on MT 1, the Anaconda–Pintler Scenic Highway (see *To See—Scenic
Drives*). This popular, high-altitude lake provides year-round recreation opportunities on its almost 3,000 surface acres and the surrounding lands. Four boat
ramps and a marina accommodate boaters, as do Forest Service campgrounds
around the lake. Fishing (brook trout, kokanee salmon, and rainbow trout) is
popular year-round, and the lake area features many miles of groomed and
marked snowmobile trails in wintertime.

⅄ **Hauser Lake, Black Sandy State Park** (406-495-3270; www.fwp.state.mt
.us/parks/parksreport.asp?mapnum=18), accessible via MT 453 northeast of Helena.
Open year-round; day-use free for residents, $5 for nonresidents; camping $13–15.
This park on the shores of Hauser Lake provides public access to the 3,720-acre
lake's recreational opportunities, including boating. Here you'll find a boat ramp
and dock, as well as the **Lakeside Marina** (406-227-6413), which has almost 100
boat slips as well as a full array of services, including a restaurant, bar, and convenience store. Year-round fishing (brown trout, kokanee salmon, perch, rainbow trout,
and walleye), hiking (1-mile trail), swimming, interpretive displays, and camping are
also available, as are ice-skating in winter. On the way to Hauser Lake, you'll drive
right by **Lake Helena,** which also offers boating and fishing opportunities (largemouth bass, mountain whitefish, rainbow trout, walleye, and yellow perch).

Holter Lake Recreation Area (406-533-7600; 406-235-4480; www.mt.blm
.gov/bdo/pages/recsites.html#holter), I-15 north of Helena to Exit 226, then

northeast 3 miles along Missouri River Road. Open year-round; $2 per vehicle for day-use or $8 per vehicle for overnight camping; fees charged mid-May through mid-October. Holter Lake Recreation Area includes three sites— **Holter Lake, Log Gulch,** and **Departure Point**—which together provide 140 campsites, two multilaned boat ramps, and three designated swimming areas. Fishing (kokanee salmon, perch, rainbow trout, and walleye), hiking, horseback riding, and wildlife viewing are also popular. The area adjoins the **Sleeping Giant Wilderness Study Area,** also managed by the Bureau of Land Management (BLM), which features hiking, primitive camping, and wildlife viewing in its 11,000 acres.

See also Dillon Field Office, Bureau of Land Management under *Camping; Fishing; Paddling/Floating;* Gates of the Mountains under *Unique Adventures;* and Beaverhead–Deerlodge National Forest, Helena National Forest, and Lincoln State Forest under *Wilder Places—Forests.*

CAMPING ⅋ **Beaverhead–Deerlodge National Forest** is south of Helena, east of Missoula, and west of Bozeman, encompassing more than 3.2 million acres of land throughout no fewer than eight counties. The forest has seven ranger districts with some 50 developed campgrounds. You can reserve sites in three of these campgrounds by using the **National Recreation Reservation System** (1-877-444-6777; www.reserveusa.com), including **Lodgepole Campground,** 11 miles south of Philipsburg on MT 1 (Anaconda–Pintler Scenic Highway; see *To See—Scenic Drives*) (open mid-May through September 30; $10); **Philipsburg Bay Campground,** 11 miles south of Philipsburg on MT 1 on Georgetown Lake Road (handicapped accessible; open mid-May through September; $12); and **Spring Hill Campground,** 11 miles west of Anaconda on MT 1 (open mid-May through September; $10). All of these campgrounds are in the **Pintler Ranger District** (Deer Lodge Office: 406-846-1770; Philipsburg Office: 406-859-3211). You'll also find a concentration of developed Forest Service campgrounds along MT 1, as well as along the Pioneer Mountains Scenic Byway (see *To See—Scenic Drives*), north and south of Butte off I-15 and I-90, along US 287 near Ennis and south of Ennis, west of Wisdom off MT 43, and south of Wisdom in the Jackson vicinity, among other locales. For more information about specific campgrounds, contact the appropriate ranger district: **Butte Ranger District** (406-494-2147), **Dillon Ranger District** (406-683-3900), **Jefferson Ranger District** (406-287-3223), **Madison Ranger District** (406-682-4253), **Wisdom Ranger District** (406-689-3243), or **Wise River Ranger District** (406-832-3178). The forest also has more than **25 rental cabins** scattered throughout its lands, available by making reservations ($15–50).

⅋ **Butte Field Office, Bureau of Land Management (BLM)** (406-533-7600; www.mt.blm.gov/bdo), 106 N. Parkmont, Butte, administers a number of campsites in this region, some handicapped accessible. Locations include seven BLM sites (and seven sites facilitated by other agencies) along the Big Hole River (see *Fishing*) between Melrose (on I-15 north of Dillon) and Wisdom (on MT 43, take Exit 102 off I-15 at Divide and head west), all of which are free except for the **Divide Bridge Campground,** which is $4 per night from May to October.

Additional sites permitting can be found in other listings in this region; see "See also" section below for references.

&. **Helena National Forest** has almost a million acres under its jurisdiction in the area surrounding Montana's capital city. The forest has three ranger districts. **Helena Ranger District** (406-449-5490) has six developed campgrounds, mainly off US 12 west of Helena, including **Cromwell Dixon Campground,** 15 miles west of Helena off US 12 (handicapped accessible; open Memorial Day through mid-September; $8). **Lincoln Ranger District** (406-362-4265) has one developed campground, the **Aspen Grove Campground,** 6 miles east of Lincoln on MT 200, then south at the sign for the campground (open Memorial Day through Labor Day; $8). **Townsend Ranger District** (406-266-3425) has one developed campground, **Skidway Campground,** 20 miles east of Townsend off US 12 (open Memorial Day through September; free). The forest also has **seven rental cabins,** available by making reservations ($20–30). (See also listing under *Wilder Places—Forests;* and Trout Creek Canyon Trail under *Hiking.*)

Dillon Field Office, Bureau of Land Management (BLM) (406-683-2337; www.mt.blm.gov/dfo), 1005 Selway Drive, Dillon, administers several camping areas, including the mostly undeveloped **Ruby Reservoir Site,** south of Alder (12 miles west of Virginia City) on MT 257 (free), which has boat ramps and decent trout fishing if the water level is high enough; and the **South Madison** sites (26 miles south of Ennis, then west 1 mile) and **West Madison** sites (7 miles south of Cameron on US 287, then south 3 miles on a BLM road) on the Madison River (see *Fishing*), which also have boat ramps and fishing access ($4).

See also Bannack State Park under *To See—Historic Landmarks, Places, and Sites;* Big Sheep Creek Backcountry Byway under *To See—Scenic Drives;* Humbug Spires Wilderness Study Area and Lewis and Clark Caverns State Park under *To See—Natural Wonders;* and Canyon Ferry Lake, Clark Canyon Reservoir, Hauser Lake, Black Sandy State Park, and Holter Lake Recreation Area under *Boating;* the Big Hole River and the Madison River under *Fishing;* Lost Creek State Park under *Wilder Places—Parks;* Lincoln State Forest under *Wilder Places—Forests;* and Red Rock Lakes National Wildlife Refuge under *Wilder Places—Wildlife Refuges and Areas.*

FISHING **The Beaverhead River** (406-994-4042/3; www.fwp.state.mt.us) originates at Clark Canyon Reservoir (see *Boating*) south of Dillon on I-15, and flows north to Dillon along I-15, then northeast along MT 41 to its confluence with the Big Hole River around Twin Bridges after 75 miles. Known for its blue-ribbon brown trout fishing, the Beaverhead's species also include mountain whitefish and rainbow trout. The river has three state fishing access sites south of Dillon on I-15, as well as one state fishing access site south of Dillon on MT 41, three of which have boat ramps but do not allow overnight camping. There are also several additional access sites south of Dillon on I-15, as well as at Beaverhead Rock State Park (see *To See—Historic Landmarks, Places, and Sites*). Floating and paddling are not particularly noteworthy on this river, due to its proximity to the interstate and its potentially low waters, though float fishing is popular on the first 16 miles of the river before the Barretts Dam.

The Big Hole River (406-994-4042 or 4043; www.fwp.state.mt.us), originates from Skinner Lake in the Beaverhead Mountains near the Idaho border, flowing north along MT 278, then east along MT 43, then south along I-15 before making a wide U-turn back north to its confluence with the Beaverhead River near Twin Bridges after a total of 153 miles. The river features blue-ribbon fishing, with species including arctic grayling, brook trout, brown trout, burbot, mountain whitefish, and rainbow trout. Four state fishing access sites (two with camping) lie along MT 43 north or northwest of Wisdom. Five state fishing access sites (four with camping) are along I-15. Three state fishing access sites (one with camping) are along MT 41. All of these access sites have boat ramps. Floating or paddling the Big Hole River is a great way to see the countryside, as the river has few, if any, rapids, none of which are difficult. (See also Butte Field Office, Bureau of Land Management under *Camping.*)

The Jefferson River (406-994-4042/3; www.fwp.state.mt.us) originates with the confluence of the Beaverhead, the Big Hole, and the Ruby rivers in Twin Bridges, and then flows northeast for 77 miles to a confluence with Madison and Gallatin to form the Missouri River at Three Forks. Fish species include brown trout, mountain whitefish, and rainbow trout, though brown trout are the primary quarry to seek here. Ten state fishing access sites lie along the river's path northeast, all with boat ramps and none with overnight camping. The river is a fine prospect for floating and paddling, though its slow flow and lack of any rapids make it not the most exciting float/paddle.

The Madison River (406-994-4042/3; www.fwp.state.mt.us) begins in Yellowstone National Park at the confluence of the Firehole and Gibbon rivers, makes its way west and then north along US 287 to Ennis Lake, and then angles northeast to its confluence with the Jefferson and Gallatin rivers to form the Missouri River at Three Forks. Fish species in this blue-ribbon fishery include brown trout, mountain whitefish, and rainbow trout. One of the most heavily fished rivers in Montana, the Madison has numerous special regulations that anglers must make themselves aware of by reading the latest booklet published by Montana Fish, Wildlife and Parks. Fishing access is easy and includes a dozen state fishing access sites: seven along US 287, all with boat ramps and three allowing overnight camping; two along MT 84, both with boat ramps and one allowing overnight camping; and three in the vicinity of Three Forks, all with boat ramps and none allowing overnight camping. The Madison is also popular with paddlers and floaters, with a 3.5-mile section of serious white water (class III–IV) just below Quake Lake (see *To See—Natural Wonders* in "South-Central Montana: Yellowstone Country"), as well as 9 miles of challenging white water (class II–V) through Bear Trap Canyon (see *Paddling/Floating*), with long stretches of more mellow water in between these sections. (See also Dillon Field Office, Bureau of Land Management under *Camping;* and Ennis on the Madison Fly Fishing Festival under *Special Events.*)

The Missouri River. See Gates of the Mountains under *Unique Adventures;* the Lower Missouri River under *Fishing* and *Paddling/Floating* in "Northeast Montana: Missouri River Country"; and the Missouri River under *Fishing* and multiple listings for the Upper Missouri National Wild and Scenic River in "North-Central Montana: Russell Country."

The Ruby River (406-994-4042/3; www.fwp.state.mt.us) originates at the confluence of its west, middle, and east forks; flows north along F.R. 100/Upper
Ruby Road to Ruby River Reservoir (see Dillon Field Office, Bureau of Land
Management under *Camping*) south of Alder; then flows northwest along MT
287 to its confluence with the Beaverhead and Big Hole rivers near Twin
Bridges for a total of 97 miles. Fish species include brown trout, mountain
whitefish, and rainbow trout. Much of the river runs through private property,
making access difficult in some portions. However, it does have several state
fishing access sites, including four located south of Alder off Ruby Dam Road
and one southwest of Sheridan on Silver Springs Road (no boat ramps or camping at any). Floating and paddling on the Ruby are easy, as it has no rapids to
speak of; however, only small, inflatable craft are recommended, as the river is
quite narrow and shallow in places.

See also Bannack State Park and Big Hole National Battlefield under *To See—
Historic Landmarks, Places, and Sites;* Big Sheep Creek Backcountry Byway and
Pioneer Mountains Scenic Byway under *To See—Scenic Drives;* Humbug Spires
Wilderness Study Area and Lewis and Clark Caverns State Park under *To See—
Natural Wonders; Boating;* Sheepshead Mountain Recreation Area and Trout
Creek Canyon Trail under *Hiking;* Diamond Hitch Outfitters and Upper Can-
yon Outfitters under *Horseback Riding;* Potosi Hot Springs Resort under *Hot
Springs; Ice Fishing* and Wade Lake Ski Trails under *Snow Sports;* Gates of the
Mountains under *Unique Adventures;* Lost Creek State Park under *Wilder
Places—Parks;* Beaverhead–Deerlodge National Forest, Helena National For-
est, and Lincoln State Forest under *Wilder Places—Forests;* Red Rock Lakes
National Wildlife Refuge under *Wilder Places—Wildlife Refuges and Areas;* Big
Horn Bed and Breakfast, Eagle Rock Hideaway Bed and Breakfast, and Litening
Barn Bed and Breakfast under *Lodging—Bed & Breakfasts;* and Old Kirby Place
under *Lodging—Lodges.*

GOLF **Anaconda Country Club** (406-797-3220), #1 Country Club Lane, Anaconda, 9 holes.

Beaverhead Country Club (406-683-9933), 1200 MT 41 N., Dillon, 9 holes.

Bill Roberts Golf Course (406-442-2191; www.helenagolfing.com), 2201 N.
Benton Avenue, Helena, 18 holes.

Butte Country Club (406-494-3383), 3400 Elizabeth Warren Avenue, Butte,
18 holes.

Deer Lodge Golf Club (406-846-1625), W. Milwaukee Avenue, Deer Lodge, 9
holes.

Fairmont Hot Springs Resort Golf Course (1-800-332-3272; 406-797-3241;
www.fairmontmontana.com), 1500 Fairmont Road, Fairmont (Exit 211 off I-90
between Anaconda and Butte), 18 holes.

Fox Ridge Golf Course (406-227-8304), 4020 Lake Helena Drive, Helena, 18
holes.

Green Meadow Country Club (406-442-1420), 2720 Country Club Avenue,
Helena, 18 holes.

Highland View Golf Course (406-494-7900), 2903 Oregon Avenue, Butte, 9 holes.

Madison Meadows Golf Course (406-682-7468), 110 Golfcourse Road, Ennis, 9 holes.

Old Baldy Golf Course (406-266-3337), Delger Lane, 1.5 miles northeast of Townsend, 9 holes.

Old Works Jack Niklaus Signature Golf Course (1-888-229-4833; 406-563-5989; www.oldworks.org), 1205 Pizzini Way, Anaconda, 18 holes.

See also Celtic House Inn under *Lodging—Other Options*.

HIKING **Blue Creek Trail** (#425) is accessible off the Pioneer Mountains Scenic Byway (Road 2/F.R. 484) north of MT 278 (west of Dillon), just south of Elkhorn Hot Springs (see *Hot Springs*). Though this 6.5-mile out-and-back trail can prove a bit hard to follow (a topographical map is a suggested item for your pack), particularly in springtime when it can be quite boggy, it provides one of the tamer outings for hikers accessible off the Pioneer Mountains Scenic Byway—hence its inclusion here. If you're looking for a shorter journey, you can just tramp out for a mile or two, enjoying the spectacular scenery of the Pioneer Mountains and the shade of the lodgepole pines.

Cherry Creek Trail (#123) is accessible via Exit 93 on I-15 at Melrose. Go west on Trapper Creek Road (Road 40) for 1.5 miles, then about 9 miles southwest on Cherry Creek Road (Road 46) to F.R. 1011, which takes you to this popular trailhead (the final mile of this drive is suitable only for four-wheel-drive vehicles). A 3.5-mile, somewhat steep jeep path takes you along Cherry Creek up to Cherry Lake, passing an old miner's cabin, with some more serious steep stretches at the end of the journey as you ascend to the lake area. If you want to push yourself, you can take a side trail (0.25 mile, on the right after the meadow) to Granite Lake, and if you want a less serious adventure, you can hike out for roughly a mile and back without too much in the way of vertical gain or loss.

Lake Louise National Recreation Trail (#168) is accessible by heading south for roughly 5 miles on MT 359 at Exit 256 off I-90. Head southwest on S. Boulder Road (F.R. 107) for about 17 miles to Bismarck Reservoir, where you'll find the trailhead. Though steep and switchbacked, the 3.5-mile ascent to Lake Louise is still fairly moderate, with no insanely challenging vertical gains—and a reward that is worth your efforts, as you'll be treated to astounding views of the lake's cirque and surrounding mountains. It's best to wait until midsummer for this hike to make sure that the snowmelt is complete. Also accessible from Bismarck Reservoir is **Lost Cabin Lake Trail** (#150), a longer but less steep 5-mile journey that takes you through similar terrain to Lost Cabin Lake, including an intimate trek through old-growth forests as well as the potential for seeing mountain goats. This trail is best suited for travel after July 1 as well.

Mount Helena City Park lies just outside of downtown Helena. From there, head south on Park Avenue to Clarke Street. Go west on Clarke, then south on Benton Avenue, then west on Adam Street to the parking area. The parking area has picnic tables as well as an informational kiosk describing the trails and the regulations. The 620-acre city park has 20 miles of trails, allowing you to plan your journey according to your needs and abilities. If you have the time and the fitness level and you want to witness an incredible panoramic view of Helena and its surroundings, you should check out one of the trails leading to the top of the mountain. These include the 70-year-old **1906 Trail,** which involves a somewhat steep ascent as it wraps around the mountainside for a bit more than 3 miles. (See also **Mount Helena Ridge Trail** under *Bicycling.*)

Nez Perce Nee–Me–Poo Trail is a designated National Historic Trail that marks the 1,170-mile historic journey taken by the Nez Perce from Wallowa Lake in Oregon to the Bear Paw Battlefield near Chinook (see *To See—Historic Landmarks, Places, and Sites* in "North-Central Montana: Russell Country"). The Nez Perce made this desperate journey during the Nez Perce War of 1877, when the Indians fled as they fought to retain their freedom from reservation living and to maintain their traditional way of living. In this region, the trail passes through the **Big Hole National Battlefield** (see *To See—Historic Landmarks, Places, and Sites*). Visitors can walk one of two self-guided interpretive trails through the battlefield (1 mile and 1.2 miles) to get a sense of the historic significance of this chapter from America's past. The trail also dips down into the northwest corner of Wyoming, where the Nez Perce traveled through Yellowstone National Park, fording the Yellowstone River near Sulphur Caldron Hot Springs in Yellowstone National Park (see also Nez Perce Creek Wayside under *To See—Historic Landmarks* in "Yellowstone National Park" in "Wyoming's Yellowstone and Grand Teton National Parks").

♿ **Sheepshead Mountain Recreation Area,** located in Beaverhead–Deerlodge National Forest, is accessible by taking I-15 about 8 miles north of Butte to Exit 138, then heading northwest on F.R. 442 for about 13 miles. This unique recreation area includes a 4.5-mile paved trail system, including a 0.75-mile trail around Maney Lake. An abundance of wildlife from elk and deer to waterfowl can be observed here frequently, and the area is surrounded by fantastic, classic Montana scenery, including mountains, meadows, and streams. The area also has wheelchair-accessible fishing access and picnic tables.

MOUNT HELENA CITY PARK

♿ **Trout Creek Canyon Trail** is accessible from **Vigilante Campground** in Helena National Forest, about 16 miles northeast of Helena via MT 280 to York, then about 8 miles northeast on F.R. 4137 (handicapped accessible; open mid-May through mid-September; $5). This easy 6-mile (round-trip) interpretive trail is wheelchair-accessible for 1 mile, with a bench at the 0.5-mile mark and a picnic table at the mile mark. Brochures at the trailhead describe the features noted by the markers along the way. This trail passes through Trout Canyon on what used to be a portion of the Figure 8 Auto Tour Route, which washed out more than 20 years ago. In addition to fishing access to Trout Creek, the trail also yields great views of beautiful limestone walls. This campground also accesses the trailhead for **Hanging Valley National Recreation Trail** (#247), a more serious 12-mile round-trip adventure that passes through incredible limestone formations, including narrow canyons and spires, as well as numerous additional scenic attractions.

See also Big Hole National Battlefield under *To See—Historic Landmarks, Places, and Sites;* Pioneer Mountains Scenic Byway under *To See—Scenic Drives;* Humbug Spires Wilderness Study Area, Lewis and Clark Caverns State Park, and Refrigerator Canyon under *To See—Natural Wonders;* Canyon Ferry Lake, Clark Canyon Reservoir, Hauser Lake, Black Sandy State Park, and Holter Lake Recreation Area under *Boating;* Potosi Hot Springs Resort under *Hot Springs;* Wade Lake Ski Trails under *Snow Sports;* Gates of the Mountains under *Unique Adventures;* Lost Creek State Park and Spring Meadow Lake State Park under *Wilder Places—Parks;* Beaverhead–Deerlodge National Forest, Helena National Forest, and Lincoln State Forest under *Wilder Places—Forests;* Red Rock Lakes National Wildlife Refuge and Mount Haggin Wildlife Management Area under *Wilder Places—Wildlife Refuges and Areas;* and Elkhorn View Lodge under *Lodging—Lodges.*

HORSEBACK RIDING **Bridger Outfitters** (406-843-5900; 406-388-4463; www .bridgeroutfitters.com), 15100 Rocky Mountain Road, Belgrade. Based in Belgrade, Bridger Outfitters offers guests the option to take one of several guided 1- or 2-hour rides around historic Virginia City (see Virginia City under *To See—Towns*). The 1-hour ride ($30 per person) will take you on a whirlwind tour around historic gold rush territory, while a 2-hour tour is a more in-depth journey that shows you the location in Alder Gulch where gold was discovered back in 1863.

Diamond Hitch Outfitters (1-800-368-5494; 406-683-4191; www.diamond hitchoutfitters.com), 3405 Ten Mile Road, Dillon. This full-service outfitter offers a number of guided horseback rides to interesting destinations, including ghost towns and hot springs, in Beaverhead–Deerlodge National Forest. You can choose a 1.5-hour ride ($30 per person) or a 3-hour ride ($45 per person) or go out for the entire day ($150), among other options. This outfitter also provides cookout rides, multiday pack trips, guided fishing trips and floats on the Beaverhead and Big Hole rivers, scenic float trips, and big-game hunts.

&. ✆ **Upper Canyon Outfitters** (1-800-735-3973; www.ucomontana.com), 24 miles south of Alder via Upper Ruby Road. This full-service outfitter and lodge also offers daily horseback rides (about $20 per person per hour) or private instructional lessons ($35 per person per hour). Children and families are welcome. Additional services include overnight pack rides, guided hunting and fishing trips, and lodging in a lodge room with a private bath (wheelchair accessible), three daily meals included ($210) or a cabin ($160–185).

See also Humbug Spires Wilderness Study Area under *To See—Natural Wonders;* Holter Lake Recreation Area under *Boating;* Potosi Hot Springs Resort under *Hot Springs;* Beaverhead–Deerlodge National Forest and Helena National Forest under *Wilder Places—Forests;* Litening Barn Bed and Breakfast and Mill Creek Lodging under *Lodging—Bed & Breakfasts;* and Sundance Lodge under *Lodging—Lodges.*

HOT SPRINGS ♿ **Boulder Hot Springs Bed and Breakfast** (406-225-4339; www.boulderhotsprings.com), 3 miles south of Boulder on MT 69. Soak away your travel weariness with a stay at this century-old inn and hot springs, now a bed & breakfast and guest accommodation. The hot springs have been a destination for more than a century, and they have had a long and checkered history, changing hands—and names—numerous times throughout the years. Now on the National Register of Historic Places, the springs and the inn provide a wonderful, peaceful escape in a pristine Montana environment. Indoor and outdoor pools afford you the chance to take a dip in the geothermal waters, whether you're an overnight guest or not (open April through October 10 AM–9 PM; shorter hours off-season). Overnight guests can choose to book simply a room ($55–89) or a bed & breakfast room ($91–129). The B&B also serves a weekly Sunday buffet and the occasional special dinner.

♿ **Elkhorn Hot Springs** (1-800-722-8978; 406-834-3434; www.elkhornhot springs.com), 13 miles north of MT 278 on the Pioneer Mountains Scenic Byway (F.R. 484). This year-round resort (accessible by car in summer months only) includes two outdoor sulfur-free mineral pools (95°–100°F) and one indoor wet sauna (102°–106°F) open to the public ($5 adults; $4 children). The resort also has lodging in cabins ($60–80) and rooms ($40 single occupancy and up), which comes with a complimentary breakfast. The restaurant serves dinner on weekends. The resort provides great access to summer and winter recreational activities in the surrounding Beaverhead–Deerlodge National Forest (see *Wilder Places—Forests*), including hiking, cross-country skiing (23K of trails), downhill skiing, and snowmobiling. The resort's rental shop rents out snowmobiles and cross-country skis.

♿ ✍ **Fairmont Hot Springs Resort** (1-800-332-3272; 406-797-3241; www .fairmontmontana.com), 1500 Fairmont Road, Fairmont (Exit 211 off I-90 between Anaconda and Butte). This full-service resort offers guests first and foremost access to its renowned pools, which include two Olympic-sized swimming pools, one indoors and one outdoors, as well as two mineral pools for soaking, one indoors and one outdoors. You can also take a slippery slide down the 350-foot enclosed waterslide. These pools are open to the public 8 AM–9:30 PM daily ($7.50 per person 11 and older, $4.25 children 10 and under, and $3.75 seniors 65 and older). Overnight guests enjoy complimentary 24-hour pool access. Rooms can be as simple as a basic hotel room with two queen beds or as fancy as a suite with two bedrooms, a kitchen, and two bathrooms ($109–435). The resort also has two restaurants—the casual Springwater Café and the fine dining Mile High Dining Room—as well as Whiskey Joe's Lounge, serving food along with your favorite beverages from a full bar and featuring live entertainment most nights. (See also Fairmont Hot Springs Resort Golf Course under *Golf.*)

🍃 **Jackson Hot Springs Lodge** (1-888-438-6938; 406-834-3151; www.jackson hotsprings.com), 43 miles northwest of Dillon on MT 278. Looking for the perfect romantic getaway without busting your pocketbook? Look no further than this charming and rustic yet clean and elegant country lodge. Nestled in the Big Hole River valley between the Pioneer Mountains and the Beaverhead Mountains, this lovely lodge offers guests and the public ($5 per person) the opportunity to soak in a natural hot mineral pool. Overnight guests can choose to stay in a cabin ($75), hotel-type room ($55), or small bedroom with a shared bath ($32), while RV travelers can hook up for the night ($25) and campers can pitch a tent ($10). The lodge also has an acclaimed fine dining establishment dedicated to incorporating local Montana produce into its creative menu.

✍ **Norris Hot Springs** (406-685-3303), MT 84 east of Norris. Open Tuesday through Sunday 10 AM–10 PM; $5. Yup, this one's just a hot springs—no resort attached! Stop in at this 107°F clean and well-kept hot springs for a soak, and you'll be delighted by its open-air charm and its fountain. It's appropriate for the kids, too, as swimsuits are required.

Potosi Hot Springs Resort (1-888-685-1695; 406-685-3330; www.potosiresort .com), 1 S. Willow Creek Road, Pony. For the ultimate in luxury, privacy, and personal attention, Montana-style, escape to this secluded resort northwest of Ennis, bordered by the Tobacco Root Mountains. Guests (a maximum of 12 at the resort at a time) can swim or soak in two hot springs pools—the larger 90°F to 92°F Cliff Pool and the more intimate 100°F to 104°F Cabana Spring. Lodging is provided in elegant streamside cabins ($200–375). You can also choose to have one, two, or three gourmet meals a day, prepared by the resort's expert chef (extra charge). Mountain Flowers Spa provides massages, spa treatments, yoga, and acupuncture (extra charge). The resort also offers an array of guided activities for an extra fee, including mountain biking, hiking, horseback riding, fly-fishing, snowshoeing, cross-country skiing, and downhill skiing. Children under 13 are not permitted here.

PADDLING/FLOATING **Bear Trap Canyon Wilderness,** managed by the Dillon Area Office of the Bureau of Land Management (BLM) (see *Camping* for contact information), encompasses some 6,000 acres of land around the Madison River northeast of Ennis. This area includes one of the region's premier white-water paddling destinations: the Bear Trap Canyon, with its 9 miles of challenging white water, including the notorious class IV and V Kitchen Sink. Only experienced, expert-level paddlers should attempt this stretch of water without a knowledgeable guide (see Yellowstone Raft Company, below, for one option). The put-in is 7 miles north of Ennis at McAllister. (See also the Madison River under *Fishing.*)

✍ **Yellowstone Raft Company** (1-800-348-4376; www.yellowstoneraft.com), based in Gardiner, offers all-day rafting adventures through the Bear Trap Canyon (see above) of the Madison River ($92 adults, $76 children), among other rafting adventures.

See also *Boating; Fishing;* Diamond Hitch Outfitters under *Horseback Riding;* Wade Lake Ski Trails under *Snow Sports;* Gates of the Mountains under *Unique Adventures;* Spring Meadow Lake State Park under *Wilder Places—Parks;*

Beaverhead–Deerlodge National Forest, Helena National Forest, and Lincoln State Forest under *Wilder Places—Forests;* Red Rock Lakes National Wildlife Refuge under *Wilder Places—Wildlife Refuges and Areas;* and Litening Barn Bed and Breakfast under *Lodging—Bed & Breakfasts.*

SNOW SPORTS

Ice Fishing

Ice fishing is a popular pastime for the patient in winter months here as elsewhere around the state. For ideas of where to go, see listings under *Boating;* Beaverhead–Deerlodge National Forest and Helena National Forest under *Wilder Places—Forests;* and Elk Lake Resort under *Lodging—Lodges.*

Ice-Skating

Ice-skating can be found around this region in wintertime on lakes and ponds, as well as at several rinks. These include the **Butte Community Ice Center** (406-490-2111), 1700 Wall Street, Butte; **United States High Altitude Sports Center** (406-494-7570) off I-90 at Continental Drive, Butte (outdoor speed skating rink); and **Rocky Mountain Ice Arena** (406-457-2817), 400 Lola Street, Helena. (See also Hauser Lake and Black Sandy State Park under *Boating;* and Spring Meadow Lake State Park under *Wilder Places—Parks.*)

Skiing

For cross-country skiing venues, see Lincoln under *To See—Towns;* Elkhorn Hot Springs and Potosi Hot Springs Resort under *Hot Springs;* Discovery Basin Ski Area, Mount Haggin Nordic Ski Area, and Wade Lake Ski Trails (below); Beaverhead–Deerlodge National Forest and Helena National Forest under *Wilder Places—Forests;* and Elkhorn View Lodge and Sundance Lodge under *Lodging—Lodges.*

✺ **Discovery Basin Ski Area** (406-563-2184; www.skidiscovery.com), 23 miles west of Anaconda on MT 1 (Anaconda–Pintler Scenic Highway; see *To See—Scenic Drives*). This day ski resort features 614 acres of skiable terrain in Beaverhead–Deerlodge National Forest, including 5K of trails for cross-country skiers. *Lifts:* three triple and three double chairlifts. *Trails:* 61 trails—20 percent beginner, 25 percent intermediate, 55 percent expert. *Vertical drop:* 1,670 feet. *Snowmaking:* on four runs. *Facilities:* full-service cafeteria-style dining room. *Ski school:* Offers ski and snowboarding lessons for all ages and ability levels. *For children:* Discovery Kinderski for ages 3–6, Kid Kruizers for ages 6–12; 2-day classes include Spike for ages 3–6, Big Horns for ages 7–12, Mountain Goats for ages 13–18. *Rates:* $30 adults, $15 children 12 and under and seniors 65 and older, children 5 and under free (with adult ticket); half-day and multiday rates available. (See also Celtic House Inn under *Lodging—Other Options.*)

✺ **Great Divide Snowsports** (406-449-3746; 406-447-1310; www.greatdivide montana.com), Exit 200 off I-15 north of Helena, then west on MT 279 (Lincoln Road) about 10.5 miles, then west on Marysville Road about 7 miles. Open Wednesday through Sunday in winter. This downhill ski and snowboarding area includes 1,600 acres of skiable terrain, including a terrain park with five rails, a tunnel, and a number of jumps. *Lifts:* five double chairlifts, one handle-tow.

Trails: 139 trails—15 percent beginner, 40 percent intermediate, 45 percent advanced. *Vertical drop:* 1,500 feet. *Facilities:* The base lodge has a cafeteria; lunch is served at the Continental Club Restaurant and Lounge and at the Sundeck Hut on weekends (weather permitting). *Ski school:* Offers ski and snowboarding lessons for all ages and ability levels. *Rates:* $19 (weekday) to $29 (weekends and holidays) adults, $14 children grades 1–5 and seniors ages 65 and older, $19 children grades 6–8, $24 children grades 9–12, preschool children free (accompanied by adult); multiday rates also available. (See also Lincoln under *To See—Towns.*)

✧ ❧ **Maverick Mountain** (406-834-3454; www.skimaverick.com), on the Pioneer Mountains Scenic Byway (F.R. 484; see *To See—Scenic Drives*) north of MT 278, in Beaverhead–Deerlodge National Forest (see *Wilder Places— Forests*). Open Thursday through Sunday in winter and daily during holiday weeks. This smaller downhill ski area provides a great getaway for the whole family, with 210 skiable acres for downhill enthusiasts, as well as access to groomed and ungroomed cross-country trails that originate from Elkhorn Hot Springs (see *Hot Springs*). *Lifts:* one double chairlift, one handle-tow. *Trails:* 24 trails—20 percent beginner, 35 percent intermediate, 45 percent expert. *Vertical drop:* 2,020 feet. *Facilities:* Dining is available at a cafeteria; Thunder Bar provides beverages of choice. *Ski school:* Offers ski and snowboarding lessons for all ages and ability levels. *For children:* Little Maverick Nursery for nonskiing children (reservations requested). *Rates:* $15 adults and juniors (weekdays); $24 adults, $16 juniors (weekends); children 5 and under free; half-day and multiday rates available.

Mount Haggin Nordic Ski Area lies 15 miles south of Anaconda. Operated by the cooperative joint efforts of Montana Fish, Wildlife and Parks and the **Mile Hi Nordic Ski Club** (406-782-4994), this area features 25K of groomed cross-country ski trails—5K easiest, 10K more difficult, 10K most difficult. About half of the trails include tracks for skate skiing as well as traditional Nordic skiing.

Wade Lake Ski Trails at Wade Lake Cabins (406-682-7560; www.wadelake .com), south on Cliff Lake Road just west of the junction of US 287 and MT 87, then 6 miles to cabins and trails. Wade Lake offers 35K of groomed trails—15K easiest and 20K more difficult—for cross-country skiing enthusiasts come wintertime at this remote locale. You actually need to ski in to your accommodations, but your food and gear will be shuttled for you while you ski. Rent a cozy, lakeside cabin ($65–100), and you'll have a warm, comfy place to hang your hat after a hard day on the trails. This is also a great location for hiking, paddling (canoe rentals available), and fishing in summertime.

Snowmobiling

Snowmobiling is incredibly popular in this region, with a prolific amount of trails accessible to snowmobilers. The 50-mile Pioneer Mountains Scenic Byway (see *To See—Scenic Drives*), closed to automobile traffic in wintertime, is a designated National Recreation Snowmobile Trail. If you need to rent a snowmobile, one place to go is Elkhorn Hot Springs (see *Hot Springs*). For more ideas of where to go, see also Lincoln under *To See—Towns;* Georgetown Lake under *Boating;*

Beaverhead–Deerlodge National Forest and Helena National Forest under *Wilder Places—Forests;* Mount Haggin Wildlife Management Area and Red Rock Lakes National Wildlife Refuge under *Wilder Places—Wildlife Refuges and Areas;* and Elk Lake Resort under *Lodging—Lodges.*

See also Lincoln under *To See—Towns;* Potosi Hot Springs Resort under *Hot Springs;* and Lincoln State Forest under *Wilder Places—Forests.*

UNIQUE ADVENTURES **Alder Gulch Short Line Railroad** (1-800-829-2969; 406-843-5247; www.virginiacity.com/steam.htm), Virginia City. Open Memorial Day through August; $10 round-trip, $6 one-way, children 6 and under free, $35 per family. The railroad never did reach Virginia City during the town's mining heyday—it stopped short a mere 10 miles, reaching Alder City to the west. Aside from this minor detail, this 1.5-mile train ride from Virginia City to Nevada City re-creates a historically accurate experience for passengers, as the train is powered on summer weekends by a restored 1910 Baldwin steam-powered locomotive. Weekday passengers will have to settle for the gas-powered C. A. Bovey train (the tracks themselves were actually laid in 1964 by Charlie Bovey).

✒ ♿ **Gates of the Mountains** (406-458-5241; www.gatesofthemountains.com), Exit 209 off I-15, 20 miles north of Helena, then 3 miles to the marina. Open Memorial Day through late September; $9.50 adults, $8.50 seniors 60 and older, $6 per child ages 4–17, children 3 and under free. Explore this area that Lewis and Clark passed through in 1805 during a 105-minute cruise aboard one of three boats—the *Pirogue,* the *Sacajawea,* or the *Hilger Rose.* Tour highlights include incredible natural scenery, potential wildlife viewing, and Indian pictographs. You can even stay for a picnic, some hiking, or fishing at the Meriwether Picnic Area and catch the rest of the tour on a later boat.

♿ **Old No. 1 Trolley Tours** (1-800-735-6814; 406-723-3177; www.butteinfo .org), 1000 George Street, Butte. Open daily Memorial Day through August or September; call for current rates and reservations. Take a 2-hour tour aboard a historic trolley to learn all about Butte's past, from its buildings to its mining. The trolley is a replica of the electric trolleys that once provided public transportation for Butte residents. Your informed driver will narrate the tour as you ride through neighborhoods and past museums and other attractions, learning to find your way around the city as you learn about the city itself.

Ranch vacations. These vacations usually allow you to participate to a certain extent in various aspects of ranch life, often including cattle herding and branding. The ratio of work time to leisure time varies from ranch to ranch, as do the additional activities and amenities offered, but most ranches include horseback riding, lodging, and meals in an inclusive package deal. In this region, providers include **Alice Creek Ranch** (406-362-4810), Lincoln; **Bannock Pass Ranch** (406-681-3229), Dillon; **Broken Arrow Lodge and Outfitters** (1-800-775-2928; 406-842-5437), Alder; **Canyon Creek Guest Ranch** (1-877-518-2407; 406-835-2207), Melrose; **CB Cattle and Guest Ranch** (June through September: 406-682-4608; October through May: 909-676-5646; www.guestranches .com/cbranch), Cameron; **Centennial Guest Ranch** (406-682-7292), Ennis;

1880s Ranch (406-491-2336), Anaconda; **Ford Creek Guest Ranch** (1-888-463-5934; 406-562-3672), Augusta; **Hidden Hollow Hideaway Guest Ranch** (406-266-3322), Townsend; **Hidden Valley Guest Ranch** (1-800-250-8802; 406-683-2929), Dillon; **Hildreth Livestock Ranch** (406-681-3111), Dillon; **Horse Prairie Ranch** (1-888-726-2454; 406-681-3155), Dillon; **Rocking Z Guest Ranch** (406-458-3890), Wolf Creek; and **White Tail Ranch** (1-888-987-2624), Ovando.

✔ **Sapphire mining.** Several locations throughout this region offer opportunities to experience the anticipation and excitement of mining for precious gems. You'll sift and possibly wash gravel in search of these unique stones, perhaps finding a treasure to take home with you as a souvenir. Try your luck at **Gem Mountain** (1-866-459-4367; 406-859-4367; www.gemmtn.com), 3835 Skalkaho Road, Philipsburg. Open Memorial Day through Labor Day 9 AM–7 PM; open Labor Day through October 10, 9 AM–5 PM; $8 per bucket o' gravel to sift and wash. Another option is **Sapphire Gallery** (1-800-525-0169; 406-859-3236; www.sapphire-gallery.com), 115 E. Broadway, Philipsburg. Open June 1 through August 31 Sunday through Friday 10 AM–6 PM; open September 1 through May 31, 10 AM–5 PM; $25 per bag of gravel for sifting. A third possibility is **Spokane Bar Sapphire Mine and Gold Fever Rock Shop** (1-877-344-4367; 406-227-8989; www.sapphiremine.com), 5360 Castles Road, Helena. Open April through October 9 AM–5 PM, by appointment off-season; $5 for a tiny sample bag of gravel or $60 for a family-sized package deal.

✔ **Wagon Ride Dinners at the Moose Meadow Tipi** (1-800-505-2884; 406-442-2884; www.lastchanceranch.biz), 2884 Grizzly Gulch, Helena. Open for dinner June through September; $59 per person includes a luxury bus ride from Helena, a wagon ride, gourmet dinner, and live entertainment. Take the whole family on a fun-filled, horse-drawn wagon ride to the Moose Meadow Tipi, courtesy of **Last Chance Ranch.** In the giant tipi, which can seat up to 50 guests, you'll sit down to a gourmet Montana dinner including an entrée of prime rib, completed with huckleberry cheesecake and cowboy coffee. A true-blue Montana musician provides live entertainment to round out your western experience.

See also Lewis and Clark Caverns State Park under *To See—Natural Wonders;* Crystal Park under *Wilder Places—Parks;* and Mill Creek Lodging under *Lodging—Bed & Breakfasts.*

✳ Wilder Places

PARKS ♿ ✔ **Crystal Park** is located in Beaverhead–Deerlodge National Forest (see *Forests*) along the Pioneer Mountains Scenic Byway (see *To See—Scenic Drives*), F.R. 484, 17 miles north of the road's junction with MT 278. Open mid-May through mid-October (depending on weather) for day-use only; $5 per vehicle. This high-elevation park allows you and the kids the chance to get down on your hands and knees and dig in the dirt for the crystals that gave the area its name. Collection is permitted by amateurs only, and hand tools are the only tools allowed. You can potentially unearth fine specimens of both quartz and amethyst scepter crystals.

&. **Lost Creek State Park** (406-542-5500; www.fwp.state.mt.us/parks/parks report.asp?mapnum=29), MT 1, 1.5 miles east of Anaconda, north on MT 273 for 2 miles, then northeast 6 miles on F.R. 635. Open for day-use and camping May 1 through November 30; free. Granite and limestone cliffs dominate the natural scenery at this park, while a short hiking trail (less than 0.5 mile) takes you to 50-foot **Lost Creek Falls.** Fishing, picnicking, and wildlife viewing (bighorn sheep and mountain goats in particular) round out the park's activities.

&. **Spring Meadow Lake State Park** (406-495-3270; www.fwp.state.mt.us/parks/parksreport.asp?mapnum=19), 930 Custer Avenue W., Helena. Open year-round for day-use only; free for residents, $5 for nonresidents. This park is a 55-acre urban recreational oasis, complete with a spring-fed lake, Spring Meadow Lake. In the lake, you can swim, paddle, and fish (largemouth bass, rainbow trout, west-slope cutthroat trout, and yellow perch). A nature trail nearly a mile long provides another outing, and picnicking is also popular. In wintertime, the lake can freeze cold enough for ice-skating.

See also Lewis and Clark Caverns State Park under *To See—Natural Wonders;* Hauser Lake, Black Sandy State Park under *To Do—Boating;* and Mount Helena City Park and Sheepshead Mountain Recreation Area under *To Do—Hiking.*

FORESTS **Beaverhead–Deerlodge National Forest** (406-683-3900; 406-683-3913; www.fs.fed.us/r1/b-d), 420 Barrett Street, Dillon. South of Helena, east of Missoula, and west of Bozeman, Montana's largest national forest encompasses more than 3.2 million acres of land that lie throughout no fewer than eight counties. Notable forest features include the **Anaconda–Pintler Wilderness Area,** part of the **Lee Metcalf Wilderness Area,** portions of the **Continental Divide National Scenic Trail** and the **Nez Perce Historic Trail,** and an abundance of natural resources, including timber, mining, and grazing. Recreational opportunities include biking on numerous trails and roads, boating, camping, cross-country skiing, fishing, hiking, horseback riding, paddling/floating, picnicking, scenic drives, snowmobiling, wildlife viewing, and more. (See also listing under *To Do—Camping;* Anaconda–Pintler Scenic Highway under *To See—Scenic Drives;* Pear Lake Trail under *To Do—Bicycling;* Georgetown Lake under *To Do—Boating;* Blue Creek Trail, Lake Louise National Recreation Trail, and Sheepshead Mountain Recreation Area under *To Do—Hiking;* and Discovery Basin Ski Area and Maverick Mountain under *To Do—Snow Sports.)*

Helena National Forest (406-449-5201; www.fs.fed.us/r1/helena), 2880 Skyway Drive, Helena. Surrounding Montana's capital, this national forest has almost a million acres under its jurisdiction. Highlights within this area include the **Scapegoat Wilderness,** northwest of Lincoln; the **Gates of the Mountains Wilderness,** northeast of Helena; the **Big Belt Mountains,** east of Helena; the **Elkhorn Mountains,** south of Helena, which includes the unique **Elkhorn Wildlife Management Unit;** and about 80 miles of the **Continental Divide National Scenic Trail.** Recreational opportunities include biking on numerous trails and roads, boating, camping, cross-country skiing, fishing, hiking, horse-back riding, paddling/floating, picnicking, scenic drives, snowmobiling, wildlife viewing, and more. (See also listing under *To Do—Camping;* Refrigerator Canyon under *To See—Natural Wonders;* Mount Helena Ridge Trail under *To Do—Bicycling;* Trout Creek Canyon Trail under *To Do—Hiking;* and Gates of the Mountains under *To Do—Unique Adventures.*)

Lincoln State Forest lies adjacent to the Scapegoat Wilderness and Helena National Forest near the town of Lincoln. The forest is one of seven state forests managed by the Department of Natural Resources and Conservation (406-542-4300; www.dnrc.state.mt.us), all of which were set aside with a twofold aim: to secure timber production and to preserve watershed coverage. Recreational opportunities include boating, camping, fishing, hiking, snow sports, wildlife viewing, and hunting.

WILDLIFE REFUGES AND AREAS **Mount Haggin Wildlife Management Area** (406-542-5500; www.fwp.state.mt.us/habitat/wma/haggin.asp), about 10 miles south of Anaconda along MT 569. This area includes more than 56,000 acres of habitat set aside mainly for mule deer and moose, as well as for outdoor recreational pursuits. These include snowmobiling in winter, abundant wildlife viewing of birds and other mammals, hunting, hiking, and more.

& **Red Rock Lakes National Wildlife Refuge** (406-276-3536; www.r6.fws.gov/redrocks), accessible via Exit 0 on I-15 at Monida, then east for 28 miles on MT 509 (Red Rock Pass Road). Visitor center open year-round, Monday through Friday 7:30 AM–4 PM, except for federal holidays. Established in 1935 with the intention of protecting habitat for the trumpeter swan, this 45,000-acre wildlife refuge provides visitors with an incredible experience in the natural world. Wildlife viewing potential includes both birds and mammals, and many visitors choose to simply drive the entirety of the Red Rocks Pass Road as a scenic drive. A stop at the visitor center provides you with more in-depth interpretive materials. Recreational opportunities include two primitive, free campgrounds—**Upper Lake Campground** (handicapped accessible) and **Lower Lake Campground;** fishing (arctic grayling, brook trout, mountain whitefish, rainbow trout, and Yellowstone cutthroat trout); paddling on Lower and Upper Red Rock lakes; hiking; cycling (roads only); snowmobiling on Red Rock Pass Road and Elk Lake Road; and hunting. (See also Elk Lake Resort under *Lodging—Lodges.*)

See also Ennis under *To See—Towns;* Humbug Spires Wilderness Study Area under *To See—Natural Wonders;* Canyon Ferry Lake, Clark Canyon Reservoir, and Holter Lake Recreation Area under *To Do—Boating;* and Sheepshead Mountain Recreation Area under *To Do—Hiking.*

✳ Lodging

BED & BREAKFASTS

Alder

🦌 ⌇ **Lynch's Lair Bed and Breakfast** (406-842-5699; www.lynchslair
.com; mailing address: 2055 28th
Street SE, Grand Rapids, MI 49508-
1582), 10 miles north of Virginia City
on MT 287. If you're looking for pre-
tentious accommodations, look elsewhere—but if you want to stay in
comfortable, cozy accommodations
with unsurpassed hospitality, this is
the place for you. This family-run
B&B features a continental breakfast
served daily for guests staying in one
of its three guest rooms (one with private bath, two with shared bath). You
can even arrange for babysitting, if
you need it. Guests enjoy a living area
with a big-screen television, plus
cookies and beverages available all
day long ($50–55).

Anaconda 59711

**Hickory House Inn Bed and
Breakfast** (1-866-563-5481; 406-563-
5481; www.hickoryhouseinn.com), 608
Hickory Street. Stay right near the scenic Anaconda–Pintler Wilderness,
enjoying easy access to the area's abundant recreational and cultural activities
while you enjoy the comfort of a room
in this restored Victorian home. The
three-story brick structure was once
the parish house for St. Paul's Church.
Today, you'll enjoy not only elegant
accommodations but also a delicious
full breakfast included in the rate
($80–110). Package deals are available
as well, both for skiing at Discovery
Basin Ski Area (see *To Do—Snow
Sports*) and for golfing at the Old
Works Golf Course (see *To Do—Golf*).

⌇ **Mill Creek Lodging** (406-560-
7666; 406-560-7676; www.millcreek
lodging.com), 11 Clear Creek Trail.
You'll get away from it all and enjoy
total privacy at this B&B, where up to
four guests (and Fido, too) can stay in
the single upstairs bedroom. The
room features a private bathroom,
and guests enjoy access to additional
amenities, including a pool table in
the basement, laundry facilities,
porches with classic Montana views,
and a full breakfast served daily
($70–100). Also available is overnight
stabling for your horses, as well as
horseback rides for experienced
riders (2-hour minimum, $25 per per-
son per hour; open to the public as
well) and guided jeep tours and hikes
($75 per day and up, depending on
the trip). If you're seeking more solitude, ask about the log cabin accommodation.

Boulder

See **Boulder Hot Springs Bed
and Breakfast** under *To Do—Hot
Springs*.

Butte 59701

♿ **Toad Hall Manor Bed and
Breakfast** (1-866-443-8623; 406-494-
2625; www.toadhallmanor.com), 1
Green Lane. Wondering about the
name of this lovely 11,000-square-foot
brick manor? It's straight out of the
children's classic *The Wind in the Wil-
lows*, and the guest rooms feature
decor in accordance with this theme.
Attention to detail is the norm here,
where guests enjoy special touches,
including down pillows and comforters, feather beds, and even a complimentary chocolate mint toad candy
paired with a beverage upon their
arrival. The manor itself embodies
hospitality and luxury blended in a
perfect recipe, with its incredible
marble and granite accents, its high-
speed hydraulic elevator serving its

five stories, and its lavish breakfasts that include a prebreakfast scone and coffee delivery right to your door. The list of services here goes on and on, including high-speed Internet, TV/VCRs and a library of movies, and even in-room massages (extra fee) ($95–165).

See also **Copper King Mansion** under *To See—Historic Landmarks, Places, and Sites.*

Dillon 59725
The Centennial Inn (406-683-4454; www.bmt.net/~centenn/inn), 122 S. Washington. This pleasant B&B in a 1905 Queen Anne–style Victorian house accommodates guests in one of four bedrooms, each with a private bathroom. Period furnishings welcome you back to a simpler day and age, complete with claw-foot bathtubs and pedestal sinks. In addition to a delectable full breakfast served daily, you can also book an afternoon tea or a gourmet dinner or browse through the gift shop for unique treasures to commemorate your stay ($79).

Ennis 59729
♿ **Eagle Rock Hideaway Bed and Breakfast** (1-866-682-5715; 406-682-5715; www.bbonline.com/mt/eagle rock), 77 Hilltop Trail. Guests choose to stay in one of three rooms, all with private bathrooms and telephones, as well as fantastic views of surrounding mountain ranges. This cozy bed & breakfast is situated on a little hill overlooking the spectacular scenery of the Madison River valley. Guests also enjoy a hot tub and a comfortable living area with a stone fireplace and a good selection of books ($55–85). You can also request a five-course gourmet meal for dinner (extra charge), or book a guided fly-fishing package.

Helena 59601

Barrister Bed and Breakfast (1-800-823-1148; 406-443-7330; http://thebarristermt.tripod.com), 416 N. Ewing. This bed & breakfast is located in a restored 1874 Victorian mansion directly across the street from the historic St. Helena Cathedral (see To *See—Historic Landmarks, Places, and Sites*). On the National Register of Historic Places, the three-story house still has its original stained-glass windows, six fireplaces, and antique furnishings. Guests stay in one of five bedrooms, all of which include queen-size beds, private bathrooms, and color televisions. A full breakfast is included in the rates ($95–110).

Carolina Bed and Breakfast (406-495-8095; www.carolinab-b.com), 309 N. Ewing. Guests stay in one of six rooms at this elegant bed & breakfast across the street from the original Governor's Mansion (see *To See—Historic Landmarks, Places, and Sites*). Constructed in 1907, the Carolina showcases the arts-and-crafts style of architecture, with attention to details throughout. A full breakfast is served daily in your choice of the main formal dining room; the intimate, private sun room; or the garden, weather permitting. Guest rooms all include private phone lines, baths, and cable television. The third floor features a two-bedroom suite, as well as a conference room that can seat up to 20 people for business travelers ($95–115).

The Sanders—Helena's Bed and Breakfast (406-442-3309; www .sandersbb.com), 328 N. Ewing. Helena's first bed & breakfast opened in 1987 in this restored 1875 mansion, which is listed on the National Register of Historic Places, and it has enjoyed critical acclaim ever since. After nearly two decades, guests are still wowed by the luxurious accommodations when they stay in one of the seven guest rooms, all of which include private baths, phone lines, televisions, and lovely decor. In addition to the full breakfast served each morning, guests also enjoy afternoon tea, including cookies and complimentary sherry ($100–120).

Ovando 59854
🐾 **Blackfoot Inn** (406-793-5555; www.blackfoot-inn.com), 722 Pine Street. Located on MT 200 northwest of Helena, Ovando retains its feeling of a late 1800s frontier town, and the Blackfoot Inn is right in the thick of things. Situated on the trail of Lewis and Clark, this B&B provides travelers with five rooms to choose from in a rustic, country inn setting. Included is a full breakfast served daily ($55–65).

Philipsburg 59858
Big Horn Bed and Breakfast (406-859-3109; www.bighornmontana.com), 31 Lower Rock Creek. Situated 15 miles west of town, this bed & breakfast offers a true escape and personalized attention. You'll stay in one of two bedrooms that share a bath, enjoy a full breakfast every morning, and feel good knowing that the B&B uses environmentally friendly products. You'll also enjoy easy access to blue-ribbon trout fishing on Rock Creek, as well as plenty of additional recreational opportunities ($69).

Quigley Cottage Bed and Breakfast (1-800-382-4519; 406-859-3812; www.philipsburgbb.com), 418 W. Broadway Street. Open April through December. Rustic country comfort with the perfect touch of elegance greets visitors to this charming English-style

cottage. Four bedrooms share two bathrooms and surround a cozy living area, perfect for relaxation in front of the fireplace. In addition to a full breakfast served each morning, guests enjoy access to a well-stocked butler's pantry all day long, complete with snacks and beverages. Winter brings the chance to take advantage of ski packages for nearby Discovery Basin Ski Area (see *To Do—Snow Sports*). In summertime, three gardens and two patios provide perfect escapes for strolling and meditation ($75–95).

Polaris
See **Elkhorn Hot Springs** under *To Do—Hot Springs*.

Sheridan 59749
🌿 **Elijah's Rest Cabins and Breakfast** (406-842-7295; www.elijahsrest.com), 8 Stagecoach NW Lane, Laurin (8 miles south of Sheridan). Open mid-May through mid-November. This unique twist on the B&B offers guests not simply a bed for the night followed by breakfast in the morning but, rather, an entire cabin for the night, with a log queen-size bed and a twin bed for a small one who might be along. Three cabins feature private porches, full private baths, log furnishings throughout, and tremendous mountain views, as well as a hearty breakfast for occupants ($95).

Townsend 59644
🌿 **Litening Barn Bed and Breakfast** (1-800-654-2845; 406-266-4554; www.ewwatson.com), 7837 US 287. This homey B&B invites guests to stay in one of two bedrooms that share a bathroom in a newly constructed home on the farm. After a full breakfast, you can to tour the historic 1900 barn, watch the horses and cattle, gather eggs from the henhouse, enjoy

abundant outdoor recreational opportunities, and then ease your sore muscles in one of two hot tubs ($65). You can also book a float trip on the Missouri River, a horseback riding adventure, a horse and buggy ride, or a guided fishing trip from this licensed and insured outfitting business.

Virginia City 59755

♪ Bennett House Country Inn (1-877-843-5220; 406-843-5220; www .bennetthouseinn.com), 115 E. Idaho. In an area rife with Montana history, you can round out your historical experience by booking a stay in this 1879 Victorian house. Six bedrooms ($75–85) and a little log cabin ($95; great for families) allow you to choose accommodations that fit your needs. You'll enjoy easy access to the historic downtown area, as well as a full breakfast served daily. A hot tub is available seasonally.

♪ Just an Experience (1-866-664-0424; 406-843-5402; www.justan experience.com), 1570 MT 287. What kind of an experience will you find at Just an Experience? A truly historic one, for certain, as you'll sleep in one of three comfortable guest rooms in the renovated 1864 log house, which has been enlarged and improved to ensure your comfort. Alternatively, you can choose to stay in a furnished cabin, with a fully equipped kitchen, private bedroom, bathroom, and additional sleeping loft. The property features a large yard and gardens. Whatever you select, you'll enjoy a hearty breakfast included with your stay ($65–100).

Stonehouse Inn (406-843-5504; www.stonehouseinnbb.com), 306 E. Idaho. Listed on the National Register of Historic Places, this 1884 Victorian house was originally the home of

a blacksmith who arrived in Virginia City by wagon train. Today, guests sleep in one of five bedrooms, all of which share baths and feature antique furnishings such as brass beds. A full breakfast is included in the rate ($70–75).

Wolf Creek 59648

Bungalow Bed and Breakfast (406-235-4276), 2020 US 287. On the National Register of Historic Places, this is not your typical Victorian mansion B&B, but rather, a lovely historic lodge constructed in 1911–13 and designed by the same architect who designed the Old Faithful Lodge. Built with cedar and logs for successful Montana entrepreneur Charles B. Power, the lodge-style B&B features antique decor, including many pieces original to the property. Four guest rooms include one with a private bath. A full breakfast is served daily ($110–125).

LODGES

Alder

See **Upper Canyon Outfitters** under *To Do—Horseback Riding*.

Anaconda 59711

Georgetown Lake Lodge (406-563-7020; www.georgetownlakelodge .com), 2015 Georgetown Lake Road. This is a great place to stay if you happen to be skiing at nearby Discovery Ski Area or snowmobiling in the surrounding area. Eleven comfortable rooms, all with two double beds and satellite television, provide you with a cozy place to rest your head after a busy day on the slopes or the trails. In summer, you'll enjoy lakeshore access to fishing and hiking trails right outside your door ($75–90). The lodge also has a full-service restaurant with great weekday specials such as $1 tacos on Tuesday.

Cameron 59720
Old Kirby Place (1-888-875-8027; www.oldkirbyplace.com), 34 miles south of Ennis via MT 287 to mile marker #15, then south to the West Fork of Madison River. Open April through October. This rustic lodge caters to trout fishermen. The original lodge was constructed in 1880, and it maintains a historic ambience while providing you with up-to-date accommodations. You'll sleep in one of two rooms in the main lodge or in one of three riverside cabins, all with private baths. Guiding services are extra. Rates include not only lodging but also three meals a day ($175 per person; 3-day minimum stay).

Clancy 59634
Elkhorn View Lodge (406-442-1224; www.elkviewbb.com), 88 Howard Beer Road. Newly constructed in 2001, the Elkhorn View Lodge features 32-foot-high ceilings in its great room, a living room for guests complete with a fireplace and a 61-inch satellite television, an outdoor hot tub, a sauna and fitness room, and 440 acres of surrounding land perfect for exploration by foot, on a bike, or on skis. You'll stay in one of four guest rooms, all of which feature a private bath. A full breakfast is included ($125–180). On-premises massages are available (extra fee).

Ennis 59729
& ❧ **Rainbow Valley Lodge** (1-800-452-8254; 406-682-4264; www .rainbowvalley.com), P.O. Box 26. Located 1 mile south of Ennis on US 287. This tidy little locally run motel-style accommodation features 24 rooms and two well-appointed cabins,

along with a heated pool, a landscaped yard, and even a horse corral. If you choose a room in the lodge, you'll have cable television, a private bath, a phone line, and a queen-size bed. Some rooms also have fully equipped kitchens ($75–110). Cabins provide more spacious accommodations ($175–210).

Jackson
See **Jackson Hot Springs Lodge** under *To Do—Hot Springs*.

Red Rock Lakes NWR
❧ **Elk Lake Resort** (406-276-3282; www.elklakeresortmontana.com), P.O. Box 1662, West Yellowstone 59758. Take Exit 0 off I-15 at Monida, then go 37 miles east on Red Rock Pass Road to Elk Lake Road, then north 6 miles to Elk Lake Resort. On the shores of Elk Lake and bordering the fantastic Red Rock Lakes National Wildlife Refuge (see *Wilder Places— Wildlife Refuges and Areas*), this phenomenal lodge-style resort gives you the opportunity to escape it all and get back to nature. Stay in one of seven cabins, each with its own distinctive style and amenities, but all with private baths, at least one queen-size bed, down comforters, and propane heaters. The resort also has a "country gourmet" restaurant, serving cold and hot continental breakfast (included in rates for overnight guests), lunch, and dinner (be sure to make reservations ahead of time if you're not staying at the lodge). Surrounding recreational activities include paddling (boat rentals available), year-round fishing, hiking, snowmobiling, and wildlife-watching ($100–120).

Wise River 59762
Sundance Lodge (406-689-3611), 4000 Lamarche Creek Road (4 miles

west of Wise River on MT 274). Cross-country skiers in particular will enjoy staying at this rustic accommodation, which features 35K of groomed ski trails, some with skate lanes. Stay in one of six lodge rooms ($69) or in a cabin ($73–79). You can enjoy additional lodge services, including a spa, dining room, and bar. In summertime, the lodge provides convenient access to nearby hiking, horseback riding, and fishing opportunities.

OTHER OPTIONS Mountain Home—Montana vacation rentals (1-800-550-4589; 406-586-4589; www .mountain-home.com), P.O. Box 1204, Bozeman 59771. Searching for just the right Montana getaway to host your family reunion? Consider the six-bedroom Mountain Lake Lodge on the shores of Georgetown Lake. Or perhaps you're looking for a cute little romantic cottage where you and your honey can enjoy some rest and relaxation? Think about the inviting R&R you'll find at Timber Wolf Cabin near Dillon. Whatever type of Montana retreat you're seeking, if you're looking for a rental home in this region, chances are that you'll find something that suits your fancy from among the choices offered by this company.

See also **Beaverhead–Deerlodge National Forest** in *To Do—Camping.*

Anaconda 59711
🍺 **Celtic House Inn** (406-563-2372; www.harppubinn.com), 23 Main Street. Right in the thick of things in Anaconda, you can stay in this 1888 two-story brick building. Enjoy a Montana microbrew or other favorite drink downstairs at the Harp Pub before you make your way to your room upstairs. All rooms include a queen-size bed, bathroom, and TV,

while some include a kitchenette as well ($40 and up). Package deals are available for skiing at nearby Discovery Basin Ski Area (see *To Do—Snow Sports*) and golfing at nearby Old Works Jack Niklaus Signature Golf Course (see *To Do—Golf*).

Ennis 59729
🛶 **El Western Cabins and Lodges** (1-800-831-2773; 406-682-4217; www .elwestern.com), 4787 US 287 N. Serving visitors since 1948, this little "resort" features all of the comforts a traveler could want, whether you're solo or traveling with the entire family. Daily housekeeping is included in all accommodations. Overnight cabins include a full bath, porch, and at least one queen-size bed ($65–90). Creekside cabins along Bear Creek feature two rooms, including a full kitchen, bedroom, full bathroom, and porch ($90–120). Deluxe cabins include two bedrooms, one or two bathrooms, a living area, a dining area, a porch, and more ($135–225). The lodges are even more spacious, providing you with a true home away from home ($250–425; weekly rates available as well).

Fairmont
See **Fairmont Hot Springs Resort** under *To Do—Hot Springs.*

Helena
See **Helena National Forest** under *To Do—Camping.*

Lincoln 59639
🛶 ♿ **Historic Hotel Lincoln** (406-362-4396; www.hotellincoln.net), 101 Sleepy Hollow Lane. No, you probably won't meet the infamous headless horseman of lore in this Sleepy Hollow, but you just might see a ghost of another sort! Rumor has it that this century-old hotel could be haunted by

a benign entity—just one of its many intriguing historical notes. This two-story log building once provided hunters with basic—and I mean basic—overnight lodging in 22 rooms, with one bathroom to each floor. Thankfully for today's visitors, the hotel has been updated and now features 14 larger guest rooms, each with a private bathroom ($59–89). Also on the premises is Miss Kitty's, an American restaurant serving dinner by the creek in summertime (breakfast, lunch, and late-night fare available upon request) and indoors in winter. There is also a bar with a fireplace.

Philipsburg 59858
& **Broadway Hotel** (1-800-877-4436; 406-859-8000; www.broadway montana.com), 103 W. Broadway. Stay the night in this recently restored (2003) 1890 hotel in the historic town of Philipsburg (see *To See—Towns*). Nine well-appointed, cleverly themed guest rooms feature queen- or king-size beds, TV/DVD players, and high-speed Internet access, among other amenities. Guests also enjoy a continental breakfast included in the rate ($64.50–114.50).

Pony
See **Potosi Hot Springs Resort** under *To Do—Hot Springs.*

Twin Bridges 59754
Kings Motel (1-800-222-5510; 406-684-5639; www.kingsflatline.com), 307 S. Main Street. This small-town, friendly hotel might just exceed your expectations with its 12 squeaky-clean rooms, all with satellite television, coffee, and a coffeemaker. Ten of the rooms feature fully equipped kitchenettes, and many "rooms" are actually suites with multiple rooms and up to five beds ($50–75).

✴ Where to Eat
DINING OUT

Anaconda
Jim and Clara's Supper Club (406-563-9963), 511 E. Park Avenue. This classic Montana supper club features steaks of all cuts, as well as fish-and-chips, salmon, and grilled lamb chops. Entrée selections are accompanied by the full meal to be expected from a supper club, including access to the salad bar, potato, pasta, shrimp cocktail, coffee or tea, and of course dessert—if you have any room. The restaurant also has a full bar and several weekly specials.

Boulder
See **Boulder Hot Springs Bed and Breakfast** under *To Do—Hot Springs.*

Butte
& **Derby Steak House** (406-723-9086), 2016 Harrison Avenue. So you're in Montana, and you want a steak . . . well, this is the place to go. This award-winning restaurant specializes in just that, featuring beef in a variety of cuts prepared to perfection just for you. Everything is guaranteed fresh, and everything that can be prepared on the premises is, from the steaks cut daily and freshly ground burgers to the smoked meats, soups, and sauces. If you're not a steak lover, you'll find fresh seafood on the menu, including salmon and lobster tail . . . but it's the steak that brings the crowds through the doors, and it's the steak that should bring you, too. A children's menu is available.

& **Lydia's Supper Club** (406-494-2000), 4915 Harrison Avenue. You'll dine at one of the oldest and finest establishments in Butte when you sit down at the table at Lydia's. Lavish full dinners include entrée choices of steaks, seafood, chicken, pork, or veal accompanied by an incredible list of side dishes. In addition to the standard dinner salad, your meal includes appetizers, homemade ravioli, bread, potatoes, coffee or tea, and ice cream. You can accompany your meal with beer, wine, or a cocktail. A children's menu is available.

Spaghettini's (406-782-8855; www .spaghettinibutte.com), 26 N. Main Street. Italian food lovers, rejoice! Here in Butte you'll sit down to a menu chockfull of your favorites, including shrimp scampi, chicken marsala, and wild salmon prepared with pesto. Vegetarians will delight in the selection they find here—no fewer than nine main entrée options are offered. Daily specials, an Italian take on buffalo, a polenta dish, and a number of additional meat, seafood, and poultry offerings round out the menu.

Uptown Café (406-723-4735; www .uptowncafe.com), 47 E. Broadway. By day, this charming little café is just that—a café, serving lunch entrées in a casual, relaxed environment. By night, however, the Uptown transforms into an elegant, fine dining destination, though it's still a great place for relaxing and unwinding after a long day of travel or work. The lunch menu includes two entrées and two soups (homemade, of course) that rotate on a daily basis, as well as a large salad bar and desserts. Dinner offerings are more expansive, with creations including pasta (vegetarian options), beef, poultry, and seafood. If you eat before 6:30, you can take advantage of the Early Dining Specials, lower-priced full dinners (including salad or soup) that will leave you full and satisfied, with

money in your pocket, too. Leave room for a homemade dessert (chocolate peanut butter pie, anyone?).

Ennis
Continental Divide Restaurant (406-682-7600), 315 E. Main Street. For more than 20 years, this restaurant has provided diners with a reliable source of a delicious meal. With European-inspired entrée selections, including influences from France and Italy, as well as purely American meal items (albeit with regional influences), you'll always find something that interests you on the menu. You'll also be certain to find just the right wine to accompany your dinner, as the restaurant has a good wine list focused on northwestern and California wines. Blending creative flair with fresh ingredients, the Continental Divide promises you a country gourmet experience that you'll remember.

Fairmont
See **Fairmont Hot Springs Resort** under *To Do—Hot Springs.*

Helena
Carriage House Bistro (406-449-6949), 234 Lyndale Avenue. You should probably make reservations to dine at this elegant, converted carriage house, now a fine dining restaurant with a small, European-style bistro menu. Selections include beef and chicken entrées, as well as lamb and pasta. Homemade, acclaimed desserts include tiramisu and ice cream, so be sure to leave some room for an after-dinner treat.

& **On Broadway** (406-443-1929; www.onbroadwayhelena.com), 106 Broadway. Located in the historic 1890 Parchen Building, once home to Parchen Drug Store and Hotel, this fine dining establishment has been serving up high-class fare for 25 years. Though the menu at one time was exclusively Italian, today the restaurant features a fusion of Italian and American cuisines. Thus you'll find eggplant parmesan and ground sirloin cannelloni offered alongside oven-roasted salmon and New York beefsteak. Vegetarians will enjoy having a weekly special prepared exactly with them in mind, as well as several suitable selections on the main menu as well.

♿ **River Grille** (406-442-1075; www.rivergrille.com), 1225 Custer Avenue. Wondering what exactly a "Montana-Euro bistro" is? The River Grille provides the answer to this question, inviting you to sit down and enjoy a comfortable and delectable upscale meal, complemented by an enormous beverage selection, including a huge collection of single-malt scotches, more than 50 martinis, and a number of microbrews and wines as well. The dinner menu features aged beef, chicken, pasta, and seafood selections, rounded out by creative daily specials, including a daily soup concoction. The garlic mushrooms are a favorite.

See also **Wagon Ride Dinners at the Moose Meadow Tipi** under *To Do—Unique Adventures.*

Jackson

See **Jackson Hot Springs Lodge** under *To Do—Hot Springs.*

EATING OUT

Anaconda

♿ **Rose's Tea Room and Parlor** (406-563-5060), 303 E. Park Avenue. Sit down for a light breakfast, snack, or lunch at this Victorian tearoom in the heart of Anaconda. Scottish scones are a house specialty, as are delicious homemade desserts. Homemade soups are also served. You can accompany your meal with a tea from the selection available or simply have a cup of tea to warm yourself up sans food. Take a moment to browse through the antiques and collectibles as well.

See also **Georgetown Lake Lodge** under *Lodging—Lodges.*

Butte

Gamer's Café (406-723-5453; www.butteamerica.com/gamer.htm), 15 W. Park Street. For down-home, reasonably priced breakfast and lunch fare, visit this café, located in historic uptown Butte. The extensive menu includes breakfast items served all day, such as 10 different omelets, homemade cinnamon rolls, pancakes, and combo plates. Lunch selections include an array of burgers, hot and cold sandwiches, chicken sandwiches, homemade soups, salads, and desserts.

Pork Chop John's (406-782-0812; 406-782-1783; www.porkchopjohns.com), 8 W. Mercury and 2400 Harrison Avenue. This local favorite has been serving up lean pork sirloin sandwiches since 1924. Originally, the sandwiches were sold from the back of founder John Burklund's wagon, with the first store opening in 1932. Take a bite of history by stepping inside one of the two locations in Butte and treating yourself to a sandwich. If you like what you taste, you'll be happy to know that even when you leave Montana, you can order pork chops delivered to your door, wherever you happen to live.

See also **Uptown Café** under *Dining Out.*

Fairmont

See **Fairmont Hot Springs Resort** under *To Do—Hot Springs.*

Helena

✦ & **Montana City Grill and Saloon**
(406-449-8890; www.montanacity
grill.com), 5 miles south of Helena at
the Montana City exit (187). This
family-friendly restaurant has one of
those extensive menus that will keep
you busy for a while as you attempt to
make up your mind about what you
want to eat. An array of entrée selections includes huckleberry barbecued
ribs and chicken; a huge assortment of
salads, steaks, seafood, and pasta items;
sandwiches and burgers; and even vegetarian entrées. This restaurant also
features a unique Just Your Size menu,
allowing you to select one of the main
menu choices in a smaller size—with a
smaller price tag, too. Dessert selections include Montana-made ice cream
and a chocolate cake iced with huckleberry cream cheese frosting. A children's menu is available.

& **Staggering Ox** (406-443-1729;
www.staggeringox.com), 400 Euclid
(in the Lundy Center). Though the
Staggering Ox now has locations in
Spokane, Washington, and in Missoula, this is where it all began. Here
you can order a sandwich made with
the shop's trademarked Clubfoot
Bun—a cool, tubular bun of bread
that your sandwich filling comes neatly stuffed into. You can choose from
tame, normal fare like ham and
cheese or turkey and cheese or select
one of the shop's more outrageous
combos that feature multiple meats,
cheese, veggies—often bearing outrageous, politically charged names as
well. Vegetarians can choose from
more than the standard (read: boring)
"veggie sandwich," with five creative
vegetarian sandwiches on the menu.
If you're not into sandwiches, the
menu also includes potato dishes, rice

dishes, soups, and salads.

Sweetgrass Bakery (406-443-1103),
322 Fuller Avenue. You'll sink your
teeth into a fine taste of Montana's
agricultural bounty when you sample
the breads baked here. The Montana
wheat flour is ground on-site, ensuring that you're experiencing the freshest baked goods possible. In addition
to bread, you can also nosh on a
whole wheat cinnamon roll, a danish,
or another sweet treat, should you
prefer a more sugary pick-me-up.

Toi's Thai (406-443-6656), 423 N.
Last Chance Gulch Street. Feeling
like Asian food? For a change from
Chinese, try this reasonably priced
restaurant. For two decades, the
owner-chef of this restaurant has daz-
zled and delighted Helena's residents
and visitors with an exotic and delicious selection of Thai foods, including classics such as pad Thai and
chicken satay—and, of course, curries. If you like it spicy—or spicier
than most Americans do, that is—just
ask, and your request will be gladly
obliged. Otherwise, you can rest
assured that your entrée's heat will
remain at a tastefully toned-down
level suitable for most palates while
retaining its overall authenticity.

Lincoln

See **Historic Hotel Lincoln** under
Lodging—Other Options.

Philipsburg

✦ & **The Sweet Palace** (1-888-793-
3896; 406-859-3353; www.sweet
palace.com), 109 E. Broadway. Open
year-round; closed on Saturday. This
restored 1890 building just might
house the largest candy store you've
ever seen. Okay, so it's not a true
restaurant, but you and the kids may
find yourselves making a meal of your

stop here anyway. For half a century, the palace has been churning out sweets of all shapes and sizes, guaranteed to delight the dessert lover in anyone. More than 750 varieties of homemade confections include 72 flavors of saltwater taffy, more than 30 varieties of fudge, Moose Drool truffles (don't ask, just try), and plenty of sugar-free selections should you be so inclined.

Red Rocks Lake NWR

See **Elk Lake Resort** under *Lodging—Lodges.*

Townsend

& ✍ **Broadwater Creamery Company** (406-266-5254), 108 N. Front Street (US 287). You've probably guessed from the name that one of the specialties at this tried-and-true favorite is ice cream—and you're right. You'll choose from 24 flavors, whether you're rounding out the delicious, American-style meal that you've eaten at the restaurant or you're just stopping in for a double dip. Celebrating its 100-year anniversary in 2004, the Broadwater Creamery Company today carries on the tradition of excellence in both food and service that has made it a mainstay on the Montana dining scene. You won't find any alcohol or gaming here but, rather, delicious American fare, including fresh Montana game and Angus beef—a great place for the whole family.

Virginia City and Nevada City

✍ & **Roadmaster Grille** (406-843-5234; www.roadmastergrille.com), 124 W. Wallace Street. Though it's not exactly the sort of historical experience you might expect from a restaurant in this former territorial capital, once a gold-mining mecca, the Roadmaster Grille provides a history lesson

from a slightly later era. Inside what was once an automobile service garage back in the 1930s, you'll find vintage automobiles as the theme. In addition to the 1950 Buick Roadmaster on display, there's a self-serve salad bar nestled in the back of a 1948 Chevrolet Thriftmaster pickup truck. And you can even sit in one of four booths, if they're not taken, made up of the front and back ends of two cars—a 1957 Chevrolet and a 1949 Cadillac. Oh yeah, and about the food . . . barbecue and rotisserie chicken are among the house specialties, and a children's menu is available.

Star Bakery Restaurant (406-843-5525), 1585 US 287. Located 1.25 miles west of Virginia City. This historic eatery brings you into intimate contact with a longtime Montana tradition. Back in the 1860s, the Star Bakery began serving miners fresh loaves of bread, beer, and vittles. In recent times, the state of Montana assumed ownership of the restaurant, leasing it to the folks who currently run it. Now diners can enjoy filling breakfasts, lunches, and dinners in this historic setting, while also taking a tour back in time. In addition to baked goods, the restaurant is known for its fine barbecue as well as its reasonable prices. Adjacent to the restaurant you'll find a display featuring olden-days candy jars and a vintage 1900 soda fountain.

Wise River

See **Sundance Lodge** under *Lodging—Lodges.*

✳ Special Events

February: **Montana Race to the Sky** (www.race2sky.com), Helena and Lincoln: annual 350-mile sled dog race from Helena to Seeley Lake.

Chocolate Festival, Anaconda: local stores are required to give away chocolates to all customers or face a fine from the constable; held in conjunction with the **Antique Quilt Exhibit and Bake Sale.**

February and March: **Winternational Sports Festival,** Butte: annual 8-week competition for athletes of all levels in sports ranging from classic winter pursuits (such as downhill skiing) to tennis, weight lifting, and more.

April: **Annual Helena Railroad Fair,** Helena: gathering of train aficionados features an incredible array of railroad-related items available for purchase, including toy trains and railroad memorabilia. **Madison River Music Festival** (www.madisonriver musicfestival.com), Ennis: 2-day musical extravaganza features a different theme each year.

June: **Gold Rush Fever Days,** Virginia City: celebration of the area's mining past includes a parade, gold panning, and more. ✍ **Governor's Cup Road Race,** Helena: premier road racing event in Helena caters to both serious runners and families, with races from 5K to full marathon, as well as music, food, and more. **Montana Mule Days,** Drummond: donkey and mule show features events pitting animals against one another in a variety of skills, as well as a parade and more.

✍ *July:* **Last Chance Stampede and Fair,** Helena: traditional cowboy rodeo includes kiddie parade, food vendors, exhibits, children's and family events, and more.

August: **Anaconda Crazy Day,** Anaconda: annual day of "craziness"

includes a tour of historic bars, watermelon eating contest, food vendors, classic car show, live music, and more. **Heritage Days and Victorian Ball,** Virginia City: celebration of historic gold-mining town's thriving past includes instructional classes on the era and a costume ball. **Beaverhead County Lewis and Clark Festival,** Dillon: weeklong festival commemorating the journey of the Corps of Discovery expedition includes historical reenactments, food, crafts, educational tours, music, and more.

September: **Beaverhead County Fair,** Dillon: annual Labor Day event includes a PRCA rodeo, art festival, parade, pancake breakfast, and more. **Ennis on the Madison Fly Fishing Festival:** weeklong celebration of the area's blue-ribbon fly-fishing. **Mining Heritage Day,** Butte: annual celebration and commemoration of Butte's historical and current ties to the mineral extraction industry. **North American Indian Alliance Pow Wow,** Butte: annual powwow featuring Native American dancing, foods, and a cultural celebration.

✍ *December:* **Victorian Christmas at Grant–Kohrs Ranch,** Deer Lodge: family-oriented holiday festivity includes children's activities, music, and decorations.

See also **Bannack State Park** under *To See—Historic Landmarks, Places, and Sites.*

SOUTH-CENTRAL MONTANA: YELLOWSTONE COUNTRY

Encompassing the land just north and west of Yellowstone National Park—and a bit of the land in the park, too—Montana's smallest travel region packs the punch of a heavyweight in the area of outdoor recreation. No matter what type of recreation you prefer, what season you visit, what age you are, or what ability level you possess, Yellowstone Country has an outdoorsy adventure in store for you. From the gentler pursuits of bird-watching and picnicking to experts-only territory like paddling class V-plus white water or ascending Montana's highest mountain—12,799-foot Granite Peak—you'll find plenty of opportunities to pursue your passions (or pick up new ones) here. Don't think it's all about warm weather, either—a visit to this region in the snowy season brings with it just as many outdoor activity options as does a summer trip—perhaps even more. And parents will be thrilled to find an abundance of tyke-to-teen-friendly activities both indoors and outside for the entire family to enjoy together.

Just how large an outdoor playground are we talking about? Consider this: the region's Gallatin National Forest contains 1.8 million acres of land within its boundaries, including two wilderness areas—the Absaroka–Beartooth and the Lee Metcalf—and six mountain ranges. Add to this the Beartooth Ranger District of Custer National Forest, as well as acres and acres of Bureau of Land Management (BLM) and state-held lands . . . not to mention six major rivers, countless streams and lakes, and three downhill ski resorts, just to mention a few items of note. Oh, and did I mention trails yet? Hundreds of trails crisscross this region, and not just the hiking type (though you'd be hard-pressed to hike all of them in your lifetime). You'll strike into a richly varied, veritable bonanza of paths to explore, no matter what type of trail user you are, with ample opportunities for mountain bikers, horseback riders, Nordic skiers, snowmobilers, and snowshoers. This variety made it difficult to select just a few trails or areas for inclusion in this guide, but what you'll find listed below should get you off to a great start.

I should tell you right now, too, that some of the outdoor activities highlighted in this section will almost certainly prove a little (or even a lot) more challenging

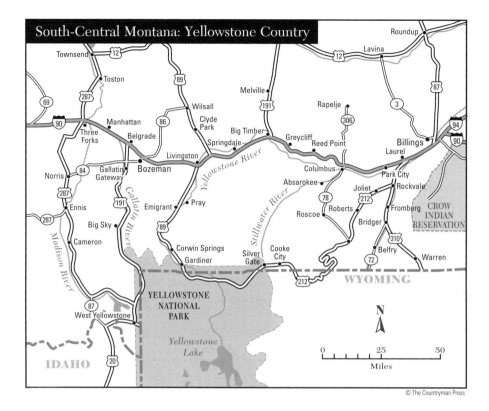

than those you'll find selected for other travel regions in this book. Their inclusion is essential to doing justice to this region's recreational offerings. Nonetheless, I've made an effort to include moderate, everyone-friendly endeavors alongside the more serious physical challenges. For the most part, I've left the truly exclusive, expert-level endeavors to the more activity-specific guidebooks—with a few notable exceptions for those features that just could not be passed by without a mention. These include both Granite Peak and the amazing white water of the ironically named Stillwater River.

Hiring a professional, qualified guide makes such adventuresome pursuits still a viable option for the relatively fit, if inexperienced, traveler. To help you out in pursuing that type of excursion, for some activities I've selected guiding services that can take you where you want to go in relative safety. Please note that these are usually not the only guide services available for that particular adventure, as there are numerous additional qualified services often competing for your business. In fact, this region is filled with professional outfitters, adventure guides, guest ranches, and working ranches that possess a staggering array of areas of expertise, including fly-fishing, horseback riding, white-water paddling, rock climbing, ice climbing, hiking, backpacking, cattle drives, Nordic skiing, snowshoeing, and more.

Don't think your vacation to Yellowstone Country needs to be a constant whirlwind of activity, though. You'll also find plenty of places and spaces to relax. Soak tired bodies at hot springs in Bozeman and Chico, both of which offer spa services, including professional massages. You can sign up the family for a dogsled adventure or a dinner hay-, sleigh-, or snowcat ride. Settle into the car for a scenic drive through the mountains on the Beartooth Scenic Byway, or travel to the remote Hailstone National Wildlife Refuge and Halfbreed Lake National Wildlife Refuge to watch wildlife and enjoy a picnic lunch. Learn how to cast for free at the one-of-a-kind Federation of Fly Fishers' Fly Fishing Discovery Center. Take the kids to a film at the Yellowstone IMAX Theatre or wow them—and yourself—with a visit to the Grizzly & Wolf Discovery Center, where you'll see these long-maligned animals in action up close, while learning about the roles they play both in the natural world and in human contexts, both current and historical.

Speaking of history, this region today continues to be influenced by its legacy of both Indian and pioneer settlement, which you can learn more about at a number of historical museums, places, landmarks, and sites throughout the area. Lewis and Clark's Corps of Discovery came across Three Forks during their travels—the place where they named the Gallatin, the Jefferson, and the Madison rivers, which combine to form the Missouri River. Today you can walk in their footsteps at Missouri Headwaters State Park and then stop by the Headwaters Heritage Museum to increase your knowledge of the area. At the Crazy Mountain Museum you'll find fascinating facts about Sweet Grass County's ties to Norway. In Bozeman, you can explore history stretching back to the very formation of the earth at the enormous Museum of the Rockies, while opportunities to narrow your focus to a more local scope await you at the Gallatin Pioneer Museum or with a tour through historic downtown Bozeman. For a fascinating glimpse at long-past Indian lives, stop at Madison Buffalo Jump State Park to learn about a traditional and very efficient hunting method once used to obtain buffalo.

Perhaps you'll catch sight of a herd of buffalo possibly descended from those same herds that the Indians hunted long ago as you journey southward into Yellowstone National Park (see "Wyoming's Yellowstone and Grand Teton National Parks" for travel guidance)—or maybe you'll become so caught up the abundance of vacationing fun to be had in this region that you'll have to save the park for your next visit. Montana's Yellowstone Country is chockfull of outdoor

MOUNTAINS JUST SOUTH OF RED LODGE IN CUSTER NATIONAL FOREST

adventures for all ages, so all you have to do is decide which ones are right for you, and then lace your shoes, strap on some skis, cinch down your saddle, put your feet to the pedals, pick up the paddle, tie on the fly, or sink in for a soak . . . whatever type of recreational vacation you're looking for, you'll almost certainly find it here.

GUIDANCE Belgrade Chamber of Commerce (406-388-1616; www.belgrade chamber.org), 10 E. Main Street, Belgrade 59714.

Big Sky Chamber of Commerce (1-800-943-4111; 406-995-3000; www.big skychamber.com), P.O. Box 160100, Big Sky 59716. The office is on Pine Drive in the Westfork Meadows complex (next to Big Sky Western Bank; watch for blue Visitor's Information sign).

Big Timber (Sweet Grass County) Chamber of Commerce (406-932-5131; www.bigtimber.com), P.O. Box 1012, Big Timber 59011. Located near Exit 367 off I-90.

Bozeman Chamber of Commerce (1-800-228-4224; 406-586-5421; www .bozemanchamber.com), 2000 Commerce Way, Bozeman 59715.

Bridger Chamber of Commerce (406-662-3651; 406-662-3388 www.valley printers.com/bridger.html), P.O. Box 99, Bridger 59014.

Cooke City Chamber of Commerce (406-838-2495; www.cookecitychamber .com), P.O. Box 1071, Cooke City 59020. The visitor center is located on the south side of US 212, on the east side of Cooke City.

Gardiner Chamber of Commerce (406-848-7971; www.gardinerchamber .com), 222 Park Street, P.O. Box 81, Gardiner 59030.

Greater Stillwater County Chamber of Commerce (406-322-4505; www .stillwater-chamber.org), P.O. Box 783, Columbus 59019. The office is situated just off I-90 at the Columbus exit.

Livingston Area Chamber of Commerce (406-222-0850; www.livingston-chamber.com), 303 E. Park Street, Livingston 59047.

Manhattan Area Chamber of Commerce (406-284-4162; www.manhattan montana.com), P.O. Box 606, Manhattan 59741.

Red Lodge Chamber of Commerce (406-446-1718; 406-446-1720; 1-888-281-0625; www.redlodge.com), 601 N. Broadway, P.O. Box 988, Red Lodge 59068.

Three Forks Chamber of Commerce (406-285-4753; www.threeforks montana.com), P.O. Box 1103, Three Forks 59752. The visitor center is housed in an old Milwaukee Railroad caboose at the south end of Milwaukee Railroad Park, which you'll see as you come off I-90 (Exit 278) and enter town.

West Yellowstone Chamber of Commerce (406-646-7701; www.westyellow stonechamber.com), 30 Yellowstone Avenue, P.O. Box 458, West Yellowstone 59758.

Yellowstone Country (1-800-736-5276; 406-556-8680; http://yellowstone .visitmt.com), 1822 W. Lincoln, Bozeman 59715.

GETTING THERE From west to east, Three Forks, Manhattan, Belgrade, Bozeman, Livingston, Big Timber, Columbus, and Park City lie along I-90 in south-central Montana. Gallatin Gateway, Big Sky, and West Yellowstone are accessible via US 191. West Yellowstone can also be reached via US 287 (and US 20). Gardiner lies on US 89 near the Wyoming border. Cooke City and Red Lodge can be reached via US 212. Bridger lies on US 310.

See also *Airports, Amtrak, Bus Service,* and *Travel Information* in "What's Where in Montana."

MEDICAL EMERGENCY **Beartooth Hospital and Health Center** (406-446-2345), 600 W. 20th Street, Red Lodge.

Bozeman Deaconess Hospital (406-585-5000), 915 Highland Boulevard, Bozeman.

Clinic at West Yellowstone (1-800-483-4762; 406-646-7668; 208-535-4691), 236 Yellowstone Avenue, West Yellowstone.

Livingston Memorial Hospital (406-222-3541), 504 S. 13th Street, Livingston.

Pioneer Medical Center (406-932-4603), 301 W. 7th Avenue N., Big Timber.

Stillwater Community Hospital (406-322-5316), 44 W. 4th Avenue N., Columbus.

✳ To See

TOWNS **Big Sky,** fewer than 50 miles from Yellowstone National Park via US 191, offers vacationers the opportunity for an incredible amount of year-round recreational opportunities, from skiing and snowmobiling to fishing, mountain biking, and hiking, in a postcard-perfect mountain setting. This small town (fewer than 1,300 inhabitants) is home to a full-service ski resort, some 25 eating establishments, and numerous shops.

Cooke City and **Silver Gate** are on US 212 near the border of Yellowstone National Park. Cooke City was born in the 1870s as a mining town, and it retains its pastoral flavor today while providing access to abundant recreational opportunities, including **Grasshopper Glacier** (see *Natural Wonders*). Farther west on US 212, alpine Silver Gate enjoys the distinction of being possibly the only U.S. town in which every single structure is made from logs or other native materials—in fact, it's a requirement for building there.

Gardiner lies on US 89 at the border of Yellowstone National Park, providing the only all-season drive-in entrance to the park. The original 1903 stone arch, dedicated by President Theodore Roosevelt and known as **Roosevelt Arch,** marks this entrance (see *To See—Historic Landmarks, Places, and Sites* in "Yellowstone National Park" in "Wyoming's Yellowstone and Grand Teton National Parks"). The town itself provides numerous services for travelers, from camping and accommodations to plenty of dining options. The **Yellowstone River** runs right through the center of Gardiner, making this a popular place for both anglers and paddlers.

Livingston lies west of Bozeman just off I-90. The original entrance town for Yellowstone National Park, historic Livingston is situated on the banks of the

Yellowstone River and is surrounded by four mountain ranges that provide seemingly endless recreational opportunities for every season. You'll also find no lack of cultural attractions, from museums and art galleries to live performances at four playhouses, and plenty of historic buildings.

Red Lodge, a historic mining town nestled on US 212 in the shadow of the stunning Absaroka–Beartooth Wilderness, possesses unbelievable recreational opportunities, including skiing, hiking, white-water rafting, golf, horseback riding, mountain biking, fishing, and more, in a breathtakingly beautiful setting, both in and around town. Plenty of shopping and dining options await your discovery in the charming, historic downtown area (walking tour maps are available from the chamber of commerce; see *Guidance*).

West Yellowstone, reached via US 191, US 287, or US 20, lies on the western border of Yellowstone National Park. This town serves not only as an entrance portal to the park but also as a destination in its own right, with numerous dining establishments, all-season recreation, lodgings, and shopping opportunities. Among its many attractions is the **Grizzly & Wolf Discovery Center** (see *For Families*).

See also **Historic Downtown Bozeman** under *Historic Landmarks, Places, and Sites.*

MUSEUMS & **American Computer Museum** (406-587-7545; www.compustory .com), 2304 N. 7th Avenue, Suite B, Bozeman. Open daily June through August, 10 AM–4 PM, until 8 PM on Thursday; open September through May Tuesday, Wednesday, Friday, and Saturday noon–4 PM, Thursday 4 PM–8 PM; closed Fourth of July, Christmas, and New Year's Day; $4 adults, $2 children ages 6–12, children 5 and under free. No longer the bastion of nerds and math whizzes, computers today play a vital role in nearly all that we do, from communication and banking to entertainment and medicine. This museum takes you all the way back to the origins of the information age some 20,000 years ago and then walks you through humanity's progression toward our current dependence on information technology—with a distinctive Montanan twist.

Carbon County Historical Society & Museum (406-446-3667), 224 N. Broadway, Red Lodge. Open Memorial Day through Labor Day Monday through Friday 10 AM–5 PM, Saturday 1 PM–5 PM; in winter, open Tuesday through Friday 10 AM–5 PM, Saturday 1 PM–5 PM; $3 adults, $2 children ages 6–17, children 5 and under free. The museum is located within the renovated 1909 three-story Labor Temple building, the first of its kind in Montana. Inside these historic surroundings you'll find exhibits detailing the origins of Red Lodge, with a particular focus on the impact that coal mining had on this area. Also on display are an extensive gun collection and the Greenough rodeo collection, as well as numerous other artifacts and memorabilia depicting Red Lodge's history, from Native American and pioneer artifacts to items related to geology and natural history.

& **Crazy Mountain Museum** (406-932-5126; www.bigtimber.com/html/local_ attractions.html#museum), south of I-90 via Exit 367 (next to the cemetery), Big Timber. Open Memorial Day through Labor Day Tuesday through Sunday

1 PM–4:30 PM; free. From the Norwegian heritage of the Sweet Grass area to its natural history, this museum covers many interesting aspects about its surroundings. Stroll through the Lewis and Clark Native Plant Garden, complete with interpretive signs about the expedition, which traveled through this area in 1806. Learn too about local ranching, rodeos, and pioneers.

& **Federation of Fly Fishers' Fly Fishing Discovery Center** (406-222-9369; www.livingstonmuseums.org/fish), 215 E. Lewis Street, Livingston. Open June through September Monday through Saturday 10 AM–6 PM, Sunday noon–5 PM; open October through May Monday through Friday 10 AM–4 PM; $3 adults, $1 children ages 7–14, children 6 and under free. No angler visiting this region should bypass a visit to this unique attraction. Under one roof, you'll find not only a complete, one-of-a-kind fly-fishing museum, including a historical account of fly-fishing's origins and development, but also educational displays about current conservation issues, living fish displays, angler-related artwork, educational programs, and a fly-fishing research library. New in 2004–2005 is the Fish of Lewis and Clark Exhibit, profiling the role that Montana's fish and rivers played in the historic expedition. Free fly-casting lessons (equipment provided) open to the public are held every Tuesday and Thursday June 1 through September 1 5 PM–7 PM.

& **Gallatin Historical Society Pioneer Museum** (406-522-8122; www.pioneer museum.org), 317 W. Main Street, Bozeman. Open May 15 through September 15 Monday through Saturday 10 AM–4:30 PM; open September 16 through May 14 Tuesday through Friday 11 AM–4 PM, Saturday 1 PM–4 PM; free. Inside the museum—an attractive, castellated, two-story brick building that used to function as the local jail—you can walk into an authentic 1870s log cabin for a real sense of what life was like in these parts back in pioneer days. Numerous additional exhibits detail local and regional history, from individuals of note (namely John Bozeman) to significant groups such as Native Americans, pioneers, ranchers, and the military. (See also **Historic Downtown Bozeman** under *Historic Landmarks, Places, and Sites.*)

GALLATIN HISTORICAL SOCIETY PIONEER MUSEUM

& **Headwaters Heritage Museum** (406-285-4778; 406-285-3644), corner of Cedar Street and Main Street, Three Forks. Open June through September Monday through Saturday 9 AM–5 PM, Sunday 1 PM–5 PM; open by appointment in May and October; free. Housed in a historic 1910 bank building, this two-story museum is filled with an amazing assortment of artifacts that together tell the tale of this area's history. Of particular note is an anvil used at the original 1810 trading post established at the Missouri Headwaters by the Missouri Fur Company. Anglers will be wowed at the largest brown trout—a 29.5-pound monster—ever pulled from the waters of Montana. The museum's second story invites you to meander through a reconstructed series of stores and buildings depicting what Three Forks might have looked like 100 years ago. Outside, you can enjoy a picnic behind the museum beside an 1860s cottonwood log cabin.

LIVINGSTON DEPOT CENTER

♿ **Livingston Depot Center** (406-222-2300; www.livingstondepot.org), 200 West Park, Livingston. Open late May through late September Monday through Saturday 9 AM–5 PM, Sunday 1 PM–5 PM; $3 adults, $2 seniors 63 and older and children ages 6–12, children 5 and under free. Built in 1902 by the Northern Pacific Railroad to serve as its station in Livingston, this majestic building has been restored and renovated, finding new life as a museum and cultural center. Changing seasonally, exhibits focus mainly on western and railroad history, while cultural attractions include performing arts, community events, and historical lectures, among varying venues. (See also **Livingston Depot Center Festival of the Arts** under *Special Events*.)

♿ **Museum of the Beartooths** (406-322-4588), 440 E. 5th Avenue N., Columbus. Open May through September Tuesday through Sunday 1 PM–5 PM; free. Learn about this area's role in Montana's history, from the early pioneer and Indian days to the present. Of particular interest is the mining history of this area, which led to the establishment of the sole platinum-palladium mine in America, run by the Stillwater Mining Company. You can also tour a 1960s red caboose donated by Burlington Northern–Santa Fe Railroad Company.

♿ ☎ **Museum of the Rockies** (406-994-2251; www.museumoftherockies.org), 600 W. Kagy Boulevard, Montana State University, Bozeman. Open daily June through Labor Day 8 AM–8 PM; open after Labor Day weekend through end of May Monday through Saturday 9 AM–5 PM, Sunday 12:30 PM–5 PM; $9.50 adults, $8.50 seniors 65 and older, $6.50 children ages 5–18, children 4 and under free. Your journey through this educational wonderland begins 4.6 billion years ago, as you learn about the formation of the earth. Then you travel through time up to relatively recent history, visiting a day in the life of the dinosaurs, some 80 million years in the past. Finally, you'll move even closer to today's world as you learn about Montana's Native American cultures and the state's pioneer experiences. Be sure to include the impressive **Taylor Planetarium** in your tour. Each summer brings with it a new exhibit as well as access to the museum's living-history farm. Special events happen at the museum year-round, so it's a good idea to call ahead or check the Web site for the latest happenings before you visit.

Yellowstone Gateway Museum of Park County (406-222-4184; www.living stonmuseums.org/pcm/default.cfm), 118 W. Chinook Street, Livingston. Open Tuesday through Saturday Memorial Day through Labor Day 10 AM–5 PM; open

September 11 AM to 4 PM, by appointment October through May; $4 adults, $3.50 seniors 65 and older, $2 children 6–12, children 5 and under free. Located within the lovely 1906 North Side School building (listed on the National Register of Historic Places), this museum houses an impressive collection of artifacts, exhibits, and items of note relating to regional archaeology and geology, Yellowstone National Park, Lewis and Clark's Corps of Discovery, pioneers, legendary figures from the Old West, the impact of the Northern Pacific Railroad, and local military history.

♿ **Yellowstone Historic Center Museum** (406-646-1100; www.yellowstone historiccenter.org), 104 Yellowstone Avenue, West Yellowstone. Open mid-May through mid-October 9 AM–9 PM; $6 adults, $5 seniors, $4 students, $15 per family (two adults and their children). Before you enter Yellowstone National Park—or after you've driven through it—consider stopping at this museum that details much of the park's unique and intriguing history, from the people who played key roles in its formation and management to the methods of transportation used to bring tourists to experience its natural wonders. Wildlife displays get you up close and personal with some of the park's more formidable inhabitants, from buffalo to grizzly bears. Learn about the railroad's impact on Yellowstone's visitation in an impressive railroad display—in fact, the museum itself is located in the historic Union Pacific depot. Gain insight into the 1988 fires through an intriguing exhibit, which helps explain the role that forest fires play in replenishing and renewing the natural world.

HISTORIC LANDMARKS, PLACES, AND SITES **Historic Crail Ranch** (406-995-2160), Spotted Elk Road (2 miles west of US 191 on MT 64, then right on Little Coyote to Spotted Elk Road), Big Sky. Open weekends July through August noon–3 PM. This historic collection of buildings, listed on the National Register of Historic Places, offers you a glimpse into the typical living quarters of those involved in ranching this land a century ago. Constructed from logs in the early 20th century, this was Big Sky's first homestead. Today, it has been restored and furnished with period-appropriate pieces. The **Crail Ranch Trail** allows you the opportunity to stroll or bike for a bit more than a mile on mostly even terrain, taking you past the historic site and along a small creek.

🐾 **Historic Downtown Bozeman** (406-522-8122; www.pioneermuseum.org), 317 W. Main Street (Gallatin Historical Society Pioneer Museum), Bozeman. Guided tours take place June through September Monday through Wednesday at 11 AM and 6 PM; free. Take a 90-minute walking tour along Main Street in Bozeman, starting at the Pioneer Museum—itself a building listed on the National Register of Historic Places (see *Museums*). Some 700 structures in the central part of the city are listed on the register as well, and your guide will take you to the ones that you shouldn't miss and fill you in on their significance. The street itself is part of the original Bozeman Trail. Also available are guided tours (free) through Bozeman's historic neighborhoods and through Sunset Hills Cemetery. Call ahead to confirm that tours are taking place.

Madison Buffalo Jump State Park (406-994-4042; www.fwp.state.mt.us/parks/parksreport.asp?mapnum=21), 23 miles west of Bozeman on I-90 to Exit

283, and then 7 miles south on Buffalo Jump Road (gravel but suitable for passenger cars). Open year-round for day-use only; free for residents, $5 per vehicle for nonresidents. Visit the location historically used by tribes of Indians to hunt buffalo in an efficient and intriguing fashion. In this area, skilled hunters would chase the buffalo on foot to the cliff's edge—and the buffalo would stampede off it, dying en masse, and thereby providing the Indians with the necessary quantity of buffalo they needed for food, shelter, and clothing. This practice lasted for some 2,000 years, until the introduction of horses, which allowed the Indians in the 1700s to abandon this method of hunting in favor of pursuit by horse and rider. Interpretive signs provide details about the use of these towering limestone cliffs, and short trails allow you to view different aspects of this historic site.

Oregon Shortline 1903 Executive Railroad Car (1-800-646-7365; 406-646-7365; www.doyellowstone.com), 315 Yellowstone Avenue (inside the West Yellowstone Holiday Inn Sunspree Resort), West Yellowstone. Open daily 8 AM–10 PM; free. This elegant railroad car has been fully restored to its original splendor. Step inside and you'll see just how much comfort and luxury rail travelers enjoyed on their journeys to Yellowstone on the Oregon Short Line in the early 20th century. (See also **Oregon Short Line Restaurant** under *Dining Out.*)

Parker Homestead State Park (406-287-3541; www.fwp.state.mt.us/parks/parksreport.asp?mapnum=23), 8 miles west of Three Forks on US 287 (passenger cars only). Open year-round for day-use only; free. History buffs and solitude seekers alike will enjoy visiting Montana's smallest state park. At this 1-acre parcel of land, you'll find a pioneer family's sod-roofed cabin from the early 20th century. While you savor the surroundings or enjoy a picnic lunch, envision just how tough these frontier folks must have been to eke out a living. There are no services at this primitive park.

See also Cooke City and Silver Gate, Gardiner, Livingston, and Red Lodge under *Towns;* Gallatin Historical Society Pioneer Museum, Headwaters Heritage Museum, Livingston Depot Center, Museum of the Yellowstone, Peaks to Plains Museum, and Yellowstone Gateway Museum of Park County under *Museums;* Raynolds Pass under *Scenic Drives;* Meeteetse Trail under *To Do—Bicycling;* Missouri Headwaters State Park under *Wilder Places—Parks;* Lehrkind Mansion Bed and Breakfast, Voss Inn, Weatherson Inn, and Yellowstone Suites Bed and Breakfast under *Lodging—Bed & Breakfasts;* Pollard Hotel and Sacajawea Hotel under *Lodging—Other Options;* the Grand

HISTORIC DOWNTOWN BOZEMAN

Hotel Restaurant under *Dining Out;* and Round Barn Restaurant and Theater under *Eating Out.*

FOR FAMILIES ✿ **Big Timber Waterslide** (1-800-455-1799; 406-932-6570; www.bigtimberwaterslide.com); Exit 377 off I-90, 9 miles east of Big Timber (1 mile west of Greycliff). Open June through Labor Day 10 AM–7 PM; $14.95 adults, $11.95 students 18 and older with ID, $11.95 children ages 3–17, children 2 and under free; $3 per spectator; half-day rates available as well. From tiny tykes to grownups, all will find that the fun comes in waves at Montana's first water park. Children under 4 feet tall can wade and play in the Tadpole Pool and slide down appropriately sized slides like the Munchkin and Frog, while older kids (and parents, too!) will no doubt delight in the bigger, wilder slides such as the Zipper, Typhoon, Hurricane, and Suicide.

✿ **Children's Museum of Bozeman** (406-522-9087; www.cmbozeman.org), 234 E. Babcock Street, Bozeman. Open Monday through Thursday 10 AM–5 PM, Friday 10 AM–8 PM, Saturday 10 AM–5 PM, Sunday noon–5 PM; $3 per person, children under 1 free (all children must be accompanied by an adult). This museum invites children and adults to engage all of their senses in an array of exhibits on a number of subjects, from pioneers and Lewis and Clark to modern-day college basketball players. You and your kids can be as loud as you want and touch whatever you want as you explore the museum, having fun learning together in a setting that encourages a hands-on, interactive educational experience. The museum hosts special seasonal events throughout the year.

✿ ♿ **Grizzly & Wolf Discovery Center** (1-800-257-2570; 406-646-7001; www .grizzlydiscoveryctr.org), 201 S. Canyon, West Yellowstone. Open daily 8:30 AM– dusk; $9.75 adults, $9 seniors ages 62 and older, $5 children 5 and older, children 4 and under free (good for 2 consecutive days). Children and adults alike are bound to be enthralled at their proximity to gray wolves and enormous grizzly bears, particularly if the bears are engaging in a playful scuffle with one another. That's not all that this not-for-profit, American Zoo and Aquarium Association–accredited center offers, though. You'll also gain a tremendous amount of knowledge and understanding about two of the historically most maligned and misrepresented predators in the United States. Even today, grizzlies and wolves often are surrounded by a frenzy of controversy and loathing. Through impressive and informative exhibits, including Bears: Imagination and Reality, you can broaden your comprehension about how vital these two species are to the ecosystems that they naturally inhabit. Kids ages 5–12 can sign up to participate in the Keeper Kids program, helping staff hide food for the bears in the bears' habitat.

✿ ♿ **Rare Earth Unlimited, Inc.** (406-646-9337; www.wyellowstone.com/ rareearth), 111 W. Yellowstone Avenue, West Yellowstone. Open May through October 9 AM–10 PM; open December through March 10 AM–6 PM. Inside this unusual gift and rock shop, the Yellowstone Mining Company offers its customers the opportunity to mine for real Montana gems, including sapphires and garnets, as well as gold, using a bona fide operational sluice. The whole family can work together in seeking to strike it rich while sharing an educational experience as they learn about how miners utilized such equipment in the past. Your success is guaranteed, so nobody will go away empty-handed. Don't want to mine? You can still browse the store's intriguing selection of fossils, rocks, and minerals—including Montana's largest amethyst geode—along with its souvenirs and gift items.

✆ ♿ **Yellowstone IMAX Theatre** (406-646-4100; www.yellowstoneimax.com), 101 S. Canyon, West Yellowstone. Showtimes vary; $8 adults, $6 children ages 3–12, children 2 and under free. Sit back, relax, and enjoy the show. If you've never experienced an IMAX theater before—or even if you have—you will likely be impressed by the enormous six-story screen and the incredible surround sound that makes the movie seem almost real. Choose from several different IMAX feature films (call ahead for current films and showtimes).

See also Museum of the Rockies under *Museums;* Big Sky Stables, Paintbrush Adventures, Inc., and 320 Guest Ranch under *To Do—Horseback Riding;* Bozeman Hot Springs under *To Do—Hot Springs;* Big Sky Resort, Bridger Bowl Ski and Snowboard Resort, Moonlight Basin Ski Resort, and Red Lodge Mountain Resort under *To Do—Snow Sports;* Absaroka Dogsled Treks, Dinner Sleigh Rides by Big Sky Stables, and Moonlight Dinners under *To Do—Unique Adventures;* Beartooth Nature Center under *Wilder Places—Wildlife Refuges and Areas;* Headwaters of the Yellowstone Bed and Breakfast under *Lodging—Bed & Breakfasts;* Lone Mountain Ranch under *Lodging—Other Options;* and Big Sky Winterfest, Christmas Stroll, Red Lodge Mountain Man Rendezvous, Running of the Sheep, and Yellowstone Ski Festival under *Special Events.*

SCENIC DRIVES **Beartooth Scenic Byway,** 64 miles on US 212 from Cooke City to Red Lodge, with much of the drive in Wyoming; closed seasonally; easily accessed in Wyoming from WY 296, the Chief Joseph Scenic Byway (see *To See—Scenic Drives* in "North Wyoming: Devils Tower–Buffalo Bill Country"). This highway has been deemed "the most beautiful highway in America" by a number of sources due to the incredible scenery and unique natural features in the surrounding Gallatin National Forest, Shoshone National Forest, and Custer National Forest. Completed in 1936, this highway provides passers-through with the opportunity to witness the transformation of the terrain outside, from a green, subalpine forest to a true alpine environment, as they climb into the Beartooth Range, a mountain range with more than 20 peaks taller than 12,000 feet and numerous glaciers. Tremendous wildlife viewing prospects and recreational activities abound along this drive, including camping, fishing, hiking, picnicking, and bicycling for experienced road riders who want a high-altitude challenge.

Raynolds Pass, via MT 87 north of Yellowstone. Drive through the same gap in the Horn Mountains through which famed mountain man Jim Bridger led a troupe of scientists back in 1860. In charge of the expedition was Captain W. F. Raynolds of the U.S. Army Corps of Engineers. If you choose to venture this way from West Yellowstone (linking up to MT 87 via US 20), you will also go over **Targhee Pass** and drive through the upper reaches of Idaho briefly, passing by **Henrys Lake** before reentering Montana. Alternatively, you can make a side trip off US 287 south on MT 87 and then backtrack back to US 287 for a shorter adventure. Raynolds Pass is also the name of the fishing access point to the **Madison River,** located on the east side of MT 87, where you'll find free primitive camping.

See also **Meeteetse Trail** under *To Do—Bicycling.*

NATURAL WONDERS Devils Slide, along US 89 north of Gardiner near Corwin Springs. This unusual geologic feature really does resemble a curved slide in a children's playground—albeit a gigantic, brightly hued one. Brilliant red fades into pink and white on this 200-million-year-old natural slide—fit only for a giant's child—that wraps down an entire hillside. This lovely example of exposed geology is visible from the highway.

Granite Peak (406-446-2103; www.fs.fed.us/r1/custer/recreation/granitepeak .shtml), 45 miles south of Columbus. At 12,799 feet, Montana's tallest mountain lies on the border of Custer National Forest and Gallatin National Forest in the Beartooth Mountain Range. There are three trails to the top, and all three require sound mountaineering skills and planning, as they cover extremely rough terrain and long distances. Rock scrambling, navigating through trail-less wilderness areas, and potentially hazardous weather conditions are just some of the factors to take into consideration when contemplating a "hike" of this mountain. It is recommended that climbers attempting this feat check in with the Beartooth Ranger Station (contact information listed above), south of Red Lodge on US 212, before embarking upon their adventure. You can also consider hiring a guide to help ensure the safety of your excursion; see **Rock Climbing and Ice Climbing** under *To Do—Unique Adventures* for details.

Grasshopper Glacier (406-446-2103; www.fs.fed.us/r1/custer/recreation/grass hopper.shtml), 2 miles east of Cooke City on US 212 to Lulu Pass–Goose Lake Road (F.R. 6493), a rough road appropriate for only four-wheel-drive vehicles with high clearance and passable only in the dry season of late July and August. The road ends at the boundary of the Absaroka–Beartooth Wilderness. Visitors must hike the remaining 4 miles to the glacier via the trail that departs from the end of the road. What you'll find at the end of the hike might just amaze you, though. Millions of grasshoppers are frozen into this 1-mile-long, 0.5-mile-wide glacier situated at 11,000 feet in the Beartooth Mountains. You should check in with the Beartooth Ranger District (see contact information listed above), south of Red Lodge on US 212, for detailed directions regarding the trail conditions before embarking

RAYNOLDS PASS

QUAKE LAKE

on your adventure. This trail is also popular with cross-country skiers in winter.

♿ **Madison Canyon Earthquake Area and Visitor Center** (406-823-6961; 406-682-7620; www.fs.fed.us/r1/gallatin/?page=recreation/visitor_center), 17 miles west of US 191 on US 287 (25 miles from the town of West Yellowstone). Open Memorial Day through mid-September 8:30 AM– 6 PM; $3 per car, $1 per hiker or biker. Overlooking the serene **Quake Lake,** this interpretive center helps explain to visitors the tumultuous events of August 17, 1959. On that date, an earthquake measuring 7.5 on the Richter scale shook the area and triggered a massive landslide, forming Quake Lake in a matter of minutes. The slide moved at 100 miles per hour, and in less than a single minute, it had dumped more than 80 million tons of rock into the narrow river valley. Known as the Hebgen Lake Earthquake, this deadly event took 28 lives. Interpretive talks and videos complement exhibits about the earthquake and general geology. Quake Lake is also open to fishing for rainbow and brown trout. (See also **Hebgen Lake** under *To Do—Boating.*)

♿ **Natural Bridge Falls** (406-932-5131; www.bigtimber.com), about 30 miles south of Big Timber via MT 298. Open year-round for day-use; free. Alas, the feature that gave these falls their name fell into the Boulder River back in 1988, but if you like waterfalls, you're still in luck. From the parking area, you can follow several paved trails along the Boulder River that show you different aspects of Natural Bridge Falls. More than 100 feet tall, the falls' appearance varies with season and water flow; depending on the time of year you visit, you may actually see three waterfalls. Interpretive signs at this state monument fill you in about your surroundings, and picnic tables invite you to sit down to enjoy an outdoor meal. The 5.5-mile (one-way), moderate **Green Mountain Trail** (#94) departs from this area, so if you want to extend your adventure into a longer hike, you have that option. (See also **the Boulder River** under *To Do—Fishing.*)

See also **Gallatin Petrified Forest** under *To Do—Hiking.*

✳ To Do

BICYCLING **Bangtail Ridge Trail,** north of Bozeman on MT 86, then east on F.R. 480 (Stone Creek Road). The road is gated at the parking area, which is located within Gallatin National Forest (see *Wilder Places—Forests*). Suitable for intermediate riders who want a challenge, this awesome, 26-mile single-track trail takes you along a ridgeline with views of not less than six surrounding mountain ranges. New in 2003, this trail also includes terrain that takes you through fields of wildflowers and fun, invigorating downhill sections. The Bozeman area has many additional excellent mountain biking trails suitable for advanced and expert riders, including **Emerald Lake Trail** and **Sypes Canyon Trail.**

For more information about local rides, stop by **Stark Raven Cycles** (406-586-1201; www.starkravencycles.com), 701 E. Mendenhall, Bozeman, a full-service bike shop offering weekly rides, repair services, and more. You can rent a bike from **Chalet Sports** (406-587-4595), 108 W. Main Street, Bozeman, for $25 a day.

Big Sky (see *To See—Towns*) could very well be your Montana destination of choice if mountain biking is your passion. In addition to the Grizzly Loop (see listing below), you can choose from numerous fire roads and single-track trails available at the **Big Sky Ski Resort** (see under *Snow Sports*), as well as a plethora of trails in the surrounding area. Your one-stop shop for all of your cycling (and outdoor activity) needs in the Big Sky area is **Grizzly Outfitters** (1-888-847-9452; 406-995-2939; www.grizzlyoutfitters.com), 145 Center Lane, Unit H, Big Sky, where you can have your own bike tuned up, rent a mountain bike for $25 a day, and get more information about local rides.

Grizzly Loop. Park at Best Western Buck's T-4 Lodge (1-800-822-4484; 406-995-4111; www.buckst4.com), US 191, Big Sky. Beginner to intermediate riders can enjoy riding at least part of this popular trail, which departs across from the parking area at Buck's. Pass through a fence and take an immediate right to pick up the moderate, single-track trail. After paralleling the Gallatin River for 2 miles, you will cross over it. Half a mile later, you will reach a parking area that marks an alternative start for a shorter, 5.5-mile loop ride (and a good place for beginners to turn around for a relatively easy 4-mile out-and-back ride). From here, the ride stays moderate for almost another mile before the advanced, strenuous portion of the trail (and the loop) begins.

Meeteetse Trail, 0.75 mile south of Red Lodge on US 212, then head east across Rock Creek onto the gravel road. You can follow this historic four-wheel-drive road for up to 19 miles if you wish, where it links up with MT 72 (and you can continue south into Wyoming via MT 72 to WY 120 for an even longer outing). Created in 1881, this road initially saw use as a supply road for the U.S. Army, becoming the first road to carry mail, goods, and settlers to this area. It ran all the way from Meeteetse, Wyoming, to Coulson (now Billings) in the north. This road earned the moniker "the 100-Mile Route," as travelers would cover that distance in the journey from Meeteetse to Red Lodge. Stagecoach service became regular within a few years after the road was established. Today, the historic road offers mountain bikers and those with four-wheel-drive vehicles the opportunity to imagine what it would be like to bounce and jostle along such a road, while also affording them the chance for viewing both scenery and wildlife. Cross-country skiers enjoy this road in winter as well. For more information about local trails, stop in at **Hellroaring Cycle & Ski** (406-446-0225; www.hellroaringbike.com), 205 S. Broadway, Red Lodge, where you can have your bike serviced, rent a bike, or even grab an espresso (see also Clarks Fork of the Yellowstone under *Paddling/Floating*).

Paradise Valley. Take US 89 south from Livingston to Free River Fishing Access Area on the Yellowstone River, pick up MT 540 (E. River Road) 0.5 mile south on US 89 from Free River, and finish at Emigrant Fishing Access Area on US 89—or at **Chico Hot Springs** on MT 572 (see *Hot Springs*). This easy, roughly 25-mile point-to-point road ride suitable for beginners offers you the chance to view spectacular Montana scenery from the seat of your bike. Take in the crisp, fresh air as you pedal along the scenic Yellowstone River, crossing numerous creeks and surrounded by national forests. When MT 540 splits, you can head right to find the Emigrant Fishing Access Area or go left to visit Chico Hot Springs, where you can soak your weary body and maybe even spend the night if you want (or need) to reverse your ride the next day.

West Yellowstone (see *To See—Towns*) offers mountain bikers and road bikers alike numerous biking opportunities in the summer months, from the **Rendezvous Ski Trails** (see *Snow Sports*) on the south side of town to numerous Forest Service roads and trails as well as paved routes around the town (not to mention the cycling opportunities in Yellowstone National Park, which you'll find listed under *Bicycling* in "Yellowstone National Park" in "Wyoming's Yellowstone and Grand Teton National Parks"). One well-liked ride begins in town south of US 20 at the intersection of Yellowstone Avenue and Iris Street. From this point, you can ride south on F.R. 1700 (in Gallatin National Forest; see *Wilder Places—Forests*) as it parallels the lovely South Fork of the Madison River. The full-service bike shop (a Nordic ski shop in winter), **Freeheel and Wheel** (406-646-7744; www.freeheelandwheel.com), 40 Yellowstone Avenue, West Yellowstone, offers bike rentals ($20 per day), tune-ups, and information on local rides, as well as a coffee shop.

See also Historic Crail Ranch under *To See—Historic Landmarks, Places, and Sites;* Beartooth Scenic Byway under *To See—Scenic Drives;* Hyalite Reservoir under *Boating;* Basin Lakes National Recreation Trail under *Hiking;* Chico Hot Springs Resort and Day Spa under *Hot Springs;* Big Sky Ski Resort, Bohart Ranch Cross Country Ski Center, and Rendezvous Ski Trails under *Snow Sports;* Custer National Forest Beartooth Ranger District and Gallatin National Forest under *Wilder Places—Forests;* Dome Mountain Ranch and Mountain Meadows Guest Ranch under *Lodging—Other Options;* and Fat Tire Frenzy and Mountain Bike and Fine Arts Festival under *Special Events.*

BOATING & **Cooney Reservoir State Park** (406-445-2326; www.fwp.state .mt.us/parks/parksreport.asp?mapnum=11), Exit 434 off I-90, then south 22 miles to Boyd, then east on access road for 8 miles. Open year-round; day-use free for residents, $5 for nonresidents; camping $13–15. This extremely popular irrigation reservoir with its 780 acres of surface area can get quite busy in summer months, but with 75 campsites and 100 picnic tables, there's usually a place to set up base camp. Three boat ramps facilitate boating and water sports, including swimming. Anglers will find the opportunity to catch walleye and rainbow trout—even in winter, when ice fishing is a popular endeavor. Cross-country skiing is also possible in winter.

& **Dailey Lake,** south on US 89 from Livingston 21 miles, then west on Chico Road at Emigrant for 1 mile, then south on MT 540 for 3 miles, then south on Sixmile Creek Road to the lake. Surrounded by mountains, Dailey Lake's 206 acres of surface area sparkle with the reflection of their splendor, inviting you to launch from the boat ramp and explore. Motorboats over 10 horsepower are not permitted. Situated at an elevation higher than 5,000 feet, this lake offers anglers the chance to catch rainbow trout, walleyes, and yellow perch. This is also a great spot for horseback riding and hiking. You'll find a free, 35-site campground with water and restrooms here as well. (See also Dome Mountain Wildlife Management Area under *Wilder Places—Wildlife Refuges and Areas.*)

Ġ **Hebgen Lake,** 8 miles west of West Yellowstone via US 20, then north on Hebgen Lake Road for 4 miles to Lonesomehurst Campground (see Gallatin National Forest under *Camping* and *Wilder Places—Forests*). At 6,500 feet, high-elevation Hebgen Lake actually a reservoir that was created in 1915. A boat launching facility enables you to get on the water quickly, but beware—due to the potential for high winds, turbulent water, and rapidly changeable weather, you should be experienced and skilled in handling your boat and ready for any conditions. Anglers will find this lake a destination of choice in all seasons, with species including brown and rainbow trout. (See also Madison Canyon Earthquake Area and Visitor Center under *To See—Natural Wonders.*)

Hyalite Reservoir, 17 miles south of Bozeman via MT 345 to F.R. 62. Popular with boaters in the warm summer months, this high-altitude reservoir also provides anglers with year-round fishing opportunities; a four-wheel-drive vehicle or a snowmobile will likely be necessary to access it during winter, however, as F.R. 62 is not plowed. Motorized boats must honor a no-wake rule. Species of fish include arctic grayling (catch-and-release only), brook trout, and Yellowstone cutthroat trout. This is also a popular place for mountain biking, camping, hiking, and cross-country skiing, with numerous trails at the reservoir and in Hyalite Canyon. (See also Gallatin National Forest under *Camping* and *Wilder Places—Forests.*)

See also Itch-Kep-Pe Park under *Camping*; and **Missouri Headwaters State Park** under *Wilder Places—Parks.*

CAMPING Carbella Recreation Site (406-533-7600; www.mt.blm.gov/bdo/pages/recsites.html#carbella), about 20 miles north of Gardiner via US 89. Open year-round; free. Up to 20 camping parties can comfortably fit at this Bureau of Land Management (BLM) recreation site on the banks of the Yellowstone River. Amenities include picnic tables, grills, toilets, and a river-access ramp. A 14-day camping limit applies. Other activities include fishing, floating, and wildlife-watching.

City Park Campground (406-662-3677), on E. Broadway 2 blocks east of US 310, Bridger. Open spring through fall. Full hookups are available at this city-park campground ($15), which can accommodate up to six RVs on a first-come, first-served basis. Tent campers and picnickers are welcome as well.

Ġ **Custer National Forest Beartooth Ranger District** (406-446-2103; www.fs.fed.us/r1/custer/recreation/D2.shtml), HC 49 Box 3420, Red Lodge. The Beartooth Ranger District has 16 campgrounds in this region, many of which provide disabled access. Six of these lie on **US 212** (see also **Beartooth Scenic Byway** under *To See—Scenic Drives*), are open May through September, and cost $9, with the exception of the **M-K Campground,** which is free. Three campgrounds lie south of Red Lodge on F.R. 71 along the West Fork of Rock Creek. Three campgrounds lie northeast of Red Lodge on F.R. 177, the road to East Rosebud Lake. Two lie on West Rosebud Road, the road to West Rosebud Lake and the Mystic Lake trailhead (see *Hiking*). Two lie on Nye Road (MT 419) in Stillwater Valley. All of these are either free year-round or charge $8 or $9 from May through September only. **Sage Creek Campground** (free) is located on F.R. 144 via F.R. 3085 north of Warren and east of Bridger. Many of these campgrounds can be reserved in advance by contacting **ReserveUSA** (1-877-444-6777; www.reserveusa.com). Many of them also provide immediate access to fishing areas. In summer, the forest also rents out **Line Creek Cabin** ($20), 66 miles south of Red Lodge.

& **Gallatin National Forest** (406-587-6701; www.fs.fed.us/r1/gallatin), P.O. Box 130, Bozeman. With five ranger districts—and 38 developed campgrounds—in this travel region, Gallatin National Forest offers a wide selection of camping opportunities, many of which provide disabled access. The **Big Timber Ranger District** (406-932-5155) has nine year-round campgrounds ranging from free to $5 per night, most of which are located at various points off the Main Boulder Road (MT 298) south of Big Timber. The exception is **Half Moon Campground** ($5), 11 miles north of Big Timber on US 191, then 12 miles west on Big Timber Canyon Road. Snow may render all of these campgrounds difficult to access or inaccessible in autumn and winter. The **Bozeman Ranger District** (406-522-2520) has 11 seasonal campgrounds (dates vary; most are mid-May through mid-September) ranging from free to $10. These are located off MT 86 north of Bozeman, along or just off US 191 south of Bozeman, or along F.R. 62 in Hyalite Canyon (see Hyalite Reservoir under *Boating* and Palisade Falls National Recreation Trail under *Hiking*). The **Gardiner Ranger District** (406-848-7375) has eight campgrounds (some seasonal, some year-round) ranging from free to $9. These are located north of Gardiner on or just off US 89, north of Gardiner via the Jardine Road, or near Cooke City on US 212 (see Beartooth Scenic Byway under *To See—Scenic Drives*). The **Hebgen Lake Ranger District** (406-823-6961) has seven seasonal campgrounds ranging from free to $18. These are located on or just off US 191 north of West Yellowstone, on or just off US 287 northwest of West Yellowstone, or on Hebgen Lake Road via US 20 west of West Yellowstone (see *Boating*). The **Livingston Ranger District** (406-222-1892) has three seasonal campgrounds ranging from free to $10. These are located off US 89 north and south of Livingston. Many of these campgrounds provide immediate access to fishing areas. (See also **Gallatin National Forest Cabins** under *Lodging—Other Options*.)

Itch-Kep-Pe Park (406-322-4505), south of Columbus via MT 78, just before crossing the Yellowstone River. Open April 1 through October 31; free (donations appreciated). Run by the City of Columbus, this park on the banks of the Yellowstone River has 30 campsites available, as well as providing opportunities for fishing and swimming. There is a boat launch, too.

See also Raynolds Pass under *To See—Scenic Drives;* Cooney Reservoir State Park, Dailey Lake, and Hyalite Reservoir under *Boating;* the Boulder River, Rock Creek, the Stillwater River, and the Yellowstone River under *Fishing;* and

MOUNTAINS JUST SOUTH OF RED LODGE IN CUSTER NATIONAL FOREST

Missouri Headwaters State Park under *Wilder Places—Parks.*

FISHING Big Timber Creek (406-247-2940; www.fwp.state.mt.us), along US 191 and Big Timber Canyon Road north of Big Timber. Flowing 31 miles from high in the Crazy Mountains to the Yellowstone River in Big Timber, Big Timber Creek's species include brook trout, brown trout, mountain whitefish, and rainbow trout. More adventuresome—and athletic—anglers can set up base camp at Half Moon Campground (see Gallatin National Forest under *Camping*), hike up trails #119 and #118 to Blue Lake, and then hop across talus to access seldom-visited Crazy Lake, an alpine lake situated at 9,150 feet.

The Boulder River (406-247-2940; www.fwp.state.mt.us), south of Big Timber on MT 298/Main Boulder Road (F.R. 6639). Originating high in the Beartooth Mountains, the 65-mile Boulder River and its many tributaries provide the opportunity for incredible fishing in an utterly spectacular wilderness setting. Bordered for much of its length by the pristine Absaroka–Beartooth Wilderness, the river flows, falls, whirls, and plummets through gorgeous mountain surroundings. Brook trout, brown trout, mountain whitefish, rainbow trout, and Yellowstone cutthroat trout are present. Numerous Gallatin National Forest Big Timber Ranger District campgrounds lie along the river's edge (see Gallatin National Forest under *Camping* and *Wilder Places—Forests*). Big Rock Fishing Access Site lies 4 miles south of Big Timber on MT 298, and overnight camping is allowed. (See also **Natural Bridge Falls** under *To See—Natural Wonders* and the listing under *Paddling/Floating.*)

The Clarks Fork of the Yellowstone (406-247-2940; www.fwp.state.mt.us), along MT 72 and US 310 south of Laurel. Designated Wild and Scenic in Wyoming (see *To Do—Fishing* in "North Wyoming: Devils Tower–Buffalo Bill Country"), this river flows from high in the Beartooth Mountains near Cooke City south into Wyoming before wrapping back north and ultimately meeting with the Yellowstone River in Montana. Species include brown trout, burbot, mountain whitefish, and rainbow trout. The Bridger Bend Fishing Access Site is 30 miles south of Laurel on US 310 to Bridger and then 13 miles south on MT 72. This is a primitive access point with no amenities and no overnight camping permitted. (See also Rock Creek, below, and the listing under *Paddling/Floating.*)

The Gallatin River (406-444-2535; www.fwp.state.mt.us), north and south of I-90 near Three Forks, then along US 191 south of Belgrade. Originating from Gallatin Lake in Yellowstone National Park at nearly 10,000 feet, the Gallatin flows for nearly 100 miles before it converges with the Madison and Jefferson rivers at Three Forks. This river is an angler's paradise, with easy accessibility, several developed Forest Service campgrounds along US 191 with easy fishing access, and top-quality fishing for species including brown trout, mountain whitefish, and rainbow trout. There are also a number of fishing access sites to the river, both along US 191 as well as just west of I-90 near Bozeman and Belgrade, and north of I-90 near Three Forks. No camping is permitted at any of these access points. (See also Gallatin National Forest under *Camping* and *Wilder Places—Forests;* and the listing under *Paddling/Floating.*)

Rock Creek (406-247-2940; www.fwp.state.mt.us), north and south of Red Lodge along US 212 and west of Red Lodge along F.R. 71. Originating in the Absaroka–Beartooth Wilderness, 62-mile Rock Creek is joined by West Rock Creek just south of Red Lodge. It then continues north to join the Clarks Fork of the Yellowstone. Anglers will find numerous access points to try their hand at catching brook trout, brown trout, mountain whitefish, rainbow trout, and Yellowstone cutthroat trout, both at Forest Service campgrounds (see Custer National Forest Beartooth Ranger District under *Camping*) and at four fishing access sites along US 212, all of which allow overnight camping and only one of which (Water Birch) requires a fee.

The Shields River (406-444-2535; www.fwp.state.mt.us), along US 89 north of Exit 340 off I-90. This 65-mile tributary of the Yellowstone River originates high in the Crazy Mountains before flowing south through more agricultural lands and meeting with the Yellowstone near Livingston. Species include brown trout, mountain whitefish, and Yellowstone cutthroat trout.

& **The Stillwater River** (406-247-2940; www.fwp.state.mt.us), southwest of Columbus on MT 78 and MT 420. Species of fish in this 70-mile tributary to the Yellowstone include brook trout, brown trout, mountain whitefish, rainbow trout, and Yellowstone cutthroat trout. Eight fishing access points lie along its banks, all of which allow overnight, free camping. Cliff Swallow Fishing Access Site, located 10 miles east of Absarokee on MT 420, offers easy accessibility for the disabled, including handicapped parking and paved access to a fishing pier and toilets. (See also the listing under *Paddling/Floating.*)

The Yellowstone River (406-247-2940; www.fwp.state.mt.us) is accessible via numerous access points along US 89 from the Wyoming border to Livingston and then just off I-90 between Livingston and Laurel. The last free-flowing river in the Lower 48 states, the Yellowstone originates in Yellowstone Lake (see "Yellowstone National Park" in "Wyoming's Yellowstone and Grand Teton National Parks") and flows unimpeded for 670 miles to its confluence with the Missouri River just over Montana's border with North Dakota. Species include brown trout, burbot, channel catfish, mountain whitefish, paddlefish, rainbow trout, sauger, smallmouth bass, walleye, and Yellowstone cutthroat trout. Many of the river's fishing access points allow free camping for up to 7 days and provide good launching places and takeouts for rafters and paddlers. (See also the listing under *Paddling/Floating.*)

See also Federation of Fly Fishers' Fly Fishing Discovery Center under *To See—Museums;* Raynolds Pass under *To See—Scenic Drives;* Madison Canyon

Earthquake Area and Visitor Center under *To See—Natural Wonders;* Cooney Reservoir State Park, Dailey Lake, Hebgen Lake, and Hyalite Reservoir under *Boating;* Carbella Recreation Site and Itch-Kep-Pe Park under *Camping;* Basin Lakes National Recreation Trail and West Rosebud Lake–Mystic Lake–Island Lake under *Hiking;* Medicine Lakes Outfitters, Inc., under *Horseback Riding;* Chico Hot Springs Resort and Day Spa under *Hot Springs; Paddling/Floating;* Big Sky Resort under *Snow Sports;* Missouri Headwaters State Park under *Wilder Places—Parks;* Custer National Forest Beartooth Ranger District and Gallatin National Forest under *Camping* and *Wilder Places—Forests;* Blue Winged Olive Bed and Breakfast, Bunkhouse Bed and Breakfast, Headwaters of the Yellowstone Bed and Breakfast, Johnstad's Bed and Breakfast and Log Cabin, Mission Creek Ranch Bed and Breakfast, Paradise Gateway Bed and Breakfast and Log Cabins, and Yellowstone Country Bed and Breakfast under *Lodging—Bed & Breakfasts;* Big EZ Lodge, Big River Lodge, Burnt Out Lodge, Gallatin River Lodge, Hubbard's Yellowstone Lodge, and Sleepy Hollow Lodge under *Lodging—Lodges;* and Dome Mountain Ranch, Lone Mountain Ranch, Mountain Meadows Guest Ranch, Rosebud Retreat, and 320 Guest Ranch under *Lodging—Other Options.*

GOLF **Big Sky Golf Course** (406-995-5780; www.bigskyresort.com), Big Sky Spur Road (2 miles west of US 191), Big Sky, 18 holes.

Bridger Creek Golf Course (406-586-2333; www.bridgercreek.com), 2710 McIlhattan Road, Bozeman, 18 holes.

Columbus Stillwater Golf Course (406-322-4298), 1203 E. 3rd Avenue S., Columbus, 9 holes.

Cottonwood Hills Golf Course (406-587-1118), 8955 River Road, Bozeman, 18 holes.

Headwaters Golf Course (406-285-3700), 225 7th Avenue E., Three Forks, 9 holes.

Livingston Country Club (406-222-1100), 44 View Vista Drive, Livingston, 9 holes.

Overland Golf Course (406-932-4297), Exit 367 off I-90, Big Timber, 9 holes.

Red Lodge Mountain Golf Course (406-446-3344; www.redlodgemountain .com/golf), 828 Upper Continental Drive, Red Lodge, 18 holes.

Riverside Country Club (406-587-5105), 2500 Springhill Road, Bozeman, 18 holes.

Valley View Golf Club (406-586-2145), 302 E. Kagy Boulevard, Bozeman, 18 holes.

See also Big EZ Lodge under *Lodging—Lodges* and Mountain Meadows Guest Ranch under *Lodging—Other Options.*

HIKING **Basin Lakes National Recreation Trail** (#61) is accessible via F.R. 71 west of Red Lodge. Breathtaking scenery awaits you just outside the town of Red Lodge on this former horse-logging road. It's about an 8-mile round-trip if you choose to hike the entirety of the trail, which gets seriously steep for only the last mile or so. You'll finish at Upper Basin Lake, where you can drop a line to fish, if angling suits your fancy, or just sit for a while and enjoy the spectacular mountain surroundings over a picnic lunch before heading back down. If you're still not tired, you can access **Timberline Trail** (#12) a little farther up the road—it's a 9-mile round-trip up to Timberline Lake and Gertrude Lake, with stunning views and great fishing. (See also Custer National Forest Beartooth Ranger District under *Wilder Places—Forests.*)

Confluence Trail departs from the campground at Missouri Headwaters State Park (see *Wilder Places—Parks*). This 4.1-mile hike brings you to the confluence of the Jefferson and Madison rivers. Interpretive signs along the way give you the opportunity to educate yourself while taking a breather. If you prefer a shorter hike, you can opt to stroll along the park's 0.4-mile **Fort Rock Trail,** another interpretive trail.

Gallatin Petrified Forest, 17 miles north of Gardiner on US 89, then southwest on Tom Miner Road (F.R. 63) to the parking area. A 0.5-mile interpretive hike begins about 1,000 feet from the parking area and guides you through the petrified remains of a forest that lived between 35 and 55 million years ago. Unlike many other petrified forests, in which the trees have long since fallen over, here you'll find trees petrified in an upright position. (See also Gallatin National Forest under *Wilder Places—Forests.*)

⚐ **Palisade Falls National Recreation Trail,** 17 miles south of Bozeman via MT 345 to F.R. 62, then east around Hyalite Reservoir (see *Boating*) on E. Fork Road for 2 miles to the trailhead. Though short—a 1.2-mile round-trip—this steep trail packs a bit of a punch for its distance. Don't be deterred, though—the trail is paved, and it takes you to view a 98-foot waterfall. With 16 interpretive signs (complete with Braille for the visually impaired, who should undertake this trail only with a sighted guide), you'll find plenty of opportunities to stop, take in the scenery, and read about your surroundings. The trail is wheelchair-accessible as well, though difficult due to the steep grade of the trail. (See also Gallatin National Forest under *Wilder Places—Forests.*)

West Rosebud Lake–Mystic Lake–Island Lake (Trail #19), accessible via MT 78 to W. Rosebud Road (F.R. 2702) southwest of Columbus. See one lake—West Rosebud—just by getting out of your car, two lakes, or all three by following this trail in the Beartooth Mountains. First, you'll skirt the south shore of Mystic Lake, the biggest lake in the Beartooths. With more than 400 acres of surface area, this lake is a popular destination for anglers. You can turn around here for a 7-mile round-trip. If you want to keep going, you'll then cross into the Absaroka–Beartooth Wilderness and head for more remote Island Lake (a 12-mile round-trip). (See also Custer National Forest Beartooth Ranger District under *Wilder Places—Forests.*)

See also Historic Crail Ranch and Madison Buffalo Jump State Park under *To See—Historic Landmarks, Places, and Sites;* Granite Peak, Grasshopper Glacier, and Natural Bridge Park under *To See—Natural Wonders;* Grizzly Loop, Meeteetse Trail, and West Yellowstone under *Bicycling;* Dailey Lake and Hyalite Reservoir under *Boating;* Big Timber Creek under *Fishing;* Paintbrush Adventures,

Inc., under *Horseback Riding;* Chico Hot Springs Resort and Day Spa under *Hot Springs;* Bohart Ranch Cross Country Ski Center under *Snow Sports;* Hailstone National Wildlife Refuge and Halfbreed Lake National Wildlife Refuge under *Wilder Places—Wildlife Refuges and Areas;* and Dome Mountain Ranch and Mountain Meadows Guest Ranch under *Lodging—Other Options.*

HORSEBACK RIDING ✎ **Big Sky Stables** (1-866-263-4396; 406-995-2972; www.bigskyhorseback.com), 5305 Spur Road, 5.5 miles east of US 191 toward Big Sky Resort. Rides offered May 15 through early October. Whether you want to ride for an hour ($32 per person) or a day ($150 per person, lunch included), Big Sky Stables has the horses (35 for riding), the guides, and the knowledge of the local trails—including access to Gallatin National Forest—to make your experience memorable. Riders must be at least 8 years old (no double riding) and weigh 250 pounds or less. Reservations are highly recommended, especially during July and August. (See also Dinner Hay or Sleigh Rides under *Unique Adventures.*)

Medicine Lakes Outfitters, Inc. (406-388-4938; www.packtrips.com), 3246 Linney Road, Bozeman. Day rides available April through September. Founded in 1973, this outfitting service promises a smoothly run, exciting daylong horseback riding adventure for adults and children ages 12 and up. Guided by an experienced husband-and-wife team, your daylong ride ($125 per person; reservations required) could take you into the Bridger, Madison, or Gallatin mountains of surrounding Gallatin National Forest—or perhaps you will choose to go into Yellowstone National Park. You can also book a multiday pack trip or a daylong guided fly-fishing trip via horseback.

Montana Horses (1-888-685-3697; 406-285-3541; www.montanahorses.com), 9700 Clarkston Road, Three Forks. If you have riding experience and want to plan your own horseback riding adventure, but you lack one key ingredient—the horse—you can lease a horse from Montana Horses. Montana Horses leases riding equipment as well, and they can also deliver horses to you. You must call ahead; rates vary according to season.

✎ 🐾 **Paintbrush Adventures, Inc.** (406-328-4158; www.paintbrushadventures .com), 86 N. Stillwater Road, Absarokee. Open year-round. Paintbrush Adventures has a permit allowing its guides to take you into the stunning Beartooth Mountains of Custer National Forest. Ride for an hour ($20 per person) up to a day ($135 per person, including lunch), or consider signing up for the Saddle and Paddle adventure ($70 adults, $45 children), which combines riding with white-water rafting for an ultra-exciting Montana experience. Paintbrush Adventures also operates wilderness pack trips and drop camp services, as well as guided day hikes. Reservations recommended.

✎ **320 Guest Ranch** (1-800-243-0320; 406-995-4283; www.320ranch.com), 12 miles south of Big Sky on US 191 at mile marker 36. Open year-round; reservations recommended. Situated close to Yellowstone National Park, this outfitter's guides log some 2,000 miles on the trail every year—so you know you're in good hands. Ride for an hour ($32 per person) or up to a day ($185 per person) through gorgeous terrain, with the potential to scale a 10,000-foot peak or perhaps ride to a mountain lake where you can try your hand at fishing. You can also book a spot on the chuck wagon barbecue in summer—a 2-hour horseback ride ($75 adults, $60 children 12 and under) or a hayride ($41 adults, $20 children 12 and under) culminates with a steak or chicken dinner under the stars. Sleigh rides are available in winter months, too, as are numerous additional guest ranch activities and amenities, including lodging in **cabins** ($95–321) and a gourmet restaurant (see **320 Ranch Steak House & Saloon** under *Dining Out*).

See also Dailey Lake under *Boating;* Chico Hot Springs Resort and Day Spa under *Hot Springs;* the Stillwater River and the Yellowstone River under *Paddling/Floating;* Big Sky Resort and Bohart Ranch Cross Country Ski Center under *Snow Sports;* ranch vacations under *Unique Adventures;* Custer National Forest Beartooth Ranger District and Gallatin National Forest under *Wilder Places—Forests;* Bunkhouse Bed and Breakfast under *Lodging—Bed & Breakfasts;* and Dome Mountain Ranch, Lone Mountain Ranch, and Mountain Meadows Guest Ranch under *Lodging—Other Options.*

HOT SPRINGS ✍ **Bozeman Hot Springs** (406-586-6492; spa: 406-522-9563), 8 miles west of Bozeman on US 191. Open daily year-round; hours and rates vary. Soak away your worries in an array of pools ranging in temperature from a cool 59°F to a steaming 104°F at this favorite destination for both locals and out-of-towners alike. These natural, chemical-free hot springs include both dry and wet saunas as well, all in an ultramodern, state-of-the-art setting. You can also make an appointment for a massage or other special treatment at the spa or get a great workout at the fitness center before soaking your sore muscles. You'll even find a day-care center for the kids and a juice bar to replenish and rehydrate your body with a healthy beverage.

Chico Hot Springs Resort and Day Spa (406-333-4933; 1-800-468-9232; www.chicohotsprings.com), 1 Old Chico Road, 31 miles north of Gardiner on US 89, then exit east in Emigrant. Open daily year-round 6 AM–midnight; rates depend on services selected; advance reservations a must. A stay here will bring you the opportunity to soak in two natural mineral pools—one averaging 104°F and one averaging 96°F—perfect for infusing your travel-weary body with relaxation. You can also opt to schedule a massage, an herbal wrap, or a spa package, including a number of treatments from the on-premises Chico Day Spa. This popular destination features a full-service resort complete with a variety of lodging options, a fine dining restaurant, a casual restaurant, and a western saloon, along with recreational activities that include horseback riding, hiking, fly-fishing, white-water rafting, mountain biking, cross-country skiing, chartered plane flights over the Absarokas, and even dogsledding (see **Absaroka Dogsled Treks** under *Unique Adventures;* see also **Chico Dining Room** under *Dining Out.*)

PADDLING/FLOATING **The Boulder River,** south of Big Timber on MT 298/Main Boulder Road (F.R. 6639). Above Natural Bridge Falls (see *To See— Natural Wonders*), the Boulder River presents an incredible stretch of river suitable only for the experienced white water enthusiast as it rolls and tumbles for literally miles of class II–IV white water. Below Natural Bridge Falls, the river becomes a mellower, tamer affair, with a few portions of class II, making it more reasonable for the less-experienced paddler and suitable for float-fishing as well. Since there is no take-out point near Natural Bridge Falls, it is imperative that anyone paddling the waters above this point does not paddle beyond Falls Creek Campground—the best landmark for this is a bridge roughly 0.25 mile upstream, where taking out is easy. For the full experience, you can put in near the river's origin at Hells Canyon Campground.

The Clarks Fork of the Yellowstone, along MT 72 and US 310 south of Laurel. The only guide service with a permit to run trips on this river is **Beartooth Whitewater** (1-800-799-3142; www.redlodge.com/btwhitewater) in Red Lodge, which offers a combination full-day 4X4 tour and river trip ($75 per person). You'll bounce along the historic Meeteetse Trail (see *Bicycling*) to the banks of the Clarks Fork, where you'll partake in a delicious barbecue lunch before embarking on your river adventure.

The Gallatin River, north and south of I-90 near Three Forks, then along US 191 south of Belgrade. Originating from Gallatin Lake in Yellowstone National Park at nearly 10,000 feet, the Gallatin flows for nearly 100 miles before it converges with the Madison and Jefferson rivers at Three Forks. No floating is permitted inside Yellowstone National Park, but the first stretch of this river from outside the park to Big Sky presents paddlers and floaters with generally calm waters and scenic terrain. This all changes after Big Sky, where the river's white water ranges from class II to class IV to the Squaw Creek Bridge—suitable for only the experienced and knowledgeable paddler. If you need to hire a guide, one option is **Yellowstone Raft Company** (1-800-348-4376; www.yellowstone raft.com), 7 miles north of Big Sky on US 191. A full day is $79 adults, $63 children. Yellowstone Raft also offers sit-on-top kayaking trips (full day $135 per person) and closed-cockpit kayaking instruction ($45 per hour).

The Stillwater River, southwest of Columbus on MT 78 and MT 420. This river is anything but still, with an abundance of challenging rapids—particularly in the wilderness section of the river, which can contain class V or harder rapids. If you want to experience a portion of this wild ride, you should either have a ton of experience or knowledge, or you should hire a guide. One option is **Adventure Whitewater** (1-800-897-3061; 406-446-3061; www.adventurewhite water.com), Red Lodge and Absarokee. A full day is $65 adults, $45 children. Adventure Whitewater also offers combination horseback riding and rafting trips ($70 per person).

The Yellowstone River, accessible via numerous points along US 89 from the Wyoming border to Livingston and then just off I-90 between Livingston and Laurel. The last free-flowing river in the Lower 48 states, the Yellowstone originates in Yellowstone Lake (see "Yellowstone National Park" in "Wyoming's Yellowstone and Grand Teton National Parks") and flows unimpeded for 670 miles to its confluence with the Missouri River just over Montana's border with North Dakota. A favorite of paddlers and floaters, for the greater part of its distance this is a beginner-friendly river, with mostly class I rapids during normal flow. For the first 20 miles after Gardiner, however, the river does have white water, usually class II and III or even class IV during higher flow times. The hardest portion is where the Yellowstone travels through Yankee Jim Canyon—which has gorgeous scenery but is appropriate for only the skilled paddler from the Joe Brown Fishing Access Site to the Carbella Fishing Access Site, 5 miles downstream. If you need to hire a guide, try **Big Sky Rafting** (1-866-848-2112; 406-848-2112; www.bigskywhitewater.com) in Gardiner, which charges $60 for adults and $50 for children for a full day; or **Wild West Rafting** (1-800-862-0557; 406-848-2252; www.wildwestrafting.com), also in Gardiner, whose rates are $75 for adults and $55 for children for a full day. **Wild West Rafting** also offers horseback rides by the hour ($30 per person) or the day ($135 per person), as well as a saddle and paddle trip ($68 per person). Big Sky Rafting also offers bike and raft rentals, as well as a bike and paddle trip ($35 per person).

See also *Boating;* Carbella Recreation Site under *Camping; Fishing;* Paintbrush Adventures, Inc., under *Horseback Riding;* Dome Mountain Ranch and Mountain Meadows Guest Ranch under *Lodging—Other Options;* and Gallatin Whitewater Festival under *Special Events.*

SNOW SPORTS

Ice-Skating
❀ ♪ **Bozeman Recreation Department's Ice Skating Rinks** (406-587-4724), located in Southside Park (S. 5th and College) and Beall Park (N. Black and Villard). Open around Christmas, closed in spring (weather dependent), Monday through Friday noon–10 PM, Saturday and Sunday 10 AM–10 PM; free. Tie on your skates and go for a spin at one of Bozeman's two outdoor ice-skating rinks, free and open to the public once the colder weather sets in for good every winter.

Skiing
♪ ♿ **Big Sky Resort** (1-800-548-4486; 406-995-5000; www.bigskyresort.com/ontheslopes), 1 Lone Mountain Trail, Big Sky. More than 150 named trails on its central mountain—11,166-foot Lone Peak—and two adjacent mountains combine to make up this ski resort's 3,600 acres, with a longest single run of 6 miles. Add to this an average annual snowfall of 400 inches, Montana's longest terrain park (1,300 vertical feet), a half-pipe, and short-to-no lift lines, and you might wonder why you haven't packed your bags yet. If you have kids, you'll really start wondering when you learn that at Big Sky, up to two children ages 10 and under per paying adult can ski and stay free at all times. Other activities and services at the resort include dinner sleigh rides, a kids' club, horseback riding, day care, snowshoeing, fly-fishing, a full-service spa, and much, much more. In summer, mountain bikers of all abilities can enjoy a number of single-track trails and fire roads. *Lifts:* one 15-passenger car, four high-speed quads, one four-person gondola, one quad, three triple chairlifts, five double chairlifts, three surface lifts. *Trails:* 150-plus trails—17 percent beginner, 25 percent intermediate, 37 percent advanced, 21 percent expert. *Vertical drop:* 4,350 feet. *Snowmaking:* 10 percent coverage. *Facilities:* The base lodge has food service and restrooms. *Snowsports school:* Available for all ages and ability levels of skiers and snowboarders. *For children:* Handprints Daycare for ages 6 months to 8 years, Small Fry Try for

ages 3–4, Mini Camp for ages 4–6, Ski Camp for ages 6–12, Teen Mountain Experience for ages 13–17. *Rates:* $61 adults, $31 seniors (67 and older), $42 juniors (14–21 with ID), $25 youths (11–13), children 10 and under free; half-day and multiday rates as well as ski-and-stay packages available. (See also **Lone Peak Tram** under *Unique Adventures.*)

Bohart Ranch Cross Country Ski Center (406-586-9070; www.bohartranch xcski.com), 16.6 miles north of Bozeman via MT 86. Located in Bridger Canyon, this ranch caters to the Nordic skier. Its regularly groomed, 15-foot-wide trails sport both classic tracks and skate lanes, taking you through scenic lands with ample opportunities for wildlife viewing. Lessons are offered in both classic and skate skiing techniques for all ability levels, and rental equipment is available as well. *Trails:* 25K, varied terrain from beginner to expert. *Rates:* $12 adults, $6 children (7–12), children 6 and under and seniors 70 and older free.

& ♂ **Bridger Bowl Ski and Snowboard Resort** (1-800-223-9609; 406-587-2111; www.bridgerbowl.com), 15795 Bridger Canyon Road, north of Bozeman via MT 26. From beginners to experts, everyone will find terrain that suits them at Bridger Bowl. Expert skiers will have an adventure exploring Bridger's Ridge area, while the rest of the crew will have fun on the tamer terrain. *Lifts:* one quad, two triple, and four double chairlifts. *Trails:* 69 trails—25 percent beginner, 35 percent intermediate, 30 percent advanced, 10 percent expert. *Vertical drop:* 2,600 feet (2,000 feet serviced by lift). *Snowmaking:* 4 percent coverage. *Facilities:* three cafeterias, a full-service bar and grill, plus food service with beer and wine available at a midmountain lodge. *Ski school:* Available for all ages and ability levels of skiers and snowboarders. *For children:* Play care for ages 18 months to 6 years, Preschool Private for ages 3–4, Mogul Mice for ages 4–6, Mighty Mites for ages 7–13, Team Extreme for ages 9–13. *Rates:* $37 adults, $31 seniors (65–71), $13 children 6–12, children 5 and under and seniors 72 and older free; also half-day and multiday rates.

♂ **Moonlight Basin Ski Resort** (406-993-6000; www.moonlightbasin.com), off MT 64, Big Sky. Montana's newest ski resort opened in 2003. Located adjacent to Big Sky Ski Resort, this lovely resort opens up more of Lone Peak to skiers, with plans for expansion continuing as it establishes itself as a player on the state's ski scene. This means that the stats listed here could quite definitely already be out of date when you read this. Moonlight is a full-service destination resort, with additional activities on the premises, including a health spa, a fitness center, dogsledding, snowshoeing, ice-skating, a hot tub, and a heated outdoor pool. *Lifts:* one six-person and two quad chairlifts, one derringer and one triple chairlift. *Trails:* 76 trails (the number grows by the season)—23 percent beginner, 41 percent intermediate, 36 percent expert. *Vertical drop:* 3,850 feet (2,070 feet serviced by lift). *Facilities:* full-service restaurant and bar at base lodge; limited food service at warming hut. *Ski school:* none. *For children:* Little Wranglers Daycare for ages 6 months to 8 years. *Rates:* $40 adults, $35 seniors (70 and older), $35 college students (with ID), $30 children 11–17, children 10 and under free; also half-day rates.

& ♂ **Red Lodge Mountain Resort** (1-800-444-8977; 406-446-2610; www .redlodgemountain.com), off US 212 in Red Lodge. With a single phone call, you can have your entire ski vacation to Red Lodge arranged, including lodging, skiing (including rentals), airfare, and car rental—so all you need to worry about is showing up and having fun. The mountain has a 0.25-mile terrain park open to both skiers and snowboarders, with features changed frequently. *Lifts:* two high-speed quad chairlifts, one triple and four double chairlifts, one handle-tow. *Trails:* 71 trails—25 percent beginner, 40 percent intermediate, 25 percent advanced, 10 percent expert. *Vertical drop:* 2,400 feet. *Snowmaking:* 40 percent coverage on terrain from base to summit. *Facilities:* two cafeterias, one full-service restaurant, two bars, espresso shop. *Ski school:* PSIA-certified instructors teach lessons for all ages and ability levels. *For children:* Kid Corral Daycare for ages 1–4, Wrangler Ski Program for ages 4–6 (private instruction for ages 3–6 available as well), Trailblazer Learn to Ski and Skillbuilder Program for ages 7–12. *Rates:* $40 adults, $31 seniors 65–69, $37 juniors ages 13–18, $15 children 6–12, children 5 and under and seniors 70 and older free; half-day and multiday passes as well as ski-and-stay packages available.

Red Lodge Nordic Center (1-800-425-0076406-446-9191;), 1 mile west of Red Lodge on MT 78, then west (left) on Fox Road for 2 miles. Enjoy cross-country skiing through the gorgeous terrain on the groomed trails of this ski center just outside Red Lodge. Lessons and rental equipment are available. *Trails:* 15K—4K easy, 7K more difficult, 4K most difficult. *Rates:* Call for this season's rates.

Rendezvous Ski Trails (406-823-6961; www.fs.fed.us/r1/gallatin/?page= recreation/cross_country_ski; www.rendezvousskitrails.com), at the intersection of Geyser Street and Obsidian Avenue, West Yellowstone. Developed in the late 1970s as a training area for the U.S. Ski Team, this network of trails lies entirely in the Gallatin National Forest (see *Wilder Places—Forests*). More than 30K of trails are professionally groomed daily to accommodate both skate skiers and classic cross-country skiers. *Trails:* 30K plus—fairly even mix from easiest to most difficult. *Rates:* $5 per person. (See also Yellowstone Ski Festival under *Special Events*).

Snowmobiling

Snowmobiling is quite popular in this region of Montana, which should come as no surprise, given the significant annual snowfalls combined with the huge amounts of public land. You should be sure to inform yourself of all rules and regulations before heading out. Popular destinations include the 135 miles of groomed trails in **Gallatin National Forest** (GNF) (406-823-6961; www.fs.fed .us/r1/gallatin/?page=recreation/snowmobile) accessible in West Yellowstone south and west of Iris Street, as well as north of Dunraven Street. Also popular are numerous GNF snowmobile trails in the **Cooke City vicinity** (406-848-7375), accessible via US 212, and numerous GNF trails in the **Bozeman** (406-522-2520) and **Livingston** (406-222-1892) vicinities. The **Custer National Forest Beartooth Ranger District** (406-446-2103; www.fs.fed.us/r1/custer/ recreation/D2.shtml) has a number of snowmobiling trails in the Red Lodge vicinity. If you need to rent a snowmobile, a couple of options include **Team Bozeman Rentals** (406-587-4671), Bozeman; and **Yellowstone Adventures** (1-800-231-5991; 406-646-7735), West Yellowstone, among many others.

See also Grasshopper Glacier under *To See—Natural Wonders;* Meeteetse Trail under *Bicycling;* Cooney Reservoir State Park, Hebgen Lake, and Hyalite Reservoir under *Boating;* Chico Hot Springs Resort and Day Spa under *Hot Springs;* Rock Climbing and Ice Climbing under *Unique Adventures;* Custer National Forest and Gallatin National Forest under *Wilder Places—Forests;* Lone Mountain Ranch and Mountain Meadows Guest Ranch under *Lodging—Other Options;* and Yellowstone Ski Festival under *Special Events.*

UNIQUE ADVENTURES ✂ **Absaroka Dogsled Treks** (1-800-468-9232; 406-222-4645; www.extrememontana.com), based at Chico Hot Springs Resort (see *Hot Springs*). Trips run Thanksgiving through Easter; call for reservations. What better way to spend a day off from skiing or winter adventuring than to rest your weary limbs and take a scenic tour—in a dogsled, no less! Load up the whole family (if you wish) for 2 hours ($90 per person), for half a day ($180 per person), or for the entire day ($240 per person), and let your experienced musher do the work of handling a team of Siberian huskies while they pull your sled through the winter wonderland of the Absaroka Mountains. If you want a more in-depth experience, you can sign up for the 3-day Musher's School and learn to drive a team of dogs yourself ($600 per person).

✂ 🐴 **Dinner Hay or Sleigh Rides by Big Sky Stables** (1-866-263-4396; 406-995-2972; www.bigskyhorseback.com), 5305 Spur Road, 5.5 miles east of US 191 toward Big Sky Resort. Hayrides run May 15 through early October; 2-hour trail ride and dinner $67 per person, 2-hour hayride and dinner $47 per person, children 6 and under with an adult ride and eat for free. Sleigh rides run December through April 15 (snow permitting); $62 per person, children 6 and under with an adult ride and eat for free. Families with young children—and families with children of any age, for that matter—are encouraged to sign up for these seasonal outings that expose children to the wonder and power of both horses and the natural world. From a seat in the hay wagon or sleigh, young children will delight in the scenery before digging into a fabulous cowboy supper with their parents (who will appreciate both the food and the free ride for their children). What's on the menu? A feast of New York steak (or chicken or salmon), baked beans, and seasonally appropriate side dishes guarantees that no rider will go home hungry.

Lone Peak Tram (1-800-548-4486; 406-995-5000; www.bigskyresort.com/onthe slopes), 1 Lone Mountain Trail, Big Sky. Even if you're not an expert skier, the 3-minute ride up the mountain in the Lone Peak Tram is likely to amaze you. This $3 million, 15-passenger tram whisks you from the base of the ski area to the elevation of 11,150 feet—almost the summit of Lone Peak (elevation 11,166 feet)—where panoramic views of your surroundings await. Extreme skiers will delight in the opportunity to experience the incredible vertical drop—4,350 feet—while the less daring will be content to simply sit back and enjoy the return ride to tamer terrain just as much as the ride up.

✂ **Moonlight Dinners** (406-995-3880; www.moonlightdinners.com), Moonlight Basin Ranch (1 mile up the road from Big Sky Mountain Resort), Big Sky. Let **Montana Backcountry Adventures** (www.skimba.com) treat you to an evening outing with a distinctively Montanan twist. You and the other guests will load up into snowcats (think giant-sized SUVs made specifically for safe, comfortable snow travel) and journey for about 20 minutes through Moonlight Basin Ranch, with views of Gallatin National Forest's Lee Metcalf Wilderness Area. You will disembark to enter into a warm, circular yurt about 30 feet in diameter, where you will be served a delicious gourmet dinner—including filet mignon—while you relax to the sounds of live acoustic music. Outside, you can enjoy sledding or hanging out by a bonfire, or if you prefer to stay inside, you can chat, relax, or play board games ($69 per person; reservations required).

Ranch vacations. These vacations usually allow you to participate to a certain extent in various aspects of ranch life, often including cattle herding and branding. The ratio of work time to leisure time varies from ranch to ranch, as do the additional activities and amenities offered, but most ranches include horseback riding, lodging, and meals in an inclusive package deal. In this region, providers include **Crazy Mountain Cattle Company** (406-222-6101; 406-932-6719), Big Timber; **G Bar M Ranch** (406-686-4423; 406-686-4216), Clyde Park; **Hawley Mountain Guest Ranch** (406-932-5791), Big Timber; **Lazy E-L Working Guest Ranch** (406-328-6858), Roscoe; **Lazy K Bar Ranch** (406-932-4449), Big Timber; **Lonesome Spur Ranch** (406-662-3460; 406-662-3357), Bridger; **Parade Rest Guest Ranch** (1-800-753-5934; 406-646-7217), West Yellowstone; **Rocking Tree Ranch** (406-932-5057), Big Timber; **S-Bar-Shepherd Ranch** (406-326-2327), Reed Point; **Sweet Grass Ranch** (406-537-4477), Big Timber; **WD Ranch** (406-537-4452), Melville; and **Yellowstone Valley Ranch** (1-800-626-3526; 406-333-4787), Livingston; among others. (See also *Lodging—Other Options.*)

Rock Climbing and Ice Climbing. Opportunities to engage in these sports are available in this region of Montana, but no technical climbing should be undertaken without proper training and experience. To help you learn the proper skills, **Beartooth Mountain Guides** (406-446-9874; www.redlodge.com/climbing) in Red Lodge offers single-day guided rock- or ice-climbing lessons for beginners (and higher levels as well) ($225–275 per person; group rates available). Other services include alpine mountaineering instruction, ski mountaineering instruction, and 4- to 5-day guided ascents of Granite Peak ($1,000 per person; see *To See—Natural Wonders*). Near Bozeman, **Reach Your Peak Guiding and Instruction** (406-578-2155; www.climbmontana.com) in Wilsall offers rock- and ice-climbing instruction ($250 per person per day) in the Bozeman area, including ice-climbing instruction in Hyalite Canyon. Other services include alpine climbing and mountaineering instruction and guided hiking and backpacking trips.

See also 320 Guest Ranch and Paintbrush Adventures, Inc., under *Horseback Riding;* the Clarks Fork of the Yellowstone, the Stillwater River, and the Yellowstone River under *Paddling/Floating;* and Lone Mountain Ranch and Mountain Meadows Guest Ranch under *Lodging—Other Options.*

✳ Wilder Places

PARKS ⟋ **Greycliff Prairie Dog Town State Park** (406-247-2940; www.fwp.state.mt.us/parks/parksreport.asp?mapnum=12), Exit 378 off I-90 between

Bozeman and Billings. Open for day-use only, April 1 through October 31; free for residents, $2 for nonresidents. With no amenities, this park's main attraction is watching and photographing the prairie dogs as they go about their daily business, popping in and out of their burrows and scurrying about to the delight of visitors. You can pack a picnic lunch and observe their antics for a while or just stop by to stretch your legs, read the interpretive signs, and get back on the road.

♿ **Missouri Headwaters State Park** (406-994-4042; www.fwp.state.mt.us/ parks/parksreport.asp?mapnum=22), Exit 283 off I-90, then east on MT 205, then 3 miles north on MT 286. Open year-round for day-use, free for residents, $5 for nonresidents; open May 1 through September 30 for camping, $12. See the place where three already-impressive rivers—the Jefferson, the Madison, and the Gallatin—come together to form the Missouri River. Walk in the footsteps of Lewis and Clark, who figured that they would eventually encounter this confluence as they worked their way across the state during their historic exploration. Two interpretive trails fill you in on your surroundings (see **Confluence Trail** under *To Do—Hiking*). Other popular activities in the park include camping, boating, and picnicking. Blue-ribbon trout fishing opportunities exist both in and around this state park. The Three Forks area has at least five designated fishing access sites, some permitting camping, along with the park itself.

See also Madison Buffalo Jump State Park and Parker Homestead State Park under *To See—Historic Landmarks, Places, and Sites;* Natural Bridge Falls under *To See—Natural Wonders;* and Bozeman Recreation Department's Ice Skating Rinks under *Ice-Skating* under *To Do—Snow Sports.*

FORESTS Custer National Forest Beartooth Ranger District (406-446-2103; www.fs.fed.us/r1/custer/recreation/D2.shtml), HC 49 Box 3420, Red Lodge. Within the boundaries of this single ranger district, you'll find four designated national recreation trails—and a plethora of additional trails, including 180 miles of maintained trails for hiking and horseback riding in this district's 345,000 acres of the 945,000-acre **Absaroka–Beartooth Wilderness.** You'll also find a portion of the **Beartooth Scenic Byway** (see *To See—Scenic Drives*) and **Red Lodge Mountain Ski Resort** (see *To Do—Snow Sports*), as well as Montana's highest peak, **Granite Peak,** on the border with Gallatin National Forest (see below and also *To See—Natural Wonders*). Recreational opportunities abound, including boating, bicycling, camping, fishing, horseback riding, paddling/floating, rock climbing, ice climbing, cross-country skiing, snowmobiling, snowshoeing, picnicking, and wildlife viewing. (See also the listings under *To Do—Camping;* Rock Creek under *To Do—Fishing;* Basin Lakes National Recreation Trail and West Rosebud–Mystic Lake–Island Lake under *To Do—Hiking;* and *Snowmobiling* under *To Do—Snow Sports.*)

Gallatin National Forest (406-587-6701; www.fs.fed.us/r1/gallatin), P.O. Box 130, Bozeman 59771. The 1.8 million acres of Gallatin National Forest provide a lifetime of outdoor recreational opportunities while protecting and preserving some of the country's finest natural areas. Six mountain ranges and two designated **wilderness areas—Lee Metcalf** and **Absaroka–Beartooth**—are among the forest's crown jewels, as well as hundreds of miles of developed trails for hiking, cross-country skiing, bicycling, horseback riding, and snowmobiling. Additional popular recreational pursuits include fishing in the forest's incredible array of streams, lakes, and rivers; camping, both at developed sites and in the backcountry; paddling/floating; boating; wildlife viewing; and picnicking. (See also Hebgen Lake and Hyalite Reservoir under *To Do—Boating;* the listing under *To Do—Camping;* Gallatin Petrified Forest and Palisade Falls National Recreation Trail under *To Do—Hiking;* Rendezvous Ski Trails and *Snowmobiling* under *To Do—Snow Sports;* and Gallatin National Forest Cabins under *Lodging—Other Options.*)

WILDLIFE REFUGES AND AREAS ♂ **Beartooth Nature Center** (406-446-1133; www.beartoothnaturecenter.org), in Coal Miners Park on 2nd Avenue E. (US 212), Red Lodge. Open daily mid-May through mid-October 10 AM–5:30 PM (weather permitting); daily mid-October through mid-May 9 AM–1 PM (weather permitting); $4 adults, $2 children. Native animal species that have either been habituated to humans or wounded by humans find refuge at this educational, nonprofit center. Animals dwelling at Beartooth include bears, bobcats, deer, elk, farm animals, foxes, mountain lions, pronghorn, and wolves, among others. Children will enjoy the petting zoo.

Dome Mountain Wildlife Management Area (406-247-2940; www.fwp.state .mt.us/habitat/wma/dome.asp), south on US 89 from Livingston for 21 miles, then west on Chico Road at Emigrant for 1 mile, then south on MT 540 for 3 miles, then 8 miles south on Sixmile Creek Road. Adjacent to Dailey Lake, this 4,680-acre area's primary focus is to protect and preserve historic winter range for elk. Year-round wildlife viewing opportunities include the chance to see not only elk but also mule deer, hawks, and waterfowl. (See also **Dailey Lake** under *To Do—Boating.*)

Hailstone National Wildlife Refuge and Halfbreed Lake National Wildlife Refuge (406-538-8706), north of Columbus via MT 306 to Rapelje, then east of Rapelje on the Molt–Rapelje Road. This complex of wildlife refuges ends in the south with the state-managed **Eastlick Pond–Big Lake Wildlife Management Area.** This is not a developed recreation area but, rather, a refuge for waterfowl and migratory birds. Bird-watching opportunities are therefore excellent, as are opportunities to glimpse other animals, including pronghorn antelope and prairie dogs. Hiking is allowed as well.

OTHER WILD PLACES See **Grizzly & Wolf Discovery Center** under *To See—For Families.*

✳ Lodging
BED & BREAKFASTS

Absarokee 59001
♿ **Brookside Bed and Breakfast**
(406-328-4757), 103 Brook Street. In the hamlet of Absarokee, you'll enjoy peace and quiet at this relaxing B&B

with easy access to the fishing and rafting opportunities afforded on the Stillwater River and hiking in the nearby Beartooth Mountains. Amenities include a large family-style common room, a hot tub, and a delectable, filling breakfast served each morning either in the dining room or on the streamside patio. You'll stay in one of four bedrooms ($75–90).

Big Timber 59011

Big Timber Inn Bed and Breakfast (406-932-4080; www.finditlocal .com/bigtimber/lodging.htm), P.O. Box 328. Take Exit 370 off I-90, then go east on the north-side Frontage Road for roughly 1.5 miles to the second house at the end of the drive. Unwind on the banks of the Yellowstone River in one of two bedrooms on the ground floor of this cozy home. You'll also enjoy access to a family room with a wood-burning stove and a television. A full breakfast is included in your nightly rate ($60).

See also **the Grand Hotel Restaurant** under *Dining Out.*

Bozeman

Fox Hollow Bed and Breakfast and Guest House (1-800-431-5010; 406-582-8440; www.bozeman-mt .com), 545 Mary Road, Bozeman 59718. Spacious, private accommodations and easy access to surrounding recreational opportunities are complemented by a full gourmet breakfast served daily. Situated on 2 acres and surrounded by open space, this modern, country-style bed & breakfast features a wraparound porch, a hot tub, and private baths for all of the five guest rooms ($89–239). You can also combine two of those rooms to rent the Guest House, a 1,200-square-foot, two-story house that sleeps six (3-night minimum stay).

Lehrkind Mansion Bed and Breakfast (1-800-992-6932; 406-585-6932; www.bozemanbedandbreakfast .com), 719 N. Wallace Avenue, Boze-

man 59715. Stay in style and modern comfort at this spectacular 1897 Queen Anne–style Victorian mansion, listed on the National Register of Historic Places. Inside, decor includes period antiques and a mélange of plant life—as well as overstuffed chairs—encouraging you to settle in and enjoy your surroundings, as well as a music parlor and library. Additional amenities include a hot tub and a full gourmet breakfast served daily ($99–159).

Voss Inn (406-587-0982; www .bozeman-vossinn.com), 319 S. Willson, Bozeman 59715. You'll stay in one of six bedrooms—all with private baths—in this restored 120-year-old Victorian mansion just three blocks from downtown Bozeman. You can choose to take your full gourmet breakfast daily in your room, or you can sit with other guests in the dining room. You can also amble through the inn's lovely Victorian rose garden and perennial gardens or take tea on the front porch ($110–130).

Emigrant 59027

Johnstad's Bed and Breakfast and Log Cabin (1-800-340-4993; 406-333-9003; www.johnstadsbb.com), 03 Paradise Lane. Gorgeous views of the surrounding mountains await guests at this newly constructed bed & breakfast that sits on 5 acres in aptly named Paradise Valley. All three of the guest rooms feature private bathrooms, and a full breakfast is included in the rate ($85–115). A short stroll from the lodging brings you to private fishing access on the Yellowstone River. The three-bedroom Log Cabin can accommodate up to six guests, with two private bathrooms, a full kitchen, and a TV/VCR ($150).

&. **Paradise Gateway Bed and Breakfast and Log Cabins** (1-800-541-4113; 406-333-4063; www.wtp .net/go/paradise), Box 84. Located 25.5 miles south of Livingston on US 89 between mile markers 26 and 27. You can really stretch your legs on this bed & breakfast's 68 acres of riverfront land along the Yellowstone River (an anglers' delight!) while enjoying views of the surrounding mountains. Each guest room has a queen bed and private bath, and you can choose from a hearty full breakfast or a healthy and light (but scrumptious) breakfast each morning ($85–120). Another option is to rent one of the two extremely private and lovely cabins, where you can enjoy a full array of modern amenities in a rustic setting ($160–225).

Yellowstone Country Bed and Breakfast (1-800-459-8347; 406-333-4917; www.yellowstonebb.com), P.O. Box 1002. Drive south of Livingston on US 89 until mile marker 28.5. Stay in a comfortable, two-bedroom log cabin on the banks of the Yellowstone River, choosing each morning to sit down to a full breakfast or to grab a continental breakfast if you're on the go. With only two guest cabins, your privacy and the attention to details are virtual guaranteed. Each cabin has a private bath, a small kitchen, and a porch with tremendous mountain views ($150, 2-day minimum).

Gardiner 59030

&. ✧ **Headwaters of the Yellowstone Bed and Breakfast** (1-888-848-7220; 406-848-7073; www.head watersbandb.com), 9 Olson Lane. Only 3.5 miles from the entrance to Yellowstone National Park you'll find this newly constructed bed & breakfast on the banks of the Yellowstone River,

which features five bedrooms in the main house as well as two private cabins, if you prefer that option. One of the rooms in the main house is especially suited for a family with children, as are the cabins. A full breakfast is served every morning, and the hosts can help you arrange recreational activities upon request ($85–150).

Yellowstone Suites Bed and Breakfast (1-800-948-7937; 406-848-7937; www.wolftracker.com/ys), 506 4th Street. Location, location, location! This bed & breakfast situates you a scant three blocks from the historic Roosevelt Arch that marks the north entrance to Yellowstone National Park. In a beautiful 1904 three-story stone house, you'll sleep in one of four guest rooms, two with private baths, and enjoy amenities that include a hot tub, gardens, a common area with TV/VCR, and a full, buffet-style breakfast served daily ($47–108).

Livingston 59047

&. **Blue Winged Olive Bed and Breakfast** (1-800-471-1141; 406-222-8646; www.bluewingedolive.net), 5157 US 89. Located 3 miles south of Livingston, this B&B sits on 10 acres of land with tremendous views of the surrounding mountains. Guests stay in one of four guest rooms with private baths and enjoy a full breakfast served daily ($90–115). Anglers in particular will find all of their needs met at this lodging, with its collection of angling books, magazines, and videos, as well as fly-tying benches and information on the region's entomology. The hosts will also gladly assist in arranging for guided fly-fishing trips, lessons, and access to private waters.

Mission Creek Ranch Bed and Breakfast (1-800-320-5007; 406-222-8290; www.missioncreekbandb.com),

10 Mission Creek Road. Get a taste of Montana's roots and history at this new bed & breakfast situated on a historic working cattle ranch. This ranch has been raising Black Angus cattle since 1869, so they probably know what they're doing by now, and it's got to be something right. You can choose to participate in ranch activities or simply observe during your stay in one of the ranch's four spacious bedrooms, all of which have private baths. Great fly-fishing opportunities are on the premises, too. A full ranch-style breakfast is included with your room rate ($90–140). Also available is the original ranch house, which has been restored and sleeps up to eight ($125–140, 2-night minimum).

Red Lodge 59068

Inn on the Beartooth (1-888-222-7686; 406-446-1768; www.bbgetaways .com/innonthebeartooth), 6648 US 212. Situated directly on the banks of Rock Creek south of Red Lodge, this lovely inn provides a perfect launching pad for your recreational activities in the surrounding mountains. Two outdoor hot tubs make a wonderfully relaxing finish to a day filled with outdoor fun—or perhaps you'll choose to sleep in the Honeymoon Suite, which features a two-person Jacuzzi ($175). A country-style breakfast is served daily, no matter which of the six rooms you stay in ($100–175).

Lazy Bear Bed and Breakfast (406-446-0303; www.lazybearbb.com), 302 S. Broadway. Just a skip and a jump from the thick of the action in Red Lodge, you'll find this well-appointed B&B. Sleep in one of three guest bedrooms, all of which have private baths and queen beds, and two of which feature spa-style bathtubs. Common areas include a large front porch, a dining area, and a parlor with books, magazines, and a TV/VCR. Wake up each morning to dine on a full and hearty mountain breakfast ($80–150).

Weatherson Inn (1-866-806-2142; 406-446-0213; www.weathersoninn .com), 314 N. Broadway. Enjoy staying in the elegance of this early-1900s Victorian home, fully restored with modern amenities, just two blocks from the hip downtown area of Red Lodge. You can stay in the West Room, which features a queen bed and private bath with spa tub, or in the Suite, which can sleep up to four guests and includes a bedroom, sitting room, and private bathroom. A full breakfast featuring fresh baked goods is served daily in the sunroom, offering fare for both hearty and lighter appetites ($79–115).

Reed Point 59069

Bunkhouse Bed and Breakfast (406-932-6537; www.bunkhouse.biz), 361 Bridger Creek Road. You and your family (even Fido is welcome) can stay in the cozy comfort of your own log cabin just a few feet from the burble of Bridger Creek in this unique bed & breakfast ($50–85). The one-room cabin features a double bed, a bunk bed, and a small child's bed, as well as a modern, private bathroom and amenities suitable for preparing basic meals. In addition to the cabin, there is a guest room available in the main house. Full breakfasts served daily may feature freshly picked berries (seasonal). Horseback riding by the hour ($18) or the day ($90) is available, as are guided fly-fishing and vacation packages (extra charge).

Silver Gate 59081

Log Cabin Café and Bed and Breakfast (406-838-2367), 1 mile

from northeast entrance to Yellowstone National Park on US 212. Open
mid-May through October 1. Stay in a
rustic cabin next to this historic café,
which has been serving travelers to
the area since 1937. The cabins, which
were built in the 1930s as well, have
been modernized. Each features two
log beds as well as easy access to restrooms and the shower house. Children must be 8 years or older. The
café, open daily, features home-style
American cooking. Breakfast is included with a stay at the cabins ($75–90).

West Yellowstone 59758

& **West Yellowstone Bed and
Breakfast** (406-646-7754; www
.westyellowstonebandb.com), 20
Crane Lane. Whether you're visiting
in summer or winter, you'll find that
this B&B's great location gives you
easy access to local attractions. Situated only 6 miles from Yellowstone
National Park's West Entrance, this
owner-built structure features three
guest rooms, all with wood floors,
private entrances, and private bathrooms. Direct access to cross-country
ski trails and snowmobiling trails is
available for winter visitors. You can
even choose your breakfast entrée
from a daily menu and specify the
time you want to have it prepared
each morning ($65–129).

See also **Mountain Meadows Guest
Ranch** under *Lodging—Other
Options.*

LODGES

Absarokee

& **Stillwater Lodge** (406-328-4899;
http://my.montana.net/stillwaterlodge;
mailing address: Theresa and Dan
Burkhart, 80 S. Fiddler Creek Road,
Fishtail 59028), MT 78. Stay in

homey comfort in one of this lodge's
six affordable guest rooms. Whatever
brings you to the area, this lodge aims
to help you keep your costs down
while still enjoying your stay in a
relaxed way—whether you need a
break from camping or you want a
place to hang your hat for a month
($52–75; weekly and monthly dis-
counted rates available).

Big Sky 59716

& **Big EZ Lodge** (1-877-244-3299;
406-995-7003; 406-995-7016; www
.bigezlodge.com), 7000 Beaver Creek
Road. Situated high in the Madison
Mountains, this lovely $12 million
lodge is sure to make your stay a
memorable one. Every night you'll
relax in the luxurious comfort of one
of 12 guest rooms—or in a separate
residential suite. If you're a golf lover,
you'll enjoy the lodge's 18-hole championship putting course. Anglers can
practice casting in the lodge's two
stocked trout ponds. The lodge can
also help organize your involvement in
additional recreational activities. Each
guest room comes with a laptop computer as well as Internet access. Room
rates include a gourmet breakfast, but
you can also opt for three meals a day
at the lodge ($315–$1,500).

& **Rainbow Ranch Lodge** (1-800-
937-4132; 406-995-4132; www.rainbow
ranch.com), P.O. Box 160336, Big Sky.
Physical location: 42950 Gallatin
Road, Gallatin Gateway 59730; 5
miles south of MT 64 on US 191.
Hospitality and the perfect combination of refinement and rusticity await
you at this historic lodge. You'll enjoy
luxurious accommodations in one of
the lodge's 16 guest rooms that surround the main lodge. Each room
comes with its own private bathroom,
including a tub with Jacuzzi jets, as

well as a private deck offering incredible forest views. Many rooms come with their own stone fireplaces. The main lodge is where you'll go to soak your sore muscles in the 12-person hot tub or to dine on incredible gourmet cuisine complemented by an award-winning wine list (see *Dining Out*). The concierge can help you coordinate your activity itinerary in any season ($155–300).

& **River Rock Lodge** (1-866-995-4455; 406-995-4455; www.riverrock lodging.com), 3080 Pine Drive. In the heart of Big Sky, this well-appointed lodge places you in close proximity to the area's attractions, from skiing to dining. Each morning you can partake of a gourmet continental breakfast available from 7 AM to 10 AM, while every evening you can relax in the comfort of a bed made up with a down comforter and wool blanket in one of the lodge's 29 rooms ($270–470).

Big Timber 59011

& **Burnt Out Lodge** (1-888-873-7943; 406-932-6601; www.burntout lodge.com), 248 Upper Deer Creek Road. Open May through November. A stay here gives you the opportunity to observe daily life on a 3,000-acre working sheep and cattle ranch that has been in the same family since 1934—but you don't need to worry about working yourself. A beautifully wrought log lodge features five bedrooms with private entrances and private bathrooms, making for the perfectly peaceful retreat you might be seeking. Anglers can fish in nearby Upper Deer Creek (which runs right by the lodge) or at the ranch's constructed pond. Included in the price of your room is a delicious breakfast served daily ($92–102).

Bozeman 59718

& **Gallatin River Lodge** (1-888-387-0148; 406-388-0148; www.grlodge .com), 9105 Thorpe Road. Situated on a 350-acre ranch, this lodge feature six suites of rooms for guests, all of which include private bathrooms with Jacuzzi-jetted baths and showers, hardwood floors, and comfortable queen or king beds. Anglers in particular will enjoy the focus on fishing at this lodge, with its private fishing pond, easy access to the Gallatin and other nearby rivers, and fishing guides (extra charge). A full-service gourmet restaurant is located on the premises, and breakfast and airport transportation are included in the lodging rate ($170–270).

Cooke City 59020

Antlers Lodge (1-866-738-2432; 406-838-2432; www.cookecityantlers lodge.com), 311 Main Street E. This year-round lodge offers guests the opportunity to stay in one of 18 cozy cabins—all with private baths—that surround the main lodge. The lodge itself is open for guests' rest and relaxation from early in the morning until late at night, offering a warm and comfortable setting with its two large stone fireplaces, a big-screen television, and a hot tub. Winter-sports enthusiasts will delight in simply stepping outside to gain access to their activity of choice, whether it's snowshoeing or wildlife-watching ($55–90).

Gallatin Canyon 59730

Big River Lodge (1-800-628-1011; 406-763-5504; www.bigriverlodge .com), 60 Squaw Creek Road, off US 191. This fine lodge on the banks of the Gallatin River is situated in the midst of verdant Gallatin National Forest. Five fully furnished, modern cabins, all of which have more than 1,500 square feet of living space, provide all of the comforts of home—and maybe even more. You can also choose to stay in a suite of rooms in the main lodge. You'll enjoy a delicious gourmet breakfast and dinner (included in your lodging rate) prepared by a talented chef—with wine and beer included. Also, you will have access to 2 miles of Story Spring Creek—private water perfect for year-round trout fishing—as well as assistance in coordinating any other activities that might pique your interest ($450–900).

Gardiner 59030

Above the Rest Lodge (1-800-406-7748; 406-848-7747; www.abovethe restlodge.com), 8 Above the Rest Lane. Located just 2 miles from Yellowstone National Park, Above the Rest Lodge has five cabins, each with a stunning view of the park and Mammoth Hot Springs. The cabins have at least one private bathroom each (the Mansion has two and a half baths!), and they sleep from one to 14 people, depending on the cabin you choose. All have fully equipped kitchens and TV/VCRs, among other amenities ($125–260).

Red Lodge 59068

&. **Chateau Rouge** (1-800-926-1601; 406-446-1601; www.chateaurouge .com), 1505 S. Broadway. Your own little mountain A-frame chalet awaits you at this darling 24-unit lodge just minutes from the Red Lodge Mountain Ski Resort. Each unit contains a fully equipped kitchen, cable television with 40 channels, and at least one queen bed. The two-bedroom units have their own hot tub and wood-burning fireplace, with free wood supplied. The main lodge has

an indoor pool and spa, as well as a large common area with a natural stone fireplace ($44–150).

West Yellowstone 59758

&. **Sleepy Hollow Lodge** (406-646-7707; www.sleepyhollowlodge.com), 124 Electric Street. Open May through October. For comfortable, affordable, and private accommodations with personal attention to your vacationing needs, you'd be hard-pressed to find a better place to sleep than Sleepy Hollow. Stay in a log cabin with a private bathroom—and most come with a complete kitchen—and enjoy a complimentary continental breakfast each morning ($69–88). Catering to fly-fishermen in particular, this lodge offers fly-tying benches, information about local fishing, a fishing library, and assistance in finding a great fishing guide. The entrance to Yellowstone National Park is merely blocks away.

Three Bear Lodge (1-800-646-7353; 406-646-7353; www.threebearlodge .com), 317 Yellowstone Avenue. You can find something as simple as a single room with a private bath and queen-size bed here—or you can take a group of family or friends and stay in a six-person suite. Every guest enjoys access to amenities that include four hot tubs, a heated pool, and easy access to the delicious food available at the on-premises **Three Bear Restaurant and the Grizzly Lounge** ($50–148).

&. **Yellowstone Lodge** (1-877-239-9298; 406-646-0110; www.yellow stonelodge.com), 250 S. Electric Street. Select a standard hotel-style room with two queens or one king bed and a private bathroom, or stay in a suite, with a microwave and refrigerator, that features up to three beds and can sleep six adults. A free continental breakfast for guests is served daily, and guests enjoy access to a heated, indoor pool and a hot tub ($49–139).

OTHER OPTIONS ♿ **Gallatin National Forest Cabins** (406-587-6701; www.fs.fed.us/r1/gallatin), P.O. Box 130, Bozeman 59771. A large number of **rental cabins** (some handicapped accessible) sleeping two to 10 people are available throughout the forest near Big Sky, Big Timber, Bozeman, Cooke City, Livingston, and West Yellowstone ($20–35). Amenities vary from extremely primitive (i.e., no vehicular access, no drinking water, no electricity) to catering to providing a full array of creature comforts (electricity, water, kitchen, drive-up access, furnishings). (See also Gallatin National Forest under *To Do—Camping* for contact information for individual ranger districts; and Gallatin National Forest under *Wilder Places—Forests.*)

Montana Vacation Homes (1-888-871-7856; 406-586-1503; www .montanavacation.com), Intermountain Property Management, Inc., 1807 W. Dickerson, Suite A, Bozeman, 59715. From West Yellowstone to Bozeman, Livingston to Gardiner, a number of well-appointed, gorgeous vacation homes await your visit. Maybe you'll pick the two-bedroom **Carpenter Rock Cabin** with its lovely masonry, just 25 miles south of Bozeman. Need something larger? How about the 3,000-square-foot **Gallatin River Haven,** a log home situated on 10 acres of land through which both the Gallatin River and Baker Creek run? Choose from a number of properties, all of which promise to serve your needs for a unique Montana hideaway.

Mountain Home–Montana Vacation Rentals (1-800-550-4589; 406-586-4589; www.mountain-home.com), P.O. Box 1204, Bozeman 59771. Searching for just the right Montana getaway to host your family reunion? Consider the seven-bedroom **Sweetwater Lodge**—with its indoor pool— in Big Sky. Or perhaps you're looking for a cute little romantic cottage where you and your honey can enjoy some rest and relaxation? Think about the cozy, secluded, one-bedroom **Hoss Creek Cabin** on a 40-acre farm in Gallatin Valley. Whatever type of Montana retreat you're seeking, if you're looking for a rental home in this region, chances are that you'll find something that suits your fancy from among the choices offered by this company.

See also **ranch vacations** under *To Do—Unique Adventures.*

Big Sky 59716
♿ 🎿 **Lone Mountain Ranch** (1-800-514-4644; 406-995-4644; www.lm ranch.com), P.O. Box 160069. Located 4.5 miles west of US 191. Open most of the year, this guest ranch provides visitors with equal—and abundant— recreational opportunities in both summer and winter. Winter visitors will enjoy access to the ranch's more than 80K of professionally groomed trails, along with opportunities for dinner sleigh rides, ski lessons, and close proximity to Big Sky Ski Resort. Summer visitors can book guided fly-fishing trips, as well as take part in horseback riding, guided tours of Yellowstone National Park, hiking, children's activities, and more. Lodging is in comfortable cabins, and three gourmet meals a day are included. Rates vary according to season and activities selected. Reservations required.

& **Mountain Meadows Guest Ranch** (1-888-644-6647; 406-995-4997; www.mountainmeadows ranch.com), 7055 Beaver Creek Road. Open all year except for May and the first half of November. In keeping with the apparent theme of this region, this nearly year-round guest ranch can provide access to a complete recreation-oriented vacation—and you'll never even have to leave the property, unless you want to. Summer activities include horseback riding, hiking, golf, fly-fishing, swimming, white water rafting, and tennis. Wintertime brings the opportunity to cross-country ski on the ranch's 30K of groomed trails, as well as sledding, snowshoeing, and sleigh rides, plus close proximity to Big Sky Ski Resort. You can choose to simply enjoy the comfortable accommodations and delicious gourmet meals while paying for your own activities, select a bed & breakfast plan, or book an all-inclusive activity-filled vacation ($150–330 per adult, depending on package selected; rates based on double occupancy). Reservations required.

See also the Grizzly Loop under *To Do—Bicycling;* **320 Guest Ranch** under *To Do—Horseback Riding;* and **Big Sky Ski Resort** and **Moonlight Basin Ski Resort** under *To Do—Snow Sports.*

Bozeman

Baxter Guest House (406-896-4910; 406-582-7523; www.baxterguest house.com), 3864 E. Baxter Lane, Bozeman 59719. If you're looking for a great place for your family to stay in Bozeman, Baxter Guest House might be just what you need. Constructed in 2002, this award-winning, country-style home sits just minutes from Bozeman's downtown area, but it surrounds you with stylish landscaping and tremendous mountain views. Some 3,700 square feet of living area will allow you to spread out, with a master bedroom suite, three additional bedrooms (all bedrooms have private baths), a living room, dining room, kitchen, family room, and game room ($1,500 per week; 3-night minimum).

🐾 **International Backpackers Hostel** (406-586-4659), 405 W. Olive Street, Bozeman 59715. You'll be hard-pressed to find a less expensive way to put a roof over your head for the night than this hostel. No-frills lodging includes bunk-style accommodations and shared bathrooms, laundry facilities, and a kitchen area—perfect for the budget-minded traveler ($16 per person). If you don't mind paying more than twice as much, privacy can be yours as well ($35).

Cooke City 59020

Big Moose Resort (406-838-2393; www.bigmooseresort.com), 715 US 212 (3 miles east of Cooke City). You'll find accommodations for three to four people in each of this small resort's cabins that lie nestled in a forest of lodgepole pines. Each cabin has a kitchenette and a private bathroom, with easy access to the surrounding recreational opportunities. Pets are permitted, and there are no televisions ($65–80).

🐾 **Cooke City Sinclair & Cabins** (1-866-700-2327; 406-838-2000; www .cookecitysinclair.com), 115 Main Street. You'll have a convenience store and gas station just a few steps away if you choose to stay in one of these two clean and snug cabins. Each cabin features its own private bathroom, two beds (a queen and a full), and complimentary coffee ($55–65).

See also **Buns 'N' Beds Deli and Cabins** and **Grizzly Pad Grill and Cabins** under *Eating Out*.

Emigrant 59027

Dome Mountain Ranch (1-800-313-4868; www.domemountainranch .com), 2017 US 89. This full-service guest ranch offers cabin accommodations and access to numerous recreational opportunities on and off the ranch, including horseback riding, mountain biking, hiking, white-water rafting, and fly-fishing at the ranch's two private trophy lakes, among other spots. Choose to book one of eight small cabins at the main lodge, which includes a dining area, a common room, and a swimming pool with a hot tub. A full breakfast is included with a stay in any of the cabins ($75–150). You can also stay in one of a number of larger guest homes that can accommodate families and groups of up to 10 people. Package deals with activities and meals included are available as well.

&. **Golden Ratio River Ranch and Spa** (1-800-310-9543; 406-333-4190; www.goldenratioriverranch.com), 2894 US 89. Heal your heart, mind, body, and soul at this exceptional and distinctive Montana guest ranch on the banks of the Yellowstone River. The brainchild of John Fanuzzi, creator of acclaimed Golden Ratio Woodworks, Inc. (products used in spas and by massage therapists worldwide), this ranch offers a full array of pay-as-you-go spa services along with professionally designed programs focused on health, fitness, wellness, and relaxation—while also offering ready access to all of the incredible outdoor activities this region of Montana is renowned for. The ranch's four guest bedrooms all have private baths, and breakfast is included in the lodging rate ($85–120).

Fishtail 59028

Rosebud Retreat (406-328-4220; 509-627-8014; www.rosebudretreat .com), 189 W. Rosebud. Fishtail is southwest of Columbus via MT 78 o Nye Rd. to West Rosebud Rd. This is truly a home-away-from-home—a four-bedroom, three-bathroom log house with a full kitchen, a living area with TV/VCR, a pool table, and laundry facilities. Your linens and dishes are supplied for you as well in this private setting. Anglers simply need to walk across the street to access trout fishing in the West Rosebud River ($225; 3-night minimum).

Gardiner 59030

Montana Buffalo Ranch Guest Cabin (1-800-267-7255; 406-848-7007; www.montanabuffaloranch .com/cabin.html), 50 Shooting Star Trail (7 miles north of Gardiner). Imagine what Montana must have looked like back when buffalo roamed throughout its lands . . . and see it for yourself, by staying at this rustic but modern log cabin on the Montana Buffalo Ranch. Constructed from logs used in an original 1800s-era cabin, this reincarnation of that pioneer-days accommodation provides an updated, luxurious version. A hot tub is just steps out the door; inside, you'll enjoy a full kitchen, a private bathroom, a propane fireplace, hardwood floors, and sleeping accommodations for up to eight guests ($100–150).

Pray

See **Chico Hot Springs Resort and Day Spa** under *To Do—Hot Springs*.

Red Lodge 59068

&. **The Pollard** (1-800-765-5273; 406-446-0001; www.pollardhotel.com),

2 N. Broadway. Built back in 1893 and known to have housed the likes of Buffalo Bill Cody and Calamity Jane, this historic hotel underwent a total renovation in 1994. Thus today's guests can enjoy the romance of yesteryear, complemented by the most modern of amenities, in this beautifully restored lodging. The 39 guest rooms and suites vary in their offerings but can include an in-room Jacuzzi, a balcony, mountain views, and a steam bath. All guests enjoy free access to the on-premises, full-service health club, as well as easy access to the hotel's on-premises restaurant, **The Dining Room** ($74–280).

Red Lodging (1-800-673-3563; 406-446-1272; www.redlodging.com), 424 N. Broadway. If you are looking to rent a private home for your stay in Red Lodge, you'll probably find one that suits your needs through Red Lodging. More than 25 properties that sleep anywhere from three to 12 people are listed with this company, providing a wide array of amenities in addition to the standard comfortable bedrooms, equipped kitchens, private bathrooms, and living areas. You might also rent a property with a hot tub, creekside setting, or on-premises laundry facilities.

See also **Custer National Forest** under *To Do—Camping* and **Red Lodge Mountain Ski Resort** under *To Do—Snow Sports.*

Three Forks 59752

♿ **Sacajawea Hotel** (1-888-722-2529; 406-285-6515; www.sacajawea hotel.com), 5 N. Main Street. Constructed in 1910 to lodge both the passengers and crew of the Milwaukee Railroad, this 31-room hotel invites guests to partake of its historic splendor. Listed on the National Reg-

ister of Historic Places, the Sacajawea Hotel provides guests with top-quality rooms furnished with period pieces, a hot continental breakfast served daily, and use of the Three Forks Athletic Club, as well as easy access to an on-premises restaurant and surrounding attractions ($75–152).

✸ Where to Eat

DINING OUT

Big Sky

♿ **Buck's T-4 Restaurant** (1-800-822-4484; 406-995-4111; www .buckst4dining.com), 1 mile south of Big Sky on US 191. Guided by the experienced, creative hand of executive chef Scott Peterson, this restaurant features entrées that cater to both the hearty steak lover and the more adventuresome or lighter eater. On the menu you'll find classic Montana fare such as a 20-ounce Black Angus T-bone steak, as well as more exotic selections including game (elk, wild boar, venison) and even pheasant and duck concoctions. Seafood lovers will not go hungry, with an assortment of selections to choose from as well.

♿ **Rainbow Ranch Lodge** (1-800-937-4132; 406-995-4132; www.rain bowranch.com), 5 miles south of MT 64 on US 191. With ingredients delivered daily to ensure that the meals served here are of the utmost quality and freshness, no matter what you choose from the menu, you're guaranteed a remarkable taste experience. From Montana-grown lamb, chicken, buffalo, beef, and pork to wild game, lobsters from Maine, and vegetarian options as well, you can choose from a wide range of entrées to suit your appetite and then select a wine from the award-winning wine list to accompany the meal. (See also the listing under *Lodging—Lodges.*)

&. **320 Ranch Steak House & Saloon** (1-800-243-0320; 406-995-4283; www.320ranch.com/restaurant .php), 12 miles south of Big Sky on US 191. Situated on a full-service guest ranch, this restaurant features a moderately priced wine list to complement all of its delectable dishes. The menu includes both tame (beef, pork, and chicken) and game (elk, bison, trout) entrées, prepared in a number of creative ways, including combinations of the two, all served with an array of side dishes.

See also **Moonlight Dinners** under *To Do—Unique Adventures.*

Big Timber

The Grand Hotel Restaurant (406-932-4459; www.thegrand-hotel.com/menu.htm), 139 McLeod Street. Built in 1890 and now listed on the National Register of Historic Places, Big Timber's Grand Hotel features not only an upscale dining experience but also a bed & breakfast and a casual, inexpensive saloon for a less fancy meal on the town. However, if you have the means, the restaurant should not be missed, with its award-winning wine list and a menu featuring original entrées fashioned with seafood (flown in fresh daily), chicken, pasta, and steaks carved tableside.

Bozeman

&. **John Bozeman's Bistro** (406-587-4100; www.johnbozemansbistro.com), 125 W. Main Street. For lunch and dinner, this elegant restaurant serves creative entrées influenced by cuisines from around the world in a lovely, historic setting in downtown Bozeman. For lighter appetites, there is a selection of entrée salads, including a walleye Caesar salad, while heartier eaters will find an array of tempting meal options, including a number of fresh seafood selections, as well as beef, chicken, pork, and lamb. A more interesting than usual children's menu includes a complimentary ice-cream sundae (and adults should know that this restaurant is a favorite dessert spot for local adults, too).

&. **Savory Olive** (406-586-8320; www .savoryolive.com), 105 W. Main Street, in the Historic Baxter Hotel. For the discerning diner with a conscience, Savory Olive is the restaurant to choose. Whenever possible, dishes are prepared with locally and regionally grown products, thus supporting Montana's agricultural endeavors while bringing diners the freshest fare possible, prepared with attention and elegant simplicity. The menu changes seasonally and will most certainly include grass-fed beef in many entrées, as well as lamb, chicken, seafood, and fresh veggies.

See also **Gallatin River Lodge** under *Lodging—Lodges.*

Cooke City

Beartooth Café (406-838-2475; 406-838-2305), at the center of town on US 212. Savor a fine dining experience at this tried-and-true restaurant in Cooke City. Choose from a traditional American menu featuring steaks, seafood, and good burgers, as well as daily specials. Diners can enjoy the rustic atmosphere inside the 1936 log building or, in nice weather, sit on the outside porch while perusing the huge selection of bottled beers and the wine list.

Gardiner

&. **Yellowstone Mine Restaurant** (406-848-7336), US 89 next to the

Best Western Hotel. You'll find traditional American fine dining selections here, including steaks, prime rib, seafood, and pasta selections, as well as salads and an assortment of appetizers and a chef's nightly special. Children can choose from a children's menu if they like. Be sure to save room for dessert creations. A full bar is available. A breakfast buffet is spread during summer months, with breakfast served year-round.

Livingston

& **Chatham's Livingston Bar & Grille** (406-222-7909), 130 N. Main Street. Renowned landscape artist Russ Chatham purchased this restaurant and completely remodeled it in the mid-1990s. Today, this hot spot invites diners to enjoy not only the great cuisine but also Chatham's lovely depictions of Montana's distinctive landscapes that add to the restaurant's refined decor. With a chic menu featuring French and European influences—and prepared with fresh, local produce whenever possible—this restaurant has become a favored hang for both locals and celebrity-types. A wine list includes international selections for every budget, and a children's menu is available.

2nd Street Bistro (406-222-9463; www.secondstreetbistro.com), 123 N. 2nd Street, in the Historic Murray Hotel. From creative entrées with French and Mediterranean influences to souped-up versions of old favorites like macaroni and cheese and meatloaf, this relative newcomer on the Livingston restaurant scene has already earned itself a place in the town's culinary spotlight. The menu also includes a well-rounded selection of soups, salads, and appetizers, as well as hand-tossed gourmet pizzas.

Pray

✔ & **Chico Dining Room** (1-800-468-9232; 406-333-4933; www.chico hotsprings.com/saloons.html), 1 Old Chico Road, 31 miles north of Gardiner on US 89, then exit east in Emigrant. Soak in Chico's hot springs (see *To Do—Hot Springs*), and then enjoy a fine meal prepared from the freshest local fare—much of which comes straight out of this resort's own garden and greenhouse. Fresh seafood is flown in daily, all baked goods are made on the premises, and the wine cellar is sure to have a selection that matches your meal and your wallet. If you're looking for something a little less fancy, simply step over to Chico's family-friendly **Poolside Grille** or the **Chico Saloon,** both of which feature choices from **E. R.'s House of Ribs,** including massive barbecue platters, as well as burgers, sandwiches, and meal salads.

Red Lodge

& **Bridge Creek Backcountry Kitchen and Wine Bar** (406-446-9900; www.eatfooddrinkwine.com), 116 S. Broadway. This fashionable dining destination is the perfect place to sit down to a delicious, bistro-style meal—or just to sip a glass of wine in the wine bar with some friends. In the morning, stop in at Bridge Creek's coffee bar, featuring all your favorites java brews as well as freshly baked pastries, muffins, and breads to get you going. Tasty lunches include salads, sandwiches, homemade soups (clam chowder is a favorite), burgers, and wraps. Dinner options include selections for both the light and the hearty appetite, with everything from entrée salads to steaks—and vegetarians will not feel left out, either. You'll also find live entertainment on some nights and a market selling some of the same gourmet products used by the chef to prepare your meal.

Three Forks

Historic Headwaters Restaurant (406-285-4511; www.headwaters restaurant.com), 105 S. Main Street. Fresh local produce, from veggies and herbs to buffalo steaks and beef, make up the menu at this restaurant, located in a restored 1908 building that was originally a restaurant. Pretty much everything is prepared on the premises, from salad dressings and soups to smoked meats and desserts—and, of course, delicious American entrées, all served with multiple side dishes. Sit outside on the patio in nice weather and sample a local microbrew while you await your feast.

West Yellowstone

& Bullwinkle's Saloon & Eatery (406-646-7974; www.wyellowstone .com/bullwinkles), 19 Madison Avenue. Choose from daily pasta, seafood, and wild game specials or from the regular menu that includes burgers and sandwiches, as well as seafood, chicken, ribs, steaks, pastas, and a good selection of original entrée salads. Sit down for a lunch or dinner on the town—or call ahead and grab a boxed lunch to go. Step into the saloon for a microbrew, a glass of wine, and/or a game of video poker before or after your meal—or just to relax anytime.

♂ & Oregon Short Line Restaurant (1-800-646-7365; 406-646-7365; www .doyellowstone.com), 315 Yellowstone Avenue. You can almost believe that you're one of the original visitors to Yellowstone when you step into this restaurant, with its turn-of-the-20th-century-themed decor. Savor a succu-

lent dinner of wild game or buffalo (or something a little more tame, if you prefer), and then relax for a drink or two in the adjacent **Iron Horse Saloon.** This restaurant serves breakfast and lunch, too—and kids 12 and under who are guests at the Holiday Inn eat for free, making it a great choice for families looking to stay the night. (See also Oregon Shortline 1903 Executive Railroad Car under *To See— Historic Landmarks, Places, and Sites.*)

EATING OUT

Big Sky

& Bambu Bar and Asian Bistro (406-995-4933; 406-580-7018), in Big Sky Mountain Village, third floor of Arrowhead Mall. Pan-Asian fusion entrées blend flavors of the Orient (Thai, Chinese, and Japanese) with one another in wonderful, healthy combinations at this trendy restaurant—but if you're like me, it's the sushi that will bring you through the doors. Yes, you can find sushi in Montana! You can also stick around after dinner on some nights for entertainment that may include a DJ, open mike, or live band.

♂ & Dante's Inferno (406-995-3999; 406-995-3998), 1 Lone Mountain Trail. With views of the ski slopes from the tables, this family restaurant welcomes the pre- and post-ski crowd with its hearty American and Italian fare. A lunch menu filled with pizza, pasta, meatball subs, burgers, nachos, wraps, and salads is sure to please. Ten beers on tap and 36 in bottles will delight the connoisseurs of such brews during the après-ski time. For dinner, you can sit down to a hand-cut Angus steak, seafood, or an assortment of pastas—and kids can choose items from a children's menu, too.

Huckleberry Café (406-995-3130), 1700 Big Sky Road. This Big Sky fixture features locally themed decor, but what really packs in the crowds is its renowned breakfast fare—served all day long. Open seasonally, this popular hang will not leave you empty for a long day on the slopes or the trails, nor will it disappoint for hearty après-ski fare.

Big Timber

See **the Grand Hotel Restaurant** under *Dining Out.*

Bozeman

🔌 ♿ **La Parilla** (406-586-2100), 1533 W. Babcock. This quick and easy Mexican joint features giant made-to-order burritos stuffed to the bursting point with your choice of filling and toppings. The organic buffalo steak filling is highly recommended. Other choices include chicken, Alaskan salmon, and beef, as well as plenty of selections for vegetarians. Beans, rice, cheese, tomatoes, lettuce, and salsas with varying degrees of heat are just some of the toppings that you can choose to add to the mix.

♿ 🔌 **Mackenzie River Pizza Company** (406-587-0055; www.mackenzie riverpizza.com), 232 E. Main Street. This is the original location of this now statewide pizza restaurant, which claims to have first introduced Bozeman to the idea of gourmet pizza back when it opened its doors in 1993. Apparently the trend caught on, as Mackenzie's now has 11 locations in Montana. Step inside for a true Montana pizza experience: the decor is purely western, and the pizzas are purely original—and delicious. You can, of course, choose one of the old standbys (cheese or pepperoni, anyone?), but why would you when you

could sample a Polynesian, Branding Iron, or Rustler, among other specialties, all of which feature unique and exotic topping combinations.

Main Street Overeasy (307-587-3205), 9 E. Main Street. This popular breakfast spot features all of the menu mainstays that you'd expect in an American breakfast restaurant—but without the greasy-spoon veneer that so often characterizes such a locale. This place is casual, comfortable, and clean, and the attentive staff at this tidy café serves you your bottomless cup of coffee right away, and your entrée follows shortly.

Pickle Barrel (406-587-2411; www .picklebarrelmt.com), 809 W. College. For the true ice-cream lover, there's practically nothing worse than going out for an ice cream and being served a minuscule scoop of the good stuff—and paying $3 for it, too! Thankfully, a trip to the Pickle Barrel is the ice-cream junkie's dream come true—a single scoop gives you an enormous helping of the Montana-made stuff for under $2. And if you're hungry for something a little heartier, the Pickle Barrel is famous for its huge, fresh sandwiches, too—both hot and cold.

Bridger

♿ **Bridger Cafe and Casino** (406-662-3201), 108 S. Main Street (MT 310). Stop in to fill your tanks up at this family-style restaurant that prides itself in serving fresh, homemade, and hearty meals to diners, along with daily soup selections and a salad bar. Broasted chicken and chicken-fried steak are particular specialties.

Cooke City

Buns 'N' Beds Deli and Cabins (406-838-2030), 201 US 212. Grab a sandwich to go from this delicious deli—or stop in and stay while you nosh. With fresh bread baked daily, tantalizing barbecue, smoked meats, and vegetarian selections, one of the sandwiches offered here will no doubt fit the bill. And if you're looking for a place to spend the night, you might as well ask about their cabins, too.

Gardiner
& **Outlaw's Pizza** (406-848-7733), US 89 (in Yellowstone Outpost Mall 1 mile from park entrance). This pizza parlor offers you more than just the average pie—here you'll find an assortment of gourmet pizza selections as well as pasta specialties and a soup and salad bar. The decor is, of course, Old West in its entirety, with fun art and memorabilia of wild days gone by. A wine list and an array of beer options are available, as are take-out orders.

Livingston
Crazy Coyote Mexican Food (406-222-1548), 206 S. 11th Street. Feeling a little bit burnt out on American food? Then step into this treasure trove of Mexican menu selections right smack-dab in the middle of steak-land. Not only will the delicious meals and fresh salsas delight your needy taste buds but also your pocketbook won't lose much of its girth in this reasonably priced establishment.

& **Pickle Barrel** (406-222-5469), 131 S. Main Street. See the listing above under *Eating Out—Bozeman.*

Pray
See **Chico Dining Room** under *Dining Out—Pray.*

Red Lodge
🍴 **Bear Creek Saloon** (406-446-3481; www.redlodge.com/bearcreek), 7 miles east of Red Lodge via MT 308. You won't find any pork on the menu at the Bear Creek Saloon—but you'll still see plenty of pigs. Join in the fun (summer season only) at this award-winning steakhouse, where your delicious dinner of beef, chicken, shrimp, or buffalo is followed by the real nightly attraction—the pig races! Since 1988, watching the pigs fly around the track has proven just as delightful as the dining experience—and these unique events have raised more than $60,000 in scholarship money for students from Carbon County.

Bogart's Restaurant (406-446-1784; www.redlodge.com/bogarts), 11 S. Broadway. Hungry? Step in to relax in the rustic, country comfort of this favorite eatery, which features an enormous menu filled with appetizing selections, including pages of American and Mexican starters, salads, and entrées, as well as a list of creative pizzas, any one of which is guaranteed to leave you stuffed to the gills. For a truly wild and unusual pizza experience, try the Kate-a-Roo—have you ever had walnuts on pizza before? Don't knock it till you've tried it! A number of local microbrews are available on tap, and margaritas are good here, too.

🍴 **Lucky Dog Wraps & Taps** (406-446-9909; www.luckydogwraps.com), 202 S. Broadway. You'll find a casual and comfortable atmosphere for eating lunch or dinner or just sipping a local microbrew at this retro, hip café. Creative wraps, burritos, homemade chili, and nachos make up the menu. Vegetarian choices extend beyond the boring norm of cheese and veggies inside a tortilla, with inspired selections including "veggie Thai peanut wrap" and a vegetarian chili option.

Round Barn Restaurant and Theater (406-446-1197; www.roundbarn restaurantandtheater.com), 2 miles north of town on US 212. For a unique, entertaining, and historical experience, stop in for a homemade buffet-style meal (complete with a 50-item salad bar)—or even just a dessert—at this former dairy barn, now listed on the National Register of Historic Places. If you do a bit of advance planning, you can make reservations not only to eat dinner but also to catch one of the Round Barn's live theater performances, which can include anything from music (country, jazz, rock 'n' roll— you name it) to standup comedy or a full-length play.

See also **the Pollard** under *Lodging—Other Options*.

Silver Gate

See **Log Cabin Café and Bed and Breakfast** under *Lodging—Bed & Breakfasts*.

Three Forks

Wheat Montana Farms Bakery & Deli (406-285-3614; www.wheat montana.com), 10778 US 287. A true Montana success story, this local farm has not only spawned franchises around the state of Montana, but it also distributes its fine flours, grains, and cereals nationwide. Sample its bounty straight from the source— choose from more than 80 varieties of fresh-baked products, from breads to pastries, made from the produce of the surrounding farm. You can also grab an espresso, fill up the gas tank, and purchase some foodstuff for gifts or later preparation to give you a tasty reminder of your Montana vacation.

See also **Sacajawea Hotel** under *Lodging—Other Options*.

West Yellowstone

& **Arrowleaf Ice Cream** (406-646-9776), 29 Canyon Street. If you want a bite to eat for lunch, Arrowleaf has all the regular stuff Americans crave— sandwiches, burgers, salads, hot dogs, homemade chili and soups, and more. But the real attraction here is the ice cream, in tons of flavors, served straight up, in a shake, in a freshly made waffle cone, or with toppings. They even have frozen yogurt and sugar-free options for those who want all of the pleasure with less of the guilt.

& **Canyon Street Grill** (406-646-7548; www.wyellowstone.com/canyon streetgrill), 22 Canyon Street. Fun for the whole family—and not too hard on the pocketbook—this '50s-style diner hearkens back to the days when you'd head to the corner restaurant for some hearty, well-made American food. No fast food will be found here; instead, Canyon Street offers made-to-order favorites like six different styles of chicken sandwiches, more than a dozen creative burgers, and five vegetarian sandwiches, as well as basket meals, salads, and, of course, malts and milk shakes in a rainbow of flavors.

 Pete's Rocky Mountain Pizza and Pasta (406-646-7820), 104 Canyon Street. Located near the west entrance of Yellowstone National Park, this family restaurant is a favorite for home-style, full-sized Italian dinners, including spaghetti and meatballs and pizza, as well as chicken entrées and salad choices. A children's menu offers smaller-sized selections for the littler folk. Adults can choose from an assortment of microbrews as well as bottled beers and wines.

See also **Three Bear Lodge** under *Lodging—Lodges*.

✳ Special Events

March: ⚘ **Big Sky Winterfest,** Big Sky: day of Nordic and snowshoe races, team races, children's activities, and live music.

June: **Gallatin Whitewater Festival,** Gallatin Gateway (1-800-943-4111): races for canoe and kayak enthusiasts.

June and July: ⚘ **Red Lodge Mountain Man Rendezvous,** Red Lodge (1-888-281-0625; 406-446-1718): annual living-history event re-creating 1830s fur-trapper encampment, with family events, costume dress, storytelling, historical seminars, and camping.

July: **Jim Bridger Day,** Bridger: annual event celebrating the town's namesake includes a parade, car show, barbecue, street dance, and more. **Livingston Depot Center Festival of the Arts,** Livingston (406-222-2300; www.livingstondepotcenter .com): annual juried art festival open to artists and craftspeople of all genres. **Fat Tire Frenzy,** Red Lodge: annual mountain biking event held on the Silver Run Trail, a technical, arduous single-track trail.

August: **Bite of Bozeman,** Bozeman (406-586-4003; 406-587-8848): restaurants deck out the downtown with samples of their culinary wizardry.

September: ⚘ **Running of the Sheep,** Reed Point (Stillwater County): Labor Day weekend festivity includes sheep running through town's main street, beauty (and not-so-beautiful) contests for sheep, a parade, vendors, a street dance, children's activities, food, and more. **Belgrade Fall Festival,** Belgrade: community festival includes a parade, barbecue, a dance, an arts-and-crafts fair, and more. **Mountain Bike and Fine Arts Festival,** Rapelje (Stillwater County): includes a 100K endurance race for mountain bikers, a shorter race for mountain bikers of all ages and ability levels, barbecue, and a costume ball with period music and dances.

November: **Feast for the Beasts,** Red Lodge: annual dinner to raise money for the Beartooth Nature Center, including a cocktail hour, a silent auction, and dancing to a live band. ⚘ **Yellowstone Ski Festival,** West Yellowstone (406-646-9427; www .yellowstoneskifestival.com): annual Nordic ski festival featuring clinics, demos, races, an indoor ski show, and children's programs.

December: ⚘ **Christmas Stroll,** Bozeman (406-586-4008): parade, caroling, activities for children, street performances, food, fireworks, hayrides, and more. **Old Saint Nick Day,** Joliet: annual celebration held the first Sunday of December, including horse-drawn wagon pulls, a chili feed, a hot dog and marshmallow roast, and more.

SOUTHEAST MONTANA: CUSTER COUNTRY

Custer Country takes its name, of course, from Lieutenant Colonel George A. Custer. On June 25, 1876, Colonel Custer, along with some 200 U.S. soldiers, died at the hands of 1,500 Lakota Sioux, Cheyenne, and Arapaho Indian warriors in the battle of Little Bighorn. Striving to defend their ancestral homelands and to preserve their traditional ways of living, the Indians struck a decisive blow on this fateful day—one that continues to resonate into the present for both those of European ancestry and Native Americans alike. In no place is the continued power of this single historical event more apparent than at the Little Bighorn Battlefield National Monument (formerly Custer National Monument; see *To See—Historic Landmarks, Places, and Sites*), where you can tour the historic battlefield, see the Indian memorial that was dedicated in 2003, and read interpretive accounts of the causes and effects of the battle. In the area surrounding the monument, you'll find numerous related attractions, including the Custer Battlefield Museum and the Reno–Benteen Battlefield. If you visit in June, you can even catch a reenactment of the day's historic events (see *To See—Historic Landmarks, Places, and Sites* and *Special Events*).

Besides the Little Bighorn Battlefield National Monument, Native Americans figure prominently in this region in other ways, both historically and in the present time. The historic Chief Joseph Trail and the Nez Perce Trail passed through this region, marking the passage of the Indians as they moved about in their final days of freedom on these lands. Today, Custer Country is home to the Crow Indian Reservation and the Northern Cheyenne Indian Reservation, where visitors can attend powwows, fish and camp (with permits from appropriate authorities), and even book tours from Indian-run companies that can provide access to areas of the reservations usually off-limits to non–Native Americans. Additionally, Chief Plenty Coups State Park, Pictograph State Park, and numerous local museums provide more insight into the history of Native Americans in this area (see *To See—Historic Landmarks, Places, and Sites* and *To Do—Unique Adventures*).

Along with Native American history, this is an area rife with pioneer history. William Clark made his return trek along the Yellowstone River in 1806 after his party split from Lewis in early July. He inscribed his name on Pompeys Pillar

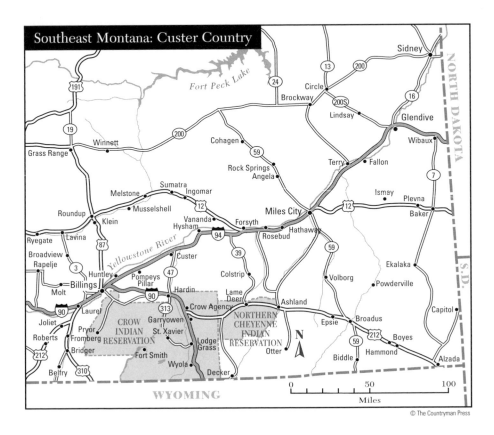

NORTH DAKOTA

Sidney

Fort Peck Lake

Circle

Brockway

Glendive

Winnett

Cohagen

Wibaux

Grass Range

Rock Springs
Angela

Terry

Fallon

Sumatra

Melstone

Ingomar

Ismay

Plevna

Roundup

Musselshell

Miles City

Baker

Klein

Vananda
Hysham

Forsyth

Hathaway

Rosebud

Ryegate

Lavina

Broadview

Custer

Ekalaka

Rapelje

Colstrip

Volborg

Powderville

Huntley

Pompeys
Pillar

Hardin

Lame
Deer

Ashland

Capitol

Billings

Molt

Crow Agency

Laurel

Garryowen

NORTHERN
CHEYENNE
INDIAN
RESERVATION

Epsie

Broadus

Joliet

CROW
INDIAN
RESERVATION

St. Xavier

N

Boyes

Roberts

Fromberg

Lodge
Grass

Otter

Biddle

Hammond

Bridger

Fort Smith

Wyola

Alzada

Belfry

Decker

WYOMING

0   50   100

Miles

© The Countryman Press

(see *To See—Historic Landmarks, Places, and Sites*), now a national monument, leaving behind the only confirmed physical evidence of the expedition's passage through Montana. The Bozeman Trail, too, passed through Custer Country, bringing more than 3,000 gold seekers this way between 1864 and 1866—and in the process, traversing through the middle of some of the last and finest of the Northern Cheyenne Indians' traditional hunting grounds in Wyoming's Powder River Basin. A number of museums throughout this region house relics and memorabilia from both the area's Native American past and its early pioneer days.

In fact, museums in this area of Montana could take up your entire vacation in and of themselves, with contents varying from the basic local and regional historical collections to unique items of note such as the O'Fallon Museum's Steer Montana, the world's largest recorded bovine; the 22,000 seashells of Mac's Museum (among other items in the collection); and the remarkable photographs taken by Evelyn Cameron in the late 1800s and early 1900s that you'll view in the Cameron Gallery. You'll even find at least two worthwhile art museums: the Custer County Art & Heritage Center in Miles City; and Billings' Yellowstone Art Museum (see *To See—Museums*).

Speaking of Billings, Custer Country's biggest city was established in 1877 as a trading post and stage stop called Coulson. The Billings area's livability was no secret—it had long been home to the Crow Indian tribe, due to the abundance of water, game, and wild fruit available there. Coulson was renamed Billings after an 1882 survey by the Northern Pacific Railroad. Billings soon became a booming railroad town, with the Chicago, Quincy, and Burlington lines joining the Northern Pacific. This legacy is evident in Billings even now, as the city remains one of Montana's leading places for shipping cattle and other agricultural products, while also supporting transportation, energy, and agricultural industries as well as medical, educational, and cultural resources. Bordered to the north by scenic rimrocks, Billings is also full of recreational opportunities as well as historical and cultural attractions. In Billings, you'll also find luxurious accommodations and dining opportunities ranging from authentic Greek food at the Athenian Greek Restaurant to top-notch nachos at Dos Machos (see *Where to Eat*).

You'll need to stay active if you want to be hungry at mealtimes, but don't worry—in Custer Country, you'll have little difficulty working up an appetite. World-class fishing opportunities await anglers visiting this region, including the acclaimed Bighorn River with its numerous access points and guide services. The Yellowstone River is a popular destination, too. In addition to this river's array of typical game fish species, in the Yellowstone, you can also fish for paddlefish, found only in the Missouri and the Yellowstone rivers in the United States and in China's Yangtze River. Ranch vacations are easy to find, too, allowing you to test your mettle at cattle herding, horseback riding, and ranch life. Plenty of additional recreational opportunities await you in Custer National Forest, the gorgeous badlands of Makoshika State Park, and Bighorn Canyon National Recreation Area, among other destinations (see *To Do—Fishing; To Do—Unique Adventures;* and *Wilder Places*).

From big-city living to wide expanses of unpopulated prairie, from historical places, museums, and guided tours to trail-less wilderness areas, Custer Country is truly a region of contrasts. Let your interests be your guide, then, in creating the Custer Country experience you want. With help from the information below, you should be able to construct a vacation chockfull of history . . . or recreation . . . or great dining experiences . . . or wildlife viewing—you get the picture!

GUIDANCE Baker Chamber of Commerce (1-866-862-2537; 406-778-2266; www.bakermt.com), 420 W. Montana Avenue, P.O. Box 849, Baker 59313.

Billings Area Chamber of Commerce and Visitor Center (406-245-4111; www.billingschamber.com), 815 S. 27th Street, Billings 59107-1177.

Carter County Chamber of Commerce (406-775-8724; 406-775-6358; www.midrivers.com/~commerce), P.O. Box 108, Ekalaka 59324.

Colstrip Chamber of Commerce (406-748-4822; www.colstrip.com), 400 Woodrose Street, P.O. Box 430, Colstrip 59323.

Crow Tribe of Indians (406-638-3700; www.crownations.net), Bacheeitche Avenue, P.O. Box 159, Crow Agency 59022.

Custer Country (1-800-346-1876; 406-778-3336; www.custer.visitmt.com), P.O. Box 1151, Baker 59313-1151.

Forsyth Area Chamber of Commerce and Agriculture (1-877-479-8468; 406-347-5656; www.forsythmontana.org), P.O. Box 448, Forsyth 59327.

Glendive, Montana Chamber of Commerce and Agriculture (406-377-5601; www.glendivechamber.com), 313 S. Merrill Avenue, Glendive 59330.

Hardin, Montana Chamber of Commerce and Agriculture (406-665-1672; www.hardinmt.com), 10 E. Railway, P.O. Box 446, Hardin 59034.

Hysham Chamber of Commerce (406-342-5457), P.O. Box 63, Hysham 59038.

Laurel Chamber of Commerce (406-628-8105; www.laurelmontana.org), 108 E. Main Street, Laurel 59044.

Miles City Area Chamber of Commerce (406-234-2890; www.mcchamber .com), 511 Pleasant Street, Miles City 59301.

Musselshell Valley Chamber of Commerce (406-323-1966; www.roundup chamber.com), P.O. Box 751, Roundup 59072-0751.

Northern Cheyenne Chamber of Commerce (406-477-8844; www .ncheyenne.net), P.O. Box 991, Lame Deer 59043. To visit the office, exit I-90 East onto US 212 in the direction of Lame Deer. The chamber is 1 block before the four-way stop on US 212.

Powder River, Montana Chamber of Commerce (406-436-2778), 119 E. Wilson Street, P.O. Box 484, Broadus 59317.

Prairie County Chamber of Commerce (406-635-4770), P.O. Box 667, Terry 59349.

Wibaux County Chamber of Commerce (406-796-2414; 406-796-2486), P.O. Box 159, Wibaux 59353.

MAKOSHIKA STATE PARK NEAR GLENDIVE

GETTING THERE Billings lies at the junction of I-90, I-94, and US 87. Laurel is west of Billings on I-90. Hardin and Crow Agency lie on I-90 southeast of Billings. Roundup is north of Billings on US 87. Hysham is east of Billings on I-94. Miles City lies on I-94 where MT 59 crosses I-94, running north to south. Miles City can also be accessed via US 12 from the east. Terry, Glendive, and Wibaux are northeast of Miles City along I-94. Baker is at the junction of MT 7 and US 12, south of Wibaux and east of

Miles City. Forsyth is west of Miles City on I-90; it can also be reached from the west on US 12.

See also *Airports, Amtrak, Bus Service,* and *Travel Information* in "What's Where in Montana."

MEDICAL EMERGENCY Big Horn County Memorial Hospital (406-665-2310), 17 N. Miles Avenue, Hardin.

Colstrip Medical Center (1-800-441-6330; 406-748-3600), 6230 Main Street, Colstrip.

Dahl Memorial Healthcare Association (406-775-8730), 225 Sandy Street, Ekalaka.

Deaconess Hospital (1-800-332-7201; 406-657-4000), 2800 10th Avenue N., Billings.

Fallon Medical Complex (406-778-3331), 202 S. 4th Street W., Baker.

Glendive Medical Center (406-365-3306), 202 Prospect Drive, Glendive.

Holy Rosary Healthcare (406-233-2600), 2600 Wilson Street, Miles City.

Powder River Medical Clinic (406-436-2333), 102 E. Morris, Broadus.

Prairie Community Medical Assistance Facility (406-635-5511), 12 MT 253, Terry.

Rosebud Health Care Hospital (406-356-2161), 383 N. 17th Avenue, Forsyth.

Roundup Memorial Hospital (406-323-2301), 1202 3rd Street W., Roundup.

St. Vincent Healthcare (406-657-7000), 1233 N. 30th Street, Billings.

✷ To See

TOWNS Baker, at the intersection of US 12 and MT 7 south of I-94, offers year-round recreational opportunities centered around **Baker Lake.** Boating, free in-town camping, fishing (and ice fishing in winter), hunting, scenic drives, and snowmobiling make this small city a haven for outdoor enthusiasts in any season.

Colstrip, located south of Forsyth on MT 39, is known as the energy capital of Montana due to its energy-producing capabilities, which include providing coal for four large coal-fired power plants. Tours are available that detail the operations of a **coal-fired power plant** and an **open-pit mine;** call the Colstrip Chamber of Commerce (see *Guidance*) for more information.

Crow Agency, located south of Hardin on I-90, serves as the tribal headquarters for the Crow Tribe of Indians, also known as the **Absaalooke Nation.** The Crow Indian Reservation encompasses almost 2.3 million acres of land in the southeastern portion of Montana. Recreational opportunities for visitors include fishing and camping. See also **Crow Country Tours** under *To Do—Unique Adventures* and **Crow Fair** under *Special Events.*

Ekalaka, the county seat of Carter County, is located south of Baker on MT 7. Home to fewer than 500 people, the town was named for the daughter of Eagle Man, an Oglala Sioux. She married David H. Russell, who was the first known white man to settle in Russell Valley. Ekalaka's modern claim to fame is that the area surrounding this tiny hamlet, known as the **Powder River Breaks,** has produced more world-champion classified bucking horses than any other single location, earning it the moniker **Bucking Horse Capital of the World.**

✍ **Hardin,** 13 miles north of the Little Bighorn Battlefield National Monument on I-90, is the county seat of Big Horn County; it's also the "big city" associated with the monument. Thus you'll find a number of amenities, including an assortment of lodging and dining options in Hardin. But don't get me wrong—this big city's population numbers fewer than 3,400 people, so we're not talking a metropolis here. Rather, you'll find small-town hospitality aplenty, plus Hardin's own local attractions, including the **Big Horn County Museum** (see *To See—Museums*), four city parks with playgrounds and picnic areas, and access to the **Bighorn River** (see *To Do—Fishing*).

Hysham, located about 75 miles east of Billings on I-94, is the county seat of Treasure County. This rural community is home to the county's museum, located on the town's main street, as well as recreational opportunities that include fishing, camping, and boating.

Lame Deer is located on US 212 south of Forsyth and east of Crow Agency and I-90, on the **Northern Cheyenne Indian Reservation.** You'll find the Northern Cheyenne Chamber of Commerce 1 block west of the four-way stop on US 212 in Lame Deer. The chamber provides visitors with area information on camping, shopping, and other activities.

Laurel is about 10 miles west of Billings on I-90. This city of about 7,000 people, also known as the Hub of Montana, boasts the largest population of any city in Montana that is not a county seat. Historic attractions include a statue of Chief Joseph and a commemorative marker for the **Canyon Creek Battlefield,** located downtown in Fireman's Park.

MUSEUMS ♿ **Big Horn County Historical Museum** (406-665-1671; www .museumonthebighorn.org), Route 1 Box 1206A (Exit 497 off I-90), Hardin. Open daily May 1 through September 30, 8 AM–8 PM; open October 1 through April 30 Monday through Friday 9 AM–5 PM; historic buildings closed October 1 through April 30; free. For an extensive view of this area's past, try to visit this museum when its historic buildings are open for touring. You can explore some 20 historic buildings on the museum's 22-acre site, including a 1911 farmhouse, an old-fashioned hospital, a country store and post office, and a one-room schoolhouse, among structures. In addition, you'll find a rotating exhibit on display in the museum's main building, as well as a gift shop and visitor center.

♿ **Carter County Museum** (406-775-6886; 406-775-6294), at the junction of MT 7 and C.R. 323, Ekalaka. Open Tuesday through Friday 9 AM–12 PM and 1 PM–5 PM, Saturday and Sunday 1 PM–5 PM; free. Exhibits on paleontology, Native Americans, and pioneers constitute the main attractions of Montana's oldest county museum, in existence since 1936. Here you'll find detailed information covering the area's prehistoric past, from the dinosaurs and their contemporaries who dwelled here some 75 million years ago to the more recent history of human inhabitation. Of particular interest are several complete dinosaur skulls and a mounted duck-billed dinosaur skeleton.

♿ **Custer Battlefield Museum** (406-638-1876; www.custermuseum.org), Exit 514 off I-90, Garryowen. Open daily Memorial Day through Labor Day 8 AM–8 PM, daily September through May 9 AM–5PM; $4 adults, $3 seniors and children 12 and older, children under 12 free. Situated on the site where the battle of Little Bighorn began on June 25, 1876, this museum features artifacts recovered from the battleground, photographic archives, the Tomb of the Unknown Soldier, artifacts from the period around the battle, a Lewis and Clark rare books and documents exhibit, and the "Peace Through Unity" Indian Memorial honoring the Lakota Sioux, Cheyenne, and Arapaho Indians who died defending their native lands and way of living during this historic event. (See also Custer's Last Stand Reenactment and Little Big Horn Days under *Special Events*.)

♿ ☘ **Custer County Art & Heritage Center** (406-232-0635; www.ccac.miles city.org), Waterplant Road (0.5 mile west of downtown Miles City off US 12; Exit 135 off I-94), Miles City. Open May through September Tuesday through Sunday 9 AM–5 PM; open September through May Tuesday through Sunday 1 PM–5 PM; closed January; free. This lovely art and heritage center displays both temporary and permanent exhibits, including photographs by local and regional photographers illustrating the area's history. Seven exhibits rotate, featuring traditional, historic, and contemporary works by artists of local, regional, and national note. The center's buildings are two former holding tanks for the Miles City Water Treatment Plant. Constructed in 1910 and 1924, they are listed on the National Register of Historic Places. The Ranger Riders Museum (see below) is just around the corner.

♿ **Frontier Gateway Museum** (406-377-8168; 406-365-4123), Belle Prairie Frontage Road (Exit 215 off I-94, then 1 mile east), Glendive. Open mid-May through mid-September Monday through Saturday 9 AM–12 PM and 1 PM–5 PM, Sunday 1–5. You'll find exhibits on fossils, wildlife, Indians, cowboys, and more modern folks in this local museum. In addition, the museum's numerous historic structures include a blacksmith shop, two country stores, a fire hall, and more.

Musselshell Valley Historical Museum (406-323-1403; www.midrivers .com/~dparrott), 524 1st Street W., Roundup. Open daily May 1 through September 30, 1 PM–5 PM; free. Exhibits include a coal tunnel, fossils, Native American artifacts, and works by local artists, as well as a one-room schoolhouse, an old-fashioned general store, an early hospital room, and more. The museum building itself is listed on the National Register of Historic Places.

O'Fallon Historical Museum (406-778-3265; www.midrivers.com/ ~bakerlo), 723 S. Main, Baker. Open Tuesday through Friday and Sunday (daily in summer) 9 AM–12 PM and

CUSTER COUNTY ART & HERITAGE CENTER

1 PM–5 PM; free. If you're interested in local Montana history, you'll find exhibits and buildings detailing that here—but really, this museum's main attraction is Steer Montana. Never heard of him? Well, now you have, and you can brag to all of your friends back home that you saw with your own two eyes the skeleton of the largest bovine ever recorded in the world. Born in 1923, this remarkable steer grew—and grew, and grew—until he reached startlingly huge proportions. He weighed in at 3,980 pounds, stood 5 feet 11 inches in height, and measured 10 feet 4 inches in length. This enormous beast traveled to more than 60 state fairs and other organized events before he died after 15 years and 4 months of life. Once you've seen Steer Montana, you'll be hard-pressed to ever look at cattle the same way! The museum's main building—the old jail—is listed on the National Register of Historic Places.

Peter Yegen Jr. Yellowstone County Museum (406-256-6811; www.pyjrycm .org), 1950 Terminal Circle, Billings. Open Monday through Friday 10:30 AM–5 PM; free. Situated across the parking lot from the main terminal at Billings Logan International Airport, this history museum brings you right back into pioneer days from the moment you walk into the log cabin that serves as its entrance. A collection of impressive exhibits illustrating local history await your perusal—and don't be fooled by the cabin's small size, as much of the museum's collection is displayed in additional space located below the floor of the cabin.

Powder River Historical Museum and Mac's Museum (406-436-2977; 406-436-2449; www.mcdd.net/museum), 102 W. Wilson, Broadus. Open Memorial Day through Labor Day Monday through Saturday 9 AM–5 PM and by appointment in the off-season; free. In this museum, you'll find an extensive collection and exhibits illustrating the area's history, including battlefield artifacts from the 1876 Reynolds Campaign, a precursor to the battle of Little Bighorn. Additional items of note include pre-1900 buggies, a restored one-room schoolhouse, Native American and pioneer artifacts, and a photo collection. Under the same roof is Mac's Museum, which represents the impressive lifelong collections of one man. These include more than 22,000 seashells, more than 1,700 arrowheads from all over the country, and many, many more unique and intriguing items.

Prairie County Museum and Cameron Gallery (406-635-5575), 101 S. Logan, Terry. Open Memorial Day through Labor Day on Monday and Wednesday through Friday 9 AM–5 PM, and Saturday and Sunday 1 PM–4 PM; open by appointment in the off-season; free. This museum complex, comprising numerous historic buildings, illustrates pioneer living as eastern Montanans experienced it. Of particular interest is the unique steam-heated outhouse, the only one known of its kind west of the Mississippi. The famous Cameron gallery features numerous photographs taken by Evelyn Cameron, a British woman, that depict the everyday life of Montanans in the late 1800s and early 1900s.

Range Riders Museum (406-232-4483; 406-232-6146), 0.5 mile west of downtown Miles City on US 12 just west of the Tongue River Bridge (Exit 135 or 138 off I-94). Open daily April 1 through October 31, 8 AM–6 PM, and by appointment in the off-season; $5 per person. Western history aficionados should not miss this impressive collection of regional relics and artifacts of all genres. You can almost feel the history come alive as you wander through the museum's brightly painted buildings filled to the brim with items of note: dinosaur bones, tools (including a large collection of broadaxes), Indian artifacts and photographs of Indians from pioneer days, photographs of former rodeo champions, an 11-building indoor frontier town, and the more than 400 firearms of the Bert Clark gun collection—to name just a few of the exhibits. The unique Custer County Art & Heritage Center (see above) is just around the corner.

RANGE RIDERS MUSEUM

Rosebud County Pioneer Museum (406-356-7547), 335 Main Street, Forsyth. Open May 15 through September 15 Monday through Saturday 9 AM–6 PM, Sunday 1 PM–6 PM; free. Local and regional everyday life for pioneers at the turn of the 20th century is the focus of this museum, located across the street from the Rosebud County Courthouse (see also *To See—Historic Landmarks, Places, and Sites*). You'll browse through collections from the area's founding families, including farm implements, Indian artifacts, and more.

🌼 ♿ **Western Heritage Center** (406-256-6809; www.ywhc.org), 2822 Montana Avenue, Billings. Open Tuesday through Saturday 10 AM–5 PM (except January); closed on Monday and on legal holidays; free. Chronicling the history of the Yellowstone Valley region, this museum's extensive collection is housed in the impressive building that formerly served as the Parmly Billings Library and is now on the National Register of Historic Places. Included in its collection are more than 16,000 artifacts, among them some 1,000 photographs of regional pertinence. The museum works closely with the Crow and Northern Cheyenne Indian tribes via its American Indian Tribal Histories Project, which has resulted not only in permanent, well-informed exhibits detailing Native American history but also in outreach projects such as Ethnobotany on Horseback.

♿ **Wibaux Museum** (406-796-9969; www.directu.com/Museum), 112 E. Orgain Avenue, Wibaux. Open May 15 through September 30 Monday through Saturday 9 AM–5 PM, Sunday 1 PM–5 PM; free. This museum is a complex of buildings of historic significance, centered around the 1892 office and house (listed on the National Register of Historic Places) of Pierre Wibaux. This young Frenchman emigrated to the United States and proceeded to become the world's most prolific cattle rancher in the late 1800s. His historic office and house have been restored and hold some of their original furnishings, as well as other items relating to local history. Also included in the museum complex are a Montana Centennial Train Car (with a mystery exhibit inside), the Old Wibaux Barber Shop, Drake Livery Stable, and the 1895 Saint Peters Catholic Church.

Yellowstone Art Museum (406-256-6804; http://yellowstone.artmuseum.org), 401 N. 27th Street, Billings. Open Tuesday through Saturday 10 AM–5 PM (until 8 PM on Thursday), Sunday noon–5 PM; closed Monday; $7 adults, $6 seniors, $3 children. Founded in 1964, this wonderful museum features both historic and contemporary art of the Rocky Mountain region. More than 4,000 works comprise the museum's permanent collection, including pieces by Will James, Charles M. Russell, and J. H. Sharp. In addition, the museum always has a number of temporary exhibitions, as well as a gift shop.

HISTORIC LANDMARKS, PLACES, AND SITES **Bell Street Bridge** (406-377-5601; www.glendivechamber.com/bridge.htm), 200 N. Merrill Avenue, Box 930, Room 1, Glendive. Walk or bicycle across this 1,300-foot-long historic steel truss structure, opened to traffic back in 1925. The bridge was closed to motorized vehicles in 1992, but a historical committee is working toward its long-term preservation as a landmark and attraction for visitors and locals alike. Today, you can take a stroll or ride a bike across the bridge and view the Yellowstone River and its banks while also appreciating the bridge for its own sake as an architectural structure of note. (See also Bell Street Bridge Day under *Special Events*.)

🚹 ♿ **Chief Plenty Coups State Park** (406-252-1289; www.fwp.state.mt.us/parks/parksreport.asp?mapnum=10), 1 mile west of Pryor (40 miles south of Billings) on the Crow Indian Reservation. Open May 1 through September 30, 8 AM–8 PM; museum open 10 AM–5 PM; free for residents, $2 adults, children 6 and under free. Plenty Coups, a Crow chief, homesteaded and farmed at this site in an effort to conform to the new lifestyle brought by European settlers. Today, you can learn about his efforts to help his people adapt to the ways of the white settlers via a small interpretive center and a walk through the grounds on a 0.6-mile trail. No camping is permitted in the park, but swimming, picnicking, and fishing are allowed. The park holds a Day of Honor on the first Saturday of each September, remembering Chief Plenty Coups with speeches, a craft fair, cultural activities, and a buffalo feast.

🚹 **Little Bighorn Battlefield National Monument** (406-638-3204; www.nps.gov/libi), on US 212 near Crow Agency. Open Memorial Day through Labor Day 8 AM–9 PM, spring and fall 8 AM–6 PM, winter 8 AM–4:30 PM; $10 per private vehicle per day or $5 per pedestrian per day. Visit the site where on June 25 and 26, 1876, Lieutenant Colonel George Custer and his more than 200 soldiers met their doom at the hands of some 1,500 Lakota Sioux, Cheyenne, and Arapaho Indian warriors striving not only to defend their lands but also to preserve their way of living and stave off the encroachment of the white settlers. Artifacts from the fields of battle are on display at the visitor center and museum. Also of interest is a self-guided auto tour connecting the Little Bighorn Battlefield with the Reno–Benteen Battlefield, several interpretive walking trails, and Custer National Cemetery.

LITTLE BIGHORN BATTLEFIELD NATIONAL MONUMENT

& Moss Mansion Historic House Museum (406-256-5100; www.mossmansion.com), 914 Division Street, Billings. Open 7 days a week with tours given on the hour (hours vary according to season, so call ahead); closed on Thanksgiving, Christmas, and New Year's Day; $7 adults, $5 seniors 62 and older, $5

LITTLE BIGHORN BATTLEFIELD NATIONAL MONUMENT

students with ID, $3 children ages 6–12, children 5 and under free. Constructed of red sandstone, this striking 1903 mansion designed by renowned New York architect Henry Janeway Hardenbergh housed the Preston Boyd Moss family in the early 20th century. Today you can see many of the original furnishings, from draperies to Persian carpets, during a 1-hour guided tour. The mansion is listed on the National Register of Historic Places. (See also Christmas at the Moss Mansion under *Special Events*.)

Pictograph Cave State Park (406-247-2940; www.pictographcave.org), 2300 Lake Elmo Drive, Billings (Exit 452 off I-90). Open May 1 through September 30, 8 AM–8 PM; free for residents, $5 per vehicle for nonresidents. A beautiful, remote locale not too far removed from the bustle of downtown Billings, this park is home to now barely visible pictographs. The pictographs date from more than 2,000 years ago and are found in three caves that humans inhabited starting at least 4,500 years ago. More than 30,000 artifacts have been recovered at this site, which also served as a burial ground for at least nine individuals. A 0.5-mile paved trail leads you through the park's three caves, including Pictograph Cave, a National Historic Landmark. You should bring binoculars to aid in viewing the pictographs here, as they will help you to discern details you might otherwise miss. No camping is permitted in the park, but picnicking facilities are available.

& Pompeys Pillar National Monument (406-875-2233; www.mt.blm.gov/pillarmon/index.html), Exit 23 off I-94, about 30 miles east of Billings. Open to drive-in traffic Memorial Day through Labor Day 8 AM–8 PM; open through September 30, 9 AM–

5 PM; closed to vehicles but open to walk-in traffic (about 0.75 mile) October through Memorial Day; $3 per vehicle. On July 25, 1806, William Clark of the Lewis and Clark expedition ascended this sandstone buttress and carved his name and the date in the rock, leaving behind the only confirmed physical evidence of his travels—and those of the Corps of Discovery—through Montana on his way back to St. Louis, Missouri. The rock also contains hundreds of petroglyphs and was of great significance to

PICTOGRAPH CAVE STATE PARK

Native Americans as well. A 0.3-mile trail takes you from the base of the tower to its top.

Rosebud County Courthouse (406-356-7318), Main Street, Forsyth. Constructed in 1912, this historic sandstone building is worth a visit before or after you stop at the Rosebud County Pioneer Museum across the street (see *Museums*). The three-story neoclassical structure features a copper dome, as well as stained glass and murals on the interior. It is listed on the National Register of Historic Places.

See also Colstrip and Laurel under *Towns;* Custer County Art & Heritage Center, Musselshell Valley Historical Museum, O'Fallon Historical Museum, Western Heritage Center, and Wibaux Museum under *Museums;* Riverside Park under *To Do—Camping;* Rosebud Battlefield State Park under *Wilder Places— Parks;* Charley Montana Bed & Breakfast and Hotel Becker Bed and Breakfast under *Lodging—Bed & Breakfasts;* Historic Jersey Lilly Bar and Café under *Dining Out;* and Caboose Saloon and Casino under *Eating Out.*

FOR FAMILIES ✐ **Folf Course** at Makoshika State Park (see complete listing under *Wilder Places—Parks*). Located in the fabulously colorful badlands of this state park adjacent to the campground you'll find a "folf"—or Frisbee golf— course, where you and the kids can stop to stretch your legs and challenge yourselves in this fun pursuit (but be sure to pack the Frisbees!).

✐ **Water parks.** In Billings, you'll find **Big Splash Water Park** (406-256-5543), 5720 S. Frontage Road (Exit 446 off I-90), and **Geyser Park** (406-254-2510), 4910 Southgate Drive (Exit 447 off I-90), among others. These easily accessed parks make for a great travel break off the interstate, and who knows? You might find yourself having just as much fun as the kids.

✐ & **ZooMontana** (406-652-8100; www.zoomontana.org), 2100 S. Shiloh Road, Billings. Open daily April 1 through October 31, 10 AM–5 PM (ticket window closes at 4 PM); open Memorial Day through Labor Day Thursday and Saturday 10 AM–8 PM (ticket window closes at 7 PM); open November 1 through March 31, 10 AM–4 PM (ticket window closes at 3 PM); $6 adults, $4 seniors 65 and older, $3 children ages 3–15. ZooMontana takes pride in the quality of its exhibits, focusing on providing its resident species with well-designed, spacious natural habitats that enable you to view the animals without disturbing them. Also distinguishing this zoo is its focus on endangered species and oft-misunderstood species, with each exhibit featuring an educational, informative write-up about its inhabitants. Completed habitats include those for the bald eagle, sika deer, eastern gray wolf, river otter, wolverine, red panda, waterfowl, Siberian tiger, and great horned owl, with addi-

ZOOMONTANA

tional plans for more species' habitats. You'll also find a 1-acre sensory garden full of native and exotic plants, designed to stimulate the senses; a children's interactive center featuring more than 11 species of domestic animals; and more. This is the only U.S. zoo that is partially funded by a grant from the Humane Society of the United States.

See also Hardin under *To See—Towns;* Two Moon Park under *To Do—Bicycling;* Riverside Park under *To Do—Camping;* Montana Fun Adventures under *To Do—Unique Adventures;* Bighorn Canyon National Recreation Area under *Wilder Places—Other Wild Places;* and Colstrip Days Celebration, Custer's Last Stand Reenactment and Little Big Horn Days, Montana Fair, and Strawberry Festival under *Special Events.*

SCENIC DRIVES **Billings to Roundup on US 87.** This 50-mile drive quickly takes you from the bustle of Billings into rolling hills and farmlands interspersed with stands of arid pine species. You'll wind through the fire-scarred **Bull Mountains,** and you'll almost certainly start to get a feel for the relative lack of population density in Montana.

Broadus to Alzada on US 212. This 60-mile stretch of highway proves to be a very enjoyable and scenic way to begin your travels through Custer Country or to exit the area, as it takes you through a wide range of scenery with little in the way of human structures to mar your enjoyment of the natural world around you. If you're just entering the state, once you get to Broadus, you can choose to go north on MT 59 to Miles City or to continue west on US 212 toward Billings. If you're leaving Montana, US 212 makes it easy to access Wyoming's **Devils Tower National Monument** (see *To See—Natural Wonders* in "North Wyoming: Devils Tower–Buffalo Bill Country"), as well as attractions in South Dakota.

Miles City to Baker on US 12. Stark, striking red hills make this 80-mile drive enjoyable, but the chance of catching sight of a **bighorn sheep** make it even more intriguing. Near the tiny town of Ismay, you may also see **zebras and llamas** grazing near the road—but as you probably already know, they are certainly not native Montanans!

Terry Badlands (406-232-7000; www.mt.blm.gov/mcfo), MT 253 to Calypso Trail northwest of Terry. The badlands outside of Terry are particularly striking due to their plethora of **multihued wind- and water-sculpted spires, hills, bridges, and buttes.** A short drive takes you right into the thick of the badlands, making for a quick jaunt off I-94 if you need a break to stretch your legs, have a picnic, or simply view the area's stunning natural scenery.

NATURAL WONDERS **Capitol Rock National Natural Landmark** (605-797-4432; www.fs.fed.us/r1/custer), 30 miles southeast of Ekalaka via MT 323, then through the Long Pines Unit of Custer National Forest (see *Wilder Places—Forests*). This enormous, white limestone uplift in Custer National Forest's Sioux Ranger District bears an uncanny resemblance to the nation's capitol building.

&. **Medicine Rocks State Park** (406-234-0900; www.fwp.state.mt.us/parks/parksreport.asp?mapnum=4), 25 miles south of Baker or 14 miles north of

Ekalaka via MT 7, then 1 mile west on a county road. Open year-round; free. Wind and water sculpted the sandstone at Medicine Rocks into latticed, pocketed arches and formations. Indians believed these rocks and the surrounding area to have "good medicine," hence the park's name. This park is a great, remote stop for picnicking, camping, wildlife viewing, and hiking on the park's 0.75-mile trail.

See also Makoshika State Park under *Wilder Places—Parks;* and Terry Badlands under *Wilder Places—Other Wild Places.*

✳ To Do

BICYCLING **Alkali Creek,** Alkali Creek Road, Billings. After you park next to the Alkali Creek School, this beginner-friendly ride will take you on a scenic, 3-mile loop with a perfect introductory section of single-track for the novice mountain biker.

BikeNet (www.bikenet.org), Billings. Billings' award-winning BikeNet Plan— also known as the Heritage Trail Plan—already has helped bring about the construction and linkage of an impressive number of bike paths, both paved and unpaved, throughout Billings, making it easy for cyclists (and pedestrians) to link much of the city together for both leisure riding and commuting purposes. In addition to Two Moon Park (listed below), you can access a BikeNet path at a number of other locations, including Coulson Park.

Custer National Forest Long Pines Unit (605-797-4432; www.fs.fed.us/ r1/custer), 30 miles southeast of Ekalaka via MT 323. Numerous Forest Service roads, solitude, ample opportunities for wildlife viewing, and ponderosa pines aplenty make this remote area a great place for the confident soloist mountain biker to get back into nature or for a romantic ride for two. Just be sure that you know what you're doing and have all of the necessities, or you could very well find yourself stranded. This is also a great place for hiking, horseback riding, and, in the winter, snowmobiling and cross-country skiing. (See also Capitol Rock National Natural Landmark under *To See—Natural Wonders;* and Custer National Forest under *Wilder Places—Forests.*)

Rimrock Trail, near Airport Road and MT 3, Billings. Pick up the trail near the intersection of US 87 and Airport Road at Boot Hill Cemetery or at Zimmerman Park. This trail system includes **Black Otter Trail** and **Zimmerman Trail East,** taking you across variable terrain from easy (suitable for novices) to difficult. Moab-esque slickrock, wild sandstone formations, and awesome views of five surrounding mountain ranges can almost make you forget the city below— except that you can still see and hear traffic (both airplanes and autos), not to mention buildings and industrial structures. Still, the relative ease with which you can access this trail system from Billings makes it a worthy destination, whether you're a novice or an expert mountain biker. If you're a novice, Zimmerman Park (west of **Zimmerman Trail**) has the best beginner-friendly trails.

⚓ **Two Moon Park,** Yellowstone River Road, Billings. A number of family-friendly trails, both gravel and paved, make this park situated on the Yellowstone River a good option for an easy 2- to 5-mile bike ride. After exploring Two

Moon's offerings, you can also hop onto the paved **Dutcher Trail,** which will take you to **Coulson Park,** also on the Yellowstone. For more details on Billings' paved bike trails, visit www.bikenet.org.

See also Bell Street Bridge under *To See—Historic Landmarks, Places, and Sites;* Pirogue Island State Park under *Paddling/Floating;* Riverfront Park under *Snow Sports;* Makoshika State Park under *Wilder Places—Parks;* Sundance Lodge Recreation Area under *Wilder Places—Other Wild Places;* and Hostetler House Bed and Breakfast under *Lodging—Bed & Breakfasts.*

BOATING **Baker Lake** (1-866-862-2537; 406-778-2266; www.bakermt.com), off US 12 in Baker. Open year-round; free. Boating isn't the only recreational opportunity at this small-town lake. Other activities include fishing (crappie, perch, pike, and walleye), swimming, and picnicking in the parks surrounding the lake.

Deadman's Basin Reservoir (406-444-2535; www.fwp.state.mt.us/parks/parks report.asp?sitenum=5509), west of Ryegate on US 12, then 1 mile north at mile marker 120. Open year-round; free. This state recreation area offers boating, camping, fishing, and swimming opportunities on the edge of Custer Country.

& **Tongue River Reservoir State Park** (406-234-0900; www.fwp.state.mt .us/parks/parksreport.asp?mapnum=2), 6 miles north of Decker on MT 314, and then 1 mile east on a county road. Open year-round for day-use (free for residents, $5 nonresidents) and camping ($15 in-season, $13 off-season). Remote and pristine, this 12-mile-long reservoir has gained quite a reputation for its excellent boating and water sports opportunities, not to mention quiet camping (106 RV-accessible sites) and excellent fishing.

See also Riverside Park under *Camping;* Lake Elmo State Park under *Wilder Places—Parks;* and Bighorn Canyon National Recreation Area under *Wilder Places—Other Wild Places.*

CAMPING **Crazy Head Springs Recreational Area** (406-477-6503; 406-477-6506), 1.5 miles south of US 212 between Lame Deer and Ashland. Located on the Northern Cheyenne Indian Reservation, this area features natural springs flowing into several ponds suitable for fishing and swimming. Camping and picnicking are popular here, too. A permit is required for overnight camping; call the Northern Cheyenne Natural Resources Department (numbers listed above) to obtain one.

Custer National Forest (605-797-4432; www.fs.fed.us/r1/custer), 1310 Main Street, Billings. The **Sioux Ranger District** near Ekalaka has four free, pack-in, pack-out campgrounds in Montana: **Ekalaka Park, Lantis Springs, Wikham Gulch,** and **McNab Pond,** which also features fishing for crappies, smallmouth bass, and rainbow trout in the stocked pond. The **Ashland Ranger District,** near Ashland, has three free, pack-in, pack-out campgrounds: **Cow Creek, Holiday Spring,** and **Red Shale;** as well as **Whitetail Cabin,** which houses up to four people for a maximum of 4 nights by permit ($30).

✔ **Riverside Park** (406-628-4796, ext. 0), Exit 434 off I-90, then south on US 212 for 0.8 mile, Laurel. Open for camping mid-May through September; small fee (call for current rate). This well-kept city park located alongside the Yellowstone River features hot showers, RV electricity hookups, fishing access, a boat ramp, and a playground. The park is of historical significance as well, having once been the site of a POW camp for German and Japanese prisoners.

Steve McClain Memorial Park (1-866-862-2537; 406-778-2266; www .bakermt.com), US 12, then south on 3rd Street W., Baker. Free overnight camping facilities at this park include barbecue grills, picnic tables, bathrooms, and dump stations (at the RV park).

See also Crow Agency under *To See—Towns;* Medicine Rocks State Park under *To See—Natural Wonders;* Deadman's Basin Reservoir and Tongue River Reservoir State Park under *Boating;* the Bighorn River, the Tongue River, and the Yellowstone River under *Fishing;* paddlefishing at Intake Dam Fishing Access Site under *Unique Adventures;* Makoshika State Park under *Wilder Places—Parks;* Pryor Mountain Wild Horse Range under *Wilder Places—Wildlife Refuges and Areas;* and Bighorn Canyon National Recreation Area under *Wilder Places— Other Wild Places.*

FISHING **The Bighorn River** (406-247-2940; www.fwp.state.mt.us), accessible via numerous access points along MT 313 and MT 47 between Custer and Fort Smith. The Bighorn is known for its excellent trout fishing opportunities along the 112-mile stretch of river from the Yellowtail Dam in the south to the Yellowstone River in the north. Other species include channel catfish, mountain whitefish, northern pike, sauger, smallmouth bass, and walleye. Many of the fishing access points allow free camping for up to 7 days and provide good launching places and takeouts for rafters and paddlers. Numerous outfitters, including **Forrester's Bighorn River Resorts** (1-800-665-3799; 406-666-9199; www .forrestersbighorn.com); **Eagle Nest Lodge & Outfitters** (1-866-258-3474; 406-665-3711; www.eaglenestlodge.com), and **Tight Lines Lodge** (406-666-2224; 406-666-2203; www.tightlineslodge.com), provide inclusive, multiday guided fishing packages. (See also the Fort Smith and St. Xavier listings under *Lodging.*)

The Musselshell River (406-234-0900; www.fwp.state.mt.us), along US 12 between Ryegate and Melstone. The Musselshell River's species include channel catfish, northern pike, sauger, smallmouth bass, and walleye.

The Powder River (406-234-0900; www.fwp.state.mt.us), 0.5 mile south of Broadus on MT 59. The Powder River's species include channel catfish, sauger, and shovel-nosed sturgeon.

&. **The Tongue River** (406-234-0900; www.fwp.state.mt.us), MT 59, 12 miles south of Miles City, then 1 mile southwest on MT 332 to 12 Mile Dam. Anglers visiting the Tongue River will find opportunities to catch channel catfish, sauger, shovel-nosed sturgeon, smallmouth bass, and walleye. The 27-acre access site also offers year-round free camping.

The Yellowstone River (406-247-2940; www.fwp.state.mt.us), accessible via numerous access points just off I-94 and I-90 between Glendive and Laurel. The last free-flowing river in the Lower 48 states, the Yellowstone originates in Lake

Yellowstone (see "Yellowstone National Park" in "Wyoming's Yellowstone and Grand Teton National Parks") and flows unimpeded for 670 miles to its confluence with the Missouri River just over Montana's border with North Dakota. Species include brown trout, burbot, channel catfish, mountain whitefish, paddlefish, rainbow trout, sauger, smallmouth bass, walleye, and Yellowstone cutthroat trout. Many of the fishing access points allow free camping for up to 7 days and provide good launching places and takeouts for rafters and paddlers. (See also Paddlefishing at Intake Dam Fishing Access Site under *Unique Adventures.*)

See also Crow Agency under *To See—Towns;* Chief Plenty Coups State Park under *Historic Landmarks, Places, and Sites;* Baker Lake, Deadmans Basin Reservoir, and Tongue River Reservoir State Park under *Boating;* Crazy Head Springs Recreational Area and Riverside Park under *Camping;* William L. Matthews Wildlife Recreation Area under *Hiking;* Pirogue Island State Park under *Paddling/Floating;* Arapooish Pond and Recreation Park under *Snow Sports;* Lake Elmo State Park under *Wilder Places—Parks;* Custer National Forest under *Wilder Places—Forests;* Bighorn Canyon National Recreation Area under *Wilder Places—Other Wild Places;* Helm River Bend Bed & Breakfast and Lakeview Bed and Breakfast under *Lodging—Bed & Breakfasts;* Kingfisher Lodge under *Lodging—Lodges;* and Absaraka Fishing Bear Cabins, Bighorn Fly & Tackle Shop, Fort Smith Fly Shop & Cabins, and Old Hookers Guesthouse at the Bighorn River under *Lodging—Other Options.*

GOLF **Briarwood Country Club** (406-245-2966), 3429 Briarwood Boulevard, Billings, 18 holes.

Circle Inn Golf Links (406-248-4202), 1029 Main Street, Billings, 9 holes.

Cottonwood Country Club (406-377-8797), Country Club Road, Glendive, 9 holes.

Eagle Rock Golf Course (406-655-4445; www.eaglerockgolfcourse.com), 5624 Larimer Lane, Billings, 18 holes.

Exchange City Golf Course (406-652-2553), 19 S. 19th Street, Billings, 18 holes.

Forsyth Country Club (406-356-7710), 3 miles west of Forsyth on Frontage Road, 9 holes.

Fort Custer Golf Club (406-665-2597), 3.5 miles north of Hardin on MT 47, 9 holes.

Lake Hills Golf Club (406-252-9244; www.lakehillsgolf.com), 1930 Clubhouse Way, Billings, 18 holes.

Lakeview Country Club (406-778-3166), Airport Road, Baker, 9 holes.

Laurel Golf Club (406-628-4504), 1020 Golfcourse Road, Laurel, 18 holes.

Miles City Town & Country Club (406-232-1500), 4th Street, Miles City, 9 holes.

Peter Yegen Jr. Golf Club (406-656-8099; www.yegengolfclub.com), 3400 Grand Avenue, Billings, 18 holes.

Pine Ridge Country Club (406-323-2880), 72 Golfcourse Road, Roundup, 9 holes.

Ponderosa Butte Golf Course (406-748-2700), 1 Long Drive, Colstrip, 9 holes.

Pryor Creek Golf Club (406-256-0626), 1292 Pryor Creek Road, Huntley, 27 holes.

Rolling Hills Golf Course (406-436-2608), 3 miles west of Broadus at the Y intersection, 9 holes.

HIKING **Diane Gabriel Trail** in Makoshika State Park (406-377-6256; www.fwp .state.mt.us/parks/parksreport.asp?mapnum=5), Snyder Avenue (follow the signs through town), Glendive. This 1.5-mile interpretive loop trail leaves from the park's campground and takes you through impressive badlands, past a fossilized hardosaur vertebra, and then through surprisingly lush grasslands. A steep side trail takes you to an impressive overlook.

Howery Island Nature Trail (406-232-7000); just off MT 311, 6 miles southwest of Hysham. Located within the Howery Island Wildlife Management Area, this easy, 1.3-mile trail takes you through a cottonwood riparian zone along the Yellowstone River. Ten interpretive signs along the path provide interesting information about your surroundings. Wildlife viewing opportunities include numerous species of waterfowl as well as deer, skunks, foxes, hawks, and bald eagles, among other fauna.

Om-Ne-A Trail in Bighorn Canyon National Recreation Area (406-666-2412; www.nps.gov/bica), Fort Smith (south Garryowen). Park your car at the Yellowtail Dam parking area to start your journey on this little-trafficked, scenic trail along the rim of the lower portion of Bighorn Canyon. The first little bit of the trail is steep, but don't worry—it levels out quickly. You can hike a total of 6 miles round-trip if you go all the way to the trail's terminus at the Ok-A-Beh Boat Ramp. This trail acquaints you with the incredible and impressive nature of Bighorn Canyon in a way that no view out a car window can.

& **William L. Matthews Wildlife Recreation Area** (406-233-2800; 406-232-7001; www.mt.blm.gov/mcfo), 7 miles east of Miles City. Open year-round for day-use only; free. This lovely 80-acre site was designed specifically with the handicapped in mind, making it easy for wheelchairs to navigate the 0.4-mile concrete trail as well as gain access to restrooms, fishing areas along the Yellowstone River, and picnic tables.

See also Chief Plenty Coups State Park, Pictograph Cave State Park, and Pompeys Pillar National Monument under *To See—Historic Landmarks, Places, and Sites;* Medicine Rocks State Park under *To See—Natural Wonders;* Billings-area listings and Custer National Forest Long Pines Unit under *Bicycling;* Pirogue Island State Park under *Paddling/Floating;* Arapooish Pond and Recreation Park, Camps Pass Ski Trail, and Riverfront Park under *Snow Sports;* Lake Elmo State Park, Makoshika State Park, and Rosebud Battlefield State Park under *Wilder Places—Parks;* Custer National Forest under *Wilder Places—Forests;* Four Dances Natural Area and Sundance Lodge Recreation Area under *Wilder*

Places—Other Wild Places; and Helm River Bend Bed and Breakfast, Lakeview Bed and Breakfast, Oakwood Lodge, and V Lazy B Bed & Breakfast and Horse Motel under *Lodging—Bed & Breakfasts.*

HORSEBACK RIDING See Custer National Forest Long Pines Unit under *Bicycling;* Pirogue Island State Park under *Paddling/Floating;* Riverfront Park under *Snow Sports;* 7th Ranch Historical Tours, Crow Country tours, ranch vacations, and Roundup Cattle Drive, Inc., Annual Cattle Roundup under *Unique Adventures;* Custer National Forest under *Wilder Places—Forests;* Bighorn Canyon National Recreation Area and Sundance Lodge Recreation Area under *Wilder Places—Other Wild Places;* and V Lazy B Bed & Breakfast and Horse Motel under *Lodging—Bed & Breakfasts.*

PADDLING/FLOATING Pirogue Island State Park (406-234-0900; www.fwp .state.mt.us/parks/parksreport.asp?mapnum=6). From Miles City, go north on MT 59 1 mile, go east on Kinsey Road for 2 miles, and then go south on a county road for 2 miles. Open year-round for day-use (closed 10 PM–5 AM daily); free. Filled with cottonwoods, this quiet state park lies on an island in the **Yellowstone River,** making it a popular spot for floaters and paddlers to visit (though it's accessible by driving a vehicle through the water during low-water season). Wildlife viewing opportunities are great here, as the park is home to bald eagles, white-tailed deer and mule deer, and many species of waterfowl. Another popular activity is searching for moss agates. Other activities include hiking, biking, horseback riding, fishing, and picnicking.

See also Riverside Park under *Camping;* the Bighorn River, the Musselshell River, the Powder River, and the Yellowstone River under *Fishing;* Frontier Adventures under *Unique Adventures;* Lakeview Bed and Breakfast under *Lodging—Bed & Breakfasts;* Kingfisher Lodge and Shamrock Lodge under *Lodging—Lodges;* and Absaraka Fishing Bear Cabins, Bighorn Fly & Tackle Shop, Fort Smith Fly Shop & Cabins, and Old Hookers Guesthouse at the Bighorn River under *Lodging—Other Options.*

SNOW SPORTS Arapooish Pond and Recreation Park (406-247-2940; www.fwp.state.mt.us), 1 mile north of Hardin off MT 47. Open year-round for day-use only; free. This fishing access site also has a developed park, complete with a 6-foot-wide trail that makes for great cross-country skiing in wintertime. The aerated, 29-acre pond offers convenient all-season fishing for smallmouth and largemouth bass and rainbow trout.

Camps Pass Ski Trail (406-842-5432; www.fs.fed.us/r1/custer), 18 miles east of Ashland on US 212. Camps Pass features two ungroomed cross-country loop trails in Custer National Forest containing 2K of easy terrain, 2K of more challenging terrain, and 6K of most challenging terrain. Also popular with hikers, this is a great spot for wildlife-watching. (See also Custer National Forest under *Wilder Places—Forests.*)

Riverfront Park (406-657-8371), S. Billings Boulevard, Billings. Open year-round for day-use only; free. This urban park on the banks of the Yellowstone

River offers cross-country skiers a quick getaway with its network of trails to explore. It's also popular with cyclists, hikers, and horseback riders.

See also Baker under *To See—Towns;* Custer National Forest Long Pines Unit under *Bicycling;* Makoshika State Park under *Wilder Places—Parks;* Custer National Forest under *Wilder Places—Forests;* Helm River Bend Bed & Breakfast, Oakwood Lodge, and V Lazy B Bed & Breakfast and Horse Motel under *Lodging—Bed & Breakfasts;* and R Lazy 4 Ranch Cabin under *Lodging—Other Options.*

UNIQUE ADVENTURES **Crow Country tours,** by **Crow Scouting Party** (406-639-2280; www.crowscoutingparty.com). Take Exit 531 off I-90 to Lodge Grass, and then take Old Highway 87 north for 6.2 miles; or by **West Fork** (406-666-2462; www.forevermontana.com), 347 Soap Creek, St. Xavier. You'll deepen your knowledge of Indian culture and traditions both past and present and get acquainted with a piece of Crow Country by booking a tour with one of these services. Your Crow—or Apsa'alooke—guides will create your adventure according to your specifications, whether you wish to explore mountains, desert areas, archaeological and historic sites, or the reservation (advance notice is required for all trips, to obtain proper permits). Trips range in length from a half-day to multiday and are priced according to activities selected. West Fork also offers horseback riding trips.

Frontier Adventures (406-748-2630; www.exploremontana.com/fa1), 4115 Prairieview, Colstrip. Trips run only in summer (call for this season's dates); $749 per person. If you're a history buff and you love rafting, then this is the adventure for you. Explore the Yellowstone River from the seat of a 15-foot raft, retracing part of Lewis and Clark's historic route. For 4 days and 3 nights, your guides will educate you about not only the famed explorers' journey but also a variety of other pertinent topics, including Native American culture, ethnobotany, and how to construct a plains tipi. You'll camp out in either a tipi or a smaller tent (whichever you prefer), enjoying delicious meals prepared by camp cooks three times a day. Reservations suggested.

✍ **Montana Fun Adventures** (1-888-618-4386; 406-254-7180; www.montana funadventures.com), 19 N. Broadway, Billings. Based out of the lobby of the **Historic Northern Hotel** (1-800-542-5121; 406-245-5121) in downtown Billings, this tour guide service offers almost any kind of tour your heart might desire, from the more standard Little Bighorn Battlefield or Lewis and Clark tours to the more whimsical Tour de Chocolate or Historic Haunting Tour. Whether you want to ride the trolley around Billings for a historic 1.5-hour tour or you want to book a custom, multiday, private family adventure, at least one of the extensive offerings available from Montana Fun Adventures is sure to excite or intrigue you.

Paddlefishing at Intake Dam Fishing Access Site (406-232-0900; www.fwp .state.mt.us), via Exit 213 off I-94 near Glendive, north on MT 16 for 16 miles, then east on C.R. 551 for 2 miles. If you're an angler—or if you want a one-of-a-kind fishing experience—don't miss out on the chance to try and catch a paddlefish here—one of the state's best-known paddlefishing destinations along the

Yellowstone River. Paddlefish are large, flat-billed, nonskeletal fish that have been around for some 70 million years and are found only in the Missouri and the Yellowstone rivers in the United States and in China's Yangtze River. Beware that your edible catch may be hefty, as paddlefish can weigh in at 100 pounds. You can even stay for a while and camp at the 40-acre site ($5).

Ranch vacations. These vacations usually allow you to participate to a certain extent in various aspects of ranch life, often including cattle herding and branding. The ratio of work time to leisure time varies from ranch to ranch, as do the additional activities and amenities offered, but most ranches include horseback riding, lodging, and meals in an inclusive package deal. In this region, providers include **Bay Horse Ranch Vacation** (406-427-5746), Biddle; **Cross A Guest Ranch** (406-639-2697), Lodge Grass; **Double Spear Ranch** (406-259-8291), Pryor; **Drga Ranch** (406-772-5715), Ismay; **The Graham Ranch** (406-639-8903; 406-639-2676), Lodge Grass; **Hougen Ranch** (406-358-2204; 406-358-2209), Melstone; **J. M. Nansel Ranch and Guest House** (406-356-7253), Forsyth; **Little Bear Skull Guest Ranch** (406-427-5724), Broadus; **Lonesome Spur Ranch** (406-662-3460), Bridger; **O Spear Guest Ranch, Ltd.** (406-427-5388; 406-427-5406), Broadus; **Pass Creek Angus Ranch** (406-343-2551), Wyola; **Powder River Cattle Drives** (1-800-492-8835); **Rose Ranch** (406-775-6204), Ekalaka; and **Runamuk Guest Ranch** (406-323-3614), Roundup.

Roundup Cattle Drive, Inc., Annual Cattle Roundup (1-800-257-9775; www.roundupcattledrive.com), P.O. Box 205, Roundup 59072. Reservations required; transportation from Billings to the ranch and back is included in the rates. Held in late August. Your participation in this annual event will provide fodder for remarkable stories to tell both family and friends. Be one of 50 guests from around the world to join in the fun as you spend 6 days assisting in rounding up hundreds of head of cattle for sorting, doctoring, and moving to a large ranch near Roundup. Additional activities range from dancing to scavenger hunts. Dine on luscious chuckwagon fare prepared by camp cooks nightly, from steaks to vegetarian meals, and then tumble into your tipi to catch some z's. Reserve your spot early! ($1,545 adults; $1,395 per adult to ride in one of 15 wooden-wheeled wagons; $1,045 children 11 and under).

7th Ranch Historical Tours (1-800-371-7963; 406-638-2438; 406-638-2459; www.historicwest.com). Take Exit 514 off I-90 at Garryowen, and then head west on Reno Creek Frontage Road for 3 miles to Reno Creek Road, where you'll find the headquarters and an RV campground. This working ranch offers you not merely the standard guest ranch experience—though if you wish to spend your vacation learning how to be a cowboy, you certainly can! Other activities include historical tours of the surrounding area on horseback or by truck, shooting instruction, horseback riding lessons, guided fishing, tipi camping, learning about Indian culture, and, of course, rest and relaxation. The ranch's collection of historical resources from printed material to memorabilia can provide hours of entertainment in and of themselves. Custom-designed, all-inclusive, upscale vacations are the standard for this company ($450 per day for one person, $300 per person per day for two people, $250 per person per day for three to six people, children under 12 $150 per day).

PARKS ♿ **Lake Elmo State Park** (406-247-2940; www.fwp.state.mt.us/parks/parksreport.asp?mapnum=8), US 87 north to Pemberton Lane and then west for 0.5 mile, Billings. Open year-round for day-use; free for residents, $5 nonresidents. This park's urban location makes it an ever-popular destination for residents and visitors alike. Activities include boating (only electric motors), hiking (1.3-mile interpretive trail), swimming, picnicking, fishing, and educational displays at the regional headquarters' interpretive center located on the lake's south shore.

♿ **Makoshika State Park** (406-377-6256; www.fwp.state.mt.us/parks/parks report.asp?mapnum=5), Snyder Avenue (follow the signs through town), Glendive. Open Memorial Day through Labor Day 10 AM–6 PM; open Labor Day through Memorial Day 9 AM–5 PM; day-use is free for residents, $5 for nonresidents, camping $10–12. *Makoshika,* meaning "bad earth, land, or spirits" in Sioux, is an appropriate name for Montana's biggest state park, where you'll find rolling badlands with sweeping vistas, as well as the fossilized remnants of some of Montana's prehistoric dinosaurs, including the formidable *Tyrannosaurus rex.* A visitor center provides interpretive materials detailing the park's geology, fossils, terrain, and human significance. Additional activities include picnicking, camping, scenic drives, hiking (3.2 miles of trails, including an interpretive trail), biking, wildlife viewing, shooting ranges (archery and rifle), snowmobiling, and a folf (Frisbee golf) course. (See also Folf Course under *To See—For Families;* and Diane Gabriel Trail under *To Do—Hiking.*)

Rosebud Battlefield State Park (406-234-0900; www.fwp.state.mt.us/parks/parksreport.asp?mapnum=3), 25 miles east of Crow Agency on US 212, turn south on MT 314 for 20 miles, and then go 3 miles west on a county road. Open for day-use year-round; free. Undulating grasslands and peaceful solitude now characterize the site where General Crook battled with Sioux and Cheyenne Indians in June 1876. This 3,000-acre park preserves the historic landscape, along with a pioneer-days homestead and ranch as well as prehistoric sites of note. Though this remote park is undeveloped and lacks trails, the open spaces allow for ample wanderings and wildlife viewing opportunities.

MAKOSHIKA STATE PARK

See also Hardin under *To See—Towns;* Chief Plenty Coups State Park and Pictograph Cave State Park under *To See—Historic Landmarks, Places, and Sites;* Medicine Rocks State Park under *To See—Natural Wonders;* Two Moon Park under *To Do—Bicycling;* Tongue River Reservoir State Park under *To Do—Boating;* Riverside Park under *To Do—Camping;* Pirogue Island State Park under *To Do—Paddling/Floating;* and Arapooish Pond and Recreation Park and Riverfront Park under *To Do—Snow Sports.*

FORESTS Custer National Forest (605-797-4432; www.fs.fed.us/r1/custer), 1310 Main Street, Billings. Altogether, Custer National Forest includes 1.2 million acres split into three ranger districts, which vary wildly not only in terrain but also in location, with one district adjacent to Yellowstone National Park (see *Wilder Places—Forests* in "South-Central Montana: Yellowstone Country"). Custer Country includes the forest's **Sioux Ranger District,** with eight separate tracts of land in Montana near Ekalaka; and the **Ashland Ranger District,** near Ashland and Otter along MT 484. The Ashland Ranger District has three areas set aside for hiking and horseback riding that don't permit any motorized vehicles: Cook Mountain, King Mountain, and Tongue River Breaks. Recreational opportunities include bicycling, camping, cross-country skiing, fishing, hiking, horseback riding, hunting, picnicking, snowmobiling, wildlife viewing, and more. (See also Capitol Rock National Natural Landmark under *To See—Natural Wonders;* Long Pines Unit under *To Do—Bicycling;* and Custer National Forest under *To Do—Camping.*)

WILDLIFE REFUGES AND AREAS Lake Mason National Wildlife Refuge (406-538-8706; http://cmr.fws.gov), 8 miles northwest of Roundup. Lake Mason is one of the Charles M. Russell National Wildlife Refuge's satellite wildlife refuges in central Montana (see the listing in "Northeast Montana: Missouri River Country"). This small refuge protects a wetlands habitat for migratory birds and waterfowl.

Pryor Mountain National Wild Horse Range (406-896-5013; www.mt.blm .gov/bifo/whb), accessible from Wyoming in the south via WY 37, or take your pick of a number of routes originating south of Billings and east of US 310 (which are not recommended for two-wheel-drive vehicles). Created in 1968, this was the first of three national wild horse ranges established thus far. From 140 to 180 wild horses range throughout this remote and pristine area. Primitive, overnight free camping is permitted, but specific rules and regulations apply. There is also a first-come, first-served cabin, Penn's Cabin, available for overnight stays on the range. Your best bet is to call ahead or visit the above Web site to adequately plan your trip to this remote and wild area.

See also Howery Island Nature Trail and William L. Matthews Recreation Area under *To Do—Hiking.*

OTHER WILD PLACES ⅙ ✐ **Bighorn Canyon National Recreation Area** (406-666-2412; www.nps.gov/bica). Yellowtail Dam Visitor Center in Fort Smith open daily Memorial Day through Labor Day 9 AM–5 PM, shortened hours May and September (call for latest hours); recreation area open year-round; $5 per vehicle per day or $30 for annual pass. More than 70,000 acres of land in Wyoming and Montana are encompassed by this national recreation area, including 60-mile-long Bighorn Lake. Popular activities include hiking, horseback riding, fishing, boating, year-round camping, wildlife viewing, and more. No roads connect the northern and southern portions of the area, so the only way to easily access both is by boat. Kids (and their families) can participate in the Bighorn Canyon's Junior Ranger Program via the completion of several fun and educational activities laid out in booklets available for purchase ($1 apiece) at the visitor center. Upon completion of the program, children earn a Junior Ranger badge. (See also Om-Ne-A Trail under *To Do—Hiking.*)

Four Dances Natural Area (406-896-5013; www.mt.blm.gov/bifo/fourdance .htm), 2 miles east of downtown Billings, east of Coburn Road and west of the Yellowstone River. Open year-round for day-use only; free. A designated Area of Critical Environmental Concern (ACEC), this 765-acre tract of land features native grassland and sagebrush, ponderosa pines, and cottonwood-studded riparian areas on the banks of the Yellowstone River.

Sundance Lodge Recreation Area (406-896-5013; www.mt.blm.gov/bifo/ sundance.htm), Thiel Road, Laurel. Open year-round for day-use only; free. Nearly 400 acres of river bottom and land irrigated for hay make up this public recreation area near the confluence of the Yellowstone River and the Clarks Fork of the Yellowstone. Formerly a working livestock ranch, since 1997 this area has been open for public use, with designated trails allowing cycling, hiking, horseback riding, and wildlife viewing.

✳ Lodging
BED & BREAKFASTS

Billings
The Josephine Bed and Breakfast (1-800-552-5898; 406-248-5898; www .thejosephine.com), 514 N. 29th Street, Billings 59101. Walk to the attractions of downtown Billings from the Josephine, and then return to enjoy the privacy and modernity offered at this luxurious bed & breakfast. Though the structure was built in 1912, you will find all of today's amenities at your fingertips, from Internet access (both wireless broadband and high-speed) to private baths for each of the five rooms. A delicious, homemade breakfast, complete with freshly ground hazelnut coffee, is served daily ($65–160).

Sanderson Inn (406-656-3388), 2038 S. 56th Street W., Billings 59106. Staying at Sanderson Inn gives you the best of both worlds Billings has to offer. Not only do you enjoy easy accessibility to the bustle of the city but you can also relax and unwind in one of this 1905 home's three lovely guest bedrooms overlooking pasturelands. Each room has differently themed decor, but all feature attention to details such as handmade quilts, restored antiques, and hardwood floors. Taking center stage at breakfast are mouthwatering homemade bread and cinnamon rolls, served daily along with other options on fine china in the dining room ($50–70).

V Lazy B Bed & Breakfast and Horse Motel (406-669-3885; 406-669-3200; www.cruising-america .com/vlazyb), 12960 Medicine Man Trail, Molt 59057 (13 miles west of Billings). Not just for travelers with horses (though they will certainly appreciate the special accommodations for their hoofed friends), this country bed & breakfast situated on a gorgeous 45-acre property was custom-designed with its future guests in mind. Constructed in 2001, it features two rooms with private baths and two with a shared bath. The surrounding scenery includes a striking canyon with nature trails perfect for horseback riding, hiking, hunting, and cross-country skiing. Breakfast is served daily ($60–110).

Broadus 59317

♿ **Oakwood Lodge** (406-427-5474), S. Pumpkin Creek Road, 25 miles west of Broadus off US 212. Oakwood Lodge's secluded location makes it a great getaway. This wheelchair-accessible bed & breakfast sits on a 1,000-acre ranch, offering guests not only comfortable accommodations with private baths, but also year-round recreation opportunities including hiking, fossil-hunting, cross-country skiing, and hunting. A complete ranch-style breakfast is served daily ($50–75).

Colstrip 59323

Lakeview Bed and Breakfast (1-888-525-3262; 406-748-3653; www.lakeviewbnb.com), 7437 Castle Rock Lake Drive. Perfect for anglers, bird-watchers, hunters, or anyone who enjoys wildlife-watching and a peaceful getaway, this five-bedroom bed & breakfast sits on the shores of lovely Castle Rock Lake. Anglers can fish for bass, bluegills, catfish, crappies, northern pike, and walleyes, either from the shores or from a pedal boat or rowboat. A 2.5-mile lakeside trail makes for great bird-watching and strolling. High-speed Internet is available at no extra charge in each room, and each room has its own private bath. Homemade breakfast is served daily ($78–95).

Forsyth 59327

Lasting Impressions (1-866-346-7067; 406-346-7067), 214 N. 13th Avenue. This appropriately named bed & breakfast will almost certainly make a lasting impression on you during your stay. Located near the Rosebud County Courthouse (see *To See—Historic Landmarks, Places, and Sites*) in Forsyth, Lasting Impressions makes its first impression with its lovely exterior—an elegant, two-story 1914

home—and continues to impress when guests come inside and experience the inn's comfortable decor and amenities (including high-speed Internet access). Breakfast, either full or take-it-with-you, is served daily ($50–75).

Glendive 59330

Charley Montana Bed & Breakfast (1-888-395-3207; 406-365-3207; www.charley-montana.com), 103 N. Douglas Street. History buffs will delight in spending the night in stockman Charles Krug's 1907 mansion, which is listed on the National Register of Historic Places. The owners have taken great care to ensure that restorations to the 25-room mansion are historically accurate, thus preserving the integrity of the experience for their guests. Even if you're not so historically inclined, one of the B&B's five bedrooms with private baths will most certainly suit your tastes, as will the delicious and hearty homemade breakfasts served daily ($65–90).

Hostetler House Bed & Breakfast (1-800-965-8456; 406-377-4505), 113 N. Douglas Street. A charming, 1912 prairie home welcomes guests to one of two comfortably furnished guest rooms. Centrally located, this B&B makes it easy for you to access outdoor recreation opportunities and in-town attractions with ease. A full gourmet breakfast is served daily on Grandma's china, and you'll enjoy relaxing in a sitting room full of books for you to peruse or in the hot tub. You can even take the tandem mountain bike for a spin to explore your surroundings ($50–75).

Hardin 59034

Hotel Becker Bed and Breakfast (406-665-2707; 406-665-3074), 200 N. Center. Only 15 miles from the Little

Bighorn Battlefield National Monument (see *To See—Historic Landmarks, Places, and Sites*), this impressive, three-story brick building, constructed in 1908 (third story added in 1917), is listed on the National Register of Historic Places. Though the entire hotel is no longer open, seven second-story rooms were renovated in 1997, along with a first-floor meeting space and lobby, creating an opportunity for overnight guests to experience a historical setting with modern comforts. Breakfast served daily; open June through September ($50–75).

Kendrick House Inn Bed & Breakfast (406-665-3035; 406-665-9090), 206 N. Custer Avenue. This lovingly restored, historic five-bedroom Victorian inn boasts lovely period furnishings, including chandeliers, pedestal sinks, and Oriental rugs. Once a boardinghouse, the building was also used as a hospital and as private apartments. Today, guests enjoy a wide selection of books in the library, an on-premises gift shop, and a full breakfast served daily. Open year-round, but may be closed for renovations in off-season so call several weeks in advance ($79–95).

Lodge Grass 59050
✿ **Wald Ranch** (406-639-2457; www.waldranch.net), HC 45 Box 809. Located on MT 463 southwest of Lodge Grass. This is not your normal bed & breakfast. Stay as a guest on this working ranch (work is not a part of your stay, though), where you'll enjoy not only a full breakfast served daily but also a homemade supper. Much of the food, from fresh garden fare to ranch-raised beef, comes from the ranch's endeavors. Added to this is the impressive number of nearby historic sites and recreational opportuni-

ties, not to mention solitude, should you seek it. Families (and pets) are welcome, too—in fact, if you book the new log ranch house for four or more people, you'll be guaranteed to have it all to yourselves ($180 per person).

Miles City 59301
Helm Bed and Breakfast (406-421-5420; www.huntmontanafree.com), HC 32 Box 4161. Located south of Miles City on MT 332. Some 7,500 acres are available for guests at this B&B, located on a working ranch on the banks of the Tongue River. Whether you want to hike, hunt (no extra fee), fish, snowmobile, or just watch wildlife, you should find ample space to do it in this remote and beautiful setting. Feel a need for some urban flavor? Miles City is a mere 15 minutes away, giving you the opportunity for a night on the town if you feel so inclined. Additional amenities include a treadmill, a hot tub, satellite television, Internet access, and breakfast ($75–90). Mobile home accommodations on the Tongue River are available as well.

Wibaux 59353
Nunberg's N Heart Ranch Bed & Breakfast Inn (406-795-2345), HC 71 Box 7315. Located 7 miles south of Wibaux on MT 7. Enjoy true country living in one of three guest rooms in this historic 1913 house. Relax in the small-town setting of Wibaux and enjoy the hospitality of the owners, who prepare a mouthwatering breakfast daily ($50–75).

LODGES

Fort Smith 59035
Kingfisher Lodge (1-800-835-2529; 406-666-2326; www.bighornking fisher.com), P.O. Box 7828. Located

off MT 313 in Fort Smith. Nestled below the Bighorn Mountains and near the Bighorn River, Kingfisher Lodge's rooms come with two double beds, private bathrooms, a small refrigerator, and air-conditioning. A main dining room serves as a central gathering area for guests to meet and share a meal together. A separate house—the Farm House—sleeps up to four people, with a private kitchen, a bathroom, a living area, and air-conditioning. Guiding services, including fly-fishing float trips and bird hunting, are available as well (call for rates and details on package deals).

St. Xavier
☙ **Shamrock Lodge** (406-665-1822; www.worldwidefishing.com/montana/b1379/index.html; mailing address: 225 W. 6th Street, Hardin 59034), at the intersection of MT 313 and the Fort Smith Road in St. Xavier. This large, furnished lodge sleeps up to 10 people in its three bedrooms (two on the main floor, one in the loft). A full kitchen, a fireplace, mountain views, and close proximity to Bighorn River fishing access points make this a great vacation place for the whole family, a group of friends, or even a corporate retreat ($125–300 depending on number of guests). Guiding services available upon request.

See also Crow Country tours under *To Do—Unique Adventures.*

OTHER OPTIONS

Baker 59313
Ringneck Rendezvous (1-888-853-5688; 406-778-2988; www.east montana.worldweb.com/BakerMT/WheretoStay/VacationHomeRentals), 4740 MT 7. You'll stay in modern comfort in this original 1908 ranch house, which is available to visitors year-round. Located 12 miles north of Baker, the vacation house sleeps up to eight people. Hunters can take advantage of the adjacent 640 acres to hunt for pheasants and grouse, while vacationers can simply relax in a peaceful setting and enjoy abundant wildlife viewing opportunities on the property as well as exploring the surrounding area ($50 for one person; $10 for each additional person).

Fort Smith 59035
Absaraka Fishing Bear Cabins (1-877-506-4676; 406-666-2304; www.bighornfishingbearlodge.com), P.O. Box 7486. Located 3 miles north of Fort Smith at 3 Mile access point on Bighorn River (see *To Do—Fishing*). Anglers in particular will delight in staying at one of four furnished duplex cabins that bunk-sleep up to four. These cabins all have air-conditioning, dish television, and a full kitchen, plus great scenery and easy fishing access to the Bighorn ($85–115). For more spacious accommodations, the larger **Overlook Cabin** has two bedrooms and two bathrooms ($150 for two or three people, $200 for four people). Guiding services, including float trips, are available as well.

Bighorn Fly and Tackle Shop (1-888-665-1321; www.bighornfly .com), 1 Main Street, has a number of year-round lodging selections available, ranging from motel-type rooms with kitchenettes ($85–95) to three-bedroom, two-bathroom Claire's Cabin ($200–250, sleeps five people) to two mobile homes that sleep five to seven people ($150–200). You can also rent equipment (including a boat) or arrange a guided fishing trip, fishing lesson(s), or a float trip from the shop, as well as book shuttle services.

Fort Smith Fly Shop and Cabins
(406-666-2550; www.flyfishingthe
bighorn.com), P.O. Box 7872. Located
just north of Fort Smith on MT 313.
Proximity to fantastic fishing opportunities in the nearby Bighorn River
aside, these cabins offer numerous
amenities, including satellite television,
air-conditioning, heat, a refrigerator,
private decks, fantastic panoramic
views, and full baths ($100–150). You
can also rent or purchase equipment
(including a boat) or book a guided
fishing trip, fishing lesson(s), or a float
trip at the nearby fly shop.

**Old Hookers Guesthouse at the
Bighorn River** (406-670-8998; 406-
254-6565; www.eastslopeoutfitters
.com; mailing address: 1130 Nugget
Place, Billings 59105), MT 313 on the
edge of Fort Smith. This large guesthouse is a perfect place for a family
getaway or reunion—especially if
at least some family members are
anglers, too! Five bedrooms (11 beds),
four bathrooms, satellite television, a
fully equipped kitchen, a private deck,
daily maid service, and the option to
have meals catered all add to the
appeal, as does the lovely, rustic setting
near the quality fishing of the Bighorn
River. Guiding services, including float
trips, are available as well (call for current rates and packages).

Miles City 59301
& **R Lazy 4 Ranch Cabin** (1-800-
685-7206, pin #6030; 406-232-4694),
Powderville Stage. Located 20 miles
east of Miles City off US 12. Constructed from timber harvested on the
R Lazy 4 Ranch, this secluded guest
cabin is 4 miles from the main house
at this working cattle ranch. You'll
have all of the privacy you could want
while staying in this fully furnished
cabin. Depending on the season,

wildlife-watching, hiking, hunting, and
cross-country skiing are all available
just by stepping outside ($100–150).

See also Custer National Forest
under *To Do—Camping;* Montana
Fun Adventures under *To Do—
Unique Adventures;* and Dude Rancher Restaurant under *Eating Out.*

✳ Where to Eat
DINING OUT

Billings
& **Athenian Greek Restaurant**
(406-248-5681), 18 N. 29th Street.
With all of the recent research and
expert kudos given to following the
Mediterranean diet for a healthier,
longer life, this restaurant just maybe
should top your list when you visit
Billings—but the real reason you
should visit is to taste the wonderful
flavors of its authentic Greek cuisine.
Imported feta, Greek wines, olives,
and olive oil promise to infuse your
dining experience with all of the
palate-pleasing pleasures of Greek
food at its finest.

George Henry's Restaurant (406-
245-4570), 404 N. 30th. Elegance and
attention to detail make any dining
experience in this historic 1882 home
wonderful—but it's the delectable
gourmet dishes that come out of its
kitchen that have earned it a remarkable reputation. Specialties include
seafood—halibut, pike, salmon, scallops, scampi, shrimp, and walleye—as
well as steaks and other meats, all
expertly prepared. Homemade
desserts are available to finish your
meal with a sweet touch.

& **The Granary** (406-259-3488),
1500 Poly Drive. This cool, upscale
restaurant is situated in a unique historic setting: a 1925 granary building

that was used by students attending Billings Polytechnic Institute (now Rocky Mountain College) to make money by producing cereal and flour. Today, patrons can still see some of the original machinery while enjoying top-quality hand-cut steak, prime rib, seafood, and chicken dishes. A large porch with lovely natural surroundings makes outdoor dining a popular option in good weather.

Q Cuisine Restaurant (406-245-2503; www.qcuisine.com), 2503 Montana Avenue. Fusion cuisine sets this restaurant apart, with a menu featuring not only steaks and seafood but also more exotic entrée selections such as chicken and wild boar fettuccine or mango shrimp. The ambience—modern blended with historic touches—provides a refined, intimate setting in which you can enjoy your meal.

The Rex (406-245-7477; www.the rexbillings.com), 2401 Montana Avenue. Housed in its original 1910 location, this restaurant once served folks like Buffalo Bill Cody, Calamity Jane, and Will James. Later, though, the decline of railroads caused the building to come within a hair of destruction in 1975. Luckily, it was saved, renovated, and restored, and it now features some of the finest dining available in Billings. The extensive menu includes hand-cut steaks, prime rib, game, chicken, pastas, salads, and seafood flown in fresh daily, among other choices.

&. **Walkers American Grill and Tapas Bar** (406-245-9291; 406-245-1534; www.walkersgrill.com), 2700 1st Avenue N. Housed in the historic Old Chamber building in downtown Billings, this critically acclaimed restaurant features a full bar and an impressive menu with European influences—and reasonable prices. Entrées of steaks, seafood, poultry, and pastas (with some options for vegetarians) are complemented by soup, Caesar salad, and/or items from the extensive tapas (little appetizer) menu. Another claim to fame: this restaurant has served up its fine fare to President Bill Clinton and Mel Gibson, among other celebrities.

Broadus
&. **Judge's Chambers Restaurant** (406-436-2002; 406-436-2576; www .broadusmontana.com/judgescham bers.htm), 101 S. Wilbur (US 212). The 1929 home of Honorable Judge Ashton Jones and his wife has been lovingly restored and converted into a remarkable restaurant serving up its own trademark cuisine—"Prairie Food." Prairie Food is made from the finest, freshest, seasonal ingredients taken from the chef's garden and local farms and sources and prepared in a fashion that blends traditional western and Native American dishes with European influences. The resulting culinary creations have brought about rave reviews. So if you're passing through—or anywhere nearby, for that matter—you should plan for a meal at this pioneering local restaurant. Who knows? Maybe someday you'll be able to brag to your friends that you tasted Prairie Food before it swept the nation.

Hardin
See **Little Big Men Restaurant and Casino** under *Eating Out*.

Ingomar
Historic Jersey Lilly Bar and Café (406-358-2278), Main Street (US 12). Housed in a building that was originally a bank (built in 1914), this restaurant, serving breakfast, lunch,

and dinner, is a favorite gathering spot for both locals and travelers. A meal in the Jersey Lilly allows you the opportunity to step back in history while you sample the restaurant's signature bean soup and steak entrées. The building is listed on the National Register of Historic Places.

Miles City

Club 519 (406-232-5133), 519 Main Street. Enjoy a scrumptious steak or seafood entrée at this hip second-floor restaurant, bar, and nightclub, which you'll find in the Professional Building. Gentle illumination and comfortable decor will help you relax and enjoy your meal.

EATING OUT

Baker

Corner Bar (406-778-3278), 1 Main Street. Charbroiled steaks are the specialty at the Corner Bar, where you'll find weekday specials for both lunch and dinner. Steaks come with fries or onion rings. A gaming area, as well as comedy and musical acts depending on the night, make for entertainment beyond just eating.

Billings

& **Artspace** (406-245-1100), 2919 2nd Avenue N. Yes, you can even find artsy, alternative hangouts in Montana. This one in Billings serves up not only a great cup of coffee but also plentiful portions of art, from poetry readings to paintings. You'll also find light, café-type fare if you're hungry for more than a hot drink.

& **Casey's Golden Pheasant** (406-256-5200; 406-259-7762; www.caseys .net), 222 N. Broadway. If you're hankering for a late-night snack, this is the place to find it in Billings. Order one (or a few) of the publicly ac-

claimed appetizers—or sit down to a full Cajun (or Mexican) meal. You can also sample drink specials and enjoy entertainment that includes live music, keno, and the 3,000-square-foot *Mural of Musicians.*

Dos Machos (406-652-2020), 980 S. 24th Street W. If you like nachos the way that I like nachos, you will not be disappointed with what you find at Dos Machos. Plenty of cheese, beans, ground beef, and more toppings (and did I mention cheese yet?) are layered *in between* crisp tortilla chips, not just on top of them. A half order is enough for one person to not go away hungry from the dinner table. And if nachos aren't your thing, don't worry—an extensive menu featuring an array of Mexican fare will almost certainly have something that strikes your fancy.

✑ & **Dude Rancher Restaurant** (406-259-5561; www.duderancher lodge.com/restaurant.htm), 415 N. 29th Street. For more than 50 years, locals and travelers alike have stopped in for breakfast or lunch (served every day) or dinner (served every day but Sunday) at this home-style restaurant (attached to the Dude Rancher Lodge), also known as the Stirrup Coffee Shop. Daily soup and entrée specials; fresh-baked breads, cinnamon rolls, and desserts; meal salads; breakfast served all day; a variety of sandwiches; and full dinners make certain that no one will leave the table hungry.

& ✑ **HuHot Mongolian Grill** (406-656-8810; www.huhot.com), 1806 King Avenue W. Kids and adults will delight in selecting individual items, including vegetables, noodles, meats, seafood, poultry, and specialty sauces, which are then grilled by one of the restaurant's cooks and returned to the diner to enjoy with wraps and rice. This great concept allows picky eaters the option to go as bland as they wish, while more adventurous types will likely come up with creative masterpieces.

&. **Montana Brewing Company** (406-252-9200), 113 N. Broadway. For fresh, local microbrews, this is the place to go. Handcrafted beers can include the "flagship beers" of Sandbagger Gold, Whitetail Wheat, and Fatbelly Amber, as well as seasonal brews. If you're not a beer drinker, you might want to try their freshly brewed root beer instead. Dinner options include a wide selection of pub fare such as wood-fired pizzas, burgers, steaks, pastas, salads, and a number of vegetarian options. Plenty of appetizers and dessert choices round out the extensive menu.

Broadus

&. ∂ **Homestead Restaurant and Lounge** (406-436-2615), 721 S. Park (US 212). This family-style restaurant has a daily lunch buffet and a children's menu as well as a prime rib special every Friday and Saturday night. Plenty of parking for RVs and a casual atmosphere make this a great place to stop and unwind. A casino is also on the premises.

Colstrip

&. ∂ **The Coal Bowl** (406-748-2695), 6111 Homestead Boulevard. The combination of a good meal and a great place for families and groups makes this local restaurant and bowling alley a favorite. You can even turn the meal somewhat educational by looking at and discussing the historic pictures hanging on the dining-room walls.

Ekalaka

Deb's Coffee Shop (406-775-8718), Main Street. Stop in for a snack or for

lunch. You'll find all of your favorite specialty coffee and tea drinks here, along with pizza by the slice, homemade soups, sandwiches, ice cream, and pie.

Forsyth

Top That! Eatery (406-356-7825), 983 Front Street. Top your salad, sandwich, pizza, or tacos just the way you like 'em at this café that promises to satiate your hunger while appealing to your particular sense of taste. Also available are homemade soups and desserts.

Glendive

Beer Jug, Inc. (406-377-9986), 313 N. Merrill Avenue. A full menu features American and German entrées priced reasonably enough for even the most sensible of pocketbooks. You'll find a comfortable, casual atmosphere and ample parking behind the restaurant, as well as an outdoor patio available for seasonal dining.

&. **The Coffee Den @ the Book N Bear Nook** (406-377-4938), 104 S. Merrill Avenue. For breakfast or lunch, this café, located in a gift shop and bookstore, offers delicious homemade favorites along with great coffee and specialty coffee and tea drinks. Breakfast selections include oatmeal, caramel and cinnamon rolls, breakfast bagels, and quiche. For lunch, you can usually choose from several soups, sandwiches, salads, baked potatoes (with toppings), and a dessert of the day, along with pies and cheesecakes.

&. ∂ **Madd Hatters Pub** (406-377-7667), 1316 W. Towne Street. Whether you're a family looking for a good place to eat with the kids or you are in search of a full-service casino to take your mind off the road for a while before you dine, Madd Hatters can serve your needs. A children's menu is available in addition to the pub fare listed on the regular menu, and you'll also find a good selection of beers and wines.

Hardin

Lariat Country Kitchen (406-665-1139), 721 N. Center Avenue. It's all about the country cookin' at this hometown restaurant, where you and the children will feel right at home as you sit back and relax to await your country feast. The kids can choose items off a children's menu if they want to.

Little Big Men Restaurant and Casino (406-665-2010), 605 N. Center Avenue. From casual fare like sandwiches and pizzas to fine dining choices such as prime rib and steaks, you can pick your own experience at this restaurant. Families will be comfortable in the restaurant proper, while those seeking an upscale experience can choose to dine in the casino. A children's menu is available.

Merry Mixer Restaurant, Lounge & Catering (406-665-3735), 317 N. Center Avenue. Serving breakfast, lunch, and dinner, this restaurant offers steaks, seafood, and pasta entrées, as well as daily homemade specials. You'll also find a selection of soups and desserts.

Purple Cow Family Restaurant (406-665-3601), MT 47. The whole family will fuel right up from eating the home cooking at this restaurant, which features a renowned salad bar and buffet. Homemade soups and pies are surefire crowd pleasers, and beer and wine are available for the bigger folks.

Laurel

Caboose Saloon and Casino (406-628-7414); 704 W. Main Street. A one-of-a-kind experience awaits you inside this recently remodeled (2004) saloon and casino that also happens to be home to an impressive collection of western art, with a focus on wildlife art. Thirty large bronze sculptures, mostly by artist Ron Raines, are on display both outside and inside the establishment. In addition, you'll find paintings, western art displays, and more memorabilia inside.

Little Big Men Pizza (406-628-8241), 220 1st Avenue S. Chicken, steaks, sandwiches, a salad bar, and (of course) pizza make this a great place for family dining or large groups, as this restaurant has a lot of space. Here you'll also find **Curt's Saloon,** a full-service bar with poker and keno machines, as well as the **Montana Motherlode Casino.** Still not busy enough? Step into the **Nine Fingers Mustard Company** for a free taste test from "Montana's Master Mustard Maker"—and try to say that five times fast!

Owl Junction Diner (406-628-4966), 203 E. Main Street. Locals have gathered at this diner serving breakfast, lunch, and dinner on the main drag for nearly a century, earning it a place in Laurel's history and lore. A house specialty has long been side pork, but you'll find plenty of other creative dishes prepared with homegrown Montana chicken, Black Angus beef, and fresh, local produce.

Miles City

& Airport Inn (406-232-9977), MT 59 north of town. This family-style restaurant is a shoo-in for fun if your child—or your inner child, for that matter—is interested in human flight. Model airplanes dangle overhead while you dine, and the 1934 Air Coupe will command your instant attention upon

arrival. The American menu consists of family standbys such as burgers, pizza, sandwiches, and homemade soups. Patio seating overlooking the Yellowstone River is available in-season, and there's even a game room for kids, along with adult gaming.

Golden Spur Sports Bar–Milestown Brewing Company (404-232-3544), 1014 S. Haynes Avenue. You can tour the brewery and then sample its microbrews while you enjoy some pub food and catch the latest sports action. Big-screen televisions, Internet access, simulcast horse and greyhound racing, and 20 video poker and keno machines promise to keep you entertained—and if you have any questions about your travels, a tourism information center will help guide you on your way.

✷ **Jewels' Steak House & Lounge** (406-232-7288), 1111 S. Haynes Avenue. This restaurant prides itself on its friendly service coupled with great American food and plenty of room for families and tour groups. Three dining rooms and a lounge ensure that everyone will have a place to sit down and enjoy their meal. Even the kids are sure to like Jewels', as the children's menu makes an effort to include selections reminiscent of familiar favorites that they eat at home. Lunch specials are offered every weekday, and a buffet is available on Sunday.

✷ � **StageCoach Station Restaurant, Casino, and BBQ Smokehouse** (406-232-2288), 3020 Stower Street. Back in the pioneer days, stagecoach riders eagerly anticipated the chance for some R & R at the next stagecoach station—a place to grab a cool beverage, dine, socialize, and enjoy some gaming. Today, that

tradition lives on at the StageCoach Station, where road-weary travelers will find the same sort of heart 'n' soul nourishment found by travelers past. Steaks, acclaimed barbecue, Mexican, and Italian selections as well as a children's menu make this a fine place to stop in for a meal, while gaming and drinks provide additional options for relaxation. Open daily for breakfast, lunch, and dinner.

Roundup
✷ ⅆ **Busy Bee Family Dining and Gift Shop** (406-323-2204), 317 1st Avenue W. An extensive salad bar complements main-course offerings that include steaks, burgers, chicken, and seafood, as well as weekly prime rib specials at the Busy Bee. Homemade pies and pastries and hard ice cream appeal to those with a sweet tooth. The Busy Bee is open for breakfast, too.

✷ **Pioneer Café** (406-323-2622), 229 Main Street. Do you love biscuits and gravy? How about chicken fried steak or homemade soup? You'll find delicious varieties of both on the full menu at the Pioneer Café, along with a casual atmosphere and welcoming service. Tasty homemade baked goods include pies, pastries, and cinnamon rolls.

✳ Special Events
May: **Buzzard Day**, Makoshika State Park: annual event celebrating the return of the turkey vultures each spring. **Living History Weekend**, Glendive: history comes alive during this event centered around explorer and Native American lifestyles during the Lewis and Clark era, with demonstrations and seminars as well as food and music. **World Famous Bucking**

Horse Sale (1-877-632-2890; 406-234-2890; ww.buckinghorsesale.com), Miles City: a rodeo, parade, trade shows, crafts shows, races, food, and, of course, the debuts of some probable future buckin' bronc rodeo stars.

June: ✿ **Strawberry Festival,** Billings (406-259-5454; www.straw berryfun.com): a pancake breakfast kicks off this annual tribute to one of the sublime symbols of summer—the strawberry. Numerous vendors sell arts, crafts, and food items, all strawberry-themed. Also includes a fun run, jazz entertainment, and children's activities. ✿ **Custer's Last Stand Reenactment and Little Big Horn Days** (1-888-450-3577; www.custerslaststand.org), Hardin (late June): annual reenactment of this famed event from the Battle of Little Bighorn, as interpreted from a script created from notes taken by Crow tribal historian Joe Medicine Crow, as well as weeklong general celebration of western heritage. Includes a quilt show, grand ball, concerts, parades, meals, and more. ✿ **Colstrip Days Celebration,** Colstrip: annual community celebration features fireworks, children's activities, parades, a golf tournament, an art show, and more.

July: **Northern Cheyenne Fourth of July Celebration,** Lame Deer: the largest powwow held on the reservation is this Independence Day event, which lasts for several days and includes dancing, fun runs, parades, vendors, and feasts of traditional Native American foods.

August: **Crow Fair Powwow and Rodeo, Crow Agency** (late August): annual celebration including powwow, rodeo, drumming and dance contests, a parade, horse races, and more.

✿ **Montana Fair,** Billings MetraPark (406-256-2400; www.metrapark.com): the largest statewide event in Montana includes rodeos, a carnival, musical performances, and midway acts, among other attractions.

September: **Bell Street Bridge Day,** Glendive: annual celebration of this historical landmark. **Medicine Rocks Black Powder Shoot,** Ekalaka: using either smokeless or black powder loads, contestants (often in period costumes) in this annual shooting contest fire muzzle-loading or cartridge rifles (circa 1860–1900) at steel silhouette targets ranging from 100 to 800 yards distant.

October: **Northern International Livestock Exposition (NILE) Stock Show, Pro Rodeo, and Horse Extravaganza,** Billings MetraPark (406-256-2495; www.thenile.org): annual pro rodeo featuring cowboys and cowgirls vying for top honors, as well as livestock exhibits, seminars, trade shows, and horse sales.

Mid-November through early January: **Christmas at the Moss Mansion,** Billings: tour the historic mansion and see a decorated Christmas tree in every room (see also *To See—Historic Landmarks, Places, and Sites*).

See also Chief Plenty Coups State Park under *To See—Historic Landmarks, Places, and Sites;* and **Roundup Cattle Drive, Inc., Annual Cattle Roundup** under *To Do—Unique Adventures.*

Wyoming

WHAT'S WHERE IN WYOMING

AGRICULTURE Agriculture played an extremely significant historic role in Wyoming's economic development. It continues to be an important component of Wyoming's economy today, more as a valuable cultural resource and tradition than as an essential contributor to the state's economic well-being, as mineral extraction and tourism are now the mainstays of Wyoming's economy. Chief agricultural endeavors include the raising of livestock—hence all that great fresh beef you'll find on menus across the state—as well as hay, grains like wheat and barley, sugar beets, and wool.

AIRPORTS **Natrona County International Airport**, or NCIA (307-472-6688; www.casperwyoming.org/airport) is centrally located in Wyoming, just 12 miles west of Casper on US 20/26. Airlines serving NCIA include **Delta Air/Skywest Airlines** (1-800-221-1212; 1-800-453-9417; www.delta-air .com), **Frontier Airlines** (1-800-432-1359; www.frontierairlines.com), **Great Lakes Aviation** (1-800-554-5111; www.greatlakes.com), and **United Airlines/United Express** (1-800-241-6522; www.ual.com).

Wyoming also has a number of regional and municipal airports with commercial flights, including **Cheyenne Regional Airport** (307-634-7071; www.cheyenneairport .com), in Cheyenne; **Jackson Hole Airport** (307-733-7695; www .jacksonholewy.net/transportation/ jh_airlines.php), in Jackson Hole; **Riverton Regional Airport** (307-856-1307; www.flyriverton.com), in Riverton; and **Yellowstone Regional Airport** (307-587-5096; www.flyyra .com), in Cody. For a complete listing of Wyoming's airports, visit www.air-nav.com/airports/state/WY.html.

AMTRAK **Amtrak** (1-800-872-7245; www.amtrak.com) has a single, unstaffed station in Wyoming, in Cheyenne. (See also *Trains* in this section.)

ANTIQUES If your travels include searching for antiques, a good resource for finding antique dealers in Wyoming is *The Antiques & Collectibles Guide* listing for Wyoming, available online at www.acguide.com/ ShopsLocWY.html. You can also get your fix in September at the **Northeast Wyoming Annual Antique Show** (307-467-5524; www.hulett.org/ antiques.htm) in Hulett, and at other annual events held around the state.

AREA CODE Wyoming has a single area code—**307.**

BEARS Many of the outdoor attractions listed in this guide are home to bears—both grizzlies and black bears. Though seeing a bear can be quite a thrill, you need to remember at all times that bears are wild animals and that you should keep your distance and respect them as such. In order to take proper precautions should you enter a bear habitat (usually, such areas are signed and have information about how you should behave), you should educate yourself about the areas where you will recreate. It is your responsibility to help keep bears wild by not habituating them to receiving food from human sources, including garbage.

BICYCLING Never heard of Wyoming as a cycling destination? Well, mark this place on your map, whether it's road riding or grinding on a mountain bike that lights your fire. Included in this guide are a number of recommended rides, most of them the short and sweet variety suitable for the novice or intermediate cyclist. However, more advanced mountain bikers should be aware that Wyoming's plethora of public lands—rife with dirt roads in varying conditions—coupled with a relative lack of regulations (though, of course, mountain bikers should strive to maintain good ethics to keep it this way) create the potential for countless fun adventures. Likewise, expert road riders will delight in the relative lack of traffic on many of Wyoming's paved roadways. A good place to start your research into mountain biking, or any bicycling in Wyoming, for that matter, is **Cycle Wyoming** (www.cycle

wyoming.org), a nonprofit organization that aims to promote cycling in the state.

BIRD-WATCHING Wyoming provides ample opportunities for bird-watchers, with nearly 400 species of birds in more than 40 families, from the state bird, the western meadowlark, to the national bird, the bald eagle. The Web site www.camacdonald.com/birding/uswyoming.htm provides a fantastic starting place as a resource for bird-watching enthusiasts visiting the state. You'll find an array of places listed in various sections throughout this book that mention bird-watching opportunities, particularly under *Wilder Places*.

BOATING The 20 reservoirs in Wyoming managed by the **United States Bureau of Reclamation** (USBR) make for popular boating locales. For the latest conditions and information, contact the **Wyoming Area Office of the Great Plains Region** of the USBR (307-261-5671; www.usbr.gov/gp/area_office_wyao.cfm). In this guide, most of the listings under *To Do—Boating* provide information on bodies of water (lakes and reservoirs) suitable for motorized watercraft in addition to human-powered craft. Listings for rivers—even those that allow motorized watercraft—will be found under *To Do—Fishing* and *To Do—Paddling/Floating*, though they are usually cross-referenced at the end of the *To Do—Boating* section.

BUREAU OF LAND MANAGEMENT (BLM) LANDS The role of **BLM Wyoming** (307-775-6256; www.wy.blm.gov) is huge: with 10 area field offices around the state, not only does it manage 18 million acres of public lands but it also manages between 20 and 30 million acres of federal mineral estate, which produce much of Wyoming's mineral wealth annually. In addition, the BLM in Wyoming is responsible for the protection, management, and control of Wyoming's wild horse population, which is estimated at about 5,000; helps manage the Wyoming Wind Energy Project; and manages a portion of the 3,100-mile-long Continental Divide National Scenic Trail, among other responsibilities.

BUS SERVICE **Greyhound** (1-800-229-9424; www.greyhound.com) and **Wind River Transportation** (1-800-439-7118; www.wrtabuslines.com) provide bus service to various destinations in Wyoming. Several Wyoming cities, including Jackson and Cheyenne, have public bus services as well. For more information, contact the **Wyoming Public Transit Association** (307-266-2524; www.wytrans.org).

BYWAYS AND BACKWAYS Wyoming has no shortage of either of these, with a total of 14 officially designated **Scenic Byways and Backways**—10 Scenic Byways and four Scenic Backways, to be exact. Taking you away from the screaming diesels and dusty monotony of the four-lane interstates, Wyoming's byways and backways offer the traveler the chance to take a breath, enjoy the scenery, and experience Wyoming at a slower pace reminiscent of times past. You'll find details about these fun side adventures, as well as a number of additional scenic drives, under *To See—Scenic Drives* in this book.

CAMPGROUNDS The majority of campgrounds listed under *To Do—Camping* in this guidebook lie on public lands, as it's my opinion that such camping adventures tend to be a little more outdoorsy and adventuresome (in keeping with that explorer's spirit) than staying at a full-service campground in a town or a city. You should know that in addition to those campgrounds listed, primitive camping is permissible on much of the public land in the state as well. Please note that often the dates given for when a campground is open mean that this is when a fee is charged to stay there and when all services (water, garbage pickup, camp hosts, restrooms) are provided. Often, free camping is permitted at these loca-

tions in the off-season as long as they are accessible, though no services are provided. Of course, Wyoming has scads of private campgrounds, too. For a free, comprehensive list of the state's campgrounds published annually in the **Wyoming Vacation Directory,** fill out the online form at www.unicover.com/cgi-bin/wtcreq, or call **Wyoming Travel and Tourism** at 1-800-225-5996.

CITIES Wyoming's state capital, **Cheyenne,** is also its largest city, with a population of about 54,000 people. **Casper** (about 50,000) and **Laramie** (about 30,000) are next on the list for biggest cities. Only eight cities total in Wyoming boast populations of more than 10,000 people.

CLIMATE With the second-highest mean elevation of any state in the country at 6,700 feet above sea level, Wyoming has a semi-arid but variable climate (above 6,000 feet temperatures seldom go above 100°F) due to its topographical diversity. Unless you love cold weather and snow sports, it's best to plan your travels for the late spring, summer, or early fall, when temperatures around the state are for the most part comfortable (between 60°F and 80°F for daytime highs). Just be aware that depending on where your travels take you and on the season when you visit, you could find yourself sweating up a storm, cursing the eternally blowing wind that plagues certain areas of the state, or dealing with a late-spring or even summer snow- or hailstorm (I've been snowed on in every single month in Wyoming except for July). Average annual precipitation is a mere 12 inches, but certain locations get much more than this, of course.

COFFEE If you need a daily dose of java (as more than 50 percent of Americans do), never fear—you will find ample places throughout the state to meet your craving, and I'm not just talking the see-the-bottom-of-your-cup variety. Wyoming is up to date and ready to serve you your coffee—or your latte, espresso, or other specialty drink—from some great coffee shops and cafés you'll find highlighted throughout this book, as well as from those little drive-through huts that are popping up everywhere you look these days. In addition, Wyoming boasts several coffee roasters of its own, including Jackson's **Cowboy Coffee** (1-877-5COWBOY; www.cowboycoffee.com), and Laramie's **Coal Creek Coffee Company** (1-800-838-7737; www.coalcreek coffee.com).

CONSERVATION GROUPS **The Wyoming Outdoor Council** (307-332-7031; www.wyomingoutdoor council.org) works "to protect and enhance Wyoming's wildlife through education and advocacy." You'll find additional links to Wyoming-based conservation groups, including **Jackson Hole Alliance, The Nature Conservancy (Wyoming),** and **Wyoming Audubon,** at www .wyomingoutdoorcouncil.org/library/ conservation.php.

COUNTIES Wyoming has 23 counties.

DUDE RANCHES Ranching is part of Wyoming's cultural and economic heritage, and though its role in the state's economy has declined, it continues to play an important role in the state's culture and identity. For a unique insight into ranching's role in Wyoming, past and present, consider

"Things to Do," and then click on "Activities and Events," where you'll find events listed seasonally; or you can use the Interactive Vacation Planner to hone in on the types of events that appeal to you.

FARMER'S MARKETS You'll find fresh fare in-season at a number of farmer's markets spread across Wyoming, from Cheyenne to Cody. For details on locations, hours, and contact information, visit www.ams.usda.gov/farmers markets/states/wyoming.htm or call 307-777-6319.

FISHING With 22 species of game fish, Wyoming is known internationally for its trout fishing, but it is also home to several species of bass, as well as numerous other species of fish. Detailed information from **Wyoming Game and Fish,** including regulations, licensing, and more, can be found at http://gf.state.wy.us/fish/index.asp or by calling 307-777-4600. **WyomingFishing.Net** (www.wyomingfishing.net) is another great online resource for anglers planning a trip to this state. Specific area recommendations for fishing spots can also be found in the ensuing chapters.

vacationing at one of Wyoming's dude ranches, many of which offer both standard ranching experiences (such as horseback riding and cattle drives) and additional activities ranging from hunting and fly-fishing to hiking and swimming. In the Ranch Vacations section under *To Do—Unique Adventures* in each region, you'll find a list of a number of dude and guest ranches offering this type of adventure. For more information, contact the **Wyoming Dude Ranchers Association** (307-455-2084; www.wyomingdra.com).

EMERGENCIES Dial **911** statewide in case of emergency. In addition, phone numbers and addresses for regional medical facilities are provided in each region of this book.

EVENTS Like most states, Wyoming has so many annual events with such a wide variety of activities that listing them all would easily fill this book—and more. In addition to those highlighted under *Special Events* in each region, you can find just what you're looking for by going to the **Wyoming Tourism and Travel** Web site (www.wyomingtourism.org). Click on

GAMBLING Gambling isn't legal in the state of Wyoming. One place you can gamble legally is at **789 Bingo** (307-856-3964 on Wind River Indian Reservation; see "Central Wyoming: Oregon Trail—Rendezvous Country"; 10369 WY 789, Riverton.

GEOGRAPHY Approximately 360 miles in length and 280 miles wide, Wyoming ranks ninth largest among the states in the nation, covering almost 98,000 square miles. It is also the second-highest state, with a mean elevation of 6,700 feet. In Wyoming, the **Great Plains** and the **Rocky Mountains** come together. In addition to these two geographic areas, Wyoming is home to a third region called the **Intermontane Basins,** which includes the **Bighorn, Powder River,** and **Great Divide basins,** among others. These relatively flat stretches of land situated between Wyoming's mountain ranges receive little in the way of precipitation compared to their mountainous neighbors. Of particular interest is the Great Divide Basin, which runs along the continental divide and is covered in part by Wyoming's **Red Desert.** This area drains neither to the Atlantic nor to the Pacific, and the little rain that falls here is quickly soaked up into the ground.

GEOLOGY If you are a geology aficionado, Wyoming will delight and amaze you to no end. Helpful signs along many state highways identify the type of rock adjacent to the road and its estimated date of birth, piquing your interest and encouraging you to delve more deeply into the state's rich geological past of glaciers, volcanic action, tectonics, and erosion by wind and water. Whether you're

interested in dinosaurs, mountains, badlands, canyons, mining, or simply different types of minerals, in Wyoming, geological attractions and one-of-a-kind formations are plentiful. In addition to what is highlighted throughout this guide, *Roadside Geology of Wyoming*, by David R. Lageson and Darwin R. Spearing (Mountain Press Publishing Company), will help take your knowledge to the next level.

GOLF COURSES Wyoming has more than 50 golf courses to choose from around the state. A free, detailed, printable guide to the state's courses is available courtesy of the **Wyoming Travel and Tourism** Web site. Go to www.wyomingtourism.org, click on "Things to Do," click on "Summer Activities," and click on "Golf." A highlighted link will appear in the text for you to click on to download the colorful 21-page guide.

GUIDES AND OUTFITTERS If you need or want a guide for your adventure of choice, you'll find no shortage of services in Wyoming, whether you want to hire animals for a pack trip, discover great fishing spots, hunt for big game, raft white water, or backpack through the mountains. The

Wyoming Outfitters and Guides Association (307-265-2376; www .wyoga.org) is good place to start the search for a qualified guide or outfitter that suits your needs.

HIGHWAYS Wyoming's major north–south routes include **US 189/191,** which runs from Yellowstone National Park to **I-80,** splitting into two separate routes midway (both of which continue to I-80); and **I-25,** which runs from **I-90** in Buffalo down to Colorado. The state's major east–west routes include I-90 to **US 14/16/20.** I-90 heads northwest into Montana, but US 14/16/20 unite in Greybull to continue west through Cody to Yellowstone. The central portions of Wyoming are transected east–west by **US 20, US 26,** and **US 287.** Wyoming's major east–west highway in the south is I-80.

HIKING Hiking in Wyoming can be a magical and marvelous experience, worthy of a book—or several—of its own. Lucky for you, there's no shortage of detailed hiking guidebooks out there for you to choose from, though some areas of the state receive more attention than others. With that in mind, I've highlighted hikes (in the *Hiking* sections) that feature particularly noteworthy attractions and hikes that are generally suited for folks of any age and fitness level.

HISTORICAL MARKERS AND TRAILS You'll see plenty of historical markers alongside Wyoming's highways, so don't be shy—take a break from driving to stretch your legs and learn a little bit about the state's past. From mammoth hunts to the Oregon Trail, the state's history comes alive via these commemorative signs and

plaques. Want to learn more? Order a copy of *A Few Interested Residents: Wyoming Historical Markers & Monuments,* by Mike Jording (self-published, 1992), which provides a complete resource for history buffs interested in locating and learning about each marker and monument in detail. If you order the book from the link on the **Wyoming State Historical Society** (www.wyshs.org/memb pubs.htm) Web page, the society receives a referral fee.

HISTORY In addition to historical markers aplenty, Wyoming's history lives on in its historic sites, museums, historic houses, and, of course, the minds of its citizens. Throughout this book you will find fascinating facts, figures, and trivia relating to Wyoming's history, as well as recommendations for selected historical attractions under *To See—Towns, To See—Museums,* and *To See—Historic Landmarks, Places, and Sites,* among other sections. For a more complete picture of this state's past, visit the **Wyoming State Historical Society** Web site (www.wyshs.org), where you will find society publications, recommended history books, photos, artwork, and more. Since its founding in 1953, the Wyoming State Historical

Society has worked toward researching and preserving Wyoming's illustrious past.

HOT SPRINGS A number of user-friendly hot springs—including **Hot Springs State Park** (307-864-2176; http://wyoparks.state.wy.us/hot1.htm) in Thermopolis, where you can soak, unbelievably, for free—invite the weary adventurer to Wyoming in for a soothing and refreshing break from traveling or, in the case of many of those hot springs located in and around Yellowstone National Park, to look in awe from a distance (because they are scaldingly hot). For a complete list of Wyoming's hot and warm springs, visit www.hotspringsenthusiast.com/WY.htm.

HUNTING An abundance of big game—**elk, mule deer, pronghorn, moose,** and more—as well as smaller game, such as **sage grouse, wild turkey, rabbits,** and others, draw hunters to Wyoming every season. Nonresident big-game hunting licenses are issued by a lottery system; hunters must apply far in advance of the season in order to have a chance at a license, since demand always vastly exceeds supply. For details on hunting rules and regulations in Wyoming, please visit the hunting section of the **Wyoming Game and Fish** Web site (http://gf.state.wy.us/wildlife/hunting/index.asp) or call 307-777-4600.

INDIAN RESERVATIONS The sole Indian reservation in Wyoming is the 2.2-million-acre **Wind River Indian Reservation** north of Lander, home to members of the **Northern Arapaho and Eastern Shoshone tribes.** Reservation headquarters are located in **Fort Washakie,** which is also home to the graves of Chief Washakie

and Sacagawea. The Wind River Indian Reservation has powwows and other events open to the public, as well as stores that cater to tourists. For details and a schedule of events, visit www.easternshoshone.net and www.northernarapaho.com. See also various related listings in "Central Wyoming: Oregon Trail–Rendezvous Country."

LEAVE NO TRACE **Leave No Trace** (1-800-332-4100; www.lnt.org) is a "national nonprofit organization dedicated to promoting and inspiring responsible outdoor recreation through education, research and partnerships." These seven principles of Leave No Trace are general guidelines for minimizing your impact on the land while you travel: "plan ahead and prepare; travel and camp on durable surfaces; dispose of waste properly; leave what you find; minimize campfire impacts; respect wildlife; and be considerate of other visitors." Detailed information on these principles, as well as other relevant information, can be found by calling the organization or visiting the Web site.

LIBRARIES Need to check your e-mail? That seems to be one of the primary functions of public libraries for travelers these days—though don't forget, libraries can be a great place to learn about local events and history, to catch up on the latest news, or just to relax and unwind with a great book. **WYLDCAT: The Wyoming Libraries Database** provides a helpful list of the state's libraries online at http://wyld.state.wy.us.

LICENSE PLATES Wyoming's distinctive license plates feature the legendary unridable bucking bronco, Steamboat, as well as one of its amazing natural features, Devils Tower. The Bucking Horse & Rider has been on the Wyoming license plate since 1936—the longest continuous use of any graphic on a license plate in the country. Its origins date back to 1918, when First Sergeant George N. Ostrom designed it to be the insignia worn by members of the Wyoming National Guard in World War I. It has since become a registered state and federal trademark for the State of Wyoming and is a much-beloved symbol to Wyomingites. Lloyd Sanderson, who retired as manager of the Wyoming Department of Transportation's Motor Vehicle Services Program in 1999, came up with the inspiration to add Devils Tower to the plates. Wyoming's license plate has been selected Best License Plate by the Automobile License Plate Collectors Association three times: in 1972, 1978, and, most recently, 2000.

The numbers on the left side of each place indicate the vehicle's county of registration. These numbers were originally assigned according the county's property valuation, but today they no longer correlate accurately.

LODGING Lodgings described in this book are focused away from traditional hotels and motels and instead feature unique offerings in each region, whether the area in question has bed & breakfasts, lodges, or other types of facilities. The reason for is that you probably already know what to expect if you book reservations at a typical hotel or motel. When you do find listings for motels, you can assume that unique or unusual lodgings are rare or nonexistent in that particular area. For a free, detailed list of lodging options around the state published

annually in the **Wyoming Vacation Directory,** fill out the online form at www.unicover.com/cgi-bin/wtcreq, or call **Wyoming Travel and Tourism** at 1-800-225-5996.

MAPS If you like to get topographically intimate with the states in which you travel (or you just like looking at detailed maps), pick up a copy of **Wyoming Atlas & Gazetteer** (DeLorme; available at www.delorme .com), which will guide you to public and private lands, back roads and byways, and even ski areas and fishing spots—and much, much more.

MICROBREWERIES
BrewPubZone.com (www.brew pubzone.com/States/Wyoming.html) lists 18 microbreweries for the state of Wyoming, including the award-winning **Snake River Brewing Company** (307-739-BEER; www .snakeriverbrewing.com), with locations in Jackson (original site) and now in Lander. With more than 85 national and international awards to its name after 10 years in business, Snake River Brewery should be on tap for your Wyoming vacation if you like sampling microbrews (a hint for dark-beer lovers: try the Zonker Stout).

MILEAGE Please remember during your trip planning that all mileages given in this book are approximate and subject to a number of inaccuracies due to differences in odometers, source errors, or pilot errors—or all three (yikes!). That having been said, to avoid future misadventures by others, the report of any gross inaccuracies you find would be greatly appreciated; if you do find yourself off in the middle of nowhere in the middle of the night, you might want to recheck your map and the directions—unless, of course, you planned it that way (which is always a possibility in Wyoming).

MUSIC Wyoming hosts musical events to meet the tastes of everyone, from classical chamber music to rock concerts, folk and bluegrass festivals to jazz. One of the biggest is Jackson Hole's **Grand Teton Music Festival** (307-733-3050; www.gtmf.org), still going strong after four decades. The festival features orchestral and chamber music as well as "spotlight" concerts (featuring tributes to particular artists, types of music, and so forth) and children's concerts. Additional selected musical events are highlighted under *Special Events* throughout this book. For an up-to-date list of musical events, go to www.wyoming tourism.org/ivc.cfm (**Wyoming Travel and Tourism's Interactive Visitor Center**) and choose "Events" and "Arts/Performance."

NATIONAL FORESTS AND GRASS-LANDS Wyoming became the first state ever to have a national forest, in 1891, with the creation of the Yellowstone Timberland Reserve, now known as **Shoshone National Forest.** Today encompassing almost 2.5 million acres in the northwest corner of the state adjacent to Yellowstone National Park, Shoshone National Forest is one of the largest of the 13 national forests in the Rocky Mountain region. In addition to Shoshone National Forest, Wyoming contains six other national forests: **Bighorn** (north-central; 1.1 million acres), **Black Hills** (northeast; 1.2 million acres), **Bridger–Teton** (west-central; 3.4 million acres), and **Medicine**

Bow–Routt (south; 1.6 million acres); two national recreation areas, the **Bighorn Canyon National Recreation Area** (near Lovell in the north; 120,000 acres, one-quarter of which is in Wyoming) and the **Flaming Gorge National Recreation Area** (near Green River in the southwest; 201,000 acres; partially in Utah); and **Thunder Basin National Grassland** (northeast; 572,000 acres).

NATIONAL PARKS AND MONU-MENTS Rack up two more firsts for Wyoming: first national park (**Yellowstone National Park,** established in 1872) and first national monument (**Devils Tower,** established in 1906). In addition to these, Wyoming is also home to **Grand Teton National Park,** just south of Yellowstone National Park, and **Fossil Butte National Monument,** near Kemmerer in the southwest.

PADDLING/FLOATING Kayaking, rafting, and canoeing enthusiasts will not be disappointed in Wyoming's offerings. Whether you're interested in a lazy day of rafting through the impressive Wind River Canyon outside

Thermopolis (where you can soak at Hot Springs State Park after your adventure, if you so wish), canoeing or kayaking in Yellowstone National Park's lakes, or bravely (or insanely) kayaking some of the state's creeks swollen with snowmelt in the late spring, there are paddling adventures of all levels aplenty in Wyoming. In this book, for the most part you'll find information for instructional services and guided rafting adventures, as well as easy paddles and floats. While instructional services exist in some locations around Wyoming—such as Jackson's **Snake River Kayak & Canoe** (1-800-529-2501; 307-733-9999; www.snakeriverkayak.com)—if you're a more experienced paddler, you may find that informational resources are slim. You can learn more about Wyoming's waters by contacting the **Jackson Hole Kayak Club** (307-733-2471; e-mail: jackson holekayak@wyoming.com) or visiting **Paddling.Net's** Wyoming page on the Web (www.paddling.net/places/WY) for starters.

PUBLIC LANDS Wyoming contains almost 15 million acres of national lands, including two national parks; more than 18 million acres of land administered by the Bureau of Land Management (BLM); and state-owned lands, including 12 state parks, a state recreation area, and numerous state historic sites. (See also *Bureau of Land Management, National Forests an dGrasslands,* and *State Parks* in this section.)

REST AREAS The **Wyoming Department of Transportation** (WYDOT) has 34 rest areas throughout the state located along interstates, and primary and secondary highways.

For a downloadable brochure with a map showing all locations as well as other relevant information, go to http://wydotweb.state.wy.us/web/e_docs/restarea.pdf.

RIVERS Wyoming counts more than 20 rivers scattered throughout the state, including one nationally designated **Wild and Scenic River, Clarks Fork of the Yellowstone River** (for more about Wild and Scenic Rivers, visit www.nps.gov/rivers/about.html), as well as scads of creeks and streams. These beautiful waterways provide fantastic recreational opportunities for anglers, paddlers, rafters, and others. They also provide drinking water for residents in some areas of the state; the **Laramie River,** for example, is the largest provider of drinking water for residents of Laramie.

ROAD REPORTS The best resource for up-to-the-minute road conditions is the **Wyoming Department of Transportation's (WYDOT) Road Report** Web site (www.wyoroad.info) or hotline (within Wyoming only: 1-888-996-7623; 307-772-0824). The site includes detailed information about closures, restrictions, and advisories, as well as images from live cameras around the state.

ROCK CLIMBING Wyoming has long been a hot spot for the nation's rock-climbing community, with attractions that simply cannot be ignored, such as **Devils Tower National Monument** in the northeast, the **Tetons** in the northwest, and **Vedauwoo** in the southeast. More recently, the state's vast quantity of quality limestone has begun to draw numerous sport climbers from around the nation and the world. The state hosts the **annual International Climbers' Festival** (www.climbersfestival.org) on the Thursday through Sunday after Independence Day. This informal festival, held in Lander, usually draws quite a crowd and features climbing-related clinics, slide shows, movies, cragging, and more—all for a nominal entry fee.

For general information on the state, visit **RockClimbing.com's** (www.rockclimbing.com) Wyoming pages. If you've never climbed before and you want to hire a guide, try **Jackson Hole Mountain Guides and Climbing School** (1-800-239-7642; www.jhmg.com), P.O. Box 7477, 165 N. Glenwood Street, Jackson, Wyoming 83002; or **Exum Mountain Guides** (307-733-2297; www.exum guides.com), Box 56, Moose, Wyoming 83012.

ROCKHOUNDING Wyoming provides ample opportunities for the rockhound, with agates, bloodstone, fossils, jade, and petrified wood, among others, so just make sure to acquaint yourself with the rules and regulations of the appropriate landowner before you help yourself to any property's bounty. One great resource that details 75 rockhounding sites across the state is *Rockhounding Wyoming,* by Kenneth Lee Graham (Falcon, 1996).

RODEOS With the **Bucking Horse & Rider** (BH&R) as a registered national and state trademark and rodeo as Wyoming's designated official state sport, it should not surprise you to discover that "the Cowboy State" hosts rodeos year-round, with one or more rodeos occurring virtually daily throughout the summer season—in fact, the **Cody Nite Rodeo** (307-587-

5155; www.comp-unltd.com/~rodeo/ rodeo.html) happens every night from June 1 to August 31. For an updated **schedule of rodeos,** visit www .wyomingtourism.org and click on "Rodeo." Another great resource is the **Wyoming Rodeo Association** (307-649-2458; www.swisherarena .com/wra).

RV PARKS If you have a home on wheels, you probably already know some of the best resources for finding RV parks around the country—the Internet is rife with listings. A great place to start your search for a place to park and hook up is the **Wyoming Campgrounds and RV Parks** Web page (www.rvpark.com/wy.htm), which provides alphabetical listings by city or town, contact information, and, sometimes, detailed information about RV parks statewide. (See also *Campgrounds* in this section.)

SNOW SPORTS If you plan to visit Wyoming in the winter, you'll find a number of snow sports to try your hand at, including snowshoeing, snowmobiling (or "snow machining"), skiing (cross-country and downhill), snowboarding, and more. In addition to the individual entries you'll find in

this book listed under *To Do—Snow Sports,* check out **Wyoming Travel and Tourism's** (www.wyoming-tourism.org) section devoted to winter sports and its free **Wyoming in Winter vacation packet,** available to order online at www.unicover.com/cgi-bin/wtcreq or by calling 1-800-225-5996.

SPEED LIMITS AND SEAT BELTS On the interstate, both day and night, the speed limit in Wyoming is 75 miles per hour, unless otherwise signed. On two-lane highways, the speed limit is 65 miles per hour, both day and night. Seat belts are required to be worn at all times by every occupant of the vehicle. Please be courteous—if you're driving exceptionally slowly (say, 10 miles per hour below the speed limit) and traffic builds up behind you, make an effort to pull over safely and allow the other drivers to pass.

STATE CAPITAL Cheyenne is the capital of Wyoming.

STATE PARKS Wyoming has 12 state parks, a state recreation area, and numerous state historic sites, all of which fall under the jurisdiction of the **Wyoming Division of State Parks and Historic Sites** (307-777-6323; http://wyoparks.state.wy.us/index1.htm). You'll find many of these parks and sites listed under various *To See* and *To Do* entries throughout this book, as they include opportunities for camping, picnicking, fishing, hiking, learning, and much, much more.

STATE THIS AND THAT Every state has them—those symbols, officially designated somethings, and nicknames that help define their identity.

Some of Wyoming's include: nicknames—**Equality State, Cowboy State, Big Wyoming**; motto—**"Equal rights"**; state registered trademark—**Bucking Horse and Rider**; state flower—**Indian paintbrush**; state mammal—**bison**; state bird—**meadowlark**; state tree—**plains cottonwood**; state gemstone—**jade**; state fish—**cutthroat trout**; state reptile—**horned toad**; state dinosaur—**triceratops**; and state sport—**rodeo**.

STATISTICS Wyoming is the ninth-largest state in area (97,914 square miles, which makes it larger than all of the United Kingdom). The state ranks 50th in population, with 498,703 residents (less than the number of people who populate the city of Denver in its southern neighbor state, Colorado). In Wyoming, there are five people per square mile (the national average is 75 people per square mile). The highest point in Wyoming is Gannett Peak at 13,804 feet; the lowest is the Belle Fourche River at 3,100 feet. Wyoming is the 44th state to be admitted to the union, on July 10, 1890.

TRAINS Wyoming's vast coal resources prompted the **Union Pacific Railroad** to construct a line across the southern part of the state in 1867–68, which largely accounted for the establishment of some of the state's first permanent settlements. Later, trains encouraged the development of tourism in the region. Today, trains are still used in Wyoming, mainly for the shipping of coal, agricultural products, and other goods made in Wyoming, as well as to bring in goods to the state from outside. For a **detailed list of Wyoming's railroads** (past and present), visit www.trainweb.org/wyomingrails/wyrr.html.

TRAVEL INFORMATION The best place to contact for overall travel information for the state of Wyoming is **Wyoming Travel and Tourism** (1-800-225-5996; www.wyoming tourism.org), which offers free vacation packets and a plethora of additional resources for travelers. For local and regional contacts to specific areas of the state, look to the *Guidance* sections of this book. Wyoming also has seven easily accessed information centers around the state: **Frank Norris Jr. Travel Center** (307-777-2883), I-25 at College Drive in Cheyenne, open daily; **Bear River Travel Information Center** (307-789-6540), I-80 East at Exit 6 in Evanston, open daily; **Jackson Information Center** (307-733-3316), 532 N. Cache in Jackson, open daily; **Summit Information Center** (307-721-9254), on I-80 at the Happy Jack exit 9 miles east of Laramie, open mid-May through mid-October; **Pine**

Bluffs Information Center (307-245-3695), along I-80 at the Pine Bluffs exit, open mid-May through mid-October; **Sheridan Information Center** (307-672-2485), located in Sheridan along I-90 at the 5th Street exit, open daily; and the **Sundance Information Center** (307-283-2440), along I-90 at the Sundance Port-of-Entry exit, open mid-May through late September.

WEATHER The most reliable resource I've found for accurate weather forecasts is the **National Weather Service** Web site (www.nws.noaa.gov). Just enter the city and state name, and you'll have an up-to-date forecast and current conditions at your fingertips. The highest temperature recorded in Wyoming was 114°F in Basin back in 1900; the lowest was –63°F in Moran in 1933. (See also *Climate* in this section.)

WILDERNESS AREAS Wyoming has 15 nationally designated wilderness areas, providing numerous recreational opportunities in pristine settings— so you need to be sure you know the rules and regulations governing each one and have the necessary outdoors skills before you visit. As a general guideline, you should practice the principles of **Leave No Trace** (1-800-332-4100; www.lnt.org; see entry in this section) when visiting wilderness areas. You can find a **complete list of Wyoming's wilderness areas** by going to www.wilderness .net, clicking on "Explore Wilderness Data," and entering *Wyoming* in the search criteria. You'll get a list of clickable links to all of Wyoming's designated wilderness areas, each of which yields detailed information about the site in question.

WILDFLOWERS Every spring brings with it the veritable multihued explosion of wildflowers to Wyoming's plains and mountains alike, from the brilliant red of the state flower, the **Indian paintbrush,** to the bright yellow **arrowleaf balsamroot** and deep indigo of **lupine,** among many others. You'll find many of these flowers— and other flora of the state—in the excellent book *Plants of the Rocky Mountains,* by Linda Kershaw, Andy MacKinnon, and Jim Pojar (Lone Pine, 1998). For those with an amateur interest in plants and flowers, *Plants of the Rocky Mountains* will be an indispensable resource, with its high-quality photography and its keys to plants and flowers, not to mention its well-written descriptions about each plant, which include interesting trivia about historical uses and more. For a state-specific guide, pick up a copy of *Wildflowers of Wyoming,* by Diantha States and Jack States (Mountain Press Publishing Company, 1999).

WILDLIFE You're almost sure to spot some of Wyoming's abundant wildlife while you're traveling around the state—even if you rarely get out of the car. It's not uncommon to see vast herds of **pronghorn** grazing adjacent to the interstates or **mule deer** crossing streets (at crosswalks, no less) en masse in the center of a Wyoming town. **Bighorn sheep, elk, moose, wild horses, and buffalo** are also viewable from behind the glass of your automobile, if you're in the right place at the right time and possess a keen eye; you might also see many of Wyoming's other furred, scaled, and feathered residents from your car. Of course, you dramatically increase your chances to see wildlife if you explore some of Wyoming's vast lands on foot, by bicycle, or on other nonmotorized modes of transportation. For more details on Wyoming's wildlife, including the official state list of birds, mammals, reptiles, and amphibians in Wyoming, contact the **Wyoming Game and Fish Wildlife Division** (307-777-4600; http://gf.state.wy.us/wildlife/index.asp).

WILDLIFE REFUGES Seven national wildlife refuges encompassing 80,776 acres of land lie within Wyoming. In addition to those refuges highlighted in this book (usually under *Wilder Places*), **detailed information about each national refuge,** including directions, recreation opportunities, contact information, and more, can be found by clicking on "WY" at http://refuges.fws.gov/profiles/bystate.cfm.

WINERIES Wyoming has at least two wineries, including **Terry Ranch Cellars** (at Terry Bison Ranch; 307-634-4171; www.terrybisonranch .com/facilities.htm) near Cheyenne and **Wyoming Wine** (307-673-0291; www.wyomingwine.com) in Sheridan.

WOMEN'S FIRSTS Wyoming's nickname, "the Equality State," comes

from the fact that Wyoming was the first state to grant women the vote, in 1869. Louisa Gardner Swain became the first woman to cast her vote in the state, in September of the following year. Wyoming was also the first state to grant women full citizenship, in 1868, when it was still a territory; the first state to have a female governor (Nellie Tayloe Ross in 1925); and the first to allow female jurors (Laramie, 1870).

ZOOS It appears that Wyoming has no bona fide zoos of its own—but if animals are your area of interest, you'll find no shortage of them in this state. Wildlife-related attractions are typically listed under *Wilder Places* throughout this book.

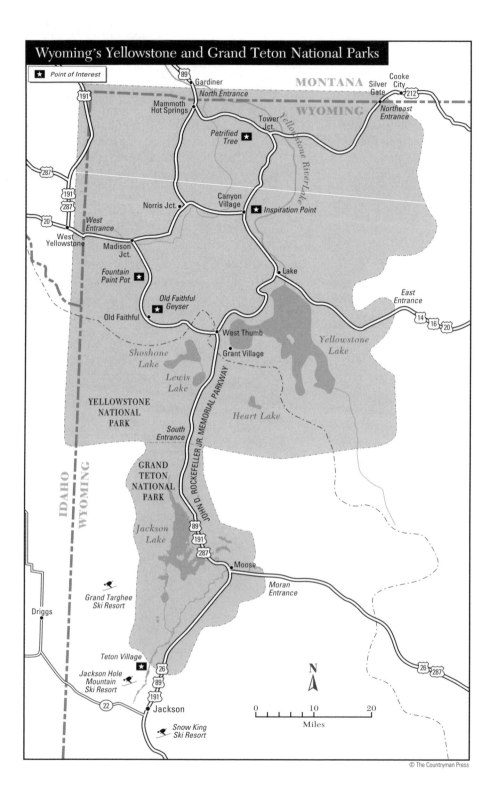

Wyoming's Yellowstone and Grand Teton National Parks

★ Point of Interest

MONTANA

WYOMING

IDAHO

WYOMING

Gardiner
North Entrance
Silver Gate
Cooke City
212

Mammoth Hot Springs
Northeast Entrance

Tower Jct.
Petrified Tree ★

Yellowstone River Lake

Norris Jct.
Canyon Village
★ Inspiration Point

West Entrance
West Yellowstone

Madison Jct.

Fountain Paint Pot ★

Old Faithful Geyser ★
Old Faithful

Lake

East Entrance
14 16 20

West Thumb
Grant Village

Yellowstone Lake

Shoshone Lake

Lewis Lake

Heart Lake

YELLOWSTONE NATIONAL PARK

South Entrance

GRAND TETON NATIONAL PARK

Jackson Lake

89 191 287

Moose

Moran Entrance

Grand Targhee Ski Resort

Driggs

Teton Village
Jackson Hole Mountain Ski Resort

26 89 191

22

Jackson

Snow King Ski Resort

JOHN D. ROCKEFELLER JR. MEMORIAL PARKWAY

89
191
287
20
287
191

N

0   10   20
Miles

© The Countryman Press

WYOMING'S YELLOWSTONE AND GRAND TETON NATIONAL PARKS

While Idaho and Montana possess small portions of Yellowstone National Park within their boundaries—1.4 percent and 7.6 percent, respectively—Wyoming lays claim to a whopping 91 percent of the park's lands. But with parts of the park in both Montana and Wyoming, what better place could there be for this book to transition from one state to the other? After all, Yellowstone National Park—and its nearby, though lesser-known, neighbor, Grand Teton National Park—is a great spot for you to transition from Montana to Wyoming or from Wyoming to Montana as well. Whether you prefer starting your adventure with Wyoming's best-known tourist attraction or you choose to finish your travels in the state with the wonders of Yellowstone, you'll no doubt be delighted and excited by the sites and sights you'll find within the borders of the world's first national park.

Yellowstone became a national park in 1872, signed into existence by President Ulysses S. Grant in an effort to preserve and protect this natural wonderland for future generations of both humans and the park's wilder inhabitants. Before it became a national park, though, Yellowstone was already an area filled with incredible phenomena, not only due to its mountains, lakes, and streams but also due to its unsurpassed concentration of geothermal features—approximately 10,000 exist within the park's 3,400 square miles. These features include hot springs, fumaroles (gas vents), mud pots, and, perhaps the most famous of all geothermal features, geysers (of which Old Faithful is one). More than 300 geysers lie within the park's boundaries, accounting for roughly 75 percent of all of the geysers in the world. These geysers fall within seven major geyser basins spread throughout the park, many of which feature interpretive trails that take you up close to observe the geysers in action.

A visit to Yellowstone and a stroll along its nature trails (see *To Do—Hiking*) will increase your knowledge of the how and why of geysers and other geothermal features (were I a scientist, I'd try to explain how they work, but I'm sure I'd get a few facts twisted or turned about, so I'll leave that job to the experts at the park). You'll also likely be wowed by the spectacular scenery, from the forested mountainsides to the areas rapidly and spontaneously rejuvenating from the devastation of the 1988 fires—areas that can be explored more closely via the park's 1,210 miles of trails or by paddling on one of its lakes. Yellowstone is packed so full of awe-inspiring sights that you'll be hard-pressed to learn about all of them during your visit, much less see them all with your own eyes (this truism accounts for the selective nature of those attractions included in this guide, which should help you pick out some of the park's more incredible offerings to include on your itinerary).

Despite Yellowstone's array of tourist-oriented sites, attractions, and activities, ranging from visitor centers to restaurants, historic sites to wayside exhibits, you might be surprised to learn that 97 percent of Yellowstone's lands remain undeveloped. In fact, the park forms the core of a much larger area—a 28,000-square-mile section—known as the Greater Yellowstone Ecosystem. This important area represents one of the largest, mostly intact temperate-zone ecosystems remaining on the planet. Thus, in spite of all of the services geared toward human visitors, Yellowstone remains committed above all to protecting, sustaining, and preserving its natural features and its wild inhabitants, both living and nonliving alike. This mission accounts for the large number of rules and regulations governing the behavior of the park's human visitors.

As a privileged visitor to the park, you must make an effort to obey the park's rules and listen and respond to the rangers should they make a request. On one of my journeys through Yellowstone, a mother black bear and her cub appeared right on the roadway—undoubtedly a cool and amazing thing to witness. Unfortunately, the experience was marred by the disrespectful behavior of the drivers around me, who parked their vehicles all over the roadway, not even bothering to pull off to the side. This resulted in an enormous traffic jam, with traffic backed up both ways. Many people proceeded to get out of their cars and approach the bears, despite the ranger yelling at them not to do so and demanding that they return to their cars. This sort of disrespectful behavior compromises the safety of both visitors and the bears, as visitors could be charged by an angered bear—particularly one with a cub; the bear would then be considered aggressive, and action against it might have to be taken as a consequence, all because of tourists not listening to a ranger.

The point of this diatribe is that Yellowstone has its rules for a reason—including the rule that you must maintain a distance of at least 100 yards from bears and at least 25 yards from all other wild animals, including bison. If you make an animal move or change its behavior due to your presence, you're too close and in violation of the park's rules. Do not stop in the road to view wildlife (unless the animal or animals are in the road, of course; in that case you should stay in your car and allow them to move off the roadway)—drive to the nearest pullout to avoid creating traffic problems. Additional rules to be aware of are the park's universal 45 mph speed limit (which the park does enforce—I've seen many a tourist pulled over), the seasonal closure of many of the park's entrance roads during wintertime, the rule against putting or throwing any objects into the park's geothermal features, including yourself or any body part, and the rule that you must stay on trails, particularly in geothermal areas. Yellowstone National Park has a number of additional rules and regulations, some of which are covered below. Upon entering the park, you will receive literature that includes this information, so to avoid any problems, be sure to read through it before embarking on any adventures.

Yellowstone National Park is linked to its less-traveled southern neighbor, Grand Teton National Park, by the John D. Rockefeller Jr. Memorial Parkway (US 89/191/287), a 50-mile road (see *To See—Scenic Drives* in "Grand Teton National Park"). In contrast with Yellowstone National Park, Grand Teton National Park has far fewer visitor services, providing an alternative for those seeking a less cattlelike vacation experience or needing a break from the crowds usually encountered (at least during the summer season) at Yellowstone's most famed attractions. Defined by its most striking feature—the incredibly distinctive Teton Range (see *To See—Natural Wonders*)—Grand Teton is a wilderness lover's playground, with opportunities to hike, fish, paddle, climb, bicycle, view wildlife, and more. Created in 1929, the park was expanded in 1950 to encompass its current area, which includes nearly 500 square miles of land. Within its boundaries lie seven morainal lakes and more than 100 backcountry lakes, the Snake River, the Teton Range, numerous species of wildlife, and a human history that includes Native Americans, ranchers, and conservationists.

Grand Teton National Park also manages the John D. Rockefeller Jr. Memorial Parkway, and the corridor that surrounds it, as a recreation area. Grand Teton has a brochure for almost every activity permissible in the park, to help you learn the necessary regulations and precautions before you undertake your recreational opportunity of choice.

Please note that many of the activities and attractions listed for each park are managed by the park itself. Therefore, if the heading in a section of this book is the name of either park (for example, Grand Teton National Park under *To Do—Boating*), then the proper contact information can be found in that park's listing under *Guidance*. In the section under the park's name, you'll find general rules, regulations, and guidance for each specific activity. Following this general overview, if a particular attraction(s) stands out, I've included a brief description. If additional contact information is necessary and/or relevant, you will find it within the individual listings. Also, please note that because many of the parks' dining establishments operate in conjunction with the lodging establishments, these listings have been consolidated into a single section.

For attractions surrounding Yellowstone National Park, see "South-Central Montana: Yellowstone Country" and "North Wyoming: Devils Tower–Buffalo Bill Country." For attractions in the area around Grand Teton National Park, see "West Wyoming: Jackson Hole–Jim Bridger Country."

YELLOWSTONE NATIONAL PARK

Welcome to one of the nation's most beloved and visited national parks in the national park system. To make the most of your trip to Yellowstone, be sure to include stops at some of the park's lesser-known spots along with those mandatory visits to its most famed attractions. You'll find an assortment of each of these listed below to help you in formulating a plan.

GUIDANCE Xanterra Parks and Resorts (307-344-7901; 307-344-7311; www
.travelyellowstone.com), P.O. Box 165, Yellowstone National Park, WY 82190.
Xanterra is the primary, National Park Service–authorized, in-park concessionaire for Yellowstone, providing camping and lodging reservations, general park
information, auto and snowcoach tour reservations, and more. Xanterra does not
charge a booking fee for its services.

&. **Yellowstone National Park** (307-344-7381; www.nps.gov/yell), P.O. Box 168,
Yellowstone National Park, WY 82190-0168. Open all day every day; $10 per
individual (7 days) or $20 per vehicle (7 days), $40 annual pass (good for
entrance into Grand Teton National Park as well). Most of the park's entrance
roads are closed to wheeled vehicles seasonally, with the exception of US 89
from Gardiner, Montana, at the North Entrance; and US 212 from Silver Gate
and Cooke City, Montana, near the Northeast Entrance. Please note that US 212
east of Cooke City is impassable to wheeled traffic during winter months (November through April). All roads south through the park are closed to wheeled
traffic in wintertime as well. In general, the park's other entrances close for the
season on the first Sunday in November. The West Entrance opens to wheeled
traffic for the season on the third Sunday in April; the South and East Entrances
open in early May. To further confuse things, even if park entrances are open,
you may not be able to travel around the park on all of its roads, particularly during spring and fall, as weather may cause closures. In addition, road construction
can thwart your efforts as well. So what's a traveler to do? Plan ahead, map your
route, and then contact the park or visit the park's Web site to ensure that your
travel plans match up to the roads currently open for travel. For details on snowmobile travel in the park, see *To Do—Snow Sports.*

GETTING THERE Yellowstone National Park is accessed from the east via US
14/16/20, from the south via US 89/191/287, from the west via US 20 from the
north via US 89 to the North Entrance Road, and from the northeast via US 212
to the Northeast Entrance Road.

See also *Airports, Amtrak, Bus Service,* and *Travel Information* in "What's
Where in Wyoming."

MEDICAL EMERGENCY Call **911;** on-duty rangers provide emergency medical
care.

Lake Clinic, Pharmacy, and Hospital (307-242-7241), in Lake Village; open
mid-May through September 30 with 24-hour emergency care.

Mammoth Clinic (307-344-7965), next to Mammoth Post Office in Mammoth
Hot Springs; open daily June 1 through September 30 8 AM–5:30 PM, closed for
lunch 1 PM–2 PM; open October 1 through May 31 Monday through Friday 8
AM–5:30 PM, closed for lunch 1 PM–2 PM and on Friday afternoon.

Old Faithful Clinic (307-545-7325), by Old Faithful; open daily early May
through mid-May 8:30 AM–5 PM, closed for lunch noon–1 PM; open daily mid-
May through mid-September 7 AM–7 PM, closed for lunch noon–1 PM; open

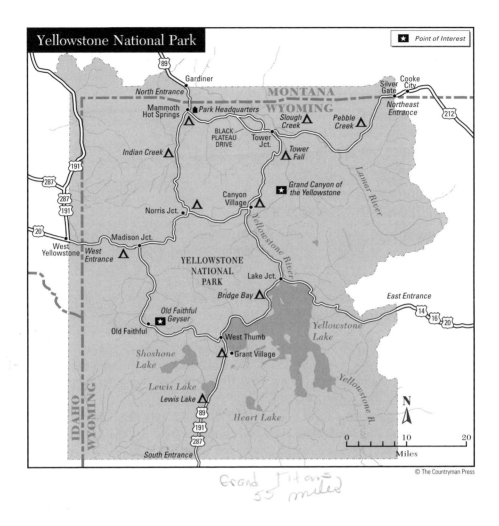

Yellowstone National Park

★ Point of Interest

89
Gardiner
North Entrance
Silver Gate | Cooke City
MONTANA
WYOMING
Mammoth Hot Springs
▲ Park Headquarters
Slough Creek ▲
Pebble Creek ▲
Northeast Entrance
212
BLACK PLATEAU DRIVE
Tower Jct.
Indian Creek ▲
191
287
287
191
Norris Jct.
Canyon Village ▲
Grand Canyon of the Yellowstone ★
Tower ▲ Fall
Lamar River
Yellowstone River
20
West Yellowstone
West Entrance ▲
Madison Jct.
YELLOWSTONE NATIONAL PARK
Lake Jct.
Bridge Bay ▲
East Entrance
14
16
20
Old Faithful Geyser ★
Old Faithful
West Thumb
Grant Village ▲
Yellowstone Lake
Shoshone Lake
Lewis Lake
Lewis Lake ▲
89
191
287
Heart Lake
Yellowstone R.
IDAHO
WYOMING
South Entrance

N

0   10   20
Miles

© The Countryman Press

Grand Titans 55 miles (handwritten)

daily mid-September through mid-October 8:30 AM–5 PM, closed for lunch noon–1 PM.

✳ To See

VISITOR CENTERS **Albright Visitor Center and Museum,** at Mammoth Hot Springs 5 miles south of North Entrance, at the northwest corner of the Grand Loop Road's upper loop. Open daily late May through early September 8 AM– 7 PM; open daily early September through late September 9 AM–6 PM; open daily October 1 through late May 9 AM–5 PM. This visitor center, museum, and the surrounding red-roofed buildings were once home to Fort Yellowstone, a U.S. Calvary post, back when the army ran the park. The buildings were turned over to the National Park Service (NPS) when it was created in 1916. Today, the exterior of these fort structures provides an excellent example of a turn-of-the-20th-century army outpost, while the interior provides up-to-date visitor information about the park in addition to a museum. Among other displays, the museum features exhibits about the park's human past, grouped by historical periods, from the time of the Native Americans before 1800 to the founding and growth of the NPS. The museum also shows Yellowstone-themed films regularly during summertime and upon request during the off-season.

& **Canyon Visitor Center** is less than 0.25 mile southeast of Canyon Junction in Canyon Village. Open late May through early September 8 AM–7 PM; open early September through late September 9 AM–6 PM; closed early October through late May. In addition to providing general visitor information, this center features an exhibit on Yellowstone bison, a joint effort of the park and the Buffalo Bill Historical Center in Cody (see *To See—Museums* in "North Wyoming: Devils Tower–Buffalo Bill Country").

& **Fishing Bridge Visitor Center and Museum** is 1 mile east of the Grand Loop Road at Lake Village, on the East Entrance Road. Open late May through early September 8 AM–7 PM; open early September through late September 9 AM–6 PM; closed early October through late May. A National Historic Landmark, this stone visitor center was constructed in 1931. Its exhibits include wildlife displays, one of which was installed in 1931 and showcases Yellowstone's birds. The Fishing Bridge itself is a historic structure as well. The original bridge was built in 1902; the current bridge, in 1937. Despite its name, you can no longer fish from the Fishing Bridge—it has been closed to anglers since 1973 in response to declining cutthroat trout populations. Nonetheless, it's still a popular tourist place to stop, stroll, take pictures, and observe wildlife.

& **Grant Village Visitor Center** is in Grant Village, 1 mile from the Grant Village Junction off the South Entrance Road on the shore of the West Thumb of Yellowstone Lake. Open late May through early September 8 AM–7 PM; open early September through late September 9 AM–6 PM; closed early October through late May. Named for Ulysses S. Grant, who signed the documentation that proclaimed Yellowstone America's first national park in 1872, this visitor center was constructed nearly 100 years later in prime grizzly habitat, making it rather controversial. Nonetheless, it stands, and it provides visitors with a comprehensive look at the 1988 fires, including a film shown regularly.

Madison Information Station is just south of Madison Junction at the Madison Picnic Area on the Grand Loop Road. Open late May through early September 9 AM–6 PM; open early September through late September 9 AM–5 PM. This National Historic Landmark was built in 1929–30. It has served many purposes since then, and it has been left empty at times. Today, it welcomes visitors to explore its resources, which include park information, a bookstore, and exhibits.

& **Old Faithful Visitor Center** is 16 miles south of Madison Junction off the Grand Loop Road, about 200 yards from Old Faithful (see *Natural Wonders*). Open mid-April through late May 9 AM–5 PM; open late May through early September 8 AM–7 PM; open early September through late September 8 AM–6 PM; open October 1 through early November 9 AM–5 PM; open December through mid-April 9 AM–5 PM. If you're headed for this visitor center, you probably already have a specific attraction in mind! The center provides visitor information, including evening ranger-led talks in summer and winter.

♿ **West Thumb Information Station** is east of the junction between Old Faithful–South Entrance Road and the Bridge Bay–Fishing Bridge–Lake Road in the West Thumb Geyser Basin. Open late May through September 9 AM–5 PM. The station provides visitor information and a bookstore.

See also **Lake Ranger Station** and **West Thumb Ranger Station** under *Historic Landmarks, Places, and Sites.*

MUSEUMS **Museum of the National Park Ranger** is on the west side of the Grand Loop Road about 1 mile north of Norris Junction at the entrance to Norris Campground. Open late May through early September 9 AM–6 PM; open early September through late September 9 AM–5 PM; closed October through late May. Though you might never have thought about park rangers and the National Park Service (NPS) in-depth before, a visit to this museum will surely pique your interest. Exhibits cover, among other topics, the origin and development of the role of park rangers as well as the NPS, including an educational film. This museum is housed in the historic 1908 Norris Soldier Station, one of the park's original structures. Interestingly, the building was taken down and then rebuilt, using as much of the original building materials as possible and re-creating as much of the original floor plan as possible.

♿ **Norris Geyser Basin Museum** is on the west side of the Grand Loop Road, 0.25 mile north of Norris Junction at the Norris Geyser Basin (see *To Do—Hiking*). An original log and stone structure constructed in 1929–30 houses this museum that introduces visitors to the geysers and geothermal features of Norris Geyser Basin. This museum's architectural style became the archetype for many of the park's facilities built in the same period.

See also **Albright Visitor Center and Museum** under *Visitor Centers.*

HISTORIC LANDMARKS, PLACES, AND SITES **Lake Ranger Station,** in Lake Village on the Grand Loop Road, was one of the first ranger stations constructed in the park after the military turned control over to the National Park Service (NPS) in 1916. Constructed in 1923, this log ranger station reflected an effort to establish structures that complemented rather than contrasted with the natural surroundings, as suggested by Steven Mather, the first NPS director.

GEOTHERMAL SIGHTS ALONG THE PORCE-LAIN BASIN LOOP IN THE NORRIS GEYSER BASIN AREA

Additional historic ranger stations include the **Northeast Entrance Ranger Station** (a National Historic Landmark) and the **Tower Ranger Station,** which is a reconstruction of the 1907 soldier station that once stood in its place.

Lamar Buffalo Ranch Historic District, along the Northeast Entrance Road east of Tower Junction, is the location of an early-20th-century bison ranching operation that continued into the 1950s in an effort to preserve the park's bison population. Four of the ranch's structures are on the National Register of Historic Places, but the facilities are not open to the public. This area is now used by the Yellowstone Association Institute for educational programs (see also *To Do—Unique Adventures*), as well as by the National Park Service (NPS) for its **Expedition: Yellowstone! Program,** an environmental education program for children in grades 4–8.

Nez Perce Creek Wayside, south of Madison Information Station and north of Fountain Paint Pot Nature Trail at Nez Perce Creek on the Grand Loop Road. At this wayside exhibit location, the Nez Perce Indians passed by in 1877 as they fled encroaching U.S. troops during the 5-month-long Nez Perce War. This is part of the historic Nez Perce Trail, a National Historic Trail that follows the 1,170-mile journey taken by the Nez Perce from Wallowa Lake in Oregon to the Bear Paw Battlefield near Chinook (see *To See—Historic Landmarks, Places, and Sites* in "North-Central Montana: Russell Country"). (See also Nez Perce Nee-Me-Poo Trail under *To Do—Hiking* in "Southwest Montana: Gold West Country.")

Obsidian Cliff, 11 miles south of Mammoth Hot Springs or 8 miles north of Norris, is a National Historic Landmark that was long used by Indians for quarrying rock, which they then fashioned into projectile points. This unusually large outcropping of obsidian rises 150–200 feet above the creek below and features the glassy, crystal-free rock favored by the Indians. Projectile points from this cliff's rock have been found as far east as Ohio. In addition to its historic significance and value as a quarry, in the 1920s Obsidian Cliff became one of the park's first places to establish a wayside exhibit to help visitors learn more about the park's resources while driving through.

Roosevelt Arch. This arch marks the park's northern entrance, on the North Entrance Road in Gardiner, Montana (see Gardiner under *To See—Towns* in "South-Central Montana: Yellowstone Country"). Constructed in 1903, this stone arch was dedicated by President Teddy Roosevelt, who placed its cornerstone. Today this historic structure continues to welcome visitors to the park year-round, as it has for more than a century.

West Thumb Ranger Station, on the way to Grant Village off the Grand Loop Road, not only provides the basic services of a ranger station (information, backcountry permits, and so forth) but also stands as a historical reminder of the park's early architectural style. Constructed in 1925, the log structure continues to serve its original purpose.

See also Albright Visitor Center and Museum and Fishing Bridge Visitor Center and Museum under *Visitor Centers;* Museum of the National Park Ranger and Norris Geyser Basin Museum under *Museums;* Old Faithful Lodge and Roosevelt Lodge under *Lodging and Where to Eat—Lodges;* and Lake Yellowstone

Hotel, Mammoth Hot Springs Hotel, and Old Faithful Inn under *Lodging and*
Where to Eat—Other Options.

FOR FAMILIES ✐ **Junior Ranger Program.** Materials are available at park visitor centers (see *Visitor Centers*); $3 per child. Designed for children ages 5–12
(and their families, of course), this fun-filled program features a 12-page activity
book (one for younger children and one for older children) called *Yellowstone*
Nature that kids complete in order to earn a Junior Ranger badge. Activities
include attending a ranger-led talk (held throughout the summer season; stop in
at a visitor center or a ranger station for a schedule), taking a hike on one of Yellowstone's many trails, and much more. Kids will also find a number of age-
appropriate, interactive, Yellowstone-oriented activities on the Web to prepare
them for their travels to the park. Just go to the main Web site (www.nps.gov/yell),
click "For Kids," and you're on your way.

✐ **Yellowstone Buddies** is offered by Xanterra Parks and Resorts (see *Guid-*
ance) from late June to late August Monday through Thursday; morning session
is 9 AM–noon (lunch included), $28 per child; evening session is 6 PM–8 PM,
$18.50 per child. This program provides children ages 6–11 the opportunity for
hands-on exploration of the Old Faithful area, under the supervision of qualified
staff. Children participating in this program will earn their Junior Ranger badge
as well (see Junior Ranger Program, above). Participants meet at the Old Faithful Inn.

See also Xanterra Parks and Resorts under *To Do—Horseback Riding;* and Old
West Cookout, Roosevelt Cookout Roundup, and Yellowstone Lake Scenic
Cruise under *To Do—Unique Adventures.*

SCENIC DRIVES **Blacktail Plateau Drive** departs the Grand Loop Road heading one-way east of Mammoth Hot Springs (about halfway to Tower–Roosevelt),
rejoining the Grand Loop Road near the **Petrified Tree** (see *Natural Wonders*).
The drive takes you away from the main road and through less-trafficked terrain
of the **Blacktail Deer Plateau,** yielding the opportunity to see wildlife and
enjoy scenery away from the regular route. This road is also open to mountain
bikes (two-way traffic).

Firehole Canyon Drive is a one-way road that departs from the Grand Loop
Road just south of the Madison Information Station, rejoining it a bit farther
south. The drive takes you along the **Firehole River** (see *To Do—Fishing*) to
view the scenic 40-foot **Firehole Falls.** The area is a popular place to swim in
the heat of summer, but there are no lifeguards, so you must use caution.

& **Firehole Lake Drive** is a one-way road that leaves the Grand Loop Road
north of the Midway Geyser Basin (north of Old Faithful) and rejoins the loop
road farther north, across from the **Fountain Paint Pot Nature Trail** (see *To*
Do—Hiking). The road leads you past the **Great Fountain Geyser,** which
features regular eruptions towering 100 feet in height and lasting for up to an
hour in length. You will see a number of additional geothermal features along
this road, including **Firehole Spring, Surprise Pool, Firehole Lake,** and
Pink Cone Geyser, among other sights.

Grand Loop Road, the park's major road, forms a figure-eight and is accessible from all five park entrances. Traveling all 142 miles of this road takes you past virtually all of the park's major natural attractions and provides access to campgrounds, picnicking facilities, visitor centers, visitor services, scenic views, and wildlife viewing opportunities. All of the other short and scenic drives listed here are accessible from the Grand Loop Road.

North Rim Drive is a one-way road that begins at the Grand Loop Road junction in Canyon Village and deposits you back on the Grand Loop Road south of Canyon Village. You can also take a spur road off the one-way road, to **Inspiration Point.** This scenic point features a tremendous view of the **Grand Canyon of the Yellowstone** (see *Natural Wonders*). Also along the one-way road, you can stop at **Grand View and Lookout Point** for views of the canyon's **Lower Falls.**

& **South Rim Drive** is an out-and-back road to **Artist Point,** accessible off the Grand Loop Road just south of Canyon Village. The drive includes a view of the spectacular 308-foot-high **Lower Falls** of the Grand Canyon of the Yellowstone (see *Natural Wonders*). You can also stop to view the 109-foot **Upper Falls** along this road. Artist Point affords a scenic overlook of the **Grand Canyon of the Yellowstone.**

Upper Terrace Drive is a one-way road that leaves the Grand Loop Road just south of Mammoth Hot Springs and returns you to the road next to your starting point. Closed in winter, the road is suitable for passenger cars only. It takes you past the multicolored, sculpturelike **limestone terraces,** giving you a quick view of their beauty and uniqueness. You can also access the **Mammoth Hot Springs Nature Trails** (see *To Do—Hiking*) from here if you'd like to take a closer look.

See also **John D. Rockefeller Jr. Memorial Parkway** under *Scenic Drives* in "Grand Teton National Park."

THE MAMMOTH TERRACES AT MAMMOTH HOT SPRINGS

NATURAL WONDERS American bison are viewable along the Grand Loop Road throughout the park; please observe the 25-yard minimum distance required by law for your own safety and that of these wild animals. More than 3,000 American bison live in Yellowstone National Park today, and visitors often see them along the roadside. You may be surprised to learn, then, that by the turn of the 20th century, the number of bison remaining in the park totaled fewer than 50. The remarkable comeback of the bison is the result of human efforts (see Lamar Buffalo Ranch Historic District under *Historic Landmarks, Places, and Sites*). The buffalo

continue to survive here in the only area of the Lower 48 states that has sustained a bison population nonstop since prehistoric times. Be aware that though somewhat cowlike, bison are truly wild animals and thus unpredictable. They are also huge—males weigh almost a ton, while females weigh "only" 1,000 pounds or thereabouts—not exactly the sort of creature you'd want to make angry!

BUFFALO ARE FREQUENTLY SEEN IN YELLOWSTONE NATIONAL PARK.

Bears, both the American black bear and the more formidable grizzly bear, make their home by the hundreds in Yellowstone National Park; please observe the 100-yard minimum distance required by law for your own safety and that of these wild animals. DO NOT FEED THE BEARS. Not at all like the friendly Yogi Bear encountered in the fictional Jellystone Park, Yellowstone's bears, while probably accustomed to varying extents to the presence of humans, are wild animals that can be extremely dangerous, and they should be treated as such. If you see a bear, keep your distance, respect the animal's space, and report the sighting to the nearest ranger station.

Grand Canyon of the Yellowstone, observable from the Canyon Village area, continues north with the Yellowstone River flowing through it to the Tower–Roosevelt Area. Originally carved out by massive erosive forces more than 10,000 years ago, this canyon features a wild environment tucked between canyon walls of soft, yellowish volcanic stone that tower 800–1,000 feet above the Yellowstone River, which continues to erode the canyon today. (See also North Rim Drive and South Rim Drive under *Scenic Drives.*)

OLD FAITHFUL IN YELLOWSTONE NATIONAL PARK

& **Old Faithful** is at the southwest corner of the lower loop of the Grand Loop Road. Probably the most-recognized of Yellowstone's attractions, this geyser erupts every 45 to 90 minutes, making it the most frequently erupting of all of Yellowstone's large geysers—one of the major facts that accounts for its popularity. You might feel like you're at a circus or theatrical production while you wait for the geyser to erupt, due to the stagelike setting, complete with ample seating to accommodate the crowds gathered to watch it, not to mention the proliferation of buildings and services surrounding it. Nonetheless, when Old

Faithful bursts forth with a fury, spewing scalding-hot water 100 to 180 feet into the air, you'll probably forget about all of the development and distractions. For a bit more solitude, you can take a hike or bike ride on the paved 1.5-mile trail (handicapped accessible) to the **Morning Glory Pool,** which includes views of other geothermal features, including **Castle Geyser** and **Crested Pool.** Hikers (but not bikers) can continue on the unpaved trail to **Biscuit Basin** from here. (See also **Old Faithful Visitor Center** under *Visitor Centers.*)

Petrified Tree is east of the Tower–Roosevelt area just off the Grand Loop Road. A 20-foot portion of this petrified redwood tree stands upright where it has stood since it grew some 50 million years ago. Volcanic activity fossilized the specimen, and you can read about this process in depth at the display area. More specimens of petrified trees, which together make up the world's most concentrated known area of petrified trees, can be viewed along the Specimen Ridge Trail, accessible from Tower Fall (see below), as well as several points along the Northeast Entrance Road east of Tower Junction.

Tower Fall is just south of Tower Junction on the Grand Loop Road. This waterfall is distinctive due to its multihued, jagged towers of eroded volcanic rock that frame the actual 132-foot waterfall made by Tower Creek. A 0.5-mile hike down steep switchbacks takes you up close for a more intimate view of this inspirational setting.

Wolves were successfully reintroduced to the park in 1995 after a human-caused absence that lasted at least 25 years and more likely 50 years; please observe the 25-yard minimum distance required by law for your own safety and that of these wild animals. That having been said, you're not likely to get that close, even if you should catch a glimpse of one of these magnificent predators—but some lucky park visitors are treated to the sight of Yellowstone's wolves each year. Wolves represent a critical piece in putting back together the somewhat shattered ecological balance in the park, considered by some to embody a microcosm of the predator-prey imbalances caused by human actions that persist outside the park.

Yellowstone Caldera, forming the central portion of the park, is an enormous, 28-mile-by-47-mile caldera, making it one of the world's largest of such formations. A *caldera* is a volcanic crater that results from either a massive eruption or the collapse of a volcano's cone. Formed by the former some 600,000 years ago, the Yellowstone Caldera continues to reverberate with the aftereffects of that event to this day, as evidenced by Yellowstone's extensive geothermal features as well as Yellowstone Lake (see below), which fills a huge portion of the caldera with its waters.

Yellowstone Lake is huge: the Grand Loop Road follows its shoreline for some 30 miles of its southeastern portion—a mere fraction of its 110 miles of total shoreline. The lake is also deep—390 feet deep at its deepest spot. It is roughly 20 miles by 14 miles in area. What do these statistics add up to? Yellowstone Lake is one of the largest alpine lakes on the planet. Visitors enjoy numerous activities centered around the lake, including fishing, boating (motorized), paddling, bicycling, hiking, swimming, and picnicking, among others.

See also Obsidian Cliff under *Historic Landmarks, Places, and Sites; Scenic Drives;* Lone Star Geyser Road under *To Do—Bicycling; To Do—Hiking;* and *To Do—Hot Springs.*

✳ To Do

BICYCLING **Yellowstone National Park** allows bicycles on park roads, in parking areas, and on certain designated trails, including those listed below, but not on backcountry trails or on boardwalks. Cyclists must obey all traffic rules. Use caution on roadways, as most are narrow, winding, and do not have shoulders, making it difficult for vehicle drivers to see cyclists. Certain park roads are open from mid-March to the third Thursday in April for bike travel (and foot travel) before they open for auto travel. Call the park or visit the Web site (see *Guidance*) for more details. You cannot rent bikes in the park. For more details on the park's bicycling regulations and opportunities, visit the Web site, click on "Activities" and then on "Biking," or call the park and request the *Bicycling in Yellowstone National Park* brochure. Several commercial outfitters are licensed by the National Park Service to provide bicycle tours in the park, including **A Personal Guide Service** (307-733-6312) and **Teton Mountain Bike Tours** (307-733-0712), among others.

Bunsen Peak Road, departing from the Grand Loop Road just south of Mammoth and north of the Upper Terrace Drive, is a 6-mile route designated for bicycle travel. You can combine the Bunsen Peak Road with the section of abandoned roadway starting in Gardiner that parallels the Yellowstone River to the park's entrance (5 miles), among other options, to lengthen your bicycle outing in this area of the park.

Fountain Flats Drive to Firehole Freight Road. On this ride, you'll leave the Grand Loop Road just south of the Nez Perce Creek Wayside (see *To See—Historic Landmarks, Places, and Sites*). Appropriate for mountain bikes, this route follows an auto road for 1.5 miles along the Firehole River and then continues for about 5.5 miles on an old service road, taking you by Goose Lake and Grand Prismatic Spring, the park's largest hot spring. The trail then rejoins the Grand Loop Road at the Midway Geyser Basin.

Lone Star Geyser Road leaves the Grand Loop Road just south of Old Faithful at the Kepler Cascades, a 125-foot, easily accessible waterfall. This route takes you on a 2-mile journey up to the Lone Star Geyser. The geyser erupts roughly every 3 hours, so if you bring a picnic lunch and have some patience (or are just lucky with your timing), you can probably catch it in action.

Riverside Trail leaves the West Entrance Road at the park entrance and rejoins it 1.4 miles later, providing a nice, albeit short, ride along the Madison River, away from automobile traffic.

See also Blacktail Plateau Drive under *To See—Scenic Drives;* and Old Faithful under *To See—Natural Wonders.*

BOATING **Yellowstone National Park** allows motorized boating on **Lewis Lake** and most of **Yellowstone Lake** (see *To See—Natural Wonders*), with the exception of the South Arm, the Southeast Arm, and a portion of the Flat

Mountain Arm. You must purchase a permit ($10 for 7 days, or $20 annually; also valid in Grand Teton National Park) in-person for each motorized watercraft (which must already have state registration as well). Permits can be purchased at Bridge Bay Ranger Station, Grant Village Visitor Center, Lewis Lake Campground, Lake Ranger Station, and South Entrance. Bridge Bay, south of Lake Village on the Grand Loop Road, serves as the park's central location for motorized boating. Here you'll find a boat launch and marina, where **Xanterra Parks and Resorts** (see *Guidance*) rents out motorized boats (first-come, first-served). (See also Yellowstone Lake Scenic Cruise under *Unique Adventures*.)

See *Paddling/Floating* for details on the use of nonmotorized watercraft in Yellowstone National Park.

CAMPING &. **Xanterra Parks and Resorts** (see *Guidance*) runs five developed campgrounds (all handicapped accessible) in the park with sites that can be reserved in advance. These include **Bridge Bay** (open late May through mid-September; $17); **Canyon** (open mid-June through mid-September; $17); **Fishing Bridge RV Park** (RVs only; open mid-May through early October; $31); **Grant** (open late June through early October; $17); and **Madison** (open early May through late October; $17).

&. **Yellowstone National Park** runs seven developed first-come, first-serve campgrounds (all handicapped accessible) and some 300 backcountry campsites. Developed campgrounds include **Indian Creek** (open mid-June through mid-September; $12); **Lewis Lake** (open mid-June through mid-November; $12); **Mammoth** (open year-round; $14); **Norris** (open mid-May through late September; $14); **Pebble Creek** (open early June through late September; $12); **Slough Creek** (open late May through late October; $12); and **Tower Fall** (open mid-May through early October; $12). Backcountry camping requires a permit, which must be obtained in-person no sooner than 48 hours before the start of your adventure in the backcountry. You can obtain a permit at most visitor centers and ranger stations. For a $20 reservation fee, you can reserve some backcountry sites in advance of your trip by mail or in person only. For a **Backcountry Reservation form,** call 307-344-2160; write to Backcountry Office, P.O. Box 168, Yellowstone National Park, WY 82190; or download the form from the park's Web site.

FISHING **Yellowstone National Park** is home to a number of prime fishing destinations, including **Yellowstone Lake** (see *To See—Natural Wonders*), **Heart Lake, Lewis Lake, Shoshone Lake,** and smaller lakes; as well as a number of rivers and streams, including the rivers described briefly below. Fishing in Yellowstone requires a park permit for those ages 12 and older. Ages 12–15 must acquire a nonfee permit. Anglers ages 16 and up must pay for the privilege to fish ($15 for a 3-day permit; $20 for a 7-day permit; $35 for an annual permit). Children 11 and under can fish without a permit under adult supervision. Permits can be purchased at visitor centers, ranger stations, and general stores throughout the park. No state fishing license is required. In an effort to preserve ecosystems and protect native fish species, Yellowstone also has a number of special rules and regulations in place regarding fishing practices, including seasonal opening and closing dates; a catch-and-release policy for all native fish species (cutthroat trout, Montana grayling, and mountain whitefish); and restrictions on bait; among others. The angler is responsible for knowing all of the current rules and regulations.

The Firehole River flows from south of Old Faithful, paralleling the Grand Loop Road north to its confluence with the Gibbon River and the Madison River. This much-loved, pristine stream is renowned among anglers for its healthy populations of brook, brown, cutthroat, and rainbow trout, as well as its scenic qualities.

The Gardner River flows from a lake on Joseph Peak east of Mammoth, first north, then south, then wraps around north again at Indian Creek Campground, where it flows north along North Entrance Road to its confluence with the Yellowstone River. Species of fish include brook, brown, cutthroat, and rainbow trout.

The Gibbon River flows from northwest of Norris along Grand Loop Road to its confluence with the Firehole River to form the Madison River at the Madison area. The mostly spring-fed Gibbon River has brook, brown, and rainbow trout, as well as Montana grayling and mountain whitefish.

The Lewis River flows from Lewis Lake south along South Entrance Road to the park's border and its confluence with the Snake River. Fish species include brook, brown, cutthroat, mackinaw, and rainbow trout.

The Yellowstone River, the park's largest and most distinctive river, flows from its origins in the mountains southwest of the park northward into the Southeast Arm of Yellowstone Lake. The river continues to flow north from the Fishing Bridge Area, angling east through the Grand Canyon of the Yellowstone (see *To See—Natural Wonders*) at Canyon Junction, before heading northwest to Gardiner, Montana, then continuing its journey through that state (see also listings under *To Do—Fishing* in "South-Central Montana: Yellowstone Country" and "Southeast Montana: Custer Country"). In the park, the portion of the river south of Yellowstone Lake is remote and difficult to access. North of the lake, the Upper Yellowstone, or the portion before the Grand Canyon between Fishing Bridge and Canyon Village, runs right along the Grand Loop Road. This portion's species of game fish is primarily cutthroat trout. The Lower Yellowstone, or the area between Tower Junction and Gardiner, Montana, is accessible via the Yellowstone River Trail and several spur trails off the Grand Loop Road, such as the Blacktail Creek Trail. This section's game fish species include brook, brown, cutthroat, and rainbow trout.

See also Yellowstone Lake under *To See—Natural Wonders;* Shoshone Lake under *Paddling;* the Snake River under *Fishing* in "Grand Teton National Park"; the Gallatin River under *To Do—Fishing* in "South-Central Montana: Yellowstone Country"; and the Madison River under *To Do—Fishing* in "Southwest Montana: Gold West Country."

HIKING & **Fountain Paint Pot Nature Trail** is accessible from the Grand Loop Road about midway between Madison and Old Faithful. This easy 0.5-mile interpretive trail is handicapped accessible only with assistance. You'll walk on one of Yellowstone's cool boardwalks for much of your journey as you pass by numerous geothermal features. These include seven geysers—Twig, Jet, Fountain, Morning, Clepsydra, Spasm, and Jelly geysers—as well as bubbling mud pots, steaming and hissing fumaroles, and hot springs, among others. This cluster of geysers features regular spouters, so you'll likely catch at least one of them in action during your trek. As always, you must stay on the trail for your safety, and please don't throw anything into any of the geothermal features or put your hands (or any other body part) in the water.

Mammoth Hot Springs Nature Trails are accessible from a parking area adjacent to Upper Terrace Drive (see *To See—Scenic Drives*) as well as from a parking area closer to the North Entrance on the North Entrance Road. This network of trails provides a variety of distances, depending on where your wanders take you and on your time constraints. You'll tour through distinctive limestone terraces, viewing unique formations that differ from geothermal areas in the rest of the park. Interpretive signs explain the geothermal processes that contribute to the formation of these intriguing travertine terraces. As always, you must stay on the trail for your safety, and please don't throw anything into any of the geothermal features.

&. **Mud Volcano Loop Nature Trail,** accessible from the east side of the Grand Loop Road northwest of Fishing Bridge. A portion of this 0.7-mile interpretive trail is handicapped accessible. This trail takes you on an easy, if somewhat steep, stroll through some of the park's murkiest, muddiest geothermal features. Though the mud in the mud pots and pools may appear to be boiling or simmering, the bubbles are actually the result of volcanic gases escaping from beneath the earth's surface. That doesn't mean that they're not hot, though. You'll see a variety of goopy wonders, including a mud geyser (though it has not been observed to erupt for more than a century), cauldrons, and pots, and the Mud Volcano. As always, you must stay on the trail for your safety, and please don't throw anything into any of the geothermal features.

FOUNTAIN PAINT POT NATURE TRAIL

&. **Norris Geyser Basin Nature Trails** are accessible from the Grand Loop Road near the Norris area. Portions of this area's various trails are handicapped-accessible. For a short journey, you can stroll through the Porcelain Basin on a 0.75-mile interpretive trail, partly a boardwalk, that loops past a number of geothermal features in an otherworldly setting. You'll see the colorful hues of heat-loving microorganisms in pools and streams as you pass by Constant

Geyser and the small but distinctive Whale's Mouth, a deep blue, calm, and cavernous little pool so clear and still that you can actually see the whale's mineral "teeth" poking above and below the water's surface. A longer (1.5-mile) journey along a part boardwalk–part dirt trail takes you through the geothermal features in the more forested Back Basin. This area is home to the world's largest geyser, Steamboat Geyser, which erupts rarely, but when it does, it shoots water 300 to 400 feet into the air. As always, you must stay on the trail for your safety, and please don't throw anything into any of the geothermal features.

GEOTHERMAL SIGHTS ALONG THE MUD VOLCANO LOOP NATURE TRAIL

Storm Point Trail is accessible from the East Entrance Road 3 miles east of the Fishing Bridge from the turnout next to Indian Pond. If you've just driven in from Cody through the East Entrance, Storm Point provides a great chance to get out of the car, stretch out your legs, and get a good look at your surroundings. This 2-mile loop trail takes you along the shore of Indian Pond, through a forest, then out to rocky Storm Point, where you may observe the marmots that live there. The trail then loops along the lakeshore and back through a forested area, where you might see bison, moose, and waterfowl, among other wildlife.

See also Old Faithful, Petrified Tree, and Tower Fall under *To See—Natural Wonders;* and Fountain Flats Drive–Firehole Freight Road and Riverside Trail under *Bicycling.*

HORSEBACK RIDING **Yellowstone National Park** allows private horse owners as well as several National Park Service–licensed concessionaires to ride horses in the park, but you should make your arrangements in advance to ensure compliance with all rules and regulations. Overnight horse trips are not allowed before July 1, due to potentially wet trail conditions and general preparedness issues. Horses are not allowed in the developed campgrounds, but they are allowed in certain backcountry campgrounds. For information and assistance in planning an overnight trip with horses, call the **Backcountry Office** (307-344-2160).

✐ **Xanterra Parks and Resorts** (see *Guidance*) has corrals at Mammoth Hot Springs, Canyon Village, and Roosevelt Lodge that offer horseback rides in Yellowstone National Park. Rides can be 1 hour ($29.50 per person) or 2 hours ($48 per person). Children 8 and older and 48 inches or taller are welcome, though children ages 8–11 must be accompanied by another rider who is at least 16 years old.

See also **Old West Cookout** under *Unique Adventures.*

HOT SPRINGS **Yellowstone National Park** obviously has an abundance of geothermal features, including a huge number of hot springs. Soaking in the springs is strictly off-limits to park visitors—and, probably, most of the park's hot springs would scald the skin off your body in seconds or make you ill due to their extreme alkalinity or acidity as well as the presence of potentially health-damaging algae and bacteria. You are not allowed to swim, bathe, or soak in any of the park's thermal waters that originate from thermal sources only. That having been said, the park does have a few places where swimming or soaking in geothermally warmed waters is allowed, though somewhat grudgingly. Popular swimming and soaking thermal sites include the swimming area on the Firehole River (see *To See—Scenic Drives*), an area of the Madison River at the Madison Campground, and the Boiling River—a popular location near Mammoth Hot Springs where a hot spring enters the Gardner River.

See also **Huckleberry Hot Springs** under *Hot Springs* in "Grand Teton National Park."

PADDLING **Yellowstone National Park** allows paddling of nonmotorized watercraft on many of its lakes, including Yellowstone Lake (see *To See—Natural Wonders*), Lewis Lake, and Shoshone Lake (see below). Paddling on all of the park's rivers and streams is strictly prohibited, with the sole exception being the channel between Lewis Lake and Shoshone Lake. You must purchase a permit ($5 for 7 days, or $10 annually; also valid in Grand Teton National Park) in person for each nonmotorized watercraft. Permits can be purchased at Bridge Bay Ranger Station, Canyon Visitor Center, Grant Village Visitor Center, Lewis Lake Campground, Lake Ranger Station, Mammoth Visitor Center, and South Entrance. **Xanterra Parks and Resorts** (see *Guidance*) offers rental boats at Bridge Bay Marina.

Shoshone Lake, located north of Lewis Lake and accessible by nonmotorized watercraft via a channel, is the largest backcountry lake in the continental United States. For paddlers looking for an incredible adventure in an unbelievably scenic setting, this lake should be high on the list. Numerous backcountry campsites dot the lake's shore, making point-to-point travel via paddled vessels a popular way to explore the lake's pristine, remote waters. You can even hike to the Shoshone Geyser Basin, northwest of the lake, via trails accessible from the lakeshore. July and August are the best times to plan a trip to Shoshone Lake, as it can still be partially covered by ice in June. Due the lake's remote location and the lack of rapid rescue services for the backcountry, a paddle in Shoshone Lake must involve careful advance planning to ensure a safe and successful adventure.

SNOW SPORTS

Skiing
Cross-country skiing is a popular winter activity in Yellowstone National Park, which has miles and miles of trails to choose from. For the most part, these trails are ungroomed, and thus you must possess the proper equipment and knowledge to make your trip a safe one. Talking with a park ranger about your plans is necessary for your safety, as he or she can update you on the latest weather conditions

and forecasts and the conditions of the trails or terrain you're interested in ski-ing—trails are sometimes closed due to severe weather or for wildlife protection. If you go into the backcountry, it is recommended that you bring a U.S. Geological Survey (USGS) map and a compass (and the knowledge of how to use them properly). A number of National Park Service–licensed concessionaires, including **Xanterra Parks and Resorts** (see *Guidance*) and **Bear Den Ski Shops** (with stores at Mammoth Hot Springs Hotel and Old Faithful Snow Lodge) offer guided cross-country skiing and snowshoeing (see also below) adventures in the park during wintertime. Bear Den Ski Shops also rents skiing and snowshoeing equipment.

See also **Old Faithful Snow Lodge** under *Lodging and Where to Eat—Lodges*.

Snowmobiling

Snowmobiling has long been a popular winter pastime in both Yellowstone and Grand Teton national parks, though in recent years, it has received national attention due to the purported ill effects—namely, pollution—of snowmobiles on the parks' ecosystems. In late 2004, a plan was approved to go into effect at least through the 2006–7 winter season. This plan allows 720 commercially guided snowmobiles daily in Yellowstone and 140 snowmobiles daily in Grand Teton. All of Yellowstone's roads, except for the North Entrance Road and Northeast Entrance Road, are usually opened to snowmobiles and other snow vehicles on the third Wednesday in December. The same general schedule applies to Grand Teton National Park, including the Continental Divide Snow-mobile Trail, Grassy Lake Road, and John D. Rockefeller Jr. Memorial Highway. These roads then remain open to snow vehicles until March, when spring plow-ing begins. For a list of National Park Service–licensed concessionaires, call the parks or go to www.nps.gov/yell/planvisit/services/wintbusn.htm#snowmobiling.

Snowshoeing

Snowshoeing, like cross-country skiing, is a great way to enjoy the beauty of Yel-lowstone National Park. You can even join a ranger for a free, ranger-led snow-shoeing tour departing from **West Yellowstone, Montana** (406-646-4403), or from **Mammoth, Wyoming** (call 307-344-2263 for reservations). For more details about snowshoeing, read the above listing on cross-country skiing. (See also **Old Faithful Snow Lodge** under *Lodging and Where to Eat—Lodges*.)

See also **Yellowstone in a Day** under *Unique Adventures*.

UNIQUE ADVENTURES ✄ **Old West Cookout,** run by Xanterra Parks and Resorts (see *Guidance*); leaves from Roosevelt Lodge. The Old West Cookout includes a steak dinner cooked cowboy style, with your choice of an accompany-ing wagon ride to the cookout spot ($45 adults; $35 children ages 5–11), a 1-hour horseback ride ($55 adults; $45 children ages 8–11), or a 2-hour horse-back ride ($65 adults; $55 children ages 8–11). Reservations are required. You can also take a stagecoach ride at Roosevelt Lodge ($8.25 adults; $7 children ages 2–11).

& **Ranger-led programs,** run by Yellowstone National Park (see *Guidance*) can involve active participation from you, such as a guided interpretive hike into an area otherwise not accessible to the public, as well as presentations in the form of a lecture, film, slide show, or other such event. Many of these activities are handicapped accessible. They can range from 20 minutes to 3 hours or longer, depending on the program, and most of them are free. For a current schedule, call the park or check at a visitor center (see *To See—Visitor Centers*) during your visit for a current schedule of events. (See also *Cross-Country Skiing* and *Snowshoeing* under *Snow Sports.*)

⚲ **Roosevelt Cookout Roundup,** run by Xanterra Parks and Resorts (see *Guidance*). Trips depart each evening mid-June through early September from a number of locations, including Bridge Bay, Canyon Lodge, Fishing Bridge RV Park, and Lake Hotel. The rates are $24 adults, $13 children ages 12–17, children 11 and under free. If you leave from Canyon Lodge, the rates are $21 adults, $11 children ages 12–17, children 11 and under free. Experienced and knowledgeable drivers load up passengers at each location and take you on a narrated auto tour through Yellowstone to the Roosevelt Lodge. At Roosevelt Lodge, you'll enjoy a delicious cookout. The drivers will then return you to the location you started from.

Yellowstone Association Institute (307-344-2293; www.yellowstoneassociation .org/institute), P.O. Box 117, Yellowstone National Park, WY 82190. Run by the Yellowstone Association, this educational institute provides a number of opportunities to have a more in-depth learning experience at Yellowstone National Park. Choose from a wide variety of programs, including field seminars, backcountry courses, lodging-and-learning programs, and "personal wildlife ed-ventures"— customized educational daylong adventures suitable for families and small groups (up to 10 people), designed to teach you about Yellowstone's large wildlife and ecology ($350 per group; make reservations in advance by calling 307-344-2294). For more information about all of the programs, call to request a course catalog, or download the course catalog from the Web site.

Yellowstone in a Day, offered by Xanterra Parks and Resorts (see *Guidance*), is one of a number of auto tours run by this park concessionaire. The Yellowstone in a Day tour leaves from Mammoth Hot Springs Hotel at 8:30 AM and returns to the hotel at 5:30 PM daily from early June to late September; $47 adults, $23 children. The daylong tour takes you in a circle around the outer loop of the park's Grand Loop Road, with stops at many of the park's major attractions, including Old Faithful and the Grand Canyon of the Yellowstone (see *To See— Natural Wonders*). You'll stop for lunch at Old Faithful, but lunch is not included in the fee. In wintertime, Xanterra and several other licensed concessionaires offer tours of the park in a snowcoach (a heated snow vehicle).

⚲ **Yellowstone Lake Scenic Cruise,** operated by Xanterra Parks and Resorts (see *Guidance*), departs from the marina at Bridge Bay. Open early June through mid-September; $10 adults, $6.50 children ages 2–11, children 1 and under free. This 1-hour boat tour offers you the opportunity to see the park's majesty and wonder from the water. Xanterra also offers guided fishing trips, shuttle boat service to backcountry camping areas, and boat rentals. (See also Yellowstone Lake under *To See—Natural Wonders.*)

✳ Lodging and Where to Eat

All of Yellowstone National Park's lodgings are run by **Xanterra Parks and Resorts** (see *Guidance*). The dining facilities, be they fine dining or fast-food (or somewhere in between), feature standard American fare for the most part, including steaks, prime rib, and seafood at the finer establishments and burgers, pizzas, pastas, salad bars, and such at the more casual eateries.

LODGES ᷓ **Canyon Lodges** are located in Canyon Village, the largest lodging complex in the park. The lodges (Canyon, Cascade, and Dunraven) are open late May through mid-September. This area also includes **Canyon Frontier/Pioneer Cabins** (open late May through late August) and **Canyon Western Cabins** (open late May through mid-September) ($51–160). Canyon Village also has a **dining room** (casual fine dining), a **cafeteria,** a "picnic shop" (fast food, light meals, and snacks), and several shops.

Lake Lodge Cabins are in Lake Village. Open early June through late September. These lodgings provide visitors with comfortable cabin-style accommodations with private baths ($65–130). Lake Lodge also has a **cafeteria** and gift shop.

🐾 **Old Faithful Lodge Cabins** are located in the Old Faithful area of the park, a National Historic District. Open mid-May through mid-September. These rustic cabins provide a more economical option when compared to most accommodations in the park ($45–95 and up). Old Faithful Lodge also has a **cafeteria,** snack shop, and gift shop.

ᷓ **Old Faithful Snow Lodge** is located in the Old Faithful area of the park, a National Historic District. Open early May through mid-October and in the winter season. The park's newest lodging facility, completed in 1999, features modern western-style lodge accommodations, complete with exposed wooden beams, high ceilings, and plenty of comfortable common areas where guests can congregate or relax. Rooms are spacious, with your choice of a hotel room or a separate cabin ($89–173). The Snow Lodge also has cross-country ski and snowshoe rentals, the **Old Faithful Snow Lodge Restaurant** (fine dining), **Geyser Grill Fast Food,** and a gift shop.

🐾 **Roosevelt Lodge Cabins** are in the Tower–Roosevelt area of the park. Open early June through early September. Want to "rough it" in style? Stay in one of the **"Rough Rider" cabins,** which have no running water and require a walk to the bathroom. If that sounds a little too rustic for your tastes, you can opt for a **Frontier Cabin** with a private bath and running water ($65–103). At this area, you'll also find the **Roosevelt Lodge Dining Room** (casual), a gift shop, and other shops, as well as nightly cookouts (see **Roosevelt Cookout Roundup** under *To Do—Unique Adventures*).

OTHER OPTIONS ᷓ **Grant Village Hotel** is in Grant Village. Open late May through early October. This is a modern hotel built in the early 1980s, with all of the amenities you'd expect from such a facility ($95–120). Grant Village also has two restaurants— **Grant Village Restaurant** (reservations required for dinner) and the **Lake House at the Grant**—as well as several shops.

♿ **Lake Yellowstone Hotel and Cabins** is in Lake Village. Open mid-May through early October. The original portion of this historic structure was completed in 1891, with additions built later. This hotel provides the most comfortable hotel room accommodations in Yellowstone and offers the additional option of staying in a well-appointed cabin ($65–200 and up). The Lake Hotel also has a **dining room** (fine dining; reservations required for dinner), deli, and gift shop. For a free historic tour of the hotel, call Xanterra Parks and Resorts (see *Guidance*) for tour times.

♿ **Mammoth Hot Springs Hotel and Cabins** are in Mammoth Hot Springs. Open early May through early October; also in winter season. Situated within view of the famous terraces of the area (see *To Do—Hiking*), this historic hotel, built in 1911, features a variety of hotel rooms with assorted amenities ranging from the basic hotel room (some with shared baths, some with private baths ($85–110) to the more luxurious suites of rooms ($315). The cabins are cozy and a bit more private—some

even have hot tubs to go with them ($70–160). The hotel also has a **dining room** (casual fine dining) and the **Terrace Grill** (casual fare), as well as several shops.

♿ **Old Faithful Inn,** a National Historic Landmark, is located in the Old Faithful area of the park, a National Historic District. Open May through September. Constructed in 1903–4, the inn is one of the few remaining log hotels in the United States. Guests stay in rooms that either share a bath or have a private bath ($86–200 and up). Since this is the park's most popular and well-known lodging facility, you should make reservations at least half a year in advance. Also at Old Faithful Inn, you'll find the inn's **Dining Room** (fine dining; reservations required for dinner), the **Pony Express Snack Shop** (casual, deli-style fare), a gift shop, and free historic tours of the inn (call Xanterra Parks and Resorts—see *Guidance*—for tour times).

See also **Flagg Ranch Resort** under *Lodging and Where to Eat—Other Options* in "Grand Teton National Park."

GRAND TETON NATIONAL PARK

If your vacation plans to Wyoming include a trip to Yellowstone National Park, they should surely include a visit to Grand Teton National Park, its southern, lesser-traveled neighbor. If you have only a few extra hours to spare, at the very least try to tack on a venture down the **John D. Rockefeller Jr. Memorial Parkway** (see *Scenic Drives*), which features views of the spectacular Tetons—as long as the weather cooperates. Driving a little bit farther will bring you to Jackson, with its many fine dining opportunities. You can round out your southerly journey by grabbing a bite to eat and then heading back north on the same day if you're crunched for time.

GUIDANCE Grand Teton Lodge Company (307-543-2811; www.gtlc.com), P.O. Box 250, Moran 83013. This National Park Service–authorized concessionaire can help organize and book the details of your stay in Grand Teton National Park, including lodging and most recreational activities.

& **Grand Teton National Park** (307-739-3300; 307-739-3611; www.nps.gov/ grte), P.O. Drawer 170, Moose 83012-0170. Open all day every day; $10 per individual (7 days) or $20 per vehicle (7 days), $40 annual pass (good for entrance into Yellowstone National Park as well); $5 per person per day mid-December through April 30 (good for entry to Grand Teton National Park only).

For locations of visitor centers and information stations, see *To See—Visitor Centers and Museums.*

GETTING THERE Grand Teton National Park is accessed from the north via US 89/191/287, from the south via US 89/191/26, and from the east via US 26/287.

See also *Airports, Amtrak, Bus Service,* and *Travel Information* in "What's Where in Wyoming."

MEDICAL EMERGENCY Call **911** in the park or 307-739-3300 for the National Park Service (NPS) dispatch.

Grand Teton Medical Clinic (307-543-2514; 307-733-8002), near the Chevron station at Jackson Lake Lodge (see *Lodging—Lodges*) near Jackson Lake Junction; open mid-May through mid-October 10 AM–6 PM.

See also **St. John's Hospital,** in Jackson, under *Medical Emergency* in "West Wyoming: Jackson Hole–Jim Bridger Country."

✳ To See

VISITOR CENTERS AND MUSEUMS & **Colter Bay Visitor Center and Indian Arts Museum** (307-739-3594), 25 miles north of Moose on US 89/191/287 on the shore of Jackson Lake. Open early May through late May 8 AM–5 PM; open late May through early September 8 AM–7 PM; open early September through early October 8 AM–5 PM; closed early October through early May. In addition to visitor information, this location includes an impressive collection of Indian artifacts collected by David T. Vernon. During the summer, guided tours, crafts demonstrations, and more are available in addition to exhibits.

& **Flagg Ranch Information Station** (307-543-2327), 2.5 miles south of the Yellowstone Park boundary and 40 miles north of Moose on US 89/191/287. Open early June through early September 9 AM–4 PM; closed early September through early June. In addition to visitor information, this station has a bookstore as well as exhibits about Greater Yellowstone and about John D. Rockefeller Jr., for whom the road connecting Grand Teton and Yellowstone was named (see *Scenic Drives*).

& **Jenny Lake Visitor Center** is 8 miles north of Moose on Teton Park Road at South Jenny Lake. Open early June through early September 8 AM–7 PM; open early September through late September 8 AM–5 PM; closed October through early June. Along with general visitor information, this visitor center includes exhibits on geology and natural features as well as a bookstore.

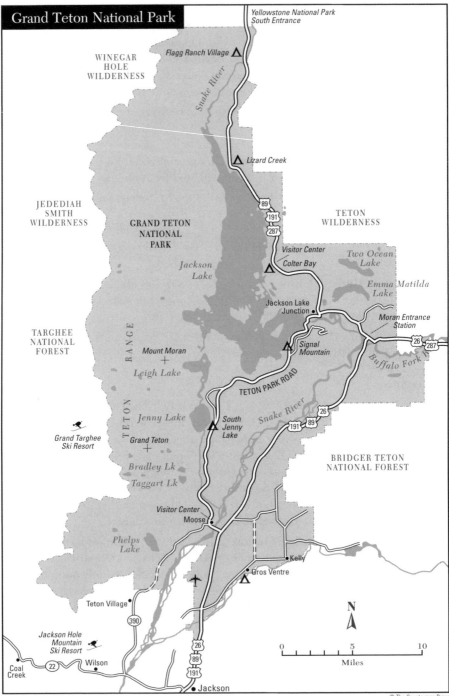

Grand Teton National Park

Yellowstone National Park
South Entrance

WINEGAR
HOLE
WILDERNESS

Flagg Ranch Village

Snake River

Lizard Creek

JEDEDIAH
SMITH
WILDERNESS

GRAND TETON
NATIONAL
PARK

TETON
WILDERNESS

Two Ocean
Lake

Visitor Center
Colter Bay

Jackson
Lake

Emma Matilda
Lake

Jackson Lake
Junction

Moran Entrance
Station

TARGHEE
NATIONAL
FOREST

R A N G E

Mount Moran

Signal
Mountain

Buffalo Fork

Leigh Lake

TETON PARK ROAD

T E T O N

Jenny Lake

South
Jenny
Lake

Snake River

Grand Targhee
Ski Resort

Grand Teton

Bradley Lk

BRIDGER TETON
NATIONAL FOREST

Taggart Lk

Visitor Center
Moose

Phelps
Lake

Kelly

Gros Ventre

Teton Village

N

Jackson Hole
Mountain
Ski Resort

Wilson

0   5   10

Coal
Creek

Miles

Jackson

© The Countryman Press

♿ **Moose Visitor Center** (307-739-3399), 12 miles north of Jackson via US 89/191/26 to Moose. Open daily year-round except for December 25, 8 AM–5 PM, until 7 PM in summer months. In addition to general visitor information, this center includes an exhibit on endangered species, a relief map model of Grand Teton National Park, a film introducing visitors to the park, and a comprehensive bookstore, among other resources.

HISTORIC LANDMARKS, PLACE, AND SITES **Menor's Ferry Trail,** accessible 0.5 mile north of Moose on Teton Park Road. This short, self-guided trail takes you on a tour back in time to the area's homesteading era. You'll see former rancher Bill Menor's cabin and country store, and if the Snake River's waters are high enough, you can even take a ride on a replica of the ferry that Menor once operated. You can also visit the historic and lovely Chapel of the Transfiguration.

See also **Jackson Lake Lodge** and **Jenny Lake Lodge** under *Lodging and Where to Eat—Lodges.*

FOR FAMILIES 🌿 **Young Naturalist Program.** Materials are available at the visitor centers (see *Visitor Centers and Museums*) or online; $1 donation per child. Children of all ages can earn a Young Naturalist patch and take a pledge to be a Young Naturalist by completing the array of activities detailed in *The Grand Adventure.* Kids must either attend two ranger-led talks in the park (stop at a visitor center to pick up a schedule) or attend a Young Naturalist program (for ages 8–12). Additional activities involve learning about the park's history, wildlife, geology, and more. Kids can also get started learning about Grand Teton by visiting the park's Web site (www.nps.gov/grte) and clicking on "For Kids."

See also Flagg Ranch Resort under *To Do—Horseback Riding;* and O.A.R.S.' Jackson Lake Kayak–Snake River Rafting Combo Trip, and Rock Climbing and Mountaineering under *To Do—Unique Adventures.*

SCENIC DRIVES **Jenny Lake Scenic Drive** is a one-way road that leaves Teton Park Road at South Jenny Lake Junction, roughly paralleling it for about 3 miles to rejoin it at North Jenny Lake Junction. The route takes you along the shores of Jenny Lake, passing by **Jenny Lake Lodge** (see *Lodging and Where to Eat—Lodges*) and **String Lake.**

John D. Rockefeller Jr. Memorial Parkway is the 50-mile scenic road that connects Yellowstone National Park with Grand Teton National Park. It starts at Moran Entrance Station, where US 287 joins US 89/191, leading you north to Yellowstone's South Entrance and along the South Entrance Road to the West Thumb of

THE TETONS, AS SEEN FROM JOHN D. ROCKEFELLER, JR. MEMORIAL PARKWAY

Yellowstone Lake. This scenic corridor takes you through classic forested terrain, including lakes, rivers, and streams.

Signal Mountain Summit Road is an out-and-back, roughly 5-mile jaunt leaving from the northern portion of Teton Park Road to the east (a few miles south of Jackson Lake Junction). This drive takes you to the summit of Signal Mountain, yielding tremendous views of the Tetons and their surroundings.

Teton Park Road loosely parallels US 89/191/26 as it journeys from Moose in the south to Jackson Lake Junction in the north for 22 miles. This alternative route takes you closer to the **Teton Range** (see *Natural Wonders*), as well as passing by **Jenny Lake** and the south end of Jackson Lake. To take a 45-mile scenic loop drive, you can start from Moose, Jackson Lake Junction, or Moran Entrance Station and drive the Teton Park Road in combination with US 89/191/26.

NATURAL WONDERS **The Teton Range** runs north–south, west of Teton Park Road and US 89/191/26, and a portion of the John D. Rockefeller Jr. Memorial Highway (see *Scenic Drives*). This breathtaking mountain range rises dramatically from the valley of Jackson Hole below. The uplift was caused by a fault that continues to push the mountains upward today. Part of the Rocky Mountains, these represent the youngest members of the range and some of its most distinctive formations; their rough and jagged cragginess create an incredibly scenic backdrop, not to mention a playground for hikers and rock climbers. The tallest mountain in the range is the majestic Grand Teton, which at 13,770 feet rises more than 7,000 feet above the valley floor.

✳ To Do

BICYCLING **Grand Teton National Park** has no designated bike paths, though bicycling is a popular activity in the park. Bicyclists must follow all rules and regulations, including remaining on only paved and unpaved roads that are open to autos. Bikes are not allowed on footpaths or in the backcountry. Bicyclists are subject to all traffic laws. The park offers a brochure, *Grand Teton Bicycling,* that explains rules and regulations.

THE TETON RANGE

Grassy Lake Road (F.R. 3261/261) is a 52-mile road that goes west from Flagg Ranch (see *Lodging and Where to Eat—Other Options*), skirting along the boundary between Yellowstone National Park and Grand Teton National Park before hitting the Idaho border and continuing in that state to Ashton. Closed in winter, the winding, hilly road is suitable for mountain bikes, taking you past a number of lakes and streams, some of which are accessible via Forest Service spur roads as well (F.R. 026 and 027 lead to Lake of the Winds). This road follows a trail historically used by Native Americans.

River Road is a 15-mile dirt road situated in between Teton Park Road and US 89/191/26. The road can be accessed in the north from just south of the Signal Mountain Road turnoff on Teton Park Road or in the south from the road linking Moose to Moose Junction. River Road parallels the Snake River as it flows through a choice wildlife habitat area (be respectful of wild animals should you encounter them, keeping your distance and leaving them in peace for your safety and theirs).

See also *To See—Scenic Drives;* Jenny Lake Lodge under *Lodging and Where to Eat—Lodges;* and Colter Bay Village and Dornan's Spur Ranch Cabins under *Lodging and Where to Eat—Other Options.*

BOATING **Grand Teton National Park** allows motorized boating on **Jackson Lake** (see listing below), as well as **Jenny Lake** (motors 10 horsepower and below only) and Phelps Lake (which has no public access). You must purchase a permit ($10 for 7 days or $20 annually; also valid in Yellowstone after check-in at ranger station) for each motorized watercraft (which must already have state registration as well). Permits can be purchased at Moose Visitor Center year-round (see *To See—Visitor Centers and Museums*) and at several other facilities seasonally. The park publishes a brochure on boating that all boaters should read before planning a boating outing in the park. It includes required and recommended gear, rules, boat launch information, and more information to make your trip an informed and safe one. The brochure is available online or by calling the park. (See also **Jenny Lake Scenic Cruise/Shuttle** under *Unique Adventures.*)

Jackson Lake is located west of the northern part of Teton Park Road and south of Flagg Ranch along the John D. Rockefeller Jr. Memorial Parkway. Jackson Lake is Grand Teton National Park's largest lake. In addition to boating, the lake is popular for waterskiing and swimming, as well as fishing (species include brown, cutthroat, and mackinaw trout). If you don't own your own motorboat or you don't want to bring it with you, you can rent a motorboat from a number of National Park Service–licensed concessionaires, including the **Colter Bay Marina** (1-800-628-9988; 307-543-3100) and the marina at **Signal Mountain Lodge** (307-543-2831; see listing under *Lodging and Where to Eat—Lodges*). (See also **O.A.R.S.' Jackson Lake Kayak–Snake River Rafting Combo Trip** under *Unique Adventures.*)

See *Paddling/Floating* for details on the use of nonmotorized watercraft in Grand Teton National Park.

CAMPING ♿ **Grand Teton National Park** has five first-come, first-served developed campgrounds in the park as well as a number of designated backcountry campsites and backcountry "camping zones." Developed campgrounds include **Colter Bay** (handicapped accessible; open late May through late September; $12); **Gros Ventre** (handicapped accessible; open May 1 through mid-October; $12); **South Jenny Lake** (handicapped accessible; open mid-May through late September; $12); **Lizard Creek** (open early June through early September; $12); and **Signal Mountain** (open early May through mid-October; $12). **Backcountry camping** is extremely popular and requires a permit. Thirty percent of permits are available by advance reservations and the rest are first-come, first-served. Reservations are highly recommended and may be made in person at the **Moose Visitor Center** (see *To See—Visitor Centers and Museums*), by fax (307-739-3438), or by mail (Grand Teton National Park, Permits Office, P.O. Drawer 170, Moose 83012).

&. **Flagg Ranch Campground** (1-800-443-2311; 307-543-2861; www.flag granch.com), located 2 miles south of the border of Yellowstone National Park and 5 miles north of the border of Grand Teton National Park along the John D. Rockefeller Jr. Memorial Parkway. The campground's dates are seasonal and dependent on the weather, so calling in advance is a must in the early and late seasons; $25 per tent, $45 per RV. This concessionaire-operated campground takes reservations (recommended, especially in summer months). (See also **Flagg Ranch Resort** under *Lodging and Where to Eat—Other Options.*)

See also **Colter Bay Village** under *Lodging and Where to Eat—Other Options.*

FISHING **Grand Teton National Park** includes a number of lakes, rivers, and streams that provide anglers with great opportunities for catching native game fish, mainly trout. These include **Jackson Lake** and **Jenny Lake** (see *Boating*), among others (see below for a few more suggestions). The park requires anglers to possess a valid state fishing license, and fishing in the park is subject to state laws and regulations (for details, including current licensing fees, go to http://gf.state.wy.us/fish/fishing/index.asp). The park publishes an informative brochure about fishing as well, which includes specific rules and regulations and the seasonal opening and closing dates of the park's waters—many of which are open year-round. Anglers are responsible for knowing all of the current rules and regulations.

Leigh Lake, north of Jenny Lake and String Lake and west of Teton Park Road, is open to fishing year-round and has cutthroat and mackinaw trout.

The Snake River flows from the mountains northeast of the park through the southern portion of Yellowstone National Park before entering Jackson Lake near the park's northern boundary, then continuing south through the park after exiting the lake at the Jackson Lake Dam near Jackson Lake Junction. The river then flows south through the valley of Jackson Hole as well. Special regulations apply to fishing the Snake River in the park, including not fishing the 150 feet of water below the dam. The river's game fish species in Grand Teton include brook and cutthroat trout. In the more remote Yellowstone portion of the river, accessible via the South Boundary Trail and the Snake River Trail, species also include brown and mackinaw trout as well as mountain whitefish. (See also the Snake River under *Paddling/Floating.*)

String Lake, just north of Jenny Lake and west of Teton Park Road, is open to fishing year-round and has cutthroat and mackinaw trout.

Two Ocean Lake, east of the John D. Rockefeller Jr. Memorial Parkway north of Jackson Lake Junction, is open to fishing year-round and has cutthroat trout.

See also Signal Mountain Lodge under *Lodging and Where to Eat—Lodges;* and Flagg Ranch Resort and Triangle X Ranch under *Lodging and Where to Eat— Other Options.*

HIKING **Colter Bay Lakeshore Trail,** accessible from the Colter Bay Visitor Center (see *To See—Visitor Centers and Museums*), is a 2-mile round-trip easy hike along the shore of Jackson Lake through ideal wildlife habitat. You might see trumpeter swans, waterfowl, moose, elk, otters, and beavers, among other inhabitants. You'll also have great views of the mountains. Additional trails, including the 3-mile round-trip **Heron Pond and Swan Lake Trail,** are accessible from this area as well; request a brochure at the visitor center for details.

Hidden Falls Trail, accessible from the Cascade Trailhead Dock on the west side of Jenny Lake, is a 1-mile round-trip, steep hike up to Hidden Falls, providing incredible scenic vistas of the lakes below. Those in search of a longer outing can continue up the **Cascade Canyon Trail,** which leads to more trails, including the trail to **Solitude Lake.** You can access the Hidden Falls trailhead via a boat shuttle (see **Jenny Lake Scenic Cruise/Shuttle** under *Unique Adventures*), by hiking a 2-mile portion of the 3.3-mile round-trip **String Lake Trail** (see below), or by hiking a 2-mile portion of the 6.6-mile round-trip **Jenny Lake Trail** (see below). Both of these lake trails are fun, relatively flat outings that wrap around the lakes. These two trails are connected as well, if you want a really long hike.

Jenny Lake Trail, accessible from the Jenny Lake Ranger Station off Jenny Lake Scenic Drive, is a 6.6-mile round-trip, relatively easy path around Jenny Lake. For more information, see Hidden Lake Trail, above.

Lunch Tree Hill Trail, accessible from Jackson Lake Lodge, is an easy 0.5-mile round-trip self-guiding trail with interpretive signs to help you learn more about your surroundings. In its short distance, the trail takes you to the top of the hill, where you'll enjoy a scenic overlook of the valley below, the lakes, and the Teton Range.

Menor's Ferry Trail. See *To See—Historic Landmarks, Places, and Sites.*

String Lake Trail, accessible from the String Lake Parking Lot off Jenny Lake Scenic Drive, is a 3.3-mile round-trip, relatively easy trail around String Lake. For more information, see Hidden Lake Trail, above. In addition, the **Leigh Lake Trail** (see *Fishing*) is a spur trail off the String Lake Trail, traveling along the eastern shoreline of Leigh Lake.

HORSEBACK RIDING **Grand Teton National Park** permits private horseback riding and overnight camping with stock subject to a number of limitations, rules, and regulations. For details and assistance in planning a horse trip, start by contacting the park and requesting the *Saddle and Pack Stock* brochure.

✿ **Flagg Ranch Resort** (307-543-2861; www.flaggranch.com), 2 miles south of the border of Yellowstone National Park and 5 miles north of the border of Grand Teton National Park along the John D. Rockefeller Jr. Memorial Parkway. Flagg Ranch is one of several National Park Service–licensed concessionaires offering horseback rides to park visitors. Rides depart hourly during the summer season ($27 per person). Children ages 8 and older are welcome. (See also Flagg Ranch Resort under *Lodging and Where to Eat—Other Options.*)

See also Jackson Lake Lodge and Jenny Lake Lodge under *Lodging and Where to Eat—Lodges;* and Colter Bay Village and Triangle X Ranch under *Lodging and Where to Eat—Other Options.*

HOT SPRINGS **Huckleberry Hot Springs** are accessible from Flagg Ranch Resort (see *Lodging and Where to Eat—Other Options*). Not technically in either park, these primitive hot springs bubble out of the ground too hot for soaking (140°F) but then blend with the cooling waters of Polecat Creek and flow into several primitive pools that are more comfortable for human skin.

PADDLING/FLOATING **Grand Teton National Park** allows paddling and float-ing of human-powered and nonmotorized watercraft on a number of its waters, including **Bearpaw, Bradley, Emma Matilda, Jackson, Jenny, Leigh, Phelps, String lakes, Taggart, and Two Ocean,** as well as on the **Snake River,** (see below for details) starting 1,000 feet below the Jackson Dam. Water-craft are prohibited on all other rivers and streams in the park. You must obtain a permit for each nonmotorized watercraft ($5 for 7 days, $10 annually; also valid in Yellowstone after check-in at ranger station). Before engaging in any pri-vate paddling or floating, be sure to read through the park's brochure on boating, available online or by calling the park. A number of National Park Service–licensed concessionaires rent out hand-propelled craft such as rowboats, canoes, kayaks, and dories (see **Jackson Lake** under *Boating;* **Signal Mountain Lodge** under *Lodging and Where to Eat—Lodges;* and **Dornan's Spur Ranch Cabins** under *Lodging and Where to Eat—Other Options*).

The Snake River is a popular river to float and paddle, starting from 1,000 feet below the Jackson Dam, near the Jackson Lake Junction. Though the river's lack of rapids makes it a relatively easy float in technical terms, floaters and paddlers should be experienced, as they must remain alert and attentive due to the high number of logjams and channel systems encountered, as well as the river's fre-quently changing flow rates and water depths. Before engaging in any private paddling or floating, be sure to read through the park's brochure on floating the Snake River, available online or by calling the park. You can also book a relaxing scenic float of one of the river's calmest sections from a National Park Service–licensed concessionaire, including **Solitude Float Trips** (1-888-704-2800; 307-733-2871; www.solitudefloattrips.com), which charges $42 per adult and $27 per child under 12 for a 10-mile trip. (See also the Snake River under *Fishing;* **O.A.R.S.' Jackson Lake Kayak–Snake River Rafting Combo Trip** under *Unique Adventures;* Jackson Lake Lodge and Signal Mountain Lodge under *Lodging and Where to Eat—Lodges;* Dornan's Spur Ranch Cabins, Flagg Ranch Resort, and Triangle X Ranch under *Lodging and Where to Eat—Other Options.*)

Cross-Country Skiing and Snowshoeing

Cross-country skiing and snowshoeing offer winter visitors a great way to explore the park's natural wonder and beauty when it's dressed in its annual shroud of white. Before embarking on a winter journey, be sure to educate yourself by obtaining a copy of the park's *Cross-Country Skiing & Snowshoeing* brochure, available online or by stopping at a visitor center (see *To See—Visitor Centers and Museums*). The brochure details the safety information and regulations that you need to know before taking part in these activities. A number of trails are groomed and marked for cross-country skiers and snowshoers, including 14 miles of **Teton Park Road** (see *To See—Scenic Drives*), which is machine groomed for skiers, snowshoers, and hikers. From this road, you can access a number of skier-groomed trails, including **Jenny Lake Trail** (see *Hiking*) and **Signal Mountain Road** (see *To See—Scenic Drives*), among others. You can even join a ranger-led snowshoe hike departing from the **Moose Visitor Center** (call 307-739-3399 for details and reservations). Several National Park Service–licensed concessionaires, including **Rendezvous Backcountry Tours** (1-877-754-4887; 307-353-2900; www.skithetetons.com), provide guided cross-country skiing and snowmobiling trips. You can rent cross-country skis or snowshoes from **Dornan's Spur Ranch Cabins** (see *Lodging and Where to Eat—Other Options*) and enjoy terrain as a guest at **Triangle X Ranch** (see *Lodging and Where to Eat—Other Options*).

Snowmobiling

See *Snowmobiling* under *Snow Sports* in "Yellowstone National Park" for details on snowmobiling in Grand Teton National Park. (See also **Flagg Ranch Resort** and **Triangle X Ranch** under *Lodging and Where to Eat—Other Options*.)

UNIQUE ADVENTURES ₺ **Jenny Lake Scenic Cruise/Shuttle** (307-734-9227; www.jennylakeboating.com). Open May 15 through 31 and September 16 through 30, 10 AM–4 PM; open June 1 through September 15, 8 AM–6 PM, with shuttles leaving every 15 minutes and scenic tours scheduled daily (call or stop by for schedule); cruises: $12 adults, $7 children ages 7–12, children 6 and under free; round-trip shuttles: $7.50 adults, $5 children ages 7–12, children 6 and under free; one-way rates also available. **Jenny Lake Boating** provides a scenic cruise around Jenny Lake or a scenic shuttle boat ride across the lake to the Cascade Trailhead Dock (see Hidden Falls Trail under *Hiking*). (See also Jackson Lake Lodge under *Lodging and Where to Eat—Other Options*.)

⚓ **O.A.R.S.' Jackson Lake Kayak–Snake River Rafting Combo Trip** (1-800-346-6277; www.oars.com). Trips depart from the Signal Mountain Public Boat Launch Ramp every day but Friday and Sunday from early June to mid-December; 2-day trip: $382 adults, $317 children; 3-day trip: $515 adults, $424 children; make reservations in advance. Children ages 4 and up are welcome in low waters, while they must be 8 or older in high waters. For an intimate view of Grand Teton National Park, you can't beat this trip. You'll paddle sea kayaks on Jackson Lake and then test your mettle by white-water rafting a portion of the

THE TETONS, AS SEEN FROM JOHN D.
ROCKEFELLER, JR. MEMORIAL PARKWAY

Snake River, all under the direction of experienced guides from O.A.R.S. (Outdoor Adventure River Specialists). In business for more than 30 years, O.A.R.S. provides some of the world's top-quality river guides. (See also Jackson Lake under *Boating* and the Snake River under *Paddling/Floating.*)

& **Ranger-led programs,** run by Grand Teton National Park (see *Guidance*), can involve your active participation. The programs include a guided interpretive hike, as well as presentations in the form of a lecture, film, slide show, or other such event. Many of these activities are handicapped accessible. They can range from 20 minutes to 3 hours or longer, depending on the program, and most of them are free. For a current schedule, call the park or check at a visitor center (see *To See—Visitor Centers and Museums*) during your visit for a current schedule of events. (See also *Cross-Country Skiing and Snowshoeing* under *Snow Sports.*)

✔ **Rock climbing and mountaineering** are popular activities in Grand Teton National Park, but neither should be undertaken without proper training and experience. If you're new to rock climbing or you'd like to try it out, Grand Teton National Park licenses two concessionaires to guide in the park: **Exum Mountain Guides** (307-733-2297; www.exumguides.com) and **Jackson Hole Mountain Guides** (1-800-239-7642; www.jhmg.com). Jackson Hole Mountain Guides offers a program called Kids Rock! that is designed for kids under 12 and their parents ($80 per person for three or more participants).

See also Menor's Ferry Trail under *To See—Historic Landmarks, Places, and Sites* and Flagg Ranch Resort and Triangle X Ranch under *Lodging and Where to Eat—Other Options.*

✳ Lodging and Where to Eat

LODGES & **Jackson Lake Lodge** (1-800-628-9988; 307-543-3100; www.gtlc.com/lodgejac.aspx; mailing address: Grand Teton Lodge Company, P.O. Box 250, Moran 83013), near Jackson Lake Junction. Open late May through early October. This National Historic Landmark serves visitors as a full-service resort, with 37 rooms available in the **main lodge,** as well as an additional 348 luxurious **guest cottages** on both sides of the main lodge ($173–575). At this lodge set atop a bluff overlooking Jackson Lake, you'll find all of the comforts required for a relaxed and elegant vacation, including a large heated outdoor swimming pool; easy access to guided activities like horseback rides, scenic lake cruises, and float trips on the Snake River; and several on-premises restaurants. These include the **Mural Room,** serving breakfast, lunch, and dinner daily in an elegant, fine dining setting with views of the Tetons as well as 80 feet of murals painted by masterful artist Carl Roters; the **Pioneer Grill,** serving lighter, over-the-counter fare for breakfast, lunch, and dinner; the **Pool Snack Bar and BBQ,** featuring sandwiches, pizzas, and salads as well as an evening all-you-can-eat barbecue (reservations required); and the **Blue Heron Lounge,** serving cocktails and snacks.

&. **Jenny Lake Lodge** (1-800-628-9988; 307-543-3100; www.gtlc.com/lodgejen.aspx; mailing address: Grand Teton Lodge Company, P.O. Box 250, Moran 83013), along Jenny Lake Scenic Drive (see *To See—Scenic Drives*). Open early June through early October. This historic 1920s lodge includes 37 **private cabins** tucked into a lovely, forested setting near Jenny Lake. To make your western vacation experience more authentic, the decor follows a western theme, and you'll find nary a radio or television in your cabin—though you can request a phone. Included in your nightly rate is breakfast; a prix fixe, five-course gourmet dinner; and horseback riding and bicycling ($475–680). Even if you are not staying as an overnight guest, you are welcome to dine at **Jenny Lake Lodge** (serving breakfast, lunch, and dinner); reservations are required for breakfast and dinner.

&. **Signal Mountain Lodge** (307-543-2831; www.signalmtnlodge.com), P.O. Box 50, Moran 83013. Located on the shores of Jackson Lake. Open early May through mid-October. You'll find the park's only true lakeside accommodations at Signal Mountain Lodge. Choose from one- or two-room **cabins** ($100–150), motel-style **lodge rooms** ($130–$180), one- or two-room **bungalows** ($145–215), **"lakefront retreat" suites** overlooking Jackson Lake with stunning mountain views ($200–215), and one three-room cabin ($255). In addition to lodging, Signal Mountain Lodge is licensed by the National Park Service to provide a number of additional activities, including Snake River float trips, boat rentals (motorized and nonmotorized), guided sailboat trips, and guided fishing trips. You'll also find several shops and restaurants, including **Leek's Marina and Pizzeria** (casual), **Trapper Grill** (casual; hearty American food), **The Peaks Restaurant** (fine dining; continental and regional cuisine), and **Deadman's Bar** (casual; full bar and appetizers).

OTHER OPTIONS &. 🐾 🛶 **Colter Bay Village** (1-800-628-9988; 307-543-3100; www.gtlc.com/lodgecbv.aspx; mailing address: Grand Teton Lodge Company, P.O. Box 250, Moran, 83013). At Colter Bay Village, you'll find a number of different accommodations to choose from. These include 166 **rustic log cabins,** including some built by homesteaders (available late May through late September; $38–140); **tent cabins,** with log walls and canvas roofs (available early June through early September; $37); and **RV camping** with hookups (available late May through late September; $27–42). Colter Bay Village has a wide range of visitor services, including a marina, a grocery store, horse corrals, a service station, gift shops, and two restaurants. These include the family-style **Chuckwagon Steak and Pasta House** (you can probably guess their specialties), open daily for breakfast, lunch, and dinner from late May to late September, and the **John Colter Café Court,** which serves up snack bar fare and boxed lunches daily from early June to early September.

✂ Dornan's Spur Ranch Cabins
(307-733-2522; www.dornans.com),
P.O. Box 39, Moose, 83012. Located
off Teton Park Road between Moose
and Moose Junction, before crossing
the Snake River. Open year-round.
This family-owned resort features
eight one-bedroom and four two-bedroom riverside duplexes, each of which
has a fully equipped kitchen and a
large living-dining area ($125–230).
While small, this resort offers numerous amenities, including gas pumps; a
wine shop; a grocery store and deli;
cross-country ski and snowshoe rentals;
Adventure Sports, which rents out
canoes, kayaks, and mountain bikes in
summer; and two restaurants. **Dornan's Pizza, Pasta Company** is open
daily in the summer season for lunch
(11:30 AM–3 PM). **The Chuckwagon,**
in operation since 1948, serves three
meals a day outside during the summer season and features an array of
classic American foods, including
steaks, burgers, and sandwiches.

&. **Flagg Ranch Resort** (1-800-443-
2311; www.flaggranch.com), P.O. Box
187, Moran 83013. Located just south
of the border of Yellowstone National
Park along the John D. Rockefeller Jr.
Memorial Highway. Open late May
through late September. You'll stay in
a **log-cabin room** with either two
queen-size beds or one king-size bed,
as well as a private bath, coffeemaker,
telephone, and patio ($145–155).
Flagg Ranch is licensed by the National Park Service to provide a number of additional activities, including
scenic float trips and whitewater rafting trips on the Snake River, camping,
horseback riding (see also Flagg
Ranch Resort under *To Do—Camping* and *To Do—Horseback Riding*),
snowmobiling, all-day interpretive

park tours of both parks, and guided
fishing trips.

Grand Teton Climbers' Ranch (June
1 through September 30 only: 307-733-
7271; www.americanalpineclub.org;
administrative offices: the American
Alpine Club, 710 10th Street, Suite
100, Golden, CO 80401), 3 miles south
of Jenny Lake on Teton Park Road.
Open mid-June through mid-September; $10 per person per night. Run by
the American Alpine Club, a nonprofit
climbing conservation and education
organization, the Climbers' Ranch has
provided climbers and their families
with an affordable lodging option since
1970. The accommodations are dormitory style in small cabins sleeping four
to eight people. Guests must bring
their own sleeping bags, pillows, gear,
food, cooking equipment, and personal
items. The ranch has a cooking area,
hot showers, and toilets. A limited
number of reservations can be taken,
though for the most part the ranch
operates on a first-come, first-served
basis.

✂ Triangle X Ranch (307-733-2183;
www.trianglex.com), 2 Triangle X
Ranch Road, Moose 83012. Open late
May through late October and late
December through March. Triangle X
is a working dude ranch. During the
summer, this family-owned and -oper-
ated ranch offers inclusive, dude
ranch–style **vacations** priced by the
week, which include lodging, meals,
ranch activities, and horseback riding
($1,270–1,485). In winter, you can
book space in a **cabin** by the night
($210). The ranch also offers a num-
ber of activities not included in the
basic rate, including guided hunting
and fishing trips, pack trips, scenic
floats on the Snake River, snowmobiling, and cross-country skiing.

NORTH WYOMING: DEVILS TOWER–BUFFALO BILL COUNTRY

Stretching across northern Wyoming from the South Dakota border to the border of Yellowstone National Park, the area known as Devils Tower–Buffalo Bill Country encompasses lands as vast and diverse in terms of topography as they are in terms of cultural and historical background. Thus within this remarkably varied region, you'll discover astonishing and breathtaking scenery, abundant recreational activities, and numerous sites of historical and cultural significance.

After leaving Yellowstone National Park—or before you get there—you'll find one great way to kick off your adventures in this broad portion of Wyoming: with a trip to the city of Cody. Here the Old West lives on, and legends and local lore about Buffalo Bill and his contemporaries abound—with good reason. Born in Iowa, William F. "Buffalo Bill" Cody (1846–1917) was not only instrumental in the founding of Cody in 1896 but also, in his day, one of the most recognized and revered figures of the American West. The creator of the famous Wild West show, which toured the country and even went overseas (1883–1913), Cody was a figure of not merely national but also international renown. Today's Cody maintains a strong bond with its historical namesake; many of the town's attractions are directly affiliated with Buffalo Bill, and many more are indirectly connected with him in one way or another.

Cody isn't all about the Old West and the frontier days, though. In addition to calling itself the Home of Buffalo Bill, Cody's other moniker, Gateway to Yellowstone Park, is of equal import. On your way to or from this one-of-a-kind national park, you'll also find plenty of opportunities to explore and enjoy the vast tracts of incredible public lands surrounding Cody, whether on horseback, guided by an expert from one of the area's many guest and dude ranches; or on foot, by boat, or on wheels, depending on your preferred mode of travel. Coming back to civilization, you'll find that downtown Cody is a veritable paradise for shoppers in search of western and Native American–themed souvenirs to remind them of their adventures. It's also home to a number of great eateries.

From Cody, head south and east to explore the rest of the Bighorn Basin, an area distinguished by fertile valleys giving way to rolling badlands, which then sweep up into the Bighorn Mountains west of Buffalo. The relatively fertile abundance of this area of Wyoming has made it a natural choice for human

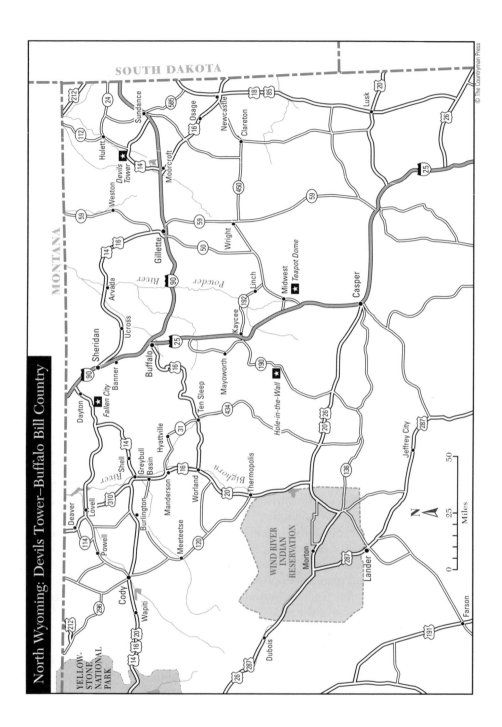

North Wyoming: Devils Tower–Buffalo Bill Country

habitation since prehistoric times (though the climate was surely different back then) and for dinosaurs and other prehistoric creatures long before humans came to exist as well. Thus you'll find ample opportunities here to explore Wyoming's wealth of dinosaur and other fossils, as well as petroglyphs, pictographs, and other relics left by the humans who dwelt in this area in the past. Modern human history is here to be explored, too, from stories of the pioneers who settled this land to those of the Native Americans that they largely displaced.

Today, the cowboy spirit lives on in the Bighorn Basin, where folks still ranch to make a living and cattle wander through the national forests to graze during certain times of the year, reminiscent of the bison that once made such forests their homes. It's not uncommon to see horses hitched at the bar or cowboys and cowgirls stomping into the post office to pick up their mail after a long day in the saddle. If you time your visit right, you can catch a rodeo or two and dance in the streets to the sounds of western music or perhaps even experience life on a working cattle ranch or participate in a cattle drive yourself.

Additional recreational opportunities include soaking in natural hot springs, exploring numerous canyons featuring fantastic rock formations carved by wind and water, and tremendous fishing, hiking, and wildlife viewing opportunities. If you're visiting in winter, you won't want to miss out on the area's incredible snowmobile trails and quaint local ski resorts.

After you pass through the Bighorn Mountains, you'll descend into northeastern Wyoming, a multifaceted land of forest, grasslands, and plains rife with history and recreational opportunities. Explore the canyons, mountains, and rivers on the east side of the Bighorns near Sheridan, Buffalo, and Kaycee on horseback, by foot, or by bike—perhaps as a guest on one of the area's guest ranches. Natural wonders like Devils Tower and Fallen City dot the scenery throughout northeastern Wyoming. You'll also find an amazing array of golf courses in this region, so be sure to pack your clubs. Walk the grounds where battles took place between the encroaching settlers and the Native Americans via the area's historic sites, or wander back to Hole-in-the-Wall, a passage where famous outlaws herded horses and cattle. You can round out your knowledge of the area's history by visiting one or more of its many western history–oriented museums.

GUIDANCE **Basin Chamber of Commerce** (307-568-3331), P.O. Box 599, Basin 82410.

Buffalo, Wyoming Chamber of Commerce (1-800-227-5122; 307-684-5544; www.buffalowyo.com), 55 N. Main Street, Buffalo 82834.

Cody Country Chamber of Commerce (307-587-2777; www.codychamber .org), 836 Sheridan Avenue, Cody 82414.

East Yellowstone Valley Chamber of Commerce (307-587-9595; www .yellowstone-lodging.com), P.O. Box 21, Wapiti 82450.

Gillette Convention & Visitors Bureau (1-800-544-6136; 307-686-0040; www .visitgillette.net), 1810 S. Douglas Highway #A, Gillette 82718.

Greybull Area Chamber of Commerce (1-877-765-2100; www.greybull.com), 521 Greybull Avenue, Greybull 82426.

Hulett Chamber of Commerce (307-467-5430; www.hulett.org), 146 Main Street, P.O. Box 421, Hulett 82720.

Kaycee, Wyoming Chamber of Commerce (307-738-2444; www.kaycee wyoming.org), P.O. Box 147, Kaycee 82639.

Lovell Chamber of Commerce (307-548-7552; www.lovellchamber.com), 287 E. Main Street, Lovell 82431.

Meeteetse Tourist Information Center (307-868-2454; www.meeteetsewy .com), 1947 State Street, P.O. Box 238, Meeteetse 82433.

Newcastle Area Chamber of Commerce (307-746-2739; 1-800-835-0157; www.newcastlewyo.com), 1323 Washington Boulevard, Newcastle 82701.

Park County Travel Council (1-800-393-2639; 307-587-2297; www.pctc.org), Buffalo Bill's Yellowstone Country, P.O. Box 2454, Cody 82414.

Powell Valley Chamber of Commerce (307-754-3494; www.powellchamber .org), P.O. Box 814, Powell 82435.

Sheridan Travel and Tourism (1-888-596-6787; www.sheridanwyoming.org), P.O. Box 7155, Sheridan 82801.

Sundance Area Chamber of Commerce (1-800-477-9340; 307-283-3411; www.sundancewyoming.com), P.O. Box 1004, Sundance 82729.

Ten Sleep Visitors Center, at the Percup Espresso Café and More (307-366-2692; www.tensleepwyoming.com), 100 2nd Street, Ten Sleep 82442.

Thermopolis Chamber of Commerce (307-864-3192; www.thermopolis.com), 119 S. 6th Street, P.O. Box 768, Thermopolis 82443.

Worland Area Chamber of Commerce/Worland–Ten Sleep Visitor's Council (307-347-3226; www.worlandchamber.com and www.tensleepworland wyoming.com), 120 N. 10th Street, Worland 82401.

GETTING THERE US 14/16/20 runs through Cody from the east and west, while WY 120 runs through Cody from the north and south. Thermopolis, Worland, and Greybull all lie along US 20, which runs north–south. Greybull can be accessed from the east or west via US 14 and Worland from the east via US 16. Sheridan, Buffalo, and Kaycee all lie along I-25, Wyoming's only major north–south interstate. Gillette lies along I-90; it can also be accessed from the north via US 14/16 or WY 59 and from the south via WY 50 or 59. Sundance lies on I-90. It can also be accessed from the northwest via US 14 and from the south via WY 585. Newcastle can be reached from the east and northwest via US 16 and from the north and south via US 85/18.

See also *Airports, Amtrak, Bus Service,* and *Travel Information* in "What's Where in Wyoming."

MEDICAL EMERGENCY **Campbell County Memorial Hospital** (307-682-8811), 501 S. Burma Avenue, Gillette.

Hot Springs County Memorial Hospital (307-864-3121), 112 E. Arapahoe Street, Thermopolis.

Johnson County Healthcare Center (307-684-5521), 497 W. Lott, Buffalo.

Memorial Hospital of Sheridan County, (307-672-1000), 1401 W. 5th Street, Sheridan.

North Big Horn Hospital (307-548-5200), 1115 Lane 12, Lovell.

South Big Horn County Hospital (307-568-3311), 388 S. US 20, Greybull.

Washakie Medical Center (307-347-3221), 400 S. 15th Street, Worland.

West Park Hospital (307-578-2375), 707 Sheridan Avenue, Cody.

Weston County Health Service, (307-746-4491), 1124 Washington Boulevard, Newcastle.

✸ To See

TOWNS **Basin.** Founded in 1896, Basin is the county seat for Big Horn County. A quiet western town on US 14/16/20 south of Greybull, Basin bustles with activity every August when it hosts the **Big Horn County Fair** (see *Special Events*).

Dayton and Ranchester are located northeast of Sheridan via I-90. Each town has a population hovering around 700 people. Nestled in the foothills of the northern Bighorn Mountains, both towns serve as gateways to the recreational opportunities therein as well as peaceful getaways from the hustle of city life. (See also *Lodging.*)

Hulett. Located north of Devils Tower National Monument on WY 24, Hulett is home to the **Northeast Wyoming Annual Antique Show** and the **Hulett Rodeo** (see *Special Events*) as well as an annual biker rally and a number of guest ranches, including the **Diamond L Guest Ranch** (see ranch vacations under *To Do—Unique Adventures*).

Kaycee is 45 miles south of Buffalo, just off I-25. Kaycee—population 249—is situated on the banks of the Powder River. Strongly rooted in the traditions of the Old West, Kaycee takes pride in being one of the smallest towns in the nation to host a professional rodeo, the PRCA-sanctioned **Deke Latham Memorial Rodeo** (see *Special Events*).

Lovell. The town of Lovell, on US 310 north of Greybull and the surrounding smaller communities of Byron, Cowley, Deaver, and Frannie serve as gateways to the **Bighorn Canyon National Recreation Area** (see *Wilder Places—Other Wild Places*) and the **Pryor Mountains.** All provide ample recreational and sightseeing opportunities (some of which are listed below). For those who love the mountains, this area of Wyoming is sure to delight.

Meeteetse. The Old West stays alive in Meeteetse on WY 120, which still boasts wooden boardwalks, hitching rails, and water troughs along its streets. Formerly the home of **Butch Cassidy,** Meeteetse was also the site of the first cattle ranching operation in the Bighorn Basin, which was established by Otto Franc in

1879. Today's Meeteetse is a charming blend of well-kept turn-of-the-20th-century structures combined with modern amenities.

Powell. Named for noted scientist and explorer John Wesley Powell, the town lies in a rich agricultural area northeast of Cody, made so by the irrigation system that virtually created Powell. Originally settled by workers brought in to create and implement a flood irrigation system for the Powell Valley, Powell and its environs today continue to rely heavily on agriculture, but with the added benefit of the recreational opportunities resulting from the Shoshone Irrigation Project, which include fishing, wildlife viewing, hunting, and more.

Shell. This tiny hamlet on US 14 east of Greybull, with a population of about 50, serves as the gateway to **Shell Canyon** and **Shell Falls.**

Story lies along I-90 between Buffalo and Sheridan near Banner in the foothills of the Bighorn Mountains. Proximity to historic sites (see *Historic Landmarks, Places, and Sites*), gorgeous ponderosa pine forests, and tons of recreational opportunities make Story a desirable place to seek accommodations (see *Lodging*).

Ten Sleep. "A little western town with a big western heart," Ten Sleep lies on US 16 just outside the mouth of **Ten Sleep Canyon,** through which runs the **Cloud Peak Scenic Byway** (See *Scenic Drives*). Ten Sleep hosts a number of great annual events (see *Special Events*).

MUSEUMS **Anna Miller Museum** (307-746-4188; www.newcastlewyo.com/anna.html), Delaware Washington Park, Newcastle. Open year-round Monday through Friday 9–5 or by appointment; free. This western history museum includes a one-room schoolhouse and the oldest structure still standing from the Black Hills Gold Rush—the Jenney Stockade Cabin—as well as numerous items of historic significance from frontier times and earlier. (See also Beaver Creek Loop Tour under *Scenic Drives.*)

Buffalo Bill Dam Visitor Center (307-527-6076; www.bbdvc.org), 6 miles west of Cody on US 14/16/20. Open May through September daily 8 AM–8 PM; free. Interpretive displays and exhibits tell the story of the dam's engineering and construction as well as the natural history of the surroundings. You'll also find gorgeous views of Shoshone Canyon, the reservoir, and an impressive overlook of the dam. A self-guided audio tour is available for purchase ($4).

Buffalo Bill Historical Center (307-587-4771; www.bbhc.org), 720 Sheridan Avenue, Cody. Open daily: in April 10 AM–5 PM; in May 8 AM–8 PM; June 15 through September 15, 7 AM–5 PM; September 16 through

BUFFALO BILL HISTORICAL CENTER IN CODY

October 8 AM–5 PM; daily except Monday November through March 10 AM–3 PM; closed Thanksgiving, Christmas, and New Year's Day; $15 adults, $13 seniors (65 and older), $4 children ages 6–17, children 5 and under 6; admission covers 2 consecutive days of access to all five museums. One of Wyoming's top attractions, the Buffalo Bill Historical Center (BBHC) is actually a collection of five world-renowned museums and a research library, so you should allot at the very least an entire day to exploring the treasure trove of exhibits held within its walls. These include the **Buffalo Bill Museum,** which celebrates and records the personal and public life of the legendary William "Buffalo Bill" Cody (1846–1917), from whom the town of Cody took its name; the **Plains Indian Museum,** which not only displays Indian objects but also places them in context and interprets their historical, cultural, and current significance; the **Cody Firearms Museum,** home to the world's largest collection of American firearms; the **Draper Museum of Natural History,** the center's newest museum, which strives to educate visitors about geology, wildlife, and human presence in the Greater Yellowstone region via interactive and engaging exhibits; the **Whitney Gallery of Western Art,** where you'll see original paintings and sculptures by artists past and present, renowned for their abilities to capture the spirit and rugged beauty of the West; and the **Harold McCracken Research Library.** (See also Buffalo Bill Historical Center & Cody Trolley Tours under *To Do—Unique Adventures.*)

OLD TRAIL TOWN IN CODY

Campbell County Rockpile Museum (307-682-5723), 900 W. 2nd Street, Gillette. Open June 1 through August 31 Monday through Saturday 9 AM–8 PM, Sunday 12:30 PM–6:30 PM; open September 1 through May 31 Monday through Saturday 9 AM–5 PM; free. Learn about the local history of Campbell County, which is portrayed through the museum's collection of western artifacts. The collection includes Native American items such as projectile points and scrapers, as well as items from frontier days such as saddles, rifles, newspapers, and more.

Crook County Museum & Art Gallery (307-283-3666), 309 Cleveland Street, Sundance. Open June through August 8 AM–8 PM; open September through May 8 AM–5 PM; free. Focused on the history of Crook County, museum collections include Indian artifacts, furniture from the 1888 courthouse where the Sundance Kid was put on trial, pioneer relics, dioramas, and historic photographs.

Greybull Museum (307-765-2444), 325 Greybull Avenue, Greybull. Open June through September Monday through Saturday 10 AM–8 PM; hours vary seasonally during rest of year; free. Exhibits include Greybull's pioneer and Native American history, as well as fossils from nearby dinosaur dig sites.

❦ **Homesteaders Museum** (307-754-9481; www.wyshs.org/mus-homesteaders .htm), 133 S. Clark Street, Powell. Open May through September Friday and

Saturday 10 AM–5 PM; open October through April Tuesday through Friday 1 PM–4 PM; free. A collection of Indian artifacts, old tools, antique farm equipment, photographs, geological exhibits, and other pertinent memorabilia walks you through the history of the settlement of Powell and the Bighorn Basin.

Hot Springs County Museum and Cultural Center (307-864-5183; www .trib.com/~history), 700 Broadway, Thermopolis. Open Memorial Day through Labor Day Monday through Saturday 9 AM–6 PM, Sunday 1 PM–6 PM; open rest of year Tuesday through Saturday 10 AM–5 PM; $4 adults, $2 seniors (over 60) and children ages 6–12, children 5 and under free; an annual family pass $20. The museum documents the history of the settlers in the Thermopolis area (1880–1930) with an extensive collection of artifacts from that period. Also on exhibit are a large collection of Native American artifacts, a log cabin from a Wyoming ghost town, some 8,000 historical photos, and a one-room school-house.

♿ **Jim Gatchell Memorial Museum and Gift Shop** (307-684-9331; www .jimgatchell.com), 100 Fort Street, Buffalo. Open daily June 1 through October 31, 9 AM–6 PM; open November 1 through May 31 Monday through Saturday 9 AM–6 PM; closed July 4th, Thanksgiving, Christmas Eve, Christmas Day, and New Year's Day; $4 adults, $2 children ages 6–16, children 5 and under free, family rate $10. Here you'll find Buffalo's frontier history kept alive and illustrated via a fine collection of roughly 7,000 artifacts, most of which came from the private collection of Jim Gatchell. Gatchell moved to Buffalo and opened a drugstore just as one of the most tumultuous eras in Wyoming's frontier history was dying down. Avidly interested in local history, Gatchell befriended and was trusted by local Indian tribes, who bestowed upon him many invaluable gifts from the frontier days in the more than 50 years that he spent in Buffalo. Following Gatchell's death in 1954, his family donated his collection to the people of Johnson County; this collection largely constitutes the museum's exhibits to this day.

🏛 **Meeteetse Bank Museum** (307-868-2423; www.wyshs.org/mus-meeteetse bank.htm), 1003 Park Avenue, Meeteetse. Open January through April Monday through Wednesday 9 AM–5 PM; open May through September Monday through Friday 9 AM–5 PM; open October through December Monday through Thursday 9 AM–5 PM; donations gladly accepted. Housed in a structure built from sun-dried bricks in 1900 for the banking firm of Hogg, Cheeseman and McDonald and now listed on the National Register of Historic Places, this museum's permanent exhibits include a banking exhibit, an exhibit on cattle and sheep ranching, and an exhibit from the ghost town Kirwin, once a mining community.

🏛 **Old Trail Town** (307-587-5302; www.nezperce.com/trltown.html), 2 miles west of Cody on US 14/16/20. Open daily mid-May through mid-September 8 AM–8 PM; $3 ages 12 and up, children 11 and under free. A collection of 26 historically significant structures dating from the late 19th century to the early 20th century, along with 100 horse-drawn vehicles, numerous Native American artifacts, and a collection of items from Wyoming's frontier days makes Old Trail Town a must-see stop if you're interested in the Old West. Highlighted are some of the area's most notorious and flamboyant personalities from the past, making this a fun and informative place to visit.

Old West Miniature Village and Museum (307-587-5362; www.imt.net/~rodeo/mini.html), 142 W. Yellowstone Avenue, Cody. Open daily mid-May through mid-September 8 AM–8 PM; open by appointment off-season; $5 adults, $3 seniors or students ages 13–18, $2 children ages 7–12, children 6 and under free, family rate $15. For a historically accurate bird's-eye view of the Old West at its wildest, this incredible collection of hand-carved figures suspended in action will not disappoint. From battles to buffalo hunts, you'll find it all captured here, along with artifacts from the Old West and items available for purchase at Tecumseh's Trading Post.

Ten Sleep Pioneer Museum (307-366-2759). 436 2nd Street, Ten Sleep. Open Memorial Day weekend through November 1, 9 AM–4 PM; free. This museum features a mishmash of historical items of local significance collected in one place, including humorous photos of pioneer days and artifacts from Ten Sleep's history.

& **Trail End State Historic Site** (307-674-4589; www.trailend.org), 400 Clarendon Avenue, Sheridan. Open daily June 1 through August 31, 9 AM–6 PM; hours vary seasonally in other months; closed December 15 through February 28; $1 adults (residents), $2 adults (nonresidents), children 18 and under free, use of grounds free. This nearly 14,000-square-foot mansion—now a historic house museum—was built in the Flemish Revival style in 1913, serving as the home for Texas-born Wyoming politician John B. Kendrick and his family. Situated on almost 4 landscaped acres, the mansion today houses an interesting collection of permanent exhibits focused on depicting everyday life for its residents during the period from 1913 to 1933, as well as temporary exhibits. (See also *For Families.*)

Washakie Museum (307-347-4102), 1115 Obie Sue (at 12th), Worland. Hours vary seasonally; free. This museum includes an interactive exhibit containing items from Worland's pioneer days, an interesting display about the prehistoric mammoth kill site unearthed near Worland, and information on the history of ranching in the area, among other exhibits.

See also Dancing Bear Folk Center–Teddy Bear Museum and Old West Wax Museum under *For Families;* and A Maverick Hotel and Historic Occidental Hotel under *Lodging—Other Options.*

TRAIL END STATE HISTORIC SITE IN NORTHEASTERN WYOMING

HISTORIC LANDMARKS, PLACES, AND SITES ✦ **Connor Battlefield State Park and Historic Site** (307-684-7629; http://wyoparks.state.wy.us/connor.htm), south of US 14 in Ranchester. Open year-round for day-use free; open May through October for first-come, first-served camping, $6 for residents, $12 for nonresidents. You'd never guess from its current incarnation as a placid camping and picnic area that this was once the scene of the 1865 battle of Tongue River, which took place between troops headed by General Patrick E. Connor and Black Bear's Arapahoe village. Aggressively attacked by Connor's troops, the Indians managed to make the soldiers withdraw and actually pursued them as they marched in retreat. Situated in an oxbow of the Tongue River, the park features shaded camping, a playground, fishing, and restrooms.

å **Fort Phil Kearny State Historic Site** (307-684-7629; http://wyoparks .state.wy.us/kearny1.htm), 20 miles south of Sheridan at Exit 44 off I-90. Open for day-use only, April through November; $1 adults (residents), $2 adults (nonresidents), children 17 and under free. Tour this historic fort, one of three constructed in 1866 to help protect travelers along the Bozeman Trail and to draw Indian attention away from the construction of the Union Pacific Railroad to the south, as well as to stave off warfare between Native American tribes. In this vicinity the Cheyenne, Sioux, and Arapahoe fought to maintain control of some of their only remaining great buffalo hunting grounds. A visitor center provides exhibits and interpretive materials, and you can take a self-guided, interpretive tour. Within 5 miles lie two historic battlefields from the era: the sites of the Fetterman Fight and the Wagon Box Fight, both of which have interpretive trails that provide both Native American and white perspectives on the events that took place. Fort Phil Kearny also hosts Bozeman Trail Days (see *Special Events*).

Legend Rock State Petroglyph Site (307-864-2176; http://wyoparks.state .wy.us/hot.htm), 30 miles northwest of Thermopolis. Check with staff at the Hot Springs State Park Headquarters (see *To Do—Hot Springs*) to get a gate key before driving to Legend Rock (they will give you precise directions, too). After parking at the end of the road, follow a trail a short distance down into a gully and then up a small rise to view this beautiful display of ancient artwork up close. Etched into the cliff faces at Legend Rock are some 300 Native American petroglyphs, including kokopellis, birds, buffalo, rabbits, humans, and numerous other animals. The petroglyphs' precise origins are unknown, but they provide a window into the past and are considered sacred by Native Americans today. As you view the petroglyphs, you'll find that it's hard to imagine just how much intricacy and precision the carving of these images required—especially when you compare them to the latter-day graffiti that some people have added to the mix. Please do your part: don't add any marks or touch the petroglyphs.

FORT PHIL KEARNY STATE HISTORIC SITE IN NORTHEASTERN WYOMING

å **Medicine Lodge State Archaeological Site** (307-469-2234; http://wyo parks.state.wy.us/mlodge1.htm), 6 miles north of Hyattville via WY 31 to Cold Springs Road. Open year-round for day-use and camping; free for day-use, overnight camping $6 for residents, $12 nonresidents. This area has drawn human visitors for more than 10,000 years to set up camp. Archaeological study has revealed more than 60 cultural levels of continuous human occupation at this site, with numerous artifacts, pictographs, and petroglyphs recovered. You can still view a plethora of pictographs and petroglyphs along with helpful interpretive signs. This site includes handicapped-accessible pit toilets and a concrete trail. Medicine Lodge also offers fishing, tremendous wildlife viewing opportunities at both the site and in the surrounding wildlife habitat management area, mountain bik-

LEGEND ROCK STATE PETROGLYPH SITE IN BIGHORN BASIN

ing, and a self-guided nature trail, among other attractions. (See also *Wilder Places—Wildlife Refuges and Areas.*)

   ♿ **Medicine Wheel National Historic Landmark** (307-674-2600; http:// wyoshpo.state.wy.us/medwheel.htm), Lovell. Open year-round for day-use only; free. Located east of Lovell just off US 14 Alternate atop Medicine Mountain in Bighorn National Forest, this site has long mystified archaeologists, who are unable to fully explain the original function and construction of this enormous medicine wheel. Measuring 75 to 80 feet in diameter and made up of stones that radiate out from a central cairn in 28 spokes, the medicine wheel is believed to have been of religious significance to Native Americans (as it still is today)—but estimates on when or exactly why it was constructed vary widely. The site includes an interpretive center and restrooms. Visitors must walk 1.5 miles to view the medicine wheel.

   ♿ **Pioneer Square.** Located along Worland's main street, Big Horn Avenue, Pioneer Square commemorates the spot where Charles H. "Dad" Worland put in a stage stop in 1900. Lovely sculptures capture the spirit of the pioneer days, while ample grass, shade trees, and benches make this a great spot for a picnic.

See also Meeteetse Bank Museum and Trail End State Historic Site under *Museums;* Beaver Creek Loop Tour under *Scenic Drives;* Lake DeSmet under *To Do—Fishing;* Hole-in-the-Wall Trail under *To Do—*

MEDICINE WHEEL NATIONAL HISTORIC LANDMARK IN THE BIGHORN MOUNTAINS

Hiking; Hot Springs State Park under *To Do—Hot Springs;* Pahaska Teepee under *Lodging—Lodges;* and Buffalo Bill's Irma Hotel and Historic Occidental Hotel under *Lodging—Other Options.*

FOR FAMILIES ✍ 🐾 **Cody Gunslingers** (1-800-745-4762; www.irmahotel.com/area.htm), 12th Street and Sheridan Avenue, Cody. Held June through September Monday through Saturday at 6 PM; free. Watch reenactments of famous gun battles and shootouts by infamous characters of the Old West, as well as historic presentations. (See also Buffalo Bill's Irma Hotel under *Lodging—Other Options.*)

✍ **Cody Nite Rodeo** (307-587-5155; www.comp-unltd.com/~rodeo/rodeo.html), Cody. Held nightly June 1 through August 31 at 8:30; $15 adults, $8 children ages 7–12, children 6 and under free. Entertaining visitors to Cody for more than 50 years, the Cody Nite Rodeo features not only PRCA-sanctioned rodeo events such as saddle bronc riding and team roping but also guaranteed kid pleasers, including a clown act and a kids' calf scramble.

✍ 🐾 **Dancing Bear Folk Center–Teddy Bear Museum and Old West Wax Museum** (307-864-9396; www.westwaxmuseum.com and www.server1.dancing bear.org), 119 S. 6th Street, Thermopolis. Open daily May 15 through September 14, 9 AM–7 PM; open September 15 through May 14 Wednesday through Saturday 10 AM–2 PM, Sunday 12 PM–4 PM; $4 adults, $3 children 4–18 and seniors 60 and older, children 3 and under free, $12 for family of four. Actually comprised of three destinations under one roof, this complex features the Old West Wax Museum, with more than 50 life-size wax features in settings that portray aspects of frontier life; the Dancing Bear Folk Center, a working textile studio with hands-on activities, including weaving and spinning thread; and the Teddy Bear Museum, a large collection of teddy bears that will delight both children and serious collectors.

✍ **Historic Bozeman Crossing** (307-684-2531; www.bozemancrossing.com), 655 Hart Street, Buffalo. Here the Bozeman Trail once crossed the Powder River's Clear Fork at its low point, providing the military and emigrants with the easiest way across. Today, you'll find attractions of a different sort: an ice-cream parlor and a restaurant (see **Colonel Bozeman's Restaurant & Tavern** under *Eating Out*), a miniature-golf course, a restored 1920s carousel, and a Ferris wheel. A stop at this collection of attractions is sure to bring a smile to the kids' faces (and maybe to yours, too).

PIONEER SQUARE IN WORLAND

✍ **Kendrick Park** (307-674-6421), adjacent to Trail End State Historic Site (see *Museums*), Sheridan. A playground, a municipal pool with a waterslide, an ice-cream vendor with lots of flavors, seasonal concerts, and acres of grass make this park a guaranteed kid pleaser. Kendrick Park is also home to a buffalo and elk refuge. This a perfect place for a picnic lunch alongside Goose Creek in the shade of the cottonwood trees.

&. ♪ **Red Gulch Dinosaur Tracksite** (307-347-5100; www.wy.blm.gov/rgdt), 5 miles south on Red Gulch–Alkali National Back Country Byway (BLM Road 1109; see also *Scenic Drives*). Open dawn through dusk; free. The Bureau of Land Management's Red Gulch Dinosaur Tracksite leads you back to prehistoric times through helpful interpretive signs along a wooden boardwalk that deposits you directly onto the surface in which the dinosaur tracks lie. Though at first they are hard to discern, tracks spring up from the stone surface all around once the eye is clued in to what to look for. Here visitors walk in the footsteps left by a number of as-yet-undetermined species of three-toed dinosaurs from the middle Jurassic period, some 160–180 million years ago. You can even keep small invertebrate fossils if you find any at the site. (See also Bureau of Land Management under *Wilder Places—Other Wild Places.*)

♪ ♘ **The Wyoming Dinosaur Center and Dig Sites** (307-864-2997; 1-800-455-DINO; www.wyodino.org), 110 Carter Ranch Road, Thermopolis. Open daily year-round; hours vary according to season; $6 adults, $3.50 children ages 4–13 and seniors 60 and older, children 3 and under free, $15 family of two adults and two children (additional children $3 each). More than 200 exhibits await exploration at the dinosaur center, including interactive exhibits, 10 full-sized mounted dinosaur skeletons, and many smaller fossils and displays. Hourly tours (additional fee) of actual dinosaur dig sites take place from 9 AM to 4 PM in the summer season, allowing you a closer look at the actual places where dinosaur fossils have been unearthed. For an unforgettable dino experience, during the summer season adults, families, or just the kids alone (ages 8–12) can partake in actual dinosaur digs at the sites (advance reservations required, call for details and current prices).

See also Connor Battlefield State Park and Historic Site under *Historic Landmarks, Places, and Sites;* Clear Creek Walking Trail and Paul Stock Nature Trail under *To Do—Bicycling;* the Shoshone River and Wind River Canyon Whitewater under *To Do—Paddling/Floating;* Antelope Butte Ski Area and Big Horn Ski Resort under *To Do—Snow Sports;* Double Rafter Cattle Drives and Float Trips by Eagle RV Park and Campground under *To Do—Unique Adventures;* Bighorn Canyon National Recreation Area under *Wilder Places—Other Wild Places;* and Lake DeSmet Fishing Derby and Northeast Wyoming Annual Antique Show under *Special Events.*

SCENIC DRIVES **Beartooth Scenic Byway,** 64 miles on US 212 from Cooke City, Montana, to Red Lodge, Montana, with much of the drive in Wyoming; closed seasonally; easily accessed in Wyoming from WY 296 (Chief Joseph Scenic Byway; see below). This highway has been acclaimed "the most beautiful highway in America" by a number of people, due to the incredible scenery and unique natural features in the surrounding **Gallatin, Shoshone, and Custer national forests.** Completed in 1936, this highway provides passers-through with the opportunity to witness the transformation of the terrain from a green, subalpine forest to a true alpine environment as they climb into the Beartooth Range, a mountain range with more than 20 peaks taller than 12,000 feet and numerous glaciers. Tremendous wildlife viewing prospects and recreational activities abound along this drive, including camping, fishing, hiking, picnicking, and bicycling for experienced road riders who want a high-altitude challenge.

Beaver Creek Loop Tour, a 50-mile loop tour around Newcastle. Stop at the Anna Miller Museum (see *Museums*) to get a map that will send you on your way to exploring 26 marked sites around Newcastle. Featuring both scenic and historic destinations, this drive's highlights include old stage stops, ghost towns, a pioneer cemetery, and scenic overlooks.

Bighorn Scenic Byway, about 50 miles on US 14, starting west of Dayton (see *Towns*) at the edge of **Bighorn National Forest** (see *Wilder Places—Forests*) and ending in the tiny town of Shell (see *Towns*). This incredible drive takes you high into the Bighorn Mountains as you wind past **Fallen City** (see *Natural Wonders*), **Steamboat Rock,** and numerous additional picturesque rock out-croppings before surmounting **Granite Pass** and beginning your gradual descent through **Shell Canyon** (see *Natural Wonders*). Numerous recreational opportunities along this drive include fishing, picnicking, hiking, and skiing. Stop on your drive at the **Burgess Junction Visitor Center,** 0.5 mile east of Burgess Junction on US 14, open daily 8 AM–5:30 PM in summer for information, exhibits, maps, and a self-guided trail.

Buffalo Bill Cody Scenic Byway, 27.5 miles stretching from 24 miles east of Cody at the border of Shoshone National Forest (see *Wilder Places—Forests*) on US 14/16/20 (Yellowstone Highway) to the eastern border of Yellowstone National Park. This drive begins at the border of the 2.4-million-acre **Shoshone National Forest** and follows the **North Fork of the Shoshone River** as it turns and twists through the rugged terrain of the Wapiti Valley, showcasing tow-ering formations of conglomerate rock and allowing abundant opportunities for wildlife viewing, fishing, hiking, camping, and picnicking, as well as access to more than 10 historic guest lodges, including **Pahaska Teepee** (see *Lodging—Lodges*).

Chief Joseph Scenic Byway, 47 miles on WY 296 starting at its intersection with WY 120 north of Cody and ending at its intersection with US 212 (Beartooth Scenic Byway; see above). A drive along the Chief Joseph Scenic Byway traverses some of the land through which Chief Joseph and the Nez Perce Indians fled as they battled defensively in the late 1870s against soldiers, civilians, and even other Indians. Spectacular natural features include the **Clarks Fork of the Yellowstone River** (see *To Do—Fishing*) and views of **Sunlight Basin** and **Sunlight Gorge.** Recreational opportunities include wildlife viewing, fishing, hiking, picnicking, and camping.

Cloud Peak Skyway Scenic Byway, about 65 miles on US 16, starting west of Buffalo and ending near the base of Ten Sleep Canyon on the other side of Pow-der River Pass. Offering travelers the only close-up view of the highest peak in the Bighorn Mountains, **Cloud Peak** (13,167 feet), this drive features gorgeous

views of **Bighorn National Forest** (see *Wilder Places—Forests*), the **Cloud**
Peak Wilderness, and the breathtaking limestone and dolomite cliffs of **Ten**
Sleep Canyon (see also *Natural Wonders*). Many pullouts and side roads afford
you the chance to step out of the car, picnic, view wildlife (moose are often seen
along this route), or gain access to numerous fishing and camping areas.

Crazy Woman Canyon, Exit 291 off I-25 south of Buffalo, then south on
WY 296 and west on C.R. 14/F.R. 33 (or via US 16 west from Buffalo, then east
on F.R. 33 to go down into the canyon). Not for RVs or trailers, this narrow, rutted dirt road joins US 16 (Cloud Peak Skyway Scenic Byway; see above) before
Powder River Pass. Travel is slow-going through Crazy Woman Canyon, but you
won't mind—the incredible, sheer canyon cliffs and the gorgeous **Crazy Wo-**
man Creek will likely have you jumping out of your car to take a closer look.
Just be sure to watch for traffic coming the other way!

Medicine Wheel Passage Scenic Byway, 27 miles east along US 14 Alternate
from the border of Bighorn National Forest east of Lovell to the junction with
US 14 at Burgess Junction (along the Bighorn Scenic Byway; above). This lovely
drive takes you by **the Medicine Wheel National Historic Landmark** (see
Historic Landmarks, Places, and Sites) and then up out of the Bighorn Basin
into higher elevations, where ponderosa pines, Engelmann spruce, lodgepole
pines, and Douglas firs are interspersed with fields of wildflowers such as lupine
and balsamroot (in the spring and summer), along with fantastic views of the
Bighorn Mountains, the **Absarokas,** and the **Bighorn Basin.** Recreational
opportunities include wildlife viewing, fishing, hiking, picnicking, and camping.

Red Gulch–Alkali National Back Country Byway, 32 miles on BLM 1111
and BLM 1109 between US 14 west of Shell 4 miles and WY 31 just north of
Hyattville. Allow 2 to 3 hours for this historic drive through red canyons and
mesas. Along this byway, there are few signs of humanity, save fences and roads,
and their relative absence creates a feeling of emptiness and isolation as you pass
sweeping vistas, sandstone buttes, and tall cairns atop hills marking a Native
American–pioneer days trail system. Do not drive this road in wet or inclement
conditions. A high-clearance two-wheel-drive vehicle (don't try to bring an RV
through) suffices, but be prepared for slow going in certain areas, and be sure to
have a spare tire in good condition, since there are no services along the drive.
Consider stopping at **Medicine Lodge State Archaeological Site** (see *His-*
toric Landmarks, Places, and Sites) and the Bureau of Land Management's **Red**
Gulch Dinosaur Tracksite (see *For Families*).

WY 434, 20–80 miles one-way south of US 16 at Ten Sleep. Turn south by the
Per Cup Espresso Café in Ten Sleep and enter rolling brush and grasslands for a
few miles, passing the monument for the **Spring Creek Raid** at around mile 7.
At mile 16, the scenery changes as the road drops into a gorgeous valley. Lush
and green in spring and early summer, the vegetation contrasts beautifully with
the brilliant red soil and sandstone buttresses reminiscent of Utah's similar formations. The pavement ends at around 20 miles, but the idyllic scenery continues if you're willing to keep going on a well-maintained gravel road, passing by
enormous **Mahogany Butte.** At this point or somewhere not too far beyond it,
you can choose to end your journey and simply turn around, or you can continue

on through more rolling hills to the tiny town of **Lysite** (70.5 miles from Ten Sleep) or the town of **Moneta** (79.5 miles from Ten Sleep), which lies on US 20/26 (see "Central Wyoming: Oregon Trail–Rendezvous Country"). Be sure to have a full tank of gas, since the "towns" of Big Trails and Nowood are simply small clusters of homes or ranches.

WINERIES **Wyoming Wine** (307-673-0291; www.wyomingwine.com), 1457 N. Main Street, Sheridan. This shop features wines made from Wyoming-grown rhubarb, chokecherries, wild grapes, cherries, plums, and apples, as well as winemaking accessories, wine-oriented gift baskets, and an assortment of Wyoming-related crafts. Wine tastings are offered at the store.

NATURAL WONDERS & **Castle Gardens Scenic Area** is accessible by traveling 1 mile west of Ten Sleep on US 16, then turning south onto a signed dirt road and following signs for about 6 miles. Open year-round; free. Managed by the Bureau of Land Management's Worland Field Office (see *Wilder Places—Other Wild Places*), Castle Gardens features sandcastlelike eroded towers and ribs of sandstone set in an isolated, windswept landscape replete with wildflowers in spring and early summer, when lilies, prickly pears, and scarlet globemallows carpet the ground. Accessible via a decent dirt road suitable for two-wheel-drive autos when not wet or snowy, this magical destination has a desert canyon feel, with its juniper and sagebrush. This area is great for hiking, wildlife-watching, and picnicking. Primitive camping is permitted at this area, but water and trash pickup are not available.

& **Devils Tower National Monument** (307-467-5283; www.nps.gov/deto), I-90 to Moorcroft or Sundance, then north on US 14 to WY 24. Open daily year-round; $10 per vehicle for 7-day pass, $12 for camping. Perhaps the most recognized feature of Wyoming's landscape, this geological wonder rises 1,267 feet above the Belle Fourche River (see *To Do—Fishing*). This towering vertical monument of religious significance to Native Americans is also a longtime favored destination of rock climbers. President Teddy Roosevelt declared Devils Tower the nation's first national monument, in 1906, and it continues to attract and amaze visitors today. Recreational opportunities include hiking, wildlife viewing, bird-watching, fishing, rock climbing, and camping. (See also Tower Trail under *To Do—Hiking*.)

Fallen City and Steamboat Rock, off US 14 between Dayton and

DEVILS TOWER NATIONAL MONUMENT IN NORTHEASTERN WYOMING

Burgess Junction. Viewable from the road, to the south of US 14, is a jumbled collection of boulders and precipices known as Fallen City. It prompts the imagination to conjure up images of the sorts of creatures who might have once dwelt within its walls. Farther to the west, you'll be overwhelmed by the enormity of the dolomite formation appropriately deemed Steamboat Rock, which juts up just at a turning point in the road, commanding all who pass this way to be staggered by its monolithic presence.

FALLEN CITY, IN NORTHEASTERN WYOMING

Shell Canyon and Falls, on US 14 east of the small town of Shell, along the Bighorn Scenic Byway (see *Scenic Drives*) in Bighorn National Forest (see *Wilder Places—Forests*). Shell Canyon's amazing walls of sandstone, limestone, and granite will impress you—but you'll be even more impressed when you stop midway up the canyon at Shell Falls, a 100-foot waterfall cut through the granite by Shell Creek that flows at a rate of 3,588 gallons per second. The **Shell Falls Interpretive Center** (open in summer 8 AM–5:30 PM; free) has restrooms, tourist information, a coffee shop, and a gift shop. A self-guided trail leads to a view of the falls and provides information about them.

Ten Sleep Canyon, on US 16 east of the small town of Ten Sleep, along the Cloud Peak Skyway Scenic Byway (see *Scenic Drives*). The canyon still retains a wild flavor that can best be appreciated by pulling off the road and stretching your legs or, better yet, staying overnight in one of a number of Bighorn National Forest campgrounds along the way (see *To Do—Camping* and *Wilder Places—Forests*) and spending a few days exploring the canyon. If you don't have the time for that, consider driving up the old highway (known by locals as Sweet 16), which parallels the paved highway but gives you the chance to get a feel for the true beauty of this magical place. Best visited in late May through June, when wildflowers bloom here in an abundant explosion of yellows, purples, pinks, and whites, US 16 can be closed due to inclement weather in the winter months. (See also Salt Lick Trail under *To Do—Hiking.*)

Tongue River Cave, in Bighorn National Forest (see *Wilder Places—Forests*), is accessed just east of Dayton via US 14 west to CR 92 (River Road to Tongue Canyon Road); the road ends in the parking lot where the trailhead departs. Take the trail from the west end of the parking lot, then drop down to cross the footbridge over the river, and you're on your way. About 1 mile of switchbacks takes you up the slope of the canyon to the cave's entrance, a small opening in a limestone outcrop. Prepare yourself well for a journey inside this 9-mile labyrinth, or simply enjoy the hike to the entrance and shine a light inside if that's as far as you want go; a true exploration of the cave requires comfort with uneven footing and narrow passages, as well as responsible planning and prepa-ration. Spelunkers will find rain rooms, bats, tiny passageways to worm through, wind tunnels, and more. Practice safe caving: be sure to bring food, water, a headlamp and extra batteries, a helmet with a chinstrap, warm clothes, a hat, gloves, and a partner—and tell someone where you're going and when you expect to be back. If you don't cross the footbridge, you can continue strolling up the lovely canyon for a mellow, gradually ascending hike, turning back when-ever you are ready to. (See also the Tongue River under *To Do—Fishing.*)

Wind River Canyon, on US 20, 4 miles south of Thermopolis, is one of the most stunning canyons that you can drive through in Wyoming. The canyon, located on the Wind River Indian Reservation, is a geological wonderland with its enormous walls of dolomite and limestone that dominate the scenery. Recre-ational opportunities include fishing and rafting (special permit required; see Wind River Indian Reservation under *Guidance* in "Central Wyoming: Oregon Trail–Rendezvous Country." See also *To Do—Fishing* and *Paddling/Floating*)

See also Crazy Woman Canyon under *Scenic Drives;* the Clarks Fork of the Yel-lowstone River under *To Do—Fishing* and Hot Springs State Park under *To Do—Hot Springs.*

✳ To Do

BICYCLING **Bearlodge Trail,** near Sundance; access via Cook Lake Recreation Area (see *Hiking*). More than 50 miles of this multiuse trail (#90) in **Black Hills National Forest** (see also *Wilder Places—Forests*) await the avid mountain biker, taking you through some of the rugged terrain and gorgeous scenery of this national forest. This is one of many multiuse trails that you'll find in Black Hills National Forest.

TONGUE RIVER CAVE IN NORTHEASTERN WYOMING

&. ⌀ **Clear Creek Walking Trail** (1-800-227-5122; 307-684-5544; www.buffalowyo.com), Buffalo. This paved trail runs for more than 11 miles along Clear Creek in Buffalo, making it perfect for a leisurely bike ride to explore your surroundings and take in some fresh air. Wildlife view-ing and scenic views abound. You'll find the trail easily—it's right along Main Street in Buffalo. Buffalo is also home to a terrific city park, complete with a playground and picnicking facilities, as well as a free outdoor pool.

⌀ **Paul Stock Nature Trail,** accessi-ble via River View Drive, Cody. Take the whole family for a fun, easy spin along this 1.3-mile, wide, gravel trail that parallels the Shoshone River just outside downtown Cody (for contact information, see Cody Country Chamber of Commerce under *Guidance*). This moderate ride winds above the cottonwood-lined banks of the river, with side trails leading down for a closer look. If you need to rent a bike or get your own bike tuned up, stop in at **Absaroka Bicycles** (307-527-5566; www.absarokabike.com), 2201 17th Street, where they can also provide information about other, more challenging rides in the Cody area.

See also Medicine Lodge State Archaeological Site under *To See—Historic Landmarks, Places, and Sites;* Beartooth Scenic Byway under *To See—Scenic Drives;* BLM campgrounds under *Camping;* Beartooth Loop National Recreation Trail, Bucking Mule Falls National Recreation Trail, and Penrose Trail under *Hiking; Cross-Country Skiing and Snowshoeing* under *Snow Sports;* Buffalo Bill State Park under *Wilder Places—Parks;* Bighorn National Forest, Black Hills National Forest, and Shoshone National Forest under *Wilder Places—Forests;* and Bureau of Land Management under *Wilder Places—Other Wild Places.*

BOATING Keyhole State Park (307-756-3596; http://wyoparks.state.wy.us/key hole1.htm), 353 McKean Road, Moorcroft, north of I-90 via Exit 165. Day-use $2 for residents, $4 for nonresidents; open for camping May through September 30; $6 for residents, $12 nonresidents. Keyhole Reservoir's nearly 15,000 acres of surface area makes this park a popular destination for boating, with its three boat ramps, as well as a privately run **marina and motel** (307-756-9529). Fishing is also popular, with species including catfish, northern pike, smallmouth bass, and walleye. At Keyhole you'll also find places to swim, hike, bird-watch, and camp, as well as snowmobiling trails in wintertime.

See also Deaver Reservoir and Newton Lakes under *Fishing;* Buffalo Bill State Park under *Wilder Places—Parks;* and Bighorn Canyon National Recreation Area under *Wilder Places—Other Wild Places.*

CAMPING ♿ **Bighorn National Forest** (see *Wilder Places—Forests*) has more than 60 developed campgrounds, some handicapped accessible, mainly located along the Cloud Peak Skyway Scenic Byway, the Bighorn Scenic Byway, and the Medicine Wheel Passage Scenic Byway (see *To See—Scenic Drives*). These campgrounds are operated by a private concessionaire, and they charge fees ($10–15) from mid-May to mid-September. Some accept **reservations** (1-877-444-6777; www.reserveusa.com), though many are first-come, first-served. For more details on campgrounds in specific areas, contact the **Tongue Ranger District** (307-674-2600), the **Medicine Wheel–Paintrock District** (in Lovell: 307-548-6541; in Greybull: 307-765-4436), or the **Powder River District** (in Buffalo: 307-684-7806; in Worland: 307-347-5105). In addition to the developed campgrounds, dispersed camping (free) is permitted throughout much of the forest.

♿ **Black Hills National Forest** (see *Wilder Places—Forests*), near Sundance off I-90. Though most of Black Hills National Forest lies within South Dakota, a portion of this forest lies in Wyoming, including four developed campgrounds— **Bearlodge** ($5), **Cook Lake** (handicapped accessible; $11–15), **Sundance** (handicapped accessible; $15), and **Reuter** ($10). All four campgrounds are located north of Sundance. Reservations are accepted at Sundance, Cook Lake, and Reuter in-season (about May through September). Sundance is closed in winter. (See also Cook Lake Trail under *Hiking*.)

♿ **BLM campgrounds** (see Bureau of Land Management under *Wilder Places—Other Wild Places*) in this region include two first-come, first-served campgrounds managed by the **Cody Field Office:** the 19-site **Five Springs Falls Campground** (handicapped accessible; open year-round; $7), located 22 miles east of Lovell on US 14 Alternate (access road not recommended for recreational vehicles of more than 25 feet in length), and the five-site **Hogan and Luce Campground** (open May 1 through December 14; free), located 18 miles north of Cody off WY 120, then 5 miles west on C.R. 7RP. The **Buffalo Field Office** has two notable areas where camping is permitted: at **Weston Hills Recreation Area,** 25 miles north of Gillette via WY 59, a jointly managed (BLM and Forest Service) recreation area offering free, primitive camping opportunities as well as 7 miles of multiuse roads and trails; and the **Middle Fork of the Powder River Recreation Area** (see *Fishing*). On the lands managed by the **Newcastle Field Office** and the **Worland Field Office,** you'll find numerous opportunities for free, undeveloped camping with limited services as well. You should also know that in general, access to campgrounds is limited to the summer season and that primitive camping is permitted on most BLM lands unless otherwise marked. For a complete list of BLM campgrounds in the area, call or stop by one of the field offices. (See also Castle Gardens Scenic Area under *To See—Natural Wonders;* Middle Fork of the Powder River Campground–Recreation Area under *Fishing;* and Five Springs Falls Trail under *Hiking*.)

♿ **Shoshone National Forest** (see *Wilder Places—Forests*) has three ranger districts in this region, with more than 20 developed campgrounds. The **Clarks**

VIEW OF BUFFALO BILL RESERVOIR FROM THE DAM AT BUFFALO BILL DAM VISITOR CENTER IN CODY

Fork Ranger District (307-527-6921) has nine first-come, first-served campgrounds near Cody (along US 212 and WY 296), with daily fees ranging from free to $10. The **Wapiti Ranger District** (307-527-6921) has nine first-come, first-served campgrounds (four handicapped accessible) near Cody (along US 14/16/20), with daily fees ranging from free to $15. The **Greybull Ranger District** (307-527-6921) has three first-come, first-served campgrounds west of Meeteetse of WY 120, all of which are free of charge. Camping season (when services like water and trash pickup are available) generally opens on Memorial Day weekend and runs through the end of September, though camping is permitted in some campgrounds during the off-season. In addition to the developed campgrounds, dispersed camping (free) is permitted throughout much of the forest.

See also Connor Battlefield State Park and Historic Site, and Medicine Lodge State Archaeological Site, under *To See—Historic Landmarks, Places, and Sites;* Devils Tower National Monument under *To See—Natural Wonders;* Keyhole State Park under *Boating;* Deaver Reservoir and Middle Fork of the Powder River Campground under *Fishing;* Float Trips by Eagle RV Park and Campground under *Unique Adventures;* Buffalo Bill State Park under *Wilder Places— Parks;* and Bighorn Canyon National Recreation Area and Thunder Basin National Grassland under *Wilder Places—Other Wild Places.*

FISHING **The Belle Fourche River** (307-672-7418; http://gf.state.wy.us/fish/ fishing/index.asp) flows from south of Gillette near WY 59 north to Keyhole Reservoir, along WY 24 between Moorcroft and Hulett, and then northeast to US 212 before arcing southeast into South Dakota. This river and its many creeks and streams offer the opportunity to catch black bullhead, channel catfish, smallmouth bass, and sunfish. The river can be easily accessed by anglers from within Devils Tower National Monument (see *To See—Natural Wonders*) and just above Keyhole Reservoir (see *Boating*), among other access points.

The Bighorn River (307-332-7723; http://gf.state.wy.us/fish/fishing/index.asp) begins at the Wedding of the Waters area (a fishing access point), where the Wind River exits the Wind River Canyon just south of Thermopolis and changes names to the Bighorn River. From there, it flows north along US 20/WY 789 to Greybull, where it continues north to empty into Bighorn Lake, in the Bighorn Canyon National Recreation Area (see *Wilder Places—Other Wild Places*). Species include brown trout, channel catfish, cutthroat trout, rainbow trout, sauger, and walleye. Numerous signed access points can be found all along US 20/WY 789 from the Wedding of the Waters to Greybull.

The Clarks Fork of the Yellowstone River (307-527-7125; http://gf.state.wy .us/fish/fishing/index.asp), located northwest of Cody along WY 120, WY 296, and US 212 in Shoshone National Forest (see *Wilder Places—Forests*). This river is known for its rainbow trout, mountain whitefish, brook trout, Yellowstone River and Snake River cutthroat trout, grayling, brown trout, and some rainbow-cutthroat trout hybrids. The 22.5-mile portion of the river that is nationally designated as Wild and Scenic (Wyoming's only such river) runs through the awe-inspiring Clarks Fork Canyon, with its dramatic, upsweeping cliffs rising more than 1,000 feet above the canyon floor. Wildlife species abound here, including moose, mountain goats, marmots, and more. (See also the Shoshone River under *Paddling/Floating.*)

Deaver Reservoir (307-261-5671), 3 miles northwest of Deaver off WY 114. Open for fishing year-round; no entrance fee. This 800-acre reservoir's fish species include catfish, trout, and walleye. The area also has picnic tables, boating (10 horsepower or less), and wildlife viewing opportunities and permits primitive camping (but no drinking water is available).

Lake DeSmet (307-672-7418; http://gf.state.wy.us/fish/fishing/index.asp), north of Buffalo off I-90 via Exits 44, 47, 51, 53, and 56a. This lake takes its name from Father DeSmet, a Belgian priest who came to Wyoming in 1840 as a missionary to the Flathead Indians. The Indians believed Lake DeSmet to be bottomless, and thus it served as the origin of many of their religious and superstitious beliefs. A monument memorializing Father DeSmet stands near the shores of the lake today. Anglers know Lake DeSmet better as a prime, year-round fishing destination (ice fishing is popular in winter), with species including brown trout, rainbow trout, rock bass, crappie, and yellow perch. (See also Lake DeSmet Fishing Derby under *Special Events.*)

The Middle Fork of the Powder River Campground–Recreation Area, accessible by taking WY 190 southwest from Kaycee for about 15 miles and then going south on the BLM Bar C road for roughly 5 miles; or, from just west of Ten Sleep on US 16, go south on WY 434 (see *To See—Scenic Drives*) for 20 miles. At Big Trails, head east on Dry Farm Road for 13 miles to Hazelton Road then go south and then west on this road for about 17 miles. Situated at 7,500 feet, the campground (open May through September; free) features restrooms, drinking water, and campfire rings. A pristine blue-ribbon trout stream (with numerous additional surrounding trout streams) is the standout attraction of this BLM-managed area (see also *Wilder Places—Other Wild Places*), which draws anglers by the hundreds annually.

&. **Newton Lakes** (307-527-7125; http://gf.state.wy.us/fish/fishing/index.asp), 5 miles northwest of Cody off WY 120. Open for fishing year-round; no entrance fee. Known for its trophy trout fishing accessible via both boat and shoreline, this area also features picnicking, swimming, wildlife viewing, and tube-floating. No drinking water is available, and no overnight camping is permitted.

The Powder River (307-672-7418; http://gf.state.wy.us/fish/fishing/index.asp) flows along WY 192 west of Kaycee and north along Upper Powder River Road into Montana. Powder River and its many creeks, streams, and forks offer tremendous trout fishing opportunities. Species include brown trout and rainbow trout. (See also Middle Fork of the Powder River Campground–Recreation Area, above.)

The Shoshone River (307-527-7125; http://gf.state.wy.us/fish/fishing/index.asp). The **North Fork** of this river flows from Yellowstone Lake in Yellowstone National Park east along US 14/16/20 west of Cody in Shoshone National Forest (see *Wilder Places—Forests*) to the Buffalo Bill Reservoir (see *Wilder Places—Parks*), eventually merging with the Bighorn River in Bighorn Lake (see Bighorn

Canyon National Recreation Area under *Wilder Places—Other Wild Places*). The river is closed to fishing from Buffalo Bill Reservoir up to and including Newton Creek from April 1 to July 1 in order to protect spawning runs of rainbow trout and Yellowstone cutthroat trout. Species include brook trout, brown trout, mountain whitefish, rainbow trout, rainbow-cutthroat hybrids, and Yellowstone cutthroat trout. The **South Fork** starts high in the Absaroka Mountains in Shoshone National Forest (see *Wilder Places—Forests*), then flows along WY 291 southwest of Cody to Buffalo Bill Reservoir. Species include brook trout, brown trout, rainbow trout, mountain whitefish, and Yellowstone cutthroat trout. Many access sites lie along the roads paralleling both forks of this river. (See also the Shoshone River under *Paddling/Floating.*)

The Tongue River (307-672-7418; http://gf.state.wy.us/fish/fishing/index.asp), in Bighorn National Forest (see *Wilder Places—Forests*), is accessed just east of Dayton via US 14, then CR 92 west (River Road to Tongue Canyon Road); the road ends in the parking lot where the trailhead departs. Take the trail from the west end of the parking lot to gain access to the river, which flows from high in the Bighorn Mountains northeast into Montana, eventually joining the Yellowstone River. The Tongue River and its many side streams and creeks present fabulous fishing prospects, with species including brook trout, brown trout, and rainbow trout. (See also Connor Battlefield State Park and Historic Site under *To See—Historic Landmarks, Places, and Sites* and Tongue River Cave under *To See—Natural Wonders.*)

Wind River Canyon (307-332-7207), on US 20, 4 miles south of Thermopolis. Located on the Wind River Indian Reservation, this easily accessed canyon and its surrounding environs are home to some of the finest brown and rainbow trout fishing in the state. A special permit is required to fish here; contact the **Wind River Reservation Fish and Game Department** at the above number for details. Another option is to contact the **Wind River Visitors Council** (1-800-645-6233; 307-856-7566; www.wind-river.org), which can advise you of local stores that sell licenses and provide you with an information packet that includes lists of guiding services and outfitters. (See also *To See—Natural Wonders;* Wind River Canyon Whitewater under *To Do—Paddling/Floating;* and the Wind River under *To Do—Fishing* in "Central Wyoming: Oregon Trail–Rendezvous Country.")

See also Medicine Lodge State Archaeological Site under *To See—Historic Landmarks, Places, and Sites;* Keyhole State Park under *Boating;* Cook Lake Trail under *Hiking;* multiple listings under *Horseback Riding;* Buffalo Bill State Park under *Wilder Places—Parks; Wilder Places—Forests;* Bighorn Canyon National Recreation Area, Bureau of Land Management, and Thunder Basin National Grassland under *Wilder Places—Other Wild Places;* and Absaroka Mountain Lodge, the Hideout and the Snowshoe Lodge at Flitner Ranch, Pahaska Tepee, and Shoshone Lodge under *Lodging—Lodges.*

GOLF **Bell Knob Golf Course** (307-686-7069), 4600 Overdale Drive, Gillette, 18 holes.

Buffalo Golf Club (307-684-5266), 2500 W. Hart, Buffalo, 18 holes.

Devils Tower Golf Club (307-467-5773), 75 Tower View Drive, Hulett, 9 holes.

Foster Gulch Golf Club (307-548-2445) 925 Lane 13, Lovell, 9 holes.

Gillette Golf Club (307-682-4774), 1800 Country Club Drive, Gillette, 9 holes.

Green Hills Municipal Golf Course (307-347-8972), 1455 Airport Road, Worland, 18 holes.

Haycreek Golf Club (307-464-0747), 1229 E. Elkhorn Drive, Wright, 9 holes.

Horseshoe Mountain Golf Club (307-655-9525), US 14, Dayton, 9 holes.

Kendrick Municipal Golf Course (307-674-8148; www.city-sheridan-wy.com/golf/golf.html), Big Goose Road, Sheridan, 18 holes.

Keyhole Golf Club (307-756-3775; www.pine-haven-wy.net/kcc), Pine Haven (off I-90 north of Moorcroft via US 14 to WY 113), 9 holes.

Legion Town & Country Golf Course (307-864-5294; www.thermopolis.com/golf.html), 141 Airport Road, Thermopolis, 9 holes.

Midway Golf Club (307-568-2255), 4053 Golf Course Road, Basin, 9 holes.

Newcastle Country Club (307-746-2639), 2302 W. Main Street, Newcastle, 9 holes.

Olive Glenn Golf & Country Club (307-587-5551; www.oliveglenngolf.com), 802 Meadow Lane, Cody, 18 holes.

Powder Horn Ranch and Golf Club (1-800-329-0598; 307-674-9545; www.thepowderhorn.com), 161 WY 335, Sheridan, 27 holes.

Powell Golf Club (307-754-7259; www.powellchamber.org/recreation.htm#Golf), 600 WY 114, Powell, 18 holes.

Sheridan Country Club (307-674-8135), 1992 W. 5th Street, Sheridan, 9 holes.

Sundance Golf Club (307-283-1191), US 14, Sundance, 9 holes.

HIKING **Beartooth Loop National Recreation Trail** (#619), in Shoshone National Forest (see *Wilder Places—Forests*), can be accessed via three trailheads—Hauser Lake Trailhead, Gardner Lake Trailhead, and Dollar Lake Trailhead (accessible via four-wheel-drive or ATV only)—all of which are just off US 212 (Beartooth Scenic Byway; see *To See—Scenic Drives*) northwest of Cody. Even hiking just a short portion of this 14.4-mile trail will bring you a little bit closer to the beautiful scenery of the rugged Beartooth Mountains. With little elevation change, this trail makes for relatively easy walking, allowing you to really enjoy the fresh mountain air and views of the surrounding mountains. Motorized vehicles, horses, and mountain bikes are also permitted on much of this trail.

Bucking Mule Falls National Recreation Trail (#53), in Bighorn National Forest (see *Wilder Places—Forests*), can be accessed via US 14 Alternate east of Lovell (Medicine Wheel Passage Scenic Byway; see *To See—Scenic Drives*). Take F.H. 11 north 3.5 miles to F.R.14. Go west on F.R. 14 for 7 miles to the parking lot at the end of the gravel road. Best to hike in July and August due to its high elevation, this 3-mile moderate out-and-back trail takes you to view the tumbling 550-foot Bucking Mule Falls. More adventurous sorts can plan to explore more of the trail, which totals about 12 miles in length. Horseback riding and mountain biking are also allowed on this trail.

Cook Lake Trail, in Black Hills National Forest (see *Camping* and *Wilder Places—Forests*), is accessible by taking Exit 165 off I-90 near Sundance and then going west about a mile before turning north (right) onto F.R. 838. Proceed north for about 7 miles before turning east (right) on F.R. 843 for about 1.7 miles, continuing on it for another 3 miles or so after it turns left. Make a left onto F.R. 842 and proceed 1 mile to find the trailhead at the campground. Day-use fee of $3 charged from May to September. This easy 1-mile trail takes you around the Cook Lake Recreation Area, a lovely, serene place great for fishing, wildlife viewing, mountain biking, and camping.

Five Springs Falls Trail involves a short, easy (less than 1 mile) nature trail that departs from the parking area at Five Springs Falls Campground (see BLM campgrounds under *Camping*). As your vehicle climbs the hill up to the camp-ground, the scenery changes from arid desert to a lush, green canyon filled with trees and plant life. In addition to the falls tumbling down a narrow, granite canyon, scenic attractions include sweeping views of the surrounding mountain ranges—the Bighorns, Pryors, and Absarokas—as well as the opportunity to view wildlife, including mule deer and elk.

Gooseberry Badlands Scenic Overlook and Interpretive Trail, located on BLM lands 23 miles west of US 20 (south of Worland) on WY 431 (see also Bureau of Land Management under *Wilder Places—Other Wild Places*). The startling scenery encountered at this area—a collection of oddly sculpted rock formations, including arches, spires, and mushrooms, together with soil that changes colors with the seasons—makes for an intriguing place to learn some-thing while you get exercise hiking the 1.5-mile interpretive trail.

High Point Lookout, in Bighorn National Forest (see *Wilder Places—Forests*), is east of Ten Sleep just off US 16 (Cloud Peak Skyway Scenic Byway; see *To See—Scenic Drives*) before Powder River Pass (look for signs). A hike to the High Point Lookout offers a spectacular panoramic view of the Bighorn Moun-tains. After leaving your vehicle at the parking area, follow a well-marked, mod-erately steep trail as it winds through a heavy evergreen forest and gorgeous dolomite boulders. A 15-minute hike brings you to the tower, which was once staffed all summer long by an individual or couple hired by the National Forest Service to watch for fires. This is a great, remote spot for picnics and views, though the cliffs nearby mean that small children should be watched closely. Also stop at **Saint Christopher's in the Bighorn Chapel for Travelers.** Located on the same road as the High Point Lookout Tower, this rustic, humble outdoor chapel lies about 0.25 mile off the highway. Episcopalian services are held on Sunday during the summer; check the sign on US 16 for details.

Hole-in-the-Wall Trail, on BLM-managed lands, is accessible by taking Exit 249 (TTT Road) off I-25 south of Kaycee and then proceeding about 14 miles south on TTT Road to F.R. 111 (Willow Creek). Take this road about 18 miles west to a junction with C.R. 105 (Buffalo Creek Road), a rough two-track road heading north that is suitable only for high-clearance vehicles during dry conditions. This road dead-ends at the trailhead (be sure to close livestock gates behind you as necessary). If you're a western history buff in decent physical shape, this long drive in to the trailhead is worth your while. Hike to one of the most-beloved hangouts of some of the most famous outlaws of the Old West—Butch Cassidy and the Wild Bunch Gang. Local lore has it that, back in the 1800s, the Wild Bunch Gang clandestinely moved horses and cattle through a notch in the Red Wall—the hole that you will see after a rugged 2.5-mile hike. No services are available, so come prepared with food, water, and proper attire. Please stay on the trail, as the land surrounding it is private.

Penrose Trail, in Bighorn National Forest (see *Wilder Places—Forests*), is accessed from the town of Story, which lies on WY 193 north of Exit 44 off I-25. In Story, take Fish Hatchery Road to the parking area on Penrose Lane. This trail leads you up into the foothills and then the mountains behind Story, ultimately depositing the serious hiker at the boundary of Cloud Peak Wilderness. You'll wind your way up through the wildflowers in the foothills into more forested terrain, where ponderosa pines give way to Douglas firs and lodgepole pines, followed by alpine meadows with granite outcrops. Stunning, sweeping views of the badlands stretch away as far as the eye can see from various vantage points on the way. This is a multiuse trail, so don't be surprised if an ATV comes barreling by.

Salt Lick Trail is located at the mouth of Ten Sleep Canyon (see *To See—Natural Wonders*) on the north side of US 16 on Bureau of Land Management land (see *Wilder Places—Other Wild Places*). This short, steep, out-and-back trail is less than 2 miles in length—but it will get your heart pumping, so take your time and enjoy the views. Park by the large black sandstone boulder and begin your journey up a trail that leads you beneath imposing, varicolored sandstone boulders that rise some 200 feet above the trail. The trail ends abruptly at a crude rock barrier, where you can turn for a stunning view of the canyon below (if you haven't already taken a peek).

Tower Trail, located at Devils Tower National Monument (see *To See—Natural Wonders*), offers a 1.3-mile paved excursion that takes you up closer to the tower for better views, enabling you to watch rock climbers should they happen to be present. With numerous interpretive signs along the way, this trail takes you through variable environments, including stands of ponderosa pine, the edges of fields, and jumbles of boulders. Benches along the way provide areas to stop and take a breather or to simply soak in the magic of this one-of-a-kind natural feature.

Trout Creek Nature Trail is located in Buffalo Bill State Park (see *Wilder Places—Parks*) near the group camping area of the North Shore Campground. Take a 0.25-mile stroll through a riparian area located on the west side of Trout Creek along the Shoshone River, observing the unique features characteristic of this type of habitat. Also at Buffalo Bill State Park, you'll find **Eagle Point Trail** (handicapped accessible), a short and easy jaunt located within the Eagle Point Day Use Area.

See also Fort Phil Kearny State Historic Site, Medicine Lodge State Archaeological Site, and Medicine Wheel National Historic Landmark under *To See—Historic Landmarks, Places, and Sites;* Bighorn Scenic Byway under *To See—Scenic Drives;* Castle Gardens Scenic Area, Shell Canyon and Falls, and Tongue River Cave under *To See—Natural Wonders;* Clear Creek Walking Trail and Paul Stock Nature Trail under *Bicycling;* Keyhole State Park under *Boating;* BLM campgrounds under *Camping;* Hot Springs State Park under *Hot Springs;* *Cross-Country Skiing and Snowshoeing* under *Snow Sports;* Wayfaring Traveler Llama Ranch under *Unique Adventures;* Bighorn National Forest and Black Hills National Forest under *Wilder Places—Forests;* Dry Creek Petrified Tree Environmental Education Area and Duck Swamp Interpretive Area under *Wilder Places—Wildlife Refuges and Areas;* and Bighorn Canyon National Recreation Area, Bureau of Land Management, and Thunder Basin National Grassland under *Wilder Places—Other Wild Places.*

HORSEBACK RIDING **Cedar Mountain Trail Rides** (307-527-4966; 307-587-7313), 39 Wall Street, Cody. You can choose from a ride as short as an hour or go for a day—or longer. Specialties include guided fishing and wildlife viewing forays. Call for current rates and to make reservations.

✔ **Ishawooa Outfitters** (307-587-9250; 1-888-801-9250; www.ishawooaout fitters.com), 2 Lone Tree Lane, Cody. An expert hunting outfitter, Ishawooa Outfitters also offers wild horse–viewing rides that take you into the Bureau of Land Management (BLM) lands (see *Wilder Places—Other Wild Places*) outside Cody for your choice of half a day ($50 per person) or all day ($95; lunch included). For families and other travelers who wish they'd planned a multiday pack trip ahead of time but didn't, Ishawooa can usually accommodate last-minute requests for overnight pack trips, departing on the following morning ($295 per person per day; 2-day minimum). Ishawooa also guides fishing trips. (See also McCullough Peaks Herd Management Area under *Wilder Places—Wildlife Refuges and Areas.*)

Little Piney Ranch (307-683-2668; www.littlepineyranch.com), 430 Wagon Box Road, Banner (near Story). This ranch has both an indoor arena and access to numerous outdoor trails, offering horseback riding lessons to novices as well as experienced riders. Your first hour-long lesson is free ($40 per hour thereafter). You can also choose to book a 2-hour trail ride ($48) or a half-day trail ride ($80), as well as longer rides.

♿ **McFadden Ranch** (307-765-9684; www.mcfaddenranch.com), 4 miles north of Greybull; call for precise directions. Not only does this ranch offer single-hour horseback riding lessons ($30), but it also offers the Body & Spirit Therapeutic Riding and Hippotherapy Program, a 2-month program designed to help with individuals' rehabilitative needs via working with well-trained horses, a riding instructor, an occupational therapist, a physical therapist, and numerous volunteers (for details, dates, and rates, contact the ranch).

South Fork Mountain Lodge & Outfitters (307-267-2609; 307-684-1225; www.southfork-lodge.com), US 16, Buffalo. Mountain trail rides depart from the lodge, situated next to Clear Creek in the Bighorn Mountains above Buffalo.

Choose from 2-hour ($48), half-day ($80), or full-day ($125, includes lunch) trail rides led by experienced guides. Overnight pack trips and fishing trips are also offered by this full-service outfitter. The lodge's dining room serves three meals a day. You can purchase activities and meals à la carte or just rent a rustic cabin on the ranch grounds ($99 per night).

❧ **Trails West Outfitters** (1-888-283-9793; www.trailswestoutfitters.com), in Bighorn National Forest, near Buffalo. Call in advance for reservations and rates. Family pack trips are one of the specialties offered by this outfitter. Each family member rides a gentle horse along trails through the Bighorn Mountains, enjoying fantastic scenery and wildlife viewing opportunities while learning about the ins and outs of trail riding in the process. Guided fishing trips are available as well ($190 per person per day).

See also Beartooth Loop National Recreation Trail, Bucking Mule Falls National Recreation Trail, and Penrose Trail under *Hiking; Cross-Country Skiing and Snowshoeing* under *Snow Sports;* Bob King's Cowboy School, Double Rafter Cattle Drives, ranch vacations, and Renegade Rides under *Unique Adventures; Wilder Places—Forests;* Bureau of Land Management under *Wilder Places— Other Wild Places;* and Absaroka Mountain Lodge, the Hideout and the Snow-shoe Lodge at Flitner Ranch, Pahaska Tepee, and Shoshone Lodge under *Lodging—Lodges.*

HOT SPRINGS & ❧ 🐾 **Hot Springs State Park** (307-864-2176; http://wyoparks .state.wy.us/hot1.htm), 220 Park Street, Thermopolis. Wyoming's unique State Bath House (open Monday through Saturday 8 AM–5:30 PM, Sunday and holidays noon–5:30 PM; free) allows you to soak in the 102°F mineral waters for 20 minutes at a time, indoors or outside. Just sign in at the desk and get a locker key from the attendant. Following a soak, showers are available free of charge as well. Also available nearby are several facilities that charge for the use of the mineral waters due to their steam rooms, waterslides, and other services. Stroll along the Terrace Walk after soaking and read about the source of the healing waters—Big Spring—which bubbles out of the ground at a steaming-hot 135°F. You'll also learn about the human history of the waters, as Indians knew of them and their healing properties long before the State Bath House came into being. This park is also home to the **Hot Springs State Bison Herd,** the state's central herd, with more than 20 animals at present. The bison can usually be viewed roaming within the boundaries of their pasture in the park (please stay in your car while viewing, since bison are wild animals and can be dangerous). Picnic tables, shade trees, and three playgrounds are available at the park, but no overnight camping is allowed. (See also Legend Rock State Petroglyph Site under *To See—Historic Landmarks, Places, and Sites.*)

PADDLING/FLOATING ❧ & **The Shoshone River** (see also *Fishing*), outside Cody, offers some of the finest and most tapped-into white water in the state of Wyoming. Cody has several guiding services that can help the less-experienced paddler plan a safe and fun family adventure on the river. These include **Red Canyon River Trips** (1-800-293-0148; 307-587-6988; www.comp-unltd.com/

~rodeo/raft.html), 1220 Sheridan Avenue, offering a **Clark's Fork of the Yellowstone** (see *Fishing*) adventure as well ($20–55 per person, depending on trip selected; group and family rates available); **River Runners** (1-800-535-7238; www.riverrunnersofwyoming.com), 1491 Sheridan Avenue ($22–60 per person, depending on trip selected; group and family rates available); and **Wyoming River Trips** (1-800-586-6661; 307-587-6661; www.wyomingrivertrips.com), Buffalo Bill Village–Holiday Inn Complex and 233 US 14/16/20 (by Wal-Mart), offering handicapped-accessible trips as well ($22–60 per person, depending on trip selected; group and family rates available).

✓ **Wind River Canyon Whitewater** (1-888-246-9343; 307-864-9343; www.windrivercanyonraft.com), 210 US 20, Suite 5, Thermopolis. This is the only outfitter permitted to guide rafters through the Wind River Canyon. Paddle exciting white water and potentially view wildlife for half a day ($35–$38 per person, depending on trip choice) or a whole day ($75, lunch included). Also available is a scenic float trip, with no white water ($25). Reservations are recommended. Children are permitted, but the age limit depends on the water level, so call in advance. Also available through this outfitter are guided fishing trips in Wind River Canyon; call for details (see also Wind River Canyon under *Fishing*).

See also Newton Lakes under *Fishing* and Float Trips by Eagle RV Park and Campground under *Unique Adventures*.

SNOW SPORTS

Cross-Country Skiing and Snowshoeing

Opportunities to cross-country ski or snowshoe are plentiful throughout this region in wintertime. In addition to many miles of ungroomed trails, you'll find numerous groomed and marked trails. These include **Carson Draw Cross-Country Ski Area,** located in Black Hills National Forest (see also *Wilder Places—Forests*) on F.R. 838, 3 miles north of US 14 outside Sundance. This 6-mile trail system is a great cross-country skiing destination; the trail is groomed weekly as snow permits from December 15 to March 30. The rest of the year it's a great place for hiking, mountain biking, and horseback riding. Another fun spot is the **Wood River Valley Ski Touring Park** (307-868-2603; www.meetrec.org/wrski/wrski.html), 22 miles southwest of Meeteetse in Shoshone National Forest (see *Wilder Places—Forests*), with roughly 15 miles of groomed and backcountry trails open October through April. (See also *Hiking;* **Sleeping Giant Ski Area** under *Downhill Skiing;* Bureau of Land Management under *Wilder Places—Other Wild Places;* and Pahaska Tepee under *Lodging—Lodges.*)

Downhill Skiing

✓ **Antelope Butte Ski Area** (307-655-9530; www.skiantelopebutte.com), on US 14 midway between Shell and Dayton in Bighorn National Forest (see *Wilder Places—Forests*). This remote downhill ski area, located in the heart of the Bighorns, is sure to make for a fun winter playground for the entire family. *Lifts:* two double lifts, one Mighty Mite. *Trails:* 24 trails—20 percent beginner, 50 percent intermediate, 30 percent advanced. *Vertical drop:* 1,000 feet. *Facilities:*

heated lodge with snack bar and pizzeria. *Ski school:* PSIA-certified ski school offers ski and snowboard lessons for all ages and abilities. Call for rates and current information; this ski area did not open for 2004–5 season.

⚓ **Big Horn Ski Resort** (1-888-244-4676; www.thebighorn.com/bhskiresort/bhskiresort.htm), on US 16 (Cloud Peak Skyway Scenic Byway; see *To See—Scenic Drives*) east of Ten Sleep before Powder River Pass in Bighorn National Forest (see *Wilder Places—Forests*). Deep powder and one of the best terrain parks in the state make the Big Horn Ski Resort a must-visit winter destination for the downhill enthusiast. The resort also rents snowmobiles (see *Snowmobiling*, below). *Lifts:* one double chairlift, one triple chairlift, one handle-tow. *Trails:* 14 trails—30 percent beginner, 40 percent intermediate, 30 percent expert. *Vertical drop:* 800 feet. *Snowmaking:* yes. *Facilities:* full-service dining lodge. *Ski school:* available for all ages and ability levels of skiers and snowboarders. *Rates:* $36 adults, $29 students (13 and older with student ID), $18 children 7–12, children 6 and under free; half-day rates also available.

Sleeping Giant Ski Area (307-587-4044), located 48 miles west of Cody on US 14/16/20. One of America's oldest ski resorts, Sleeping Giant has been around since 1936–37. Standout attractions include ample natural snowfall, great temperatures, and little wind. Snowboards permitted on all trails. *Lifts:* one double chairlift, one rope tow. *Trails:* 17 trails—20 percent beginner, 60 percent intermediate, 20 percent advanced. *Vertical drop:* 500 feet. *Facilities:* a heated day lodge with a snack bar. *Ski school:* offers lessons for all ages and ability levels. **Cross-country skiing available as well.** Call for rates and current information; this ski area did not open for 2004–5 season. (See also Pahaska Tepee under *Lodging—Lodges*.)

Ice Climbing

Ice-climbing opportunities of the finest caliber begin in Cody as early as October and last as late as April. Hundreds of waterfalls in the South Fork Canyon of the Shoshone River (see *Fishing*) freeze up and form climbs, so if ascending frozen waterfalls is one of your favorite pastimes, Cody will not disappoint. For more information about ice climbing, as well as about current conditions (in-season), stop by Cody's latest and greatest addition to its outdoor-oriented businesses: **Core Mountain Sports** (1-877-527-7354; www.coldfear.com) on 15th Street just north of Sheridan Avenue. You can also visit www.codyice.com, or call **Sunlight Sports** (307-587-9517) or the climbers' hostel, **Bison Willy's Basecamp** (307-587-0629), both in Cody. (See also Waterfall Ice Roundup under *Special Events*.)

Ice Fishing

Ice fishing is a popular sport on many of this region's frozen lakes and ponds come wintertime. For ideas about where to go, see listings under *Boating* and *Fishing*.

Ice-Skating

Ice-skating opportunities can be found throughout this region, particularly in wintertime. In Cody, go to the **Victor J. Riley Public Arena** (307-587-1681; www.codyicearena.com), 1400 Heart Mountain Street ($3.50 per person, $1.50

for skate rentals); call for hours and season. In Sheridan, head for the **Whitney**
Community Ice Rink (307-674-9423; www.sheridanice.org), 475 E. Brundage
Street; call for current rates, hours, and season.

Snowmobiling

Snowmobiling is popular in this region, with incredible trail systems located
throughout its three national forests (see *Wilder Places—Forests*). Another plus
is the close proximity of the snowmobiling trails in Yellowstone National Park
(see *Snowmobiling* under *Winter Sports* in "Yellowstone National Park"). You'll
find numerous places to access the nearly 400 miles of trails that make up the
Bighorn Mountain–North-Central Wyoming trail system (almost 350 of which
are groomed snowmobile trails) along the scenic drives through the Big Horn
Mountains (see *To See—Scenic Drives* and Bighorn National Forest under
Wilder Places—Forests). Snowmobile rentals are available at the **Big Horn Ski
Resort** (see *Downhill Skiing*, above), among other places. You can also plan a
full-scale snowmobiling vacation with **the Hideout and the Snowshoe Lodge
at Flitner Ranch** or **Pahaska Tepee** (see *Lodging—Lodges*). In the northeastern portion of the state, you can snowmobile on the **Sundance Snowmobile
Trail,** accessible from Reuter Campground in Black Hills National Forest (see
Camping and *Wilder Places—Forests*). Take I-90 to Exit 185, go north 1 mile on
US 14, then north on F.R. 838 for 2 miles to the campground. You'll find 62
miles of groomed trails (weekly grooming as snow permits) open for snowmobiling December 15 through March 30. For detailed trail reports, call 1-800-225-
5996 or go to http://wyotrails.state.wy.us/snow, the **Wyoming Snowmobile
Trails** Web site, which provides information about rules, rental agencies, trails
around the state, and more as well. (See also Bearlodge Trail under *Bicycling;*
Keyhole State Park under *Boating;* and Bureau of Land Management under
Wilder Places—Other Wild Places.)

UNIQUE ADVENTURES **Bob King's Cowboy School** (1-866-771-7358; 307-
736-2236; www.cowboyschool.net), Arvada (on US 14/16 between Buffalo and
Gillette), reservations required. So you want to learn to be a cowboy—really?
Then saddle up for a 5-day adventure packed with learning the ropes, customized
to your preferences. You'll ride a horse chosen according to your ability level and
enjoy days of hands-on instruction. Meals and comfortable accommodations are
included ($1,525 per 5-day course, $5,000 for month-long course).

Buffalo Bill Historical Center & Cody Trolley Tours (307-587-4771; www
.bbhc.org/tours/trolleytours_01.cfm), 720 Sheridan Avenue, Cody. $25 adults and
seniors, $10 children 6–17; price includes admission to the center. Spice up your
visit to the Buffalo Bill Historical Center (see *To See—Museums*) with this interpretive 1-hour, 24-mile trolley tour that spotlights historical sites, geological sites,
wildlife, and more, complete with hands-on objects of interest and two live nar-
rators.

Dinosaur Safaris, Inc. (1-800-367-7457; www.dinosaursafaries.com), Shell. Dig
season is usually July and August; reservations required; $100 per day for adults,
$50 children ages 16–18, children 10–15 free, no children under 10 permitted
unless by special permission. Dig with experts for a day—or a few days—for

dinosaur bones and other fossils on this private, active dig site. Dinosaur Safaris provides you with the proper tools and training, educates you about the types of dinosaur fossils you'll likely encounter, teaches you about casting fossils you unearth (so that you can take away a permanent reminder of your findings), and provides you with lunch and transportation to and from the dig site. (See also the Wyoming Dinosaur Center and Dig Sites under *To See—For Families.*)

✎ **Double Rafter Cattle Drives** (1-800-704-9268; 307-655-9539; www .doublerafter.com), Ranchester. June through September; $995–1,935 adults (depending on the trip), $595 children (children permitted only on Cow Camp Trip); reservations required. For a real western living experience, sign up for a 6-day adventure at the historic Double Rafter Ranch, the first ranch known to bring cattle to graze in Bighorn National Forest (see *Wilder Places—Forests*). Since 1895, the Double Rafter has been raising cattle for beef, and since 1989, it has been inviting vacationers in pursuit of a down 'n' dirty western adventure to join in on its 6-day, 6-night cattle drives. Don't expect this to be a relaxing, dude-ranch experience, though—you'll be working hard to earn your chuck wagon meals every day. The **Cow Camp Trips** (5 days, 4 nights) offer a slightly less breakneck pace that enables children to accompany parents on these adventures.

🐟 ✎ **Float Trips by Eagle RV Park and Campground** (1-888-865-5707; 307-864-5262; www.eaglervpark.com/river%20float%20trips.htm), 204 US 20, Thermopolis. $7 per tube rental for 2.5- to 3-hour float, includes transportation upriver to put-in point; $5 per tube for group of six or more; reservations recommended. Get downright intimate with the beautiful Bighorn River by seeing it close up as you float in your inner tube—a perfect way to while away a summer day and to grow a little closer to nature while you're at it. You can also grab a site at the campground (open year-round; $15 tent site; $21 RV site; $31 cabin). This privately owned RV park and campground allows easy access to attractions around Thermopolis and provides more than 100 large shade trees, a play-ground, and a pet walk area.

Ranch Vacations. These vacations usually allow you to participate to a certain extent in various aspects of ranch life, often including cattle herding and brand-ing. The ratio of work time to leisure time varies from ranch to ranch, as do the additional activities and amenities offered, but most ranches include horseback riding, lodging, and meals in an inclusive package deal. In this region, providers include, among others, **Klondike Ranch** (1-800-362-2982), Buffalo; **Paradise Guest Ranch** (307-684-7876), Buffalo; **the Ranch at Ucross** (1-800-447-0194; 307-737-2281), Clearmont; **Crossed Sabres Ranch** (307-587-3750), Cody; **Ranger Creek Guest Ranch** (1-888-817-7787; 307-272-5107), Greybull; **Dia-mond L Guest Ranch** (1-800-851-5909; 307-467-5236), Hulett; **Willow Creek Ranch at the Hole-in-the-Wall** (307-738-2294), Kaycee; **Kedesh Guest Ranch** (1-800-845-3320; 307-765-2791), Shell; **Spear-O-Wigwam Ranch** (1-888-818-3833), Sheridan; and **Little Piney Ranch** (307-683-2668), Story.

Renegade Rides (1-888-307-2689; 307-366-2689; www.renegaderides.com), 280 WY 434, P.O. Box 575, Ten Sleep 82442. Reservations required in advance; $1,595–1,795; children under 8 not permitted. For a horseback riding adventure above and beyond just your average western trail ride, Renegade Rides provides several options to make your Wyoming experience a memorable one. These include participating for a week in a real **cattle drive** at the Mahogany Butte Ranch, participating for a week in a **horse drive,** or going on a 100-mile-plus **weeklong ride.**

Wayfaring Traveler Llama Ranch (307-762-3536; www.tctwest.net/~wtr), 1100 Lane 38, Burlington (east of Cody just off US 14/16/20). For the simplest llama trekking experience, "renting" a llama (which comes with a prepared lunch for two) will run you $45 (for two people) for the day if you wish to hike to the top of nearby Table Mountain to take in the scenic Bighorn Basin below. The Wayfaring Traveler offers several more extensive **llama rentals and excursions,** a **guesthouse** available for rent, and additional adventure packages.

Wyoming Nature Tours (307-527-6306; www.wyomingnaturetours.com), Cody. For $300 a day (for one to two people, $75 for each additional participant), you can hire Wyoming Nature Tours to customize a private adventure to your liking, whether you're interested in learning more about petroglyphs, the Old West, Wyoming's wildlife, geology, or a variety of other subjects. Owned and operated by wildlife biologist Sean Sheehan, Wyoming Nature Tours provides the opportunity to dig deeper into topics that interest you. Tours are limited to a maximum of seven participants; tour rates include an interpreter, a guide, a driver, a vehicle, and use of binoculars, spotting scopes, and reference books. A healthy lunch and liquid refreshments are also included in the fee. Tours originate in Cody.

See also **Spahn's Big Horn Mountain Bed & Breakfast** under *Lodging—Bed & Breakfasts.*

✳ Wilder Places

PARKS ♿ **Buffalo Bill State Park** (307-587-9227; http://wyoparks.state.wy.us/buffalo1.htm), 47 Lakeside Road, Cody. Open year-round for day-use and camping; day-use $2 (residents), $4 (nonresidents); camping $6 (residents), $12 (nonresidents). Located about 9 miles west of Cody on US 14/16/20 (Yellowstone Highway), Buffalo Bill State Park provides visitors with an array of recreational opportunities including camping, hiking, fishing, windsurfing, boating (three boat ramps), wildlife viewing, scenic vistas, picnicking, and bicycling, to name a few. Surrounded by mountains and including Buffalo Bill Reservoir, with its 40 miles of shoreline, the park is an outdoor lover's paradise. The lake, with its 8,000 acres of surface area, contains brown trout, cutthroat trout, mackinaw trout, and rainbow trout, with easy access from roads along the shoreline. The park also has two **campgrounds**—North Shore Bay Campground, open year-round; and North Fork Campground, open April 1 through October 31. (See also Trout Creek Nature Trail under *To Do—Hiking.*)

See also Connor Battlefield State Park and Historic Site under *To See—Historic Landmarks, Places, and Sites;* Clear Creek Walking Trail under *To Do—Bicycling;* Keyhole State Park under *To Do—Boating;* and Hot Spring State Park under *To Do—Hot Springs.*

FORESTS Bighorn National Forest (307-548-6541; www.fs.fed.us/r2/bighorn/index.shtml), east of Greybull (US 14) and east of Worland (US 16). Notable in

EXPLORE WYOMING'S PETRIFIED PAST AT DRY CREEK PETRIFIED TREE ENVIRONMENTAL EDUCATION AREA

part for its incredible canyons (see *To See—Natural Wonders*), Bighorn National Forest encompasses 1,115,073 acres of land, including the 189,000-acre **Cloud Peak Wilderness Area.** It is also home to the headwaters of the **Bighorn River** (see *To Do—Fishing*), from which it got its name. This national forest provides an abundance of recreational opportunities, including boating, camping, fishing, hiking (on more than 1,500 miles of trails), horseback riding, bicycling, snowmobiling, wildlife viewing, and more. (See also Bighorn Scenic Byway, Cloud Peak Skyway Scenic Byway, Crazy Woman Canyon, and Medicine Wheel Passage Scenic Byway under *To See—Scenic Drives;* Shell Canyon and Falls, Ten Sleep Canyon, and Tongue River Cave under *To See—Natural Wonders; To Do—Camping;* the Tongue River under *To Do—Fishing;* Bucking Mule Falls National Recreation Trail, High Point Lookout, and Penrose Trail under *To Do—Hiking;* Antelope Butte Ski Area, Big Horn Ski Resort, *Cross-Country Skiing and Snowshoeing* and *Snowmobiling* under *To Do—Snow Sports;* and Double Rafter Cattle Drives under *To Do—Unique Adventures.*)

Black Hills National Forest (307-283-1361; 307-746-2782; www.fs.fed.us/r2/blackhills), near Sundance off I-90 and Newcastle off US 85/18. Though most of Black Hills National Forest lies within South Dakota, a portion of this forest lies in Wyoming. Recreational opportunities include camping, fishing, hiking, horseback riding, bicycling, snowmobiling, wildlife viewing, and more. (See also Bearlodge Trail under *To Do—Bicycling; To Do—Camping;* Cook Lake Trail under *To Do—Hiking;* and *Cross-Country Skiing and Snowshoeing* and *Snowmobiling* under *To Do—Snow Sports.*)

Shoshone National Forest (307-578-1200; 307-527-6241; www.fs.fed.us/r2/shoshone), 808 Meadow Lane, Cody. Created in 1891 as the Yellowstone National Reserve, Shoshone National Forest enjoys the distinction of being not only America's first national forest but also one of the largest national forests in the Rocky Mountain region. The forest encompasses more than 2.4 million acres, stretching from the northern border of Wyoming south to Lander and bordering Yellowstone National Park on the west. This forest includes portions of the Absaroka and Beartooth Mountain ranges in the area surrounding Cody, as well as part or all of five designated **wilderness areas.** Recreational opportunities abound, including hiking, fishing, camping, picnicking, horseback riding, wildlife viewing, boating, snowmobiling, and more. (See *To Do—Camping;* the Clarks Fork of the Yellowstone River and the Shoshone River under *To Do—Fishing;* Beartooth Loop National Recreation Trail under *To Do—Hiking;* and *Cross-Country Skiing and Snowshoeing, Ice Climbing,* Sleeping Giant Ski Area, and *Snowmobiling* under *To Do—Snow Sports.*)

WILDLIFE REFUGES AND AREAS **Dry Creek Petrified Tree Environmental Education Area,** located 13 miles southeast of Buffalo via I-90 to Exit 65 (Red Hills Road) and then north on Tipperrary Road about 6 miles to the Petrified Tree access road (all-weather gravel). Explore Wyoming's petrified past at this remote and intriguing natural area located in the middle of the badlands and managed by the Bureau of Land Management (BLM; see *Other Wild Places*). A 0.8-mile interpretive **loop trail** fills you in on the formative processes of the petrified trees and the way this land used to look some 60 million years ago when these very same trees—the giant metasequoias—covered the landscape.

Duck Swamp Interpretive Area, located about 3 miles north of Worland on WY 433, on the east side of the road. At this 81-acre Bighorn River oxbow marsh and lake, managed by the Bureau of Land Management (BLM; see *Other Wild Places*), you'll discover an environment replete with wildlife, particularly waterfowl. Bird species include great blue herons, kingfishers, and numerous ducks, while beavers and muskrats are commonly sighted as well. Hike a 1-mile interpretive **loop trail** to learn more about the area. Restrooms, drinking water, and picnic facilities are available, but overnight camping is not permitted.

McCullough Peaks Herd Management Area is located between 12 and 27 miles east of Cody along US 14/16/20. This BLM-managed Herd Management Area (HMA; see Bureau of Land Management under *Other Wild Places*), one of a number in Wyoming, is home to an estimated 450 wild horses. Encompassing nearly 110,000 acres, the HMA also contains the **McCullough Peaks Wilderness Study Area.** Even if you don't see any of the horses, be sure to bring along your camera to take some photos of the desolate, yet somehow strikingly beautiful badlands of the Wilderness Study Area and stop at the **Wild Horse Interpretive Site** along US 14/16/20 several miles before the intersection with WY 32 to learn a little more about Wyoming's herds. (See also Ishawooa Outfitters under *To Do—Horseback Riding* and Bighorn Canyon National Recreation Area under *Other Wild Places.*)

MCCULLOUGH PEAKS HERD MANAGEMENT AREA

Medicine Lodge Wildlife Habitat Management Area (307-469-2234; http://wyoparks.state.wy.us/mlodge .htm), 6 miles north of Hyattville via WY 31 to Cold Springs Road. This area surrounds the Medicine Lodge State Archaeological Site (see *To See—Historic Landmarks, Places, and Sites*), encompassing more than

12,000 acres. Managed by the Wyoming Game and Fish Department, this area was purchased in 1972 in an effort to protect winter grazing lands for the Bighorn Mountains' elk herds, among other species. Accessible to the public via the state archaeological site, the habitat management area allows great opportunities for viewing wildlife, including elk, mule deer, beavers, jackrabbits, marmots, porcupines, and bobcats, among many others.

✎ **Nature Conservancy's Ten Sleep Preserve** (307-366-2671; www.tnc wyoming.org/where/tensleep.shtml), east of Ten Sleep via US 16 to Rome Hill Road (WY 436); advance reservations required, call for rates. The Ten Sleep Preserve lies along 12 miles of the stunningly hued sandstone cliffs that rise above Canyon Creek. With eight plant communities and abundant wildlife, including 120 species of birds as well as mountain lions, black bears, mule deer, elk, and the spotted bat, the preserve works to educate visitors while protecting the environment contained within its 8,500 acres. Structured programs, including **conservation projects** (appropriate for children ages 11 and up when accompanied with an adult) and child-oriented **discovery programs,** are available for those who wish to visit and spend some time in this remarkable natural setting.

Wyoming Bird Farm (307-674-7701), south of Sheridan via WY 335 to Bird Farm Road. Open May through September. The Wyoming Game and Fish Department operates this farm where some 16,000 ring-necked pheasants are raised annually for release into habitats around the state. Visitors can stop at an information center, which provides exhibits and educational material about the birds, as well as view the birds on the premises.

See also **Kendrick Park** under *To See—For Families* and **Hot Springs State Park** under *To Do—Hot Springs.*

OTHER WILD PLACES ♿ ✎ **Bighorn Canyon National Recreation Area** (307-548-2251; www.nps.gov/bica), Bighorn Canyon Visitor Center, located at 20 US 14 Alternate E., Lovell. Open Memorial Day through Labor Day 8 AM–6 PM; open Labor Day through Memorial Day 8:30 AM–5 PM; $5 per vehicle per day or $30 for annual pass. This national recreation area encompasses more than 70,000 acres of land in Wyoming and Montana, including 60-mile-long Bighorn Lake. Popular activities include hiking, fishing, boating, year-round camping, wildlife viewing, and more. Boats are available for rent during the summer season at the **Ok-A-Beh Marina,** located within the recreation area. You might even glimpse wild horses from the Bureau of Land Management's **Pryor Mountain Wild Horse Range** along WY 37 in this recreation area. The Bighorn Canyon Visitor Center has a wheelchair-accessible **nature trail** with a reflection pond. Kids (and their families) can participate in the Bighorn Canyon's Junior Ranger Program via the completion of several fun and educational activities laid out in booklets available for purchase ($1 apiece) at the visitor center. Upon completion of the program, children earn a Junior Ranger badge.

Bureau of Land Management (BLM) has four field offices in this region: the **Buffalo Field Office** (307-684-1100; www.wy.blm.gov/bfo/index.htm), 1425 Fort Street, managing almost 800,000 acres of public lands and almost 1.5 million

acres of mineral estate; the **Cody Field Office** (307-578-5900; www.wy.blm
.gov/cyfo/index.htm), 1002 Blackburn Avenue, managing 1.1 million acres of
public lands and 1.5 million acres of federal mineral estate; the **Newcastle**
Field Office (307-746-6600; www.wy.blm.gov/nfo/index.htm), 1101 Washington
Boulevard, managing almost 300,000 acres of public lands and 1.6 million acres
of federal mineral estate; and the **Worland Field Office** (307-347-5100; www
.wy.blm.gov/wfo/index.htm), 101 S. 23rd Street, managing more than 2 million
acres of public lands and mineral estate. Much of the lands administered by the
BLM are open to recreational pursuits, including bicycling, boating, camping
(both primitive and developed; most developed campgrounds are handicapped
accessible), fishing, hiking (portions of the 3,100-mile-long **Continental Divide**
National Scenic Trail pass through sections of Wyoming's BLM land; see www
.cdtrail.org for details; see also *To Do—Hiking* in "South Wyoming: Medicine
Bow–Flaming Gorge Country"), horseback riding, paddling, rock climbing, wildlife viewing (including wild horses), and snow sports, including snowmobiling
and cross-country skiing. BLM lands tend to be the most unregulated of public
lands, meaning that most typical outdoor recreational pursuits are allowed on
most BLM lands, guided by the dictates of **Leave No Trace** (1-800-332-4100;
303-442-8222; www.lnt.org) outdoor ethics. To find out more general information about the BLM lands in this region, including maps, developed campgrounds,
and other recreational pursuits, contact the appropriate field office. (See also
Red Gulch Dinosaur Tracksite under *To See—For Families;* Red Gulch–Alkali
National Back Country Byway and WY 434 under *To See—Scenic Drives;* Castle
Gardens Scenic Area under *To See—Natural Wonders; To Do—Camping;*
Middle Fork of the Powder River Campground–Recreation Area under *To*
Do—Fishing; Five Springs Falls Trail, Gooseberry Badlands Scenic Overlook
and Interpretive Trail, Hole-in-the-Wall Trail, and Salt Lick Trail under *To Do—*
Hiking; Ishawooa Outfitters under *To Do—Horseback Riding;* and Dry Creek
Petrified Tree Environmental Education Area, Duck Swamp Interpretive Area,
and McCullough Peaks Herd Management Area under *Wildlife Refuges and*
Areas.)

&. **Ralston Reservoir Facilities** (307-527-7125; www.usbr.gov/gp/recreate/
bbrrec.htm), 15 miles northeast of Cody off US 14 Alternate. A walkway and
bridge provide access to tremendous wildlife viewing opportunities. Wetland
species and waterfowl, including sandhill cranes, pelicans, and ducks, are particularly abundant here. This area has no overnight camping, restroom facilities, or
drinking water.

Thunder Basin National Grassland (307-358-4690; www.fs.fed.us/r2/mbr),
located mostly south of I-90 and north of I-25 between Gillette and Douglas and
accessible via WY 59 and WY 450. This national grassland lies in the Powder River
Basin between Bighorn National Forest and Black Hills National Forest in northeastern Wyoming, extending south almost to Douglas (see Central Wyoming:
Oregon Trail–Rendezvous Country). Managed by the Douglas Ranger District of
the Medicine Bow and Routt national forests, the grassland provides numerous
recreational opportunities, including hiking, fishing, camping (undeveloped), and
wildlife viewing.

BED & BREAKFASTS

Buffalo 82834

Clear Creek Bed and Breakfast
(1-888-865-6789; 307-684-2317;
www.clearcreekbb.com), 330 S. Main
Street. One of the oldest B&Bs you'll
find in Wyoming, this house was built
in 1883 and boasts a fossil and stone
fireplace, a wraparound porch, and a
full, delicious breakfast served to
guests daily. Relax and unwind in the
comfortable white wicker of the two-
room Sagebrush Suite or the western
pine furnishings of the Highland
Retreat, both of which have queen-
size beds and private baths. You can
also opt for Miss Lottie's Room or the
Penrose, both with queen-size beds,
which share a bath ($65–85).

Cody 82414

Angels' Keep (1-877-320-2800; 307-
587-6205; www.angelskeep.com),
1241 Wyoming Avenue. Billed as "the
most fun you've ever had in church,"
Angels' Keep offers its guests lodging
in a 1930s church just four blocks
from downtown Cody. Rates include a
gourmet country breakfast and fresh-
baked cookies served daily ($85–125).

The Lambright Place (1-800-241-
5310; 307-527-5310; www.lambright
place.com), 1501 Beck Avenue. Constructed in 1924 for Cody Mayor P. E.
Markham, this beautiful B&B has
three guest rooms that come with
queen-sized beds and private baths,
as well as a separate bunkhouse that
sleeps five (a queen-size bed and
three single beds). You can enjoy a
hearty breakfast served in the dining
room or grab a speedy breakfast if
you're rarin' to go ($95–160).

The Mayor's Inn Bed & Breakfast
(1-888-217-3001; 307-587-0887; www
.mayorsinn.com), 1413 Rumsey
Avenue. Sleep in the very same
house—or, rather, mansion—that was
built from 1905 to 1909 for Cody's
first elected mayor, Frank L. Houx.
Moved to its present location in 1997
and restored to its full historical
splendor with modern amenities, this
B&B offers five guest rooms that
come with a full breakfast included in
the rate. Among the guest rooms is a
detached carriage house behind the
main building ($65–205). (See also
Dining Out.)

Parson's Pillow Bed & Breakfast
(1-800-377-2348; 307-587-2382; www
.cruising-america.com/parsonspillow),
1202 14th Street. "It's okay to sleep in
church," according to Parson's Pillow
B&B, which occupies a wood-framed
1902 church building. You choose
where to rest your head from among
five distinctly different guest bedrooms, all with queen-size beds and
private baths, and all come with a
delicious full breakfast ($65–95).

Robin's Nest Bed & Breakfast
(1-866-723-7797; 307-527-7208; www
.robinsnestcody.com), 1508 Alger
Avenue. Getting away from the hustle
and bustle of Cody's downtown is easy
if you stay at the Robin's Nest, where
two blocks make a world of differ-
ence. Stepping inside this B&B brings
you in touch with the West through
numerous vintage photographs, Indian weavings, and other such trappings,
many of which are available for purchase. Three guest rooms all include
private baths and a full breakfast
($115–135).

Dayton 82836

✐ **Four Pines Bed and Breakfast**
(1-866-366-2607; 307-655-3764; www
.fourpines.com), 114 Dayton E. Road.
Pets are permitted at this B&B located

conveniently near the Bighorn Mountains just a mile outside the small western town of Dayton. Enjoy the opportunity to unwind with Fido and partake of a hearty breakfast every morning before you embark on your day's activities, whether they include shopping for souvenirs or hiking in the mountains ($65–89; children under 10 sharing a room with parents stay free).

Gillette 82718
Jost House Inn Bed & Breakfast (1-877-685-2707; 307-687-1240; www.josthousebb.vcn.com), 2708 Ridgecrest Drive. This charming two-story B&B with its white-columned front porch, sky-blue shutters, and lovely, well-kept gardens offers fine hospitality. Delicious full breakfasts are prepared every morning and served in its cozy dining room. Choose from a suite with a private bath or an individual room (call for current rates).

Newcastle 82701
EVA—Great Spirit Ranch Bed & Breakfast (307-746-2537; www.wyomingbnb-ranchrec.com/EVAGreatSpirit.html), 1262 Beaver Creek Road. Hardwood floors and high ceilings, not to mention its lovely natural surroundings, distinguish this B&B. Set in Black Hills National Forest (see *Wilder Places—Forests*), this getaway provides a full homemade breakfast every day (included in the rate), complete with fresh-baked bread and other baked goods topped with homemade jams and jellies. Three spacious guest rooms come with private baths ($55–80).

Sheridan
Spahn's Big Horn Mountain Bed & Breakfast (307-674-8150; www.bighorn-wyoming.com; mailing address: P.O. Box 579, Big Horn 82833), 15 miles from Sheridan. Built by its owners, this lovely, solar-powered log home and its surrounding cabins bring with them incredible 100-mile views of the Bighorn Mountains. Whether you stay in the main house or in a cabin, you'll have a private bath and a queen-size bed, as well as a full breakfast every morning ($100–140). For $35, on Monday and Thursday nights you can enjoy this B&B's trademark Moose Safari, which includes a full steak dinner and a four-wheel-drive wildlife viewing tour.

Story 82842
Hitchin' Post Lodge (307-683-3039; 719-328-9207; www.storybnb.com), 12 Ridgecrest Drive, P.O. Box 141. Enjoy creekside accommodations and beautiful grounds at this B&B in Story, where you can either rent the entire three-bedroom guesthouse (your home away from home), complete with kitchen, dining room, and living room ($225–275), or simply rent a room, with or without a private bath, depending on your needs ($65–135).

♿ **Piney Creek Inn Bed & Breakfast** (307-683-2911; www.pineycreekinn.com), 11 Skylark Lane. Escape to this secluded spot in the Bighorn Mountains and relax every night in the hot springs spa on the back patio or around the evening campfire. Rates include a full breakfast and snacks daily. You'll sleep either in a guest room or a suite with private bath, coffeemaker, refrigerator, and deck access or in one of two cabins, both of which have a gas grill, kitchen or kitchenette, and more ($85–195).

Sundance 82729
Sundance Mountain HideAway Bed and Breakfast (1-877-838-0063; 307-283-3766; www.sundancemountain hideaway.com), 42 Sundance Mountain Road (WY 585 via Exit 187 off I-90). Three log cabins (all with private baths)—the Getaway Cabin, the Wildlife Cabin, and the Romantic Getaway—offer you a choice of luxurious amenities, including private decks, TV/VCRs, a Jacuzzi, and more. A gourmet, mouth-watering, full breakfast is included in the rate ($80–125).

Thermopolis 82443
Nuss Broadway Inn (307-864-2786; www.nussbroadwayinn.com), 342 Broadway Street. Four bedrooms, each with a queen bed and private bath, are available at this charming 1900s B&B in Thermopolis, situated just 1 block from downtown. Guests can use the kitchen and dining area as they please. Rates include a light breakfast of fruit, coffee, juices, fresh muffins and/or bread ($65–75).

LODGES

Buffalo
See **South Fork Mountain Lodge & Outfitters** under *To Do—Horseback Riding.*

Cody 82414
🔹 **Absaroka Mountain Lodge** (307-587-3963; www.absarokamtlodge .com), 1231 Yellowstone Highway. Built in 1910, Absaroka's historic lodge offers a central gathering place for the activities available here, which include horseback riding, trout fishing (specializing in fly-fishing), and more. The full packagen includes lodging,

THE HISTORIC OCCIDENTAL HOTEL IN NORTHEASTERN WYOMING

three meals a day, and 4 hours of horseback riding daily ($142 adults, $110 children ages 13–17, $76 children ages 5–12, children 4 and under free; cabin rentals only, $76–157).

Pahaska Teepee (1-800 628-7791; 307-527-7701; www.pahaska.com), 183 Yellowstone Highway. Included on the National Register of Historic Places, Buffalo Bill's original 1904 hunting lodge today offers visitors all of the amenities of a modern guest ranch, including guided trail rides, fishing trips, overnight trips, and more. You can stay in a guest room in one of the lodge's two-, four- or six-room cabins ($69.95–139.95), among other lodging options. Also on the premises you'll find a restaurant, a gift shop, and an antique bar that dates to 1872. Pahaska Teepee also has a 20K groomed cross-country ski trail system connecting the lodge with the Sleeping Giant Ski Area (see *Downhill Skiing* under *To Do—Snow Sports*). In addition, the lodge offers snowmobile rentals and guided snowmobile excursions through the East Entrance of Yellowstone National Park.

✿ **Shoshone Lodge** (307-587-4044; www.shoshonelodge.com), 349 Yellowstone Highway. Lodge activities include horseback riding, fishing, rockhounding, square dancing, and hiking. Meals are available for moderate prices in the main lodge, and children can play on the on-premises playground. Reserve a one-, two- or three-bedroom log cabin—rustic on the outside, modern on the inside, each with a private bath—and then either pick and choose from among the various activities offered by the lodge, paying for them separately from your lodging, or purchase a package deal, which includes lodging,

three meals a day, and 2 hours of horseback riding daily ($200 adults, double occupancy; $250 adults, single occupancy; $120 children ages 6–12; $50 children ages 5 and under with no horseback riding; cabin rentals only, $90–280).

See also **Wayfaring Traveler Llama Ranch** under *To Do—Unique Adventures.*

Shell 82441

The Hideout and the Snowshoe Lodge at Flitner Ranch (1-800-354-8637; www.thehideout.com), 3170 Road 40.5, P.O. Box 206, Shell (15 miles from Greybull); call for directions. Along with private cabins and gourmet ranch dining nightly, this 300,000-acre ranch offers numerous additional activities, including airboat rides, horseback riding, fishing, trapshooting, and guided hiking. Winters bring loads of snow to the Bighorn Mountains, making for tremendous snowmobiling opportunities. The ranch provides easy access to the nearly 400 miles of trails that make up the Bighorn Mountain–North-Central Wyoming trail system (almost 350 miles of which are groomed snowmobile trails). Reservations required. Six-night summer cowboy adventure package: $2,400 per adult or $3,100 for single occupancy, $1,500 for children under 12; call for current rates and packages. Winter rates: $100–165 per night for two people. Also available are snowmobile rentals, three meals a day, and package deals.

OTHER OPTIONS

Buffalo 82834

Historic Occidental Hotel (307-684-0451; www.occidentalwyoming.com), 10 N. Main Street. Step back in time at this 120-year-old hotel where the likes of Buffalo Bill, Butch Cassidy, and Calamity Jane all stayed. The hotel's Grand Lobby houses the free Occidental Hotel Museum, bringing you a little bit closer to the Old West with its photographs and other memorabilia from days gone by. Fully restored with modern amenities, the Occidental Hotel today nonetheless retains much of its original decor, including the original embossed ceilings in the lobby and bar, plus antique period furniture in each individually decorated room or suite. All accommodations include a private bathroom, a king- or queen-size bed, and a complimentary continental breakfast ($75–165). (See also **the Virginian Restaurant at the Historic Occidental Hotel** under *Dining Out.*)

Cody 82414

Buffalo Bill's Irma Hotel (1-800-745-4762; 307-587-4221; www.irma hotel.com), 1192 Sheridan Avenue. Named in honor of Buffalo Bill Cody's youngest daughter, the Irma was constructed in 1902 from local building materials, including sandstone quarried from nearby Beck Lake. Listed on the National Register of Historic Places, today's Irma Hotel gives you the best of both worlds, offering rooms with modern amenities in a one-of-a-kind historical setting—if you want, you can even reserve Buffalo Bill's own suite! Centrally located in downtown Cody just off the main drag, the Irma makes for a great place to start your exploration of the Old West ($70.50–130). Also on the premises, you can dine at the **Irma Restaurant Grill,** where you'll find tasty western fare served for breakfast, lunch, and dinner.

Cody Lodging Company (1-800-587-6560; www.codyguesthouses .com), 927 14th Street. An assortment of cozy getaways from cottages to vacation homes, as well as bed & breakfast accommodations, is available through Cody Lodging Company. One option in Cody is **Moose Alley Lodging** (1-877-511-4438; 307-587-6159; www.moosealleylodging.com), 1407 Wyoming Avenue, a cute, private, and quiet second-story studio apartment (the first story is storage space) beautifully furnished with a gas fireplace that will keep you warm on the coldest of nights. Much of this guidebook was written in the cozy comfort of Moose Alley Lodging ($79–110).

Greybull 82426

A Maverick Motel (307-765-4626; www.greybull.com/restlodge/adpages/ AMaverikMotel/index.html), 625 N. 6th Street. Staying at the Maverick is almost like having your own cottage: every room has its own kitchenette. The motel also features a free Mini Western and Ranch Antique Museum with more than 550 items on display. Pets are permitted in all rooms, and continental breakfast is included in rates from June 1 to September 1 ($45 or thereabouts, depending on season; weekly and monthly rates available).

Hyattville 82428

Diamond S Retreat (307-469-2204; www.tctwest.net/~kr), P.O. Box 18; off WY 31 outside Hyattville (north of Ten Sleep). A large country cabin set in an amazing location perfect for fly-fishing, hiking, wildlife viewing, or just relaxing, Diamond S sleeps up to seven people in its rustic, comfortable, handmade pine log beds. The cabin is fully furnished and comes with a full-service kitchen (but no television or phone, to help preserve that sense of truly getting away from it all). Reservations are required ($100, $20 for each additional person.)

Ten Sleep 82242

Log Cabin Motel (307-366-2320; www.tensleepwyoming.com/log cabin), 314 2nd Street (US 16). Clean and affordable, the Log Cabin Motel has one-, two-, and three-bedroom accommodations, some with kitchenettes. Call or e-mail for current rates (senior discounts and off-season rates available).

Meadowlark Lake Resort/Deer Haven Lodge (1-888-244-4676; www.thebighorn.com/meadowlark/ meadowlark.htm; mailing address: Big Horn Mountain Resorts, P.O. Box 86, Ten Sleep 82442), east of Ten Sleep on US 16 before Powder River Pass and situated adjacent to the Big Horn Ski Resort (see *Downhill Skiing* under *To Do—Snow Sports*) and Meadowlark Lake. A stay in the beautiful setting of **Meadowlark Lake Resort** gains you access to numerous recreational opportunities in the surrounding area. Motel rooms, cottages, cabins, and RV sites are available ($23–143). Under the same ownership, **Deer Haven Lodge** is a little ways back toward Ten Sleep on US 16, offering a Swiss chalet ($188–209) or a ranch house ($315–350; accommodates 12–14), as well as motel rooms, cabins, and RV sites ($18–98). Both facilities have on-premises bars as well as restaurants serving up tasty fare.

Thermopolis 82443

Star Inn (307-864-3499; www.rt connect.net/~starinn), 401 Park Street. Just a mile from Hot Springs State Park, this motel's already low prices include free tickets to the Star Plunge Water Park as well. Clean rooms come with a kitchenette ($35, $5 for each additional person).

See also **Float Trips by Eagle RV Park and Campground** under *To Do—Unique Adventures.*

Worland 82401

Herzberg Hideaway Country Guest House (307-347-2217; www .herzberghideaway.com), 1365 Airport Road. For a different sort of home-away-from home experience, rent this charming, two-story, 1930s adobe home nestled 3 miles south of Worland on an acre of wooded land. Adults only, 2-night minimum stay, barn for horse or llamas available by prearrangement ($85 single occupancy, $10 for each additional person up to five people).

& **The Wild Sage Inn** (307-347-2222; www.wildsageinn.com), 1895 Big Horn Avenue. Totally smoke-free, this motel's rooms are newly remodeled and come with data ports, voice mail, coffeemakers, and a complimentary continental breakfast. There is one kitchenette available and a Jacuzzi suite as well. Lovely landscaping and parking in front of each room add to the appeal of this locally owned and locally operated motel on Worland's main street ($30–75; weekly rates available as well).

See also **Wagon Box Restaurant & Cabins** under *Dining Out.*

✳ Where to Eat
DINING OUT

Buffalo

The Virginian Restaurant at the Historic Occidental Hotel (307-684-0451; www.occidentalwyoming .com), 10 N. Main Street. Steaks, seafood, and prime rib are the specialties at this beautifully restored restaurant located within the Historic Occidental Hotel (see *Lodging— Other Options*). This elegant dining experience is complemented by exceptional service and impeccable decor.

Cody

Cassie's Supper Club & Dance Hall (307-527-5500; www.cassies .com), 214 Yellowstone Avenue. A Cody fixture since 1922, Cassie's is the place in Cody to go for a delicious aged-to-perfection and cut-to-order steak or prime rib, served with a relish tray, homemade bread, and a soup of the day or a fresh garden salad, as well as your choice of baked potato, steak fries, rice, or pasta. Other menu items include seafood and chicken selections. Three levels of dining space, three bars, and a large dance floor incorporate parts of the club's original structure and decor. West the Band, which includes Steve Singer— the owner, operator, and head chef of Cassie's—among its members, plays Friday and Saturday nights starting at 10 PM throughout the year.

Maxwell's Fine Food and Spirits (307-527-7749), 937 Sheridan Avenue. Expect the finest at Maxwell's, where the well-dressed waitstaff will show you to your table and allow you time to peruse the extensive menu. Among the choices are pizzas and pastas, as well as full entrées of seafood, prime rib, and steak, which come with a host of sides. Plenty of appetizers to start the meal and desserts to finish it are available as well.

The Mayor's Inn Dinner House (307-587-0887; www.mayorsinn dinnerhouse.com), 1413 Rumsey

CASSIE'S SUPPER CLUB & DANCE HALL IN CODY

Avenue. Located with the historic **Mayor's Inn Bed & Breakfast** (see *Lodging*), this elegant restaurant serves meals Friday through Sunday, with seating beginning at 6 PM (reservations required). Entrée selections can include buffalo ribeye steak, wild sockeye salmon, and roasted duckling. Delectable appetizers and desserts, and an extensive selection of wine and spirits, make this a perfect choice for a romantic meal.

See also **Buffalo Bill's Irma Hotel** under *Lodging—Other Options*.

Greybull

Lisa's Fine Food & Spirits (307-765-4765; www.lisasfinefoods.com), 200 Greybull Avenue. Serving up delicious and creative entrées for breakfast, lunch, and dinner with a Southwestern flair, as well as native Wyoming favorites (think steak), for more than a decade, Lisa's is a favorite both with locals and passers-through. Southwestern specialties include enchiladas and fajitas, while steaks are available prepared in a variety of ways. The menu also includes pastas, stir-fries, and heart-healthy options.

Sheridan

The Empire Grill (307-674-4300; www.theempiregrill.com), 5 E. Alger

Street. An elegant dining experience awaits you at the Empire Grill. Fine wines complement a dinner menu that includes items from the grill such as steaks, chicken, pork tenderloin, salmon, and shrimp, as well as meal salads, pastas, and specialty pizzas.

Story

Wagon Box Inn Restaurant & Cabins (1-800-301-3120; 307-683-2444; www.wagonbox.com), 108 North Piney Creek. Known for its fabulous fare by both locals and visitors, this fantastic restaurant offers western dining at its finest. Specialties are seafood and steaks, and a variety of menu items combine the two. Other options include chicken, pastas, and burgers. Entrées come with a ton of sides. Kids' and seniors' menus are offered. Larger cuts of meat than those listed on the menu are available if you so desire. Patio dining in summer yields potential for viewing white-tailed deer that often graze on the grounds at dusk. (You can also grab a cabin or a room for the night for $40–99.)

EATING OUT

Buffalo

✍ **Colonel Bozeman's Restaurant & Tavern** (307-684-2531; www.bozeman crossing.com/restaurant.htm), 655 Hart Street. This large, family-oriented restaurant is the centerpiece for a veritable village of entertainment options (see Historic Bozeman Crossing under *To See—For Families*). The restaurant offers a large menu with options for all types of eaters, including terrific specialty salads and burgers done a number of ways, and steaks, prime rib, and buffalo.

Winchester Steak House (307-684-8636), 117 US 16. With daily specials and a great menu focused on (what else?) steaks, this restaurant is guaranteed to please in the meat department. The prime rib makes an excellent choice, but you really can't go wrong with any of the meat selections.

Cody

The Beta Coffeehouse (307-587-7707), 1132 12th Street. Just off the main drag and across the street from the Irma Hotel sits the finest coffee joint in town. Run by avid rock climbers Mike and Meg Snyder (look for portraits of both Snyders in action on the walls), the Beta serves not only coffee, tea, smoothies, and specialty drinks but also fantastic baked goods, and homemade soup in winter. Enjoy the rotating exhibitions of artwork by local and regional artists, or grab a seat on the couch and flip through a magazine while you sip your brew.

The Breadboard (307-527-5788), 1725 17th Street. For a quick, fresh-lunch, stop in at the Breadboard, where a huge selection of sub sandwiches is sure to make your mouth water, from the meatiest of meaty to vegetarian options. Soups, espresso, and bagels are also on the menu.

✍ **Granny's Restaurant** (307-587-4829), 1550 Sheridan Avenue. Perfect for families, this restaurant serves hearty breakfasts all day long, as well as lots of other American diner fare. Everyone will find something that suites their tastes on the extensive menu, while those on a budget will appreciate the moderate prices.

Peter's Café Bakery (307-527-5040; www.codynetwork.com/_includes/ menus/petersbakery.asp), 1191 Sheridan Avenue. Dine-in or take-out breakfast, lunch, and dinner. Peter's 150 menu items (give or take a few) include omelets, pancakes, buffalo burgers, unique sub sandwich combinations in three different sizes, an assortment of baked goods, and a delicious selection of ice-cream flavors.

Gillette

Las Margaritas (307-682-6545), 2107 S. Douglas Highway. If you're not in the mood for fast food or steaks tonight, then try a relatively authentic Mexican experience—right in the heart of Wyoming. Las Margaritas features all of your favorites, taking you south of the border with both its festive decorations and its menu.

✎ **Sanford's Grub and Pub** (307-682-0100), 408 W. Juniper Lane. Though Sanford's is not for everyone, most kids will probably dig this Wyoming–South Dakota restaurant chain, with its junkyard decor (remember the television show?) and its plethora of televisions tuned to all different channels. Beer aficionados will appreciate the enormous beer list, and if you're really hungry, you won't be overwhelmed by the supersized pub entrées, served with plentiful sides on oversize platters to be eaten with oversize silverware. The huge menu includes salads, burgers, sandwiches, and all sorts of entrée selections—you'll have to see it to believe how large and extensive it is.

Greybull

✎ **Buffalo Rose Restaurant** (307-765-4718), 601 N. 6th Street. If you can, catch the prime rib special on Friday and Saturday nights, but if you miss it, don't worry. The Buffalo Rose has plenty of other entrée selections available at reasonable prices to make the whole family happy. You'll feel right at home here—a comfortable and relaxing venue serving breakfast, lunch, and dinner.

✎ **Wheels Inn Restaurant & Gift Shop** (307-765-2456), 1336 N. 6th Street (US 16, main street through town). Open 24 hours, this restaurant specializes in what seems to be Wyomingites' unofficial favorite dessert: homemade pie. Grab yourself a slice anytime, day or night, or sit down for a full meal. A salad bar is available daily, and a buffet is served every Sunday. As an added attraction, the Wheels Inn Restaurant has a 50-foot dinosaur mural.

Newcastle

The Hop (307-746-2585), 1114 W. Main Street. Remember the '60s? Well, even if you don't, you'll get to dine like you're living in a bygone era at the Hop. In addition to breakfast, lunch, and dinner served daily, you can also sip a fabulous malt or milk shake or eat a hand-dipped ice-cream cone. Try the house specialty: a 10-ounce, hand-battered chicken-fried steak.

Isabella's Italian Restaurant (307-746-3500), 12 S. Sumner Avenue. Italian-food lovers, beware—you will have a wide selection of all of your favorites to choose from at this eatery. Choices range from pastas of all shapes and types, topped with a variety of sauces, to strombolis, pizzas, Italian subs, salads, and more.

Shell

✎ **Dirty Annie's Country Store** (307-765-2304; www.dirtyannies.com), 1669 US 14. This is a great place to stop for some old-fashioned, hand-dipped hard ice cream. Let the kids explore the store's authentic sheep wagon while you stretch your legs before beginning your journey up the Bighorn Scenic Byway (see *To See—Scenic Drives*).

Sheridan
❧ **Sanford's Grub and Pub** (307-674-1722), 1 E. Alger Street. Super-sized pub entrées, served with plentiful sides on oversized platters to be eaten with oversized silverware. The huge menu includes salads, burgers, sandwiches, and all sorts of entrée selections—and an enormous beer list. (See complete description under the town of Gillette.)

Ten Sleep
Dirty Sally's (307-366-2319), 2nd Street. If you like ice cream, no visit to Ten Sleep would be complete without a stop at Dirty Sally's. Not only is the store filled to the brim with souvenirs and items of local interest, but it also serves the best ice cream in town, in quantities so vast that you won't believe your eyes. Try a waffle cone (made right in the shop) with two scoops—$3 with tax will give you a belly full of rich, flavorful ice cream that will bring you back for more if you're in town for a few days.

L&L's Hitchin' Post Inn (307-366-2696), 201 2nd Street. Though some of the prices can be higher than those at other restaurant options in town, this restaurant does feature inexpensive menu choices alongside its delicious entrée selections, which include ribeye steak, a center-cut pork chop, and a 1-pound hamburger steak. The L&L does meat right, so if you're in the mood for a big hunk of protein, this is the place to go.

❧ **Percup Espresso Café and More** (307-366-2692), 100 2nd Street. Also the visitor center for the tiny town of Ten Sleep, the Percup is owned and

TEN SLEEP RODEO IN TEN SLEEP

run by friendly local Janna Hampton, who has grown her business into a central spot for locals and passersby to grab a cup of coffee or a smoothie; to sample delicious homemade pastries, muffins, and pies; or to sit down for an inexpensive meal with family or friends. The Percup also sometimes hosts jams with local musicians, so don't be shy about asking if anything's shaking when you stop in.

Thermopolis
❧ ✿ **Granny's Bakery, Ice Cream & Grill** (307-864-2809), 200 N. 6th Street. For thick, delicious hamburgers and hearty helpings of curly fries, you can't beat Granny's. Daily specials are a good option, too, as are the homemade soups and sandwiches. For dessert, choose from more than 20 flavors of ice cream, served up in huge portions.

❧ **Pumpernicks Family Restaurant** (307-864-5151), 512 Broadway Street. If the weather permits, have a seat on the enclosed patio and take some time to peruse the large menu at this family-run restaurant—unless it's Friday or Saturday night. As long as you're a meat eater, the prime rib special is all you need to satisfy your hunger. Deli sandwiches are recommended as well. Be sure to save room for a slice of one of Verna's homemade pies, brownies, or carrot cake.

Worland

🍴 **Cross Bow Restaurant** (307-347-8296), 1110 Big Horn Avenue. For inexpensive family fare, the Cross Bow has a great selection, including a salad bar and burgers. You'll also find a selection of homemade pies to choose from to top off your tanks after the main event.

🍴 **The Office Lounge** (307-347-8171), 1515 Big Horn Avenue. Traditional American fare is what you'll find at the Office Lounge, prepared with excellence in a tavernlike setting. Homemade foods include steaks, chicken, and specials, with homemade pie and an assortment of other goodies on the menu for dessert.

See also **Meadowlark Lake Resort/Deer Haven Lodge** under *Lodging—Other Options.*

✳ Special Events

February: **Waterfall Ice Roundup** (307-527-4326; www.southforkice .com), Cody: ice climbers from around the world gather annually on Presidents' Day Weekend to celebrate the fantastic ice climbing in the South Fork of the Shoshone. (See also *Ice Climbing* under *To Do—Snow Sports.*)

🍴 *May:* **Lake DeSmet Fishing Derby** (1-800-227-5122; 307-684-5544), Buffalo: on Memorial Day weekend, anglers of all ages can com-

pete for prizes at this community-oriented event. (See also Lake DeSmet under *To Do—Fishing.*)

June: **Bozeman Trail Days** (www .bozemantrail.org/bozemantraildays .html), Fort Phil Kearny State Historic Site, Story: 3-day event with living history demonstrations, symposiums, and tours of historic battlefields. **Days of 49,** Greybull: annual local celebration includes a barbecue, rodeo, parade, western street dance, and more. **Hulett Rodeo** (www .hulett.org), Hulett Rodeo Grounds, Hulett: traditional rodeo and associated festivities. **Plains Indian Museum Powwow** (307-587-2297; www .bbhc.org/events/powwow.cfm), Cody: annual competition that draws dancers and drummers from around North America to compete for more than $15,000 in prize money.

July: 🍴 **Buffalo Bill Cody Stampede Rodeo** (1-800-207-0744; 307-587-5155; www.codystampederodeo .org), Cody: for more than 85 years, the Buffalo Bill Cody Stampede Rodeo has been a major annual happening—a 4-day extravaganza complete with parades, rodeos, fireworks, and family entertainment. 🍴 **Fourth of July Parade, Ten Sleep Rodeo and Street Dance,** Ten Sleep: the whole town comes out to celebrate this annual 2-day bash, featuring fireworks, a rodeo, dancing, live entertainment, food, and more. **Yellowstone Jazz Festival** (307-587-2777; www.tctwest.net/~yellowstone jazz), Cody: 2-day annual event attracts great jazz musicians and performers each year, with some free performances and some performances requiring ticket purchase.

July and August: **Park County Fair** (307-754-5421), Powell: a traditional county fair with a 4H competition, carnivals, livestock, food, exhibits, and more.

August: **Big Horn County Fair** (307-568-2968; www.tctwest.net/~bhfair), Basin: traditional county fair. **Nowoodstock Music Festival** (www.nowoodstock.com), Ten Sleep: 3-day outdoor music festival featuring local musicians and special guests. **Gift of the Waters Pageant,** Thermopolis: taking place the first full weekend of August annually; Indian ceremony reenacts the legend of the hot springs being given to Wyoming.

Washakie County Fair and Parade, Worland: traditional county fair and events. **Johnson County Fair and Rodeo,** Johnson County Fairgrounds, Buffalo: traditional county fair and events.

September: ✿ **Northeast Wyoming Annual Antique Show** (307-467-5524; www.hulett.org/antiques.htm), Hulett Rodeo Grounds, Hulett: includes children's activities, tractor races, and antiques. **Deke Latham Memorial PRCA Rodeo** (307-738-2444; www.dekelathamrodeo.com), Kaycee: 4-day PRCA rodeo.

WEST WYOMING: JACKSON HOLE–JIM BRIDGER COUNTRY

When you think of Jackson Hole, one thing probably comes to your mind: skiing. The town of Jackson and the valley surrounding it, Jackson Hole, together embody the term *ski town*, having developed into one of America's premier winter sports destinations during the 20th century. Today Wyoming's three largest ski resorts are here: Jackson Mountain, Grand Targhee, and Snow King, Wyoming's oldest ski area.

Jackson hasn't always been known as a ski town, however; in fact, it didn't begin to develop this identity until the establishment of Snow King Ski Resort in 1939. Before that time and before the time of the first white settlers, Native Americans had inhabited the Jackson Hole area continuously for centuries. Mountain men constituted the first known travelers of European descent to leave written accounts of the area, passing through during the first half of the 19th century when, for a short period, beaver fur represented the pinnacle of high fashion both in America and in Europe. These early trappers found a verdant area rife with wildlife, including coveted beavers, though they didn't establish any permanent settlements in the valley at that time. These trappers included such notable and legendary figures of America's past as Jim Bridger, Jedediah Smith, and David Jackson, for whom the town of Jackson was named.

By the mid-1840s, the "beaver boom" had passed, and the valley was pretty much left to its own devices for the remainder of the 19th century—Native Americans still stayed there, explorers passed through, and a few hale and hardy pioneers dug in by homesteading the land, attempting to ranch and grow crops in an area not exactly perfect for such endeavors due to its rather harsh climate and short growing season. It was some of these early settlers who turned to the trades that would become a mainstay of Wyoming's economy: outfitting and guiding. Both helped to bring in more money when it became evident that ranching and farming would not be profitable enough to sustain the settlers through the years ahead. The 1872 creation of Yellowstone National Park just north of Jackson helped the dude ranching business grow and prosper, as the American public became more familiar with this isolated area of Wyoming. Nonetheless, the actual population of permanent settlers remained small.

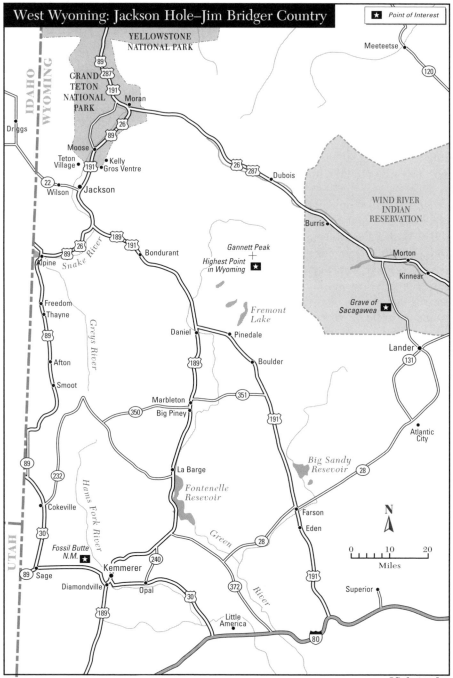

West Wyoming: Jackson Hole–Jim Bridger Country

★ Point of Interest

YELLOWSTONE NATIONAL PARK

Meeteetse

120

89
287
GRAND
TETON
NATIONAL
PARK
191
Moran

IDAHO
WYOMING

26

89

Driggs

Moose

26
287
Dubois

Teton
Village
191
Kelly
Gros Ventre

22
Wilson
Jackson

WIND RIVER
INDIAN
RESERVATION

Burris

189
191
Bondurant

Gannett Peak
+
Highest Point
in Wyoming ★

Morton

Kinnear

Alpine
89
26
Snake River

Grave of
Sacagawea ★

Freedom
Thayne

Greys River

Fremont
Lake

Daniel
Pinedale

Lander
131

89

Afton

189
Boulder

Smoot

Marbleton
350
Big Piney

351

191

Atlantic
City

La Barge

Big Sandy
Resevoir
28

89
232

Ham's Fork River

Fontenelle
Resevoir

N

Cokeville

Farson

Eden

0   10   20
Miles

UTAH

30

Fossil Butte
N.M. ★

Green
River

28

240
Kemmerer

191

89 Sage

Diamondville
Opal
30
372

Superior

189

Little
America

80

© The Countryman Press

As the late 1800s gave way to the 20th century, the town of Jackson sprang up in response to the growth of the dude ranching and cattle ranching operations in the valley. Dubbed Jackson in 1894, the town soon had services; streets and wooden sidewalks followed in their wake. Tourism continued to sustain the area, with big-game hunting and fishing taking top spots on the itineraries of many visitors to Wyoming's early dude ranches. A desire to preserve and protect the area's natural resources resulted in the formation of the National Elk Refuge in 1912 and Grand Teton National Park in 1929, as well as the inclusion of much of the land surrounding the valley in Bridger–Teton National Forest. Such moves were not without conflict, though: in particular, Grand Teton National Park's 1950 expansion to its current size was a controversial move that put some of the valley's ranching families at odds with those responsible for such legislation, as it seriously impacted the amount of land available for cattle grazing.

Nonetheless, the tourism industry that had begun to take off in the early days of Jackson had supplanted cattle ranching and other endeavors as the valley's chief industry, and it is the industry that continues to define and shape the area today. With the establishment of Snow King in 1939, Jackson started its journey toward capturing one of the preeminent positions in the psyche of the nation's downhill skiers, who would later be joined by snowboarders as well. Today, Jackson Hole is a thriving ski town, but even the slightest peek under the surface reveals that the area has so much more to offer its visitors, whether they come primarily to ski or whether it's another pursuit that draws them.

In addition to its proximity to Grand Teton National Park and Yellowstone National Park, Jackson Hole and its surrounding environs contain a lifetime's worth of outdoor recreational pursuits, from the endless number of trails to explore by foot, bike, horseback, snowshoe, ski, or snowmobile (among other modes of travel) in Bridger–Teton National Forest to the countless streams and lakes that offer top-quality fishing. But that's not all—in the wake of the growth of dude ranches and other services aimed at providing first-rate outdoor adventures, a plethora of complementary services has evolved to support such endeavors. Thus the visitor to Jackson Hole will find plenty of arts and cultural institutions and events, shopping, spas, fine dining and casual eateries, and lodging options ranging from basic to luxurious.

JACKSON'S TOWN SQUARE

What's more, a journey to the "Jim Bridger" portion of this travel region, south of Jackson Hole, will yield even more opportunities for outdoor adventures—minus the crowds. The small town of Pinedale, nestled on the western side of the Wind River Range, Wyoming's highest, offers a full array of recreational pursuits for all seasons. There you'll find White Pine Ski Area and Resort, Fremont Lake and its surrounding neighbor lakes, the Green River and the New Fork River, and a huge swath of land also included in Bridger–Teton National Forest, with more public lands managed by the Bureau of Land Management (BLM). This is the location where the mountain men held one of their famed "rendezvous" trading events annually for several years during the 1830s— happenings that are commemorated at Pinedale's Green River Rendezvous Days each July and at other such events.

To the west, from Alpine in the north to Kemmerer in the south, you'll find even more remote and less traveled terrain ripe for exploring, including the local Pine Creek Ski Area by Cokeville and the fishing, hiking, biking, and horseback riding opportunities in both the national forest and on BLM lands. Here, too, you can learn about the area's prehistoric times with a visit to Fossil Butte National Monument, showcasing an incredible concentration of quality fossils. You can visit offbeat attractions like the Tri-State Monument and Names Hill. You can walk or ride in the footsteps of the early pioneers who passed this way on historic trails, including the Overland Trail, the Oregon Trail, and the Mormon Trail. You can fish the Greys River and the Salt River or their tributaries or float or paddle portions of them. You can camp at numerous spots, many of them free of charge, and enjoy the opportunity to get away from it all in this remote portion of the state that beckons with its mystical charm to the adventurer within.

Wherever you go, whatever you do, in this region you should take care to remember that wildlife abounds here and must be respected. Up in and around Jackson and anywhere near the mountains, you must take particular care to maintain a clean camp to avoid potentially hazardous encounters with bears (interactions can pose a danger to both yourself and to the animals, as they can end up with a death sentence if they become a persistent problem). Many campgrounds provide on-site information and helpful tools, such as bear-proof trash cans and food storage containers, to enable you to avoid any sort of conflict with a little extra effort on your part. Be smart, educate yourself, and do your part to help these areas maintain a harmonious state of coexistence with their wild inhabitants—after all, it was their home before it was ours, and we all need to make an effort to help them survive.

GUIDANCE **Big Piney Chamber of Commerce** (307-276-3554; www.bigpiney .com), P.O. Box 70, Big Piney 83113.

Cokeville Chamber of Commerce (307-279-3200; www.cokevillewy.com), 110 N. US 30, P.O. Box 358, Cokeville 83114.

Jackson Hole Central Reservations (1-800-443-6931; 307-733-4005; www .jacksonholewy.com), 140 E. Broadway, P.O. Box 2618, Jackson 83001. This company can not only book lodging for you at a variety of locations in Jackson and the surrounding area but also hook you up with vacation activities, often wrapped into package deals.

Jackson Hole Chamber of Commerce (307-733-3316; www.jacksonhole chamber.com), 990 W. Broadway, P.O. Box 550, Jackson 83001.

Kemmerer–Diamondville Chamber of Commerce (1-888-300-3413; 307-877-9761; www.kemmererchamber.com), 800 Pine Avenue, Kemmerer 83101.

La Barge Chamber of Commerce (307-386-2541), P.O. Box 96, La Barge 83123.

Marbleton Chamber of Commerce (307-276-3815), P.O. Box 4160, Marbleton 83113.

Star Valley Chamber of Commerce (1-800-426-8833; 307-883-2759; www.starvalleychamber.com), Box 1097, Afton 83110.

Sublette County Chamber of Commerce (1-888-285-7282; 307-367-2242; www.pinedalechamber.com or www.visitsublettecounty.com) and **Visitor Center,** 26 N. Tyler Street, P.O. Box 176, Pinedale 82941.

GETTING THERE Jackson is accessed from the north via US 26/89/191 through Grand Teton National Park, from the southwest via US 26/89 through Alpine, from the southeast via US 189/191 through Bondurant, and from the west via WY 22 to Idaho. Pinedale can be reached from the north and south via US 191 or via US 189 to WY 351 from the south. Kemmerer can be accessed from the north and south via US 189 and from the east and west via US 30.

See also *Airports, Amtrak, Bus Service,* and *Travel Information* in "What's Where in Wyoming."

MEDICAL EMERGENCY **St. John's Medical Center** (307-733-3636), 625 E. Broadway, Jackson.

South Lincoln Medical Center (307-877-4401), 711 Onyx Street, Kemmerer.

Star Valley Medical Center (307-885-5864), 110 Hospital Lane, Afton.

✳ To See

TOWNS **Afton** is located along US 89 in **Star Valley** just east of Wyoming's border with Idaho. At close to 2,000 inhabitants, it is the largest of Wyoming's towns in the Star Valley area. Other towns (south to north) include **Smoot, Fairview, Auburn, Grover, Bedford, Thayne, Freedom, Etna,** and **Alpine.** All of these towns are part of Lincoln County, which is rife with year-round outdoor recreational pursuits for those seeking an out-of-the-way destination. Afton is home to the annual **Lincoln County Fair,** held in early August, but its real claim to fame is the **World's Largest Elkhorn Arch,** an 18-foot structure containing more than 3,000 elk antlers. Be sure to stop in at the famed **Star Valley Cheese Factory** in Thayne on your journey.

Jackson is south of **Grand Teton National Park** on US 26/89/191. Jackson is the biggest (almost 9,000 people) and most well known town in the valley called Jackson Hole, a 15-mile-wide and 80-mile-long wonderland bursting with outdoor recreational opportunities coupled with virtually all of the finest tourist amenities imaginable. Named for a founder of the Rocky Mountain Fur Company, David E. Jackson, the town of Jackson today is perhaps best known for its proximity to the world-renowned **Jackson Hole Ski Resort** (See *To Do—Snow*

Sports). Jackson has much more to offer than skiing, though—in addition to the abundance of outdoor recreational pursuits surrounding it, the town also features an elegant, centrally located Town Square with distinctive antler arch entrances at each of its four corners, along with dozens of art galleries, massage and spa services, shopping, elegant lodging, fine dining, museums, cultural attractions, and special events held throughout the year. Other Jackson Hole towns include **Kelly, Moose, Moran Junction, Teton Village,** and **Wilson.**

Kemmerer lies at the intersection of WY 233, US 30, and US 189. This town serves as a gateway to **Fossil Butte National Monument** (see *Natural Wonders*), one of Wyoming's two national monuments (the other being Devils Tower). The town's nickname, "the Fossil Fish Capital of America," echoes this role, as do several commercial dig sites on the way to the monument, which allow you to try your hand at uncovering fossils (for a fee). Kemmerer, population 2,651, is also home to the original **JCPenney** (bet you didn't know that it all started in Wyoming) and the **Fossil Country Frontier Museum** (see *Museums*). The town has a tent camping area on WY 233 near City Hall.

⚓ **Pinedale,** on US 191 10 miles east of Daniel and the junction of US 189/191, is one of Wyoming's true unsung gems. Situated at the southern entrance to the **Wind River Mountains,** this town of 1,400 is surrounded by incredible mountain scenery and offers ample opportunities for year-round recreation. The **Pinedale Town Park** has a kids' fishing pond and picnic areas. Pinedale is also home to the **Museum of the Mountain Man** (see *Museums*), and it hosts the annual **Green River Rendezvous Days** (see *Special Events*), commemorating the 1830s mountain man rendezvous that occurred in this area. The **Upper Green River Rendezvous–Trapper's Point National Historic Site,** 6 miles west of Pinedale on US 191 at the Cora Junction, commemorates these events as well.

MUSEUMS Fossil Country Frontier Museum (307-877-6551; www.hamsfork .net/~museum), 400 Pine Avenue, Kemmerer. Open late May through early September Monday through Saturday 9 AM–5 PM; open early September through late May Monday through Friday 10 AM–4 PM; free. This museum's exhibits capture the local history and interpret it for visitors. You'll see a prehistoric dinosaur footprint, an exhibit on the area's coal mining heritage, bootlegging equipment from Prohibition, and even (gulp!) a two-bodied lamb.

Green River Valley Museum (307-276-5343; www.grvm.com/home.htm), 206 N. Front Street, Big Piney. Open June 15 through October 15 Tuesday through Saturday noon–4 PM; free. In the tiny mountain town of Big Piney (population 408), this museum has provided visitors with insight into the area's past since its construction in

COLORFUL, HISTORIC BUILDINGS IN HISTORIC DOWNTOWN JACKSON

JACKSON HOLE HISTORICAL SOCIETY AND MUSEUM

the early 1990s. Featured exhibits cover the area's history, including Indians, ranching, mining (coal, oil, and gas), and pioneers and homesteads, including a restored homesteader's cabin. The museum's building was constructed after another building—the old jailhouse—burned to the ground in 1948, with the exception of the metal jail cell, which continued to be used for a while to house prisoners—this despite the lack of a surrounding building. The new building was constructed around the old cell, and today you can take a peek inside and imagine what it might have been like to be imprisoned in the cell.

🔹 **Jackson Hole and Greater Yellowstone Visitor Center** (307-733-3616; www.fs.fed.us/jhgyvc/welcome.html), 532 N. Cache Street, Jackson. Open daily Memorial Day weekend through September 30, 8 AM–7 PM; open October 1 through Memorial Day 9 AM–5 PM; closed Thanksgiving and Christmas; free. Though it's called a visitor center, what you'll find inside—and outside, too—stretches beyond the norm for a typical visitor center (which is why it's listed under *Museums*). Operated through interagency cooperation among eight separate local and regional agencies, this center features an overload of free visitor information in the form of brochures, maps, and helpful staff. The center also features wildlife displays and exhibits, a viewing area overlooking the adjacent National Elk Refuge (see *Wildlife Refuges and Areas*) and beautiful Flat Creek, a bookstore and retail shop, informational films, educational and interpretive programs, a picnic area, a pet exercise area, and much, much more. You can also purchase national park passes and state hunting and fishing licenses here, among other passes and permits available.

Jackson Hole Historical Society and Museum (museum: 307-733-2414; historical society: 307-733-9605; www.jacksonholehistory.org), 105 N. Glenwood Street (museum), Jackson; 105 Mercill Avenue (Historical Society Research Center), Jackson. **Museum** open last Friday in May through first week of October Monday through Saturday 9:30 AM–6 PM, Sunday 10 AM–5 PM; $3 adults, $2 seniors, $6 per family, $1 students; free on season's opening day. **Historical Society Research Center** open year-round Monday through Friday 8 AM–5 PM; free. The Jackson Hole Museum interprets the area's history for you with an impressive collection that includes some 7,000 historic photographs; Indian artifacts, including weapons, pottery, and stone tools; artifacts from the fur trade, pioneer days, homesteading, and ranching; and exhibits on Grand Teton and Yellowstone national parks, among other attractions. The Historical Society Research Center houses a tremendous array of resources for researching the area's history, as well as a small exhibit space with historic photographs. The museum's staff also provides **walking tours** of historic downtown Jackson in summertime ($2 adults, $1 seniors and students, $5 per family).

Museum of the Mountain Man (1-877-686-6266; www.museumofthe mountainman.com), 700 E. Hennick, Pinedale. Open daily May 1 through September 30, 9 AM–5 PM; open October Monday through Friday 10 AM–noon and 1 PM–3 PM; $5 adults, $4 seniors, $3 children ages 6–12. Learn all about the history and times of the notorious mountain men who made their livings in the fur trade during the early 1800s. The museum features numerous additional exhibits detailing other aspects of the area's past, including Native American artifacts and clothing and women's historic role in dude ranching, among other subjects.

♿ ♪ **National Museum of Wildlife Art** (1-800-313-9553; 307-733-5771; www .wildlifeart.org), 2820 Rungius Road (3 miles north of Town Square on US 191 across street from National Elk Refuge), Jackson. Open daily in summer and winter 9 AM–5 PM; open daily in spring and fall Monday through Saturday 9 AM–5 PM, Sunday 1 PM–5 PM; closed Thanksgiving and Christmas; $8 adults, $7 seniors 60 and older, $7 children 6 and older and students, children 5 and under free; $16 per family (two adults with one to two children). If you're both a wildlife lover and an art aficionado, be sure to set aside time to stroll through the galleries of this unique fine art museum while you're in Jackson. Children will delight in the hands-on discovery area. You'll likely find yourself captivated by the scope of the museum's collection, which includes 3,000 pieces of artwork by more than 200 artists from around the world. Exhibits of western wildlife art, including pieces by such notable artists as **Charles M. Russell, Carl Rungius, Albert Bierstadt,** and **John J. Audubon,** are on permanent display. The museum also features several temporary exhibits at any given time. In wintertime, the museum's **Wapiti Gallery** hosts an interpretive display for the National Elk Refuge (see also Sleigh Rides on the National Elk Refuge under *To Do—Unique Adventures*).

HISTORIC LANDMARKS, PLACES, AND SITES **J. C. Penney Homestead and Historical Foundation** (307-877-3164), 107 J. C. Penney Drive, Kemmerer. Open May through September Monday through Saturday 9 AM–6 PM, Sunday 1 PM–6 PM; free. Most customers who walk through the doors of one of the many JCPenney stores around the nation probably don't realize that the original "Mother Store" was—and still is—in the small western town of Kemmerer, Wyoming. Opened in 1902 under the name Golden Rule Store by one James Cash Penney, the store enjoyed a virtual overnight success. A decade later, more than 30 Golden Rule Stores were in operation, and in 1913 the decision was made to change the stores' names to

THE NATIONAL MUSEUM OF WILDLIFE ART

J. C. Penney. Today, visitors can stroll through the original J. C. Penney Homestead; the six-room cottage decorated with authentic period pieces is a National Historic Landmark. Kemmerer's Mother Store is still open for business as well for those wanting to shop where it all started.

Names Hill is 6 miles south of LaBarge, just west of US 189. At this location, you'll find inscriptions of two sorts in the sandstone cliffs: Native American petroglyphs from long ago, and more recent inscriptions made by some 2,000 pioneers who passed this way traveling west on the Overland Trail via the Sublette Cutoff. The pioneers' inscriptions date to 1827, and included among them is the signature of the famed mountain man, James "Jim" Bridger.

Tri-State Monument, accessible by driving 8.5 miles south of Cokeville on WY 207 and then turning west onto WY 208. Continue 5 miles to reach the monument. No, it's not the Four Corners Monument . . . but it is Wyoming's less visited version of a place where one can stand in multiple states at once. After a short walk, you'll arrive at that spot, located in Idaho, Utah, and Wyoming. This is one of those attractions that the true explorer of this area must visit. After all, do you know anyone who has visited the Tri-State Monument? I didn't think so.

See also Pinedale under *Towns;* Wagons A+cross Wyoming under *To Do— Unique Adventures;* Bureau of Land Management under *Wilder Places—Other Wild Places;* the Chambers House Bed and Breakfast under *Lodging—Bed & Breakfasts;* and the Log Cabin Motel and the Wort Hotel under *Lodging— Other Options.*

FOR FAMILIES 🐾 𝒮 **Putt Putt Miniature Golf Course,** on the corner of Park Street and 1st Street in Cokeville (just east of Town Park); free. At the Country Shopper on Main Street, you can check out clubs and balls for this free family attraction. After you play a round with the kids, you can also let them play on the playground equipment in adjacent Town Park.

See also Pinedale under *Towns;* National Museum of Wildlife Art under *Museums;* Fossil Butte National Monument under *Natural Wonders;* Teton Mountain Bike Tours, LLC, under *To Do—Bicycling;* BLM Campgrounds under *To Do— Camping;* Granite Creek Hot Springs under *To Do—Hot Springs;* Grand Targhee Ski Resort, Jackson Hole Mountain Resort, Snow King Ski Resort, and White Pine Ski Area and Resort under *To Do—Snow Sports;* "Llamaneering" with Jackson Hole Llamas, Sleigh Rides on the National Elk Refuge, Wagons A+cross Wyoming, and Wyoming Balloon Adventures under *To Do—Unique Adventures;* and Mountain Days under *Special Events.*

SCENIC DRIVES **Big Springs Scenic Backway** is a 68-mile journey on partially paved, partially graveled, and dirt roads, starting in Kemmerer. Go north on WY 233 (Hams Fork Road), which changes to oiled gravel just north of Lake Viva Naughton and then to just plain gravel when you enter **Bridger–Teton National Forest** (on F.R. 10062). Follow F.R. 10062 as its winds around to its junction with WY 232 and then follow this road south to **Cokeville** and the official terminus of the backway. To avoid becoming lost, it's helpful to get a map from the **Kemmerer Ranger Station** (307-877-4415), 308 US 189, Kemmerer. This winding, scenic backway could be driven in about 2 hours—but what would be the point? You'll be better off scheduling a day (or more) to explore all of the scenic, historic, and recreational highlights you'll encounter on this drive that crosses a portion of the historic **Oregon Trail.** You'll pass by **Lake Viva Naughton** (see *To Do—Boating*), numerous old **homesteaders' cabins, Mayfield and Nugent Park Winter Sports Area** (popular with Nordic skiers and snowmobilers), numerous creeks, and several developed campgrounds in Bridger–Teton National Forest (see *To Do—Camping*), among other attractions.

Wyoming Centennial Scenic Byway is a 155-mile U-shaped journey that begins (or finishes) in Dubois (see *To See—Towns* in "Central Wyoming: Oregon Trail–Rendezvous Country"). Head northwest on US 26/287 to Moran Junction. Go southwest on US 26/89/191 through Jackson Hole to Hoback Junction. Head southeast on US 189/191 to Pinedale. This lengthy journey could be split up into several days of travel, since you'll pass by so many of the attractions covered in this region of Wyoming. Key features include the impressive **Togwotee Pass** (9,658 feet; see *To Do—Snow Sports*) and the beautiful **Pinnacle Buttes,** encountered on US 26/287 west of Dubois, and the **Jackson Hole** area (see *Towns*), among other sites.

NATURAL WONDERS ♿ ❀ **Fossil Butte National Monument** (307-877-4455; www.nps.gov/fobu), roughly 15 miles west of Kemmerer on US 30. Open June through August 8 AM–7 PM; open September through May 8 AM–4:30 PM; closed on winter holidays; free. While you've undoubtedly heard of Wyoming's other national monument (Devils Tower), this one should be included in your travel plans, too, if you happen to be in the area. Not only is it free (yes, free!), but Fossil Butte is also home to one of the world's most extensive collection of freshwater fossils. Some 50 million years ago a huge lake existed at Fossil Butte, as the plentiful fossils discovered here show. At the visitors center you can view more than 80 of these specimens up close, and receive educational and interpretive information about them as well. If you have time to spare, you can watch a film to learn even more about the fossils or attend a ranger-led talk. If you're lucky (or you plan ahead), you can also go along on a ranger-guided hike and then help the staff dig for fossils at the monument's active quarrying area. Remote and beautiful, the monument's cold, high desert environment sustains an abundance of wildlife as well, which you might view if you walk along one of two **interpretive trails**—the 2.5-mile Historic Quarry Trail or the 1.5-mile Fossil Lake Trail. Children ages 5–15 can participate in a Junior Ranger Program (free) to earn a Junior Ranger badge. Overnight camping is not allowed. Cross-country skiing is a

TOGWOTEE PASS

popular activity here in winter. Bikes and horses are allowed in the monument, but not on the trails.

Grand Canyon of the Snake River, along US 26/89 east of Alpine and south-west of Hoback Junction. Scenic pullouts enable you to stop and take a closer look at this incredible canyon, which features immense cliffs framing the popular white water of the Snake River below. You might even be lucky enough to watch paddlers in action—or perhaps you'll be one of those paddlers that others are watching from the pullouts above. (See also the Snake River and Snake River Kayak & Canoe under *To Do—Paddling/Floating.*)

Gros Ventre Slide Geological Area lies in the Gros Ventre Wilderness of Bridger–Teton National Forest (see *Wilder Places—Forests*) off Gros Ventre Road (F.R. 30410) near Lower Slide Lake. This area changed radically in 1925 when an entire mountainside—some 50 million cubic yards of sandstone—cut loose in a massive landslide, resulting in a huge, naturally formed lake (Lower Slide Lake) in mere minutes. Part of the dam broke two years after the slide, causing huge, but brief, floods, and destroyed the town of Kelly. Today you can still view dramatic evidence of the power of natural forces by walking a 0.25-mile-long self-guided interpretive trail.

Periodic Geyser, also known as **Intermittent Spring,** lies in the Salt River Range of Bridger–Teton National Forest, just east of Afton. Take F.R. 10211 east of Afton to the trailhead for Periodic Spring Trail (which allows mountain bikes). An 0.8-mile hike (one-way) takes you to the spring, North America's only known cold-water geyser and one of only three such phenomena known to exist in the world. The spring's cycle of starting and stopping is most pronounced in late summer and early fall, but the reasons why it does this are unknown. Another trail, #35, also leaves from the parking area; it links up with other trails, should you wish to explore the surrounding terrain a bit more.

See also **Clear Creek Trail** under *To Do—Hiking.*

✳ To Do

BICYCLING ♿ **Jackson Hole Community Pathway System** is an 8-mile net-work of trails in Jackson Hole and includes Indian Springs Trail, Melody Ranch Trail, Road Pathway, Russ Garaman Trail, School Trail, Teton Pines–Teton Vil-lage Trail, and the Wilson Centennial Trail. The trail system is also open to walk-ing, running, horseback riding, and in-line skating—and cross-country skiing in winter. If your bike needs a tune-up or you want to rent a bike, stop by **Teton Cycle Works** (307-733-4386; www.tetoncycleworks.com), 175 N. Glenwood, Jackson. Open March through October Monday through Saturday. The friendly folks there can also recommend great road and mountain bike rides suitable to your ability level.

♂ **Teton Mountain Bike Tours, LLC** (1-800-733-0788; 307-733-0712; www .tetonmtbike.com), P.O. Box 7027, Jackson; call for reservations and directions. With rides suited to all ability levels, this bicycling outfitter offers half-day, full-day, multiday, and customized tours, with prices varying according to the selected tour ($75 per person for a 7-hour adventure gives you an idea of this activity's price tag). You'll be outfitted with a mountain bike, a helmet, appropriate gear, a free water bottle (to take with you), a lunch for full-day tours, and an expert, knowledgeable guide who will give you tips on mountain biking and fill you in on your surroundings. Families are welcome here—kids ages 8 and up can ride their own bike, while kids 5–7 can ride a nifty Adams Trail-a-Bike, adding their pedaling power to yours. Children 1–4 can ride along in a child trailer that attaches to your bike.

See also Periodic Geyser under *To See—Natural Wonders;* Fremont Lake under *Boating;* Cache Creek Trail, Lake Alice Trail, Lake Barstow Trail, and Lost Lake Trail under *Hiking;* Granite Creek Hot Springs under *Hot Springs;* Grand Targhee Ski Resort, Jackson Hole Mountain Resort, and White Pine Ski Area and Resort under *Snow Sports;* Bridger–Teton National Forest in *Wilder Places—Forests;* Bureau of Land Management under *Wilder Places—Other Wild Places;* and Tour de Wyoming under *Special Events.*

BOATING **Big Sandy Recreation Area,** managed by the **Bureau of Reclamation** (307-273-9566; 801-379-1000; www.recreation.gov/detail.cfm?id=1229), is located 8 miles north of Farson along US 191. This recreation area is home to **Big Sandy Reservoir,** with 2,500 acres of surface area, which offers opportunities not only for boating (boat launch) but also for swimming, hunting, camping (free), and fishing (species include brown trout, channel catfish, cutthroat trout, and rainbow trout). South of Big Sandy Reservoir is **Eden Reservoir,** accessed by taking WY 28 east of Farson 4 miles and then going north on Farson 2nd E. Road (Eden Reservoir Road) for 7 miles. This reservoir also permits fishing (species include cutthroat trout and rainbow trout).

& **Fontenelle Reservoir** is located on US 189 15 miles south of LaBarge (see Bureau of Land Management under *Wilder Places—Other Wild Places* for contact information). This reservoir, with 8,000 acres of surface area, offers opportunities not only for boating (boat launch) but also for swimming, fishing (species include brown trout, cutthroat trout, rainbow trout, and smallmouth bass), and camping (see BLM campgrounds under *Camping*).

& **Fremont Lake** (www.visitsublettecounty.com/destinations/fremontlake.htm) is accessible by taking Fremont Lake Road 3.2 miles northwest of Pinedale. Fremont is the largest of several lakes situated west-northwest of Pinedale, and it is the second-largest natural lake in Wyoming. This glacially formed lake—the largest (11 miles long) and deepest (up to 600 feet deep) of its kind in the Green River Basin—lies partially in Bridger–Teton National Forest (see *Wilder Places—Forests*). For boaters, the lake has boat launches, a marina, and several providers of boat rentals. The lake is famed for its mackinaw trout fishing; other game fish species here include brown trout and rainbow trout. Additional nearby lakes with both boating access and fishing in this area include (from north to south) **New Fork Lakes, Willow Lake, Half Moon Lake, and Boulder Lake.** You can fish in numerous additional nearby lakes, including **Long Lake, Soda Lake, Fayette Lake, and Burnt Lake.** Overnight camping is available at several developed campgrounds (see BLM campgrounds and Bridger–Teton National Forest under *Camping*), and hiking trails abound in the area. On the way to Fremont Lake, you'll also find a number of Civilian Conservation Corps ponds (handicapped accessible) with trails around them for fishing access as well as for strolling and biking. Several fishing derbies are held annually on these lakes, which are also popular for ice fishing in winter. (See also Lakeside Lodge under *Lodging—Lodges.*)

Viva Naughton Reservoir lies on WY 233 about 14.5 miles north of Kemmerer (see Bureau of Land Management under *Wilder Places—Other Wild Places* for contact information). This reservoir offers opportunities not only for boating (boat launch) but also for fishing (species include brown trout, cutthroat trout, rainbow trout, splake, and whitefish). Just south of this reservoir is **Kemmerer Reservoir,** which also permits fishing (species include brown trout, cutthroat trout, rainbow trout, and whitefish).

CAMPING & **Bridger–Teton National Forest** encompasses more than 3.4 million acres of land around three sides of Jackson Hole, extending south in two large "peninsulas" of land as well. The forest has six ranger districts with 37 developed campgrounds, some handicapped accessible, and most first-come, first-served. **Big Piney Ranger District** (307-276-3375) has two developed campgrounds, both of which lie west of Big Piney via WY 350/Middle Piney Road (Road 111/F.R. 10024): **Middle Piney Lake** (open early July through late September; free) and **Sacajawea Campground** (open mid-June through late September; $7). The ranger district also has **two guard stations** available for rent ($30 per night). **Greys River Ranger District** (307-885-3166) has seven developed campgrounds, five of which lie along F.R. 10138 on the Greys River and two on the Star Valley Front, including **Swift Creek,** just east of Afton off US 89 on 2nd Avenue to C.R. 138 to F.R. 10211 (open mid-May through mid-October; $5). **Kemmerer Ranger District** (307-877-4415) has three developed campgrounds: **Allred Flat,** 20 miles south of Afton on US 89 (handicapped accessible; open late May through late October; $5); **Hobble Creek,** located on F.R. 10070 northeast of Cokeville 34 miles—follow WY 232 northeast 12 miles to a Y where the pavement ends, then go right, continuing 20 miles on graveled F.R. 10062, 10066, and 10193 to 10070 (open early June through late October; $5); and **Hams Fork,** 38 miles north of Kemmerer on Hams Fork Road (open late May through late October; $5). The ranger district also has **three rental cabins** ($30 per night). The **Pinedale Ranger District** (307-367-4326) has nine developed campgrounds (some free), five of which are in the area around Fremont Lake (see *Boating*), including **Fremont Lake** (mid-May through mid-September; $10) and **Narrows Campground** (mid-May through mid-September; $10), at which you can reserve sites in advance by contacting the **National Recreation Reservation System** (1-877-444-6777; www.reserveusa.com). The forest's **Teton Division** includes the **Buffalo Ranger District** (307-543-2386) and the **Jackson Ranger District** (307-739-5400), which together have some 20 developed campgrounds, including **Box Creek,** 46 miles northeast of Jackson via US 26/287 to F.R. 30500 (Buffalo Valley Road), then left (northeast) to the campground (handicapped accessible; open mid-May through mid-September; $10); and **Granite Campground** (near Granite Hot Springs; see *Hot Springs*), accessed by taking US 189 south of Hoback Junction for 10 miles, then going north on F.R. 30500 for about 9 miles (handicapped accessible; open mid-May through mid-September; $15). For more information, contact the appropriate ranger district. (See also Gros Ventre River and Snake River under *Fishing*.)

& ✍ **BLM campgrounds** (see Bureau of Land Management under *Wilder Places—Other Wild Places*) in the area include four developed facilities near Fontenelle Reservoir (see *Boating*) that are managed by the **Kemmerer Field Office: Fontenelle Creek Campground,** 10 miles south of LaBarge on the west side of Fontenelle Reservoir (handicapped accessible; $5), which also has a playground and information about surrounding recreational opportunities; **Slate Creek Campground,** 4 miles south of the reservoir (free); **Tail Race Campground,** 0.25 mile south of the reservoir (free); and **Weeping Rock Campground,** 1 mile south of the reservoir (free); among others. The **Pinedale Field Office** manages several campgrounds as well, including **Boulder Lake North**—from US 191 by Boulder, go 7 miles northeast on BLM 5106 (free); **Upper Green River,** 30 miles north of Pinedale along WY 352 (free); **New Fork River,** on WY 351 12 miles west of its junction with US 191 (free); **Scab Creek,** about 15 miles northeast of Boulder via WY 353 to BLM 5423 (free); **Stokes Crossing,** about 5 miles north of Boulder via Boulder North Road (free); and **Warren Bridge Campground,** 20 miles northwest of Pinedale on US 191 (free). You should also know that in general, access to campgrounds is limited to the summer season and that primitive camping is permitted on most BLM lands unless otherwise marked. For a complete list of BLM campgrounds in the area, call or stop by one of the field offices. (See also Green River under *Fishing*.)

& **Caribou–Targhee National Forest** (see *Wilder Places—Forests*), while mostly in Idaho, also has a small portion in northwest Wyoming, including land below the southwestern border of Yellowstone National Park south and west of Grand Teton National Park. In this area, managed by the **Teton-Basin Ranger District** (208-354-2312), you'll find six developed campgrounds, including **Teton Canyon,** 9 miles east of Driggs, Idaho, on F.R. 009 (handicapped accessible; open early June through mid-September; $10); and **Trail Creek Campground,** located west of Jackson on WY 22 just before the Idaho border (handicapped accessible; open mid-May through early October; $8). Reserve sites in advance by contacting the **National Recreation Reservation System** (1-877-444-6777; www.reserveusa.com).

See also Kemmerer under *To See—Towns;* Big Sandy Recreation Area under *Boating;* the Gros Ventre River under *Fishing;* and Lake Alice Trail under *Hiking.*

FISHING **The Green River** (307-367-4352; http://gf.state.wy.us/fish/fishing/index.asp) originates from the Green River Lakes in the Bridger Wilderness of the Wind River Range, in Bridger–Teton National Forest (see *Wilder Places—Forests*). The river arcs south and continues for 730 miles, eventually emptying into the Colorado River in Utah. This upper portion of the Green River is popular for fishing, including float fishing. You'll find access points in the national forest portion of the river, as well as additional access sites for public fishing and boat launching, including the Warren Bridge BLM Campground (see *Camping*). Game fish species include brook trout, brown trout, cutthroat trout, Mackinaw trout, mountain whitefish, and rainbow trout. (See also the Green River under *To Do—Fishing* in "South Wyoming: Medicine Bow–Flaming Gorge Country."

The Greys River (307-777-4600; http://gf.state.wy.us/fish/fishing/index.asp) flows right alongside F.R. 10138 southeast of Alpine in Bridger–Teton National Forest (see *Camping* and *Wilder Places—Forests*). Game fish species in the Greys River include cutthroat trout. Numerous streams in this area provide great fishing opportunities as well. Five developed Forest Service campgrounds lie along F.R. 10138, providing easy access to the river. Kayakers enjoy paddling portions of this river in springtime's higher waters, often putting in at an area 4 miles from Alpine along F.R. 10138.

The Gros Ventre River (307-777-4600; http://gf.state.wy.us/fish/fishing/index.asp), northeast of Jackson and formed by the confluence of several creeks flowing from the Wind River Mountains to the west (including Fish Creek and its forks), flows west through Bridger–Teton National Forest (see *Wilder Places—Forests*) along Gros Ventre Road (F.R. 30400). On its way, it passes through Upper Slide Lake, the Gros Ventre Slide Geological Area (see *To See— Natural Wonders*), and Lower Slide Lake (which has boating access) before angling southwest to join the Snake River (see below) near Jackson. The river can be accessed in the forest at various sites along the road, among which are a number of Forest Service campgrounds. Game fish species include cutthroat trout, mountain whitefish, and rainbow trout.

The Hams Fork River (307-777-4600; http://gf.state.wy.us/fish/fishing/index .asp) has a state fishing access site on WY 233 north of Kemmerer (follow the signs). Game fish species include brook trout, brown trout, cutthroat trout, rainbow trout, and whitefish.

The New Fork River (307-367-4352; http://gf.state.wy.us/fish/fishing/index.asp) originates in the New Fork Lakes (see Fremont Lake under *Boating*) 24 miles north of Pinedale. The river then flows south to join the Green River (see above) just south of WY 351. This New Fork is popular for both fishing and floating. Game fish species include brook trout, brown trout, mountain whitefish, and rainbow trout. The river has numerous signed and unsigned public access sites along US 191 starting in Pinedale, where the river becomes large enough for floating. The most popular of these sites is the Boulder Bridge access point (signed) just off US 191 in Boulder. Another popular access site run by the Bureau of Land Management is at the Piney Cutoff area on WY 351, right where the river crosses the road.

The Salt River (307-367-4352; http://gf.state.wy.us/fish/fishing/index.asp) begins on the western slope of the Salt River Range west of Afton and then flows north along US 89 through Star Valley to the Palisades Reservoir (which is mostly in Idaho, with a small portion in Wyoming). The river is popular for both fishing and floating—and especially the two combined—with flat water and tremendous scenery making it great for scenic floats and paddles as well. Easy access is a bonus for users of this river, which has numerous signed state access points along US 89. Game fish species include brook trout, brown trout, cutthroat trout, mountain whitefish, and rainbow trout.

The Snake River (307-777-4600; http://gf.state.wy.us/fish/fishing/index.asp) originates in the Teton Wilderness of Bridger–Teton National Forest (see *Wilder Places—Forests*), flows through the southern portion of Yellowstone National Park before entering Jackson Lake in Grand Teton National Park (see the Snake River under *To Do—Fishing* and *Paddling/Floating* in "Grand Teton National Park"), and then flows south out of the lake through the valley of Jackson Hole before curving west to travel alongside US 26/89 just south of Jackson, following this road as it angles southeast through the **Grand Canyon of the Snake River** (see *To See—Natural Wonders*). This river is popular for fishing and floating—and both together, since access can be tough, particularly the closer you are to Jackson. South of Hoback Junction along US 89, you'll find a several Forest Service campgrounds, state access areas, and designated boat launches that provide places for boat launching and fishing. Game fish species include brown trout and cutthroat trout. (See also the Snake River under *Paddling/Floating.*)

See also Pinedale under *To See—Towns; Boating; Hiking;* National Elk Refuge under *Wilder Places—Wildlife Refuges;* Bureau of Land Management under *Wilder Places—Other Wild Places;* Big Sandy Lodge LLC, Boulder Lake Lodge, Box Y Lodge and Guest Ranch, and Triple Peak Guest Ranch and Lodge under *Lodging—Lodges;* and Cow Cabins under *Lodging—Other Options.*

GOLF **Aspen Hills Golf Course** (307-883-2899; www.starvalleywy.com/svra/golf.htm), Star Valley Ranch, 1800 Cedar Creek Drive, Thayne, 9 holes.

Cedar Creek Golf Course (307-883-2230; www.starvalleywy.com/svra/golf.htm), Star Valley Ranch, 1800 Cedar Creek Drive, Thayne, 18 holes.

Jackson Hole Golf and Tennis Club (1-800-628-9988; 307-733-3111; www.gtlc.com/golf.aspx), 5000 Spring Gulch Road, Jackson, 18 holes.

Kemmerer Field Club (307-877-6954), WY 233 N., Kemmerer, 9 holes.

Rendezvous Meadows Golf Club (307-367-4252), 55 Clubhouse Drive, Pinedale, 9 holes.

Teton Pines Resort and Country Club (1-800-238-2223; 307-733-1733; www.tetonpines.com), 3450 N. Clubhouse Drive, Jackson, 18 holes.

Valli Vu Golf Club (307-885-3338; www.vallivu.com), US 89, Afton, 9 holes.

HIKING **Cache Creek Trail** is accessible from the end of Cache Creek Drive on the east side of Jackson. Located in Bridger–Teton National Forest (see *Wilder Places—Forests*), this extremely popular 6-mile trail features easy access from the town of Jackson, gentle grades, and creekside access. Opportunities for viewing wildlife abound, and you can choose to walk a portion of the trail or the entire distance—or try it on a mountain bike. Horseback riding is also a possibility on this trail; in winter, it's popular for cross-country skiing and snowshoeing. The **Tiny Hagen Trail** and the **Putt-Putt Trail** are accessible from this area as well.

Clear Creek Trail (#184), in Bridger–Teton National Forest, is accessible via WY 351 to F.R. 10091, 52 miles northwest of Pinedale to the Green River Lakes. The 8-mile round-trip Clear Creek Trail takes you along the western shore of Upper Green River Lake (species include cutthroat trout and rainbow trout) before turning east into the Bridger Wilderness. The trail then takes you to a natural wonder: a natural bridge formed where Clear Creek wore a passageway through stone, an impressive demonstration of the persistent, erosive power of water. You can continue for another 2 miles to Clear Lake if you wish, though this trail is not maintained. This is one of several popular trails accessible from the Green River Lakes area, including **Trail #144,** which skirts the western shore of Upper Green Lake, and **Trail #094,** which takes you along the eastern shore of Lower Green Lake. Horseback riding is also popular here.

Lake Alice Trail (#025) departs from Hobble Creek Campground (see Bridger–Teton National Forest under *Camping*). A moderate 1.5-mile hike takes you to the south shore of Lake Alice, a lovely, unspoiled lake with fishing opportunities. The trail continues along the lakeshore, should you wish to explore further. There are a number of primitive, hike-in, tent-only, free campsites at Lake Alice. Formed by a landslide that dumped a mile of debris into Poker Creek, 3-mile-long Lake Alice reaches depths up to 200 feet. Because the lake's outlet flows beneath the natural dam, the cutthroat trout population was effectively trapped and isolated by the landslide, and this is the only species you'll find in the lake. Horseback riding and mountain biking are also popular here.

Lake Barstow Trail (#088) is accessible by taking F.R. 10138 southeast from Alpine, then going west on F.R. 10043 to the trailhead. This easy 3-mile round-trip in Bridger–Teton National Forest (see *Wilder Places—Forests*) takes you along Three Forks Creek to Lake Barstow in the Salt River Range. Off-road motorized vehicles are allowed on this trail as are foot traffic, horses, and mountain bikes.

Lost Lake Trail is accessible by taking US 26/287 east from Moran Junction 26 miles, turning left onto F.R. 30200, and then taking F.R. 30200 to the parking area (where the road ends). From here, a short, moderately steep, 1-mile trail leads to Lost Lake. The lake is situated below the Breccia Cliffs, which are home to bighorn sheep that you might spot with a good pair of binoculars. The deeply turquoise-hued lake lies just outside the Teton Wilderness in Bridger–Teton National Forest (see *Wilder Places—Forests*). Fish species include cutthroat trout and mountain whitefish. Horseback riding and mountain biking are also allowed.

See also Fossil Butte National Monument, Gros Ventre Slide Geological Area, and Periodic Geyser in *To See—Natural Wonders;* Fremont Lake under *Boating;* Granite Creek Hot Springs under *Hot Springs;* "Llamaneering" with Jackson Hole Llamas under *Unique Adventures;* Grand Targhee Ski Resort, Jackson Hole Mountain Resort, Snow King Ski Resort, *Snowshoeing,* and White Pine Ski Area and Resort under *Snow Sports;* and Bureau of Land Management under *Wilder Places—Other Wild Places.*

HORSEBACK RIDING Green River Outfitters (307-367-241; www.greenriver outfitters.com), P.O. Box 727, Pinedale; call for reservations and directions. Ride for half a day ($115) or a full day ($190) in the Gros Ventre Mountains 35 miles south of Jackson. You'll enjoy the peaceful solitude of your surroundings, far from the normal tourist beat of the Jackson Hole area. Full-day riders will be treated to a western-style barbecued lunch, cooked for you on an open fire. Longer trips are available as well.

Hidden Basin Outfitters (1-866-900-HUNT; 307-733-7980; www.hiddenbasin .com), 7895 Cowboy Way, Jackson. In addition to guided hunting trips, this outfit-ter offers full-day rides (10 AM–4:30 PM) into the Teton range ($125; children must be 10 or older). You can also book a longer horseback riding adventure, including a combination trip that includes white-water rafting and a rodeo.

See also *Hiking;* Goosewing Ranch, Grand Targhee Ski Resort, Snow King Ski Resort, and White Pine Ski Area and Resort under *Snow Sports;* Bridger–Teton National Forest under *Wilder Places—Forests;* Bureau of Land Management under *Wilder Places—Other Wild Places;* Pole Creek Ranch under *Lodging— Bed & Breakfasts;* Big Sandy Lodge LLC, Boulder Lake Lodge, Box Y Lodge and Guest Ranch, and Triple Peak Guest Ranch and Lodge under *Lodging— Lodges;* and Cow Cabins under *Lodging—Other Options.*

HOT SPRINGS ♨ **Granite Creek Hot Springs** lie in Bridger–Teton National Forest (see *Wilder Places—Forests*) and can be accessed by taking US 189 south of Hoback Junction for 10 miles, then going north on F.R. 30500 for about 10 miles. There you'll find a pool perfectly engineered to capture the springs' 103° to 108°F waters (in winter; in summer the temperature is only about 93°F); open daily 10 AM–8 PM; fee (contact Jackson Ranger District for current rates). A campground just south of the hot springs makes this a fun destination for the family (see also Bridger–Teton National Forest under *Camping*). The **Granite Falls Hot Springs** feature a number of more primitive soaking pools, which you can access by hiking the 2-mile trail that begins where Swift Creek meets Gran-ite Creek south of the developed pool; it then follows the east bank of Granite Creek north to the developed pool. Granite Creek Hot Springs are also a popu-lar destination for **mountain bikers,** who can bike the distance from the turnoff on US 189 up F.R. 30500 for a fun, moderate ride. This road also provides access to Trail #018 (no bikes allowed), which follows Granite Creek into the Gros Ventre Wilderness and links up with other trails in the wilderness. In win-ter, the springs are a popular destination for adventuresome snowshoers, cross-country skiers, and snowmobilers. **Jackson Hole Snowmobile Tours** (1-800-633-1733; 307-733-6850; www.jacksonholesnowmobile.com), 516 N. Cache, P.O. Box 11037, Jackson Hole, 83002, offers a hot springs adventure (minimum driver age is 13), which includes a day of snowmobile riding, a grilled steak lunch, and, of course, soaking in the hot springs ($185 per driver; $70 per child ages 5–12 riding along).

PADDLING/FLOATING **The Snake River** (see *Fishing*) offers something for everyone seeking a little river adventure, from scenic floats through flatter waters to the notorious class III and IV rapids of the Grand Canyon of the Snake River (see *To See—Natural Wonders*). Whether you're floating or paddling, rafting or kayaking, you're probably best off hiring a knowledgeable and experienced guide service to coordinate the details of your trip on this river, as it can be tricky even through the flat sections. Luckily for you, there are many services to choose from, including **Barker–Ewing River Trips** (1-800-448-4202; 307-733-1000; www.barker-ewing.com), Jackson Hole; **Jackson Hole Whitewater** (1-800-700-7238; 307-733-1007; www.jhww.com), P.O. Box 125, Jackson 83001; and **Snake River Kayak and Canoe** (1-800-529-2501; 307-733-9999; www.snakeriverkayak.com), P.O. Box 4311, Jackson 83001; contact all three for directions.

See also *Boating;* the Green River, the Greys River, the New Fork River, and the Salt River under *Fishing;* Hidden Basin Outfitters under *Horseback Riding;* Bureau of Land Management under *Wilder Places—Other Wild Places;* and Boulder Lake Lodge under *Lodging—Lodges.*

SNOW SPORTS

Cross-Country Skiing

Cross-country skiing opportunities abound in this region on both groomed and ungroomed trails. With the tremendous amount of lands and trails in Bridger–Teton National Forest (see *Wilder Places—Forests*) and Bureau of Land Management lands (see *Wilder Places—Other Wild Places*), you will find a lifetime's worth of Nordic skiing throughout this region. To get you started, near Jackson you'll find two groomed trails: Cache Creek Trail (see *Hiking*) and Game Creek Trail, accessible by going south from Jackson for 7 miles on US 89/191, then turning east on F.R. 30455. For other ideas of where to go in this region, see also Fossil Butte National Monument under *To See—Natural Wonders;* Big Springs Scenic Backway under *To See—Scenic Drives;* Granite Creek Hot Springs under *Hot Springs;* Grand Targhee Ski Resort, Jackson Mountain Ski Resort, and White Pine Ski Area and Resort under *Downhill Skiing* (below); and *Snowshoeing* (also below).

Downhill Skiing

✍ ♿ **Grand Targhee Ski Resort** (1-800-TARGHEE; 307-353-2300; www.grandtarghee.com), on F.R. 025 northeast of Driggs, Idaho; P.O. Box SKI, Alta 83422. High in the Teton Range of Caribou–Targhee National Forest (see *Wilder Places—Forests*) you'll discover this full-service ski resort. Two mountains provide more than 2,000 acres of lift-served skiable terrain, including a terrain park—plus 1,000 acres served by snowcats—that see some 500 inches of champagne powder each season. The resort also offers **cross-country skiing** on 15K of groomed and tracked trails ($10 adults; $5 seniors and juniors). You'll find information about additional adventures at the resort's Activity Center, located in the main plaza, including dogsledding, snowshoeing, sleigh ride dinners, ice-skating (free rink), snow tubing, and more. In summer, the resort offers an array of recreational activities, including hiking, mountain biking, horseback riding, Folf (Frisbee golf), and more. *Lifts:* three quad chairlifts, one double chairlift, one "magic carpet." *Trails:* 75 trails—10 percent beginner, 70 percent intermediate to intermediate-advanced, 20 percent advanced. *Vertical drop:* 2,400 feet. *Facilities*: four restaurants and a bar located in the base area, as well as three ski-in, ski-out lodges. *Ski school:* offers ski and snowboard lessons for all ages and ability levels. *For children:* Kids' Club (day care with optional ski lesson) for ages 2 months to 5 years, Little Deer for ages 4–5, Powder Scouts for ages 6–12 (skiing) and 8–12 (snowboarding), and Teen Adventures for ages 13–16. *Rates:* $53 adults, $34 seniors (ages 62 and older), $33 juniors (ages 6–14), children 5 and under ski free with an adult; half-day and multiday rates also available.

& ✄ **Jackson Hole Mountain Resort** (1-888-DEEP-SNO; 307-733-2292; www.jacksonhole.com), 3395 W. Village Drive, Teton Village. Undoubtedly Wyoming's best-known ski resort, Jackson Hole Mountain's reputation has been gained for good reason. Only 12 miles northwest of the town of Jackson via WY 22 to WY 390, this resort's two mountains include 2,500 acres of in-bounds ski-able terrain and 3,000 additional acres of gate-accessed backcountry terrain—but it's the 4,139 feet of vertical drop that might just knock your skis off. That's the biggest continuous vertical drop you'll find at any ski area in the United States, in case you were wondering. Complementing its remarkable downhill skiing and snowboarding (including a terrain park and half pipe), the resort offers a wide range of winter activities, including dogsledding, ice-skating, snowshoeing, dinner sleigh rides, heli-skiing, snowcat skiing, snowmobiling, and more. The resort also has **cross-country skiing** on 12K of groomed and tracked trails ($10 person). In summer, visitors can enjoy a sightseeing ride on the resort's aerial tramway, as well as hiking and mountain biking opportunities, among other activities. *Lifts:* one aerial tram, one gondola, six quad chairlifts, one triple and one double chairlift, one "magic carpet." *Trails:* 74 trails—10 percent beginner, 40 percent intermediate, 50 percent expert. *Vertical drop:* 4,139 feet. *Snowmaking:* covering 160 acres. *Facilities:* Corbets Cabin at the top of the mountain; Nick Wilson's Cowboy Café at the Tram Tower building for breakfast, lunch, and après-ski; Casper Restaurant at the base of the Casper Chairlift offers a full menu; Thunder Café at the base of Thunder Chairlift offers ski-in, ski-out quick eats; Bridger Bagels at the base of the Gondola offers bagels, coffee, and other such goodies. You'll find numerous additional eateries and bars in Teton Village. *Ski school:* offers a full range of skiing and snowboarding lessons for all ages and ability levels. *For children:* Kids Ranch offers age-appropriate activities for kids ages 6 months to 17 years, including Wranglers (day care) for ages 6 months to 2 years, Rough Riders for ages 3–6, Little Rippers for ages 5–6, Explorers for ages 7–14, and Team Extreme for ages 12–17. *Rates:* $67 adults, $54 young adults (ages 15–21), $34 juniors and seniors (14 and younger or 65 and older); half-day and multiday rates also available.

Pine Creek Ski Area (307-279-3201; www.pinecreekresort.com), 4061 Pine Creek C.R. 204, Cokeville. Open Friday through Sunday in-season. Situated in the Tunp Mountain Range 7 miles east of Cokeville, this little ski area might be off the beaten path, but its terrain packs a punch without leaving you broke. The area has a terrain park and a half pipe, too. *Lifts:* one quad chairlift. *Trails:* 30 trails—30 percent beginner, 35 percent intermediate, 35 percent advanced. *Vertical drop:* 1,200 feet. *Rates:* $25 adults, $20 juniors and seniors.

✄ 🐾 **Snow King Ski Resort** (1-800-522-5464; 307-733-5200; www.snowking .com), 400 E. Snow King Avenue, Jackson Hole. Just 6 blocks from downtown

Jackson, you'll find Wyoming's first ski area—Snow King, founded in 1939. Every winter season since that time, Snow King has continued to draw skiers from around the world to test their mettle on its worthy terrain. Always changing with the times, the resort welcomes snowboarders to its slopes as well, inviting them to ride in its terrain park, too. Families in particular seem drawn to try out a different sort of snow ride in Snow King's separate area for snow tubing (lift-served); $14 for 2 hours, adults; $10 for 2 hours, children 5 and older; children under 5 not allowed. In summer, the resort operates an alpine slide, a scenic chairlift, and a miniature golf course and also provides opportunities for hiking and horseback riding, among other activities. *Lifts:* one triple chairlift, two double chairlifts, one handle-tow. *Trails:* 20 trails—15 percent beginner, 25 percent intermediate, 60 percent advanced. *Vertical drop:* 1,571 feet. *Snowmaking:* 150 acres. *Facilities:* base lodge has a cafeteria and an indoor ice-skating rink, plus hotels and condos. *Ski school:* Great American Ski School offers lessons for all ages and ability levels. *Rates:* $35 adults, $25 juniors and seniors (14 and younger or 60 and older); nighttime, 2-hour, half-day, and multiday rates available as well.

✍ **White Pine Ski Area and Resort** (307-367-6606; www.whitepineski.com), P.O. Box 1420, Pinedale, 82941. Located 10 miles northeast of Pinedale via Fremont Lake Road in Bridger–Teton National Forest (see *Wilder Places—Forests*). This resort, nestled just above the lovely small town of Pinedale (see *To See—Towns*), includes many of the elegant amenities you might expect from a larger ski area—without all of the crowds and the hefty price tag. **Cross-country skiers** can access more than 35K of trails (free) from the resort's parking area, 9K of which are groomed with both classic and skating lanes (additionally, the surrounding area has some 60K of marked, groomed trails). In summer, the resort's activities include scenic chairlift rides, mountain biking, hiking, and horseback riding. *Lifts:* two triple chairlifts. *Trails:* 25-plus trails—25 percent beginner, 45 percent intermediate, 30 percent advanced. *Vertical drop:* 1,100 feet. *Facilities:* three-story base lodge includes family-style dining at White Pine Grill, as well as a ski and rental shop; plus new in 2004–5, duplex cabins available for rental near the lodge. *Ski school:* offers ski and snowboard lessons for all ages and abilities. *For children:* Mountain Explorer and Junior Racer for ages 6–12. *Rates:* $26; half-day rates available as well.

Ice-Skating

In and around Jackson, ice-skating can be enjoyed at numerous places, including Grand Targhee Ski Resort, Jackson Hole Mountain Resort, and Snow King Ski Resort (see *Downhill Skiing,* above). The **Teton County Parks and Recreation Department** (307-733-5056) also allows public skating at outdoor hockey rinks at Snow King and in Wilson (call for times), as well as at a small rink at the elementary school in Jackson at 155 E. Gill. You can also ice-skate farther south in this region at the **Cokeville Ice Skating Rink** (outdoors in Cokeville Town Park on Main Street), among other places.

Snowmobiling

Snowmobiling, like cross-country skiing, is very popular in this region, and the possibilities are virtually endless, from the area around Togwotee Pass northeast of Jackson along US 26/287 to the Wyoming Range north of Kemmerer. For detailed **trail reports,** call 1-800-225-5996 or go to http://wyotrails.state.wy .us/snow, the **Wyoming Snowmobile Trails** Web site, which also provides information about rules, rental agencies, trails around the state, and more. If you're a novice or you want some expert guidance on your adventure, you should hire a guide, such as **Goosewing Ranch** (1-888-733-5251; 307-733-5251; www.goosewingranch.com), **Jackson Hole Snowmobile Tours** (1-800-633-1733; 307-733-6850; www.jacksonholesnowmobile.com), or **High Country Snowmobile Tours** (1-800-524-0130; www.hcsnowmobile.com). Such services can help you learn the tools of the trade, while acquainting you with the proper etiquette, rules, and regulations. For more snowmobiling ideas, see Big Springs Scenic Backway under *To See—Scenic Drives;* Granite Creek Hot Springs under *Hot Springs;* Jackson Hole Mountain Resort under *Downhill Skiing* (above); Bridger–Teton National Forest under *Wilder Places—Forests;* Bureau of Land Management under *Wilder Places—Other Wild Places;* Box Y Lodge and Guest Ranch, Triple Peak Guest Ranch and Lodge, and Togwotee Mountain Lodge under *Lodging—Lodges;* Maverick Snowmobile Hill Climb under *Special Events;* and Continental Divide Snowmobile Trail under *To Do—Snow Sports* in "Central Wyoming: Oregon Trail–Rendezvous Country."

Snowshoeing

Snowshoeing, like cross-country skiing and snowmobiling, is a great way to see this region in wintertime, with so many places to go that you would need more than a lifetime to explore all of them. **The Hole Hiking Experience** (1-866-733-4453; www.holehike.com), P.O. Box 7779, Jackson 83002, can coordinate a snowshoeing adventure for you, led by a knowledgeable botanist who can help interpret your wintry surroundings (half-day $70 adults, $55 children; full day $100 adults, $85 children, includes lunch; minimum four people per trip). Hole Hiking also guides cross-country skiing trips and hikes in warmer months. For more ideas, see also Cache Creek Trail under *Hiking; Cross-Country Skiing* (above); Grand Targhee Ski Resort and Jackson Hole Mountain Resort under *Downhill Skiing* (above); Bridger–Teton National Forest under *Wilder Places—Forests;* and Bureau of Land Management under *Wilder Places—Other Wild Places.*

See also **Fremont Lake** under *Boating.*

UNIQUE ADVENTURES ✄ **"Llamaneering" with Jackson Hole Llamas** (1-800-830-7316; 307-739-9582; www.jhllamas.com), P.O. Box 12500, Jackson 83002. Open May through October. Want to take a day hike with a unique, four-footed companion? Let a llama carry your gear while you hike unencumbered through the gorgeous terrain surrounding Jackson, accompanied by an experience llama handler and guide. Gentle and strong, the llamas will carry along water, a huge lunch (provided by the outfitter), and all of your gear for the day ($95). Children are welcome. Jackson Hole Llamas also offers multiday llama-neering adventures. Call for details and reservations.

Ranch vacations. These vacations usually allow you to participate to a certain extent in various aspects of ranch life, often including cattle herding and branding.

The ratio of work time to leisure time varies from ranch to ranch, as do the additional activities and amenities offered, but most ranches include horseback riding, lodging, and meals in an inclusive package deal. In this region, providers include **Darwin Ranch** (1-866-733-5588; 307-733-5588), Jackson; **Fort William Guest Ranch** (307-367-4670), Pinedale; **Goosewing Ranch** (1-888-733-5251; 307-733-5251), Jackson; **Historic DC Bar Guest Ranch** (1-888-803-7316; 307-367-2268), Pinedale; and **R Lazy S Ranch** (307-733-2655), Teton Village. (See also **Box Y Lodge and Guest Ranch** and **Triple Peak Guest Ranch and Lodge** under *Lodging—Lodges.*)

&. ♪ **Sleigh Rides on the National Elk Refuge** (1-800-313-9553; 307-732-5425; http://nationalelkrefuge.fws.gov/nersleighrides.html). Rides depart from the National Wildlife Museum (see *To See—Museums*). Open mid-December through early April (depending on weather and herd conditions); closed Christmas; rides leave three to four times per hour 10 AM–4 PM; $15 adults, $11 children ages 6–12, children 5 and under free, family $48 (two adults and one to two children ages 6–12); combination sleigh ride and museum entry passes available as well; reservations taken only for groups of 20 or more. Bundle up for this exciting 1-hour ride in a horse-drawn sleigh right into the thick of the hundreds to thousands of elk that winter here each year. (See also National Elk Refuge under *Wilder Places—Wildlife Refuges and Areas.*)

♪ **Wagons A+cross Wyoming** (1-888-818-3581; 307-859-8629; 307-733-3045; www.wagonsacrosswyoming.com), P.O. Box 132, Daniel 83115. About three 5-day, 4-night wagon trips per summer season; $950 adults, $750 children 14 and under. Want to have an authentic pioneer experience? Then go ahead and take a step back in time with Wagons A+cross Wyoming. Your journey will follow the Lander Cutoff portion of the historic Oregon Trail, which starts in Big Piney. You'll cover 10 miles on days one and two, and then take a rest day before covering the same distance on days three and four, as you head back to where you started. Ride in historic wagons pulled by draft horses, and experience camping, cooking, and incredible scenery while learning firsthand a little more about the trials and travails of this kind of travel. When your trip is finished, you'll most likely have a deeper understanding of and appreciation for the boldness and tenacity of the people who traveled these routes as pioneers.

&. **Wild West Jeep Tours** (307-733-9036; www.wildwestjeeptours.com/wyoming tours.htm), P.O. Box 7506, Jackson 83002. Open summer months only; $45 adults, $35 children ages 12 and under. Let your knowledgeable guide do all of the driving, from the moment he or she picks you up from your lodgings to the moment you're dropped off at your home away from home 3 hours later. You'll get a real feel for the terrain as you tour through the backcountry areas outside Jackson. Your guide's informed interpretive narration about both the natural and cultural history of the area will provide you with a deeper and more intimate understanding of this incredible locale.

♪ **Wyoming Balloon Adventures** (307-739-0900; www.wyomingballoon.com), P.O. Box 2578, Jackson 83001. $225 adults, $175 children ages 6 and up (children 5 and under not allowed). Imagine yourself floating high above Jackson Hole, with incredible, bird's-eye views of the Teton Range and the surrounding natural splendors—sound like a dream? Well, you can make this fairy-tale image become a reality during your visit to Jackson—and be back in time for breakfast, too! Wyoming Balloon Adventures will pick you up at around 6 AM to get you started on your adventure. You'll spend about an hour in flight in a balloon piloted by an FAA-certified pilot, enjoying the morning sun on the Tetons and the potential to see wildlife as well. Your friendly guides will then have you back by around 9:30 AM.

See also Hidden Basin Outfitters under *Horseback Riding;* Granite Creek Hot Springs under *Hot Springs;* and Grand Targhee Ski Resort, Jackson Hole Mountain Resort, Snow King Ski Resort, White Pine Ski Area and Resort, *Snowmobiling,* and *Snowshoeing* under *Snow Sports.*

✳ Wilder Places

PARKS See "Wyoming's Yellowstone and Grand Teton National Parks."

FORESTS **Bridger–Teton National Forest** (307-739-5500; www.fs.fed.us/btnf), P.O. Box 1888, Jackson 83001. Covering more than 3.4 million acres of land, Bridger–Teton National Forest surrounds Jackson Hole on three sides, extending south in this region like two huge, wide arms, embracing much of the area's lands within its grasp. Encompassed within these lands are three pristine, untrammeled wilderness areas—**Bridger, Gros Ventre,** and **Teton**—which together comprise 1.2 million acres. The lands of this national forest make up a large portion of the more than 12-million-acre **Greater Yellowstone Ecosystem,** the Lower 48 states' largest remaining intact temperate ecosystem, of which **Yellowstone National Park** and **Grand Teton National Park** are the cores. With its numerous mountains, including the Gros Ventre, Salt River, Wind River, and Wyoming ranges; its abundance of rivers, lakes, and streams; and its 30,000 miles of developed roads and trails, this national forest provides not only abundant wildlife habitat but also endless recreational opportunities. These include mountain biking, boating, camping, fishing, horseback riding, hot springs, paddling/floating, snow sports, picnicking, hunting, and wildlife-watching, among other activities. (See also Grand Canyon of the Snake River, Gros Ventre Slide Geological Area, and Periodic Geyser under *To See—Natural Wonders;* Fremont Lake under *To Do—Boating; To Do—Camping;* the Green River, the Greys River, and the Snake River under *To Do—Fishing; To Do—*

JACKSON'S TOWN SQUARE

Hiking; Granite Creek Hot Springs under *To Do—Hot Springs;* White Pine Ski Area and Resort under *To Do—Snow Sports;* and Boulder Lake Lodge and Togwotee Mountain Lodge under *Lodging—Lodges.*)

Caribou–Targhee National Forest (208-524-7500; www.fs.fed.us/r4/caribou -targhee), 1405 Hollipark Drive, Idaho Falls, ID 83401. The more than 3 million acres of lands in this forest lie primarily in Idaho. A small portion in northwest Wyoming includes lands below the southwestern border of Yellowstone National Park south and west of Grand Teton National Park, including the **Jedediah Smith Wilderness,** a portion of the **Teton Range,** and a portion of the **Snake River Range.** Recreational opportunities in this area include camping, fishing, horseback riding, snow sports, and wildlife-watching, among other activities. (See also *To Do—Camping* and Grand Targhee Ski Resort under *To Do—Snow Sports.*)

WILDLIFE REFUGES National Elk Refuge (307-733-3616; http://nationalelk refuge.fws.gov) comprises 25,000 acres along the west side of US 26/89/191 just north of Jackson. The **Jackson Hole and Greater Yellowstone Visitor Center** (see *To See—Museums*) is a great place to start your exploration of the National Elk Refuge, one of the nation's largest ranges for wintering elk. Each year, some 7,500 of these grand animals make this area near Jackson their seasonal abode, and both visitors and residents alike delight in their presence. During the wintertime, when conditions become extremely harsh, the elk enjoy a supplementary feeding program for 2 to 3 months that helps them to make it through the season without an abnormally high rate of mortality. This human intervention is an effort to right a human-caused wrong: due to human habitation and cattle grazing, the elk do not have access to nearly as much forage and safe range as they once did. In response to this problem, the National Elk Refuge was established in 1912. Of interest to anglers is lovely Flat Creek, currently Wyoming's sole fly-fishing-only stream (for cutthroat trout), which flows through the refuge. (See also Sleigh Rides on the National Elk Refuge under *To Do—Unique Adventures* and ElkFest under *Special Events.*)

THE NATIONAL ELK REFUGE

OTHER WILD PLACES & **Bureau of Land Management** (BLM) has two offices in this region: the **Pinedale Field Office** (307-367-5300; www .wy.blm.gov/pfo/index.htm), 432 E. Mill Street, Pinedale, managing 912,000 acres of federal surface land and mineral estate and almost 300,000 acres of private surface land and mineral estate; and the **Kemmerer Field Office** (307-828-4500; www.wy.blm .gov/kfo/index.htm), 312 US 189 N., Kemmerer, managing 1.6 million

acres of surface land and 250,000 acres of mineral estate. Much of this land is
open to recreational pursuits, including bicycling, boating, camping (both primitive and developed; most developed campgrounds are handicapped accessible),
fishing, hiking, horseback riding, paddling, and snow sports, including snowmobiling and cross-country skiing. BLM lands tend to be the most unregulated of
public lands, which means that most typical outdoor recreational pursuits are
allowed on most BLM lands, guided by the dictates of **Leave No Trace** (1-800-
332-4100; 303-442-8222; www.lnt.org) outdoor ethics. Of particular interest to
history buffs are the **historic trails,** including the Lander Trail, Sublette Cutoff,
Oregon Trail, Mormon Trail, and Overland Trail, each of which has portions running throughout this region on BLM land. For more detailed information about
these trails, visit the **National Historic Trails Center** in Casper (see *To See—
Museums* in "Central Wyoming: Oregon Trail–Rendezvous Country"). To find
out more general information about the BLM lands in this region, including
maps, developed campgrounds, and other recreational pursuits, contact the
appropriate field office. (See also Fontenelle Reservoir and Viva Naughton
Reservoir under *To Do—Boating;* BLM campgrounds under *To Do—Camping;*
and the New Fork River under *To Do—Fishing.*)

✳ Lodging

& **Jackson Hole Central Reservations** (1-800-443-6931; 307-733-4005;
www.jacksonholewy.com), 140 E.
Broadway, Jackson. This company can
not only book lodging at a variety of
locations in Jackson and the surrounding area but also hook you up with
vacation activities, often wrapped into
package deals.

BED & BREAKFASTS

Jackson Hole
& **Bentwood Inn Bed and Breakfast** (307-739-1411; www.bentwood
inn.com), 4250 Raven Haven Road,
P.O. Box 561, Jackson Hole 83001.
Sink into the divinity of your own private hot tub and then curl up in front
of a cozy, private fireplace in any one
of the five guest rooms at this award-
winning, critically acclaimed bed &
breakfast. All rooms also feature cable
television, a telephone, a private bath,
and a deck or balcony. The elegant
5,800-square-foot log inn itself was
constructed in 1995 with much of its

wood salvaged from the famous Yellowstone National Park fires of 1988.
Inside, you'll find a charming blend
of fine English antiques and country
western furnishings. You'll also enjoy a
hearty breakfast in the morning and
afternoon refreshments as well
($215–325).

Grand Victorian Lodge (1-800-584-
0532; 307-584-0532; www.grand
victorianlodge.com), 85 Perry Street,
P.O. Box 464, Jackson Hole 83001.
You'll know you're staying in style
from the moment you pull up in front
of this Victorian B&B on the north
side of Jackson. The elegant exterior is
complemented by the exquisite interi-
or, which features well-matched furnishings throughout. All 11 guest
rooms feature cable television, wireless Internet access, and telephones,
while some also include private hot
tubs, private baths, fireplaces, and
canopied king-size beds. You'll enjoy a
full gourmet breakfast prepared daily
and served either directly to you in

your room or in the dining room—your choice. Afternoon coffee and tea service—with homemade cookies, too—is standard as well ($99–325).

☞ 🐾 ♿ **Sassy Moose Inn** (1-800-356-1277; 307-733-1277; www.sassymoosejacksonhole.com), 3859 Miles Road, Jackson Hole 83014. With the Tetons as your backdrop, you can simmer in the serenity of this rustic log inn's outdoor hot tub before you settle into the soothing comfort of your guest room, perhaps reading a story to the children in front of the crackling fireplace before you slip off to slumber. Four of the five guest rooms offer views of Jackson Hole Mountain Resort to tantalize your imagination when you're not actually on the slopes. All rooms feature private baths, views of the Tetons, down comforters, and cathedral ceilings. A full breakfast is included in the rates, and children 11 and under stay for free ($79–189).

A Teton Treehouse (307-733-3233; www.cruising-america.com/tetontreehouse), 6175 Heck of a Hill Road, P.O. Box 550, Wilson 83014. If you read the contact information closely for this entry, you probably already have a bit of an idea of the lighthearted and playful spirit you'll find infused in every nook and cranny of this lovingly handcrafted B&B. Located on Heck of a Hill Road, the inn itself is a product of the owner-innkeeper's efforts to create a wonderful, whimsical mountainside haven for himself and his family—and for you, too! You'll get your exercise in every day as you walk up the 95 steps that lead to the front door—but don't worry, they're not all that steep, just enough to get your heart rate up a little and to slow you down a bit from the hurried pace of the outside world. You'll relax in the comfort of one of six guest rooms, all of which feature private baths, decks, views, and window seats. You can also enjoy an outdoor hot tub, and you'll start each day with a healthy and delicious breakfast ($155–385).

Wildflower Inn (307-733-4710; www.jacksonholewildflower.com; mailing address: P.O. Box 11000, Jackson 83002), 3725 Teton Village Road, Jackson 83001. This award-winning inn welcomes you in style, whether you're in search of the spot for a perfect romantic getaway or a comfortable, elegant place to relax after a hard day playing on the slopes or in the woods. Situated on 3 acres of land tucked back in the trees, this log lodging offers privacy and solitude aplenty as you rest in one of four guest rooms or in the suite. Rooms all feature down comforters on hewn-log beds, private baths, charming decor, private decks, and televisions. Elegant, country western comfort beckons to you from every corner of the B&B, from

THE GRAND VICTORIAN LODGE

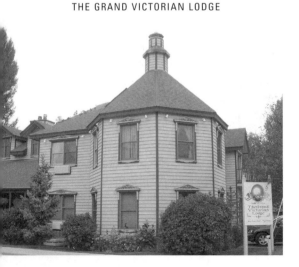

the cozy easy chairs to the stone fireplace. Freshly prepared breakfasts with something for everyone, from light appetites to hearty ones, greet you every morning ($200–350).

Pinedale 82941

🐾 ♿ **The Chambers House Bed and Breakfast** (1-800-567-2168; 307-367-2168; www.chambershouse.com), 111 W. Magnolia Street, P.O. Box 753. Built in 1933 by one of Pinedale's pioneers, this historic, renovated log structure combines the flavor of the past with the comforts of modernity to weave you an exquisite lodging experience. Throughout the inn and in the five guest rooms, decor features family antiques and handmade quilts. Some guest rooms have private baths, and two have private fireplaces as well. Homemade breakfast served daily is included in the rate. The kids are welcome here, as is Fido ($75–125).

🐾 ♿ **Pole Creek Ranch** (307-367-4433; www.bbonline.com/wy/pole creek), 244 Fayette Pole Creek Road, P.O. Box 278. Rustic, ranch-style accommodations and adventures can be found year-round at Pole Creek Ranch. Choose to stay in one of three rooms, one with a private bath and two with a shared bath, or go for the out-of-the-ordinary and book a night or two in the ranch's tipi. You and the kids ($10 extra apiece) will find plenty of activities to keep you occupied, from horseback riding to buggy rides or horse-drawn sleigh rides in wintertime—and if you're traveling with a horse, boarding is also available. Soaking in the hot tub can help relax the most tired of muscles after a day of play. You'll enjoy a full ranch breakfast served each morning ($65).

🐾 🍴 **Bridger View Bed and Breakfast** (307-886-5666; www.starvalley wy.com/BridgerviewB&B), C.R. 400, #79, Afton 83110. Perfect for you and the kids, this neat country inn offers accommodations for up to four people. Amenities include a king-size bed, cable television, a living area, a refrigerator and microwave, hot breakfast served daily, laundry facilities, a private bath, and homemade cookies ($75, includes up to two kids). You can also book the B&B for an Anniversary Special, which includes a romantic, candlelit dinner for two in addition to the above amenities ($100).

🐾 🍴 **Cottonwood Cottage Bed and Breakfast** (307-886-9348; http://home.silverstar.com/~halls/cotton wood_cottage.htm), 78391 US 89, Smoot 83126. This B&B offers you two choices, both with lovely views of the Salt River Range. Your first option is the large suite, which includes a king-size bed, an indoor Jacuzzi, a gas fireplace, a private bathroom, satellite TV/VCR, and a sofa hide-a-bed ($85). Your other option, the Country Charm Room, features a queen-size bed, hide-a-bed, television, and private bath ($75). Each child staying with you is only $5 more. A full country breakfast is served daily in the dining room, except on Sunday, when a continental breakfast is served instead.

♿ 🍴 **The Inn at Deer Run** (307-883-3444; www2.silverstar.com/steadman/DeerRun.html), 102293 US 89, Thayne 83127. Situated on a 160-acre ranch, this B&B is an authentic, Old West–style lodging with 10 well-appointed rooms that include pine furniture and private baths. A central room features television and space for relaxing, chatting, playing games, or reading. A full country breakfast is served each morning ($60–75).

LODGES

Big Piney 83113

Triple Peak Guest Ranch and Lodge (1-866-302-7753; 307-276-3408; www.triplepeak.com), HCR 3000. At this remote and rustic guest ranch and lodge, you can have it all (reservations required). Whether you are just looking for a place to rest your weary head or you want a coordinated ranch-style vacation, Triple Peak can help you out. Eight guest bedrooms with private baths are available by the night ($70)—and you can add in three home-cooked meals a day for not much more ($120). The ranch also offers horseback riding, pack trips, guided fly-fishing trips and lessons, snowmobiling, hunting trips, and inclusive "cowboy vacations."

Jackson Hole

Buckrail Lodge (307-733-2079; www.buckraillodge.com), 110 E. Karns Avenue, P.O. Box 23, Jackson 83001. You'll enjoy true country comforts at this 12-room lodge situated among mature trees and grassy lawns at the base of Snow King Ski Resort. Within walking distance of downtown Jackson, the lodge itself is a step removed from this scene, offering you a convenient escape into solitude, should you need one. Each room features western red cedar logs in its construction. Cathedral ceilings create spacious accommodations, which also include furniture made from native pine. Each room has cable television and a large bathroom. Guests also enjoy access to a large outdoor Jacuzzi, plus free morning newspapers and coffee and tea served in the lobby ($52–112 plus).

✔ **Jackson Hole Lodge** (1-800-604-9404; 307-733-2992; www.jackson holelodge.com), 420 W. Broadway, Jackson Hole 83001. This lodge has been a fixture on the Jackson lodging scene since 1942. You can rest assured that your needs will be cared for at this lovely place, just three and a half blocks from the heart of downtown. Lodging options range from basic, cozy lodge rooms with hotel-style amenities to two-bedroom condos. Also available to guests are a 40-foot heated pool, two hot tubs, a sauna, a children's pool, a game room, free Internet access, and a free nightly movie rental, among other features. Combination deals with activities are frequently offered; ask for details when you call to make reservations ($49–200 plus).

♿ **Snake River Lodge and Spa** (1-800-445-4655; www.snakeriver lodge.rockresorts.com), 7710 Granite Loop Road, P.O. Box 348, Teton Village 83025. Completely remodeled in 2002, this ski-in, ski-out full-service resort at the base of Jackson Hole Mountain Ski Resort features an array of amenities that can't be surpassed. You'll stay in one of 88 rooms or 40 suites, all featuring thoughtful and elegant amenities that range from the practical (such as Internet access and in-room movies) to the luxurious (including fluffy robes and granite countertops in the bathrooms). You can recharge your engine in the heated indoor pool, heated outdoor pool, hot tubs, sauna, or on-site health club or at the on-site full-service Avanyu Spa, depending on your needs and energy level. A fine dining restaurant, the GameFish, means you don't have to go far to fill your belly. The lodge often has ski 'n' stay packages, so be sure to check for details when making reservations (room: $349–459; suite: $1,500 plus).

Teton Mountain Lodge (1-800-801-6615; 307-734-7111; www.teton lodge.com), 3385 West Village Drive, P.O. Box 564, Teton Village 83025. Located slopeside at Jackson Hole Mountain Ski Resort. This new lodge features 129 elegant guest rooms and suites—including a drop-dead-gorgeous penthouse suite—with all of the amenities you'd expect from a luxury accommodation. On the premises, you'll also find the Mountain Lodge Spa, fine dining and cocktails at the Cascade Grill House and Spirits, and much, much more. Staying at the lodge gives you easy access to Jackson Hole Mountain Ski Resort as well as to Grand Teton National Park ($109–$1,000).

✦ ✎ **Togwotee Mountain Lodge** (1-800-543-2847; 307-543-2847; www .togwoteelodge.com), P.O. Box 91, Moran 83013. Located about 17 miles east of Moran Junction on US 26/287. A snowmobiler's paradise, Togwotee Mountain Lodge sits in Bridger–Teton National Forest (see *Wilder Places—Forests*), allowing its visitors easy access to the 2.5 million acres of terrain in an area that regularly receives 600 inches of powder in a season. The 35 rooms in the lodge proper feature basic hotel-style amenities, including private baths and cable television. Cabins include more room to spread out, as well as two televisions, a kitchenette, and full bathrooms. The lodge also has hot tubs, a saloon, and a full-service dining room serving three meals daily. The package rate includes breakfast and dinner, a predinner cocktail and appetizer hour, a group snowmobile tour

guide, and airport transportation ($286–406; children 12 and under, $40 per child).

✦ ✎ ✿ **The Virginian Lodge** (1-800-262-4999; 307-733-2792; www .virginianlodge.com), 750 W. Broadway, P.O. Box 1052, Jackson Hole 83001. Founded for hunters by a hunter, this lodge has been serving Jackson Hole's visitors since 1965. Today the large lodge features 170 units designed to meet the needs of any visitor. Rooms range from basic motel- or hotel-style rooms to rooms that include a Jacuzzi or a kitchenette. In summer, guests enjoy an outdoor, heated swimming pool. A saloon with old-fashioned swinging doors, a liquor store, a convention center, and a restaurant serving three meals daily are all on the premises as well. Children ages 12 and under stay for free in their parents' room ($55–185).

See also **the Alpenrose** and **Wild Sage Restaurant** under *Dining Out.*

Pinedale

Big Sandy Lodge LLC (307-382-6513; www.big-sandy-lodge.com; mailing address: #8 Spotted Trail Circle, Rock Springs 82901), 44 miles southeast of Boulder at 1050 Big Sandy Opening Road (ask for directions when you make reservations). Open late May through early October. Situated at the Big Sandy entrance to the Wind River Mountains, this remote mountain lodge offers you the supreme getaway or a great jumping-off point for your mountain adventure. In operation since 1929, the rustic lodge sits at 9,100 feet, providing guests with a place to dine on family-style meals and relax in front of a massive stone fireplace. You'll sleep in one of 10 rustic, one-room log cabins with wood-burning stoves, kerosene lamps, and no electricity or phone lines—but never fear, modern bathroom facilities are just a short walk out of your door ($55–85; meals extra), as are tremendous fishing opportunities. The lodge offers package deals, horseback riding, pack trips, and gear drops.

✍ **Boulder Lake Lodge** (1-800-788-5401; 307-537-5400; www.boulder lake.com; mailing address: P.O. Box 1100, Pinedale 82941), 48 Bridger Drive, Boulder. Located in Bridger–Teton National Forest (see *Wilder Places—Forests*), this lovely lodge features the pristine scenery most people only dream of seeing, let alone spending time in. You'll enjoy the modern comfort of your lodge room and private bath, while also spending some time in the lodge's central area, where three delicious meals are served family-style every day ($70; meals and activities not included). Lodge activities include guided horseback riding, fishing trips, hunting, and float trips on the Green River and/or the New River. Ask about inclusive package deals. (See also Fremont Lake under *To Do—Boating.*)

Lakeside Lodge, Resort, and Marina (1-877-755-5253; 307-367-2221; www.lakesidelodge.com; mailing address: P.O. Box 1819, Pinedale 82941), 99 F.S. 111, Fremont Lake. Stay in a basic, rustic cabin ($60–65) or a luxury cabin ($75–129) at this resort on the shores of Fremont Lake (see *To Do—Boating*)—or if you want to, just pull up in your RV and camp at one of the resort's campsites ($18–20), enjoying the same access to the bathhouse as guests staying in the rustic cabins. The lodge also features a dining room, a marina, and access to the abundance of recreational opportunities in the surrounding environs.

Star Valley

✍ **Box Y Lodge and Guest Ranch** (307-654-7564; www.boxylodge.com), P.O. Box 3051, Alpine 83128; call for directions and reservations. Situated between the majestic Wyoming and Salt River ranges, this ranch gladly provides you with overnight lodging, should that be all you desire. Guests stay in one of eight private cabins that sleep two to six people and include full baths, satellite phones, and satellite Internet. The main lodge has satellite television, a large common area, and a casual dining room where home-cooked meals are served. Summer activities include horseback riding, fishing, hiking, mountain biking, and more. Snowmobiling is popular in winter ($220, includes dinner and breakfast; $400 for guest ranch activities; children's and multinight rates available).

OTHER OPTIONS See also **Bridger–Teton National Forest** under *To Do—Camping.*

Jackson 83001

&. 🐾 **Antler Inn** (1-800-483-8667; 307-733-2535; www.townsquareinns .com), 43 W. Pearl Street, P.O. Box 1948. Location, location, location. This charming motel gives you a front-row seat to all of the action happening in Jackson. A single block separates you from the center of it all—Town Square—and you'll enjoy the ease of your access to all things Jackson. That's not to say that the rooms at the Antler aren't noteworthy—the cozy, cedar log rooms conjure up the feeling of being inside a log cabin, with their deep, earthy tones and warm lighting. You'll enjoy access to a hot tub, a sauna, and fitness equipment, as well as cable television ($50–165).

🏄 **Bunkhouse Hostel** (1-800-234-4507; 307-733-3668; www.anvil motel.com/bunkhouse.htm), 215 N. Cache, P.O. Box 486. If you're traveling solo and trying to do Jackson on a budget, you probably won't find anywhere cheaper to stay than the Bunkhouse. Located on the bottom level of the Anvil Motel, the Bunkhouse offers dormitory-style, semiprivate, clean and tidy accommodations—including a communal kitchen with a microwave and refrigerator, a ski waxing room with ski lockers, a common room with cable television, men's and women's showers (soap, shampoo, and towels provided), laundry facilities, and 25 bunk beds, each with its own locker (bring your own lock or borrow one for a $5 refundable deposit). Children under 16 are not allowed—but neither is smoking or alcohol. The price tag? $25 per person per night. If you're traveling with another person, you might want to check on the hotel's rates upstairs before you decide on the Bunkhouse, but solo travelers won't find a better deal in Jackson.

🎣 **Hoback River Resort** (307-733-5129; www.hobackriverresort.com), 11055 S. US 89. Where the Snake River meets the Hoback River, that's where you'll find this charming, family-run lodging. You can choose to stay in a motel-style room with basic amenities, including a full bathroom and a queen-size bed ($40–80), or you can rent a furnished cottage or a cabin (open June through September). Cottages include one or two bedrooms, fully equipped kitchens, full bathrooms, and picnic

ANTLER INN

tables with barbecue grills ($135–155; 3-night minimum). Cabins include two studios and two one-bedroom cabins, all of which include fully equipped kitchens, bathrooms, and a common picnic table and barbecue area ($110–155; 3-night minimum). The resort features great views of the Snake River, as well as a sandy beach and easy fishing access.

♿ **The Trapper Inn** (1-888-771-2648; 307-733-2648; www.trapper inn.com), 235 N. Cache, P.O. Box 1712. A scant one and a half blocks from downtown Jackson, the Trapper Inn is an established Jackson lodging, in business since 1970. You'll enjoy access to two hot tubs—one indoors and one outside—perfect for soaking away that soreness in your muscles after a hard day on the slopes. The inn caters to its skiing clientele in winter, providing daily shuttle service to the "big three"—Grand Targhee, Jackson Hole Mountain, and Snow King—as well as ski lockers on the premises. A variety of rooms and suites are available for you to choose from ($58–231).

The Wort Hotel (1-800-322-2727; www.worthotel.com), Glenwood and Broadway, P.O. Box 69. This historic hotel, listed on the National Register of Historic Places, has graced Jackson's downtown since 1941, embodying the dream of one of the area's original homesteaders, Charles J. Wort. The hotel's Silver Dollar Bar, built in 1950, quickly became a favorite for both travelers and locals, defined by its cool bar inlaid with more than 2,000 uncirculated silver dollars from Denver's Federal Reserve. Today travelers can stay in one of 60 modern rooms or three suites, all of which feature country lodgepole pine furnishings, goosedown comforters, western decor, comfy bathrobes, and cute Silver Dollar Sam teddy bears ($160–550).

Kemmerer 83101

&. ✐ **Fossil Butte Hotel** (307-877-3996; www.fossilbuttemotel.com), 1424 Central Avenue. Kemmerer may not have much in the way of fancy accommodations, but if you're looking for somewhere tidy and modern to call home for a night, this little motel should do nicely. Recently renovated rooms feature queen-size beds, in-room coffeemakers, microwaves, refrigerators, cable television, phones with voice mail, and more. Children and pets are welcome ($50–100).

Pinedale 82941

✐ **Cow Cabins** (307-367-2428; www.cowcabins.com), P.O. Box 1397. Located 45 miles from Jackson and 30 miles from Pinedale off US 191. Stay in one of two log cabins on a private ranch property of more than 2,000 acres. Breathtaking views of the surrounding mountains and secluded privacy make these cabins a destination in and of themselves—not to mention their central location between two charming Wyoming towns. At the Cow Cabins, you'll enjoy immediate access to all of the outstanding recreational opportunities afforded by your surroundings. The larger of the cabins, set in an open area, is a ranch-style house with three bedrooms and one and a half baths, as well as satellite television, a fully equipped kitchen, and a washer and clothesline ($200). The smaller cabin, set back in the woods, has three single beds, a kitchenette, a full bathroom, and a loft with a double bed ($120). Both cabins can be rented together ($300), and weekly rates are available as well. You can also pay extra to fish on the property's waters or to board your horse.

The Log Cabin Motel (307-367-4579; www.thelogcabinmotel.com), 49 E. Magnolia. Open June 1 through September 30. Listed on the National Register of Historic Places, this 1929 motel offers the privacy of your own historic cabin right in the classic mountain town of Pinedale. The 10 cabins are the real deal—the original cabins constructed by local shop owner and businessman Walter Scott to provide travelers with overnight accommodations. Throughout the years since they have served additional purposes, including housing Civilian Conservation Corps (CCC) workers, and they have changed names several times. Nonetheless, they have been renovated several times and today stand restored and beautifully cared for, offering travelers comfortable and homey accommodations, including bathrooms, in-room coffee, covered front porches, and cable television ($85–120).

See also **Half Moon Lake Resort** under *Dining Out.*

Star Valley

✐ **Old Mill Cabins** (307-886-0520; www.silverstar.com/oldmill), 3497 Dry

Creek Road, Afton 83110. For spacious, private cabin accommodations in Star Valley, Old Mill Cabins can't be beat. Choose one of four log cabins to suit your needs. The Aspen, Cottonwood, and Lodgepole cabins all feature two queen-size beds, private baths, private porches, access to the hot tub, gas fireplaces, cable television, and minifridges ($69 and up). The larger Willow farmhouse features three bedrooms, sleeping up to eight people, as well as a full kitchen, a washer/dryer, a private porch, a private picnic area, cable television, a private bathroom, and access to the hot tub ($175 and up).

✳ Where to Eat

DINING OUT

Jackson Hole

The Alpenrose (307-733-3462; www.alpenhoflodge.com), next to the clock tower, P.O. Box 288, Teton Village 83025. Situated inside the elegant, Austrian **Alpenhof Lodge,** the Alpenrose invites you to sample its delectable German-inspired cuisine. For the adventurous, there is a five-course wine and food tasting menu called Taste of the Alps. The main menu features specialties such as wiener schnitzel, rabbit loin, elk loin, and duck breast. Fondues, both cheese and chocolate, are also popular menu selections. This restaurant is a winner of the prestigious *Wine Spectator* Award of Excellence. Also at the Alpenhof Lodge, you'll find the popular après-ski hot spot, the **Alpenhof Bistro,** which offers a more casual dining experience as well as a European-style bar and often live entertainment.

Nani's Genuine Pasta House (307-733-3888; www.nanis.com), 242 N. Glenwood. Authentic, acclaimed Italian fine dining awaits you at Nani's—this ain't no pizza 'n' pasta joint! Using the finest and freshest of ingredients available, often from local and regional sources, Nani's always includes on its menu a number of favorites from the 20 regions of Italy. These include handmade ravioli and fettuccine, veal marsala, and *frutti del mare,* among many others. In addition, each month the menu features specialty dishes from Italy's regions as well, providing repeat customers and newcomers alike with culinary adventures to keep their taste buds intrigued and delighted. The homemade desserts are fantastic, from the tiramisu to the biscotti.

Nikai Asian Grill and Sushi Bar (307-734-6490; www.nikaisushi.com), 225 N. Cache. Despite your rather substantial distance from any ocean, you can be sure that the sushi is always fresh here. Fish is flown in daily from around the globe to meet the needs of Nikai's customers. Start your meal with miso soup and *edamame* (steamed and salted soybeans—very yummy, if you haven't tried them), then select from the sushi menu. Not a big raw fish fan? Never fear—Nikai also offers a classic Asian grill menu that includes such favorites as chicken teriyaki, vegetable tempura, seared sea scallops, and ahi tuna salad, among other options. A full-service bar offers you whatever drink (sake, anyone?) your heart desires to accompany your meal.

✻ **Nora's Fish Creek Inn** (307-733-8288; www.jacksonholenet.com/noras), 3859 Miles Road, Wilson 83014. Acclaimed by locals and visitors alike, Nora's offers you a fine dining experience in a log building filled with country western charm. The menu features a delicious array of steaks, seafood, and poultry entrées, as well as pork, pastas, and lamb, each served with a full complement of classic side dishes. Burgers, sandwiches, and salads are also options for those not seeking quite so much food. Nora's even has several vegetarian items. A children's menu is available. You can select a drink from the restaurant's full bar that is well stocked with microbrews and wines and top of your tanks with a homemade dessert.

& **Snake River Grill** (307-733-0557; www.snakerivergrill.com), 84 E. Broadway, Town Square. This award-winning, critically acclaimed restaurant has received both the Award of Excellence from Distinguished Restaurants of North America and the *Wine Spectator* Award of Excellence. Inspired entrées feature organic produce, fresh fish, and free-range meats, put together in creations designed to please the palate. Choose from the tame (such as steak, chicken, salmon, and burgers) to game (such as elk, buffalo, pheasant, and venison), all prepared with unique and intriguing complementary ingredients. Dessert choices include made-to-order soufflés among other house-made options. In addition to the award-winning wine list, the bar also offers a full array of cocktails and beers.

Wild Sage Restaurant (1-800-458-2004; 307-733-2000; www.rusty parrot.com), 175 N. Jackson. Situated inside the **Rusty Parrot Lodge and Spa,** the Wild Sage Restaurant features an elegant, comfortable atmosphere in which you'll find one of Jackson's premier fine dining experiences. The exhibition-style kitchen allows you to watch as your food is prepared while you relax by the lovely stone fireplace. The seasonal menu includes regional cuisine as well as fish flown in daily, with entrée selections ranging from beef and pork tenderloins to stuffed quail and elk racks. Presentation is an art form at the Wild Sage, and your dinner will be served in a visually appealing and tantalizing fashion—but the delicious blend of creative ingredients is likely to surpass even the artistry of the presentation. A full wine list is available to complement your meal.

See also **Snake River Lodge and Spa** and **Teton Mountain Lodge** under *Lodging—Lodges.*

Pinedale

Half Moon Lake Resort (307-367-6373; www.halfmoonlake.com), take Fremont Lake Road northeast of Pinedale to the signed dirt entrance road on right. On the shores of Half Moon Lake northeast of Pinedale, a unique fine dining experience is in store for you. Sit down in a pine log chair and take in picturesque views of the lake's pristine waters visible through the restaurant's huge windows. Enjoy a cocktail while you peruse the menu, which features a classic array of American favorites, including steaks, seafood, poultry, and pastas. Generous portions ensure that you'll leave the table satisfied. You can even choose to sit on the deck, weather permitting, for an even more intimate lakefront dining experience. Reservations preferred.

EATING OUT

Jackson Hole

♪ **Chili Pepper Grill** (307-734-6574), 380 W. Pearl Avenue. Fun and relaxed, the Chili Pepper Grill serves up generous platters of Southwestern and Mexican favorites. You'll find all of the standards here—burritos, chimichangas, enchiladas, and tacos—plus some creative twists, such as bourbon baby back ribs, the Tostada That Ate Jackson Hole, and fish tacos. Vegetarians won't be left out, with options including a fresh vegetable burrito and enchiladas. Desserts include deep-fried ice cream and apple chimichanga, but if you're like me, you'll head straight for the chocolate Kahlua mousse pie (who cares if it's not Mexican?).

Jedediah's House of Sourdough (307-733-5671), 1 block east of Town Square on E. Broadway. Sourdough is served all day long at Jedediah's, whether you're stopping for breakfast, lunch, or dinner. In the morning, it takes a leading role in the sourjack pancakes; at lunchtime, it jumps in to hold the sandwiches together. At dinnertime, the grilled steaks, chicken, and seafood options come with sourdough biscuits, while the burgers are served on sourdough buns. You'll even find sourdough in the desserts, with both carrot cake and brownies made from the divine dough. A hint to breakfast eaters: if you're a granola aficionado, don't pass up the chance to try Jedediah's homemade granola, too.

Million Dollar Cowboy Steakhouse (307-733-4790), Town Square. Downstairs from the Million Dollar Cowboy Bar (a Jackson experience unto itself), you can sit down to a full 'n' fancy cowboy dinner in the steakhouse. The full-service bar features an extensive wine list as well as beers and cocktails. The menu includes aged, hand-cut beef prepared to perfection in a number of ways—but that's not all. You can also choose

from a wide range of other items, including game (venison, buffalo, duck, and elk), chicken, lamb, pork, pastas, seafood, and more. In the tradition of the Old West, the Million Dollar Cowboy Steakhouse strives to make your dining experience a friendly and delicious one.

✔ **Mountain High Pizza Pie** (307-733-3646), 120 W. Broadway. Reasonably priced and excellent, this is the spot to go when you need something filling and fast. Choose from the creative pizzas topped with ingredients ranging from standard (such as pepperoni, Canadian bacon, and mushrooms) to offbeat (such as corn, broccoli, and spinach), or create your own from the nearly 30 toppings available. You can also choose a calzone, sub, sandwich, or salad if pizza just isn't your favorite. Dine inside or on the patio in summer, or just call to have a pizza delivered to your door.

✔ **Snake River Brewpub** (307-739-2337; www.snakeriverbrewing.com/pub.htm), 265 S. Millward. Stop in for happy hour to sample the award-winning brews of Jackson's own Snake River Brewpub, and grab some cheap appetizers while you're at it. You'll probably wind up staying for dinner. The pub-style fare includes pastas, pizzas, burgers, salads, and sandwiches, all served in a nonsmoking environment. Kids are welcome and can choose from their own menu. During football season, you can catch up to eight different games playing on the satellite televisions.

✔ **Thai Me Up** (307-733-0005), 75 E. Pearl Street. If you like Thai food, you're not likely to be disappointed with a meal at this popular restaurant. Reasonable prices, a wide selection of vegetarian and vegan dishes, and a full bar add to the appeal, but it's the delicious, classic Thai entrées and sides that make this restaurant so good. Choose from two different pad Thai dishes, an assortment of curries, fried rice, stir-fries, and salads, among other options. The restaurant also has a children's menu and welcomes take-out orders.

See also **the Alpenrose** under *Dining Out*.

Pinedale

✿ **Cafe on Pine** (307-367-3111), 807 W. Pine. Whether you're craving American or Italian fare, you'll find a delicious meal here in both departments. Freshly prepared pastas, seafood, and steaks are the dinner menu's mainstays. Lunchtime brings lighter fare, including wraps, salads, sandwiches, and soups. You can even find fresh Alaskan salmon here. The kids can choose from their own menu. Everyone should leave room to at least share a homemade dessert creation by the chef. Patio seating is available in-season.

Pitchfork Fondue (307-367-3607; 307-367-8264; www.pitchfork fondue.com), at the Pinedale Rodeo Grounds, 9888 US 191. Open mid-June through September. Watch as experienced chefs prong choice steaks on the tines of a pitchfork and then cook them to perfection in mere minutes. That's the experience you'll find when you reserve your place at Pitchfork Fondue. To accompany your cauldron-sizzled steak, you'll choose from a number of sauces and enjoy salad, rolls, and dessert. Seating is at covered pine picnic tables for up to 240 diners.

See also **White Pine Ski Area and Resort** under *To Do–Snow Sports* and **Lakeside Lodge, Resort, and Marina** under *Lodging—Lodges*.

Star Valley

Bull Moose Restaurant and Saloon (1-877-498-7993; 307-654-7593; www.bullmoosesaloon.com), 91 US 89, Alpine. Stop in for smoked prime rib, steak, or salmon, or select from less-expensive pub-style fare, including an assortment of burgers and sandwiches. You can also choose just a couple of appetizers and nosh for a quick pick-me-up during your travels. To experience a truer western flair, step into the saloon with its moose and elk chandeliers, wood-paneled walls, and animal mounts. The Bull Moose also has a liquor store, a gift shop, and, sometimes, live music.

✿ **Kringle's Birdhouse Cafe and Catering** (1-888-900-5072; 307-654-7536; www.kringlescafe.com), 161 US 89, Alpine. It's not often that you'll find a restaurant owned and run by a European master chef in a tiny Wyoming town—but that's exactly what you'll find at Kringle's. With a long and illustrious cooking career under his belt, John Jensen, along with his wife, Francene, now delivers the fruits of his talents to the fine folks of Alpine. Kringle's serves breakfast, lunch, and dinner, featuring American favorites such as baked meatloaf, country fried steak, grilled chicken, and more. Desserts are a particular decadence here, with the favorites being the homemade carrot cake and the homemade chocolate cake. A separate children's menu is available as well.

See also **Box Y Lodge** under *Lodging—Lodges*.

✳ Special Events

November through February: **All–American Cutter Races,** Afton: yearly series of modern chariot races culminating in Wyoming state championship.

February: **Cowboy Ski Challenge,** Jackson: cowboys compete for top honors at roping, riding, and skiing events to the delight and awe of spectators. ✍ **Green River Valley Winter Carnival,** Pinedale: winter festival includes children's games, arm wrestling competitions, an ice-water swimming challenge, and more frozen fun. **Maverick Snowmobile Hill Climb,** Grover (Star Valley): annual snowmobile competition with prize money.

April: **Aniel Daniel Chili Cook-Off,** Daniel: cooking competition pits chili wizards against one another in a tasting extravaganza. **Pole-Pedal-Paddle,** Jackson: individual athletes and teams (some serious, some silly) compete in a multisport endurance race that includes skiing, mountain biking, and paddling.

May: **ElkFest,** Jackson: festival centered around Jackson Hole Boy Scout Elk Antler Auction, the auctioning of antlers shed by wintering elk at the National Elk Refuge. **Old West Days,** Jackson: celebration of the Old West includes mountain man rendezvous, arts and crafts, food, entertainment, and more.

✍ *June:* **Mountain Days,** Alpine: annual celebration of western and mountain heritage held over Father's Day weekend; events include dutch-oven cook-offs, black powder shoots, and children's activities, among others.

June through September: **Grand Teton Music Festival** (307-733-3050; www.gtmf.org), Jackson: concerts held nearly all summer long Tuesday through Sunday at 8 PM.

July: ✍ **Green River Rendezvous Days,** Pinedale: annual mountain man celebration includes a pageant reenacting the 1830s rendezvous that happened annually in this area, as well as camping, children's activities, lectures, and more. **Oyster Ridge Music Festival** (www.oysterridge musicfestival.com), Kemmerer: annual free music festival featuring local and regional artists. **Tour de Wyoming** (307-742-5840; www .cyclewyoming.org): annual event bringing cyclists together for a 360-mile, 6-day, fully supported tour to benefit Cycle Wyoming; the tour starts and ends in Kemmerer. Sign up early to ensure participation; limited to 250 entrants.

August: **Annual Microbrew Festival,** Jackson: sample brews from more than 30 breweries for $15; inexpensive eats and free music are part of the fun, too.

September: **Jackson Hole Fall Arts Festival,** Jackson: annual event that celebrates not only visual arts but also culinary arts, music, and poetry.

See also Afton under *To See—Towns* and Fremont Lake under *To Do—Boating.*

CENTRAL WYOMING: OREGON TRAIL–RENDEZVOUS COUNTRY

Experts estimate that during the middle of the 19th century, more than 500,000 people traveled along Wyoming's nearly 500 miles of the 2,000-mile-long Oregon Trail; most of those 500 miles lie in Wyoming's Oregon Trail–Rendezvous Country. In addition, some 300,000 Mormons traveled west en masse through Wyoming between 1846 and 1869 on the Mormon Trail (following a route similar to that of the Oregon Trail), seeking a new place to dwell far from the religious persecutions and general hostility they had endured during their tenure in more "civilized" areas of the United States. The historic movement of such massive numbers of people through the region has ensured this area of Wyoming a place of significance in the history books and in the collective memory of the nation as a whole.

What began as a journey undertaken by a few venturesome souls in the middle of the 1830s became a full-scale river of emigration in less than a decade; the first large wagon train of 1,000 wagons began the journey on the Oregon Trail in 1843. The news spread quickly—moving west offered the prospect of abundant, open lands and the potential to leave the past behind and reinvent oneself. The discovery of gold in California in 1848 only increased the traffic, as gold seekers began rushing in hordes to California the following year, starting a boom 'n' bust cycle that would characterize selected areas of the West throughout the 19th century as more gold was discovered elsewhere.

One in 10 of the emigrants on the Oregon Trail died on the journey westward, succumbing to sickness, exhaustion, hunger, thirst, accidents, or the occasional skirmish with Native Americans (which accounted for fewer deaths than you might think). For about 25 years, the emigration by wagon train continued at a somewhat steady clip, until it was brought back down to a trickle by the completion of the transcontinental railroad in 1869 and finally dried up entirely by the early 20th century. But the pioneers had left their mark on the terrain for future generations, both in the now fading physical remains of their passage—such as names carved in rocks and ruts left by the wheels of thousands of wagons—and in the legacy of the unstoppable tide of humanity that permanently displaced the Native American population, disrupting their traditional ways of living forever and introducing new ways of living to the land.

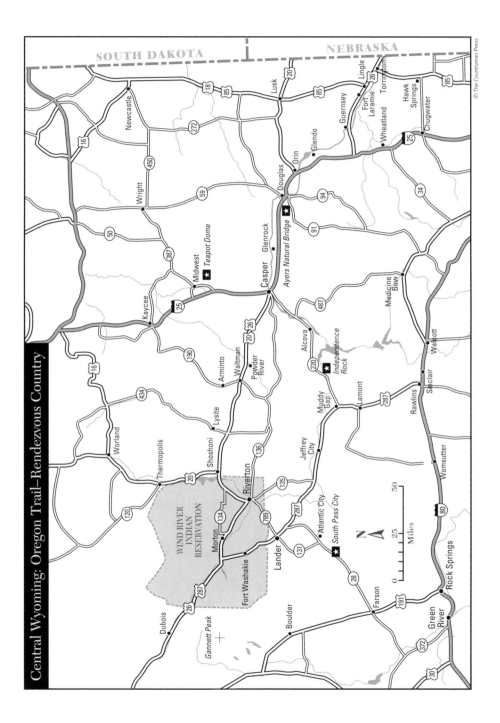

Central Wyoming: Oregon Trail–Rendezvous Country

SOUTH DAKOTA

NEBRASKA

© The Countryman Press

Newcastle
Wright
Kaycee
Midwest
Teapot Dome
Casper
Glenrock
Douglas
Orin
Glendo
Ayers Natural Bridge
Lusk
Guernsey
Fort Laramie
Wheatland
Torrington
Lingle
Hawk Springs
Chugwater
Medicine Bow
Worland
Thermopolis
Shoshoni
Lysite
Arminto
Waltman
Powder River
Alcova
Independence Rock
Muddy Gap
Lamont
Jeffrey City
Rawlins
Sinclair
Walcott
Wamsutter
Rock Springs
Green River
Farson
Lander
Atlantic City
South Pass City
Boulder
Dubois
Gannett Peak
Fort Washakie
Morton
Riverton

WIND RIVER INDIAN RESERVATION

N

Miles
0   25   50

When you plan a visit to this region today, you almost have to include time in your plans to explore at least a few of the many museums and historical landmarks, places, and sites that document the passage of these hardy emigrants, bent on and determined, come hell or high water, to make it through this harsh and unforgiving terrain in search of the promised land. You can start with a drive over South Pass—the easiest passage found through the Rocky Mountains, traveled by thousands in wagon trains. Stop to walk through South Pass City State Historic Site, home to a well-preserved Wyoming gold-mining town, and then explore the surrounding historical and natural attractions (see *To See—Historic Landmarks, Places, and Sites*). Farther south and east, you can follow in the footsteps and wagon ruts of the pioneers who journeyed on the Oregon Trail, the Mormon Trail, and other historic trails as you follow the passage of the Sweetwater River (see *To Do—Fishing*). You'll see the natural and constructed landmarks, such as Independence Rock, Devil's Gate, Split Rock, Ayre's Natural Bridge, Fort Fetterman, Fort Laramie, Register Cliff, and Laramie Peak, among others, that helped these travelers stay on track and chart the progress of their journey (see multiple listings under *To See*). You can even immerse yourself completely in an emigrant experience by riding on a wagon train with Adventures West Tours and Spiritrider Wagon Train Adventures (see *To Do—Unique Adventures*), or you can experience the fast-paced excitement of the Pony Express, used briefly for carrying mail by the U.S. Postal Service, on a Pony Express Re-Ride (see *To Do—Horseback Riding*).

Should you wish to learn about the emigrants' lives in a more traditional way, you'll find numerous museums throughout this region housing artifacts and exhibits that help interpret and explain the various hardships and realities of life as an emigrant. First and foremost among these is Casper's National Historic Trails Interpretive Center (see *To See—Museums*), which is dedicated to bringing this vital piece of the nation's history to life for today's visitors. In addition, along with the other museums listed in this book, you'll discover that nearly every small town in this area, including Chugwater, Glenrock, Guernsey, Lingle, and Lusk, among others, has at least one historical museum, if not two or three. Such museums usually feature collections of artifacts, documents, and photographs detailing local histories and legends. Most of these museums are free of charge and operate seasonally.

Not to be forgotten are the other peoples who have strong traditional ties and histories associated with this area—the Native Americans. Wyo-

AYERS NATURAL BRIDGE

ming's sole Indian reservation, the 2.2-million-acre Wind River Indian Reservation, lies in this region. In addition to the Indian artifacts and histories documented at many of the museums and historical attractions throughout this region, the reservation itself is home to several museums endeavoring to chronicle the past of the reservation's two distinctively different tribes: the Eastern Shoshone and the Northern Arapaho (see Fort Washakie under *To See—Towns*). The Eastern Shoshone received the reservation—their cultural and traditional homeland—through the Fort Bridger Treaty, negotiated by the great leader Chief Washakie in 1868. Thus they became the sole Indian tribe to actually remain on their traditional homelands—every other tribe in this region and elsewhere was placed on a reservation that did not include its original and familiar lands. Such was the fate of one of the Eastern Shoshone's historic enemies, the culturally distinctive Northern Arapaho, who joined them on the Wind River Reservation in 1878 in what was supposed to be a temporary arrangement—but which nonetheless became a permanent one. The two tribes have struggled to live together on this land ever since, attempting to find harmony while still retaining their unique cultural histories and traditions.

In addition to the Native American and emigrant trail heritage found in this region, you'll also discover attractions of historical interest from both before and after this pivotal time in American history. Here, too, lived much more ancient peoples, who left their marks at Castle Gardens (see *To See—Historic Landmarks, Places, and Sites*). Dinosaurs also dwelt here, and you can find fossil evidence on display at Glenrock Paleontological Museum (see *To See—Museums*) and Tate Geological Museum (see *To See—For Families*), among other sites. And before the first emigrants came through, mountain men trapped here and held some of their annual rendezvous here, celebrated annually in reenactments such as the 1838 Mountain Man Rendezvous in Riverton (see *Special Events*). From the postemigrant times, this area includes historical evidence of the Tie Hack industry (see Tie Hack Memorial under *To See—Historic Landmarks, Places, and Sites*), a presidential scandal (see Teapot Dome under *To See—Natural Wonders*), and the work of the Civilian Conservation Corps (see Guernsey State Park under *To See—Historic Landmarks, Places, and Sites*).

In the veritable sea of historical attractions concentrated throughout this region, its incredible year-round outdoor recreational opportunities should not be overlooked. These range from snowshoeing and snowmobiling in winter to rock climbing and hiking in summer. Here you'll find the state's highest mountain, Gannett Peak (13,804 feet), situated on the continental divide in the Wind River Mountains of Shoshone National Forest (see *Wilder Places—Forests*). An abundance of adventures awaits you in these mountains, whether you choose to explore them yourself or perhaps under the guidance of an instructor from the National Outdoor Leadership School (NOLS; see *To Do—Unique Adventures*), headquartered in the charming town of Lander (see *To See—Towns*). Some of the state's most well-known rock-climbing destinations—Sinks Canyon and Wild Iris among them—are within a half-hour's drive of Lander, accounting for the annual International Climbers' Festival hosted by the town (see *Special Events*). In winter, Lander serves as the southern terminus of the state's acclaimed Continental Divide Snowmobile Trail (see *To Do—Snow Sports*), which stretches northwest past Dubois (see *To See—Towns*), ultimately reaching its northern terminus in West Yellowstone, Montana. Free or inexpensive camping is easy to find both in Lander and throughout the region, with an array of town parks offering a place to rest your weary head, along with the abundant lands of the Bureau of Land Management (BLM), state parks, and the national forests (see *To Do—Camping*). And anglers will delight in this region's tremendous fishing opportunities, which include first and foremost the Miracle Mile of the North Platte River (see *To See—Natural Wonders* and *To Do—Fishing*).

The enormous North Platte River flows through the eastern half of this region, running right through the center of its "big city"—Casper. With about 50,000 residents, Casper is Wyoming's second-largest city, smaller than Cheyenne by roughly 3,000 people. In addition to providing the familiar array of hotels and eateries one would expect to find in a large urban area (large by Wyoming standards, anyhow), Casper is also home to a number of distinctive cultural and historical attractions of interest, including the Nicolaysen Art Museum and Discovery Center (see *To See—Museums*) and the Fort Caspar Museum and Historic Site (see *To See—Museums*), as well as the National Historic Trails Center, mentioned above. In addition, Casper is home to the lovely Platte River Parkway (see *To Do—Bicycling*) and Casper Whitewater Park (see *To Do—Paddling*), providing visitors and residents with several ways to easily enjoy the North Platte River's proximity. Families, too, will find plenty of fun places to explore here, from the Casper Planetarium (see *To See—For Families*) to Edness K. Wilkins State Park (see *Wilder Places—Parks*), among other sites.

From its parks to its planetarium, from its prehistoric peoples to its pioneer paths and its presidential scandal, Wyoming's Oregon Trail–Rendezvous Country will undoubtedly provide you with plenty of places to pique your interests while you pick your own path through the region's attractions.

GUIDANCE Casper Area Convention and Visitors Bureau (1-800-852-1889; 307-234-5311; www.casperwyoming.info), 330 S. Center, Suite 420, Casper 82601.

Casper Chamber of Commerce (1-800-852-1889; 307-234-5311; www.casper wyoming.org), 500 N. Center, Casper 82602.

Converse County Tourism and Promotional Board (www.conversecounty tourism.com), P.O. Box 1212, Douglas 82633.

Douglas Area Chamber of Commerce (307-358-2950; www.jackalope.org), 121 Brownfield, Douglas 82633.

Dubois Chamber of Commerce (307-455-2556; www.duboiswyoming.org), 616 W. Ramshorn Street, P.O. Box 632, Dubois 82513.

Glenrock Chamber of Commerce (307-436-5652; www.glenrockchamber .com), 506 W. Birch Street, P.O. Box 411, Glenrock 82637.

Goshen County Chamber of Commerce (307-532-3879; www.torrington territory.com), 350 W. 21st Avenue, Torrington 82240.

Lander Chamber of Commerce (1-800-433-0662; 307-332-3892; www.lander chamber.org), 160 N. 1st Street, Lander 82520.

Niobrara Chamber of Commerce (1-800-223-5875; 307-334-2950; www.lusk wyoming.com), P.O. Box 457, Lusk 82225.

Platte County Chamber (307-322-2322; www.plattechamber.com), 65 16th Street, Wheatland 82201.

Riverton Chamber of Commerce (1-800-325-2732; 307-856-4801; www .rivertonchamber.org), 213 W. Main Street, Riverton 82501.

Shoshoni Chamber of Commerce (307-876-2556; 307-876-2513; www .windrivercountry.com/other/shoshonifrontpage.html), 212 Idaho Street (City Hall), P.O. Box 324, Shoshoni 82649.

Wind River Indian Reservation. Eastern Shoshone Tribal Offices (307-332-3532; www.easternshoshone.net), 15 North Fork Road; Northern Arapaho Tribal Offices (307-332-6120; 307-856-3461; www.northernarapaho.com), 533 Ethete Road. The reservation comprises 2.2 millions acres in northwest-central Wyoming (see also **Fort Washakie** under *To See—Towns*).

Wind River Visitors Council (307-856-7566; www.wind-river.org, also www .windrivercountry.com), P.O. Box 1449, Riverton 82501.

GETTING THERE US 287 leads to Lander from the northwest and the southeast. WY 28 reaches Lander from the southwest. WY 789 reaches Riverton and Lander from the north and south and is the main road connecting the two cities. US 26 reaches Riverton from the east and west. I-25 runs through Casper, Douglas, Wheatland, and Chugwater from the north to the east. US 287 to WY 220 reaches Casper from the southwest. US 26 reaches Torrington and Casper from the east. US 20 reaches Lusk and Casper from the east.

See also *Airports, Amtrak, Bus Service,* and *Travel Information* in "What's Where in Wyoming."

MEDICAL EMERGENCY **Community Hospital** (307-532-4181), 2000 Campbell Drive, Torrington.

Glenrock Diagnostic and Treatment Center (307-436-9206), 925 W. Birch, Glenrock.

Lander Valley Medical Center (307-335-6365), 1320 Bishop Randall Drive, Lander.

Memorial Hospital of Converse County (307-358-2122), 111 S. 5th Street, Douglas.

Niobrara Memorial Hospital (307-334-2901), 921 Ballancee Avenue, Lusk.

Platte County Memorial Hospital (307-322-3636), 201 14th Street, Wheatland.

Riverton Memorial Hospital (1-800-967-1646; 307-856-4161), 2100 W. Sunset Drive, Riverton.

Wyoming Medical Center (1-800-822-7201; 307-577-7201), 1233 E. Second Street, Casper.

✳ To See

TOWNS Douglas, on I-25 east of Casper and north of Wheatland, has the distinction of being included in the book *The 100 Best Small Towns*, by Norman Crampton (Douglas was in 72nd place). The town also has a unique statue of a jackalope that can't be missed if you're visiting for any period of time. In addition to **Riverside Park** (see *To Do—Camping*), you'll find a paved pathway alongside the **North Platte River,** great for walking, jogging, and biking. For those interested in history, in addition to the **Wyoming Pioneer Memorial Museum** (see *To See—Museums*), the town has a self-guided historic walking tour, starting at the **Douglas Railroad Interpretive Center** (307-358-2950), 121 Brownfield Road; open Monday through Friday Memorial Day through Labor Day. If you're hungry, you'll find several restaurant options, including nationwide chains and some local hangouts, off I-25.

Dubois, pronounced "due boys," is situated between the Wind River Mountains to the southwest and the Absaroka Mountains to the northeast. It lies along US 26/287 southeast of Togwotee Pass (see the listing in "West Wyoming: Jackson Hole–Jim Bridger Country"). With nearly 1,000 inhabitants today, Dubois traces its history of settlement back to the mid-1800s, when a family from Iowa built a cabin on the banks of the Wind River near the town's present location. For a time, Dubois thrived on the railroad tie hack industry (see **Tie Hack Memorial** under *Historic Landmarks, Places, and Sites*), but today the mainstays of its economy are the area's livestock ranches and dude ranches, as well as the **terrific fishing and big-game hunting,** as well as other recreational opportunities that draw visitors. The largest known herd of **Rocky Mountain bighorn sheep** on the planet inhabits the surrounding area, hence the town's **National Bighorn Sheep Interpretive Center** (see *Museums*), among its other museums.

Fort Washakie, northwest of Lander on US 287, serves as the headquarters for the 2.2 million acres of the **Wind River Indian Reservation,** Wyoming's sole Indian reservation. Established in 1868, the reservation is home to two tribes, the **Northern Arapaho** (www.northernarapaho.com) and the **Eastern Shoshone** www.easternshoshone.net). Having once served as a U.S. military post, Fort Washakie is home to many historic buildings and is listed on the National Register of Historic Places. Fort Washakie is also home to the **Eastern Shoshone Tribal Culture Center** (307-332-9106), 1st Street; open Monday through Friday 8 AM–4:45 PM. Here you can learn more about this tribe's culture, history, and present-day situation (see also **Fort Washakie Tours** under *To Do— Unique Adventures*). Nearby, you'll

DUBOIS TOWN PARK

also find the graves of **Sacagawea** and **Chief Washakie.** The towns of **Ethete,**
Arapahoe, and **St. Stephens** to the east of Fort Washakie are mainly home to
members of the Northern Arapaho tribe. You'll find the **Northern Arapaho**
Cultural Museum (307-332-2660) at the old **St. Michael's Mission** in Ethete
and the **North American Indian Heritage Center** (307-856-7806) at St.
Stephen's Mission in Arapahoe. To take advantage of the **tremendous fishing**
opportunities on the reservation—including more than 1,000 miles of streams
and more than 250 lakes—you'll need a permit from the Tribal Fish and Game
Department (307-332-7207), which you'll find at the old BIA building in Fort
Washakie, open regular business hours. Both tribes hold **annual powwows** that
are open to the public (see *Special Events*). (See also **the Wind River** under *To*
Do—Fishing.)

Lander, situated along US 287 just north of the junction with WY 789 and WY 28,
is an interesting Wyoming town in that it apparently thrives on its unique blend of
cowboy culture and environmental activism. Lander serves as the national headquarters for the **National Outdoor Leadership School** (NOLS; see *To Do—*
Unique Adventures), which probably has a lot to do with this interesting mix.
NOLS brings in numerous outsiders to Lander regularly as they filter through the
town on their way to their outdoor educational experience—and many of them
keep on coming back or end up staying in Lander. Hence Lander's mix that
includes traditional Wyomingites such as ranchers, farmers, and cowboys as well as
the "granola" contingent, folks who sport the finest in outdoor tech-wear, pursue
outdoor recreational activities with abundant enthusiasm, and possess extensive
knowledge of human impact on the environment. The results? Among other
noticeable effects, Lander can sustain places like the **Global Café and the Mag-**
pie (see *Eating Out*) as well as more traditional spots like **the Hitching Rack** (see
Dining Out). In addition to the attractions you'll find listed below, Lander is also
home to the **One Shot–Evans–Dahl Memorial Museum** (1-800-768-7743; 307-
332-3356; www.waterforwildlife.com), 545 Main Street; open in summer Monday
through Friday 10 AM–5 PM; and the **Eagle Bronze Foundry** (307-332-5436),
130 Poppy Street, where many of the town's bronze sculptures were forged. (See
also **Annual One Shot Antelope Hunt** under *Special Events.*)

Riverton is located on the Wind River Indian Reservation, northeast of Lander
at the junction of WY 789 and US 26. This town of nearly 10,000 people is home
to a regional airport with daily flights to and from Denver, Colorado. In addition
to **Wind River Heritage Center** (see *Museums*), Riverton is home to the
Riverton Museum (307-856-2665), located at 7th E. and Park Avenue; open
Tuesday through Saturday 10 AM–4 PM; free. Housed in a historic building, the
museum maintains a collection of items and artifacts detailing the pioneer history of the local area. You'll find a plethora of inexpensive motel-style lodging
options in Riverton, as well as a Wal-Mart and two (handicapped-accessible) privately run campgrounds: **Owl Creek Kampground** (307-856-2869), 11124 US
26/WY 789; and **Wind River RV Park** (1-800-528-3913; 307-857-3000), 1618
E. Park Avenue.

Torrington is located at the junction of US 26 and US 85 in southeastern
Wyoming. Back in pioneer times, Torrington was on or near the path of many

of the area's historic trails, including the **Oregon Trail** and the **Mormon Trail,** and you'll find evidence of early travelers and former settlements both in and around the Torrington. Today, this town of almost 6,000 people welcomes visitors to explore its historic downtown area with a self-guided **walking tour** that will bring you a greater understanding of this area's past. You can also stop for a picnic lunch in Torrington—in addition to **Pioneer Park** (see *To Do—Camping*), the city has five other parks, including a skate park. Joggers and cyclists will enjoy the 10-block paved **Grassroots Trails** that go through residential areas of town. Dining options in Torrington include a number of restaurants along US 26 and Main Street, mainly serving traditional American food, as well as Mexican and Chinese. North of Torrington on US 85 about halfway to Lusk, you'll find the **Jay Em Historic District,** listed on the National Register of Historic Places, which affords you another chance to explore the pioneer history of this region.

Wheatland, the first big town north of Cheyenne on I-25, is the county seat of Platte County and has about 3,500 inhabitants. Here you'll find an array of visitor services as well as easy access to the surrounding recreational opportunities, including the **Laramie Mountains in Medicine Bow National Forest** (see *Wilder Places—Forests*). History buffs and architecture aficionados should schedule a visit to the **Platte County Courthouse,** which was built in 1911, as well as the **Laramie Peak Museum** (307-322-2052), 1601 16th Street; open May through September Monday through Friday 1 PM–4 PM. This history museum features collections and exhibits illustrating the history of the local area.

MUSEUMS **Fort Caspar Museum and Historic Site** (307-235-8462; www .fortcasparwyoming.com), 4001 Fort Caspar Road, Casper. Museum open October through April Monday through Friday 8 AM–5 PM, Sunday 1 PM–4 PM (fort buildings closed). Museum open May and September Monday through Saturday 8 AM–5 PM, Sunday noon–5 PM; fort buildings open Monday through Saturday 8:30 AM–4:30 PM, Sunday 12:30 PM–4:30 PM. Museum open June through August Monday through Saturday 8 AM–7 PM, Sunday noon–7 PM; fort buildings open Monday through Saturday 8 AM–6:30 PM, Sunday 12:30 PM–6:30 PM. $2 adults, $1 children ages 6–17, children 5 and under free; admission half-price when fort buildings closed. At this city-run museum and historic site, you can explore a piece of Wyoming's military and pioneer past. The authentically furnished fort buildings—listed on the National Register of Historic Places—are reconstructions of the actual buildings, built in 1865, which sat on this site and served as a trading outpost established by the U.S. Army. The strategically placed outpost lay along the path of many of the pioneer trails passing through this region, including the Mormon Trail, the Oregon Trail, and the Pony Express Trail. In 1847, Mormon leader Brigham Young and his followers crossed the North Platte River near here via a ferry, setting a precedent followed by future wagon trains until the establishment of toll bridges provided a more suitable alternative. A replica of the ferry—two dugout canoes joined by planks—is on the grounds, as are the remains of one of the toll bridges—the Guinard Bridge. In addition to the ferry, bridge, and fort buildings, the Fort Caspar Museum features exhibits covering aspects of central Wyoming history, including the history of the area's Indian residents and the history of oil development in the region. The grounds also include a city park, which is a great place for a picnic. (See also Fort Caspar Chautauqua under *Special Events*.)

Glenrock Paleontological Museum (307-436-2667; www.paleon.org), 506 W. Birch Street, Glenrock. Open Memorial Day through Labor Day Monday through Saturday 1 PM–5 PM; open Labor Day through Memorial Day Tuesday and Thursday 1 PM–5 PM, Saturday 10 AM–5 PM; free. If your children love dinosaurs (or you do), plan a stop at the Glenrock Paleontological Museum. Here you can not only view specimens of some of the world's most notorious dinos, such as a triceratops discovered near the town of Glenrock in 1994, but you can also watch scientists actually prepare the specimens in the lab for preservation and presentation. For a more in-depth prehistoric experience, inquire about the day and/or overnight dinosaur digging excursions that the museum offers.

Homesteaders Museum (307-532-5612; www.torringtonterritory.com/tourism/ ?page_code=homestead), 495 Main Street, Torrington. Open Labor Day through Memorial Day Monday through Friday 9:30 AM–4 PM; open Memorial Day through Labor Day Monday through Wednesday 9:30 AM–4 PM, Thursday and Friday 9:30 AM–7 PM, Saturday noon–6 PM, Sunday noon–4 PM; donations gladly accepted. Situated in the historic Union Pacific Railroad depot, this local history museum features relics and artifacts detailing the area's past. Included are exhibits on the history of the local Indians, the pioneers, ranching, military service, and more. Of particular interest is a shack, constructed by one Ben Trout in 1910, which viscerally illustrates some aspects of the difficulties of eking out a living in this area in the early 20th century.

Museum of the American West (307-332-4137; www.amwest.org), 1445 W. Main Street, Lander. Open Monday through Friday 9 AM–noon; free. At the time of this book's publication, this museum was still in its development phase, so you should be sure to call in advance for the latest information about the hours of operation and the status of construction efforts. Currently, museum exhibits can be seen at Community First Bank (303 Main Street) in Lander. Ultimately, the Museum of the American West aims to include the **Lander Children's Museum** (see *For Families*), the **Pioneer Museum,** the **Pushroot Living History Village,** the **Native Americans of the Central Plains and Rockies Museum,** and an adjoining living-history display, all in the same location. This will provide visitors with a wonderfully extensive and informative historical destination that will include places of interest for the whole family. The museum also offers self-guided tours and guided tours as well as weekly Native American powwow dance exhibitions.

National Bighorn Sheep Interpretive Center (1-888-209-2795; 307-455-3429; www.bighorn.org), 907 W. Ramshorn Street, Dubois. Open daily Memorial Day through Labor Day 9 AM–8 PM; open daily after Labor Day through Memorial Day 9 AM–5 PM; $2 adults, $.75 children 12 and under, $5 per family. Learn more about this majestic and mysterious mountain-loving creature with a visit to this marvelous museum, where a full-size bighorn sheep display gives you an intimate view of this animal's natural beauty. Start or complete your journey with a walk along the paved trail outside the center, which guides you through some of the hazards faced by these large mammals as they struggle to survive in a changing world. Nearby, the **Whiskey Mountain Habitat Area** serves as home to the largest known herd of wintering Rocky Mountain bighorn sheep in the nation. The museum offers guided 3- to 5-hour tours of this area from November to March ($25, 24-hour advance reservations required), providing you with the potential opportunity to view the resident bighorns up close.

  ♿ **National Historic Trails Interpretive Center** (307-261-7700; www.wy.blm .gov/nhtic), 1501 N. Poplar, Casper (I-25 at Exit 189). Open daily April through October 8 AM–7 PM; open November through March Tuesday through Saturday 9 AM–4:30 PM; closed Thanksgiving, Christmas, New Year's Day, and Easter; $6 adults, $5 seniors age 60 and older, $4 students over age 18 with valid ID, $3 children ages 6–17, $1 children ages 3–5, children 2 and under free. If you're interested in the historic pioneer trails that crisscrossed Wyoming in the 1800s, you should certainly plan a visit to this museum. Interactive exhibits bring you along on the journeys taken by pioneers and others on the Bozeman, Bridger, California, Mormon, Oregon, and Pony Express trails. The uniquely constructed center also incorporated its actual construction materials into the exhibits themselves, thus drawing you even closer to the people who traveled this way in the past. These include tiles engraved with entries from diaries as well as illustrations of the various hardships and obstacles pioneers faced along the trails. Native American history, particularly in relation to the trails, is incorporated as well. (See also Pony Express Re-Ride under *Special Events.*)

  ✎ **Nicolaysen Art Museum and Discovery Center** (307-235-5247; www .thenic.org), 400 E. Collins Drive, Casper. Open Tuesday through Saturday 10 AM–5 PM, Sunday noon–4 PM; $2 adults, $1 children, $5 per family. An art museum that won't bore the kids to tears? You bet—the Nicolaysen Art Museum will keep their little hands and minds busy with its cool and fun hands-on Discovery Center. There they'll learn all about the various forms of media used by artists in creating their masterpieces (and perhaps they'll even create some masterpieces of their own!). The art museum's exhibits feature not only pieces by Wyoming and regional artists but also works by national and international artists of note, which are displayed in its seven galleries. Exhibits change frequently, so repeat customers are likely to find something new to engage them during each visit.

Wind River Heritage Center (307-856-0706; www.1838rendezvous.com/ wind_river_heritagecenter.htm), 412 E. Fremont Street, Riverton. Open Monday through Saturday 10 AM–6 PM; donations gladly accepted. The central attraction of this local history museum is the Jake **Korell Wildlife Collection.** This collection includes life-size displays of local and regional wildlife positioned in active, realistic settings, giving the visitor a sense of the area's ecological diversity. Also included in the exhibits are animal traps dating to the early 1800s, as well as additional fur-trade-era artifacts.

Wind River Historical Center (307-455-2284; www.windriverhistory.org), 909 W. Ramshorn Street, Dubois. Open daily Memorial Day through October 15, 9 AM–4 PM; $1 adults, $.50 children 6–12, children 5 and under free. This extensive museum details the natural and cultural history of the local and regional surroundings, including a main museum building with a variety of historical exhibits, as well as several historical structures surrounding the main building. The historical structures include the **Tie Hack Interpretive Center,** which helps explain the tie hack industry's historical significance in the area (see also **Tie Hack Memorial** under *Historic Landmarks, Places, and Sites*). Exhibits in the main museum include the history of the local mountain Shoshone, or "Sheep Eater" Indians, legendary hunters of the Rocky Mountain bighorn sheep; displays about the area's pioneers and homesteaders; and natural history exhibits; as well as rotating exhibits that relate to the region's history. The museum's partner, the **Lucius Burch Center for Western Tradition,** provides educational opportunities, such as historical lectures, in addition to funding and promoting historical and archaeological research, among its other endeavors.

Wyoming Pioneer Memorial Museum (307-358-9288; www.wyshs.org/mus -wypioneer.htm), 400 W. Center Street, Douglas. Open Monday through Friday 8 AM–5 PM, and in summer Saturday 1 PM–5 PM; donations gladly accepted. This extensive pioneer museum, situated on the state fairgrounds, features an enormous collection of relics and artifacts from the early days of the country's westward expansion. Of course, the focus of the museum centers on Wyoming's early pioneer families and homesteaders. You'll also enjoy viewing the museum's collection of western artwork. The museum houses a research library that includes relevant historical documents as well as genealogies, photographs, and books.

See also Lander, Riverton, and Wheatland under *Towns;* **Lander Children's Museum** and **Tate Geological Museum** under *For Families;* and Guernsey State Park under *Historic Landmarks, Places, and Sites.*

HISTORIC LANDMARKS, PLACES, AND SITES **Atlantic City Mercantile** (307-332-5143; http://wyoshpo.state.wy.us/atcitym.htm), 2 miles off WY 28 (look for signs to Atlantic City). Open year-round. Listed on the National Register of Historic Places, this 1893 structure hearkens back to this area's booming gold rush days. Back in the late 19th and early 20th centuries, both Atlantic City and nearby South City were destinations for those willing to seek their fortunes in this area of Wyoming's high country. The mercantile served not only as a place for locals to stock up on supplies but also as one of the town's social centers where people could catch up on the latest news and gossip from around the town. The store closed in 1929 after the death of its original owner, Lawrence Giessler. It remained closed until 1964, when it was purchased by a new owner and reopened as a bar. Since then, it has remained open, though its ownership and functions have changed over the years. Today, the mercantile houses a local history museum, a bar, and a steakhouse and also offers cabins for rent should you want to spend the night.

Castle Gardens (307-332-8400; www.wy.blm.gov/lfo/cultural/castlegardens .htm), roughly 45 miles east of Riverton; take WY 136 (Gas Hills Road) about 35 miles to a left turn (signed), proceed about 6 miles to a right turn (signed), and proceed about 5 miles to the site. This drive—particularly the last few miles—is best made in summer months, when the dirt road has had ample opportunities to dry out. At Castle Gardens, you'll be swept into the area's prehistoric past via the impressive array of petroglyphs found carved into the rocks here. Unlike pictographs, or paintings on the rocks, petroglyphs are actually carved into the rocks' surfaces, often a laborious process for the carver. The petroglyphs at Castle Gardens feature shields and warriors bearing shields, among other distinctive artwork, and many were colored with dyes after being carved into the stone. A footpath takes you among the petroglyphs, but please only look and don't touch—they've already seen more than their fair share of damage from vandals throughout the years. Managed by the Lander Field Office of the Bureau of Land Management (BLM), Castle Gardens is listed on the National Register of Historic Places (see also Bureau of Land Management under *Wilder Places— Other Wild Places*).

& **Fort Fetterman State Historic Site** (307-684-7629; http://wyoparks.state.wy .us/fetter1.htm), 752 US 93, Douglas (Exit 140 off I-25). Open Memorial Day through Labor Day; visitor center and Ordnance Building open 9 AM–5 PM; grounds open from sunrise to sunset, closed in winter; $1 adults (residents), $2 adults (nonresidents), children 17 and under free; overnight camping $6 per vehicle (residents), $12 per vehicle (nonresidents); call for reservations in advance (two sites). Located at the intersection of the Bozeman Trail and the Oregon Trail, this once critical military supply site preserves and interprets a crucial slice of Wyoming's frontier history. Established by the U.S. military at the close of the Civil War in 1867, the outpost served as a military base of operations for supplies and as a starting point for actions taken against the Indians, who were struggling to keep their cultures and lands intact during this time. It also became known as a relatively safe haven for the pioneers passing through on the road to westward expansion. You'll tour through two of the fort's original buildings, which house exhibits on historic Fort Fetterman City, local Native Americans and their history, and the military's role in the development of the frontier. A 1-mile **interpretive trail** guides you to several significant points of interest, and picnic tables provide a great place for stopping to eat while reflecting on the past.

& ✐ **Fort Laramie National Historic Site** (307-837-2221; www.nps.gov/fola), 965 Gray Rocks Road, Fort Laramie. Visitor center open daily mid-May through late September 8 AM–7 PM; open daily late September through mid-May 8 AM– 4:30 PM; closed Thanksgiving, Christmas, and New Year's Day; grounds open daily until dusk; $3 per person ages 16 and up (7-day permit), children 15 and under free. This is the site of one of the earlier outposts established in Wyoming, dating back to 1834, when it was built as a trading and supply post for fur traders. At that time, the Cheyenne and Arapaho Indians frequented the post and interactions were, for the most part, friendly. In 1849, when the trickle of emigrant traffic had turned into a sweeping wave of pioneers flooding the Oregon Trail in hopes of striking it rich out west, the post became a military fort. In that capacity, it served not only as a crucial place to stop for supplies but also as a base of operations for planning military actions against the Indians. During this time, the Indians had grown increasingly violent and resistive to being forced onto reservations, which was due not only to the encroachment of the increasing numbers of pioneers but also to the repeated making and breaking of treaties and the refusal to allow them to remain on their ancestral homelands, among other factors. The fort closed in 1890 after all was said and done, having served its purpose—the removal of the Indians, making way for permanent white settlements and future westward expansion. The fort remains today as a testament to the struggle for the West, a struggle that ultimately and permanently displaced the many Indian tribes who had long made these lands their homes, disrupting their traditional ways of living for good. Visitors can tour through some 50 restored rooms of the fort, furnished with authentic period pieces; watch a video presentation; tour the fort with an audio tour; and attend interpretive programs. Children can participate in a Junior Ranger program and receive a Junior Ranger badge.

  ♿ **Guernsey State Park** (307-836-2334; http://wyoparks.state.wy.us/guern1 .htm), 15 miles east of I-25 on US 26 to C.R. 317, then 1.5 miles north to the park entrance. Open year-round for day-use and camping, limited facilities in winter; day-use $2 per vehicle (residents), $4 per vehicle (nonresidents); camping $6 per vehicle (residents), $12 per vehicle (nonresidents). A National Historic Landmark that is listed on the National Register of Historic Places, Guernsey State Park showcases the work of the Civilian Conservation Corps (CCC) that was performed here throughout the 1930s. Here you'll find structures, including the park's museum, the "castle," and a number of other picnic shelters, all of which were constructed through the hard work of the CCC and illustrate the architectural and planning abilities of those involved in this extensive project. Additionally, the CCC put in much of the park's network of **trails** (17 miles). Camping is available in seven campgrounds, five of which are on the lakeshore of the Guernsey Reservoir. Boating is also a major focus at this park, with its nearly 2,400 surface acres of water and three boat ramps to provide easy access. Other popular water sports here include swimming and fishing.

  ♿ **Independence Rock State Historic Site** (307-577-5150; http://wyoparks .state.wy.us/irock1.htm), located northeast of Muddy Gap and southwest of Casper on WY 220. Open year-round in daylight hours (no overnight camping); free. Also known as the Register of the Desert, a name given to this huge granite outcropping by Father Peter J. DeSmet way back in 1840, Independence Rock served as an iconic landmark for nearly all of those traveling on the Oregon Trail and other historic trails—as well as a place to leave a mark of their passage for some. Here, though erosion has worn away many inscriptions, you'll still find some of the names and dates inscribed by a number of the more than half-million or so pioneers who passed by this very spot on their journeys to points westward. Christened Independence Rock by William Sublette on the Fourth of July in 1830, the 6,208-foot monolith serves as a silent witness to the veritable flood of pioneers who once traveled through this stark landscape in pursuit of their own versions of the already legendary and elusive American dream. You are welcome to walk around the rock (the distance is more than a mile around at the base) or even on top of it, but please leave the rock itself as you find it, so that future generations can enjoy this piece of history just as much as you do. (See also Devil's Gate under *Natural Wonders.*)

Register Cliff and Oregon Trail ruts (307-777-7697; http://wyoshpo.state .wy.us/trailsdemo/register_cliff.htm), 2 miles south of Guernsey via the well-signed roads that guide you to the sites. Listed on the National Register of Historic Places, the 100-foot-high Register Cliff provided pioneers on the Oregon Trail with a ready-made place to leave behind evidence of their travels. This rock precipice, made up of soft stone, towered over the popular camping spot that was a day's journey beyond Fort Laramie (see above). As pioneers rested and rejuvenated for another day on the trail, many of them found time to carve their names, the date, from whence they came, and/or their hoped-for destinations. An interpretive kiosk provides information about the site, and a walkway enables you to stroll along the cliff. Please do your part in protecting this historical place, which has already been the site of vandalism. You can see the tracks of the Oregon Trail passing by this way. Just 0.5 mile south of Guernsey off US 26 are some of the more prominent remaining trail ruts that lie scattered throughout this region, evidence of the passage of thousands of wagons in trains as they made their way westward more than a century ago.

South Pass, located 10 miles southwest of South Pass City and about 45 miles southwest of Lander on WY 28. This National Historic Landmark proved to be the key to unlocking westward travel for pioneers along the Oregon Trail. The easiest passage through the Rocky Mountains, South Pass witnessed the flood of emigrants traveling by wagon train through this barren country from 1843 to 1912. Today, South Pass still serves as a key travel route for residents of Lander and Riverton traveling to Utah; but trust me—unless you need to, you do *not* want to travel this route at any time of year except in summer. I've witnessed some of the most treacherous and terrible driving conditions of my entire life along WY 28 over South Pass, including a brilliant combination of pea soup fog, horizontal sleet, snow-covered roads, and high winds—in May. Just imagine enduring such conditions in a covered wagon without a well-marked highway dotted with reflectors to guide you! (See also Bureau of Land Management under *Wilder Places—Other Wild Places.*)

&. 🎣 **South Pass City State Historic Site** (307-332-3684; http://wyoparks .state.wy.us/south1.htm), 125 South Pass Main, 2 miles off WY 28 (35 miles south of Lander). Open daily May 15 through September 30, 9 AM–6 PM; $1 adults (residents), $2 adults (nonresidents), children 17 and under free. This is a must-see site for anyone interested in the gold rush or just the general history of pioneers in this area. A fully restored gold rush town allows you intimate access into some 30 structures, which feature period furnishings and plenty of interpretive materials to guide your way. Stroll through town and take it in, learning

SOUTH PASS CITY STATE HISTORIC SITE (RIVERTON–LANDER AREA)

about the strike that originally brought people to the area in 1867, as well as the unique characters who left a long-term legacy for the generations to come. Prominent residents of South Pass City included among others William Bright, who penned a women's suffrage bill that was passed into law in Wyoming in 1869, making Wyoming the first state to allow women the right to vote and hold political office. Another South Pass City citizen, Esther Morris, would become the first woman to exercise the right to hold office when she was appointed a justice of the peace the following year. The initial boom had subsided by 1872, and fewer than 100 people remained by 1875, though the town would continue to see resurgences of population growth well into the early 20th century with reports of more gold strikes. Additional attractions at this site include an operational general store with items for sale, a 3-mile **hiking trail** along Willow Creek, and access to the **Continental Divide National Scenic Trail,** which runs right through town. To complete your South Pass experience, stop at the former mining towns of Miner's Delight and Atlantic City (see Atlantic City Mercantile, above), which can be accessed via the same turn off WY 28, before journeying over South Pass. Want to stay nearby? Try **Miner's Delight Bed and Breakfast** in historic Atlantic City (see *Lodging—Bed & Breakfasts*). (See also Gold Rush Days under *Special Events.*)

Tie Hack Memorial, located 15 miles west of Dubois along US 26/287. This picturesque setting overlooking the beautiful and peaceful Wind River seems somehow suitable for this simple commemorative structure. The memorial pays tribute to the people, many of Scandinavian, German, and Eastern European origin, who eked out their livings by hand-hewing railroad ties from the timber surrounding Dubois. The industry began in this region with the construction of the Chicago and North Western Railroad in the early 20th century and continued for three decades. The "tie hacks" became intimately acquainted with the forests north of Dubois, where they lived in temporary camps as they created the railroad ties with their own hands. The ties were then floated down the Wind River to the Riverton tie yards, about 100 miles to the southeast. (See also Wind River Historical Center under *Museums.*)

TIE HACK MEMORIAL

See also Douglas, Torrington, and Wheatland under *Towns;* Fort Caspar Museum and Historic Site under *Museums;* South Big Horn–Red Wall Scenic Backway under *Scenic Drives;* Ayres Natural Bridge Park, Devil's Gate, Hell's Half Acre, and Teapot Dome under *Natural Wonders;* Glendo State Park under *To Do—Boating;* Laramie Peak Trail under *To Do—*

Hiking; Pony Express Ride under *To Do—Horseback Riding;* Adventures West Tours, Fort Washakie Tours, and Spiritrider Wagon Train Adventures under *To Do—Unique Adventures;* Shoshone National Forest under *Wilder Places— Forests;* Blackbird Inn Bed and Breakfast, Blue Spruce Inn, Delfelder Inn Bed and Breakfast, Hotel Higgins, Morton Mansion Bed and Breakfast, and the Sager House Bed and Breakfast under *Lodging—Bed & Breakfasts;* Twin Pines Lodge and Cabins under *Lodging—Lodges;* Outlaw Cabins and Sleeping Bear Ranch RV Resort and Café under *Lodging—Other Options;* Cowfish under *Dining Out;* and Gannett Grill under *Eating Out.*

FOR FAMILIES ✐ **Casper Planetarium** (307-577-0310; http://ncsdweb.ncsd .k12.wy.us/planetarium/index.html), 904 N. Poplar Street, Casper. Open for nightly shows June 10 through Labor Day at 7:30 PM; show starts at 8 PM; also open for public shows some nights in the off-season (call for schedule); $2.50 per person, not recommended for children under 6. Explore *The Stars Tonight* first, and then sit back to take in another themed show. Topics range from today's hottest astronomical developments to historic and prehistoric themes, including dinosaurs. The planetarium also does laser light shows set to contemporary popular music.

✐ **Lander Children's Museum** (1-800-332-1341; 307-332-1341; www.lander childrensmuseum.org), 445 Lincoln Avenue. Open June through August Tuesday and Thursday 10 AM–4 PM; open September through May Tuesday and Friday 10 AM–1 PM, Saturday 10 AM–4 PM; $2 per person ages 3 and up. Geared toward children ages 3–12, the Lander Children's Museum offers an array of hands-on exhibits designed to stimulate children's innate curiosity about the world around them. Learning becomes fun through interactive exhibits that provide children with ample opportunities to explore not only the disciplines of math and science but also art, music, reading and more. The Lander Children's Museum is scheduled to move at some point in the future to the campus of the Museum of the American West (see *Museums*).

✐ 🐾 **Tate Geological Museum** (307-268-2447; www.caspercollege.edu/tate/ webpage.asp), 125 College Drive (at Casper College), Casper. Open Monday through Friday 9 AM–5 PM, Saturday 10 AM–4 PM; closed Sunday and most major holidays; free. Children are particularly welcome at Tate, where the mineral exhibits include a visually stimulating black room, showcasing minerals that glow in the dark. Additional displays include meteorites, Indian artifacts, dinosaur fossils and other fossils (the majority of which are from Wyoming), and crystals. Children (and adults, too) can touch all they want at the museum's "touch tables," where mineral specimens are set out to help further their knowledge of the world of minerals through direct interaction.

See also Glenrock Paleontological Museum, Museum of the American West, National Bighorn Sheep Interpretive Center, and Nicolaysen Art Museum and Discovery Center under *Museums;* Fort Laramie National Historic Site under *Historic Landmarks, Places, and Sites;* Sinks Canyon State Park under *Natural Wonders;* Boysen State Park, Glendo State Park, and Hawk Springs State Recreation Area under *To Do—Boating;* Lander City Park under *To Do—Camping;*

Casper Whitewater Park under *To Do—Paddling;* Hogadon Ski Area and *Ice-Skating* under *To Do—Snow Sports;* Adventures West Tours, Lander Llama Company, and Spiritrider Wagon Train Adventures under *To Do—Unique Adventures;* Dubois Town Park and Edness Kimball Wilkins State Park under *Wilder Places—Parks;* and Fort Caspar Chautauqua, Wild West Winter Carnival, Winterfest, Gold Rush Days, 1838 Mountain Man Rendezvous, Pageant of the Old West and Rodeo, Riverton Rendezvous, Buffalo BBQ Weekend, Wyoming State Fair, and Wyoming State Winter Fair under *Special Events.*

SCENIC DRIVES **Seminoe to Alcova Scenic Backway** is a journey of about 70 miles that starts at Alcova, roughly 30 miles southwest of Casper off WY 220. The adventure takes you south from this small town along C.R. 603/407 to C.R. 291 to BLM 3159 to C.R. 351 (Seminoe Road), depositing you at its terminus in Sinclair, near Rawlins. Highlights of this remote, backcountry journey include **Fremont Canyon,** popular with rock climbers; the **Miracle Mile of the North Platte River** (see *Natural Wonders*); **Seminoe State Park** (see *To Do—Boating* in "South Wyoming: Medicine Bow–Flaming Gorge Country"); the **Pedro Mountains;** and the **Seminoe Mountains.** This area is rife with streams, springs, and bodies of water, making it a tremendous destination for anglers.

South Big Horn–Red Wall Scenic Backway takes you on a 100-mile journey, beginning about 15 miles west of Casper via US 20/26 to C.R. 125 (Bucknam Road). The trek winds northwest on 33-Mile Road (C.R. 110) to C.R. 109 (Bighorn Mountain Road) to C.R. 105 (Buffalo Creek Road) to C.R. 104 (Arminto–Waltman Road), depositing you back onto US 20/26 at Waltman, west of your starting point. This mostly graveled backcountry drive should be undertaken only in good weather conditions and in a suitable vehicle (that is, if you're in an RV, you might want to consider spending the day elsewhere). You'll drive through country used historically by some of the first ranchers to inhabit this area, who drove both sheep and cattle to the pastures of the higher ground of the **Bighorn Mountains.** Along the way, you may see antelope, among other wildlife, as they make their homes on Wyoming's windswept prairies such as those found here. You'll pass by **Roughlock Hill,** where emigrants along the Oregon Trail locked their wagon wheels and simply slid down the steep slope to the valley below, rather than try to negotiate the hill with rotating wheels—certainly a more dangerous prospect. You can also access the **Hole-in-the-Wall Trail** (see *To Do—Hiking* in "North Wyoming: Devils Tower–Buffalo Bill Country") from this drive by taking Buffalo Creek Road (C.R. 105) north instead of south.

See also **South Pass** under *Historic Landmarks, Places, and Sites.*

NATURAL WONDERS ᕁ **Ayres Natural Bridge Park** (307-3858-3532), 208 Natural Bridge Park, 12 miles west and 5 miles south of I-25 at Exit 151 (near Douglas). Open April through October dawn through dusk (some overnight camping); free. The lovely red rocks of this park surround the parking area, but it's the top-heavy natural arch of stone over La Prele Creek that gives the park its name. Easily accessed for viewing, the arch is made up of 150 acres of stone and is purportedly one of the few known natural bridges that still have water flowing beneath them. Early pioneers along the Oregon Trail visited the arch during their journeys west, marveling at its solidity, enormity, and beauty. Today the park surrounding the arch offers opportunities for picnicking, hiking, camping, and wildlife viewing—but pets are absolutely prohibited; if you get caught with Fido or Fluffy on the grounds, you're in for a sizable fine.

Devil's Gate, situated southwest of Casper on WY 220 just southwest of Independence Rock (see *Historic Landmarks, Places, and Sites*), features a dramatic canyon cut by the Sweetwater River. Here where the river turns, it worked through the granite wall, leaving a 330-foot-deep canyon that spans 400 feet at its rim, narrowing to a mere 30 feet across where the river flows through it. You'll find a convenient scenic turnout offering you views of this natural phenomenon, which appears much the same as it did to the emigrants who passed this way on the Oregon, Mormon, and Pony Express trails. This was one of many distinctive natural landmarks that lay along the journey westward through Wyoming.

Hell's Half Acre (307-235-9311; www.casperwyoming.info/parks.html) can be found 45 miles west of Casper just south of US 20/26 before Waltman. Closer to 320 acres in size, this pocket of dramatic, multihued badlands-esque terrain earned its name from adventurers who passed this way in the 1830s. These travelers noted not only the area's odd appearance but also the even odder phenomenon of the sulfuric smoke rising from the ground—the result of the smoldering coal fires that lay beneath the surface, unbeknownst to them at the time. If this terrain seems strangely familiar to you during your visit, then perhaps you actually have seen it before—this is where the 1996 film *Starship Troopers* was shot. After all, it does look like the perfect sort of place where we'd imagine aliens would feel right at home, doesn't it? Indians also once used this area as a place to hunt and trap buffalo.

Miracle Mile of the North Platte River—actually about 5.5 miles in length—spans the section of the river that lies between Kortes Reservoir and Pathfinder Reservoir (see *To Do—Fishing*) and is accessible by driving a portion of the **Seminoe to Alcova Scenic Backway** (see *Scenic Drives*). If you're an avid fisherman, you probably have already heard of this blue-ribbon trout fishing stream, which has gained national renown for the high quality of its fishing. This section of river tends to be home to unusually large concentrations of brown, rainbow, and cutthroat trout of unusually large size (both in terms of weight and in terms of length). (See also the North Platte River under *To Do—Fishing*.)

& ✇ ✿ **Sinks Canyon State Park** (307-332-3077; http://wyoparks.state.wy.us/sinks1.htm), 3079 Sinks Canyon Road, Lander. Open year-round; day-use free; camping $4 per vehicle (residents), $8 per vehicle (nonresidents); visitor center open daily Memorial Day through Labor Day 9 AM–6 PM. This park's biggest attraction gave the canyon its name. On your first visit, drive right by the signs marking "the Rise" and start your exploration of the park at "the Sinks," which is accessible by a short trail (not handicapped accessible) by the visitor center. A walk down the trail brings you to the remarkable cave complex known as the Sinks, where the Popo Agie River (see *To Do—Fishing*) plunges into a latticed network of limestone caverns beneath the surface, disappearing entirely until it resurfaces 0.25 mile downcanyon in a placidly bubbling pool known as the Rise, having worked its way through the underground tunnels and back to the surface. The Rise is home to enormous trout that visitors feed by purchasing fish food from a nearby dispenser—but alas, no fishing is permitted at the Rise, which accounts for their enormity, no doubt! In addition to the Sinks and the Rise, Sinks Canyon State Park provides visitors with opportunities for bicycling (on-road only), camping, hiking (1-mile and 4-mile trails depart from the suspension bridge at the Popo Agie Campground), picnicking, playing on playground equipment, fishing,

"THE SINKS" AND THE POPO AGIE RIVER IN SINKS CANYON STATE PARK (RIVERTON–LANDER AREA)

wildlife viewing (with Rocky Mountain bighorn sheep sometimes grazing right along the road), and rock climbing, among other popular endeavors. (See also Baldwin Creek Road–Squaw Creek Road Loop under *To Do—Bicycling* and Popo Agie Falls Trail under *To Do—Hiking.*)

Teapot Dome, situated in the Salt Creek Oil Fields about 25 miles north of Casper via I-25 to WY 259, is the very formation that gave the notorious Teapot Dome Scandal of the early 1920s its name. This distinctively shaped butte received national attention not merely for being shaped like a teapot but also because it was the defining feature of the richly endowed oil fields surrounding it—fields that lay at the very heart of the scandal. The Teapot Dome area came under controversy and great scrutiny in its connection with the administration of President Warren G. Harding. The president himself was unaware of the shady goings-on, which involved the illegal conveyance of the oil rights to these and other fields by one of his appointees, Secretary of the Interior Albert Fall, to the oil magnate Harry F. Sinclair. Though the "spout" and the "handle" of the teapot were destroyed by a storm in the 1960s, the butte still stands today, not only as a unique natural feature but also as a symbol of the scandal that rocked the country in 1923.

See also **Shoshone National Forest** under *Wilder Places—Forests.*

✳ To Do

BICYCLING **Baldwin Creek Road–Squaw Creek Road Loop** is a 10.6-mile ride that starts on the west end of Main Street in Lander and is best done on a road bike. From the starting point, you'll head left (west) on Baldwin Creek Road for 5.3 miles, climbing gradually out of town and then winding through sparsely inhabited lands, with some BLM- and state-owned lands on the south side of the road (great for mountain biking). After 5.3 miles, the road angles sharply southeast (left), looping as it becomes Squaw Creek Road. Continue your journey through undulating, winding terrain for another 5.2 miles before you reach the intersection with Sinks Canyon Road (WY 131). From there, you can complete the loop by following Sinks Canyon Road to 9th Street. Go left on 9th Street, and then left on Main Street, and pedal back to your starting point—or stop in at one of the restaurants on Main Street to refuel. For a longer ride, you can tack on an out-and-back journey along Sinks Canyon Road to Sinks Canyon State Park (see *To See—Natural Wonders*) by turning right instead of left off Squaw Peak Road. It's about 6 miles to the park's entrance from the intersection of Squaw Peak Road and Sinks Canyon Road.

&. **Platte River Parkway** (307-577-1206; www.platteriverparkway.org), a paved trail open to nonmotorized traffic only, runs for about 10 miles along the North Platte River in Casper, from the North Casper Soccer Complex (at K Street and Beverly Street) to Paradise Valley Park (at the end of Paradise Drive where it bends into Riverbend Road). In addition, numerous side trails connect the main trail to a variety of recreational areas and parks throughout the city. These parks include Casper Park, Crossroads Park, and North Platte Park. Mountain bikers and hikers will find an abundance of trails shooting off the main trail in the section between the North Casper Soccer Complex and the Historic Trails Overlook Shelter to the west. Fishing access, several boat ramps, and the Casper Whitewater Park (see *Paddling*) can be found along the trail as well. (See also the North Platte River under *Fishing*.)

&. **Wyoming Heritage Trail** is a rails-to-trails project that takes you from Riverton to Shoshoni, with about 5 miles paved with asphalt and the remaining 17 miles of trail featuring rather rough terrain. You'll have to do a little searching to find the trailhead, since it's not well marked (unless things have changed recently). From Riverton, head west on US 26 toward Dubois, keeping your eyes out for the old railroad depot, now home to a Mexican restaurant (appropriately deemed the Depot). The trail begins across the street from this location. From there, you'll head northeast through town on a paved surface until you reach the edge of Riverton—and then, you're on your way through the wilder, wackier terrain of Wyoming's wetlands and prairies, which can be rocky and rutted at times. You'll probably enjoy total solitude, unless you count the jackrabbits, antelope, mule deer, birds, and other fauna you'll potentially encounter as you ride. Bring plenty of water, food, and an adventuresome spirit on this ride. The trail terminates in the tiny town of Shoshoni. Hikers and four-wheelers also enjoy this trail, as do snowmobilers and cross-country skiers in winter.

See also Douglas and Torrington under *To See—Towns;* Guernsey State Park under *To See—Historic Landmarks, Places, and Sites;* Sinks Canyon State Park under *To See—Natural Wonders;* Boysen State Park under *Boating;* BLM campgrounds under *Camping;* Laramie Peak Trail, Muddy Mountain Environmental Education Area National Recreation Trail, and Popo Agie Falls Trail under *Hiking;* Casper Mountain Park under *Wilder Places—Parks;* Medicine Bow National Forest and Shoshone National Forest under *Camping* and *Wilder Places—Forests;* and Bureau of Land Management under *Wilder Places—Other Wild Places.*

BOATING &. ✍ **Boysen State Park** (307-876-2796; http://wyoparks.state.wy.us/boysen1.htm), accessible via US 20/WY 789 north of Shoshoni and just south of Wind River Canyon (see *To See—Natural Wonders* in "North Wyoming: Devils

Tower–Buffalo Bill Country") and via points off US 26 west of Shoshoni. Open year-round for day-use and camping, limited facilities in winter. Day-use $2 per vehicle (residents), $4 per vehicle (nonresidents); camping $6 per vehicle (residents), $12 per vehicle (nonresidents). The almost jarring visual dissonance created by Boysen Reservoir results from the presence of such an enormous body of water—nearly 20,000 acres—covering an area that at one point probably featured mainly arid prairies. The first damming of the Wind River took place here in 1908 under the directorship of a Danish immigrant, Asmus Boysen. That dam ceased operations in 1925. The present dam was built in 1951. Today, visitors enjoy easy access from a number of points to the reservoir's abundance of water-oriented recreational opportunities, including not only boating (five boat ramps), but also waterskiing, swimming, and fishing (species include brown trout, crappie, cutthroat trout, ling, perch, rainbow trout, sauger, and walleye, among others). Additional recreational opportunities include playgrounds, bicycling, hiking, camping (11 campgrounds), picnicking, and wildlife viewing. The marina is near the entrance of Wind River Canyon just off US 20 (watch for signs). (See also the Wind River under *Fishing*.)

  Glendo State Park (307-735-4433; http://wyoparks.state.wy.us/glendo1 .htm), 397 Glendo Park Road, off I-25 at Glendo. Open year-round for day-use and camping, limited facilities in winter. Day-use $2 per vehicle (residents), $4 per vehicle (nonresidents); camping $6 per vehicle (residents), $12 per vehicle (nonresidents). For water lovers, Glendo State Park is a popular destination. Boaters will find a marina and boat ramps, along with ample room on the 14-mile-long reservoir for waterskiing and fishing. A sandy beach invites swimmers to test the waters as well, and windsurfers enjoy the reservoir frequently. A great place for families, Glendo also has a plethora of campsites, a playground, 500 picnicking sites, and 4 miles of trails (handicapped accessible) near the reservoir. History buffs will find that though the 1957 completion of the earthen dam forming the reservoir covered up some of the tracks of the historic trails that passed this way, including the Oregon Trail, the area still shows evidence of earlier human activities. Not only have indications of pioneer passage been found here but evidence of Indian inhabitation, including tipi rings, can also still be found in and around the park.

  Hawk Springs State Recreation Area (307-836-2334; http://wyoparks .state.wy.us/hawk1.htm), 3 miles east of US 85 via C.R. 186, about 39 miles south of Torrington. Open year-round for day-use and camping, limited facilities and access in the winter. Day-use $2 per vehicle (residents), $4 per vehicle (nonresidents); camping $6 per vehicle (residents), $12 per vehicle (nonresidents). This remote destination in the southeastern corner of the state features great opportunities for boating and fishing alike. Boaters will enjoy the opportunity to explore more remote areas of the reservoir not accessible by land (as only a relatively small portion of the shore is publicly accessible). In particular, the south end of the reservoir affords the potential for viewing blue herons, among other birds in the area. Fish species include black crappie, channel catfish, largemouth bass, walleye, and yellow perch. Additional recreational opportunities include camping, playground equipment, and picnicking.

Louis Lake, in Shoshone National Forest (see *Wilder Places—Forests*) south-west of Lander, is accessible by taking Sinks Canyon Road southwest out of town, through Sinks Canyon State Park (see *To See—Natural Wonders*) and then up the canyon, where its name changes to Louis Lake Road. From here it switchbacks up Fossil Hill and leads you back to this remote yet accessible alpine lake. Situated nearby is **Louis Lake Lodge** (see *Lodging—Lodges*), which provides an array of services, including boat rentals if you don't have your own boat with you. Situated near the border of the Popo Agie Wilderness, the lake is a great place to start a boating or fishing adventure. You can easily access numerous other nearby lakes, including **Fiddlers Lake,** where boating is also permitted. In addition, this area is rife with trails great for hiking, cross-country skiing, snowmobiling, and more. (See also the Popo Agie River under *Fishing.*)

♾ **Pathfinder Reservoir and Alcova Reservoir** lie on lands managed by the Bureau of Land Management (BLM; see Bureau of Land Management under *Wilder Places—Other Wild Places*) and are accessible by taking WY 220 about 30 miles southwest of Casper. For Alcova Reservoir, go south on C.R. 407 or C.R. 406. For Pathfinder Reservoir, go south on C.R. 408 or C.R. 410. Pathfinder Reservoir, the larger of the two bodies of water, is situated in the Pathfinder National Wildlife Refuge (see *Wilder Places—Wildlife Refuges and Areas*). Three boat ramps gain you access to the enormous reservoir. In addition to boating, recreational opportunities include fishing (brown trout, cutthroat trout, Ohrid trout, rainbow trout, and walleye), camping (three campgrounds), a 1.7-mile interpretive hiking trail, and an interpretive center. Alcova Reservoir, though smaller, also features numerous recreational opportunities, including boating (with a marina, boat ramps, and rental boats). Sailboating and windsurfing are popular here, as are swimming, fishing, and ice fishing (brown trout, cutthroat trout, rainbow trout, and walleye). The reservoir also has a short, interpretive dinosaur trail, camping areas, and picnicking facilities. Also managed by the BLM, **Goldeneye Wildlife and Recreation Area** (29 miles northwest of Casper just off US 20/26) offers boating and fishing opportunities.

See also Guernsey State Park under *To See—Historic Landmarks, Places, and Sites;* Platte River Parkway under *Bicycling;* the North Platte River under *Fishing;* Shoshone National Forest under *Wilder Places—Forests;* and Bureau of Land Management under *Wilder Places—Other Wild Places.*

CAMPING ♾ **BLM campgrounds** (see Bureau of Land Management under *Wilder Places—Other Wild Places*) in this area include two (handicapped accessible) developed campgrounds that are managed by the **Casper Field Office** inside the Muddy Mountain Environmental Education Area (see *Hiking*): **Rim** and **Lodgepole campgrounds,** which together have 22 campsites ($3 day-use; $5 camping). The **Lander Field Office** manages **Cottonwood Campground** ($6), accessible by taking US 287/WY 789 east of Jeffrey City to BLM 2411 (Green Mountain Road), then going south for 11 miles to the campground (on the east loop of Green Mountain Road). Green Mountain Road is also a good mountain biking loop (31 miles total). Wild Horse Point Picnic Area is on the east loop of Green Mountain Road as well, 17 miles from US 287. The Lander

Field Office also manages two campgrounds near South Pass: **Atlantic City Campground** (handicapped accessible; $6), on the west side of the road to Atlantic City just 1 mile south of WY 28; and **Big Atlantic Gulch Campground** ($6), located on Fort Stambaugh Loop Road, 0.25 mile from its intersection with Atlantic City Road. Great roads for mountain biking are accessible from both campgrounds. (See also Pathfinder Reservoir and Alcova Reservoir under *Boating* and Bureau of Land Management under *Wilder Places—Other Wild Places*.)

☙ ✐ ⚅ **Lander City Park** (307-332-4647), 405 Fremont Street, Lander. Open year-round; free. Lander's city park should be a model for all small towns in America. You can stay and camp for up to 3 days in the shade of giant cottonwood trees next to a pleasant, gurgling stream. The park also has picnic tables, flush toilets, and large grassy areas, as well as a playground, a baseball diamond, and, in winter, an ice-skating rink. I've spent many a night in this park, and though local kids might cruise through looking for excitement, they rarely find anything going on here besides sleeping campers.

Larson Park Campground–RV Park (307-836-2255; www.golfandcamp.com), 100 S. Guernsey Road, Guernsey. Open seasonally; $13 (weekly rates available as well). This municipal park, adjacent to the city's Trail Ruts Golf Club (see *Golf*), has campsites for both tent campers and RVs. Facilities include drinking water, hot showers, and hookups. The city offers a special golf and camp rate; call for details.

Medicine Bow National Forest (see also *Wilder Places—Forests*) has one ranger district in this region, the **Douglas Ranger District** (307-358-4690), which has four first-come, first-served developed campgrounds as well as plentiful opportunities for dispersed camping (free). All of the developed campgrounds provide access to trails suitable for both hiking and mountain biking, while some also have opportunities for fishing, horseback riding, rock climbing, and off-road vehicle use as well. **Campbell Creek** (open June 1 through October 15; $15) is accessible by taking WY 91 southwest of Douglas 20 miles and then going 13 miles southwest on C.R. 24. **Curtis Gulch** (open June 15 through October 15; $10) is accessible by taking WY 91 southwest of Douglas 20 miles, then going south for 14 miles on C.R. 16 and then east for 4 miles on F.R. 658. **Esterbrook** (open May 15 through October 15; $10) is accessible by taking WY 94 south of Douglas 17 miles, going 11 miles south on C.R. 5, and then heading 3 miles east on F.R. 633. **Friend Park** (open June 1 through October 15; $10) is accessible by taking WY 94 south of Douglas 17 miles, then going 11 miles south on C.R. 5, then 15 miles southwest on F.R. 653, and then 3.5 miles southeast on F.R. 671. From here turn left at the sign for the campground and proceed another 1 mile to reach it. This campground is also the access point for the Laramie Peak Trail (see *Hiking*). The district also rents out the **LaPrele Guard Station,** a two-bedroom Civilian Conservation Corps (CCC)–built log cabin, to overnight visitors ($60; 1-877-444-6777 for reservations; www.reserveusa.com).

Natrona County Roads, Bridges, and Parks Department (307-235-9311) runs a number of public campgrounds and recreation areas in the Casper area. Day-use free; camping $7. These include **Beartrap Meadow** (7 miles south of town on Casper Mountain Road (WY 251), **Casper Mountain** (8 miles south of town on Casper Mountain Road (WY 251), **Gray Reef Reservoir** (26 miles west of town on WY 220), and **Ponderosa Park** (10 miles south on WY 1301). (See also **Casper Mountain Park** under *Wilder Places—Parks.*)

❦ **Riverside Park** (307-358-9750), 420 W. Grant, Riverside. This park is run by the City of Douglas. Campers are allowed to stay for a maximum of 48 hours (free). The park has 20 campsites, water, showers, restrooms, and picnic tables.

❦ **Pioneer Park** (307-532-5666), W. 15th Avenue, Torrington. This free municipal park includes a dump station, restrooms, and picnic tables. You can also camp nearby at the **Goshen County Fairgrounds** (307-532-2525), 7078 Fairgrounds Road, which includes hot showers, restrooms, a dump station, and horse boarding facilities.

♿ **Shoshone National Forest** (see also *Wilder Places—Forests*) has two ranger districts in this region that together have 11 first-come, first-served campgrounds, most of which are not handicapped accessible. Dispersed camping (free) is also available in many places throughout both districts. The **Washakie Ranger District** (307-332-5460) has six developed campgrounds (most $8 per night), mostly in the area southwest of Lander in and around Sinks Canyon, including **Sinks Canyon** (handicapped accessible; open Memorial Day through Labor Day; $8), accessible by taking Sinks Canyon Road southeast out of Lander and through Sinks Canyon State Park, then watching for signs to the campground. The **Wind River Ranger District** (307-455-2466) has five developed campgrounds ($5–10) in the area of the forest surrounding Dubois, including **Horse Creek** (handicapped accessible; open seasonally; $5), which is accessible by going north off US 26/287 just west of Dubois on Horse Creek Road (F.R. 285) for 10 miles or so to reach the campground. (See also the Popo Agie River under *Fishing.*)

❦ **Wheatland City Park–Lewis Park** (307-322-2962), 600 9th Street, Wheatland. This free city park offers overnight camping, including a dump station, electrical hookups, showers at the adjacent municipal pool (fee), restrooms, drinking water, picnic tables, and grills. The park can be loud at times, but you can't beat the price!

See also Riverton under *To See—Towns;* Guernsey State Park under *To See—Historic Landmarks, Places, and Sites;* Ayres Natural Bridge Park and Sinks Canyon State Park under *To See—Natural Wonders;* Boysen State Park, Glendo State Park, and Hawk Springs State Recreation Area under *Boating;* the North Platte River under *Fishing;* Louis Lake Lodge under *Lodging—Lodges;* and Sleeping Bear Ranch RV Resort and Café under *Lodging—Other Options.*

FISHING **The North Platte River** (307-473-3400; http://gf.state.wy.us/fish/fishing/index.asp) originates in northern Colorado, flowing north over the Wyoming border along WY 230 and WY 130 before reaching Seminoe Reservoir, then Kortes Reservoir, then Pathfinder Reservoir, and then Alcova Reservoir. The 5.5-mile stretch between Kortes and Pathfinder is known as the **Miracle Mile of the North Platte River** (see *To See—Natural Wonders*) due to its abundance of trout. The North Platte is one of Wyoming's most renowned blue-ribbon fishing streams. From Alcova Reservoir, the river arcs east, flowing along-side WY 220 to Casper, through Casper, and then roughly along I-25 to Glendo Reservoir and Guernsey Reservoir, making a slow turn toward the south to flow southeast along US 26 past Torrington before crossing the border into Nebraska. In addition to access at the reservoirs and the Miracle Mile section, numerous additional state-run access points can be found along the river's course, some with boat ramps and camping facilities. Species vary depending where you fish the river but can include brown trout, catfish, cutthroat trout, rainbow trout, and walleye. The river is also popular for floating, float fishing, and white-water pad-dling, with a number of access points suitable for these endeavors as well. (See also Platte River Parkway under *Bicycling;* Pathfinder Reservoir and Alcova Reservoir under *Boating;* Casper Whitewater Park under *Paddling;* Edness K. Wilkins State Park under *Wilder Places—Parks;* House on the Mile under *Lodging—Other Options;* and the North Platte River under *To Do—Fishing* in "North Wyoming: Medicine Bow–Flaming Gorge Country."

The Popo Agie River (307-332-7723; http://gf.state.wy.us/fish/fishing/index .asp), pronounced "Puh-*poh* zha" (meaning "headwaters" in Crow Indian), lies in Shoshone National Forest (see also *Wilder Places—Forests*). The Popo Agie has three forks: the North Fork, flowing from the Wind River Mountains through the North Fork Canyon northwest of Lander; the Middle Fork, flowing from the Wind River Mountains through Sinks Canyon southwest of Lander; and the Lit-tle Popo Agie River, flowing from the Wind River Mountains through Little Popo Agie Canyon south of Sinks Canyon. The Middle and North forks meet just north of Lander, along with Baldwin Creek, Squaw Creek, and several other creeks. The Little Popo Agie joins them around Hudson, northeast of Lander along WY 789. The river then flows northeast a few more miles to its confluence with the Little Wind River, which empties into the Wind River shortly thereafter in Riverton. The **North Fork**'s species include brook trout, hybridized Yellow-stone cutthroat, rainbow trout, and mountain whitefish in its upper reaches, giv-ing way to brook trout, brown trout, burbot, mountain whitefish, rainbow trout, and sauger in the midway and lower portions. This fork is accessible by taking US 287 northwest of Lander and then heading southwest out of Fort Washakie on Trout Creek Road (C.R. 294) to F.R. 329—you must stay on these roads and follow this itinerary or risk a hefty fine from the tribal police. A free Forest Ser-vice campground (Dickinson Creek) on F.R. 329 offers access to trails that lead to the river. The **Middle Fork**'s species include artic grayling, golden trout, Snake River cutthroat trout, and Yellowstone cutthroat trout in the upper reaches, with brown trout, brook trout, mountain whitefish, and rainbow trout throughout. This fork is accessible by taking Sinks Canyon Road (WY 131) southwest from Lander into the canyon (see also Sinks Canyon State Park under *To See—Natural Wonders*) and by hiking the Popo Agie Falls Trail (see *Hiking*). The **Little Popo Agie**'s species include brook trout, golden trout, and Snake River cutthroat trout in the upper regions, with brown trout, burbot, rainbow trout, and sauger throughout. To access the Little Popo Agie, follow the direc-tions for the Middle Fork, but continue on F.R. 300 (Louis Lake Road) at the end of WY 131, switchbacking up Fossil Hill toward Fiddlers Lake and Louis Lake (see also Louis Lake under *Boating*). Paddling portions of the Middle Fork of this river is possible as well.

The Sweetwater River (307-332-7723; http://gf.state.wy.us/fish/fishing/index .asp) flows south from its origins in the Wind River Mountains southwest of Lander before turning east and flowing by South Pass (see *To See—Historic Landmarks, Places, and Sites*) northeast to Sweetwater Station (along US 287/WY 789 southeast of Lander), then making its way east past Split Rock (a distinctive natural feature recognized as a landmark by emigrants on the Oregon Trail and other historic trails), Devils's Gate (see *To See—Natural Wonders*), and Independence Rock (see *To See—Historic Landmarks, Places, and Sites*), before emptying into Pathfinder Reservoir of the North Platte (see *Boating*). Species include brook trout, brown trout, cutthroat trout, and rainbow trout. Much of the river flows through private lands, making access somewhat difficult, though the state game and fish department has leased some lands for access from ranchers and other landowners. You'll find a couple of these points around South Pass, as well as five access points near Sweetwater Station, including two access points by taking C.R. 233 (Graham Road) northwest of US 287/WY 789 just west of Sweetwater Station.

The Wind River (307-332-7723; http://gf.state.wy.us/fish/fishing/index.asp; 307-332-7207 for the section on the Wind River Indian Reservation managed by the Tribal Fish and Game Department) flows from its origins on Togwotee Pass northwest of Dubois alongside US 26/287 and then roughly parallels US 26 through the Wind River Indian Reservation to its confluence with the Little Wind River in Riverton. From there, it turns northeast, flowing roughly parallel to US 26/WY 789 into Boysen Reservoir (see *Boating*) and then north out of the reservoir through the Wind River Canyon (see *To See—Natural Wonders* and *To Do—Fishing* in "North Wyoming: Devils Tower–Buffalo Bill Country"), where its name changes to the Bighorn River (see *To Do—Fishing* in "North Wyoming: Devils Tower–Buffalo Bill Country") just south of Thermopolis. Species include brook trout and rainbow trout, as well as walleye and sauger in the Wind River Canyon vicinity. Access to the river can be found northwest of Dubois at various points in Shoshone National Forest (see also *Wilder Places—Forests*), as well as at various signed points off US 26/287 around Dubois. To fish on the reservation, a special tribal permit is required; upon purchasing the permit, you can also ask for information about access points on the reservation. (See also Dubois Town Park under *Wilder Places—Parks.*)

THE WIND RIVER

See also Fort Washakie under *To See—Towns;* Guernsey State Park under *To See—Historic Landmarks, Places, and Sites;* Seminoe to Alcova

Scenic Backway under *To See—Scenic Drives;* Sinks Canyon State Park under
To See—Natural Wonders; Boysen State Park, Glendo State Park, Hawk Springs
State Recreation Area, and Louis Lake under *Boating;* Popo Agie Falls Trail
under *Hiking; Ice Fishing* under *Snow Sports;* Medicine Bow National Forest
and Shoshone National Forest under *Camping* and *Wilder Places—Forests;*
Pathfinder National Wildlife Refuge under *Wilder Places—Wildlife Refuges and
Areas;* and Bureau of Land Management under *Wilder Places—Other Wild
Places.*

GOLF Antelope Hills Golf Club (307-455-2888), 107 Country Club Drive,
Dubois, 9 holes.

Casper Country Club (307-265-0767), 4441 E. Country Club Road, Casper, 18
holes.

Casper Golf Club (307-234-2405; www.casperwy.gov/Content/Leisure/golf/
golf.asp), 2120 Allendale Boulevard, Casper, 27 holes.

City of Torrington Municipal Golf Course (307-532-3868; www.city-of-
torrington.org/golf_course.htm), W. 15th Street and Golf Course Road, Torrington, 18 holes.

Douglas Community Golf Club (307-358-5099), 64 Golf Course Road, Douglas, 18 holes.

Glenrock Golf Course (307-436-5560), 933 W. Grove Street, Glenrock, 9 holes.

Lander Golf and Country Club (307-332-4653), 1 Golf Course Drive, Lander, 18 holes.

Niobrara Country Club (307-334-2438; www.luskwyoming.com/ncc.html), 2
miles west of Lusk on US 20, 9 holes.

Paradise Valley Country Club (307-234-9146), 70 Magnolia Street, Casper, 18
holes.

Renegade Golf Course (307-857-0117), 12814 US 26 W., Riverton, 9 holes.

Riverton Country Club (307-856-4779), 4275 Country Club Drive, Riverton,
18 holes.

Salt Creek Country Club (307-437-6207), WY 387, Midwest, 9 holes.

Three Crowns Golf Club (307-472-7696; www.threecrownsgolfclub.com),
2435 King Boulevard, Suite 300, Casper, 18 holes.

Trail Ruts Golf Club (307-836-2255; www.golfandcamp.com), 100 S. Guernsey
Road, Guernsey, 9 holes. (See also Larson Park Campground under *To Do—
Camping.*)

Wheatland Golf Club (307-322-3675), 1253 E. Cole, Wheatland, 9 holes.

HIKING Laramie Peak Trail, (#602), in Medicine Bow National Forest (see
Camping and *Wilder Places—Forests*), is accessible from Friend Park Campground. Take WY 94 south of Douglas 17 miles, going 11 miles south on C.R. 5,
then 15 miles southwest on F.R. 653, and then 3.5 miles southeast on F.R. 671,
turning left at the sign for the campground and proceeding another 1 mile to

reach it. You must pay a $5 per vehicle fee to use the trail, which involves a steep, somewhat arduous 10-mile round-trip to reap the reward: panoramic views from atop 10,772-foot Laramie Peak, the tallest mountain for miles around. Not only will you enjoy the fantastic scenery of this Rocky Mountain peak, but you should also know that for emigrants heading west on the Oregon Trail and other historic trails, this very peak served as a significant landmark indicating their arrival at the Rocky Mountains. For many of these pioneers, this was also the first real mountain they had seen in their lives. So when you hike Laramie, you're not only getting a great workout and taking in fabulous views, but you're also hiking to the summit of a piece of American history. The trail is also open to use by mountain bikers, horseback riders, and ATVs.

Lee McCune Braille Trail is in Casper Mountain Park (see *Wilder Places— Parks*), accessible by taking WY 251 (Casper Mountain Road) 6 miles south of Casper and parking in the Skunk Hollow area. This unique, 0.3-mile interpretive nature trail includes 36 signs, all of which are written in Braille as well as standard print. The trail also includes guide ropes lining the pathway to help ensure the safety of its visually impaired visitors. Sighted visitors will enjoy the short interpretive walk as well. (See also Natrona County Roads, Bridges, and Parks Department under *Camping* and Casper Mountain Park under *Wilder Places— Parks.*)

&. **Muddy Mountain Environmental Education Area National Recreation Trail** is accessible by taking WY 251 south of Casper 9 miles to the top of Casper Mountain and then heading south on C.R. 505 for roughly 6 miles (3 paved, 3 graveled). Turn east on Circle Drive and proceed another 4 miles to access the area and the trail. This is an easy 2-mile interpretive trail open to foot traffic only and situated in the 1,260-acre Muddy Mountain Environmental Education Area (EEA), managed by the Bureau of Land Management (see *Wilder Places—Other Wild Places*). The trail connects the two campgrounds (Rim and Lodgepole) in the area, offering great views of the valley below, as well as potential for viewing wildlife such as antelope and mule deer. Though this trail is limited to foot traffic, the EEA features numerous additional trails, some of which are limited to foot traffic, mountain bikes, and horseback riders and some of which permit off-road motorized vehicles, including snowmobiles in wintertime. (See also BLM campgrounds under *Camping*.)

Popo Agie Falls Trail, in Shoshone National Forest (see *Wilder Places— Forests*) south of Lander, can be accessed by going south on Sinks Canyon Road from Lander, proceeding through Sinks Canyon State Park (see *To See—Natural Wonders*) to Bruce's Parking Area. From there, start your hike by crossing the footbridge over the Middle Fork of the Popo Agie River and turning left (west). The 3-mile round-trip features a moderate gain in elevation as it takes you through forests, passing granite outcrops, and then through an open area with great views of the canyon below and behind you. Finally, you'll reach the falls themselves. In spring and early summer, they can appear as roaring cascades up to 60 feet in height, with pools that local teenagers can often be seen frolicking in. By mid- to late summer and early fall, the falls usually have dwindled in size and scope, though they are still lovely. In winter, viewing the falls can be just as awesome as seeing them in the tumultuous raging beauty of the spring thaw. You'll likely have the place all to yourself while you observe the white and deep-blue hues of the frozen falls set against the bleak and harsh winter landscape. This trail is very popular not only with hikers but also with trail runners, mountain bikers, and horseback riders. (See also the Popo Agie River under *Fishing.*)

See also Castle Gardens, Guernsey State Park, and Independence Rock State Historic Site under *To See—Historic Landmarks, Places, and Sites;* Ayres Natural Bridge Park and Sinks Canyon State Park under *To See—Natural Wonders;* Platte River Parkway and Wyoming Heritage Trail under *Bicycling;* Glendo State Park, Louis Lake, and Pathfinder Reservoir and Alcova Reservoir under *Boating;* Lander Llama Company and National Outdoor Leadership School under *Unique Adventures;* Dubois Town Park and Edness Kimball Wilkins State Park under *Wilder Places—Parks;* Medicine Bow National Forest and Shoshone National Forest under *Camping* and *Wilder Places—Forests;* Bureau of Land Management under *Wilder Places—Other Wild Places;* and Louis Lake Lodge under *Lodging—Lodges.*

HORSEBACK RIDING Pony Express Ride (1-888-9-TRAILS; www.hidden trails.com/usa/rt/wy-pony.htm), Lander. Take a whirlwind, fast-paced tour along the same historic route taken by the 183 riders of the Pony Express, which for a short time—18 months in 1862–63—served the U.S. Post Office as its fastest overland mail carrier. An experienced and knowledgeable guide will lead you on this historic journey for a total of 6 days of riding along the Sweetwater River (see *Fishing*), following the tracks of the Pony Express and the Oregon Trail. Experienced riders will enjoy the challenge of long days in the saddle, lots of open land for lengthy canters, and, of course, the incredible, open scenery of the terrain. The rate includes 2 nights in a hotel (in Lander), 5 nights camping, all meals, and 6 days of riding ($1,410 per person). A ride suited to beginners is available as well, including all of the same amenities in the package ($1,460 per person). Call the above number or visit the Web site for trip dates and reservations.

See also Pioneer Park under *Camping;* Laramie Peak Trail, Muddy Mountain Environmental Education Area National Recreation Trail, and Popo Agie Falls Trail under *Hiking;* ranch vacations under *Unique Adventures;* Medicine Bow National Forest and Shoshone National Forest under *Camping* and *Wilder Places—Forests;* Bureau of Land Management under *Wilder Places—Other Wild Places;* Tea Kettle Bed and Breakfast under *Lodging—Bed & Breakfasts;* Louis Lake Lodge and Powderhorn Ranch under *Lodging—Lodges;* and Deer Forks Ranch under *Lodging—Other Options.*

PADDLING/FLOATING ⚲ Casper Whitewater Park (307-577-1206; www .platteriverparkway.org/whitewater.htm) is a free city-owned and city-operated park for white-water enthusiasts that runs for a distance of 0.5 mile on the North Platte River (see also *Fishing*) in Casper. The park parallels 1st Street from Wyoming Boulevard to just east of Poplar Street. It features four rock structures in the river, constructed and designed with beginner and intermediate-level boaters in mind. If you want to experience the excitement of this white-water park on the North Platte River under the watchful eye of an experienced guide, **Platte River Raft n' Reel** (307-267-0170; www.raftnreel.com), 17,000 WY 220, Casper 82604, runs daily 40-minute float trips through the park ($17 adults, $15 children ages 12 and under; make reservations in advance). This guide service also offers longer scenic and white-water rafting trips on the North Platte as well as guided fishing trips; call for details and reservations. (See also Platte River Parkway under *Bicycling*.)

See also *Boating;* the Popo Agie River under *Fishing;* Edness Kimball Wilkins State Park under *Wilder Places—Parks;* Bureau of Land Management under *Wilder Places—Other Wild Places;* and Wind River Canyon Whitewater under *To Do—Paddling/Floating* in "North Wyoming: Devils Tower–Buffalo Bill Country."

SNOW SPORTS

Cross-Country Skiing

Cross-country skiing opportunities are virtually limitless in this region, with miles and miles of trails for the both the fit and seasoned skier as well as the novice to explore. A good place to start is the **Casper Nordic Center** (307-235-9325; www.caspernordic.com), located in Casper Mountain Park (see *Wilder Places— Parks*) and accessible by driving south on WY 251 (Casper Mountain Road) for 8 miles. The center features 42K of trails groomed for skate skiing, cross-country skiing, and snowshoeing, including a 1.2K lighted loop trail for night skiing ($5 for access to all trails). You can purchase a ski pass, rent skis, and get more information on area trails from **Backcountry Mountain Works** (307-234-5330), 4120 S. Poplar Street, Casper; or **Mountain Sports** (307-266-1136), 543 S. C Street, Casper. You'll also find 10K of groomed trails accessible near **South Pass** (see *To See—Historic Landmarks, Places, and Sites*), south of Lander. In town, **Freewheel Ski and Cycle** (307-332-6616), 378 Main Street, Lander, offers ski rentals and can give you advice about where to ski in the area.

For more ideas about where to cross-country ski in this region, see also Sinks Canyon State Park under *To See—Natural Wonders;* Wyoming Heritage Trail under *Bicycling;* Louis Lake under *Boating;* Muddy Mountain Environmental Education Area National Recreation Trail under *Hiking;* Medicine Bow National Forest and Shoshone National Forest under *Wilder Places—Forests;* Bureau of Land Management under *Wilder Places—Other Wild Places;* Miner's Delight Bed and Breakfast under *Lodging—Bed & Breakfasts,* and Louis Lake Lodge under *Lodging—Lodges.*

Downhill Skiing

✦ **Hogadon Ski Area** (307-235-8499; www.casperwy.gov/content/leisure/ hogadon/hogadon.asp; mailing address: 1800 E. K Street, Casper), Casper Mountain Park, 11 miles south of Casper via WY 251. Open Wednesday through Sunday in-season. Owned and managed by the city of Casper, this small, family-oriented ski area features easy access from the city and terrain suitable for all ability levels. The area welcomes snowboarders as well as skiers. Daily ski rentals are available at **Mountain Sports** (307-266-1136), 543 S. C Street, Casper. *Lifts:*

two double chairlifts, one Poma lift. *Trails:* 15 trails—20 percent beginner, 40 percent intermediate, 40 percent expert. *Vertical drop:* 600 feet. *Snowmaking:* 50 percent. *Facilities:* full-service restaurant and snack bar. *Ski school:* offers lessons for all ages and ability levels. *For children:* Age-specific lessons are available; on-premises childcare is not available. *Rates:* $29 adults (19 and older), $25 students (12–18), $16 children (5–11), $12 for Poma lift only; half-day rates available as well.

Ice Fishing

Ice fishing opportunities can be found in this region at a number of its lakes and reservoirs. Throw your line in at Boysen State Park, Hawk Springs State Recreation Area, and Pathfinder Reservoir and Alcova Reservoir (see *Boating*), among other popular spots. Also look for smaller mountain lakes in the Wind River Mountains (see Shoshone National Forest under *Wilder Places—Forests*).

Ice-Skating

Ice-skating on rinks, as well as on frozen lake and ponds, provides a fun diversion and a great workout. Test your skill on the blades in this region at **Lander City Park** (see *Camping*), which has a regulation hockey rink open to the public during wintertime (skate rentals available for a small fee). In Casper, you can skate at the **Casper Ice Arena** (307-235-8484; www.casperwy.gov/content/leisure/cia/ice.asp), 1801 E. 4th Street. Public skating $1.50 weekdays, $2.50 weekends; skate rentals are $1 weekdays, $1.50 weekends (call for public skating hours in advance). (See also Louis Lake Lodge under *Lodging—Lodges.*)

Snowmobiling

The **Continental Divide Snowmobile Trail** (1-877-996-7275; 307-777-7477; http://wyotrails.state.wy.us/snow/divide.htm) is a 365-mile trail roughly paralleling the continental divide. It runs from Lander northwest to West Yellowstone, Montana, passing by the areas around Pinedale, Dubois, Togwotee Pass, and Yellowstone National Park. The trail passes over the divide four times, and it also gains you access to hundreds of miles of side trails, both groomed and ungroomed, along its way. Consistently ranked as one of the nation's premier snowmobiling destinations by enthusiasts of the activity, the trail features incredibly remote and scenic terrain as well as an array of visitor services spread out along its length.

Overall, snowmobiling opportunities in this region are incredible. In addition to the showpiece Continental Divide Snowmobile Trail, the trail by which all others can be judged, among the many trails throughout the region are 46 miles of signed, groomed trails located just south of Casper in **Casper Mountain Park** (see *Wilder Places—Parks*). For detailed **trail reports** on this and other trails, call 1-800-225-5996 or go to http://wyotrails.state.wy.us/snow, the **Wyoming Snowmobile Trails** Web site, which also provides information about rules, rental agencies, trails around the state, and more. If you want to rent a snowmobile or hire a guide, you'll find a number of outfitters in this region, including **Louis Lake Lodge** (see *Lodging—Lodges*), near Lander. Many of the area's guest ranches provide snowmobiling packages in the winter as well (see **ranch vacations** under *Unique Adventures*).

For more ideas about where to snowmobile, see also Wyoming Heritage Trail under *Bicycling;* Louis Lake under *Boating;* Lee McCune Braille Trail and Muddy Mountain Environmental Education Area National Recreation Trail under *Hiking;* Medicine Bow National Forest and Shoshone National Forest under *Camping* and *Wilder Places—Forests;* Bureau of Land Management under *Wilder Places—Other Wild Places;* and Miner's Delight Bed and Breakfast under *Lodging—Bed and Breakfasts.*

Snowshoeing

Snowshoeing is a great way to explore this region's abundance of developed trails in wintertime. You'll find plenty to keep you busy and warm in Medicine Bow National Forest and Shoshone National Forest (see *Wilder Places—Forests*), as well as in the state parks (see Guernsey State Park under *To See—Historic Landmarks, Places, and Sites* and Sinks Canyon State Park under *To See—Natural Wonders*) and in lands managed by the Bureau of Land Management (see *Wilder Places—Other Wild Places*). (See also Louis Lake under *Boating;* Muddy Mountain Environmental Education Area National Recreation Trail and Popo Agie Falls Trail under *Hiking; Cross-Country Skiing,* above; Casper Mountain Park under *Wilder Places—Parks;* and Louis Lake Lodge under *Lodging—Lodges,* where snowshoe rentals are available.

UNIQUE ADVENTURES ✍ **Adventures West Tours** (1-877-868-7996; 307-577-1226; www.usatouring.com), 4486 Moonbeam Road, Casper. Let Adventures West be your guide to all things western! This tour company can provide a number of unique and interactive western adventures. You can take a 6-hour wagon train journey on the historic Oregon Trail, learning about the pioneers who passed this way from your costumed guide while you ride ($100 adults, $40 children 2–12, children under 1 free). You'll also enjoy a meal cooked the old-fashioned way—in a dutch oven, on the campfire. This package also includes admission to the Fort Caspar Museum and Historic Site and National Historic Trails Interpretive Center (see *To See—Museums*). Adventures West Tours also does multiday wagon train rides, among its other western adventures.

Fort Washakie Tours (307-332-9106; 307-332-3177; www.easternshoshone.net/easternshoshoneculture.htm), 1st Street, Fort Washakie. Take an in-depth tour with a Native American guide to delve more deeply into this area's Indian heritage. Choose from a 1-hour ($30), 2.5-hour ($60), or 4-hour ($150) walking adventure, during which your knowledgeable guide will interpret sites that include Sacagawea's grave, Chief Washakie's grave, historic structures, and more, depending on the length of your tour. For a more authentic experience, add an Indian meal of flatbread and berry pudding ($5). If you time your visit right, you can also be an observer at an annual powwow (see *Special Events*).

✍ **Lander Llama Company** (1-800-582-5262; 307-332-5624; www.llamahiking .com), 2024 Mortimore Lane, Lander. Hire a llama to do the work of ferrying your loads while you hike alongside this beast of burden in the Wind River Mountains, the Absaroka Mountains, or Wyoming's Red Desert. You'll start your llama rental experience with a mandatory 3- to 4-hour introductory course (for first timers) to backpacking with a llama ($25 adults, free for children), which you can schedule anytime before your trip. Then rent a pair of llamas (you must rent at least two llamas, as they are social animals) for a minimum of 3 days ($100 per day for first pair of llamas; $50 per day for each additional llama). The llamas come with their packs and gear; transporting the llamas to and from the trailheads will cost you extra (cost dependent on trailhead locations). Sound too complex? Then consider taking a guided trip, on which experienced llama handlers lead you and the llamas through Wyoming's lovely terrain for anywhere from 3 days to a week ($600–1,400 per person). Either way, you must call in advance to make reservations, so you can consider all of your options then. (See also the Bunk House under *Lodging—Bed and Breakfasts.*)

National Outdoor Leadership School (NOLS) (1-800-710-NOLS; www.nols .edu), 284 Lincoln Street, Lander. One of the nation's top outdoor educational institutions, NOLS runs a wide variety of courses in Wyoming and around the world throughout the year and covers an array of disciplines. Courses—including some that count for college credits—range in length from 10 days to an entire school semester and can include such activities as backpacking, skiing, rock climbing, paddling, camping, environment education, caving, snowboarding, horsepacking, and more. Many courses do not require that you have any previous experience in the discipline taught. Courses in Wyoming include Absaroka Backpacking, a 30-day course open to ages 16 and up ($3,180); Wind River Wilderness—the original NOLS course—a 30-day hiking adventure open to ages 16 and up ($3,275); and Rock Climbing, a 21-day course that takes place in the Lander vicinity and is open to ages 16 and up ($3,325). Contact NOLS for a complete course catalog and additional information about the application process.

Ranch vacations. These vacations usually allow you to participate to a certain extent in various aspects of ranch life, often including cattle herding and branding. The ratio of work time to leisure time varies from ranch to ranch, as do the additional activities and amenities offered, but most ranches include horseback riding, lodging, and meals in an inclusive package deal. In this region, providers include **Allen's Diamond 4 Ranch** (307-332-2995), Lander; **Bear Mountain Riding Ranch** (307-834-2492), Torrington; **Bitterroot Dude Ranch** (1-800-545-0019; 307-455-3363), Dubois; **Bucking S Working Cattle and Guest Ranch** (307-325-6280), Casper; **Cheyenne River Ranch** (307-358-2380), Douglas; **CM Ranch** (1-800-455-0721; 307-455-2331), Dubois; **Crooked Creek Guest Ranch** (1-888-238-2647; 307-455-2815), Dubois; **Deer Forks Ranch** (307-358-2033), Douglas; **Mill Iron 4 Mill Iron Guest Ranch** (1-888-919-6627; 307-455-3478), Dubois; **Ogalalla Wyoming Cattle Ranch** (307-358-0161), Douglas; **Powderhorn Ranch** (307-358-0549), Douglas; **Sand Creek Ranch Outfitters** (307-234-9597), Sand Creek; **Triangle C Ranch** (1-800-661-4928; 307-455-2225), Dubois; **Twin Creek Ranch and Lodge** (307-335-7485), Lander; **Two Creek Ranch** (307-358-3467), Douglas; and **Wapiti Ridge Ranch** (307-322-3220), Wheatland.

✔ **Spiritrider Wagon Train Adventures** (1-866-373-9397; 307-472-5361; www.spiritrider-wagontrain.com), 5897 S. 12 Mile Road, Casper. Get back to a simpler way of life by joining a western wagon train for the ride of a lifetime.

You'll travel along historic paths, including the historic Oregon Trail, that once served as the thoroughfares for pioneers making their weary ways westward. Your journey can be as short as an hour ($46 adults; $12 children ages 7–17; $6 children ages 6 and under; meals $10 extra per person) or as long as 4 nights and 5 days ($1,079 adults; $599 children ages 7–17; $359 children ages 6 and under; meals included), with lots of options in between as well. Families are welcomed, as are groups. Spiritrider also runs a number of specialty tours such as a women's wellness retreat and corporate team-building; call for details.

See also Glenrock Paleontological Museum and National Bighorn Sheep Interpretive Center under *To See—Museums* and Pony Express Ride under *Horseback Riding.*

✳ Wilder Places

PARKS Casper Mountain Park (307-235-9311; www.casperwyoming.info/parks .html), located just south of Casper via WY 251, along with adjacent **Beartrap Meadow Park,** is a 3,000-acre area managed by the Natrona County Roads, Bridges, and Parks Department. The area features all sorts of recreational opportunities, including bicycling (mountain biking trails), camping, hiking, off-road vehicles, snow sports, and more. (See also Natrona County Roads, Bridges, and Parks Department under *To Do—Camping;* Lee McCune Braille Trail under *To Do—Hiking;* and *Cross-Country Skiing,* Hogadan Ski Area, and *Snowmobiling* under *To Do—Snow Sports.*)

✔ **Dubois Town Park,** located next to the National Bighorn Sheep Interpretive Center (see *To See—Museums*), is a charming little town park (day-use only) that makes for a great place to have a picnic if you're stopped in the area. The park has a paved walkway that gains you access to the Wind River (see *To Do—Fishing*), as well as posted informational material about this natural area. The park also has a playground.

♿ ✔ **Edness Kimball Wilkins State Park** (307-577-5150; http://wyoparks.state .wy.us/edness1.htm), 6 miles east of Casper on US 20/26/87. Open for day-use only; $1 for residents, $2 for nonresidents. This 315-acre park is a popular place for family outings in summertime—for good reason. Three playgrounds, a pond with a sandy beach, numerous picnic areas, and 2.8 miles of paved, handicapped-accessible trails are just some of the park's attractions. The park also features a boat ramp perfect for launching canoes and rafts, bird-watching opportunities aplenty, and fishing in the North Platte River (see *To Do—Fishing*).

See also Fort Caspar Museum and Historic Site under *To See—Museums;* Guernsey State Park under *To See—Historic Landmarks, Places, and Sites;* Sinks Canyon State Park under *To See—Natural Wonders;* Platte River Parkway under *To Do—Bicycling;* Boysen State Park and Glendo State Park under *To Do—Boating;* and Lander City Park, Larson Park Campground, Pioneer Park, Riverside Park, and Wheatland City Park–Lewis Park under *To Do—Camping.*

FORESTS Medicine Bow National Forest (307-745-2300; www.fs.fed.us/r2/ mbr), 2468 Jackson Street, Laramie. Though most of this forest's lands lie south of this region (see listing in "South Wyoming: Medicine Bow–Flaming Gorge Country"), this region is home to those lands managed by the **Douglas Ranger District** (307-358-4690), 2250 E. Richards Street, Douglas. The central feature of this district is the Laramie Mountains, which run from just southeast of Casper on a southeastern slant to just northwest of Wheatland, with I-25 arcing around them. In and around the Laramie Mountains, you'll find numerous recreational opportunities, including fishing (LaBonte Creek is a popular spot), hiking, mountain biking, camping, picnicking, rock climbing (LaBonte Canyon has technical routes), off-road vehicle travel (ATVs and snowmobiles), horseback riding, snow sports, hunting, wildlife viewing, and more. The Douglas Ranger District also manages the **Thunder Basin National Grassland,** situated northeast of Casper (see *Wilder Places—Other Wild Places* in "North Wyoming: Devils Tower–Buffalo Bill Country." See also *To Do—Camping* and Laramie Peak Trail under *To Do—Hiking.*)

Shoshone National Forest (307-578-1200; 307-527-6241; www.fs.fed.us/r2/shoshone), 808 Meadow Lane, Cody. The 2.4 million acres of land in this forest—America's first national forest—lie partially in this region and partially in the region covered by "North Wyoming: Devils Tower–Buffalo Bill Country" (see Shoshone National Forest under *Wilder Places—Forests*). In this region, Shoshone National Forest includes lands around Dubois and Lander, managed by two ranger districts: the **Washakie Ranger District** (307-332-5460), 333 E. Main Street, Lander; and the **Wind River Ranger District** (307-455-2466), 1403 W. Ramshorn, Dubois. This land includes the Fitzpatrick, Popo Agie, and Washakie wildernesses, as well as the Wind River Mountains, home to Wyoming's highest mountain—Gannett Peak, standing 13,804 feet above sea level along the continental divide. Recreational opportunities include biking, boating, camping, fishing, hiking, horseback riding, rock climbing (Sinks Canyon and Wild Iris, near Lander, are popular spots), off-road vehicle travel (ATVs and snowmobiles), snow sports, hunting, wildlife viewing, and more. (See also Louis Lake under *To Do—Boating; To Do—Camping;* the Popo Agie River and the Wind River under *To Do—Fishing;* and Louis Lake Lodge under *Lodging—Lodges.*)

BIGHORN SHEEP IN SINKS CANYON STATE PARK (LANDER AREA)

WILDLIFE REFUGES AND AREAS

Pathfinder National Wildlife Refuge (970-723-8202; http://refuges.fws.gov/profiles/index.cfm?id=65523), accessible by taking WY 220 southwest of Alcova for 20 miles to C.R. 410 (Buzzard Road) or turning off earlier at C.R. 409 (Pathfinder Road). Open dawn to dusk; free. This unstaffed national refuge was created by an executive order in 1928. Actually made up of four separate tracts of land, the refuge totals 16,807 acres, set aside mainly to protect and provide habitat for migratory waterfowl. Wyoming Audubon assists with the management of this refuge and helped to create the interpretive signs and overlook for visitors. Additional wildlife viewing opportunities include small mammals such as cottontail rabbits, as well as mule deer and antelope, among other animals. Fishing and hunting are also popular activities. (See also Pathfinder Reservoir and Alcova Reservoir under *To Do—Boating*.)

🐾 **Sybille Conservation Education Center** (307-322-2571; http://gf.state.wy .us/admin/regional/sybille.asp), 2362 WY 34, 35 miles southwest of Wheatland. Open daily May 1 through September 15, 8:30 AM–4:30 PM; free. This public education center is run in conjunction with the Sybille Wildlife Research and Conservation Education Unit. In operation since 1952, this research center is one of the oldest of its type in the country. The center's focus is on practical research into the pertinent and critical topics facing the state's wildlife managers today, such as managing the diseases impacting wildlife, managing habitats, and fostering the recovery of endangered species, among other efforts. The visitor center includes exhibits detailing the human impact on Wyoming's wildlife and some of the center's research projects, such as the black-footed ferret project, which helped this near-extinct species recover its chances of survival.

See also National Bighorn Sheep Interpretive Center under *To See—Museums;* Pathfinder Reservoir and Alcova Reservoir under *To Do—Boating;* and Muddy Mountain Environmental Education Area National Recreation Trail under *To Do—Hiking.*

OTHER WILD PLACES & **Bureau of Land Management** (BLM) has two field offices in this region: the **Casper Field Office** (307-261-7600; www.wy.blm .gov/cfo/index.htm), 2987 Prospector Drive, Casper, managing 32,531 square miles of public lands and mineral estate combined; and the **Lander Field Office** (307-332-8400; www.wy.blm.gov/lfo/index.htm), 1335 Main Street, Lander, managing 2.5 million acres of public lands and 2.7 million acres of federal mineral estate. Of particular interest to history aficionados exploring BLM land are the historic sites around **South Pass,** including South Pass City, Atlantic City, and Miner's Delight, as well as Castle Gardens (see *To See—Historic Landmarks, Places, and Sites*) and the historic **emigrant trails** that passed this way (see National Historic Trails Center under *To See—Museums*). Much of the lands administered by the BLM are open to recreational pursuits, including bicycling, boating, camping (both primitive and developed; most developed campgrounds are handicapped accessible), fishing, hiking (portions of the 3,100-mile-long **Continental Divide National Scenic Trail** pass through sections of Wyoming's BLM land; see www.cdtrail.org for details; also see Continental Divide National Scenic Trail under *To Do—Hiking* in "South Wyoming: Medicine Bow–Flaming Gorge Country"), horseback riding, paddling, rock climbing, wildlife viewing (including wild horses), and snow sports, including snowmobiling and cross-country skiing. BLM lands tend to be the most unregulated of public lands, which means that most typical outdoor recreational pursuits are allowed on most BLM lands, guided by the dictates of **Leave No Trace** (1-800-332-4100; 303-442-8222; www.lnt.org) outdoor ethics. To find out more general information about the BLM lands in this region, including maps, developed campgrounds, and other recreational pursuits, contact the appropriate field office. (See also Pathfinder Reservoir and Alcova Reservoir under *To Do—Boating;* BLM campgrounds under *To Do—Camping;* and Muddy Mountain Environmental Education Area National Recreation Trail under *To Do—Hiking.*)

See also **Hawk Springs State Recreation Area** under *To Do—Boating.*

✳ Lodging

BED & BREAKFASTS

Atlantic City 82520
Miner's Delight Bed and Breakfast (1-888-292-0248; 307-332-0248; www.wyomingbnb-ranchrec.com/MinersDelight.html), 290 Atlantic Road. You'll enjoy a true old-time gold rush experience by staying in one of this B&B's three hotel rooms or one of its four historic log cabins. Situated in a historic 1895 former log hotel and surrounded by the historic setting of Atlantic City—once the site of a flourishing gold rush town, but now a mere ghost of its former incarnation—this lodging lies conveniently close to another former boomtown: South Pass City State Historic Site (see *To See—Historic Landmarks, Places, and Sites*). The lodging also provides convenient access to the area's abundant snowmobiling and cross-country skiing opportunities, should you happen to stay in wintertime ($60–75).

Casper
✦ ⅃ **Casper Mountain Bed and Breakfast** (307-237-6712; www.caspermountainbnb.com), 4471 S. Center Street, Casper 82601. You'll feel right at home in this unpretentious B&B, situated in a peaceful residential neighborhood in Casper. Stay in one of two clean, comfortable guest rooms that share a bathroom. Enjoy access to the lovely deck and

the yard with mountain views. Every morning you'll be treated to a delicious, homemade breakfast ($60–65).

⅃ **Ivy House Inn Bed and Breakfast** (307-265-0974; www.ivyhouseinn.com), 815 S. Ash Street, Casper 82601. A BnBfinder.com "Property of Distinction," this historic, Cape Cod–style house accommodates travelers in one of five well-appointed, uniquely themed guest rooms or suites. Both suites—the masculine Fir Tree Lodge and the whimsical island feel of the Palm Tree Court—include private bathrooms, kitchenettes, and private entrances. The three guest rooms on the main floor share a guest kitchen and two bathrooms in the hall. Additional amenities include a hot tub and Internet access in each room. A full breakfast is served daily, with the option for a continental breakfast as well ($50–105).

Red Butte Ranch Bed and Breakfast (307-472-3784; www.casperwyoming.org/redbutteranch), 8550 S. Bessemer Bend, Casper 82604. Privacy, solitude, and the grandeur of nature will define your stay at Red Butte Ranch. Your private cottage (sleeping up to six people) rests on the shores of the North Platte River, with the splendor of Bessemer Mountain's red rock formations as your backdrop. Furnished with rustic log furniture, the cottage has a full kitchen and a full bath. Access to the river is a few short steps out your door. Breakfast is included ($130).

Douglas 82633

Carriage House Bed and Breakfast (307-358-2752; www.wyoming bnb-ranchrec.com/CarriageHouse .html), 413 Center Street. This historic B&B served as a stable in the past—but don't worry. In place of horse stalls and hay, you'll find instead three comfortable, modern guest rooms, with either private or shared baths. The inn is only a few short blocks from the Wyoming Pioneer Memorial Museum (see *To See— Museums*). A continental breakfast is served daily (less than $50).

Morton Mansion Bed and Breakfast (307-358-2129; www .mortonmansion.com), 425 E. Center Street. Listed on the National Register of Historic Places, this 1903 Queen Anne Victorian mansion features an elegant formal parlor and dining room, a wraparound porch, and beautiful antiques throughout. Guests stay in one of four guest rooms, all of which include private bathrooms, phones, and cable television. For those needing more space, the B&B also has an attic suite, which has two bedrooms, a private bath, a full kitchen, a living room, phone, and cable television. The mansion is situated in close proximity to local attractions, including the Wyoming Pioneer Memorial Museum (see *To See— Museums*). A full breakfast is served each morning on French Castle furniture from the 1860s ($65–125).

Dubois 82513

Jakey's Fork Homestead (307-455-2769; www.frontierlodging.com),
11 Fish Hatchery Road, P.O. Box 635. On the banks of Jakey's Fork, a trout stream, this rustic homestead welcomes guests to one of two bedrooms that share a bath in the main house. Also available are rooms in the historic Simpson bunkhouse, a three-room cabin (available June through September). The house rests on 22 acres of beautiful Wyoming country, allowing guests access to the lovely landscape surrounding them. Guests enjoy a full breakfast served daily ($70–135). You can also rent out the entire main house or the entire bunkhouse, if you're interested.

The Stone House (307-455-2555; www.duboisbnb.com), 207 S. 1st Street, P.O. Box 1446. Open May through October. This beautiful, historic stone home invites you to stay in a private three-room cottage or a two-room suite, both with private baths, or in one of two guest rooms that share a bath. The cottage has two queen-size beds, a refrigerator, a microwave, and a coffeemaker. The suite has a queen-size bed, a sofa hide-a-bed, and a fireplace. A full breakfast is included in the rates ($50–100).

Glenrock 82637

Hotel Higgins (1-800-458-0144; 307-436-9212; www.hotelhiggins .com), 416 W. Birch Street, P.O. Box 741. Hotel Higgins has been restored to its former, early-20th-century grandeur and is listed on the National Register of Historic Places. Guests stay in one of six rooms, all with private baths. The decor features antique period pieces, including brass beds, iron beds, and oak and walnut dressers, which fit in nicely with the deep mahogany and stained oak woodwork of the interior. Guests enjoy a complimentary continental breakfast served daily ($50–100 plus). Also on the premises is the acclaimed fine dining establishment the Paisley Shawl, as well as the full-service Highlander Bar and Lounge.

Lander 82520

✔ ♿ **Baldwin Creek Bed and Breakfast** (307-332-7608; www .wyomingbandb.com), 2343 Baldwin Creek Road. You can enjoy the beauty of Red Butte Canyon on the outskirts of Lander while also enjoying convenient access to town at this B&B. Town proper is a short drive or bike ride away (see Baldwin Creek Road to Squaw Creek Road Loop under *To Do—Bicycling*), but you will enjoy the peace and quiet of this 34-acre country retreat, with access to literally thousands of acres of state lands just outside your door. Accommodations are in one of four cabins or two guest rooms in the main house, all with private bathrooms. Lodging rates include early-morning coffee, a full breakfast served daily, and even afternoon treats ($70–95).

♿ **Blue Spruce Inn** (1-888-503-3311; 307-332-8253; www.bluespruce inn.com), 677 S. 3rd Street. Tucked among the stately houses and statuesque trees of one of Lander's nicest neighborhoods, you'll find this lovely B&B, listed on the National Register of Historic Places. Constructed in 1919 by a prosperous rancher, the inn itself is shaded by five enormous blue spruce trees. Inside, you'll find lovely architectural touches from the arts and crafts style, as well as four uniquely decorated guest rooms, all with private baths. The inn also has a game room, a sunroom, gorgeous gardens, and a porch swing. A full breakfast is served every morning ($70–85).

✔ **The Bunk House** (307-332-5624; www.wyomingadventure.com/fbunk house.html), 2024 Mortimore Lane. The Bunk House is located at the headquarters of the Lander Llama Company (see *To Do—Unique Adventures*). The rustic lodgepole lodging can sleep up to five people, and you'll also find an equipped kitchenette and a shower bath. You can see all of the llamas just outside the doors and windows, making it a fun spot for families—particularly if your kids like animals. Guests enjoy a complimentary, make-it-yourself breakfast each morning, which includes homemade cinnamon rolls ($95).

✔ **Cottage House of Squaw Creek** (307-332-5003; www.cottagehouseof tails.com), 72 Squaw Creek Court. This log cabin on Squaw Creek, 5 miles from Lander, is situated on a working ranch—a working llama ranch, that is. The private cabin can sleep up to six people and includes a fully equipped kitchen, a private bath, laundry facilities, a wood-burning stove, a TV/VCR, and a phone, among other amenities. Children and pets are welcome—guests' pets can even enjoy a complimentary stay in the pet boarding area also on the property while guests explore Lander. The cottage can be rented as a B&B ($98) or as a guesthouse ($78).

Lusk 82225

The Sager House Bed and Breakfast (1-800-435-2468; 307-334-2423; www.sagerhouse.com), 310 S. Main Street. Luxury and elegance await you at the turn-of-the-20th-century Sager House, an inn of distinction. This well-appointed B&B features six guest rooms, all with private, tiled bathrooms. Guests enjoy special touches, including down comforters, robes, slippers, fresh flowers, and ironed sheets. The inn's common areas include a library, living room, dining room, exercise room, and game room. Lovely antiques make up much of the interior decor (call for current rates).

Riverton 82501

& **Delfelder Inn Bed and Breakfast** (1-877-901-3100; 307-857-3100; http://w3.trib.com/~delfeld), 222 S. Broadway. If you're a history lover, you'll love staying in the Delfelder Inn, one of the oldest homes in Riverton that still stands. Constructed in 1907, this lovely Victorian house features off-street parking, a large yard, and easy access to the town—a mere two blocks' walk from the door. Inside, you'll find a sunporch, a dining room, and four well-appointed, differently themed guest rooms, some with private baths and some with shared baths. A full breakfast is served in the morning (call for rates).

Torrington 82240

& ♪ **Tea Kettle Bed and Breakfast** (307-532-5375; www.wyomingbnb-ranchrec.com/teakettle.html), 9634 Van Tassell Road. Thirteen miles north of Torrington on a plateau overlooking its scenic surroundings, you'll find this charming bed & breakfast. New in 2001, the house includes four guest bedrooms that share baths; also available are a pool table, table tennis, and three decks. The B&B has horse boarding facilities, as well as more than 1,800 acres of land perfect for exploring on horseback (or on foot). Rates include a full breakfast served daily ($60–74).

Wheatland 82201

♪ **Blackbird Inn Bed and Breakfast** (307-322-4540; www.wheatland wy.com/blackbird.htm), 1101 11th

Street. Constructed in 1910, this gracious Victorian B&B provides guests with a choice of four bedrooms sharing three bathrooms or a third-story suite of rooms with a private bath. The rooms are all distinctively themed, featuring antiques as centerpieces of the decor. The front porch makes a great place for relaxing after a day of adventures, with its wicker furniture, rocking chairs, and porch swing ($70–104).

LODGES

Douglas 82633

& ♪ **Powderhorn Ranch** (307-358-0549; www.powderhornranch.com), 2345 Cold Springs Road. You can stay in a western-style lodge room at this working cattle ranch, whether or not you want to partake of its array of guided activities. The luxurious **Powderhorn Lodge** features a gourmet kitchen, Jacuzzi, Internet access, satellite television, and more ($250). You can also rent out a room in a more rustic cabin or bunkhouse ($25–50) or an entire **cabin or bunkhouse** for a family or a group, if that's what you're looking for ($100–150). You'll enjoy full run of all of the unguided opportunities on the ranch's property, such as hiking, fishing, and rock climbing, among other sports. The ranch can also provide you with guided activities (fee), including horseback riding, cattle drives, rock climbing, mountaineering, and more.

Dubois 82513

& **The Sawmill Lodge** (1-866-472-9645; 307-455-2171; www.thesaw mill.org), 1 Fir Road. This gorgeous and remote lodge on Union Pass offers year-round recreational opportunities right outside your door.

Situated on the northeast side of the Wind River Mountain Range, the Sawmill Lodge features four different styles of accommodations to suit your needs. The **two-room suites** feature private baths with Jacuzzi tubs, an upstairs loft, and a downstairs room, sleeping up to six total. The **studios,** sleeping four, also have Jacuzzi tubs. In the main lodge, the **bunkroom** can sleep up to 15, with couches, tables, beds, and two shower baths. The **family room,** also in the main lodge, sleeps six ($75–115 plus). The Sawmill also has an on-premises restaurant, serving breakfast, lunch, and dinner, as well as a game room and a full-service bar.

Twin Pines Lodge and Cabins (1-800-550-6332; 307-455-2600; www .twinpineslodge.com), 218 W. Ramshorn Street. This distinctive lodge and cabins, listed on the National Register of Historic Places, were constructed with incredible craftsmanship and many unique design and architectural features in the early 20th century. Today, you can stay in the very same accommodations that housed earlier travelers to the lodge—with some improvements and modernizations for your comfort and convenience. You can stay in a **lodge room** or individual **cabin,** both of which include cable TV/VCR, refrigerators, in-room coffee, and a complimentary continental breakfast ($48–73).

Lander

♪ **Louis Lake Lodge** (1-888-422-2246; 307-332-5549; www.louislake .com), 1800 Louis Lake Road. This remote and rustic lodge, accessible via Sinks Canyon Road to Louis Lake Road southwest of Lander, provides a wonderful, wholesome place for a family vacation. The lodge, situated in Shoshone National Forest (see *Wilder*

Places—Forests), provides year-round recreational opportunities, including horseback riding, canoeing, fishing, and hiking in summertime and snowmobiling, cross-country skiing, and snowshoeing in winter (the lodge is on the groomed Continental Divide Snowmobile Trail; see *To Do—Snow Sports*). You'll stay in a one- or two-room cabin ($65–155). Most cabins share a common bathhouse. The lodge also welcomes campers. You can rent canoes, motorized fishing boats, horses, human guides, and snowmobiles by the hour, half-day, or full day. (See also Louis Lake under *To Do—Boating.*)

Lusk 82225

Big Pines Retreat and Lodge (307-334-3144; www.bigpinesretreat.com), 4039 W. US 20, 0.5 mile from Lusk. This luxury lodge provides a perfect getaway for a family gathering or an executive retreat or just a relaxed yet elegant place to stop in your travels and rejuvenate for a day or two. You'll enjoy the classic, upscale furnishings of this private accommodation for two to 11 people. Leather furniture, a big-screen television, a formal living area, wood paneling, and comfortable bedrooms are just some of the amenities you'll find. The owners will provide food and beverage service for you and your guests upon request as well (call for rates).

OTHER OPTIONS

Alcova 82620

House on the Mile (307-325-6491; www.woodenrifleoutfitters.com/id27 .htm), P.O. Box 77, Alcova; call for directions. Stay in your own private fishing haven at this rustic, three-bedroom vacation home. On the banks of Sage Creek right next to the

North Platte River's famed Miracle Mile area (see Miracle Mile of the North Platte River under *To See— Natural Wonders*), this home provides the perfect place to get away from it all and spend your days fishing to your heart's content. The house can sleep up to nine people, and it has a bathroom, a fully equipped kitchen, a wood-burning stove, laundry facilities, and 2 miles of private stream and reservoir fishing for you to savor ($50–75).

Atlantic City

See **Atlantic City Mercantile** under *To See—Historic Landmarks, Places, and Sites.*

Douglas 82633

☞ **Deer Forks Ranch** (307-358-2033; www.guestranches.com/deerforks), 1200 Poison Lake Road. Deer Forks offers guests lodging in its two well-appointed log guesthouses. The houses both include fully equipped, modern kitchens, two bedrooms (one with queen-size bed), private bathrooms, and a living room. Linens are provided, so guests just need to bring food. Guests can also request to partake in family-style breakfasts and dinners in advance (extra fee) or to join in on horseback rides (extra fee). Otherwise, participation in other ranch activities is included in the cost ($100).

See also Medicine Bow National Forest under *To Do—Camping.*

Dubois 82513

☞ **Branding Iron Inn** (1-888-651-9378; 307-455-2893; www.branding ironinn.com), 401 W. Ramshorn Street. These handmade Swiss Cope log cabins were constructed in the 1940s. Today they can provide you with an authentic, rustic vacation lodging—with all of the modern com-

forts and amenities you need. The cabins' rich and lustrous wood-paneled interiors almost glow with warmth, and inside each one, you'll find a king- or queen-size bed (or beds), cable television, and a private bathroom. Some units include kitchenettes and adjoining rooms as well. Children under 12 stay free in their parents' room. Horse corrals make this a great spot to stop if you're traveling with horses. Plenty of parking accommodates RVs in the summertime and snowmobilers in winter months ($35–100).

Lander 82520

☞ **Outlaw Cabins** (307-332-9655; www.outlawcabins.com), 2415 Squaw Creek Road. Two private, handcrafted log cabins resting near Squaw Creek accommodate guests at this location. One of the cabins was constructed from downed wood on the surrounding ranch's property. A local sheriff constructed the other cabin in the 1890s—but the inside is brand spanking new, with all of the modern amenities you'd expect to find. Both cabins include a queen-size bed as well as a loft perfect for children, with two twin beds. Guests enjoy the fixings for breakfast already stocked in the cabins' kitchens, including coffee, cereal, cocoa, tea, and so forth. You'll also enjoy the VCR, with free movies available at the ranch house, and the kids will have fun on the swings ($80–110).

&. ☞ **Sleeping Bear Ranch RV Resort and Café** (1-888-757-2327; 307-332-5159; www.sleepingbearrv park.com), 7192 WY 789/US 287. Not just a spot for RVs, this cool campground 9 miles south of Lander also offers seven **cabin rentals** ($45). The cabins themselves, as well as other buildings on the property, were moved here from the Dallas, Wyoming, ghost town. The campground is situated on a historic, century-old ranch, providing guests with plenty of acres for roaming and relaxing, including a playground for children. The café serves up complimentary coffee, as well as meals. Tent campers are also welcome here.

✳ Where to Eat

DINING OUT

Atlantic City
See **Atlantic City Mercantile** under *To See—Historic Landmarks, Places, and Sites.*

Casper
303, Inc. (1-866-610-0303; 307-233-4303; www.303grill.com), 303 S. Wolcott, Casper. The latest newcomer on Casper's dining scene is sure to make a splash with its elegant atmosphere, world-influenced cuisine, and incredible selection of wines handpicked from around the globe. Housed in the historic Prairie Publishing Company Building, the restaurant has breathed new life into the walls that have been empty for more than a decade. The menu features a wide selection of inspired and creative items—including a number of intriguing vegetarian options. Even the most basic of entrées here has a special, unique twist, such as an espresso-crusted filet mignon or a mac 'n' cheese prepared with gouda cheese and lobster. Give your taste buds a treat and try out the 303, a restaurant delivering the diverse and eclectic tastes of the world straight into the mouths of the diners of central Wyoming.

Dubois
See **The Sawmill Lodge** under *Lodging—Lodges.*

Glenrock
See **Hotel Higgins** under *Lodging— Bed & Breakfasts.*

Lander
Cowfish (307-332-8227; www.lander bar.com), 128 Main Street. Situated in the historic Coalter Block of buildings, the Cowfish itself is housed in an elegantly renovated 1888 structure. Here you'll find the only true New American cuisine available in Lander, including delicious and creative full entrées (featuring—what else?—beef and fish, with some chicken and pastas thrown in for good measure) and savory salads, appetizers, and desserts. Fish tacos are a tasty choice, but you'll probably be happy with most anything you order in this stylish, hip hangout. Inside the Cowfish you'll also find the award-winning **Snake River Brewpub,** with locally crafted microbrews. The Cowfish is connected by an outdoor deck to the more casual **Gannett Grill** (see *Eating Out*) and **Lander Bar.**

The Hitching Rack (307-332-4322), 785 E. Main Street. This well-respected Lander establishment specializes in one thing: steaks, cooked to perfection, however you prefer them. This is the place where locals go to impress their dates, in the true tradition of wowing them with a pricey steak dinner. The cozy ambience complements the delicious, melt-in-your-mouth entrées, which don't disappoint in either taste or size. Desserts are yummy too—if you have any room left after dinner.

EATING OUT

Casper
Metro Coffee Company (307-472-5042; www.metrocoffeeco.com), 241 S. David. The dark hues of the Metro

Coffee House's spacious and inviting interior evoke a European coffee-house. Step up to the counter and select from an array of coffee specialty drinks or just have a cup of the house brew—or a smoothie, if you prefer. Choose a delicacy or light snack to accompany your beverage, with options including pastries, muffins, bagels, ice cream, and desserts. Then you can saunter back to find the perfect seat to enjoy your treat—maybe a couch, or an over-stuffed chair? You never know . . . even though you are in the middle of Wyoming, you might end up caught in the middle of an intellectual debate as the sensations of the Continent infuse your soul. The Metro hosts live entertainment and other events as well.

*Poor Boys Steak House** (307-237-8325; www.poorboyssteakhouse .net), 739 N. Center Street. Want a big ole steak? Love huge portion sizes? Then head on over to Poor Boys, where they guarantee that you won't ever leave the table hungry. You can dine in the main restaurant, or choose to have your meal in the **Pump Room,** a western bar with an array of microbrews on tap, which serves the full dinner menu (and permits smoking, too). Along with steaks in more than a dozen varieties (and up to 20 ounces in size), you can also choose from an assortment of salads, chicken dishes, pork, pastas, ribs, seafood, burgers, and sandwiches. Desserts are rich, varied, and extravagant. A children's menu is available.

*Sidelines Sports Bar–Banjo Bob's Barbecue** (307-234-9444; www.sidelines.us), 1121 Wilkins Circle. You'll find everything you'd expect to find at this sports bar—so if you're looking to catch a sporting event during your travels and to grab some food and fun with it, look no farther than here. The 12,000-square-foot facility has no fewer than 25 televisions, including five big-screen TVs. At 10 PM Wednesday through Saturday, the sports bar transforms into a hopping nightclub, with a deejay and dancing until 2 AM. If you're hungry for a meal, the extensive menu features an array of sandwiches, burgers, pub-style appetizers, salads, soups, sandwiches, and full entrées with all of the fixings. If you love meat, you can even treat yourself to a multi-meat plate (you'll see what I mean). A children's menu is available.

See also **La Costa Mexican Restaurant,** below.

Douglas

La Costa Mexican Restaurant (307-358-2449), 213 Teton Way. In the mood for some south-of-the-border fare? Step into La Costa, and you're there! Nacho lovers will rejoice when they read the seven different nacho options on the menu—if you're like me, you're always happy to substitute this substantial appetizer for an entrée. If you're not such a cheese fiend, you'll certainly find another Mexican dish on the extensive menu that suits your desire for spicy food, whether you prefer a burrito, fajitas, a taco salad, enchiladas, or a combination plate. Generous sides accompany each main dish, and the prices are reasonable as well. La Costa also has a **Casper location** (307-266-4288), 400 W. F Street.

Dubois

Village Cafe and Daylight Donuts (307-455-2122), 515 W. Ramshorn Street. Whether it's an early breakfast, a midday meal, or dinner you're in search of, this casual and comfortable restaurant should fit the bill. You'll find an array of American favorites, including steaks, chicken, burgers, and pizza. Doughnut lovers will be delighted with this find—a doughnut shop with the tasty, sweet treats baked fresh daily in a number of varieties.

Lander

✿ **Big Noi Family Restaurant** (307-332-3102), 8125 WY 789. The folks at Big Noi were probably smart to include a wide selection of traditional American favorites on their menu, including burgers—but if you're going to eat here, you should really come for the Thai food. Though they may not be as spicy as you might find in a more urban setting, the Thai entrées at Big Noi are really pretty good, considering that you're in the middle of Wyoming. If you're a hot-food lover, you can always request that the heat be turned up in your choice of entrée. You'll find a great selection of traditional Thai favorites, including pad Thai, curries, and spring rolls, among other selections.

🍴 ✿ **Gannett Grill** (307-332-8228; www.landerbar.com), 126 Main Street. Situated in the historic Coalter Block, the Gannett Grill provides the best deal in town for good food at great prices. Whether you're in search of a giant burger with all the fixings or you prefer a salad, this is the place to go. The Gannett doesn't skimp in either department—salads are served in a veritable trough of a bowl, with fresh, crispy greens, ample toppings, and soft pita triangles. Add in some grilled chicken to the "Green and Greener"; it's awesome. Burgers feature half a pound of beef, organic if you choose, topped with a variety of

condiments ranging from grilled mushrooms to jalapeño peppers. The Gannett also offers pizza, appetizers, sandwiches, and specials that are usually quite tasty as well. The outdoor deck is a popular hangout in warmer months, and the adjacent **Lander Bar** is one of the most hopping nightspots in town. The Gannett Grill is connected by an outdoor deck to the more upscale **Cowfish** (see *Dining Out*).

✿ **Global Café** (1-866-312-7900; 307-332-7900; www.landerglobalcafe .com), 360 Main Street. Undoubtedly one of the coolest new places to hit Lander in years, the Global Café features an alcohol-free, smoke-free environment that is anything but boring. This worldly hangout features a full range of coffee drinks and accompanying treats, as well as daily meal specials usually including a meat entrée, vegetarian entrée, and chicken dish. Soups, salads, and other goodies are also on the menu. The café has an intimate performance area where you can catch live acts, including music of all genres, standup comedy, and other gigs by local, regional, and national performers. Upstairs you'll find a game room with a pool table, table tennis, and foosball. An enclosed courtyard outside is a great place to relax over a cup of coffee in warmer weather or to catch an act on the outdoor stage.

The Magpie (307-332-5565), 159 N. 2nd Street. Creaky hardwood floors and high ceilings, plus comfy couches and tables tucked by the windows, make this coffeehouse a cool place to sit back and enjoy a bottomless cup of java while you read the papers, meet with a friend or business associate, or just plan out your day of adventure. The shop usually has four different types of coffee "on tap," so you can refill your mug with a different flavor each time you go back. You can also find an array of fresh-baked goods to go with your joe, as well as more substantial light-meal fare around lunchtime.

✍ **Tony's Pizza** (307-332-3900), 637 Main Street. The brightly lit, colorful, checkerboard sign outside calls you to step inside Tony's, the locals' favorite place to go for a pizza dinner. Tony's offers pizzas in both basic flavors and more creative pies, depending on what you're in the mood for. You can also opt for a cheesy stromboli, a veggie bread-bowl salad, a pasta creation, or a chicken dish, among other menu selections. In warmer weather, the roof deck is one of the most happening places in the town of Lander, as folks flock to share drinks and meals while perched above the main drag.

See also **Sleeping Bear Ranch RV Resort and Café** under *Lodging— Other Options.*

Riverton

✍ **The Bull Restaurant** (307-856-4728), 1100 W. Main Street. "Where the locals go," the Bull Restaurant serves up steaks and other down-home fare in good-sized portions for both lunch and dinner. The restaurant features reasonable prices on entrée selections that include chicken and seafood as well as beef. Lunches, served on weekdays, include three daily specials in addition to the regular menu. The restaurant also has a special seniors' menu and a children's menu.

✍ **QT's Restaurant** (1-877-857-4834; 307-856-8100), 900 E. Sunset Boulevard. This family-style fine dining establishment is located inside River-

ton's Holiday Inn. Here you'll find well-prepared, traditional American food, with dinner entrée selections including beef, seafood, chicken, and more. If you're staying at the hotel, your kids 12 and under eat for free from the children's menu, making it easy on the pocketbook and satisfying for the belly. In summertime, the restaurant is open early for breakfast (6 AM) and late for dinner (10 PM), making it a surefire option for off-hours dining needs.

Wheatland

✍ **Casey's Timberhaus Family Restaurant and Lounge** (307-322-4932), 1803 16th Street. Serving up three hearty meals a day, this moderately priced, family-style restaurant has an extensive menu that is sure to have something to please everyone. Breakfast choices include numerous egg combos, specialty pancakes, omelets, and more. Lunch options include both an array of menu selections and sack lunches to go, with one or two sandwiches—your choice. Dinner selections range from a simple hamburger to fancier affairs like shrimp scampi, lobster tail, and prime rib on Friday and Saturday nights. And if you're looking for a place to sample those infamous Rocky Mountain oysters, you'll find 'em on the menu here. Casey's serves breakfast, lunch, and dinner anytime. A children's menu is available.

&. ✍ **Vimbo's Dusty Boots Restaurant** (1-800-577-3842; 307-322-3725; www.vimbos.com), 203 16th Street. This restaurant, adjacent to the motel and lounge of the same name, is a family-owned operation that serves breakfast, lunch, and dinner. You'll find traditional American food here. Breakfasts include several omelet selections, fresh-baked goods, and hearty combinations. Lunches include a weekday buffet and sack lunches to go, as well as sandwiches and salads. Dinnertime brings with it steak done in a number of cuts and styles, as well as seafood, daily specials, burgers, sandwiches, and more. A long list of desserts, including pies, pies, and more pies, among other options, means you should certainly leave room for a slice (or two!). A children's and seniors' menu is available as well.

Wheatland Inn (307-322-9302), 86 16th Street. I love places like the Wheatland Inn—they serve breakfast and dinner anytime. Being one of those folks who just can't seem to stomach much in the morning, I usually miss out on all of the goodies that go with a hearty start-of-the-day meal—pancakes, waffles, omelets, bacon, and sausage, to name a few. But at the Wheatland Inn, you can have breakfast whenever you feel like it. And if you want dinner in the morning, they'll do that, too. The menu features a great diversity of breakfast offerings, such as eggs, pork chops, and Belgian waffles. Lunch and dinner offerings are extensive as well, ranging from burgers and sandwiches to seafood and steaks.

✳ Special Events

February: **Cowboy State Games Sports Festival,** Casper: five-weekend event featuring competitions between amateur athletes from around the state for top honors; sports include power lifting, gymnastics, indoor soccer, and figure skating. *Wild West Winter Carnival,* Riverton: celebration of the coldest season of the year includes ice sculptures, casino nights, tethered balloon rides, and more. *Winterfest,* Dubois: a winter celebration that includes sled dog races, skijoring, a soup cook-off, a snowman-building contest, and more.

February and March: **Wyoming State Winter Fair,** Lander: fair features a livestock show, a horse show, a trade show, and food vendors.

June: **Eastern Shoshone Indian Days,** Fort Washakie: annual pow-wow celebration drawing hundreds of dancers and drummers to compete for prizes; also includes concessions, arts and crafts, and more. **Pony Express Re-Ride,** Atlantic City, Casper, Douglas, and Torrington: annual reenactment of the entire Pony Express ride from Missouri to California, performed by the National Pony Express Association. Contact the National Historic Trails Interpretive Center (see *To See—Museums*) for details.

July: **Annual Ethete Celebration Powwow,** Ethete: one of a number of annual spring and summer powwows held by the Northern Arapaho Tribe, includes dancing, arts and crafts, and additional festivities. *1838 Mountain Man Rendezvous,* Riverton: annual celebration featuring historical reenactments of mountain man gatherings, including food, entertainment, dancing, and games. *Fort Caspar Chautauqua,* Fort Caspar Museum and Historic Site (see *To See—Museums*): annual historical celebration featuring reenactments, period dress, food booths, children's activities, and music. *Gold Rush Days,* South Pass City: yearly celebration on the last Friday, Saturday, and Sunday of July, includes food, drinks, games (including a vintage baseball game), contests, and interpretive programs.

International Climbers' Festival, Lander: annual gathering of rock climbers from around the world, taking place the Thursday through Sunday after the Fourth of July; includes clinics, climbing, slide shows, movies, food, socializing, fun competitions, and more.✒ **Pageant of the Old West and Rodeo,** Lander: Lander's annual celebration of the Fourth of July began way back in 1894, and the tradition continues today with a multi-day celebration. Activities include a road race, pancake breakfast, parade, rodeo, barbecue, and more. ✒ **Riverton Rendezvous,** Riverton: yearly celebration of the city's founding in 1906; includes a hot-air balloon rally, Arts in the Park, a rodeo, a street dance, and more.

August: ✒ **Buffalo BBQ Weekend,** Dubois: annual celebration includes a rodeo, a quilt show, chariot races, and—what else?—a buffalo barbecue. ✒ **Wyoming State Fair** (1-800-464-5167; 307-358-2398; www.wystatefair.com), Douglas: traditional state fair featuring food vendors, booths, livestock, entertainment, and more.

September: **Annual One Shot Antelope Hunt,** Lander: taking place for more than 60 years, this yearly hunt allows licensed teams of hunters (drawn by lottery) a single shot each to take down an antelope. (See also Lander under *To See—Towns.*)

SOUTH WYOMING: MEDICINE BOW–FLAMING GORGE COUNTRY

Perhaps more than anything else in this region, the transcontinental transportation corridor running through the entire southern portion of Wyoming has defined and shaped Wyoming's role and identity in the modern world. This role hearkens back to the emigrant trails that began the massive movement of people west in the early to mid-1800s, when portions of the Oregon Trail, the Mormon Trail, the Pony Express Trail, and other such trails passed through parts of this region. These first trails traversed the far western portion of this region after running northward over South Pass (see *Historic Landmarks, Places, and Sites* in "Central Wyoming: Oregon Trail–Rendezvous Country"), arcing south to the area around present-day Green River. But in 1862, Ben Halladay, a.k.a. "the Stagecoach King," created an alternative route that came to be known as the Overland Trail, a route that, though short-lived in its incarnation as a stagecoach route, would nonetheless have long-lasting repercussions for this desolate, windswept Wyoming landscape.

With the establishment of the Overland Trail as a stagecoach mail route through southern Wyoming in 1862, a precedent for all future trans-state transportation routes was set. The Overland Trail proved to be a safer way to traverse Wyoming than were the more northerly trails, both in terms of terrain and in terms of being better protected from the agitated Indians, who at that point were still struggling wholeheartedly to resist the veritable invasion of pioneers and soldiers attempting to force them off their homelands and on to reservations. The heyday of the Overland Trail lasted only seven years, but during that time, it became the main route westward for emigrants despite continued threats of Indian attacks as well as the general hardships of traveling in those times.

The Overland Trail's precedence as a travel route ended with the completion of the transcontinental railroad in 1869, when the Union Pacific and Central Pacific ends of the railroad met at Promontory Point in Utah. Running the railroad through Wyoming was pretty much a no-brainer for Union Pacific, given not only the suitability of the terrain but also the discovery of plentiful coal deposits in the vicinity of the railroad's path through the state. Nonetheless, the railroad was not constructed without difficulties. The Indians were understandably displeased (to say the least) with this latest invasion of their historic territories, coupled with all of the additional conflicts and unpleasant interactions

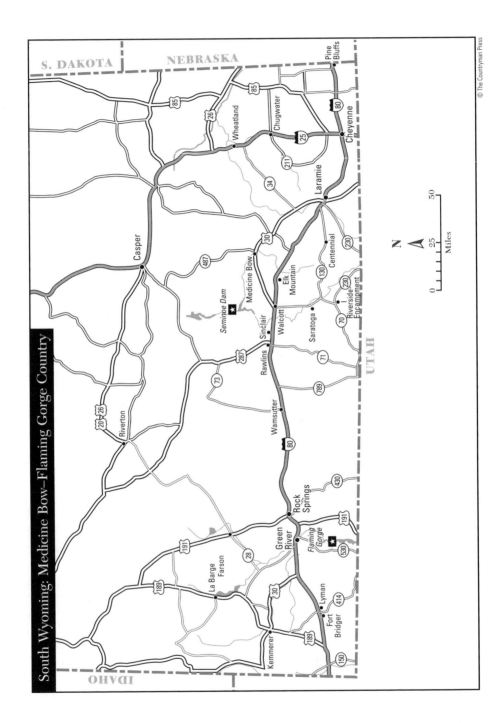

South Wyoming: Medicine Bow–Flaming Gorge Country

they'd already had with the newcomers to this land, and they did manage to dis-
rupt the railroad's progress on several occasions. More military forts followed in
the wake of such attacks, helping to further secure the unstoppable progression
of the railroad across the landscape. Upon its completion, the railroad virtually
immediately transcended all other forms of transport westward, becoming the
preferred and safest mode of travel by emigrants who ventured this way.

Following the precedent set by both the Overland Trail and the transcontinental railroad, the almost 3,400-mile Lincoln Highway—the nation's first
east–west transcontinental highway—marched into being in the state of Wyoming in 1913. The vision of industrialist Carl Fisher, the Lincoln Highway
stretched from New York to San Francisco, passing through 13 states. It would
take years for the entirety of the road to be paved, but the official establishment
and designation of this road set the tone for America's future interstate roadways, designed to accommodate travel by automobile. The original Lincoln
Highway in Wyoming followed the same basic route as today's I-80; the major
exception was the stretch from Laramie to Walcott Junction. That portion originally arced north along the path of today's US 30/287, passing the town of Medicine Bow (see *To See—Towns*).

Though many travelers journey through Wyoming along I-80 today, probably
a scant few of them realize the historical significance of this travel route not only
to the history of the state but also to the entire nation. As you travel along I-80,
delving more deeply into Wyoming's transportation history is as simple as exiting
the interstate to visit the cities and their historical and cultural attractions.

Starting in the east, you'll enter Wyoming along I-80 in the small border town
of Pine Bluffs (see *To See—Towns*), a historic railroad town, and then it's on to
Cheyenne. Cheyenne—Wyoming's capital city and its largest city as well—owes
its very existence to the coming of the transcontinental railroad in the late 1860s.
Recognizing the need to provide a hometown for those working on the railroad,
the Union Pacific Railroad selected Cheyenne's location in 1867, officially founding the town on the Fourth of July. The establishment of Fort D. A. Russell—
today F. E. Warren Air Force Base—followed shortly thereafter, with the U.S.
Army providing military protection for the railroad construction, mainly against
antagonistic Indians (see also *To See—Historic Landmarks, Places, and Sites*).

Cheyenne is full of museums and historical attractions, promising to keep you
busy for weeks of exploration if the history of the taming of the western frontier
interests you. By far the city's most popular annual event is Cheyenne Frontier
Days, known as the Daddy of 'Em All (see *Special Events*), which includes
incredible action-packed rodeos, a parade, free pancake breakfasts, and more—
turning the entire city of Cheyenne into one big celebration at the end of July.
Each year, the festivities include headlining acts by famous entertainers that sell
out early, so be sure to check long in advance on who's playing—and be aware
that most lodging accommodations charge premium rates during this popular
event. Among its many other attractions, Cheyenne has 17 municipal parks (see
Lions Park under *Wilder Places—Parks* for details), so it's easy to find a place for
picnicking or other outdoor recreation.

After Cheyenne, continue westward toward Laramie, taking Happy Jack
Road (see *To See—Scenic Drives*) for a slower, more scenic journey. Just east of

Laramie, you can visit the Lincoln Monument at the Summit Information Center (see *Guidance*), accessible via Exit 323 off I-80. Laramie, Wyoming's third-largest city, is home to the University of Wyoming, which has several free museums (see University of Wyoming Art and Geological Museums and the American Heritage Center under *To See—Museums*). More than 10 city parks lie within city limits, providing ample opportunities for urban recreation, ranging from the Laramie River Greenbelt (see *To Do—Bicycling*) to LaBonte Park, home to the Wyoming Children's Museum and Nature Center (see *To See—For Families*).

You can stay on I-80 to go west from Laramie, but why not mix it up a bit? West of Laramie off WY 130 (Snowy Range Scenic Byway; see *To See—Scenic Drives*) and southwest off WY 230, you'll find the concentrated recreational opportunities of the Medicine Bow Mountains and the Sierra Madre Mountains in Medicine Bow National Forest (see *Wilder Places—Forests*). A number of charming, small towns lie in this area, including Centennial, Encampment–Riverside, and Saratoga (see *To See—Towns*). Another option is to head northwest from Laramie on US 30/287, tracing the historic path of the Lincoln Highway and visiting the historic attractions in the town of Medicine Bow (see *To See—Towns*).

You'll rejoin I-80 near Sinclair (see *To See—Towns*) and Fort Fred Steele State Historic Site (see *To See—Historic Landmarks, Places, and Sites*). Your journey continues past Rawlins, another historic railroad town, which got its name from General John A. Rawlins, a surveyor for the Union Pacific Railroad. Seeking to quench his thirst during a surveying trip to this area, he discovered a spring and declared it to be the finest water he'd ever tasted. The county seat of Carbon County, Rawlins, situated on the eastern edge of the Great Divide Basin (see *To See—Natural Wonders*), has a number of historic and natural attractions. These include the Wyoming Frontier Prison (see *To See—Historic Landmarks, Places, and Sites*) and wild horses (see *To See—Scenic Drives*).

From Rawlins, you'll continue east through the Great Divide Basin, arriving in Rock Springs and then Green River, both historic railroad towns. Stop at the Rock Springs Historical Museum (see *To See—Museums*) for a lesson on the town's ties to both mining and the railroad. From here, you can also access the one-of-a-kind Flaming Gorge National Recreation Area (see *Wilder Places—Other Wild Places*), taking a scenic loop tour on the Flaming Gorge–Green River Basin Scenic Byway (see *To See—Scenic Drives*). If you're shorter on time, you can also potentially see wild horses north of the city (see *To See—Scenic Drives*) or take a journey to the Killpecker Sand Dunes, one of the largest active dune systems in the country (see *To See—Natural Wonders*). Green River offers a unique in-town recreational opportunity at the Green River Whitewater Park (see *To Do—Paddling/Floating*), one of 26 parks found in the city. Continue west from Green River to Fort Bridger State Historic Site (see *To See—Historic Landmarks, Places, and Sites*) before your final destination in Wyoming—Evanston.

As with practically every other town or city along the I-80 corridor, Evanston's ties to the railroad defined its past and continue to define it in the present day as well. Begin your stay here with a stop at the Bear River State Park and Travel Information Center (see *Wilder Places—Parks*), where you can view captive herds of bison and elk, take a walk along Bear River, and gather information about the area (especially noteworthy if you're starting your journey here and heading east).

Explore Evanston's history at Historic Depot Square (see *To See—Historic Land-marks, Places, and Sites*), including the history of the Chinese emigrants who came here to work on the railroad and to mine the coal to fuel the trains. More than 15 city parks lie scattered throughout Evanston, many of which can be accessed from both Historic Depot Square and Bear River State Park via the BEAR (Better Environment And River project) Parkway (see *To Do—Bicycling*).

I would be remiss to leave you to your travels without mentioning that though I-80 is an interstate highway and one of the country's major east–west transportation routes, traveling on I-80 during inclement weather conditions can be a hair-raising and even life-threatening event. High winds blow semis off the roadway at times (I've seen this), and I've driven for miles upon miles holding the steering wheel sideways and thinking that my car's alignment must be off, only to realize that I've been compensating for the winds all along. And if it snows, well, you'd better be good at dealing with slick, slippery surfaces and blinding, blowing snow—not to mention semis screaming by you at 70 or 80 miles per hour, seemingly impervious to the horrendous conditions of the roadway. Don't be scared, though—just be prepared, and use good judgment and postpone your travels if need be. If you do encounter bad weather, perhaps you'll even feel a little bit of kinship with the emigrants who braved this harsh and unforgiving environment with drastically fewer resources than we have today—after all, they couldn't just call it quits and grab a hotel room for the night.

GUIDANCE **Albany County Tourism Board** (1-800-445-5303; 307-745-4195; www.laramie-tourism.org), 210 Custer Street, Laramie 82070.

Bear River Travel Information Center (307-789-6540), Exit 6 off I-80 in Evanston; open daily.

Bridger Valley Chamber of Commerce (307-787-6738; www.bridger valleychamber.com), 100 E. Sage St. (town government), P.O. Box 1506, Lyman 82937.

Cheyenne Area Convention & Visitors Bureau (1-800-426-5009; 307-778-3133; www.cheyenne.org), 1 Depot Square, 121 W. 15th Street, #202, Cheyenne 82001.

Cheyenne Chamber of Commerce (307-638-3388; www.cheyenne chamber.org), 1 Depot Square, P.O. Box 1147, Cheyenne 82003.

City of Evanston (1-866-783-6300; www.evanstonwy.org), 1200 Main Street, Evanston 82930.

Evanston Chamber of Commerce (1-800-328-9708; 307-783-0370; www .etownchamber.com), 36 10th Street, P.O. Box 365, Evanston 82931.

Frank Norris Jr. Travel Center (307-777-2883), Exit 7 off I-25 at College Drive, Cheyenne; open daily 8 AM–5 PM.

Green River Chamber of Commerce (1-800-354-6743; 307-875-5711; www .grchamber.com), 541 E. Flaming Gorge Way, Suite E, Green River 82935.

Laramie Chamber of Commerce (1-866-876-1012; 307-745-7339; www .laramie.org), 800 S. 3rd Street, Laramie 82070.

Medicine Bow (307-379-2225; www.medicinebow.org), P.O. Box 156, Medicine Bow 82329-0156.

Pine Bluffs Chamber of Commerce (307-245-3746; www.pinebluffs.org), 206 Main Street, P.O. Box 486, Pine Bluffs 82082.

Pine Bluffs Information Center (307-245-3695; www.pinebluffs.org), Exit 401 off I-80 in Pine Bluffs; open daily mid-May through mid-October.

Rawlins–Carbon County Chamber of Commerce (1-800-935-4821; 307-324-4111; www.wyomingcarboncounty.com or www.rawlinscarboncounty chamber.com), 519 W. Cedar Street, P.O. Box 1331, Rawlins 82301.

Rock Springs Chamber of Commerce (1-800-GO-DUNES; 307-362-3771; www.rockspringswyoming.net), 1897 Dewar Drive, P.O. Box 398, Rock Springs 82902-0398.

Saratoga–Platte Valley Chamber (307-326-8855; www.saratogachamber.info), 106 N. Street, P.O. Box 1095, Saratoga 82331.

Summit Information Center (307-721-9254), Exit 323 off I-80 south of Laramie at Happy Jack; open mid-May through mid-October.

Sweetwater County Joint Travel and Tourism Board (307-354-6457; www .tourwyoming.com), 79 Winston Drive, #236, P.O. Box 38, Rock Springs 82901.

Wyoming Game and Fish Department Headquarters and Visitor Center (307-777-4600; http://gf.state.wy.us/fish/fishing/index.asp), 5400 Bishop Boulevard, Cheyenne 82006.

See also **Bear River State Park and Travel Information Center** under *Wilder Places—Parks.*

GETTING THERE Cheyenne lies at the crossroads of Wyoming's two major interstates, I-25 and I-80. Laramie lies on I-80. It can also be accessed from the north and south via US 287. Saratoga is south of I-80 via WY 130 between Laramie and Rawlins. Rawlins lies along I-80, Wyoming's major southern east–west highway. Rawlins can also be accessed from the north via US 287 and from the south via WY 71. Rock Springs lies southwest of Rawlins on I-80 where US 191 crosses the interstate. Green River, Lyman, and Evanston are all west of Rock Springs on I-80.

See also *Airports, Amtrak, Bus Service,* and *Travel Information* in "What's Where in Wyoming."

MEDICAL EMERGENCY **Evanston Regional Hospital** (307-789-3636), 190 Arrowhead Drive, Evanston.

Ivinson Memorial Hospital (307-742-2141), 255 N. 30th Street, Laramie.

Memorial Hospital of Carbon County (307-324-2221), 2221 Elm Street, Rawlins.

Memorial Hospital of Sweetwater County (307-362-3711), 1200 College Drive, Rock Springs.

United Medical Center–West (307-634-2273), 214 E. 23rd Street, Cheyenne.

TOWNS **Centennial,** 35 miles west of Laramie on WY 130, is the closest town to this region's sole ski area, the **Snowy Range Ski Area** (see *To Do—Snow Sports*), but its origins have nothing to do with the ski industry. Like so many of the population centers in this region, this town came about as a result of the construction of the transcontinental railroad, serving as a hub for the tie hack industry—the cutting of railroad ties. Less than a decade later, in 1875 Centennial was also home to a gold strike, which brought gold-hungry hopefuls to the area as well. Named in honor of the country's 100th birthday, the town of Centennial today is appropriately home to about 100 permanent residents, providing an array of services for the outdoor recreation lovers who pass this way, as well as being home to the **Nici Self Museum** (see *To See—Museums*).

Encampment–Riverside, situated about 90 miles west of Laramie via WY 130 to WY 230, are also accessed by taking Exit 235 off I-80 at Walcott and then heading south past Saratoga on WY 130. Encampment, with its population of roughly 440 people, and neighboring Riverside, population 85, lie less than a mile apart from one another on the other side of the Snowy Range from Centennial. In these two small towns, you'll find an array of visitor services, including river access points (see **Encampment River** under *To Do—Fishing*), parks, lodging, and restaurants, aimed particularly at those adventuring into nearby **Medicine Bow National Forest** (see *Wilder Places—Forests*). This was the area known to the fur trappers of the mid-1800s as the Grand Encampment, a location historically used by numerous Indian tribes as a gathering spot to hunt buffalo and other game animals. Find out more at Encampment's **Grand Encampment Museum** (307-327-5308), 817 Barnett Avenue. Open late May through early September Monday through Saturday 10 AM–5 PM, Sunday 1 PM–5 PM; free. It features exhibits detailing local history, including the area's ties to the mining, timber, and agriculture industries. Don't miss Encampment's **Woodchopper's Jamboree and Rodeo** (see *Special Events*).

Medicine Bow is accessed by taking US 30/287 northwest out of Laramie or by taking Exit 235 northeast off I-80 at Walcott. The town, the river, the mountains, and the national forest—they all go by the name Medicine Bow, a name taken from the Cheyenne and Arapaho Indians, who found that this area of Wyoming had particularly "good medicine"—that is, top-quality resources—for the making of bows. With a population of fewer than 300 people, the town of Medicine Bow and its immediate environs nevertheless have not only one but, rather, several claims to fame that just might intrigue you enough to entice you to make a side journey this way. Medicine Bow provided author Owen Wister with much of the inspiration for the famous novel *The Virginian,* published in 1902. The **Historic Virginian Hotel** (307-379-2377), built in 1911 and now on the National Register of Historic Places, pays tribute to Wister's use of this area in his novel. You can still stay there today (for about $50 a night) while you explore other area attractions, including the **Owen Wister Cabin and Monument** and the **Medicine Bow Museum** (307-379-2383), which are located right across the street from the Virginian. The museum is in the restored **Union Pacific Railroad depot,** which is listed on the National Register of Historic Places. About 10 miles east of town is the site of **Como Bluff,** a National Natural Landmark, where in 1877, railroad employees first discovered this place that would ultimately yield thousands of nearly perfectly preserved dinosaur bones. Though visible from the road, at this time the site is closed to the public. Learn more about this site by stopping at the nearby **Como Bluff Fossil Cabin Museum** (open in summer months), constructed entirely of dinosaur bones, which is about 8 miles east of Medicine Bow. In town you'll find a number of visitor services, including gift shops, lodging, and dining facilities.

Pine Bluffs welcomes you to Wyoming with its information center, accessible via Exit 401 off I-80, just after you cross the border with Nebraska. The center provides not only information but also **nature trails** that allow the weary traveler an opportunity for some movement and fresh air after long hours in the car. Like so many towns in this region, Pine Bluffs—formerly known as Rock Ranch—came into being thanks to the arrival of the Union Pacific Railroad in 1867. Before that time, the bluffs that gave the town its name served as favored camping grounds for Indians, who chose them not only for the tremendous vantage point they gave but also for their abundance of firewood and close proximity to ample fresh water and food sources. After the coming of the railroad, Pine Bluffs became a hub of the **Texas Trail,** which was used to move thousands upon thousands of head of cattle from Texas north to Wyoming for shipping during the 1870s and 80s. Learn more about this at the **Texas Trail Park and Museum** (307-245-3713), 201 W. 3rd Street; open Memorial Day through Labor Day Monday through Saturday 11 AM–5 PM. Additional attractions in Pine Bluffs include Wyoming's largest sculpture, the 40-foot **Our Lady of Peace Shrine,** by Robert Fida (on US 30 and visible from I-80), as well as the free, seasonal **University of Wyoming Archaeology Lab and Visitor Center** (307-245-9372) at 2nd and Elm and its corresponding **Dig Site,** situated by the information center off I-80.

Saratoga, easily accessed by going south on WY 130 off I-80 at Exit 235 at Walcott, is perhaps best known for its free, 24/7 hot mineral pool—the **Hobo Pool** (see Saratoga Hot Pool under *To Do—Hot Springs*). In fact, the town took its name from New York's renowned Saratoga Springs. Additional attractions include blue-ribbon fishing on the **North Platter River** (see *To Do—Fishing*); the **Saratoga Museum** (307-326-5511), 104 Constitution Avenue, open Memorial Day through Labor Day 1 PM–5 PM, housed in a historic railroad depot; Saratoga Lake, which features boating (boat dock), all-season fishing (rainbow trout; see also **Ice Fishing Derby** under *Special Events*), and camping (small fee); and the **Saratoga National Fish Hatchery** (307-326-5662; http://saratoga .fws.gov), 4 miles north of town on C.R. 207, open daily Memorial Day through Labor Day 8 AM–4 PM, Labor Day through Memorial Day Monday through Friday 8 AM–4 PM; free. The town itself, with its population of nearly 2,000, is replete with visitor attractions and services, including gift shops and many lodging accommodations (see listings under *Lodging*). You'll also find a number of eateries, both fine dining establishments and more casual hangouts such as the **Mexican-American Lazy River Cantina** (307-326-8472), 110 E. Bridge Avenue, and **Lollypop's** (307-326-5020), 107 E. Bridge Avenue (next to the

Wolf Hotel; see *Lodging—Other Options*), an ice-cream parlor and coffee shop.

Sinclair, just west of Rawlins off I-80 at Exit 221, will likely either repulse you or fascinate you—or maybe a little bit of both (like me)—depending on who you are. This town's defining landmark is the enormous **Sinclair Refinery,** which can be seen from I-80, often spitting an eerie flame from one of its stacks.

MUSEUMS **Carbon County Museum** (307-328-2740), 9th and Walnut, Rawlins. Open June through August Monday through Friday 1 PM–8 PM, Saturday 1 PM– 5 PM; open September through May Monday through Friday 1 PM–5 PM; free. This county museum strives to preserve the history of the surrounding region with unique exhibits, including a 1920 fire truck—and shoes made from the skin and skull of a notorious criminal! You'll also find an array of artifacts and documents explaining and interpreting the roles of various peoples and industries, including Indians, pioneers, mining, ranching, and the railroad, in shaping this region.

Cheyenne Depot Museum (307-632-3905; www.cheyennedepotmuseum.org), 1 Depot Square, 121 W. 15th Street. Open Monday through Friday 9 AM–5 PM, Saturday 10 AM–5 PM, Sunday noon–5 PM (hours slightly longer in summer); donations gladly accepted. Learn all about the area's strong ties with the railroad, starting with the construction of the transcontinental railroad by Union Pacific, which prompted the establishment of Cheyenne in 1867. Housed in a painstakingly renovated 1929 Union Pacific Railroad depot graced with a beautiful and distinctive clock tower, this museum documents the role played by the railroad both in the establishment of Wyoming's capital city and in the city's ensuing development, as well as the history of the depot building itself. The Cheyenne Depot Museum became the city's newest cultural center when it opened in 2004, and it provides an array of visitor services and information as well. (See also Cheyenne Street Railway Trolley under *To Do—Unique Adventures.*)

Cheyenne Frontier Days Old West Museum (307-778-7290; www.oldwest museum.org), 4610 N. Carey Avenue, Cheyenne. Open Monday through Friday 9 AM–5 PM, Saturday and Sunday 10 AM–5 PM, with extended hours in summer; closed Thanksgiving, Christmas, New Year's Day, and Fourth of July; $5 adults, children 11 and under free. This museum strives to help visitors learn about this area's history, from its ties to the Union Pacific Railroad to its legacy of cowboys and rodeos that lives on today in the annual Cheyenne Frontier Days (see *Special Events*). Particular attention is given to western art, ranching history, and the history of the Frontier Days celebration itself.

Chinese Joss House Museum (307-783-6320; www.wyshs.org/mus-josshouse .htm), 920 Front Street (in Historic Depot Square; see *Historic Landmarks, Places, and Sites*), Evanston. Open Monday through Friday 8 AM–7 PM (summer); call for winter hours; free. You might not know about the history of southwestern Wyoming's Chinese immigrants and their descendents, but you'll learn about it with a visit to this unique museum. Housed in a replica of the Joss House, a Chinese temple that stood in Evanston from 1874 until it burned down in 1922, the museum exhibits unique and rare work on the construction of the transcontinental railroad. Exhibits include collections of artifacts unearthed in Chinatown, photographs, decorations, and more.

Community Fine Arts Center (307-362-6212; www.cfac4art.com), 400 C Street, Rock Springs. Open Monday through Thursday 10 AM–6 PM, alternate Fridays and Saturdays 10 AM–5 PM; free. View exhibits featuring works by some of the finest western artists of the 20th century, including Grandma Moses and Norman Rockwell, among other notable figures. The center also features works by local and regional contemporary artists of note, as well as hosting an array of rotating exhibits and art-related community events throughout the year.

F. E. Warren A.F.B. Intercontinental Ballistic Missile (ICBM) and Heritage Museum (307-773-2980; www.pawnee.com/fewmuseum), 7405 Marne Loop, Building 210, FE Warren AFB, Cheyenne. Open Monday through Friday 8 AM–4 PM; closed holidays; free. Visitors must follow certain procedures to gain entry to this museum, as it's situated on the F. E. Warren Air Force Base; it's best that you call in advance to ensure that you can gain entry. Housed in the former U.S. Army commanders' headquarters used in the early 20th century, this military museum includes exhibits depicting the daily lives of early military personnel, the history of missiles, the 90th Space Wing, and more. This active air force base was originally an army base (Fort D. A. Russell), established in 1867 to protect the new city of Cheyenne and the workers building the intercontinental railroad. The air force took command of the base in 1947, and it retains command of the base today. The base, which still has many of its original redbrick buildings, is listed on the National Register of Historic Places.

The **Laramie Plains Museum** at the **Historic Ivinson Mansion** (307-742-4448; www.laramiemuseum.org), 603 Ivinson, Laramie. Open year-round Tuesday through Saturday; call for hours (vary by season and events); $4.25 adults, $3.25 children, children 5 and under free, $12.50 per family. Your tour of this Victorian mansion, listed on the National Register of Historic Places, begins when you arrive. You'll be led through this exquisitely restored 1892 structure, once the home of prominent Laramie banker Edward Ivinson and his wife, Jane. The mansion contains numerous artifacts and items of historical significance, including period furnishings, historical photographs, and many more relevant pieces that help illustrate Laramie's past. Also on the neatly landscaped grounds you'll find a one-room schoolhouse and a cowboy line cabin.

CHINESE JOSS HOUSE MUSEUM

&. **Nelson Museum of the West** (307-635-7670; www.nelsonmuseum .com), 1714 Carey Avenue, Cheyenne. Open June through August Monday through Saturday 8 AM–5 PM; open September through May Monday through Friday 8 AM–noon and 1 PM–5 PM; $3 adults, $2 seniors, children 11 and under free. A must-see for anyone interested in the frontier history of Wyoming, this museum is dedicated to the preservation of all things Western with a capital *W*. This means you'll find both Indian and cowboy memorabilia, collectibles, and artifacts as well as a tremendous collection of fine western art on display. Additional exhibits include antique firearms, sculptures, wildlife trophies (both from Wyoming and international specimens), and more.

Nici Self Museum (307-742-7158; 307-634-4955), 2740 WY 130, Centennial. Open mid-June through Labor Day 1 PM–4 PM; free. Hearkening to this region's railroad roots, a portion of this museum is situated in a restored 1907 Hahn railroad depot, giving you a sense of history through its very structural composition in addition to its contents. Another train exhibit features a Union Pacific caboose that dates to 1944. The museum's focus is on the history of the settlement of the Centennial Valley environs, with exhibits detailing the impacts of the mining, ranching, farming, railroad, and lumber industries on the area.

Rock Springs Historical Museum (307-362-3138; www.wyshs.org/mus-rock springshist.htm), 201 B Street, Rock Springs. Open summer Monday and Wednesday 10 AM–8 PM; Tuesday, Thursday, and Friday 10 AM–5 PM; Saturday 11 AM–4 PM. Open winter Wednesday through Saturday 10 AM–5 PM. Free. The museum's exhibits are centered around the history of the Rock Springs area, particularly focused on the period beginning with the coming of the transcontinental railroad (1868) onward. Learn about not only the impact of the railroad but also the area's ties to the coal mining industry. The museum itself is housed in the old City Hall.

Sweetwater County Historical Museum (307-872-6435; 307-352-6715; www .sweetwatermuseum.org), 3 E. Flaming Gorge Way, Green River. Open Monday through Saturday 10 AM–6 PM; free. Dedicated to the historical preservation and presentation of the history of the local and regional area, this county museum features exhibits on prehistoric inhabitants of the area, the Native Americans, early explorers, mountain men and fur trading, the historic trails that passed this way (including the Oregon Trail and the Overland Stagecoach Trail), the transcontinental railroad, coal mining, and more. Situated in a historic building itself—a restored 1931 U.S. Post Office building—the museum's collection also includes a remarkable number of historical photographs.

🐾 ♿ **University of Wyoming Art and Geological Museums** and the **American Heritage Center.** *Geological Museum* (307-766-2646; www.uwyo.edu/ geomuseum), Department 3006, 1000 E. University Avenue, University of Wyoming; in the S. H. Knight Geology Building (northwest corner of campus), Laramie. Open Monday through Friday 8 AM–5 PM, Saturday and Sunday 10 AM– 3 PM; closed state and national holidays; free. *Art Museum* (307-766-6622; www.uwyo.edu/artmuseum), 2111 Willett Drive (the Centennial Complex), Laramie. Open year-round Monday through Saturday 10 AM–5 PM; open June through August Monday through Friday 10 AM–7 PM, Saturday 10 AM–5 PM, Sunday 1 PM–5 PM; closed state and national holidays; free. *American Heritage Center* (307-766-4114; http://ahc.uwyo.edu), 2111 Willett Drive (the Centennial Complex), Laramie. Open June through August Monday through Friday 7:30 AM– 4:30 PM, Saturday 11 AM–5 PM; open September through May Monday through Friday 8 AM–5 PM, Saturday 11 AM–5 PM; closed state and national holidays; free. If you visit one of these attractions, you should make an effort to visit the other two, as they are all free and all explore different aspects of Wyoming's history and heritage. The geological museum's exhibits provide an in-depth look at Wyoming's geology, past and present, including dinosaur skeletons (allosaurus and apatosaurus, among others), other fossils, mineral specimens, and more. The art museum displays rotating exhibits in nine galleries, with a collection of more than 7,000 pieces of art from around the world, including many works by local and regional artists, past and present. The American Heritage Center strives to preserve Wyoming and western history with exhibits that include photographs and artifacts; it also houses an extensive quantity of reference materials and archives.

Wyoming Arts Council Gallery (307-777-7742; http://wyoarts.state.wy.us/vagall.html), 2320 Capitol Avenue, Cheyenne. Open Monday through Friday 8 AM–5 PM; closed holidays; free. Inside the historic Kendrick Building's restored carriage house, this gallery showcases the work of contemporary artists living and creating artwork in Wyoming. Artwork on exhibit is usually available for purchase as well.

🎭 🖉 ♿ **Wyoming State Museum** (307-777-7022; http://wyomuseum.state .wy.us), Barrett Building, 2301 Central Avenue, Cheyenne. Open May through October Tuesday through Saturday 9 AM–4:30 PM; November through April Tuesday through Friday 9 AM–4:30 PM, Saturday 10 AM–2 PM; closed on state and federal holidays; free. Dedicated to preserving both the human and the natural aspects of Wyoming's history, the official state museum is a treasure trove for history buffs. Here you'll find on display all things Wyoming, with permanent exhibits that include a timetable illustrating Wyoming's natural and human past, Wyoming wildlife, Wyoming's mining industry, the state's dinosaur discoveries, and much, much more. Younger visitors will find plenty to keep their little hands busy—and their brains learning—in the Hands-On History Room, an interactive area that encourages kids to engage in learning about the state's history by allowing them to touch and examine relevant items, including a child-size tipi into which they can go. In addition to the permanent exhibits, the museum always has numerous temporary and traveling exhibits as well.

See also Encampment, Medicine Bow, Pine Bluffs, and Saratoga under *Towns;* Fort Bridger State Historic Site, Historic Depot Square, and Wyoming Frontier Prison under *Historic Landmarks, Places, and Sites;* Wyoming Children's Museum and Nature Center under *For Families;* and Cheyenne Street Railway Trolley under *To Do—Unique Adventures.*

HISTORIC LANDMARKS, PLACES, AND SITES ♿ **Fort Bridger State Historic Site** (307-782-3842; http://wyoparks.state.wy.us/bridger1.htm), 3 miles off I-80 via Exit 34 between Evanston and Green River. Grounds open daily year-round 8 AM–sunset; museum open daily May 1 through September 30, 9 AM–4:30 PM; open October 9 AM–4:30 PM; $1 per vehicle (residents), $2 per vehicle (nonresidents), children 17 and under free. **Bridger–Vasquez Trading Company** open daily May 1 through September 30, 9 AM–4:30 PM. Established in 1843 by two of the most famed mountain men of the 19th century, Jim Bridger and Louis Vasquez, Fort Bridger's original incarnation was to serve those traveling on the

Oregon Trail as a place to purchase more supplies. After changing hands, becoming first the property of the Mormons and then the U.S. military in 1858, the fort was abandoned by 1890. Nearly half a century later, efforts were made to restore the historic fort, and in 1933 it was declared a Wyoming Historical Landmark. Today, you can tour through the beautifully restored fort grounds and buildings. In some structures, you'll even find friendly guides dressed in period dress, ready to tell you all about the building's purpose. You can even "trade" with the traders at the Bridger–Vasquez Trading Post (a gift shop) and view related historical artifacts on display at the museum located at the site. For the full-scale mountain man experience, plan to attend the **Mountain Man Rendezvous** (see *Special Events*). Much of the site is includes Braille signs.

Fort Fred Steele State Historic Site (307-320-3013; http://wyoparks.state .wy.us/steele1.htm), north a few miles at Exit 228 off I-80, just east of Sinclair and Rawlins. Open daily May 1 through September 15, 9 AM–7 PM; free. Perhaps even more so than the developed historic sites of this region, Fort Fred Steele gives you a real sense of the utter isolation and desolation that newcomers to this area must have felt when stationed here. Constructed in 1868 to protect the Union Pacific Railroad from Indian attacks, this outpost saw U.S. military occupation for less than two decades. Following that, it experienced brief periods of vibrancy, first with the timber industry and then with the sheep ranching industry. Today, most of what remains at this undeveloped site are the foundations of the old fort buildings, as well as access to fishing on the North Platte River (see *To Do—Fishing*).

✒ 🌿 **Historic Depot Square** (307-783-0370; www.etownchamber.com), 36 Front Street, Evanston. Anchoring **Historic Downtown Evanston** (a National Historic District), Historic Depot Square is home to several historical attractions, all set in a beautifully landscaped and organized setting. Here you'll find the **Uinta County Museum** (307-789-8248), open daily Memorial Day through Labor Day 9 AM–5 PM; open Labor Day through Memorial Day Monday through Friday 9 AM–5 PM; free. The museum, situated in Evanston's historic Carnegie library building, strives to preserve the county's history with exhibits on the railroad, ranching, Indians, Chinese, pioneers, and more; the building also houses the chamber of commerce. Depot Square is also home to the **Chinese Joss House Museum** (see *To See—Museums*) and a restored **Union Pacific passenger railroad depot,** as well as a children's play area and sand volleyball courts. (See also BEAR [Better Environment And River project] Parkway under *To Do—Bicycling* and Pine Gables Inn Bed and Breakfast under *Lodging—Bed & Breakfasts.*)

FORT BRIDGER STATE HISTORIC SITE

Historic Governors' Mansion (307-777-7878; http://wyoparks.state.wy .us/govern1.htm), 300 E. 21st Street, Cheyenne. Open Tuesday through Saturday 9 AM–5 PM; free. You'll pass through a doorway framed by four enormous white columns to enter into the brick mansion that served as Wyoming's first official governors' residence. This elegant three-story home was constructed in 1904 under the guidance of architect Charles Murdock, who designed a Colonial Revival house that segued nicely into the middle-class neighborhood surrounding it. Designed to be large and comfortable—with plenty of room for entertaining guests and for comfortable living—the mansion lacked all ostentation or pretentiousness, particularly in comparison with the enormous homes being constructed by the wealthiest Wyomingites of the time. The mansion continued to serve as the home of a total of 19 of Wyoming's governors until 1976, when a new residence was completed in Frontier Park. You can either take a guided tour of the house or simply wander through this historic residence on your own.

Historic Lakeview Cemetery (307-637-6402; www.cheyennecity.org/ cemetery.htm), 2501 Seymour Avenue, Cheyenne. Grounds open daily; office hours Monday through Friday 8 AM–4:30 PM except city holidays; free. You can take a free, self-guided walking (or driving) tour through this quiet cemetery, a bit off the beaten path but still easily accessed from downtown Cheyenne. Learn interesting bits and pieces of local history during your stroll, which includes stops at 22 different spots on the grounds.

Reliance Tipple (307-872-6435; 307-352-6715; www.sweetwatermuseum.org/ reliance_tipple.htm), 5 miles north of Rock Springs via US 191 to Reliance Road (C.R. 42); open dawn to dusk daily; free. View one of the few such structures that remain intact. Used to sort and grade coal and then to load it into railroad cars for transport, the tipple today stands as a testament to this area's strong historical ties to both the railroad and the mining industries. A self-guided interpretive tour is available, enabling you to learn more about the tipple during your visit.

Wyoming Frontier Prison (307-324-4422; www.wyomingfrontierprison.com), 500 W. Walnut Street, Rawlins. Open daily April through October 8:30 AM– 6:30 PM; open November through March Monday through Friday 9 AM– 5 PM; free. Guided tours available daily Memorial Day through Labor Day 8:30 AM–4:30 PM; shortened hours off-season (call for details); guided tours leave every hour on the half hour; $4.25 per adult, $3.75 per child or senior. Step into Wyoming's criminal past at this former state penitentiary that operated for 80 years from 1901 to 1981, which is listed on the National Register of Historic Places. Affectionately deemed Old Pen, the prison is now home to a

HISTORIC GOVERNORS' MANSION

museum that displays historical exhibits about the prison, including inmate-made weapons and an exhibit about the 1987 movie *Prison,* filmed on the premises. You're best off not merely visiting the museum but also shelling out the cash for the guided tour, which takes you through the former prisoners' quarters, gas chamber, gallows, and solitary confinement area, among other such cheery locales. Rumored to be haunted, the prison also holds special Halloween tours as well as fun-filled overnight lockdown events, in which participants pay nearly $100 to be incarcerated in a prison cell for a night. Also on the premises, you'll find the **Wyoming Peace Officers Museum** and an interpretive trail that takes you to the prisoners' cemetery.

Wyoming State Capitol Building and grounds (307-777-7220; http://wyo shpo.state.wy.us/capitol.htm), Capitol Avenue and 24th Street. Open Monday through Friday 8:30 AM–4:30 PM; free. A National Historic Landmark, Wyoming's State Capitol dates to 1887, when the cornerstone for this majestic architectural masterpiece was laid. The building features sandstone quarried from the area around Fort Collins to the south in Colorado, as well as around Rawlins to the northwest. Inside, you can view murals and legislative chambers; outside, the grounds feature lovely landscaping and several statues of note.

Wyoming Territorial Prison State Historic Site (307-745-6161; www.wyo prisonpark.org), 975 Snowy Range Road, Laramie. Open daily April 1 through October 30, 9 AM–6 PM; November 1 through March 30 weekends (and by appointment); closed Christmas and New Year's Day; $1 per vehicle (residents), $2 per vehicle (nonresidents). Constructed in 1872, this former prison is listed on the National Register of Historic Places. You can take a self-guided tour through the old prison complex, which includes stops at the dining area, guard's quarters, infirmary, women's quarters, and Lawmen and Outlaw Gallery. Also on the premises, you'll find an extensive ranching exhibit, as well as the warden's house and a historic boxcar. On weekends costumed volunteers in period dress make your experience that much more authentic. You can also participate in special events at the prison, including a dinner theater; call for details and reservations.

See also *Towns;* Cheyenne Depot Museum, F. E. Warren A.F.B. Intercontinental Ballistic Missile (ICBM) and Heritage Museum; and the Laramie Plains Museum at the Historic Ivinson Mansion under *Museums;* Cheyenne Street Railway Trolley under *To Do—Unique Adventures;* Curt Gowdy State Park and Lions

WYOMING STATE CAPITOL BUILDING AND GROUNDS

Park under *Wilder Places—Parks;* the Brick Bed and Breakfast, Brooklyn Lodge Bed and Breakfast, the Hood House Bed and Breakfast, Nagle Warren Mansion Bed and Breakfast, Old Depot Bed and Breakfast, Pine Gables Inn Bed and Breakfast, Rainsford Inn Bed and Breakfast, and Vee Bar Guest Ranch Bed and Breakfast under *Lodging—Bed & Breakfasts;* Snowy Mountain Lodge under *Lodging—Lodges;* Elk Mountain Hotel, Historic Woods Landing Resort, Mountain View Historic Hotel, the Plains Hotel, and Wolf Hotel under *Lodging— Other Options;* the Whipple House under *Dining Out;* and the Pantry Restaurant under *Eating Out.*

FOR FAMILIES ✐ **IKON Ice and Events Center** (307-433-0024; www.ikon center.com), 1530 W. Lincolnway, Cheyenne. Open year-round; daily May through August; weekends September through April; rates and hours vary according to activity. The kids will thank you for a trip to this multiactivity center, a virtual palace of fun. Treat them to a day here for good behavior—or just for fun. Activities include laser tag, ice-skating, drop-in ice hockey, and miniature golf on a course that features some of Wyoming's top attractions in miniature, including Devils Tower and Old Faithful.

✐ **Wyoming Children's Museum and Nature Center** (307-745-6332; www .wcmnc.org), 968 N. 9th Street, Laramie. Open Tuesday through Thursday 9 AM– 4 PM, Saturday 10 AM–4 PM; $2 adults, $3 children ages 3 and up, children 2 and under free. Whether your kids love animals, history, or both, they'll enjoy themselves at this interactive museum and nature center. Exhibits include pioneer-themed activities such as dressing up in old-fashioned clothes and exploring tipis and cabins. The nature center includes living animal exhibits. For hands-on fun designed with little ones in mind, the children's museum and nature center are a sure bet. The museum is situated in Laramie's **LaBonte Park,** a perfect place for a family picnic before or after you tour the museum. LaBonte Park also has playground equipment, a short walking and jogging path, and a skateboard park.

See also Wyoming State Museum under *Museums;* Historic Depot Square under *Historic Landmarks, Places, and Sites;* Laramie River Greenbelt under *To Do— Bicycling;* Seminoe State Park under *To Do—Boating;* Saratoga Hot Pool under *To Do—Hot Springs; Ice-Skating* and Snowy Range Ski and Recreation Area under *To Do—Snow Sports;* High Plains Outdoor Institute under *To Do—Unique Adventures;* Bear River State Park and Travel Information Center, Cheyenne Botanic Gardens, Curt Gowdy State Park, and Lions Park under *Wilder Places— Parks;* and Carbon County Fair, Cheyenne Frontier Days, Cheyenne Gunslingers, Flaming Gorge Days, Happy Jack Music Festival, Ice Fishing Derby, Platte Valley Festival of the Arts, and Wyoming's Big Show under *Special Events.*

SCENIC DRIVES **Flaming Gorge–Green River Basin Scenic Byway** is a journey that can be taken as a 160-mile loop, from US 191 to WY 530 with a brief passage through Utah on UT 44, or as a one-way, 70- to 90-mile journey entering or exiting Wyoming via US 191 or WY 530. Begin the loop by exiting at Exit 99 off I-80 just west of Rock Springs and head south on US 191 for about 70 miles to Dutch John, passing over the **Flaming Gorge Dam** shortly thereafter. Watch for signs for UT 44 and head west, then northwest for about 40 miles to Manila, Utah, which is right on the border. From there, head north on WY 530, a journey of about 50 miles. If you choose to do the entire loop, you'll get a remarkably complete overview of the beautiful **Flaming Gorge National Recreation Area** (see *Wilder Places—Other Wild Places*). Just don't expect your drive to be a quick one, as some of the roads are windy and slow—plus, the dramatic scenery will likely compel you to make more than one stop. Another caveat: like many Wyoming roads, this route can be dangerous, even if it's not officially closed due to inclement weather, so use good judgment.

Happy Jack Road, or WY 210, makes for a great and rather quick 40-mile scenic drive—as long as the weather's good. Take WY 210 out of Cheyenne (easily accessible from both I-80 and I-25), and you're on your way for a tour that will take you past **Curt Gowdy State Park** (see *Wilder Places—Parks*) and then into the gorgeous rock formations of the **Vedauwoo Recreation Area of Medicine Bow National Forest** (see *Natural Wonders* and *Wilder Places—Forests*). The road will deposit you conveniently at Exit 321 off I-80, where you can stop to get your bearings at the **Summit Information Center** (see *Guidance*).

Mirror Lake Scenic Byway, or WY 150/UT 150, is about an 80-mile drive that is mostly in Utah, though it has a brief span of about 20 miles in Wyoming. Begin by exiting I-80 at Exit 5 in Evanston, heading south toward Utah on WY 150. This portion of the journey takes you over the **Bear River** and passes by **Sulphur Creek Park** (see *To Do—Boating*). Upon entering Utah, simply stay on UT 150 as it continues south and then heads west, through beautiful **Wasatch–Cache National Forest.** The byway officially terminates in Kamas, Utah, and is closed seasonally.

Snowy Range Scenic Byway takes you on an awe-inspiring journey through the Snowy Range (also known as the **Medicine Bow Mountains**) west of Laramie and east of Saratoga along WY 130. Though the byway officially begins about 30 miles west of Laramie, for most travelers this journey is likely to start or end in Laramie, with the other terminus being Saratoga, for a total distance of about 80 miles. You'll traverse some of the most breathtaking scenery of **Medicine Bow National Forest** (see *Wilder Places—Forests*), passing the wide range of outdoor recreational opportunities found therein. **Lake Marie,** situated just off the road high in the mountains, is a beautiful place to stop and take in the scenic vistas, including windswept alpine peaks. Also here is the access to **Lake Marie Falls Trail** (see *To Do—Hiking*) and **Medicine Bow Trail,** a challenging 6-mile round-trip excursion that gains more than 1,500 feet to reach the ridgeline.

Wild horse tours provide a fun adventure in this region, as you search to see some of Wyoming's bona fide wild horses while traversing windswept prairies and open terrain on back roads. One designated loop tour through the area with the largest population of wild horses in Wyoming—the Bureau of Land Management's (BLM's) **White Mountain Herd Management Area**—departs from just north of **Rock Springs.** Take US 191 north for 14 miles to C.R. 14 and then go west, following signs for the tour. Head south on C.R. 53 (White Mountain Road) as it arcs around the base of **Pilot Butte,** a defining natural landmark, and deposits you in the town of Green River. Another wild horse herd lives near **Rawlins,** in an area managed by the BLM's Rawlins Field Office. The designated wild horse viewing tour involves taking C.R. 63 west off US 287 north of Rawlins and then heading north on C.R. 23 to Jeffrey City on US 287. Interestingly enough, this intersection is considered to be the exact center of the **Great Divide Basin** (see *Natural Wonders*). For both of these adventures, please respect the wild horses (it's illegal to chase them), and be sure you are prepared—this means having a spare tire and plenty of water and paying attention to the weather, since back roads can quickly become quagmires in poor driving conditions. Both of these drives take place on BLM lands (see also *Wilder Places—Other Wild Places*).

See also **Seminoe to Alcova Scenic Backway** under *To See—Scenic Drives* in "Central Wyoming: Oregon Trail–Rendezvous Country."

WINERIES See **Terry Bison Ranch Resort** under *Lodging—Other Options.*

NATURAL WONDERS Great Divide Basin, roughly bordered by US 287 to the northeast, by WY 28 to the northwest, by US 191 to Rock Springs to the west, from near Rock Springs to Rawlins along I-80 to the south, and jutting out near Seminoe Reservoir to the east, is a topographic feature that is truly unique to the state of Wyoming. Here water flows neither east nor west—in fact, the 3,100-mile continental divide splits in two, encircling the basin. And the water that drops here? It stays right here, in this 90-mile-wide, 2.5-million-acre basin, which has no river outlet that allows water to escape. Not that much falls here anyhow—this area forms a rather large portion of Wyoming's incredible Red Desert (see below). You'll pass through the basin, managed by the Bureau of Land Management (see *Wilder Places—Other Wild Places*), if you drive from Rawlins to Rock Springs. For a closer look at the incredible vast and stark terrain of the basin, which includes a prolific amount of animal life, see wild horse tours under *Scenic Drives.* (See also **Continental Divide National Scenic Trail** under *To Do—Hiking.*)

Killpecker Sand Dunes, part of the Red Desert (see below), lie on the southwestern side of the Great Divide Basin (see above) on the other side of the continental divide. Accessed by driving north from Rock Springs on US 191 for about 12 miles and then heading northeast on C.R. 17 (Chilton Road), these dunes are among the largest active dune systems in North America. Towering up to 150 feet in height, the dunes constantly shift in shape and size due to the winds blowing them eastward. They measure 75 miles in length and are 3 miles wide. A particularly intriguing feature of the dunes is the phenomenon known as eolian ice cells, in which layers of sand blow over banks of snow on the dunes in colder months, keeping them frozen until summer's heat begins to melt them. As they melt, they form pools of water at the base of the dune—true oases in this desert environment. Part of this area is designated by the Bureau of Land Management (BLM) as the **Killpecker Sand Dunes Open Play Area,** open to motorized off-road vehicles (see www.wy.blm.gov/rsfo/rec/dunes.htm for details). Use care, whether you're exploring on foot, on horseback, or on an off-road vehicle, to keep track of where you are, as the uniformity of the terrain can lead to confusion and disorientation (a compass is recommended). This area is managed by the BLM's Rock Springs Field Office (see *Wilder Places—Other Wild Places*).

Red Desert encompasses an enormous, 8-million-acre tract of BLM-managed lands (see *Wilder Places—Other Wild Places*) in southern Wyoming, including the Great Divide Basin and Killpecker Sand Dunes (see above). This desert, with its brilliantly hued red sands (hence the name), is one of the country's few remaining relatively undisturbed high desert ecosystems. Home to the largest migratory herd (50,000 animals) of pronghorn antelope in the Lower 48 states, the Red Desert sustains numerous additional species of animals, including the largest herd of desert elk, rare birds, and more—350 species of animals, all told. The desert is home to the unique natural features mentioned above, along with other distinctive natural features, including the **Oregon Buttes.** Historical features include portions of the **Oregon Trail, Overland Trail, Mormon Trail,** and **Pony Express Trail,** as well as Native American cultural sites. The future of the desert as an intact ecosystem has been threatened in recent years by oil and gas mining interests. For more information about this issue, as well as detailed background information on the Red Desert, contact the **Wyoming Outdoor Council** (307-332-7031; www.wyomingoutdoorcouncil.org).

Vedauwoo Recreation Area, located in Medicine Bow National Forest (see *Wilder Places—Forests*), is accessible via Exit 329 off I-80 about 20 miles east of Laramie. This area's chief feature is its remarkable jumble of granite rocks, which range from large to absolutely enormous in size. *Vedauwoo* means "earthborn spirits" in Arapaho, and the Native Americans believed these rocks were created by fun-loving spirits, both human and animal. You'll see balanced rocks, odd-shaped rocks, and just plain gorgeous rocks here—and perhaps some rock climbers, too, as the area is quite popular with these vertically inclined adventurers. For a short walk among the rocks, with great views of your surroundings, hike the 0.6-mile round-trip **Vedauwoo Glen Trail** (#790), accessible from the parking lot of the same name. Camping is also allowed here (early May through late October; $10). (See also High Plains Outdoor Institute under *To Do—Unique Adventures.*)

See also Medicine Bow and Pine Bluffs under *Towns;* wild horse tours under *Scenic Drives;* and Flaming Gorge National Recreation Area under *Wilder Places—Other Wild Places.*

✳ To Do

BICYCLING ♿ **BEAR (Better Environment And River project) Parkway** (307-779-1770; www.evanstonwy.org/parkrec/parks_bear.asp), along Bear River Drive, Evanston. This 2.3-mile system of paved trails connects with the trail system at Bear River State Park (see *Wilder Places—Parks*). Winding along the pathway of the Bear River, the trails are popular not only for bicycling but also for running, strolling, skating, and, in wintertime, cross-country skiing. Situated along the pathway are also two ice-skating ponds (seasonal), fishing and boating access, an interpretive center, and easy access to many of Evanston's parks and attractions, including Historic Depot Square (see *To See—Historic Landmarks, Places, and Sites*).

♿ **Greater Cheyenne Greenway** (307-637-6423; www.cheyennecity.org/greenway.htm) is an award-winning 10-mile paved pathway that runs along both Crow Creek and Dry Creek in Cheyenne, offering a fun and easy recreational adventure not only for bicyclists but also for runners, walkers, and skaters. It is also open to wheelchairs. Accessible from a number of parks (see Lions Park under *Wilder Places—Parks*), the Greenway also connects neighborhoods, shopping areas, and schools. Along the path you'll discover lovely landscaping, birdhouses and bat boxes, and interpretive signs. Plans are in the works to extend the Greenway's scope in the future, adding more miles of paved trails for the benefit of alternative commuters and outdoor enthusiasts alike.

♿ **Laramie River Greenbelt** (307-721-5269; www.ci.laramie.wy.us/recreation/parks) is a 5.75-mile trail along the Laramie River in Laramie, offering recreational opportunities for bicycling, as well as for walking, running, and skating. It is also open to wheelchairs. Along the Greenbelt, you'll find benches where you can stop for a rest or a snack, as well as playground equipment and restroom facilities. **Optimist Park,** located off Cedar Street in southwest Laramie, has a trailhead that provides access to the Greenbelt, as well as playground facilities and fishing access to the Laramie River (see *Fishing*).

See also Vedauwoo Recreation Area under *To See—Natural Wonders;* Bear River State Park and Travel Information Center and Lions Park under *Wilder Places—Parks;* Medicine Bow National Forest under *Wilder Places—Forests;* Flaming Gorge National Recreation Area and Bureau of Land Management under *Wilder Places—Other Wild Places;* A. Drummond's Ranch Bed and Breakfast and Windy Hills Bed and Breakfast under *Lodging—Bed & Breakfasts;* and Harrison's Guest House and Guide Service, and Platt's Guides and Outfitters Rustic Mountain Lodge under *Lodging—Lodges.*

BOATING **Hog Park Reservoir,** accessible by taking Hog Park Road (C.R. 353 to F.R. 550) southwest off WY 70 just west of Encampment for about 25 miles to F.R. 496, lies in Medicine Bow National Forest (see *Wilder Places—Forests*). This small reservoir features a boat ramp and allows motorboats. Fishing for brook trout, brown trout, cutthroat trout, rainbow trout, and splake is popular here, and this is a great place to access the Encampment River (see *Fishing*). Here you'll also find the **Lake View Campground** (open June 15 through September; $10), as well as access to a completed portion of the **Continental Divide National Scenic Trail** (see *Hiking*). You can also access the shorter Hog Park Trail (#475), about 1.3 miles in length, which links up with the Encampment River Trail (see *Fishing*). Horseback riders are welcome on this trail as well.

Lake Hattie–Twin Buttes Reservoirs lie about 18 miles west of Laramie and are accessible by taking WY 230 7.5 miles southwest to C.R. 422 (Pahlow Road) and then proceeding west to C.R. 45 (Lake Hattie Road). This series of reservoirs, partially managed by the Bureau of Land Management (see *Wilder Places—Other Wild Places*), provides opportunities for boaters and anglers alike. You'll find several boat ramps here, as well as camping facilities. Fish species include brown trout, cutthroat trout, and rainbow trout.

✒ **Seminoe State Park** (307-320-3013; http://wyoparks.state.wy.us/seminoe1
.htm), accessible by taking Exit 219 off I-80 at Sinclair and then proceeding
northeast for about 34 miles via C.R. 351 (Seminoe Road) to the park. Open
year-round; day-use $2 per vehicle (residents), $4 per vehicle (nonresidents);
camping $6 per vehicle (residents), $12 per vehicle (nonresidents). Here you'll
find the enormous **Seminoe Reservoir,** offering boaters more than 20,000 surface acres of water with almost 200 miles of shoreline—the largest reservoir in
the entire state park system. In addition to the park's three boat ramps, you'll
also find launching facilities, as well as fuel, supplies, and state fishing licenses,
at the nearby marina operated by the **Seminoe Boat Club** (307-320-3043), 10
miles southeast of the park. Along with boating and water sports, this reservoir is
popular for swimming (several sandy beaches), fishing (brown trout, cutthroat
trout, rainbow trout, and walleye), and camping (three campgrounds). You'll also
find playgrounds and picnicking facilities, as well as ample opportunities for
viewing both wildlife and gorgeous natural scenery, including sand dunes. (See
also Seminoe to Alcova Scenic Backway under *To See—Scenic Drives* in "Central
Wyoming: Oregon Trail–Rendezvous Country.")

Sulphur Creek Park (307-789-1770; www.evanstonwy.org/parkrec/parks_
sulphur.asp?id=251), 12 miles south of Evanston on WY 150. Open year-round
for day-use only; free. The park's main feature, Sulphur Creek Reservoir, is a
popular destination for boaters and anglers alike. The area has a boat dock as
well as developed picnic facilities, including a grill. Restrooms are available, but
there is no running water. Windsurfing is popular here as well.

See also Saratoga under *To See—Towns;* BEAR (Better Environment And River
project) Parkway under *Bicycling;* Curt Gowdy State Park and Lions Park under
Wilder Places—Parks; Medicine Bow National Forest under *Wilder Places—
Forests;* Flaming Gorge National Recreation Area and Bureau of Land Management under *Wilder Places—Other Wild Places;* Windy Hills Bed and Breakfast
under *Lodging—Bed & Breakfasts;* Fontenelle Reservoir under *To Do—Boating*
in "West Wyoming: Jackson Hole–Jim Bridger Country"; and Pathfinder Reservoir and Alcova Reservoir under *To Do—Boating* in "Central Wyoming: Oregon
Trail–Rendezvous Country."

CAMPING ♿ **BLM campgrounds** (see Bureau of Land Management under
Wilder Places—Other Wild Places) in this region include six developed campgrounds managed by the **Rawlins Field Office.** Two of these are **Bennett Peak**
(handicapped accessible; open June 1 through November 15; $7) and **Corral
Creek** (open June 1 through November 15; free), accessible by taking Exit 235
off I-80 and going south on WY 130 about 40 miles to Riverside and then east on
WY 230 for about 4 miles. Go left (northeast) on C.R. 660 for about 12 miles,
and then go left (northwest) on BLM 3404 for about 6 miles to reach Corral
Creek and 7 miles to reach Bennett Peak. This beautiful area lies on the banks
of the North Platte River (see *Fishing*), providing great fishing access complete
with a boat ramp for floating access, as well as opportunities to hike, horseback
ride (bring your own horses—but they're not allowed in Bennett Peak Campground), picnic, and view wildlife. The **Rock Springs Field Office** manages

several campgrounds and recreation areas as well, including **Three Patches Recreation Area,** a popular spot for picnicking that also allows primitive camping (free), accessible by taking WY 430 southeast out of Rock Springs to Aspen Mountain Road (C.R. 27) and following this south for about 10 miles to reach the area. (See also Lake Hattie–Twin Buttes Reservoirs under *Boating;* the Encampment River under *Fishing;* and Bureau of Land Management under *Wilder Places—Other Wild Places.*)

&. **Medicine Bow National Forest** (see also *Wilder Places—Forests*) has two ranger districts in this region. The **Brush Creek–Hayden Ranger District** has two offices, one in **Saratoga** (307-326-5258) along WY 130 and one in **Encampment** (307-327-5481) at 204 W. 9th Street. This ranger district manages 14 developed campgrounds and provides plenty of opportunities for dispersed camping (free). **Lincoln Park** (handicapped accessible; open June 15 through October; $10), a first-come, first-served campground, is easily accessed by going east on WY 130 from Saratoga for about 20 miles and then north on F.R. 100 for less than 3 miles. Eight more developed campgrounds lie just off WY 130 east of Saratoga (some are in the Laramie Ranger District). A number of additional developed campgrounds can be accessed off WY 70 southwest of Encampment, including **Bottle Creek** (open June through October; $10), a first-come, first-served campground accessed by taking WY 70 southwest from Encampment for 7 miles and then going south on F.R. 550 for about 0.25 mile. Visitors can find information about the district, including campgrounds, by calling the **Brush Creek Visitor Center** (307-326-5562). The **Laramie Ranger District** (307-745-2300), 2468 Jackson Street, Laramie, manages more than 20 developed campgrounds in this region and offers plenty of opportunities for dispersed camping (free). Some of these campgrounds lie along or just off WY 130 (see above). Additional campgrounds lie southwest of Laramie and are accessible off WY 230. You'll also find a couple of developed campgrounds just off I-80 at Exit 323, southeast of Laramie, then north on WY 210 or F.R. 712. Almost all of the campgrounds in this ranger district are open seasonally and charge a $10 per night fee. (See also Vedauwoo Recreation Area under *To See—Natural Wonders;* Hog Park Reservoir under *Boating;* the Medicine Bow River under *Fishing;* Platte River Trail under *Hiking;* and Flaming Gorge National Recreation Area under *Wilder Places—Other Wild Places.*)

See also Saratoga under *To See—Towns;* Seminoe State Park under *Boating;* Curt Gowdy State Park under *Wilder Places—Parks;* and Elk Mountain Hotel and Terry Bison Ranch Resort under *Lodging—Other Options.*

FISHING **The Encampment River** (307-745-4046; http://gf.state.wy.us/fish/fishing/index.asp) flows from the Rockies across the Colorado border north through the Encampment Wilderness of Medicine Bow National Forest (see *Camping* and *Wilder Places—Forests*), eventually joining the North Platte River (see below). You can access the Encampment River via the Encampment River Trail (#470) by taking F.R. 496 south from F.R. 550 at Hog Park Reservoir (see *Boating*). This trail, closed to motorized vehicles, takes you through the Encampment Wilderness Area along the banks of the Encampment River, running for about 15 miles to a point just south of the town of Encampment (see *To See—Towns*). At that end, the trail and the river are accessible via BLM 3407 off C.R. 353. The trailhead departs from the BLM-managed **Encampment River Campground** (open June 1 through November 15; $7), which provides great fishing and floating access. Fish species include brown trout and rainbow trout.

The Green River (307-367-4352; http://gf.state.wy.us/fish/fishing/index.asp) originates from the Green River Lakes in the Bridger Wilderness of the Wind River Range, in Bridger–Teton National Forest (see *Wilder Places—Forests* in "Central Wyoming: Oregon Trail–Rendezvous Country"). The river arcs south and continues for 730 miles, eventually emptying into the Colorado River in Utah. In this lower portion of the Green River, before it enters Flaming Gorge Reservoir, it flows through the town of Green River, where you'll find easy access from numerous parks along the river's banks, including Evers Park, Expedition Island Park, Green Belt Nature Area, and Scotts Bottom Nature Area. The nature areas also include unpaved trails with interpretive signs. Fish species include brown trout, catfish, cutthroat trout, kokanee salmon, and rainbow trout. (See also Green River Whitewater Park under *Paddling/Floating;* Flaming Gorge National Recreation Area under *Wilder Places—Other Wild Places;* and the Green River under *To Do—Fishing* in "West Wyoming: Jackson Hole–Jim Bridger Country.")

The Laramie River (307-745-4046; http://gf.state.wy.us/fish/fishing/index.asp) flows from the Rocky Mountains in Colorado north through Laramie, continuing north to eventually join the North Platte River. Much of the river flows through private land, making access for the most part difficult. In addition to the Laramie River Greenbelt (see *Bicycling*), you can access the river from several signed Wyoming Game and Fish Department designated access sites off WY 230 and WY 130 southwest of Laramie. Fish species include brown trout and rainbow trout.

The Medicine Bow River (307-745-4046; http://gf.state.wy.us/fish/fishing/index.asp) flows from the Medicine Bow Mountains in the south, north to the town of Medicine Bow, where it arcs to the west and flows into Seminoe Reservoir (see Seminoe State Park under *Boating*). Much of the river flows through private land, making access difficult, with the exception of the portions that are found in Medicine Bow National Forest (see *Wilder Places—Forests*). Probably the easiest access comes by taking Exit 255 off I-80 and heading south past Elk Mountain, then proceeding south for about 16 miles on F.R. 101 (Medicine Bow Ranger Station Road) to **Bow River Campground** (open June through October; $10).

The North Platte River (307-473-3400; http://gf.state.wy.us/fish/fishing/index.asp) originates in northern Colorado, flowing north over the Wyoming border along WY 230 and WY 130 before reaching Seminoe Reservoir, then Kortes Reservoir, then Pathfinder Reservoir, and then Alcova Reservoir. From Alcova Reservoir, the river arcs east, flowing alongside WY 220 to Casper, through Casper, and then roughly along I-25 to Glendo Reservoir and Guernsey Reservoir, making a slow turn toward the south to flow southeast along US 26 past Torrington before crossing the border into Nebraska. Fish species include brown trout, cutthroat trout, rainbow trout, and walleye. In this region you'll find numerous river access points, most of which include launching facilities for those interested in floating or paddling as well. Most of these access points are signed by the Wyoming Game and Fish Department, allow overnight camping, and can be found off WY 230 south of Saratoga, off WY 130 north of Saratoga, and near the Fort Fred Steele State Historic Site exit off I-80 (see *To See—Historic Land-marks, Places, and Sites*). (See also Saratoga under *To See—Towns;* BLM camp-grounds under *Camping;* the Encampment River, above; Platte River Trail under *Hiking;* Medicine Bow National Forest under *Wilder Places—Forests;* Harrison's Guest House and Guide Service, and the River Cottages under *Lodging—Other Options;* and the North Platte River under *To Do—Fishing* and *To Do—Paddling/Floating* in "Central Wyoming: Oregon Trail–Rendezvous Country."

See also BEAR (Better Environment And River project) Parkway under *Bicy-cling;* Hog Park Reservoir, Lake Hattie–Twin Buttes Reservoirs, Seminoe State Park, and Sulphur Creek Park under *Boating;* Bear River State Park and Travel Information Center, Curt Gowdy State Park, and Lions Park under *Wilder Places—Parks;* Medicine Bow National Forest under *Wilder Places—Forests;* Bureau of Land Management and Flaming Gorge National Recreation Area under *Wilder Places—Other Wild Places;* Windy Hills Bed and Breakfast under *Lodging—Bed & Breakfasts;* Platt's Guides and Outfitters Rustic Mountain Lodge under *Lodging—Lodges;* Mountain View Historic Hotel and Terry Bison Ranch Resort under *Lodging—Other Options;* and Ice Fishing Derby under *Special Events.*

GOLF **Airport Golf Course** (307-637-6418; www.cheyennecity.org/golf.htm), 4801 Central Avenue, Cheyenne, 18 holes.

Cheyenne Country Club (307-637-2230; www.cheyennecountryclub.com), 800 Steiner Road, Cheyenne, 18 holes.

F. E. Warren AFB Golf Club (307-773-3556), 7103 Randall Avenue, Suite 103, Cheyenne, 18 holes.

Jacoby Golf Club (307-745-3111), 30th and Willett, Laramie, 18 holes.

Kingham Prairie View (307-637-6420; www.cheyennecity.org/golf.htm), 3601 Windmill Road, Cheyenne, 9 holes.

Laramie Country Club (307-745-8490), 489 WY 230, Laramie, 9 holes.

Leaning Rock Golf Course (307-245-3746), Beech Street, Pine Bluffs, 9 holes.

Little America Cheyenne Golf Course (1-800-235-6396; 307-775-8400; www.littleamerica.com/cheyenne), 2800 W. Lincolnway, Cheyenne, 9 holes.

Old Baldy Club (307-326-5222), E. Pic Pike Road, Saratoga, 18 holes.

Purple Sage Golf Course (307-789-2383), 19th and Country Club Road, Evanston, 18 holes.

Rochelle Ranch Public Golf Course (307-328-4573), 2808 E. Rochelle Drive, Rawlins, 18 holes.

Rolling Green Country Club (307-875-6200), Country Club Road, off Covered Wagon Road 3 miles west of Green River, 9 holes.

Saratoga Inn Golf Course (1-800-594-0178; 307-326-5261; www.saratogainn .com), 601 E. Pic Pike Road, Saratoga, 9 holes.

Sinclair Golf Club (307-324-7767), R.R. 1, Sinclair, 9 holes.

White Mountain Golf Course (307-352-1415), 1501 Clubhouse Drive, Rock Springs, 18 holes.

HIKING **Continental Divide National Scenic Trail** is a projected 3,100-mile trail that will run from the Canadian border to the border with Mexico along the entire continental divide, passing through lands managed by several organizations. At this time, the trail is still in the process of being constructed and/or restored to a usable standard. In this region of Wyoming, you can access a portion of the trail from Hog Park Reservoir (see *Boating*), where it departs from the campground, heading north through the Sierra Madre Mountains of Medicine Bow National Forest (see *Wilder Places—Forests*). This portion of the trail can also be accessed to the north by taking WY 70 southwest out of Encampment to Battle Pass. The majority of this trail lies in the Huston Park Wilderness, which means that you won't encounter any motorized vehicles on your journey. You'll also find a large portion of the trail on Bureau of Land Management (BLM) lands in Wyoming (see www.wy.blm.gov/Recreation/cdnst/index .htm and *Wilder Places—Other Wild Places*), as it passes right by Rawlins and then arcs around the northern edge of the Great Divide Basin (see *To See—Natural Wonders*). For more information about the trail, contact the **Continental Divide Trail Alliance** (1-888-909-CDTA; 303-838-3760; www.cdtrail.org), P.O. Box 628, Pine, CO 80470.

Lake Marie Falls Trail (#290), an easy, 0.2-mile loop trail, can be accessed by taking WY 130 south from Saratoga for 7.5 miles and then going east on WY 130 for almost 27 miles to the parking area along the Snowy Range Scenic Byway (see *To See—Scenic Drives*). This is a great place to enjoy a picnic lunch either before or after you explore the lovely alpine setting surrounding you. Take a casual stroll along the trail, which brings you closer to Lake Marie's outlet. If you're driving this way, this trail should be on your itinerary, as it's a perfect stopping point for stretching your legs and taking a closer look at the Snowy Range.

Platte River Trail (#473), in Medicine Bow National Forest (see *Camping* and *Wilder Places—Forests*), is accessible by taking WY 230 southeast from Riverside 26 miles to F.R. 492. Go east for about 2 miles to **Six Mile Gap Campground** (open May 15 through October; $10). From here, you can access the North Platte River (see *Fishing*) for both fishing and floating, as well as hiking along the river's shore in the Platte River Wilderness. The 5-mile trail (one-way) involves a steep descent to the river, but then it is fairly level and moderate as you follow the river's course.

See also Pine Bluffs under *To See—Towns;* Wyoming Frontier Prison under *To See—Historic Landmarks, Places, and Sites;* Snowy Range Scenic Byway under

To See—Scenic Drives; Killpecker Sand Dunes and Vedauwoo Recreation Area under *To See—Natural Wonders;* BEAR (Better Environment And River project) Parkway and Greater Cheyenne Greenway under *Bicycling;* Hog Park Reservoir under *Boating;* the Encampment River and the Green River under *Fishing;* Curt Gowdy State Park and Lions Park under *Wilder Places—Parks;* Medicine Bow National Forest under *Camping* and *Wilder Places—Forests;* Bureau of Land Management and Flaming Gorge National Recreation Area under *Wilder Places—Other Wild Places; Lodging;* and Platte Valley Festival of the Birds under *Special Events.*

HORSEBACK RIDING See Killpecker Sand Dunes under *To See—Natural Wonders;* Seminoe State Park under *Boating;* BLM campgrounds under *Camping;* Curt Gowdy State Park under *Wilder Places—Parks;* Medicine Bow National Forest under *Wilder Places—Forests;* Bureau of Land Management and Flaming Gorge National Recreation Area under *Wilder Places—Other Wild Places;* Platt's Guides and Outfitters Rustic Mountain Lodge under *Lodging—Lodges;* and Harrison's Guest House and Guide Service, and Terry Bison Ranch Resort under *Lodging—Other Options.*

HOT SPRINGS ✍ 🐾 **Saratoga Hot Pool** (307-326-8855; www.saratogachamber .info/hotpool.html), just off WY 130, Saratoga. Open 24 hours daily; free. This hot mineral pool—also known as the Hobo Pool—and its healing powers were known to numerous tribes of Native Americans long before the first pioneers set foot in this area. In the 1930s the Civilian Conservation Corps (CCC) constructed the stone pool that you'll find here today. Restrooms and changing areas are located on the premises as well, and the pool welcomes families.

See also **Saratoga Inn** under *Lodging—Other Options.*

PADDLING/FLOATING **Green River Whitewater Park** (1-800-FL-GORGE; 307-875-5711), on the Green River in the town of Green River, features several drops designed and constructed by Coloradoan Gary Lacy. With exciting names like the Electrocutioner, Powell's Plunge, and Castle Falls, these U-drop features are fun for the white-water enthusiast, whether you're a kayaker or a canoeist. Access is easy, particularly from Evers Park and Expedition Island Park (off 2nd Street). (See also the Green River under *Fishing.*)

See also *Boating;* the Encampment River and the North Platte River under *Fishing;* Platte River Trail under *Hiking;* High Plains Outdoor Institute under *Unique Adventures;* Curt Gowdy State Park and Lions Park under *Wilder Places—Parks;* Medicine Bow National Forest under *Wilder Places—Forests;* Bureau of Land Management and Flaming Gorge National Recreation Area under *Wilder Places— Other Wild Places;* Windy Hills Bed and Breakfast under *Lodging—Bed & Breakfasts;* Harrison's Guest House and Guide Service, and the River Cottages under *Lodging—Other Options;* Platte Valley Festival of the Birds under *Special Events;* and the North Platte River under *To Do—Fishing* and *To Do—Paddling/Floating* in "Central Wyoming: Oregon Trail–Rendezvous Country."

Cross-Country Skiing

Cross-country skiing opportunities can be found throughout this region, particularly in **Medicine Bow National Forest** (see *Wilder Places—Forests*), which offers several groomed trails in wintertime ($5). These include a trail system with loops of varying distances and varying levels of difficulty that are easily accessed by taking Exit 323 off I-80 east of Laramie. Trails depart from both the Summit Information Center (see *Guidance*) and from the Tie City Trailhead on WY 210. A **snowshoe trail** can be found here as well. Contact the **Medicine Bow Nordic Association** (www.medbownordic.org) for details, or pick up a free map of the trails from **Cross Country Connection** (307-721-2851), 222 S. 2nd Street, Laramie. For more ideas of where to don your skis, see BEAR (Better Environment And River project) Parkway under *Bicycling; Hiking;* Bear River State Park and Travel Information Center under *Wilder Places—Parks;* Medicine Bow National Forest under *Wilder Places—Forests;* Bureau of Land Management under *Wilder Places—Other Wild Places;* A. Drummond's Ranch Bed and Breakfast, Brooklyn Lodge Bed and Breakfast, and Windy Hills Bed and Breakfast under *Lodging—Bed & Breakfasts;* Platt's Guides and Outfitters Rustic Mountain Lodge, and Snowy Mountain Lodge under *Lodging—Lodges;* Mountain View Historic Hotel and Rainbow Valley Resort under *Lodging—Other Options;* and Sierra Madre Winter Carnival and Snow-Cross Games under *Special Events.*

Downhill Skiing

✧ **Snowy Range Ski and Recreation Area** (1-800-GO-2-SNOW; 307-745-5750; www.snowyrange.com), just west of Centennial off WY 130 in Medicine Bow National Forest (see *Wilder Places—Forests*). Call for hours and days open. Take to the slopes at this lovely local ski area, where you'll find plenty of fun for both skiers and snowboarders, including a half pipe and a terrain park (2004). *Lifts:* one triple chairlift, three double chairlifts, one surface lift. *Trails:* 27 trails—30 percent beginner, 40 percent intermediate, 30 percent expert. *Vertical drop:* 990 feet. *Facilities:* At the base you'll find a new (2004) day lodge with seating for more than 800 people, serving cafeteria-style food. *Ski school:* offers both ski and snowboard lessons for all ages and abilities. *For children:* all-day and half-day ski–snow play programs for kids ages 4–12. *Rates:* $35 adults, $21 children (ages 6–12), $21 seniors (ages 60–69), 70 and older and 5 and under free (child must be accompanied by paying adult); half-day and multiday rates also available.

Wondering where to stay while you ski? See Brooklyn Lodge Bed and Breakfast under *Lodging—Bed & Breakfasts;* Snowy Mountain Lodge under *Lodging—Lodges;* and Mountain View Historic Hotel and Rainbow Valley Resort under *Lodging—Other Options.*

Ice Fishing

Ice fishing opportunities can be found in the many lakes and reservoirs in this region. For ideas of where to go, see Saratoga under *To See—Towns; Boating;* Curt Gowdy State Park under *Wilder Places—Parks; Wilder Places—Forests; Wilder Places—Other Wild Places;* and Ice Fishing Derby under *Special Events.*

Ice-Skating

✍ Ice-skating can be found at a number of locations in this region. In Cheyenne, try the **IKON Ice and Events Center** (see *To See—For Families*). At the **Laramie Community Ice Arena** (307-721-2161; www.ci.laramie.wy.us/recreation/icerink/index.html), 3510 Garfield Street, Laramie, you can skate from October 1 to early March ($3.15; skate rental $2.10). The **Rock Springs Family Recreation Center Ice Arena** (307-352-1445; www.rswy.net/departments/frc_icearena.htm), 3900 Sweetwater Drive, Rock Springs; and **Green River Recreation Center** (307-872-0511; www.cityofgreenriver.org/parksnrec/reccenter.asp), 1775 Hitching Post Drive, Green River, also both offer seasonal ice-skating for a minimal fee. Evanston has a number of outdoor ponds that freeze hard enough for ice-skating as well. (See also Windy Hills Bed and Breakfast under *Lodging—Bed & Breakfasts.*)

Snowmobiling

Snowmobiling opportunities abound in this region, particularly in the Snowy Mountain Range of Medicine Bow National Forest (see *Wilder Places—Forests*), which includes more than 300 miles of designated trails known as the **Snowy Range Trail System. Snowy Mountain Adventures** (1-800-291-5959; www.ridethesnowies.com), 21 Brandt Lane, Foxpark. Foxpark is southwest of Woods Landing (southwest of Laramie via WY 230). It offers guided snowmobile tours as well as snowmobile rentals ($160–210 per driver per day). You can also rent a snowmobile from **Albany Lodge** ($150–180 per driver per day; see *Lodging—Lodges*); they also offer guided tours. (See also Bureau of Land Management under *Wilder Places—Other Wild Places;* Brooklyn Lodge Bed and Breakfast under *Lodging—Bed & Breakfasts;* Platt's Guides and Outfitters Rustic Mountain Lodge, and Snowy Mountain Lodge under *Lodging—Lodges;* and Mountain View Historic Hotel and Rainbow Valley Resort under *Lodging—Other Options.*)

Snowshoeing

Snowshoeing is a great way to explore this region in wintertime, particularly in Medicine Bow National Forest (see *Wilder Places—Forests;* and *Cross-Country Skiing*, above, for details). For more ideas of where to go, check out *Hiking;* Bear River State Park and Travel Information Center under *Wilder Places—Parks;* Medicine Bow National Forest under *Wilder Places—Forests;* Bureau of Land Management and Flaming Gorge National Recreation Area under *Wilder Places—Other Wild Places;* Brooklyn Lodge Bed and Breakfast under *Lodging—Bed & Breakfasts;* Snowy Mountain Lodge under *Lodging—Lodges;* and Mountain View Historic Hotel and Rainbow Valley Resort under *Lodging—Other Options.*

UNIQUE ADVENTURES Cheyenne Street Railway Trolley (1-800-426-5009; 307-778-3133; www.cheyenne.org/trolley.asp), departs from Cheyenne Depot Museum (see *To See—Museums*). One-hour tours run mid-May through mid-September Monday through Friday 10 AM–4 PM, departing on the hour, plus Saturday at 10 AM and 1:30 PM (1.5-hour tour), Sunday at 1:30 PM (1.5-hour tour); $8 adults, $4 children ages 2–12. Whether you don't have a ton of time or you just want to get a quick overview of Cheyenne's historical attractions before exploring them more on your own, this narrated trolley tour provides a convenient introduction to the city. Stops include the Big Boy Steam Engine (the world's largest steam engine), Cheyenne Botanic Gardens, Cheyenne Frontier Days Old West Museum, Nelson Museum of the West, Wyoming State Capitol building, and Wyoming State Museum. The trolley also operates in late October for a historic ghost tour and in late December for a tour of holiday lights; call for details, pricing, and tickets. Narrated horse-drawn carriage rides are available as well.

✔ **High Plains Outdoor Institute** (307-742-0932; www.hpoiadventure.com), 1522 Barratt, Laramie. Whether you're interested in rock climbing at Vedauwoo Recreation Area (see *To See—Natural Wonders*), learning to kayak, or rafting the North Platte River (see *Fishing*), High Plains Outdoor Institute offers a lesson for you. Welcoming total novices as well as those with some experience, this outdoor educator provides instruction on these and other outdoor adventures in this region. Reasonable prices, small student-to-teacher ratios, and incredible scenery and terrain await those interested in learning the basics of these popular extreme sports. The institute also offers guided hikes and backpacking trips, as well as teen-specific lessons and adventures.

Ranch vacations. These vacations usually allow you to participate to a certain extent in various aspects of ranch life, often including cattle herding and branding. The ratio of work time to leisure time varies from ranch to ranch, as do the additional activities and amenities offered, but most ranches include horseback riding, lodging, and meals in an inclusive package deal. In this region, providers include **Brush Creek Ranch** (1-800-726-2499; 307-327-5241), Saratoga; **Bucking S Ranch** (307-325-6250), Rawlins; **Elk Mountain Ranch** (307-348-7440), Elk Mountain; **Kingfisher Bend Ranch** (307-789-4938), Evanston; **Ladder Ranch** (307-383-2418), Savery, which is east of Baggs (on WY 789) and west of Riverside on WY 70 near the Colorado border; **Medicine Bow Lodge and Guest Ranch** (1-800-409-5439; 307-326-5439), Saratoga; **Mountain Meadow Guest Ranch** (307-742-6042), Centennial; **Sierra Madre Guest Ranch** (307-326-5261), Saratoga; **Two Bars Seven Ranch** (307-742-6072), Laramie; and **Vee Bar Guest Ranch** (1-800-483-3227; 307-745-7036), Laramie.

See also **A. Drummond's Ranch Bed and Breakfast** under *Lodging—Bed and Breakfasts* and **Terry Bison Ranch Resort** under *Lodging—Other Options.*

✳ Wilder Places

PARKS ♿ 🐾 ✔ **Bear River State Park and Travel Information Center** (307-789-6547; http://wyoparks.state.wy.us/bear1.htm), 601 Bear River Drive, Evanston (via Exit 6 off I-80). *Park:* Open April 1 through October 31, 8 AM–10 PM; open November 1 through March 31, 8 AM–8 PM. *Visitor center:* Open April 1 through September 30, 8 AM–5 PM; open October 1 through March 31, 9 AM–5 PM; free. If you're looking for a quick place to stop, stretch your legs, and learn a little bit about Wyoming—or you're in search of a longer recreational outing, perhaps involving some wildlife viewing, picnicking, bicycling, cross-country skiing, or fishing (cutthroat trout)—Bear River State Park and Travel Information Center has what you seek. Easily accessed from I-80, the park features two protected, captive herds of Wyoming native mammals—**bison and elk**—as well as a helpful information center. Nearly 3 miles of trails (1.2 miles paved) afford hiking, biking, and cross-country skiing opportunities, linking into the Evanston Parks and Recreation Department's BEAR Parkway system of trails (see *To Do—Bicycling*). Children will enjoy playing on the playground equipment as well. (See also Bear River Rendezvous under *Special Events*.)

& ✐ ❀ **Cheyenne Botanic Gardens** (307-637-6458; www.botanic.org), 710 S. Lions Park Drive, Cheyenne. Gardens open daily dawn to dusk; conservatory open weekdays 8 AM–4:30 PM, weekends 11 AM–3:30 PM; donations gladly accepted. Both outside and inside, this tribute to all things verdant stimulates your senses with a rainbow of colors and scents. Stroll through perfectly maintained outdoor gardens, including a xeriscape garden, rose garden, herb garden, cactus garden, and a cool, interactive sensory garden. The indoor exhibits thrive on renewable energy—the conservatory is heated entirely by solar power, and half of its electricity is derived from solar power as well. The majority of the gardens' upkeep comes from the work of volunteers, including senior citizens, children, and the handicapped. (See also Lions Park, below.)

✐ & **Curt Gowdy State Park** (307-632-7946; http://wyoparks.state.wy.us/curt1 .htm), 1351 Hynds Lodge Road, 24 miles west of Cheyenne and 23 miles east of Laramie via WY 210 (Happy Jack Road). Open year-round for day-use and camping; day-use $2 per vehicle (residents), $4 per vehicle (nonresidents); camping $4 per vehicle (residents), $8 per vehicle (nonresidents). This state park sits on grounds long used by multiple Indian tribes as camping grounds when scouting for buffalo. In addition to this historical tie, the park is also home to **Hynds Lodge,** listed on the National Register of Historic Places, which was built in 1922–23 for the Boy Scouts. Today the structure can be reserved for group events, as it includes a kitchen, sleeping facilities, a dining area, and a covered porch (contact the park for information). The park has opportunities for boating (two ramps), fishing (handicapped-accessible pier), paddling, and swimming on **Granite Lake Reservoir** and **Crystal Lake Reservoir.** Additional attractions include hiking trails (6.2 miles), two playgrounds, picnicking, horseback riding trails, camping, and wildlife-watching. (See also Happy Jack Bluegrass Festival under *Special Events*.)

BEAR RIVER STATE PARK

& ✐ ❀ **Lions Park** (307-637-6429; www.cheyennecity.org/ park_facility_ guide.htm), 8th Avenue and Carey Avenue, Cheyenne. Lions Park is one of 17 municipal parks managed by the City of Cheyenne Parks Division. This showpiece of the parks system includes a bike path, a beach and lake, fishing, boating (canoes and paddleboats for rent), an indoor swimming pool with a waterslide, picnicking facilities, a handicapped-accessible fitness trail, the **Cheyenne Botanic Gardens** (see above), miniature golf, playground equipment, and athletic facilities. The park is also home to Engine 1242, the oldest locomotive in Wyoming. The engine was built in New Jersey in 1890. Following its retirement in the mid-1950s, it was donated to the city of Cheyenne by the Union Pacific Railroad.

See also Wyoming Children's Museum and Nature Center under *To See—For Families;* Seminoe State Park and Sulphur Creek Park under *To Do—Boating;* and the Green River under *To Do—Fishing.*

FORESTS **Medicine Bow National Forest** (307-745-2300; www.fs.fed.us/r2/mbr), 2468 Jackson Street, Laramie. With the exception of the area managed by the **Douglas Ranger District** (see listing in "Central Wyoming: Oregon Trail–Rendezvous Country"), this region lays claim to the portions of the nearly 3 million acres of land included in the jointly managed Medicine Bow–Routt national forests that lie north of the Colorado border: Medicine Bow National Forest.

Included in Medicine Bow National Forest are several relatively small wilderness areas: **Encampment River Wilderness, Huston Park Wilderness, Platte River Wilderness,** and **Savage Run Wilderness.** Chief features of the forest in this region include the **Snowy Range** (part of the Medicine Bow Mountains), the **Sierra Madre Mountains,** and **Vedauwoo Recreation Area** (see *To See—Natural Wonders*). The forest's recreational opportunities include boating, fishing, hiking, mountain biking, camping, paddling/floating, picnicking, rock climbing, off-road vehicle travel (ATVs and snowmobiles), horseback riding, snow sports, hunting, wildlife viewing, and more.

See also Hog Park Reservoir under *To Do—Boating; To Do—Camping;* the Encampment River, the Medicine Bow River, and the North Platte River under *To Do—Fishing; To Do—Hiking; To Do—Snow Sports;* Flaming Gorge National Recreation Area under *Other Wild Places;* Brooklyn Lodge Bed and Breakfast under *Lodging—Bed & Breakfasts;* Snowy Mountain Lodge under *Lodging—Lodges;* and Historic Woods Landing Resort, Mountain View Historic Hotel, and Rainbow Valley Resort under *Lodging—Other Options.*

CHEYENNE BOTANIC GARDENS

WILDLIFE REFUGES AND AREAS Bamforth, Hutton Lake, and Mortenson Lake National Wildlife Refuges (970-723-8202; http://arapaho.fws.gov) are small refuges located west of Laramie. (Bamforth and Mortenson refuges are currently closed to the public.) Hutton Lake, located about 8 miles southwest of Laramie via C.R. 34 (Sand Creek Road), provides the visitor with the opportunity to view wildlife daily from dawn to dusk (free) at the five lakes included in the refuge. Migratory waterfowl, shorebirds, and raptors are often seen, and several white-tailed prairie dog towns inhabit this area as well.

Seedskadee National Wildlife Refuge (307-875-2187; http://seedskadee.fws .gov), accessible by taking WY 372 northwest from Green River for 27 miles, is a tremendous place for wildlife viewing and solitude. Situated on a 35-mile stretch of the Green River, this 22,000-acre wildlife refuge is home to antelope, moose, and mule deer, as well as hundreds of bird species, including trumpeter swans, golden eagles, and sage grouse. You might also stumble upon the ruins of a pioneer cabin or two, as this area was briefly inhabited by pioneers in the late 1800s.

See also Saratoga under *To See—Towns.*

OTHER WILD PLACES & **Bureau of Land Management (BLM)** (307-775-6256; www.wy.blm.gov), 5353 Yellowstone, P.O. Box 1828, Cheyenne 82009. Responsible for managing more than 18 million surface acres of land in the state of Wyoming, along with more than 23 million acres of federal mineral estate, the Wyoming BLM is headquartered in this region. The **Wyoming Information Desk** (phone number above) operates Monday through Friday 7:45 AM–4:30 PM. Also on the premises is the **Public Room,** open Monday through Friday 9 AM–4 PM. In addition, two field offices are located in this region: the **Rawlins Field Office** (307-328-4200; www.wy.blm.gov/rfo/index.htm), 1300 N. 3rd, Rawlins, responsible for managing 3.5 million acres of public lands and 4.5 millions acres of federal mineral estate; and the **Rock Springs Field Office** (307-352-0256; www.wy.blm.gov/rsfo/index.htm), 280 US 191 N., Rock Springs, responsible for managing more than 3.6 million acres of public lands and more than 3.5 million acres of federal mineral estate. On BLM lands in this region, you'll find a number of natural wonders, including the **Great Divide Basin, Killpecker Sand Dunes, Red Desert** (see *To See—Natural Wonders*), and **wild horses** (see **wild horse tours** under *To See—Scenic Drives*), as well as portions of the historic emigrant trails that passed this way (see **National Historic Trails Center** under *To See—Museums* in "Central Wyoming: Oregon Trail–Rendezvous Country"). Much of the lands administered by the BLM are open to recreational pursuits, including bicycling, boating, camping (both primitive and developed; most developed campgrounds are handicapped accessible), fishing, hiking (see also **Continental Divide National Scenic Trail** under *To Do—Hiking*), horseback riding, paddling, rock climbing, wildlife viewing (including wild horses), and snow sports, including snowmobiling and cross-country skiing. BLM lands tend to be the most unregulated of public lands, which means that most typical outdoor recreational pursuits are allowed on most BLM lands, guided by the dictates of **Leave No Trace** (1-800-332-4100; 303-442-8222; www.lnt.org) outdoor ethics. To find out more general information about the BLM lands in this region, including maps, developed campgrounds, and other recreational pursuits, contact the appropriate field office. (See also **Lake Hattie/ Twin Buttes Reservoirs** under *To Do—Boating; To Do—Camping;* and **the Encampment River** under *To Do—Fishing.*)

&. **Flaming Gorge National Recreation Area** (435-784-3445; www.fs.fed.us/ r4/ashley/recreation/flaming_gorge/index.shtml), along WY 530 south of Green River. Open year-round; day-use $2 per day in managed areas; see information about camping below. **Green River Flaming Gorge Visitor Center** (307-875-2871; southwest on WY 530) is open Monday through Saturday 8 AM–4:30 PM. Managed by Ashley National Forest (which is mostly in Utah), the Flaming Gorge National Recreation Area offers several recreational opportunities in an area of land that straddles the Wyoming and Utah border, with the majority of developed services in Utah. The chief feature of this area is the enormous **Flaming Gorge Reservoir,** with its 42,000-acre surface area, 300 miles of shoreline, and its length of 91 miles, which was created in the early 1960s by the construction of the **Flaming Gorge Dam,** damming the Green River. Flaming Gorge itself received its name from the famed explorer John Wesley Powell, who deemed it thus upon viewing the brilliantly hued sandstone walls of the canyon during his 1869 exploration of the area. Popular activities include fishing (brown trout, channel catfish, cutthroat trout, kokanee salmon, mackinaw trout, rainbow trout, and smallmouth bass), boating (in Wyoming, numerous access sites for launching located at the end of dirt roads off WY 530, including **Buckboard Marina,** 25 miles southwest of Green River off WY 530, which also rents boats), and camping. Some sites are reservable by calling 1-877-444-6777 or visiting www.reserveusa.com, including **Buckboard Campground** (handicapped accessible; $14), located 23 miles southwest of Green River via WY 530 to F.R. 009, then 1.5 miles southeast to the campground; and **Firehole Campground** (handicapped accessible; $14), located 23 miles south of Rock Springs on US 191. Hiking, biking, horseback riding, picnicking, and snow sports are also permitted in the area. For more information, contact the **Flaming Gorge Corporation** (435-784-3483) or visit them online at www.flaminggorge.com. (See also the Green River under *To Do—Fishing* and **Flaming Gorge Days** under *Special Events.*)

See also **Terry Bison Ranch Resort** under *Lodging—Other Options.*

✳ Lodging

BED & BREAKFASTS

Centennial 82005

Brooklyn Lodge Bed and Breakfast (307-742-6916; www.brooklyn lodge.com), 3540 WY 130. Situated in a historic mountain lodge high in the Snowy Mountains of southern Wyoming, this B&B provides luxurious western comfort and personal attention to your every need. The lodge accommodates a maximum of two couples per night in its two guest rooms, each featuring satellite television, a king-size bed, a DVD player, western decor, and cedar closets. From the enormous, filling ranch breakfast served fireside each morning to the afternoon's fresh-baked cookies and the delectable chocolates that greet you at bedtime, you will be delighted by the food. As for the views and the solitude, they are simply enchanting—the lodge rests between two trout streams, with views of mountain meadows and ample opportunities for wildlife-watching. Constructed by two of Buffalo Bill Cody's sidekicks, this lodge is listed on the National Register of Historic Places ($150).

Cheyenne

A. Drummond's Ranch Bed and Breakfast (307-634-6042; www.adrummond.com), 399 Happy Jack Road, Cheyenne 82007. Creating an out-of-the-ordinary bed & breakfast experience, this unique accommodation includes 120 acres of land situated near thousands upon thousands of acres in Medicine Bow National Forest (see *Wilder Places—Forests*). You'll enjoy one of four guest rooms, which include access to peaceful outdoor hot tubs and decks, as well as complimentary snacks and beverages. If you're interested, the B&B can coordinate unique adventures that can include llama trekking, bottle feeding llama babies, cross-country skiing, mountain biking (rentals available), and more. Or you can plan your own adventures and just enjoy the luxurious accommodations and delicious breakfasts served on fine china each morning ($70–160).

✍ **Howdy Pardner Bed and Breakfast** (307-634-6493; www.howdypardner.net), 1920 Tranquility Road, Cheyenne 82009. Just 10 minutes from the hustle and bustle of downtown Cheyenne, you'll find this hillside retreat, promising you the best of both worlds. Enjoy quick access to all of the capital city's attractions, but start and end each day of your vacation in the comfort and peace of the Howdy Pardner. The three guest rooms all include queen-size beds, private baths, TV/VCR, phones, and western decor throughout. For the more adventurous of spirit, an Old West sheepherder's wagon can provide your overnight accommodation as well, with easy access to restroom facilities in the main house. A full ranch breakfast is included in the rates ($65–115).

&. **Nagle Warren Mansion Bed and Breakfast** (1-800-811-2610; 307-637-3333; www.naglewarrenmansion.com), 222 E. 17th Street, Cheyenne 82001. Built in 1888 for Erasmus Nagle, this incredible Victorian mansion also was the home of Wyoming notable Francis E. Warren, who served as the state's governor and as a U.S. senator. A complete renovation and restoration of this architectural icon was finished in 1999. Today it provides a full range of modern amenities to its guests while retaining a historic authenticity throughout. Twelve luxuriously furnished guest rooms—six in the main house and six in the adjacent carriage house—all include private baths, private phones, televisions, and access to a hot tub. Guests enjoy a full gourmet breakfast served daily, and an English high tea—complete with the staff dressed in 19th-century costumes—is served on Friday and Saturday ($99–168).

&. ✍ 🐾 **Rainsford Inn Bed and Breakfast** (307-638-2337; www.rainsfordinnbedandbreakfast.com), 219 E. 18th Street, Cheyenne 82001. Listed on the National Register of Historic Places, this charming Victorian home is conveniently situated right in the middle of Cheyenne's Rainsford Historic District. It's a great base if you're exploring the city's many historical attractions, as you'll be staying in one of them! Each of the inn's seven rooms includes period decor, a private bath, cable television, and a private phone line. Guests also enjoy a full homemade breakfast served daily ($40–85.50).

&. ✎ **Windy Hills Bed and Breakfast** (1-877-946-3944; 307-632-6423; www.windyhillswyo.com), 393 Happy Jack Road, Cheyenne 82007. Overlooking Granite Lake, this lovely mountain retreat lies at 7,200 feet in the Snowy Range between Cheyenne and Laramie. You'll have a number of options about where you sleep, ranging from multibedroom private homes to suites in the main house (all of which feature private entrances as well). Two unique spa houses include private steam rooms, outdoor Jacuzzis, and see-through ceiling domes that create a romantic way to sleep under the stars in cozy comfort. Whatever accommodation you choose, you'll enjoy access right outside your door to numerous recreational opportunities, including hiking and mountain biking trails, fishing, cross-country skiing, paddling, boating, ice-skating, and more ($75–200).

See also **the Plains Hotel** under *Other Options*.

Encampment–Riverside 82325
✎ **Grand & Sierra Bed and Breakfast** (307-327-5200; www.wyoming bnb-ranchrec.com/GrandSierra.html), 1016 Lomax, P.O. Box 312, Encampment. Stunning scenery and vast solitude welcome you at this modern log B&B, where you'll stay in one of five locally themed guest rooms (two with

private baths) that hearken to the area's mining history. You'll enjoy access to the outdoor hot tub, plus tremendous views of the Encampment River Canyon and the Sierra Madre Mountains. You can relax in your own room or in the comfortable den with its pool table, rock fireplace, and television. A full country breakfast is included in the rates ($50–99).

✎ **Old Depot Bed and Breakfast** (1-877-619-6677; 307-327-5277; www.oldedepot.com), 201 N. 1st Street, Riverside. Housed in a meticulously renovated train station, this B&B accommodation lets you get up close and intimate with the area's historic ties to the railroad—while you enjoy the relaxed comfort of one of three guest rooms, all with private baths. You'll enjoy the property's amenities, too, which include an on-site fitness center, a hot tub, and a lovely wraparound deck. A full breakfast served daily is included in the rate ($50–100).

See also **Platt's Guides and Outfitters Rustic Mountain Lodge,** and **Spirit West River Lodge** under *Lodges*.

Evanston 82930
Pine Gables Inn Bed and Breakfast (307-789-2069; www.pine gablesinn.com), 1049 Center Street. Graceful Victorian splendor awaits you at this beautifully appointed B&B, constructed in 1883 for notable businessman Anthony V. Quinn. Each meticulously appointed and renovated guest room—six in total—includes a private bathroom with a pedestal sink, a TV/VCR, and a telephone. Three of the rooms have working fireplaces as well, and all include carefully chosen period decor. Listed on the National

Register of Historic Places, the B&B is part of Historic Downtown Evanston (a National Historic District). You'll enjoy a full gourmet breakfast served daily in the dining room ($75–155). *Note:* This property was for sale at press time, so be sure to call for the latest information.

Laramie
The Brick Bed and Breakfast
(1-800-788-4626; 307-745-4390; www .wyomingcompanion.com/thebrick bb), 102 S. 5th Street (at University), Laramie 82072. In a 1905 foursquare brick house, you'll enjoy staying in a historic Laramie residence, complete with four comfortable, cozy bedrooms (shared baths) featuring rustic yet luxurious decor. The house situates you within easy walking distance of both the University of Wyoming campus and Laramie's historic downtown. Guests enjoy a full breakfast served daily, as well as brownies and beverages served upon their arrival ($89–109).

Home Ranch Bed and Breakfast
(307-745-6010), 15 Millbrook Road, Laramie 82070. On a ranch near the lovely Snowy Mountains, you'll find this peaceful country house—a perfect, restful retreat to make your home away from home. Four non-smoking guest rooms (some with shared baths, some with private baths) are offered, and a continental breakfast is included in the rates. You'll enjoy seclusion and ample opportunities for wildlife viewing ($50–100).

⅍ ✐ Vee Bar Guest Ranch Bed and Breakfast
(1-800-483-3227; 307-745-7036; www.veebar.com), 2091 WY 130, Laramie 82070. Listed on the National Register of Historic Places, the Vee Bar Guest Ranch serves as both a bed & breakfast accommodation and an inclusive ranch vacation proprietor. B&B guests stay in one of six riverside suites or in one of three cabins, enjoying a full breakfast, access to the hot tub, and catch-and-release fishing privileges. The riverside suites each feature two bedrooms and a full bathroom, while each of the cabins has two or three sleeping areas, plus a full bathroom ($100–150). B&B guests can also make reservations to dine at the ranch for lunch and dinner.

Rawlins 82301
Rimrock Lodge
(1-877-995-6343; 307-324-8857), 717 Scarlet Drive. This B&B stresses its Christian environment to its guests, offering three bedrooms with shared baths in a setting of pastoral comfort. Guests are welcome to spend time in the various common areas in the three-story log home, including an exercise room, a living area with a fireplace, a hot tub, and the "entertainment room," with its big-screen television. From the home's perch, you can take in beautiful views of Elk Mountain and the surrounding environment of Wyoming's Red Desert. A buffet breakfast is served every morning ($75–100 plus).

Rock Springs
✐ Spring Creek Ranch Bed and Breakfast
(307-350-3005; www .quickbyte.com/springcreek; mailing address: P.O. Box 199, Dutch John, UT 84023), 550 US 191, Minnies Gap (south of Rock Springs near the Colorado border). Open April 1 through November 1. This working ranch offers you the opportunity to enjoy a bona fide country experience while still savoring the comforts of a homey and welcoming western atmosphere.

Treat yourselves and the kids to a TV-free vacation accommodation, whether you stay in the cabin, which includes a private bath, double bed, and bunk bed ($100), or one of seven rooms in the lodge that share baths ($80). You'll enjoy a full, home-style breakfast served daily, and this B&B also offers chuck-wagon cookouts every Friday and Saturday night.

Saratoga 82331
 The Hood House Bed and Breakfast (307-326-8901; www .hoodhousebnb.com), 214 N. 3rd Street. Built in 1892, this charming Victorian B&B also happens to be one of the oldest homes in Saratoga. The four comfortably decorated guest bedrooms share two bathrooms, with guests enjoying access to all of the B&B's facilities, including the kitchen. You are also welcome to play croquet in the yard or go for a bike ride on one of the B&B's bicycles. A full breakfast is served daily and included in the rate ($90–100).

LODGES

Albany
 Albany Lodge (307-745-5782; www.albanylodge.com; mailing address: 1148 WY 11, Laramie 82070). Located at 1148 WY 11, 35 miles southwest of Laramie and 12 miles south of Centennial. Situated at the foot of the Snowy Mountain Range, this rustic lodge, new in 2003, includes nine comfortable guest rooms with private bathrooms ($70), as well as one cabin with a kitchenette sleeping up to four ($100) and a two-bedroom, two-bathroom house ($350). An on-premises restaurant serves up home-cooked fare for breakfast, lunch, and dinner. Albany Lodge also rents snowmobiles and offers guided

tours (see *To Do—Snow Sports*), providing easy access to nearby snowmobile trails.

Centennial 82055
 Snowy Mountain Lodge (1-866-GO-SNOWY; 307-742-7669; www .snowymountainlodge.com), 3474 WY 130. Constructed in 1927, this historic log lodge features 9,000 square feet of majestic mountain beauty, harmonizing with its wild surroundings in Medicine Bow National Forest. Once used as a science camp by the University of Wyoming, this lodge and its cabins were transformed into comfortable visitor accommodations, beginning in 2001. With three styles of cabins to choose from, ranging from basic to luxurious, the Snowy Mountain Lodge caters to its outdoor-loving visitors year-round. All of the cabins were newly remodeled and redecorated late in 2004 ($50–100). The lodge rents out snowmobiles, has fueling services, and offers guided snowmobile tours as well. You can also dine at the on-premises Three Horned Rhino Eat'n Place Restaurant, serving upscale western fare for breakfast, lunch, and dinner.

Encampment–Riverside 82325
 Platt's Guides and Outfitters Rustic Mountain Lodge (307-327-5539; www.plattoutfitting.com/cabinlo.htm), Star Route Box 49, Encampment. Located 12 miles southeast of Encampment off WY 230. You have a number of options when you stay at this beautiful working ranch near the Colorado border. You can choose a bed 'n' breakfast experience, booking one of the three large guest rooms in the modern log lodge that share two private baths ($65). Also available is a separate, private cabin, complete with all of the

modern amenities a traveler could wish for: two bedrooms, a full kitchen, a living room, and a bathroom (but no television or phone—you want to get away, right?). The cabin is available by the week ($1,380). You can also take advantage of the lodge's experienced outfitting service, which can provide guided horseback rides (minimum 2 hours; advance reservations required), pack trips, hunting, fishing, and more. Additional recreational opportunities include trails suited for hiking, biking, cross-country skiing, and snowmobiling.

Spirit West River Lodge (1-888-289-8321; 307-327-5753; www.spiritwestriverlodge.com; mailing address: P.O. Box 605, Encampment). Located 0.25 mile east of Riverside. On the banks of the Encampment River (see *To Do—Fishing*), you'll find this hidden escape from the daily rat race, which offers you a bed & breakfast experience in a one-of-a-kind setting. Here you'll stay in one of four rooms in a rustic, one-story log lodge, all of which feature carefully chosen western decor, two entrances apiece, and private bathrooms. Not only does a complete breakfast (served outside if the weather allows it) come with your stay, but you'll also be served a delectable selection of hors d'oeuvres every evening. Guests enjoy easy access to the abundant recreational opportunities surrounding this beautiful property ($85).

Rawlins 82301

& ♫ **The Lodge at Rawlins** (1-877-729-5467; 307-324-2783; www.thelodgeatrawlins.com), 1801 E. Cedar. This is really a hotel rather than a true country lodge, but it's nonetheless a good option if you're staying in Rawlins. More than 130 newly

remodeled hotel-style rooms and suites, which include private bathrooms and cable television, welcome guests to relax and get a good night's sleep ($45–80). In warmer weather, two outdoor pools offer recreation, as do complimentary passes to the Rawlins Recreation Center, available for all hotel guests. The Fat Boys Bar and Grill, located on the premises, serves home-style American food for breakfast, lunch, and dinner.

OTHER OPTIONS

Centennial 82055

& ♫ **Mountain View Historic Hotel** (1-888-400-9953; 307-742-5476; www.mtnviewhotel.com), WY 130 (6 miles from Snowy Range Ski Area and 27 miles west of Laramie), P.O. Box 328. Constructed in 1907, this historic hotel has been fully restored to ensure the comfort of its guests in modern accommodations while retaining its vibrant history. You'll sleep in a hand-peeled log bed in a traditional hotel room, complete with private bath, direct television, VCR, and refrigerator ($55–100). Easy access to the ski area is a bonus, as is the access right out your door to more than 300 miles of snowmobile trails in Medicine Bow National Forest (see *Wilder Places—Forests*), as well as plenty of trails for snowshoeing and cross-country skiing. Also on the premises you can enjoy homemade meals (breakfast and lunch) in the café and coffee shop, which can even pack you a lunch to go.

♫ **Rainbow Valley Resort** (307-745-0368; www.rainbowvalleyresort.com), 75 Rainbow Valley Road, P.O. Box 303. This mountain resort features six individual cabins that vary in size and price, but all include TV/VCR, a fully equipped kitchen, a private bathroom, and a propane grill. Options range from the one-room Aspen Cabin (similar to a hotel room) to the 1,100-square-foot Saratoga Cabin, which includes two bedrooms (five queen-size beds total) and two full bathrooms ($75–210). Nearby you'll find the Snowy Range Ski Area, as well as easy access to the more than 300 miles of snowmobile trails in Medicine Bow National Forest (see *Wilder Places—Forests*), as well as plenty of trails for snowshoeing, cross-country skiing, hiking, and mountain biking.

See also **Prospector Dining Room at the Old Corral Hotel and Steakhouse** under *Eating Out*.

Cheyenne
& **The Plains Hotel** (1-866-275-2467; 307-638-3311; www.theplains hotel.com), 1600 Central Avenue, Cheyenne 82001. This historic hotel, constructed in 1911, once housed cattle barons and other upscale visitors passing through the city. Today you can revisit the splendor in the newly remodeled version of this mainstay of Cheyenne's lodging facilities, situated right in the heart of Cheyenne's historic downtown. Across the street from the hotel, you can start your explorations with Cheyenne Depot Museum (see *To See—Museums*), housed in the old Union Pacific Railroad depot. Stay in one of 100 luxurious hotel rooms with custom-designed western decor, or choose from one of 30 suites and spread out a little more ($49–259). Package deals, including bed & breakfast packages, spa packages, and theater packages, are available. You'll enjoy access to an on-site fitness center and business center, Adora Spa (a full-service day spa), the Trail Coffee Shoppe (serving

Starbucks coffee), and the Capitol Grille, serving fine western cuisine for breakfast, lunch, and dinner.

& ☙ **Terry Bison Ranch Resort** (307-634-4171; www.terrybison ranch.com), 51 I-25 Service Road E., Cheyenne 82007. Not your typical vacation destination, the Terry Bison Ranch offers the unique opportunity to stay and play on a 27,500-acre working buffalo ranch. Accommodation options include cabins, a bunkhouse, RV campsites, and tent campsites (call for current pricing; overnight stays available year-round). The ranch's amenities and attractions include Wyoming's first winery (situated on the premises), the Brass Buffalo Saloon and Senator's Restaurant specializing in—appropriately—buffalo entrées (with other menu items featuring steaks, seafood, poultry, and more), weekly summer rodeos, chuck-wagon dinners, horseback riding, pony rides for children, wagon rides, guided wagon tours or 1-hour motorized driving tours of the buffalo ranch (which is also home to emus, ostriches, and peacocks, among other animals), and trout fishing on a private lake (that list should keep you busy for a while, no?). The Terry Trading Post sells bison meat and wine from the winery, among other items.

Elk Mountain 82324
& **Elk Mountain Hotel** (1-888-348-7774; 307-348-7774; www.elk mountainhotel.com), 102 E. Main Street. Listed on the National Register of Historic Places, this restored 1905 Victorian Folk hotel features luxurious accommodations in each of its 12 uniquely themed guest rooms, all decorated with period antiques and all with full, private bathrooms. Situated conveniently just off I-80 between Laramie and Rawlins, the

hotel affords a distinctive place to stop and spend the night (or 2 or 3 . . .). Also on the premises, the "1905" Dining Room offers fine American dining (complete with a terrific wine list), providing you with a complimentary, hot American breakfast for each night that you stay ($80–155). The hotel also has spaces for RV travelers ($30 with electricity; $20 without), as well as a separate three-bedroom, two-bathroom guesthouse with a full kitchen, dining area, and living room ($150).

Jelm 82063
Historic Woods Landing Resort (307-745-9638; www.woodslanding .com), #9 WY 10, Jelm. Located 25 miles southwest of Laramie via WY 230. Stay in one of two new cabins, which include private baths and limited kitchenettes ($85–95); one of six rustic cabins, which include access to a shared bathhouse ($35–45); or a tipi, which includes access to a shared bathhouse ($25), or just drive your RV or bring a tent ($20 per site includes access to bathhouse) to this rustic and historic resort, situated with easy access to the tremendous recreational opportunities found in the Medicine Bow Mountains of Medicine Bow National Forest (see *Wilder Places— Forests*). The Woods Landing Café serves breakfast, lunch, and dinner daily from Memorial Day to mid-November, offering breakfast on weekends only and lunch and dinner daily during the rest of the year. The dance hall, listed on the National Register of Historic Places, hosts live entertainment (and dancing, of course) on most Saturdays.

Medicine Bow
See Medicine Bow under *To See— Towns.*

Saratoga 82331
✍ **Harrison's Guest House and Guide Service** (April through October: 303-298-0848; 307-326-6079; www.northplattefishing.com), 14 Deer Haven. Stay in one of three bedrooms in this lovely guesthouse on the banks of the North Platte River—an angler's dream come true. You'll either have your own private bath or share a bath with one other room while enjoying access to a fully equipped kitchen and a huge deck as well. If you're a fly-fisherman—or you aspire to become one—you can hire a guide along with your lodging. Harrison's also offers scenic float trips and can help arrange a number of additional recreational activities that you might have a hankering to explore, including mountain biking, hiking, hunting, and horseback riding. You can also order up meals prepared by a gourmet chef, if you prefer not to cook for yourself.

The River Cottages (307-326-8750; www.grmo.com/lodging.html), 216 E. Walnut Street. The lodging properties of Great Rocky Mountain Outfitters, a fly shop and fishing outfitter (offering scenic float trips, too), these remodeled cabins sit right near the North Platte River, next door to the Saratoga Hot Pool (see *To Do—Hot Springs*). Truly, you'll find a home away from home here, as each cabin includes a full kitchen, a living area, satellite television, a deck, a gas fireplace, and a private bathroom, plus plenty of places to hang your gear. Year-round recreational opportunities nearby include not only blue-ribbon fishing but also access to all of the nearby fun to be found in Medicine Bow National Forest (see *Wilder Places—Forests*) ($75–125).

🚣 **Saratoga Inn** (1-800-594-0178; 307-326-5261; www.saratogainn.com), 601 E. Pic Pike Road. Relax and unwind at this hot springs resort, which allows guests unlimited, complimentary use of its 70-foot hot mineral pool, renowned for its high mineral content and its relative lack of rotten-eggish odors that can so often taint a natural soaking experience. If you like, you can add a spa treatment from the on-premises Healing Waters Spa, such as a warm stone massage or a mud wrap. Guests enjoy access to the resort's 9-hole golf course, complimentary use of resort bicycles, and easy access to the abundance of recreational opportunities available in nearby Medicine Bow National Forest (see *Wilder Places—Forests*). The resort can book adventures for guests with its sister property, **Brush Creek Ranch** (a working cattle and guest ranch), such as fishing, snowmobile rentals and tours, and horseback riding. The Saratoga Inn is also home to the Silver Saddle Restaurant, featuring the perfect atmosphere of elegant yet casual dining. Rooms are comfortable and private, fresh-baked chocolate chip cookies are included in the rate, and children 12 and under stay for free ($79–179).

♿ 🚣 **Wolf Hotel** (307-326-5525; www.wolfhotel.com), 101 E. Bridge Street. This historic property, built in 1893 and listed on the National Register of Historic Places, was once home to a stage stop. Today, it is home to a lovely guest accommodation featuring nine restored rooms and suites for you to choose from, all with private bathrooms ($52–110). Also on the premises, you'll find a sociable saloon with a pool table, as well as a dining room serving lunch and dinner (reservations recommended for dinner). The menu includes traditional American favorites cooked-to perfection, including burgers, sandwiches, steaks, salads, seafood, poultry, and even options for vegetarians. Excellent service rounds out the pleasant dining experience.

✳ **Where to Eat**

DINING OUT

Centennial
See **Snowy Mountain Lodge** under *Lodging—Lodges*.

Cheyenne
Little Bear Inn (307-634-3684), 1700 Little Bear Road. Treat yourself to an authentic, western-style, fine dining experience at this locally owned and operated establishment, a Cheyenne fixture since 1958. In a world rife with chain steak houses, this restaurant is an original, one-of-a-kind destination, featuring top-notch cuisine in an unsurpassable atmosphere of cozy and elegant western hospitality. But be forewarned: you might find it hard to select just one of the chef's creations from the menu, with choices such as buffalo top sirloin, northern walleye pike, salmon in parchment paper, or bourbon blackjack steak, to name a few. For the more adventurous palate, the restaurant also has offbeat selections, including fried frog legs and Rocky Mountain oysters.

The Whipple House (307-683-3551), 300 E. 17th Street. A taste of the continent—in Cheyenne, Wyoming? You bet! That's just what you'll find at the elegant and historic Whipple House, a Victorian mansion constructed in 1883 and listed on the

National Register of Historic Places. The restaurant specializes in gourmet lunches and dinners, including filet mignon, duck a l'orange, and seafood linguini, aimed to please the sophisticated palate. On Friday and Saturday nights, the Whipple House is a great romantic destination, where you can wow your date with an order of cheese fondue or chocolate fondue. Sunday brunch is a weekly happening as well. During summer, dining outdoors is an option.

See also **the Plains Hotel** and **Terry Bison Ranch Resort** under *Lodging—Other Options*.

Elk Mountain

See **Elk Mountain Hotel** under *Lodging—Other Options*.

Laramie

The Library Restaurant and Brewing Company (307-742-0500; www.library-odwyers.com), 1630 E. Grand Avenue. Located next door to O'Dwyers Grub and Pub (see *Eating Out*) and under the same ownership, this upscale restaurant and brewery makes a fine place to go for a meal on the town. While you savor one of the tasty microbrews from the brewery, you can sit back in the wood-paneled, library-themed dining room and peruse a menu filled with gourmet palate pleasers. In the mood for a steak? Try a bigger-than-average filet mignon—or perhaps you'd prefer rosemary dijon lamb, prime rib, or an entrée of three lobster tails, among other choices. Save room for dessert—they've got all of the tasty tempters, like fresh berry pie, a dreamy peanut butter 'n' chocolate concoction, key lime cheesecake, tiramisu, six-layered chocolate cake, and more.

Rawlins

Aspen House Restaurant (307-324-4787), 318 5th Street. Acclaimed as the finest restaurant in Rawlins, this favorite eatery is open every day but Sunday for both lunch and dinner. Here you'll find a menu with not only expertly prepared, traditional American favorites (steaks, seafood, poultry, and pastas) but also entrées influenced by Cajun cuisine and Singapore cuisine. Great service and a fine wine list complement this excellent dining experience.

Saratoga

See **Saratoga Inn** and **Wolf Hotel** under *Lodging—Other Options*.

EATING OUT

Albany

See **Albany Lodge** under *Lodging—Lodges*.

Centennial

Prospector Dining Room at the Old Corral Hotel and Steakhouse (1-866-OLD-CORRAL; 307-745-5918; www.oldcorral.com), 2750 WY 130. This western restaurant in the Snowy Mountains is known for its huge and marvelous creations. If you want to kick back and enjoy a steak after a long day of playing in the snow, you'll find an assortment of sizes and styles on the menu to suit your fancy, right up to a 32-ounce monster steak. Open daily for breakfast, lunch, and dinner, with menu selections for all types of appetites, not just the supersized (though no one will go away from the table hungry). If you're looking for a place to stay, you'll also find 35 hotel-style rooms for overnight travelers.

See also **Mountain View Historic Hotel** under *Lodging—Other Options*.

Cheyenne

💎 🐚 **Avanti Ristorante Italiano** (307-634-3432; 307-638-0912), 4620 Grandview Avenue. This Italian restaurant may not compare to the fine dining establishments you'll find in bigger urban areas—but it can certainly fit the bill if you're in the mood for some spaghetti, lasagna, fettuccine alfredo, or other classic Italian entrées. You can order an individual item off the menu, such as gnocchi, spicy shrimp alfredo, or chicken abruzzo, among other offerings, or you can choose to sample a number of entrées by ordering the buffet (available for both lunch and dinner, Monday through Saturday). This is a great option for families with children, as the kids can partake of the buffet as well—but at special, reduced rates.

🐚 💎 **Casa de Trujillo** (307-635-1227), 122 W. 6th Street. Popular with locals, this Mexican restaurant has all of the favorites you would expect to find on the menu—plus some interesting creations and combination plates of its own. Broaden your south-of-the-border horizons by ordering the red chili burger, a chili relleno or chorizo omelet, or a stuffed sopapilla; or if you like, stick with an old standby like a platter including tacos, burritos, guacamole, or tostadas. Most dinner entrées come with Mexican refried beans and rice. The prices at Casa de Trujillo are extremely reasonable, while the serving sizes are generous. A children's menu is available.

💎 **The Pie Lady** (307-637-8838), 3515 E. Lincolnway (in Cheyenne Plaza). Okay, I admit it: I love the name of this restaurant, which conjures up images of the welcoming, grandmotherly type, baking up a storm in preparation for the arrival of her grandkids—and really, that isn't too far from the truth of what you'll discover at this family-friendly diner. A menu of down-home-cooking selections features an array of homemade soups, incredible chili and cornbread, sandwiches, quiche, cinnamon rolls, potpies, salads, and of course, pies, pies, and more pies, with the selection varying daily. Devour a slice—à la mode if you like—or take home a whole pie (you may find yourself doing both) to enjoy later.

💎 **Sanford's Grub and Pub** (307-634-3381), 115 E. 17th Street. Though the Wyoming–South Dakota restaurant chain known as Sanford's is not for everyone, most kids will probably dig it, with its junkyard decor (remember the television show?) and its plethora of televisions tuned to different channels. Beer aficionados will appreciate the enormous beer list, and if you're really hungry, you won't be overwhelmed by the supersized pub entrées, served with plentiful sides on oversize platters to be eaten with oversize silverware. The huge menu includes salads, burgers, sandwiches, and all sorts of entrée selections—you'll have to see it to believe how large and extensive it is.

Zen's Bistro (307-635-1889), 2606 E. Lincolnway. Whether you just want a good cup of coffee or tea or you want to sit down and nosh for a while, Zen's Bistro offers you a comfortable and casual atmosphere to enjoy a hot beverage, a hearty sandwich, or a light snack. Breakfasts include a healthy fruit parfait served with a whole-grain muffin or, for the heartier appetite, a breakfast bagel piled high with goodies like eggs, cheese, and honey ham.

Creative salads and sandwiches are offered later in the day, filled with delicious ingredients that will leave you smacking your lips.

See also **the Plains Hotel** and **Terry Bison Ranch Resort** under *Lodging—Other Options.*

Evanston

Bear River Brewing (307-444-6274), 1012 Main Street. Stop in to taste a locally brewed, award-winning microbrew at this small, pub-style restaurant attached to the brewery. Menu selections include sandwiches, prime rib, seafood, and more. For the avid beer aficionado traveling through the state, this restaurant will fill you up and please your palate with its microbrews . . . especially if you've been spending time in nearby Utah, where the beer is—how to put it delicately?—not quite the same.

Kelly's Roadhouse Grill (307-783-7464; www.kellysroadhouse.com), 240 Bear River Drive. Whether you're a biker on the way to or from Sturgis or you're just an average traveler in search of some good grubbin', Kelly's will fill your belly and have you back on the road in no time. Pick from an assortment of half-pound burgers— including, of all things, a peanut butter burger (they swear it's tasty . . .), or if you're in the mood for something bigger, try a 16-ounce steak. Kelly's also offers an assortment of sandwiches, teriyaki chicken, and for all those french fry fanatics out there, a 1-pound order of fries.

Green River

China Garden Restaurant (307-875-3259), 190 N. 5th E. For a good selection of classic Chinese entrées, all at reasonable prices, this restaurant fits the bill. Mongolian beef, sesame chicken, egg foo young—you'll find all of your favorites here, plus a number of less mainstream options. You can even please those in your party who are not interested in ethnic food, as the restaurant also serves some American fare for less adventurous diners. If you want to catch that important sporting event, this is a likely place to watch it, as the restaurant has a sports bar as well.

🍴 **Krazy Moose Restaurant** (307-875-5124), 211 E. Flaming Gorge Way (in the **Red Feather Bar**). The entire family is welcome to sit down and enjoy a hearty, delicious meal at this Green River establishment. Open for breakfast, lunch, and dinner, the restaurant features traditional American fare served just the way you like it, from hearty burgers and sandwiches to steaks (8 ounce to 24 ounce), seafood, and chicken entrées. Top off your meal with a delectable homemade dessert. A children's menu is available.

Sage Creek Bagels (307-875-4877), 36 E. Flaming Gorge Way. If you're in the mood for a bagel with a smear of cream cheese for breakfast or lunch, you'll find that at Sage Creek, along with other fresh-baked goods. Sage Creek also serves up an array of sandwiches and soups (including a soup of the day), plus coffee, tea, and other beverages.

Jelm

See **Historic Woods Landing Resort** under *Lodging—Other Options.*

Laramie

Coal Creek Coffee Company (1-800-838-7737; 307-745-7737; www.coalcreekcoffee.com), 110 Grand Avenue. This local establishment enjoys a well-earned regional reputation for its excellent coffee, which it distributes to numerous locations throughout the American West. Sample some of the stuff right from the source by stepping into the original store in Laramie. Here you'll find expertly prepared coffee beverages made from the finest of beans, as well as teas, hot chocolates, and shakes. If you're hungry, you can order a freshly prepared sandwich, homemade soup, or a salad or just nosh on one of the assorted baked goods that tempt patrons daily. What else? Well, this cool hangout also features art shows with works by local and regional artists displayed on the walls, and it hosts live entertainment several times each month, usually on Friday and Saturday nights.

Grand Avenue (307-721-2909), 301 Grand Avenue. On a busy corner of Laramie's historic downtown, you can sit down at a window-side table and watch the goings-on outside, if you like, while you peruse the menu. Gourmet pizzas are a favorite here, with original creations such as buffalo chicken, Thai pie, and, of course, the Grand Avenue, all of which feature unique combinations of toppings. You can get a more standard pie, too, if you wish. Not a pizza lover? No worries. The menu also includes more than 10 salad creations, more than 10 pasta dishes, more than 10 sandwiches, and more than 10 calzones (can you say "variety"?). If you're wondering, "what's with the 10 theme?" here's your answer: almost everything on this menu is under $10, making it easy on the wallet while satisfying your hunger for good food.

Jeffrey's Bistro (307-742-7046; www.jeffreysbistro.com), 123 E. Ivin-son Avenue. Serving lunch and dinner in a corner location in historic downtown Laramie, Jeffrey's takes pride in offering up deliberately healthy fare, with most of its menu items being meatless, as well as being prepared using heart-healthy canola oil. Creative meal salads, served with bread baked fresh on the premises, include a create-your-own salad option with 20 add-ins possible to top off the bistro's special blend of five different leafy greens. Each day features several homemade soups. The menu also includes an array of sandwiches and entrée items such as potpies, enchiladas, burritos, and pastas. The restaurant even gives you the option of ordering your entrée à la carte or with all of the yummy "extras," which include coffee or tea, soup or salad, and your choice of a homemade dessert (highly recommended). A children's menu is available as well.

O'Dwyers Grub and Pub (307-742-3900; www.library-odwyers.com), 1622 E. Grand Avenue. Located next door to and under the same ownership as the Library Restaurant and Brewing Company (see *Dining Out*), this sports bar and restaurant serves healthier than average pub-style fare with an Irish twist, along with an assortment of microbrews from the brewery. This means that in addition to the traditional deep-fried selections on the menu, such as wings, mozzarella sticks, and fish-and-chips, there's also an array of salads and wraps. O'Dwyers' menu also has burgers, pizzas, steaks, and sandwiches. You can order up an Irish special, too—depending on the day of the week, you may get corned beef and cabbage, shepherd's pie, or seafood potato patties, among other dishes.

 Teriyaki Bowl (307-742-0709), 3021 E. Grand Avenue. If you're in the mood for Asian food or you just need something fast—but you can't stomach the idea of fast food—try Teriyaki Bowl, where you can eat in or take out. I love places like this, where the entrée menu features a list of "bowls," all of which provide a complete and rather healthy meal unto themselves—for about $5 a bowl. Choose from a chicken teriyaki bowl, beef teriyaki bowl, combo bowl (both chicken and beef), or vegetable bowl, among others, all of which include rice and an assortment of steamed vegetables.

Rawlins

 Huckleberry's Juice, Java, and Ice Cream (307-324-4758), 509 W. Cedar Street. In the mood for an espresso—or an ice-cream cone? Either way, you've come to the right place if you stop at Huckleberry's, where you'll find not only an assortment of specialty coffee drinks and ice-cream treats but also more filling, meal-making fare. Breakfast is served all day long, but if you want something else, you'll also find soup, sandwiches, and other light fare on the menu as well.

The Pantry Restaurant (307-324-7860), 221 W. Cedar Street. In an elegant 1881 Victorian house, you can sit down to a wonderful and generously portioned American meal. Be sure to include either the homemade bread or the homemade soup (or both) in whatever you pick to order—the restaurant makes this easy, with menu selections including soup, sandwich, and "all you care to eat," which includes soup, salad bar, and sourdough roll—and for an extra buck, a slice of homemade pie (another house

specialty). Heartier appetites need not fear; complete dinners are also available, including an array of steaks, chicken, and seafood, all of which come with lots of tasty sides.

 Rustler's Family Restaurant (307-324-5539), 1800 E. Cedar Street. Serving breakfast, lunch, and dinner daily, this family-style restaurant will serve you from the breakfast menu anytime of day. Breakfasts range from big to huge, with pretty much every traditional American morning repast you can imagine available on the menu. Meanwhile, the prices for these hearty dishes hover in the $5 range, meaning you'll get a lot for your money. Lunch choices include burgers, sandwiches, and salads. Dinner choices include steaks, fried chicken, seafood, and more, all served with all-you-can-eat homemade cornbread with honey butter. Delectable homemade desserts await those diners who can still fit something in their tummies.

See also the Lodge at Rawlins under Lodging—Lodges.

Rock Springs

 Bitter Creek Brewing (307-362-4782; www.bittercreekbrewing.com), 604 Broadway. Above-average pub fare in a comfortable, welcoming atmosphere is what you'll find at this local establishment, which serves up several microbrews crafted in the brewery on the premises, including Red Desert Ale and Mustang Pale Ale, among others. The kids can even sample a microbrew, too—a root beer, that is! The extensive menu includes something for everyone, including burgers and sandwiches, steaks, pastas, and pizzas, plus salads and appetizers. Unique creations include Thai chicken nachos and chicken and portobello mushroom linguini, among others. Vegetarians will find a few choices to suit their dietary restrictions. Be sure to save room for dessert—the microbrew root beer float shouldn't be missed.

✐ **Log Inn Supper Club** (307-362-7166), 12 Purple Sage Road, Exit 99 off I-80. Specializing in serving up traditional yet upscale American entrées in a casual and relaxed atmosphere, this restaurant features an array of steaks and seafood options. House specials include deep-fried lobster tail, prime rib, and mesquite-broiled chicken with black-bean salsa, among many other dishes. Vegetarians will even find several menu options, such as pasta primavera and linguini alfredo. The restaurant is open for dinner Monday through Saturday; entrées tend to be pricey for "eating out," but the casual, family-friendly atmosphere is welcoming to all.

✐ **Sands Chinese and American Restaurant** (307-362-5633; www .sandschinese.com), 1549 9th Street. Withstanding the toughest test of all—the test of time—this restaurant has served its fine Chinese and American food for more than half a century, establishing itself as a local favorite. Here you'll find a complete array of all of your favorite Chinese entrées, including cashew chicken, moo shu pork, kung pao shrimp, and lo mein. You'll also find a delicious selection of traditional American favorites, also expertly prepared, including pastas, steaks, seafood, burgers, and sandwiches. Portion sizes are generous, while prices are reasonable. Sands has a seniors' menu for more mature patrons, plus an extensive dessert menu featuring an incredible "death by chocolate" chocolate cake.

Saratoga
See Saratoga under *To See—Towns.*

✱ Special Events

January: ✐ **Ice Fishing Derby,** Saratoga: family-friendly competition includes thousands of dollars in prize money and children's fishing contests as well. (See also Saratoga under *To See—Towns.*)

February: **Sierra Madre Winter Carnival and Snow-Cross Games,** Encampment: 2-day winter sports competition includes casino night, sled dog races, homemade-sled races, cross-country skiing races, and more.

June: ✐ **Flaming Gorge Days** (307-875-5711; www.flaminggorgedays .com), Green River: annual 4-day event includes a rodeo, children's entertainment, a parade, concerts, and more. **Platte Valley Festival of the Birds,** Saratoga: festivities include a guided scenic float of the North Platte River, speakers, bird-watching, a banquet with a guest speaker, and guided bird-watching hikes. **Woodchopper's Jamboree and Rodeo,** Encampment: annual event for more than four decades; includes wood chopping competitions, a rodeo, entertainment, and a barbecue. **Wyoming Brewer's Festival** (307-432-5395), Cheyenne: sample more than 40 microbrews brewed in the state of Wyoming and the Front Range area during this 2-day festival held in mid-June.

June and July: ✐ **Cheyenne Gunslingers,** Cheyenne: Monday through Friday at 6 PM and Saturday at noon; witness old-time western fun at Old Town Square with skits, gunfights, and more.

June through August: **Pine Bluffs Night Rodeo,** Pine Bluffs: every Friday at 7 PM, you can catch the buckin' broncos in action, as well as all of the other exciting rodeo events.

July: ✑ **Cheyenne Frontier Days** (www.cfdrodeo.com), Cheyenne: known as the Daddy of 'Em All, this annual 10-day celebration, running since 1897, includes rodeos, a parade, free pancake breakfasts, and big-name entertainers. ✑ **Platte Valley Festival of the Arts,** Saratoga: annual juried art competition; also includes an Old West shootout reenactment, a Fourth of July parade, a children's art show, live entertainment, food, fireworks, and dancing.

July and August: ✑ **Wyoming's Big Show,** Rock Springs: southwestern Wyoming's summer festival includes carnival rides, livestock shows, a rodeo, entertainment, an art show, and more.

August: **Bear River Rendezvous,** Evanston: celebration the weekend before Labor Day at Bear River State Park (see *Wilder Places—Parks*); includes reenactments of traditional 19th-century "mountain man" rendezvous events, with costumed competitors engaging in powder shoots and other competitions. ✑ **Carbon**

County Fair, Rawlins: traditional county fair includes livestock exhibitions, 4H, a rodeo, food, children's activities, a demolition derby, a street dance, and more. ✑ **Happy Jack Music Festival** (303-471-6282; www.happyjackfestival.com), Curt Gowdy State Park (see *Wilder Places—Parks*): 3-day festival in mid-August includes Friday and Saturday bluegrass, folk, old-time, and country music; plus free gospel music all day Sunday.

September: **Cheyenne Cowboy Symposium and Celebration** (307-635-5788; www.cheyennecowboy symposium.com), Cheyenne: celebrates the spirit of the cowboy through poetry, music, a trade show, and more. **Greek Festival** (307-638-2000), Cheyenne: 2-day festival includes Greek food, dancing, and entertainment. **Mountain Man Rendezvous,** Fort Bridger State Historic Site (see *To See—Historic Landmarks, Places, and Sites*): annual Labor Day weekend event includes costumed actors re-creating historical rendezvous activities; includes games, entertainment, food, and more.

See also **Wyoming Frontier Prison** under *To See—Historic Landmarks, Places, and Sites.*

INDEX

continued on next page

X/Y

Z

Follow The Countryman Press to your favorite destinations!

Discover more when you travel with our EXPLORER'S GUIDES:

NORTHEAST
Berkshire Hills & Pioneer Valley of Western Massachusetts
Cape Cod, Martha's Vineyard & Nantucket
Connecticut
Hudson Valley & Catskill Mountains
Maine
New Hampshire
New York City
Rhode Island
Vermont
Western New York
MID-ATLANTIC
The Blue Ridge & Smoky Mountains
Maryland
New Jersey
The Shenandoah Valley & Mountains of the Virginias
SOUTHEAST
Orlando, Central & North Florida
WEST
Montana & Wyoming
Oregon

Savor the best these regions have to offer with our GREAT DESTINATIONS series:

NORTHEAST
The Adirondack Book
The Berkshire Book
The Coast of Maine Book
The Finger Lakes Book
The Hamptons Book
The Hudson Valley Book
The Nantucket Book
MID-ATLANTIC
The Chesapeake Bay Book
SOUTHEAST
The Charleston, Savannah, & Coastal Islands Book
The Sarasota, Sanibel Island & Naples Book
Palm Beach, Miami & the Florida Keys
WEST & SOUTHWEST
Big Sur, Monterey Bay & Gold Coast Wine Country
The Napa & Sonoma Book
The Santa Fe & Taos Book
The Seattle & Vancouver Book
The Texas Hill Country Book

General Travel
American Rock
Bouldering USA
The 100 Best Art Towns in America
NORTHEAST
Adirondack Odysseys
Chow Maine
The Colors of Fall
Covered Bridges of Vermont
Dog-Friendly New England
Dog-Friendly New York
Eating New England
A Guide to Natural Places in the Berkshire Hills
In-Line Skate New England
Hudson River Journey
Hudson Valley Harvest
Maine Sporting Camps
New England Seacoast Adventures
New England Waterfalls
The Other Islands of New York City
The Photographer's Guide to the Maine Coast
The Photographer's Guide to Vermont
Shawangunks Trail Companion
Touring East Coast Wine Country
Weekending in New England
Weekend Walks Along the New England Coast
Weekend Walks in Historic New England
MID-ATLANTIC
Dog-Friendly Washington D.C. and the Mid-Atlantic States
52 Weekends in New Jersey
New Jersey's Great Gardens
New Jersey's Special Places
Waterfalls of the Mid-Atlantic States
SOUTHEAST
Eating New Orleans
Fly Fishing the Louisiana Coast
WEST
The California Coast
The Photographer's Guide to the Grand Canyon
The Photographer's Guide to the Oregon Coast
Wild Weekends in Utah
INTERNATIONAL
Bicycling Cuba
Switzerland's Mountain Inns

We offer many more books on hiking, fly-fishing, travel, nature, and other subjects. Our books are available at bookstores and outdoor stores everywhere. For more information or a free catalog, please call 1-800-245-4151 or write to us at The Countryman Press, P.O. Box 748, Woodstock, Vermont 05091. You can find us on the Internet at www.countrymanpress.com.